AFRICAN-AMERICAN ART

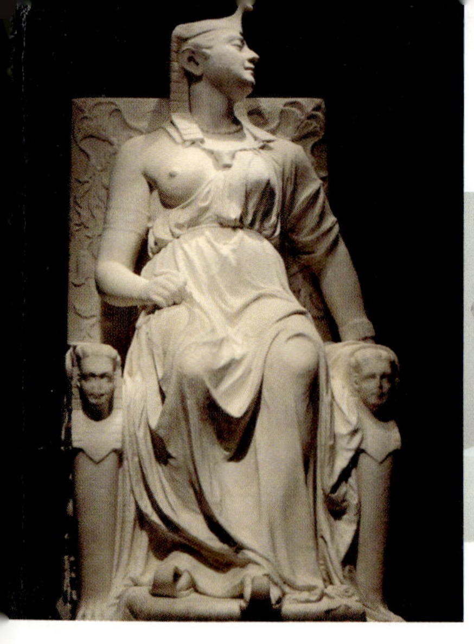

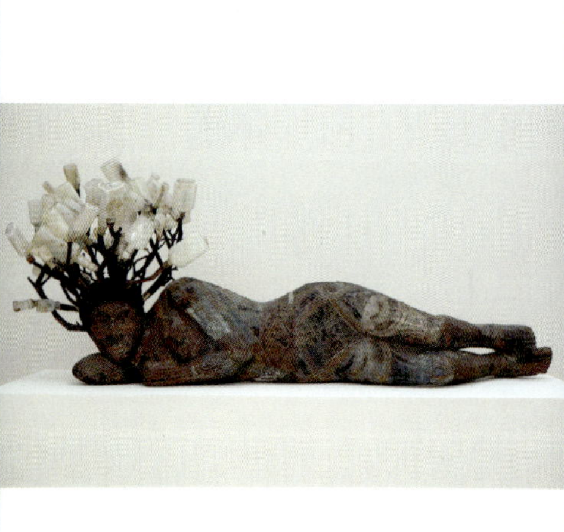

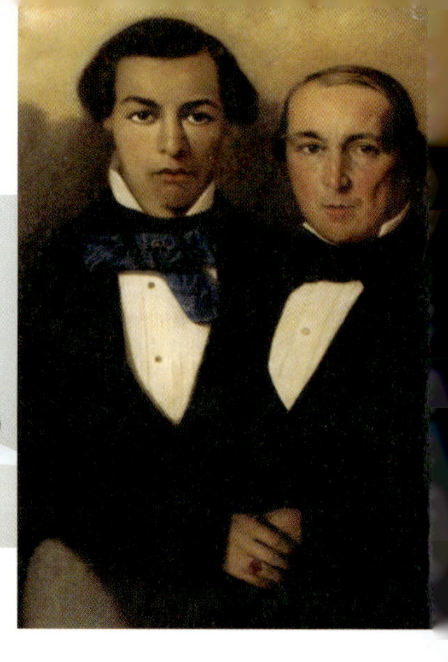

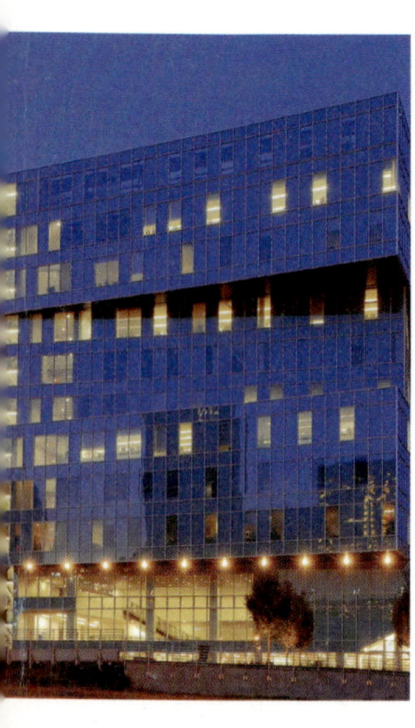

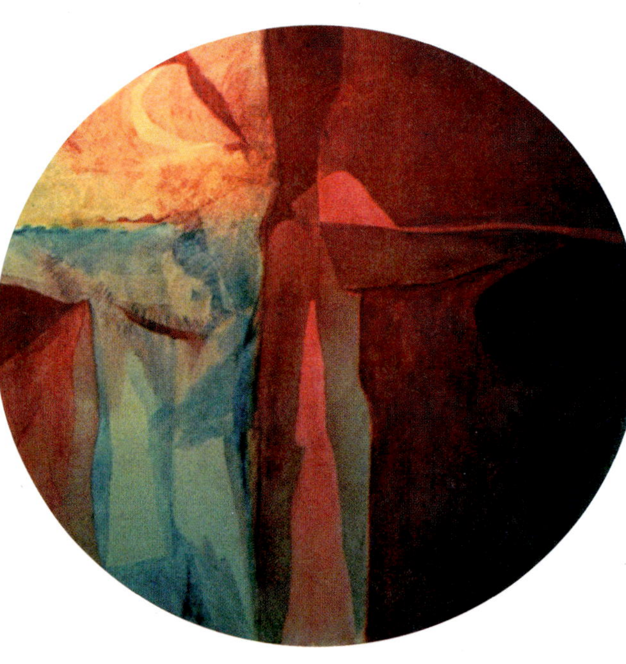

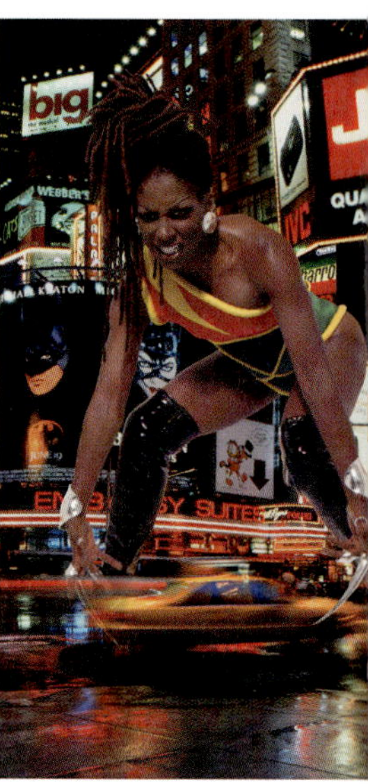
big
JVC

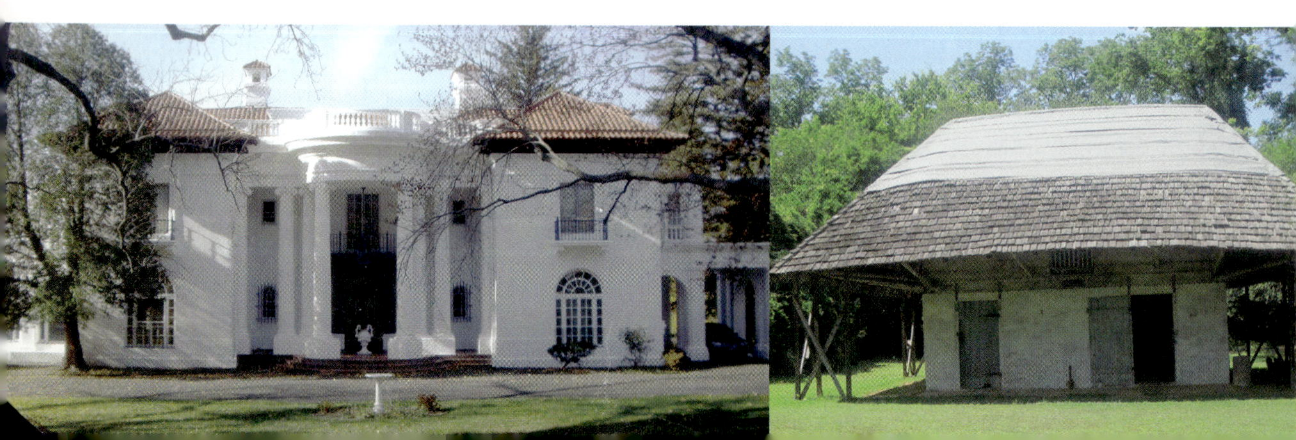

AFRICAN-AMERICAN ART

A Visual and Cultural History

Lisa Farrington
John Jay College of Criminal Justice, City University of New York

New York Oxford
OXFORD UNIVERSITY PRESS

Oxford University Press is a department of the University of Oxford. It furthers the University's objective of excellence in research, scholarship, and education by publishing worldwide.

Oxford New York
Auckland Cape Town Dar es Salaam Hong Kong Karachi
Kuala Lumpur Madrid Melbourne Mexico City Nairobi
New Delhi Shanghai Taipei Toronto

With offices in
Argentina Austria Brazil Chile Czech Republic France Greece
Guatemala Hungary Italy Japan Poland Portugal Singapore
South Korea Switzerland Thailand Turkey Ukraine Vietnam

For titles covered by Section 112 of the US Higher Education Opportunity Act, please visit www.oup.com/us/he for the latest information about pricing and alternate formats.

Published by Oxford University Press
198 Madison Avenue, New York, New York 10016
http://www.oup.com

Library of Congress Cataloging-in-Publication Data

Farrington, Lisa E., author.
African-American art: a visual and cultural history / Lisa Farrington, John Jay College of Criminal Justice.
pages cm
Includes bibliographical references and index.
ISBN 978-0-19-999539-4 (pbk.: alk. paper) 1. African American art—Textbooks. I. Title.
N6538.N5F265 2016
700.89'96073—dc23
2015033237

Printing number: 9 8 7 6 5 4 3 2 1

Printed in the United States of America
on acid-free paper

In memory of my mentors, Tritobia Hayes Benjamin and Laurie Adams, outstanding teachers, art historians, and women

CONTENTS

PREFACE

The African-American creative impulse has a long and venerable history, from the making of ceramics, textiles, and wood carvings in the 17th century to the avant-garde installation art and architecture of the 21st century. Much of this creativity has been shaped by traditional African aesthetics—which, arguably, gives art made by African Americans a quality distinct from that of their Euro-American peers (although it is no less intrinsically American). Africans were among the very first nonindigenous residents of the New World, arriving on the shores of North America as early as 1526, within a few short decades of Columbus. Over the centuries, the growth of the African-American population paralleled that of the European colonizers and immigrants, particularly in the slaveholding states of the South, where blacks made up more than 30 percent of the population at the time of the Civil War. By this time, most southern blacks no longer had any immediate African-born relatives but, rather, had become fourth- and fifth-generation Americans themselves. However, nearly 90 percent of this population was enslaved and lived in poverty.

The disadvantages to black Americans resulting from slavery would continue for centuries. As a result, many generations of black artists had limited access to art schools, clients, patrons, and professional advancement. Not only was the ability of blacks to function as artists hindered (restricting their art-making pursuits, for the most part, to the creation of utilitarian objects, at least until the 19th century), but the art that blacks did produce was marginalized or wholly dismissed by critics, collectors, and historians, who saw art produced by slaves and their descendants as unworthy of notice.

African-American Art: A Visual and Cultural History joins the ranks of a number of books written by scholars since the mid-20th century that have addressed this marginalization through a thorough survey of this art from colonial times to the present. Its two key objectives are (1) to provide a foundation in the analysis of visual language and (2) to build on that foundation an understanding and appreciation of African-American art. Visual literacy, as a primary goal, is imparted in each chapter through the analysis of works of art, architecture, painting, sculpture, photography, and design. Individual works are given careful aesthetic, historical, and contextual consideration, so that readers may understand African-American art in microcosm as well as macrocosm—just as one must understand individual words in order to appreciate an entire novel.

The exploration of art by people of African descent in America allows us to gain deeper knowledge of the artists, their identities, their experiences and aesthetics, and issues of art patronage and, beyond this, of the changing nature of the African-American experience over nearly half a millennium. Taken as a whole, the study of African-American art "reads" like a grand epic and provides an enlightening account of Africans and their descendants. Viewed individually, each work becomes an episode in the larger narrative, offering insights into the ways and means of African-American artists, and into the nature of art as language.

Through a carefully selected collection of creative works and accompanying analyses, *The History of African-American Art* addresses crucial gaps in the scholarly literature and breaks new ground in several areas. It is the first comprehensive survey on the subject to be published in more than a decade, and it is one of the only art surveys (on any subject) to include nearly 40 percent women artists. This book also integrates photography and architecture—genres that have been minimally represented in African-American art histories—into its discussion of the 19th and 20th centuries.

THE BOOK AND ITS CONTENTS

African-American Art: A Visual and Cultural History consists of 14 chapters with highlighted key words (defined at the end of each chapter) and concludes with a chapter summary and questions and topics designed to stimulate thought and discussion. The chapters are grouped into four chronological sections: **Part 1** considers the 18th to 19th centuries; **Part 2** comprises the first half of the 20th century and emphasizes modern art trends; **Part 3** examines the second half of the 20th century and the reaction against Modernism (i.e., Postmodernism); and **Part 4** focuses on the 21st century.

Chapter 1 introduces some key methods of viewing art that have been developed by historians over the last hundred years. This is meant not to be a comprehensive examination but rather to introduce the reader to some tools that will be used throughout the text to analyze and interpret the artists' works. By using common tools, it is hoped that the work of African-American artists can be understood both as a unique cultural expression and as an integral part of the mainstream development of American art.

Chapter 2 is devoted to the presence of African aesthetics in art produced by enslaved Africans over several generations. Although separated from their African origins by an ocean and by decades—even centuries—African continental art-making methods persisted in the New World. In particular, the profound influence of African aesthetics on architecture, utilitarian objects, and textiles created by enslaved Africans is reviewed. Also featured in this chapter is the work of Scipio Moorhead, one of the first professional African-American artists known to history, whose drawings were preserved as engravings in 19th-century books.

Chapter 3 continues the journey with an in-depth look at late 18th- and early 19th-century architecture and design. Influenced greatly by classical Greco-Roman and contemporary European trends, Federal-style architecture is rarely attributed to black builders even though, in fact, much of this construction and even design was the work of African Americans. Special attention is given to *gens de couleur* (men of color)—a French term commonly used in the Louisiana Territory (which comprised what is today the entire midwestern United States from the Gulf of Mexico to Canada and from Idaho to Illinois) beginning in 1682. The designation "men of color" referred to members of a privileged sector of the black population who gained socioeconomic status through their patrimony, as the children of wealthy white landowners and merchants and their enslaved mistresses. The phrase aptly describes some of the first African-American professional architects and designers. Among these were free black architect Charles Paquet of Louisiana; John Hemings, who created furniture at the Monticello home of President Thomas Jefferson; and several highly successful New Orleans cabinetmakers. Examinations of wood, metal, and ceramic sculpture as well as early quilting traditions conclude the chapter.

Chapter 4 addresses the rise of the neoclassically trained sculptors and painters in the late 18th and early 19th centuries. Working in the main as portraitists and sculptors of funerary monuments, these artists of color benefitted from the escalating abolitionist movement as the era of slavery drew to a close. The period marked increased opportunities for artists of color, whose work was supported by antislavery groups. A special focus of Chapter 4 is the continuing circumstance of miscegenation, which afforded a number of artists of color access to a wealthy white clientele and to financial support for study at home and abroad. A key example is Robert S. Duncanson, who, because of his fair complexion, was presumed by many to be the biracial son of a white father. This chapter also highlights distinguished portrayals of people of color by their artist-peers, such as engraver Patrick Reason's portraits of black dignitaries. Central to this discussion is internationally renowned Neoclassical sculptor Edmonia Lewis, an expatriate artist who left the United States in search of creative freedom and professional success abroad.

Nineteenth-century Romantic landscape painting is the chief focus of **Chapter 5**, which features African-American artists of the Hudson River School. Until the latter 20th century, art historical scholarship on the Hudson River School tended to overlook the artists of color who worked in the genre. Responding to this gap in the literature, the discussion in Chapter 5 places Romantic artists of color within the larger framework of Western landscape traditions in both the United States and Europe. The chapter also reviews the growing number of academically trained artists who flourished prior to, and after, the Civil War, who created their art in tandem with European movements such as Neoclassicism, Realism, Impressionism, Symbolism, and Post-Impressionism. While framing the art of this period within various Western art movements, the discussion also addresses the many iconographic tributes that the artists paid to their African-American heritage. This chapter likewise reviews the important work of 19th-century black photographers and Gilded Age architects—most notably, Julian Francis Abele (1881–1950), the first black graduate of the Department of Architecture at the University of Pennsylvania.

The dawn of artistic Modernism in the United States and the age of the Harlem Renaissance are the themes of **Chapter 6**. It begins with a discussion of the demographic population shift known as the Great Migration: the exodus of more than one million blacks from the rural South to the urban North, particularly New York City. During the 1920s, the city's then outlying district of Harlem was transformed from an all-white neighborhood into a mecca for the "New Negro"—a term popularized by black social critic Alain Locke that referred to talented black visual artists, literati, dancers, actors, musicians, and intellectuals. These New Negroes converged on Harlem along with many southern migrants, transforming the neighborhood into a vibrant artistic and cultural center; this resulted in an age of artistic creativity unprecedented in U.S. history. Artists highlighted in this chapter include, among others, precisionist painter Aaron Douglas, cubist artist Lois Jones, and modernist sculptor Richmond Barthé (one of a rare few black artists who exhibited at the Whitney Museum as early as 1934).

Chapter 7 is devoted to Social Realist art and the age of the Great Depression. This discussion focuses on the financial and political shifts that set the stage for this new artistic trend. Social Realism was a style of painting and printmaking that glorified the working class and signified a conscious rejection of Early Modernist abstraction in favor of realistic imagery with a socialist agenda. Government-sponsored programs like President Franklin Roosevelt's New Deal and the WPA (Works Progress Administration) also influenced art production, while encouraging more inclusion of African Americans and women artists into mainstream art circles. Further consideration is given to the influence of the Mexican Muralist Movement on black art styles, and on women movers and shakers of the period, such as sculptors Augusta Savage and Selma Burke.

Chapter 8 examines the reversion of national interest from veneration of the worker and community achievement to regard for exclusivity and individual achievement. This trend is seen through the lens of a canonical art historical debate that took place in the 1930s between art theorists Walter Benjamin and Clement Greenberg about the role of art in society. The two disagreed on the relative hierarchy and centrality of form over content in art, a divergence that placed Social Realism at odds with renewed abstract trends. Included in this chapter are those artists who persevered with figurative art and socially committed content against the grain of the rise in reputation of abstraction and nonrepresentational art. Abstract Expressionism rapidly overtook Social Realism in popularity as socialist and communist sentiments waned during and after World War II. In particular, the atmosphere of anticommunism embodied in the HUAC (House Un-American Activities Committee) during the McCarthy era inspired a retreat from social action in the arts.

The art of painter and printmaker Jacob Lawrence shows how a talented artist overcame these seemingly irreconcilable trends. A major visual arts player of the period, Lawrence's works fused both figurative and abstract forms with content that venerated the minority poor and the history of African Americans, thus straddling both Social Realist and midcentury modernist sensibilities. This unique fusion of otherwise opposing methods brought Lawrence to the forefront of the mainstream art world. Chapter 8 concludes with a discussion of three additional mid-20th-century developments: the Surrealist impulse in African-American art, influenced by the dream interpretations of the founding father of psychoanalysis, Austrian neurologist Sigmund Freud (1856–1939); the fine arts photography of Gordon Parks and Roy DeCarava; and finally the burgeoning Vernacular Art Movement, which includes folk artists who worked outside of academic traditions and established art circles.

The achievements of African-American artists after World War II are the subject of **Chapter 9**. Included in this chapter is a clarification of the differences among figurative, abstract, and nonrepresentational art: that is, respectively, art that represents nature, art that distorts natural forms, and art that does not reference nature in any way. This chapter continues the discussion begun in Chapter 8 of the effects of the changing political and economic climate in the United States on the formerly inclusive policies of the WPA years, as Abstract Expressionist art solidified its status as the preferred art form in America. The paths of abstract artists are traced over the next decades—including the spectacular success of Washington Color School artist Alma Thomas and other abstract movements in the postwar decades. Finally, Chapter 9 includes a review of Hard-Edge and Minimalist painting, which emphasized flat, unmodulated color and clean edges.

The agitprop art of the Civil Rights and Black Power Movements of the 1960s and 1970s is the focus of **Chapter 10**. Just as black Americans across the country began to engage in a nonviolent political battle to gain rights equal to those of white Americans, black artists used the visual arts to protest social oppression. African-American artists formed new art groups, such as Spiral (founded in New York City by artist Romare Bearden and others in 1963), in response to the nationwide call of the Civil Rights Movement. Spiral marked the first organized response to the national bid for equal rights on the part of black artists.

The nonviolent social protests of the civil rights era evolved into the more militant age of black power and black liberation by the late 1960s. This chapter takes a look at this volatile decade as well, as African-American artists became more militant in their agendas. The artists of this era expressed a profound interest in African art patterns and palettes, and a desire to return to the socialist art of the 1930s. In 1970, CONFABA (the Conference on the Functional Aspects of Black Art) laid the groundwork for the Black Arts Movement—the visual arts arm of the Black Power Movement. The formation of artists' collectives such as the Harlem group WEUSI (Swahili for "blacks") and AfriCOBRA (the Chicago-based African Commune of Bad Relevant Artists) brought together politically minded artists who sounded a call for public art (particularly murals) that was accessible to the "masses" and the incorporation into black visual art of African formal elements such as polyrhythmic patterns inspired by African textiles, intense color schemes, readily recognizable forms (rather than abstraction), and content directly related to the history, concerns, and achievements of Africans in the diaspora.

Chapter 11 surveys black feminist art, which evolved in response to the Black Arts and the Women's Art Movements. African-American women faced compelling issues regarding race and gender. As blacks, they felt a need to join the Black Arts Movement; as women, they were drawn to the Women's Art Movement. Unfortunately for them, these two factions had little, if anything, in common. This chapter explores the creative works of the few brave black feminist artists who grappled with this dilemma, such as Faith Ringgold, who is considered a leading light of black feminist art. Initially a staunch activist in the Black Arts Movement, the patriarchal and, at times, misogynistic impulses of some of its players (who discouraged and marginalized female participants) convinced Ringgold to shift allegiances to the Women's Art Movement. The latter group, however, although supportive of women artists, was essentially a middle-class white collective with little or no interest in the racial and economic concerns of minority women artists. Nevertheless, Ringgold found her place within the Women's Art Movement and became its first major black contributor.

Chapter 12 surveys the black participants in the many iterations of Postmodernism in the 1980s and 1990s. Postmodernism sprang both from and rejected Modernism. Quintessential modern art was marked by compositional purity, single-medium works (mainly painting and sculpture), abstraction or nonrepresentation, and a foregrounding of form over content. Postmodern art, by contrast, preferred unorthodox compositional structures, multimedia and alternative media works, and word-based conceptual art. This chapter reviews Conceptualism, Post-Minimalism, Earth Art, assemblage, and installation art. Many of these styles reject the idea of the art "object" as a permanent, unchangeable, or even necessary component of art. Because Postmodernism dismissed much of the artistic conventions set in place by artistic traditions of the past, photography, which is also discussed, became a flexible medium that could be coupled with texts, sounds, collage techniques, installation, and other methodologies to create an entirely new form of expression.

Chapter 13 examines the persistence of two midcentury traditions as the 20th century came to a close. The first is figurative art in the form of Neo-Expressionism and related representational trends. Exponents of the late 20th-century figurative impulse include Kara Walker and Robert Colescott, whose works incorporate elements of black caricature and satire in order to subvert the very stereotypes that these caricatures once promoted. As proponents of the figurative and the political, their works look backward to the Black Arts Movement and to a resistance to change while, at the same time, embracing new approaches to black art that are less didactic than those of the past. The flip side of the figurative coin, and equally persistent at the close of the 20th century, is abstraction, as seen in works such as the jazz-inspired paintings of colorist Gaye Ellington—granddaughter of the famed jazz musician Duke Ellington—or the ethereal abstractions of Danny Simmons—brother of art patron and famed music producer Russell Simmons. The chapter concludes with a renewed look at architecture. The relative dearth of African-American architecture prior to the latter 20th century is superseded by an abundance of projects by gifted black designers in a variety of styles, including neomodern, neohistoricist, and postmodern.

African-American Art: A Visual and Cultural History concludes in **Chapter 14** with an eye to the future. Presented in this final chapter are artists who gained national and international attention in the most recent years of the New Millennium. "Post-Black" as a term that defines changing and increasingly nuanced representations of race in visual art is a central theme, as are "Afrofuturism," performance, "intervention" art, and alternative media abstraction. Tentative conclusions are drawn as to where (and in how many new directions) the next generation of African-American artists may be heading.

DON'T CALL ME AFRICAN-AMERICAN

One advance reader of this book questioned whether the descriptor "African-American" was appropriate for the book's title. Certainly the decision as to whether to use "African-American" or "black" in the title posed a dilemma. The infamous Gibré George Facebook page "Don't Call Me African American" is one sign of this quandary. It highlights a conundrum with which Americans of African descent have been grappling since the 16th century. Since that time, literally dozens of names have been associated with African Americans: from "African" and "Colored" to "Negro" and "black," and from "high yellow" and "red" to "biracial" and "mixed," ad infinitum. Indeed, few other American ethnic groups have had more identifiers as have African Americans. These many titles suggest not so much the lack of a clear sense of identity—which is hardly the case—but rather the infinitely varied character and ever-mutable sociopolitical status of African Americans. They have risen from slaves to indentured servants, from migrant workers to urban dwellers, and from politically voiceless to president of the United States, within just a few centuries.

The complex and sometimes convoluted collection of appellations for African Americans has been in flux since 1526, when enslaved Africans were first brought to the Carolinas by the Spanish explorers. From then until the early 19th century, blacks in the United States self-identified as "African." Whites, on the other hand, particularly in the South, preferred terms such as "black," "mulatto," "quadroon," and "octoroon" (borrowed from the French Code Noir penned by Louis XIV in 1685) to differentiate among full-blooded, mixed-race, enslaved, and free Africans in America. After the abolition of slavery at the end of the Civil War, the most commonly used term was "Freedman."

During the latter part of the 19th century and the early 20th century, new titles came into use, including, most notably, "Negro" and "Colored." The latter was used popularly for the first time during the Civil War and was later affirmed as the politically correct term by the NAACP (National Association for the Advancement of Colored People) when that association was formed in 1909. Some 15 years later, in the mid-1920s, "Negro" was endorsed by the cultural elites of the Harlem Renaissance. This privileged group identified themselves as New Negroes or, more specifically, as urbane recreations of the southern "Old Negro," the latter of whom was embodied in the stereotype of the illiterate black farmworker.

Replacing the popular "Negro," the term "black" was popularized 40 years later, in the late 1960s and early 1970s, coincident with the Black Power Movement. As a racial designation, "black" suggested pride in skin complexion, in Africa and African customs, and in a new ideal of beauty. Memorialized in the popular phrase "black is beautiful," this new ideal embraced and honored African physical features—broad noses, full lips, dark skin, and "woolly" hair (to use the description of fifth-century B.C.E. Greek historian Herodotus)—rather than rejecting these features as unattractive, as they had historically been in the West. The popularization of the term "black" came into common use simultaneously with the founding of black militant groups such as the Black Panthers, and the term "black" became associated with revolutionary action against oppression.

The label "African-American" replaced "black" as the preferred politically correct appellation in the late 1980s. The timing of this shift corresponded with 1988 legislation that apologized to Japanese Americans for their racially motivated interment during World War II, leading to the payment of $1.6 billion in reparations. It also coincided with the passing of the Indian Gaming Regulatory Act of the same year, which protected and supported the Native-American gambling industry. The moment seemed appropriate for the redesignation of blacks as African Americans. This action had, among many effects, the consequence of allying African Americans with other hyphenated Americans who, likewise, had been the long-suffering victims of sanctioned social, economic, and political oppression. The term "African-American," in a similarly timely fashion, also linked oppressed African Americans with black South Africans, who were in the final throes of the war against apartheid.

Referred to as the "1989 cultural offensive to build an African-American identity," the campaign to replace "black" with "African-American" was spearheaded by Rev. Jesse Jackson and was intended to strengthen the link between blacks in Africa and those in America. In 1988, at the time of his bid for presidential candidacy, Jackson argued before several hundred attendees at a PUSH (People United to Save Humanity) meeting that the word "black" was no longer tenable, because the skin color of Africans in the diaspora varied from white to tan to brown to black and everything in between. After all, "black" was a racial rather than cultural designation, and cultural identity was, in fact, what African Americans ultimately shared. In response to the Jackson campaign, by the end of 1989 the major black press and sociopolitical organizations had officially adopted "African-American."

Despite widespread acceptance of the African-American designation, there remain dissenters who feel that the use of the word "African" is misleading. Critics argue that the unique culture created by the descendants of Africans in America has little or nothing to do with Africa today. They reason that the African component of the African-American experience is an artificial construct, a myth of the motherland created by a group that has little or no firsthand knowledge of its African origins (unlike more recent African and Afro-Caribbean immigrants, who are only first- or second-generation Americans). This is not to suggest that "old" African Americans (descended from the slave-era population) are any less culturally unique than "new" African Americans (recent immigrants). However, the former's identity is a product of the group's multicentury history as an oppressed minority in America. Complicating the discussion is the fact that the growing numbers of African and Afro-Caribbean immigrants themselves have vastly differing cultural practices, depending on their country of origin.

African immigrant trends aside, the mutable identity of "old" (or *anciens*, to use a term popularized during the Haitian Revolution) African Americans continues to evolve. Prior and subsequent to the turn of the New Millennium, the terms "biracial," "multiracial," and "mixed-race" came into common use. Many African Americans chose to assert a fact that has long been true of America's black population: they are a mixture, both genetically and culturally, of black and white, African and European. Resulting from centuries of institutionalized slave rape as well as consensual sexual encounters between the races, nearly one-third of African Americans whose DNA has been tested have been proven to be, at least in part, of European ancestry. Of the total population of African Americans, it is estimated that the great majority have no less than 12 percent European ancestry. Of this group, 20 percent are estimated to be one-quarter to one-half white.

A shift in perception toward a more inclusive and complex definition of what it means to be African-American is evident in the art of the Afrofuturist Movement (see Chapter 14). Its exponents prefer to question rather than to define issues of race, and to express shared human experience across ethnic boundaries. This mutability was most eloquently expressed in the 2013 Los Angeles Museum of Contemporary Art traveling exhibition *Blues for Smoke*, a collection of works of art by artists "across race and generations," all of whom were inspired by a single theme—the blues—as both a musical and conceptual phenomenon. *Blues for Smoke* artists were given the freedom to respond to the exhibit's theme in any way they chose. They could interpret the blues as an expression of African-American culture, American culture, or an individual artist's response to the music.

Whether the term "black," "African-American," or some as-yet-unidentified designation will take precedence in the years to come is anyone's guess. The decision to use "African-American" to describe the content of this book errs on the side of caution. It also acknowledges President Obama's preference for the term because it so aptly describes his white American and black African parentage. Nevertheless, throughout the pages of this book, a fluidity of descriptive terms has been employed, depending on the era and the content being addressed, and indicative of the changeling history of African-American-ness.

ACKNOWLEDGMENTS

The publication of *African-American Art: A Visual and Cultural History* was made possible by the generous support of a great many artists, collectors, galleries, and museums, to whom I would like to express my heartfelt appreciation. Also vital to the production of this book was my colleague Dr. Benjamin Bierman (who first brought my proposal for *African-American Art: A Visual and Cultural History* to the attention of Oxford University Press) and Oxford University Press executive editor Richard Carlin, who so graciously embraced the idea of this book, and who has supported my endeavors throughout this project. Also at the Press I wish to thank assistant editor Meredith Keffer, permissions coordinator Natalie Russell, senior production editor Barbara Mathieu, and copyeditor Laura Wilmot. As always, the love of my family sustains me—and I would like to thank my brother, Duane Farrington, and my sisters, Dr. Leslie Farrington-Griggs, Denise Farrington, and Constance Delaigle, for always standing by me. Finally, my deepest gratitude goes to William Mazzella for his steadfast love and support.

Additional support for this project has come from many quarters, including the following, to whom I extend my sincere thanks:

Laurie Adams
Norma Broude
Andrea Barnwell Brownlee
Cynthia Collins
CUNY Research Foundation
Gwendolyn H. Everett
Freida High
John Jay College
Amy Kirschke
Akua McDaniel
Susy Mendes
PSC-CUNY
Faith Ringgold
Moira Roth
Beverly Guy Sheftal
Marta Reid Stewart
Roberto Visani

I also wish to thank the manuscript reviewers: W. Ian Bourland, Maryland Institute College of Art; Lana A. Burgess, University of South Carolina; Alison C. Fleming, Winston-Salem State University; Denise Rogers, San Diego Mesa College; Paul Niell, University of North Texas; Naurice Frank Woods, University of North Carolina, Greesnboro; and three anonymous reviewers.

AFRICAN-AMERICAN ART

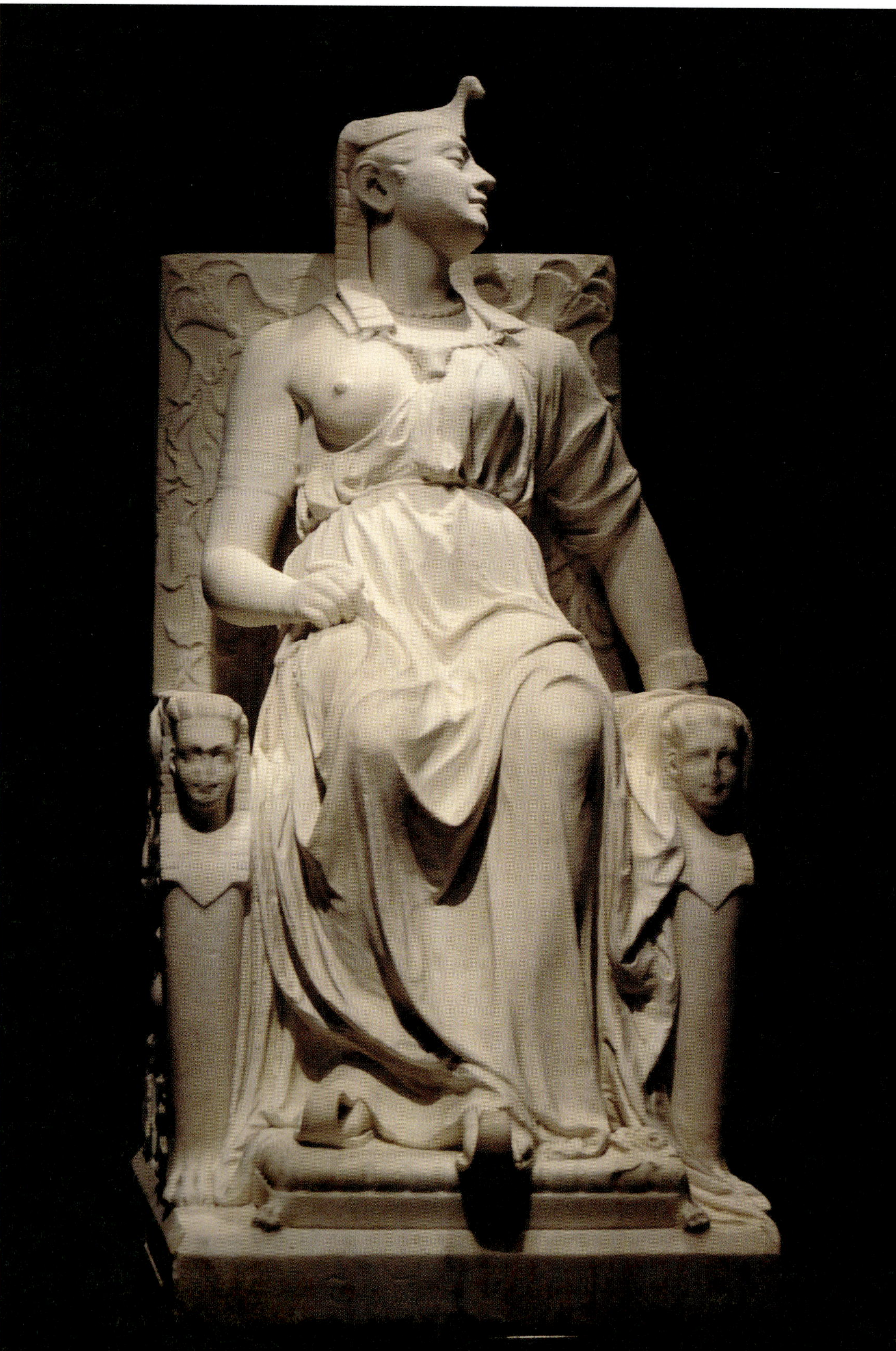

THE ART OF PERCEPTION: HOW ART COMMUNICATES

1

In order to study art, you must first understand that art is a language—a visual language with the power to impart information with as much insight and complexity as written or verbal language. From the icons on our computers to the video games that occupy our free time, and from the movies, news programs, and television shows that we watch to the visual realities that play out before our eyes—"live"—every day, we are constantly looking. But although we may be *looking*, we are not necessarily *seeing*. As one of the only fields of study devoted entirely to analyzing visual images and objects, art is vital in developing our ability to critically analyze and understand what we see.

THE PRIMARY SOURCE

Visual literacy, as the phrase suggests, describes the ability to "read" images—that is, to understand how images communicate and what they are saying. Art, as a nuanced and complex visual language, has the potential to speak volumes about the history, experiences, culture, and philosophies of artists and of their societies. Indeed, in many cases, art provides us with as much, or more, information about human history than written language. What we know about ancient Egyptian society, religion, politics, and history, for example, is imparted to us through architectural monuments—pyramids and temples; through sculpture, both **in-the-round** and in **relief**; and through **hieroglyphics**. The visual art of ancient Egypt is the **primary source**—a source of information that has not been altered—from which historians have gleaned considerable knowledge about the worldview of this venerable African culture. The term "primary source" refers specifically to original and unmodified objects, documents, or other materials produced by a particular culture at a particular time and place. Historians routinely study primary sources such as works of art in order to best understand a given time, place, and ethos.

As unmodified and unfiltered **texts** (objects or documents that communicate information), primary sources have the potential to provide the most accurate and direct information about the people who produced them. Examples of primary sources include original plays, law codes, letters, interviews, and, of course, works of art. Primary source documents stand in stark contrast to **secondary sources**, which alter, adulterate, extract from, expand on, or in some way modify the primary source. This gives the visual arts a distinct advantage over the written word, because art, by nature, is almost always a primary source, existing principally in its original form.

◀ Edmonia Lewis, *Death of Cleopatra,* 1876, marble.

Smithsonian American Art Museum, gift of the Historical Society of Forest Park, IL. Photo: Caroline Léna Becker. Creative Commons, CC 1.0 Universal Domain Dedication

Even this book—which relays the ideas of other historians, scientists, authors, and artists—must be considered a secondary source. It is redeemed, however, by the inclusion of accurate images of the artwork—the primary sources—in question, which readers may examine to determine the validity of the related discussions. Although they are not the original works themselves, reproductions offer a relatively unadulterated view of the primary source. Whenever possible, however, it is imperative to view original works of art in person (in museums, galleries, and public and private collections). In situ, one is able to experience the scale of the artwork and examine its textures, colors, brushstrokes, and so on, with the naked eye rather than through a reproduction. One can compare this experience (or lack thereof) to hearing a recording of a concert versus experiencing a live musical performance; the former cannot compare to the latter.

A similar conundrum occurs with the study of African-American visual culture, which has historically been disseminated via a particular type of secondary source: the media. As most of us are aware, media outlets are able to manipulate our perceptions of both people and events by selective omission, inclusion, and emphasis or de-emphasis of subject matter and imagery. In the United States, this phenomenon is especially evident in representations of Americans of African descent. Because society gleans most of its perceived insights into the "black experience" from the media, and because the vast majority of media outlets are neither owned nor controlled by African Americans, the information imparted by these conduits is suspect.

Persuasively exaggerated and distorted pop culture images—from the **Jim Crow** caricatures of past centuries to the gangster rappers of late 20th-century music videos—have made it virtually impossible for the world to perceive African Americans in any holistic or unbiased way. The result is a skewed vision of African Americans as seen through the eyes of others. The drawback of learning about African-American (or any) culture through representations created by others is that one's knowledge is derived from an illegitimate secondary source. The only authentic sources for information about African Americans—that is, the only true primary sources—are African Americans themselves. Because it has been established that art provides a nearly foolproof form of primary source documentation, we turn to art for knowledge about the "black experience" in America. Hence, just as we study Greek sculpture and architecture to understand classical Greek culture, Egyptian pyramids and monuments for insights into the ancient Egyptian psyche, and Gothic architecture for an understanding of medieval Europe, we study African-American art to better know African Americans.

HOW TO LOOK AT ART: A CASE STUDY

Just as there are preferred sources—namely, art—from which to glean insight into human culture, there are also tried-and-true methods for analyzing those sources. The field of art history offers several acknowledged methodologies or modes of analysis that enable viewers to accurately "read" works of art—to understand their meaning and how that meaning is constructed. The two most salient of these methods are iconography and formalism. **Iconography** (from the Greek word *eikon* for "image" and *graphe* or "writing") is the study of the content, meaning, and symbolism of a work of art—in other words, the story behind the image. Formal analysis, or **formalism**, is the study of the composition or design of an art object. The former method informs the latter and vice versa; that is to say, the way a work of art is composed or designed determines how and what it will communicate, and the information an artist hopes to impart determines how he or she will design a work.

In addition to formalism and iconography, there exist four more key methods of art analysis:

1. *Biography* (including autobiography) informs and extrapolates from works of art using facts from the artist's life.
2. *Psychoanalysis* attempts to access the subconscious agenda of the artist via methods of image and dream analysis developed by Freud, Lacan, Winnicott, and other influential psychoanalysts.
3. *Contextual analyses* consider gender, sociopolitics, economics, ethnicity, and culture when investigating the meaning of an artwork.
4. *Semiotics* rejects the importance of the artist in conferring meaning. Instead, this method seeks to identify universal meaning within an image that exists independently of the image itself and is defined by a broadly conceived "social consciousness."

Any one, or combination, of these methods may be applied to a single work of art. The more methods one employs, the more insights one might potentially gain into a work of art.

Iconography

Each method employed by art historians reveals something different about a work of art. To demonstrate how various methods can be applied to a single work of art, let us examine the sculpture *Death of Cleopatra* (1876), by 19th-century Neoclassical sculptor Edmonia Lewis (see chapter-opening image). This work is ideal for iconographic analysis because there is a well-known story behind the image: the life of the Egyptian queen Cleopatra and her death by suicide in 30 B.C.E. An iconographic reading of the sculpture tells us that it is a portrayal of the famed queen at the moment of her death. This identification is confirmed by several tells that are visible in the work. For example, Cleopatra's identity as a pharaoh of Ptolemaic descent is made evident by her Greek-style clothing; the manner of her death is made apparent by her bared right breast, where the asp (visible in Cleopatra's right hand) has bitten and poisoned her; and her pharaonic identity is apparent in her Egyptian-style crown, jewelry, and elaborate throne.

A comparison of multiple sculptures by Lewis has the potential to lead to more profound conclusions than does the examination of a single work alone. We could potentially compare Lewis's *Death of Cleopatra* to her other sculptures that depict legendary historical figures, such as Lewis's representations of the Native-American leader Hiawatha, whose biography (like that of Cleopatra) is shrouded in mystery and myth. Cleopatra used her intellect and charisma to refute the military might of Rome, to protect her kingdom, and to maintain her political status. This can be compared to Hiawatha's legend, in which he, a renowned pacifist, also used charisma and diplomacy to unite the Iroquois nations. An iconological study (analyzing more than one work of art in tandem) of both sculptural subjects implies an interest on Lewis's part that would not be as apparent if only one work were studied.

Lewis sculpted another related work: a portrait bust of Henry Wadsworth Longfellow, author of the 1855 epic poem *The Song of Hiawatha*. The bust was carved while Longfellow was visiting the artist's expatriate hometown of Rome in 1872. Like Hiawatha, Longfellow, too, was a pacifist, and one can assume that Lewis's interests and those of the poet are related. An iconological study of Lewis's three subjects—Hiawatha, Cleopatra, and Longfellow—reveals Lewis's admiration for persuasive and powerful leaders, and her interest in pacifism and nonviolent political negotiation. The larger the program of works studied, the greater their revelatory potential. This makes iconology a profound and in-depth form of iconography.

Formalism

Formal analysis entails an examination of the material and design elements of a work of art. The materials or media (medium, in the singular) that are used to make three-dimensional works may include marble (used by Lewis in her *Death of Cleopatra*), granite and other stones, bronze and various metals, clay, wood, plastic and other synthetic materials, fiber, and, indeed, almost any solid material. Two-dimensional works of art (drawings, paintings, collages, photographs, and prints) may be created on paper, canvas, wood panels, walls (as is the case with murals), or other surfaces, using pencil, chalk, crayon, ink, and all manner of paints, from oil to watercolor to acrylic. Artistic compositions or designs created using the various media comprise formal elements including line, shape, space, volume, mass, texture, light (either actual or implied), color, **symmetrical** and **asymmetrical balance**, proportion, pattern, and rhythm.

In the case of *Death of Cleopatra*, a formal analysis would entail a discussion of such elements as the following:

1. The artist's emphasis on verticality in the lines of the throne and the powerful neck of the deceased queen
2. The **closed form** or shape (lacking in open, extending, or **negative space**)
3. The massive size and volume of the figure
4. The smooth texture of the marble
5. The effect of light on the gleaming white surface of the stone
6. The symmetry of the design, resulting from the centering of Cleopatra's body and the flanking stone heads of the throne

7. The idealized proportions of the figure (based on the classical Greek models)
8. The repeated curvilinear patterns incised in relief into the chair

Taken as a whole, these formal elements create the style of the work. In this case, Lewis's figurative style is Neoclassical due to its similarity to the art of classical Greece and Rome. Neoclassicism in the visual arts began in France in the 1760s and is marked by such features as **naturalism** (also referred to as **illusionism** or **representational art**), symmetry, decorative austerity, the use of white marble as the preferred sculptural medium, and the dispassionate nature of the presentation. Also indicative of Neoclassicism is the artist's use of **wet drapery** to reveal the contours of the figure and the classical Roman features of the queen's face (borrowed by Lewis from antique Roman coins).

The formal elements of a work of art almost invariably affect its iconographic meaning. For example, in *Death of Cleopatra*, the verticality and mass of the composition serve as metaphors for the rigidity and power of the pharaoh herself. The closed form of the figure suggests the timelessness of the queen's history, legend, and culture. The use of polished white marble and figurative naturalism is reminiscent of ancient Greek statuary and hence of the time in which the queen lived. Thus, Lewis has made several formal choices that deepen the iconographic meaning of the sculpture and add to the viewer's experience.

Biography

Biographical and autobiographical analyses take into account those aspects of an artwork that reveal something about the artist's life (and sometimes the life of those associated with the work, such as the **patron** or **sitter**). Knowledge of the biography of the artist can lead to a better understanding of the art. Lewis's interest in Cleopatra's difficulties as a Greek ruler of an African land under Roman rule is enriched by the knowledge that Lewis, too, lived as an outsider in a foreign land (an American expatriate in Rome). Also like Cleopatra, she functioned as a woman in a man's world: the world of the professional artist. Other biographical information is equally telling, such as the fact that Lewis was of mixed race—African and Native-American—a detail that informs her Native-American sculptures. In addition, Lewis's struggles against racial bias and violence while a student at Oberlin College in Ohio (discussed in chapter 4) support the theory that she was a pacifist, augment our understanding of her pacifist works, and inform an understanding of her famed 1867 abolitionist sculpture, *Forever Free* (see the chapter-opening image in Chapter 4).

Semiotics

Semiotics is the study of signs (symbols within a work of art). A sign includes a **signifier** (the form the sign takes) and that which is **signified** (the meaning of the signifier). Semiotics studies both the significance of a sign and how that significance is constructed. Initially intended as a way to study the changeable relationship between words and ideas, semiotics has expanded to include such signs as sounds, gestures, objects, and images, as well as their signifiers. Simply put, a sign is anything that stands for something other than its literal self. For example, the "buster" sign is comprised of two parts: the signifier—a red circle with a backslash line through it—and that which it signifies—"no," or "prohibited." Even the letters *N-O*, which constitute two signs, when placed together signify a negative response to a particular statement or situation. A grouping of many signs together creates a text, and a text is anything that imparts information while existing separately from its maker (a book, a sculpture, a piece of music, a film, etc.).

A key classification of semiotics, known as **structuralism**, identifies broadly understood signs in cultural expression, beyond those which the creator may have intended. Structuralism is at play in Lewis's *Death of Cleopatra*, which can be interpreted as a text made up of many signs. For instance, the crown of the queen signifies royalty in a broad sense (rather than "Cleopatra" in a narrow sense) because crowns, in general, signify kingship. The same can be said of the relief carving of a griffin—a lion with an eagle's wings—on the side of the throne, which signifies kingship because both lions and eagles are considered the kings of their species. Furthermore, unlike formalism and style, which group works of art together based on appearance, semiotics classifies art based on signs. For example, Lewis's sculpture is identified as Neoclassical because it shares various formal elements with other works of this style and time period. Alternatively, semiotics would link Lewis's *Death of Cleopatra* to other depictions of royalty, from any time period and in any medium or style, so long as the works share in common certain signs, such as crowns, thrones, and other references to kingship.

Another sign is the bared breast of Cleopatra, which, while iconographically suggestive of the location where the asp bit the pharaoh, from a semiotic vantage point might also signify motherhood and fertility, even though this was not likely the artist's intent. Indeed, a group of French scholars known as **Post-Structuralists**, who came to prominence in the 1960s, entirely rejected the intentions of the artist as a source of study. Post-Structuralists believe that the viewer's perceived understanding of a work of art—not the artist's intended meaning—is of primary importance. The artist is, in fact, seen by Post-Structuralists as an unreliable source for discerning meaning in an artwork, because any perception of the artist's objectives is a construction rather than a fixed and discernible reality. Post-Structuralists theorize that the relationship between a text or work of art and its meaning is subjective and eminently changeable over time and place, as well as with each viewer. For example, one viewer might interpret Lewis's sculpture as a representation of female empowerment, whereas another might view it as a representation of death and defeat.

A variant of semiotics known as **deconstruction** takes Post-Structuralism a step further. The goal of deconstruction is to broaden rather than limit meaning, to question rather than to assert signification. A deconstructionist reading of Lewis's *Death of Cleopatra* would look for those signs (such as her bared breast) that contradict the convention of the queen's royal and empowered status. Her bared breast might signify vulnerability rather than power, motherhood rather than kingship, or femininity rather than masculinity.

Psychoanalysis

The psychoanalytic method of art analysis shares several points of interest with semiotics. An area of psychology developed by Freud in the 1890s, psychoanalysis is well suited to the study of visual art because it depends on images as primary investigative tools—in particular, dream imagery or subconscious visions that have the capacity to reveal much about the dreamer's (and artist's) psyche. Psychoanalysts reason that the instinctive motivations of artists (whose very modi operandi are predicated on the creation of imagery) may well be revealed in their art.

Psychoanalysis, therefore, views a work of art as having the capacity to tell us much about the artist (and his or her patron and culture, as perceived by the artist's mind). If one were to psychoanalyze Lewis's *Death of Cleopatra*, one would look for elements that shed light on the artist's subconscious state of being. The most obvious element, in this instance, is the poisonous asp, which is held firmly in Cleopatra's right hand, rather than being curled around her wrist or against her bared breast, as had been a common convention for centuries.

The snake may represent, among many concepts, fertility and sexual desire, as both a phallic and umbilical form; rebirth, due to its ability to shed its skin; and medicine or evil, because of the positive and negative chemical properties, respectively, of its venom. Snakes appear as metaphors for these and other universal ideas such as guardianship, retribution, and infinity in the beliefs of cultures from around the globe and throughout the ages—from Asian to Nordic climes, from Native America to Mayan societies, and from ancient Egyptian to Christian belief systems.

If viewed as a phallic symbol, Lewis's snake could be interpreted as a symbol of the artist's ability to control (because her hand grips and thus controls the snake) and possibly avert a phallic/sexual assault. This interpretation is supported by our knowledge of Lewis's biography (essential to a psychoanalytic reading): she was kidnapped and brutalized by a group of white male bigots in Ohio in January of 1862. One might alternatively interpret Lewis's snake as being symbolic of her own phallic or masculine energy as a sculptor—considered then a man's profession—because Cleopatra holds the snake in the same hand with which Lewis sculpts. This leads to another interpretive methodology: contextual analysis, a form of investigation that considers such issues as feminism and race.

Contextual Analyses

Contextual approaches to art analysis take into consideration the political, socioeconomic, ethnocultural, and sexual milieu in which an artwork is created and/or consider these contexts as lenses through which to view a work. Political analysis explores such concerns as the politics of the artist (for example, Lewis's perceived pacifism) or pivotal political events that occurred in tandem with the making of a work of art or the development of an artist (such as the Civil War and post-Reconstruction eras, in Lewis's case). A socioeconomic approach would concern itself with the financial and class status of the artist, her audience, and her patrons, or even the status of her subject (such as Cleopatra's royal and even sacred standing in Egyptian society).

Ethnocultural analysis would take into account Lewis's genealogy and upbringing as both Native- and African-American. Sexual or gender analysis would acknowledge the artist's sexual orientation, as this might have influenced her art; or it might re-examine a work of art from the point of view of feminism. This latter approach—the re-examining and revising of past conventions and assumptions about a work of art or artist—is known as **revisionism**. A feminist revision of Lewis's sculpture, for example, would include a discussion of the artist's gender alignment. Some historians have speculated that Lewis was a lesbian, because she never married, did not have children, was reported to cross-dress, and was associated with a circle of American expatriate lesbians in Rome. Such a reading would explore the possible effects of Lewis's lifestyle on her representation of Cleopatra.

Integral to the study of African-American art is a type of ethnocultural contextual analysis that considers the construct of racial identity in art analysis. **Racial iconography**, as this method is termed, is especially relevant to the study of African-American art because race has historically affected so many aspects of African-American existence: from cultural and religious practices to social and economic standing, and from the microcosm of private and personal life to the macrocosm of public and political life. We've already discussed Lewis's interest in black and Native-American subjects. Other potential discussions in this vein would include the artist's decision to leave the United States after a period of racial persecution (and the effect of that decision on her art) and her reputation abroad as an exotic persona who many believed (because of her race and her gender) was perpetrating a hoax and was not, in fact, responsible for sculpting her own art. (Lewis responded to these charges by giving live demonstrations of her carving skills in her Rome studio.)

Although racial iconography is, without doubt, an essential tool for understanding the content of much African-American art, as well as the struggles of artists of color, it remains only one of many ways in which to analyze art. For many African-American artists today, race has become a social construct that they may choose to embrace or reject and is not, they feel, essential to an appreciation of their art. Indeed, numerous African-American artists today much prefer to be known for their art rather than their race.

In the chapters to follow, equal emphasis is placed on all of these methodologies, to obtain the most exhaustive understanding of African-American art, history, and culture.

Summary

Art, like writing, is a language. Understanding that language is defined as visual literacy and is vital in our contemporary culture, where so much information is exchanged through images. The best sources for accurate cultural and historical information are primary ones such as original works of art or unaltered texts, because these are direct reflections of their makers. Likewise, information about African-American culture can most accurately be gleaned from art and other cultural productions created by African Americans themselves. A number of methods are used to analyze visual art. Among these are

- Iconography: the study of meaning
- Formalism: the study of composition and design
- Biography: analysis of an artwork through awareness of the artist's life
- Psychology: studying the artist's psyche through his or her art
- Contextual methods: interpreting art through the lenses of gender, race, politics, economics, or society
- Semiotics: the analysis of universal signs and symbols within an artwork

Key Terms

asymmetrical balance: the property of an artwork that is irregular or unbalanced in composition or form

closed form: a self-contained shape or composition that does not extend into the surrounding space

deconstruction: questioning accepted meanings of an artwork and seeing multiple interpretations as equally valid

formalism: refers to the design or composition of an artwork

hieroglyphics: an ancient Egyptian alphabet consisting of letters and icons, or picture symbols

iconography: the study of the meaning of art and artistic symbols

icons: symbolic images

illusionism: see naturalism

in the round: sculpture created for viewing from all sides

Jim Crow: refers to the era in the 1880s and 1890s when a series of southern U.S. state laws were passed to enforce racial segregation

naturalism: realistic portrayals of forms and figures; art that replicates forms in nature or that creates an impression or illusion of physical reality, particularly two-dimensional art that simulates the three-dimensional world

negative space: areas of a composition that are left untouched, empty, or open

patron: a financial supporter of the arts or of a particular artist

Post-Structuralism: a philosophy that sees social, behavioral, moral, verbal, and visual structures as changeable constructions rather than fixed truths or realities

primary source: unaltered original, firsthand, or direct evidence concerning a specific topic

racial iconography: the study of racial meaning and symbolism in art

relief: sculpture that projects from, or is carved into a flat two-dimensional background surface

representational art: see naturalism

revisionism: the revising or modifying of previously accepted theories, principles, or viewpoints

secondary source: a document or object that provides secondhand knowledge of an artwork or topic

semiotics: the study of signs and symbols, and their meaning and construction, within a universal rather than narrowly defined or individual context

signified: the object of the meaning of a symbol or sign

signifier: a sign or symbol

sitter: one who poses for a portrait

structuralism: the analysis of cultural structures such as art, language, literature, anthropology, and society through an examination of binaries or opposing elements within each structure

symmetrical balance: balance created when two sides or halves of a form or composition are equivalent or corresponding

text: in semiotic terms, any object or document that communicates information and exists independently of its creator

visual literacy: the ability to identify, interpret, and evaluate information presented in image form

wet drapery: a sculptural technique developed by the ancient Greeks that creates the appearance of clothing clinging to the body

Questions for Further Study and Discussion

1. Identify several examples of visual communication and translate their messages into words.
2. List several visual messages you received today and describe what type of information they imparted to you.
3. Identify a primary source document that has been dramatically altered in subsequent versions. Detail the alterations and discuss why they might have been made.
4. Select a political event or crime recently covered in the news media. Review how this event is represented in two or more different news media outlets. Discuss these differences in representation and how they might reveal the agenda of each media outlet.
5. List several stereotypes associated with African Americans. Then list several characteristics of an African American whom you know personally. Compare the lists and discuss how they differ.

6. Choose a work of art by an African-American artist who has a documented biography or autobiography. How might elements of the biography enhance an understanding of the artwork?
7. Debate: Should racial identity be integral to the study of African-American art? Why and why not?
8. Identify which terminology best describes your ethnicity or cultural orientation. Discuss why you prefer the term you chose.

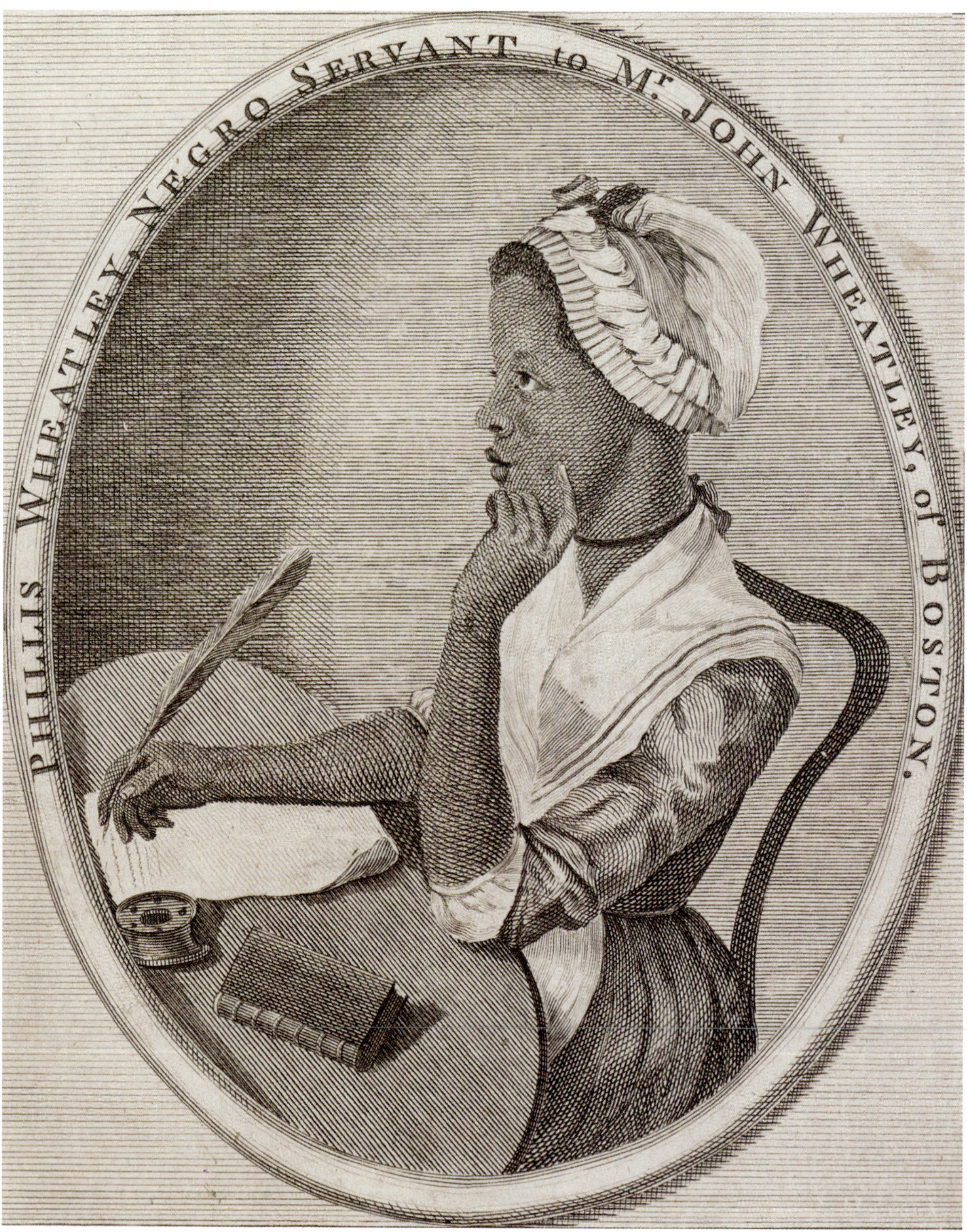
PHILLIS WHEATLEY, NEGRO SERVANT to Mr. JOHN WHEATLEY, of BOSTON.

ART AND DESIGN IN THE COLONIAL ERA

2

African artists first arrived in America in the 1500s. The earliest record of a black presence in America dates to 1526, when a group of African captives was brought from Hispaniola (present-day Haiti and the Dominican Republic) to coastal South Carolina or to Georgia's Sapelo Sound. Over the next century, a quarter of a million European settlers came to the Americas determined to colonize the New World. With them, they brought to the Native-American population death in millions from disease and violence. The reduction in the indigenous population created a demand for a massive, low-cost labor force. This need fueled the transatlantic slave trade, which grew exponentially. No less than 12.5 million Africans were displaced to the Caribbean and North, South, and Central America between 1500 and the 1860s. West-central Africa yielded the largest number (5.7 million), followed by Benin (2 million), Biafra (1.6 million), Ghana (1.2 million), Senegambia (755,500), southeastern Africa (543,000), Sierra Leone (390,000), and the Ivory Coast (337,000). Of this number, an estimated 1.5 million lost their lives during the grueling 3- to 12-week journey across the Atlantic known as the **Middle Passage**. African deaths were caused by everything from murder, starvation, and disease to drowning, suicide, and suffocation in the cramped, unsanitary, and nearly airless cargo holds of the slave ships.

In the United States alone, the African population reached more than 4 million by the 1860 census: 12 percent of the country's entire population and 90 percent of all Africans in America were enslaved. Restricted by their enslaved status, black artists in America were limited to making utilitarian art objects, for the most part, until well into the 18th century. Their creative output included handwoven baskets, ceramics, metalwork, musical instruments, clothing, textiles, wood carvings, furniture, and architecture. Most of these categories—with the exception of architecture—have historically been considered craftwork: that is to say, "low" rather than "high" art, requiring technical skill but not necessarily artistic genius. As a result, until the late 20th century, much of the art produced by enslaved Africans was marginalized by scholars who considered craftwork unworthy of in-depth art historical research, discussion, and analysis.

In the 1980s, however, the "decorative arts"—the design and decoration of functional objects—came to be reclassified as equivalent in aesthetic value to painting and sculpture. Played out in museums, galleries, and on the pages of art journals, the high-low debate questioned not only the notion of so-called high art but also the factors of gender and class that had shaped its perception. For example, quilts, lace, clothing, dolls, and other "domestic" objects—because they were produced in the main by women—were

◀ Scipio Moorhead, *Phillis Wheatley* (Drawing Engraved by Archibald Bell), 1773, engraving.

Library of Congress, Rare Books and Special Collections Division, illus. in PS866.W5 1773, LOC Catalog Number 2002712199.

considered women's work and thus devalued. Similarly, art created by those who were poor and untrained (including the enslaved) was deemed "folk," "naïve," "vernacular," or "outsider" art and thus also underappreciated and marginalized.

This was not the case in traditional sub-Saharan Africa, where Western hierarchies of high and low art did not apply. Despite variations in style and media from one area, group, and time period to another, art was regarded, by and large, as functional and integral to life, rather than as exclusive and isolated from it. Traditional African art, by its very nature, was utilitarian. Masks and figure sculptures—key forms of African art—were created for religious, civil, political, and social purposes. Textiles, vestments, vessels, instruments, headrests, thrones, jewelry, staffs, doors, and a multitude of other objects were woven, painted, printed, carved, molded, and designed for both use and beauty. Multiple art objects were often used in tandem during ceremonial performances such as youth initiations, weddings, funerals, the conferring of rank, and religious services wherein utility and aesthetics were not mutually exclusive. African gender-based labor divisions also tended to differ from those in European society. For instance, West African men wove textiles using portable foot-pedal looms, whereas women dominated ceramic production, masonry, and, in nomadic societies, tent construction.

AFRICANISMS IN THE NEW WORLD

Hailing from so many geographical locations was a broad spectrum of cultural groups—the Akan, Bakongo, Baoule, Beti-Pahuin, Dan, Edo, Ewe, Fon, Igbo, Mande, Mandinka, Mende, Senufo, and Yoruba—who brought with them to America a rich aesthetic tradition and wide-ranging artistic practices. However, western aesthetic standards were applied to African artists once they reached the New World, as were American Western divisions of labor, and slave-produced artifacts were seen as functional objects of no particular artistic value. Yet despite being dislocated from their homeland and subject to rigidly enforced **slave codes** that restricted or forbid African cultural practices such as the creation of art objects, enslaved artists in America retained a great deal of their cultural memory and creative skills, which they expressed through the utilitarian objects that they were obliged to make. Slave ship rolls and insurance records indicate that the enslaved Americans came from more than a dozen countries in West and Central Africa.

Architecture

African traditions and practices were nowhere more evident than in colonial architecture. Africans were a driving force in the design and construction of both domestic and public architecture during the colonial era. This was especially true in Louisiana and South Carolina, where Africans were the majority population, and in Georgia, Alabama, Florida, Maryland, Mississippi, North Carolina, and Virginia, where they were a significant minority of 40 percent. From entire building projects to smaller individual tasks such as foundation digging, brick making and bricklaying, carpentry, window glazing, and chimney building, black workers left their mark on the

American architectural landscape. In fact, they were the labor force behind the construction of both the White House and the Capitol Building.

Africans constructed Spanish-Colonial buildings as early as the 1560s in St. Augustine, Florida—a mecca of the Spanish slave trade and the location of the first documented slave birth on January 3, 1606. The Spanish-Colonial style comprised "board houses" (one-room, thatched-roof bungalows) and whitewashed two-storied "common houses" that featured airy verandas. Enslaved laborers toiled in Maryland and Virginia on southern colonial-style buildings, marked by large parlors and central corridors. Africans also built French-Colonial structures with steeply pitched roofs and open **galleries** in Louisiana and along the Mississippi as far north as Missouri.

Often left to their own devices, enslaved builders were sometimes able to pattern their architectural creations after African designs. West and Central African architectural forms were first introduced into Brazil and Hispaniola (where similar house construction still exists today) by way of the Portuguese slave industry in the 1600s.These forms spread to the French, English, and Spanish colonies of North America by the next century. Over time, their designs—an aggregate of African and European features—became standard in many parts of the United States. Built in the 1790s or early 1800s, the Bequette-Ribault House (Figure 2.1) on St. Mary's Road in Ste. Geneviève, Missouri, is one of the oldest remaining examples of a French-Colonial-style home that incorporates architectural elements from West and Central Africa. Built as the residence of French Canadian settler Jean Baptiste Bequette (whose slaves lived and worked on the abutting property), the house is typical of the **creole** style. Constructed of rot-resistant red cedar timbers that are sealed with mud and grass **chinking** or ***bousillage***, the house features lime-whitewashed walls fashioned with vertically placed logs (unlike the typical horizontal log cabin style used elsewhere in the colonies). The home integrates a raised floor and pole-support design known as **poteaux-en-terre** (posts-in-earth), which comprises evenly spaced timbers anchored deeply into the earth to support an extended **hipped roof** and to create a 360-degree veranda. The year 1723 marks the earliest recorded poteaux-en-terre structures in the United States. Particularly in the Louisiana Territory, it was used to construct homes, slave quarters, and public buildings alike. The Bequette-Ribault House is one of only three of this type in Ste. Geneviève and five in the country that still stand.

▼ 2.1 *Bequette-Ribault House*, c. 1800. Ste. Geneviève, Missouri.

Photo: Jack E. Boucher, Library of Congress, Prints and Photographs Division, Historic American Buildings Survey HABS MO, 97-SAIGEN,14–18 (CT).

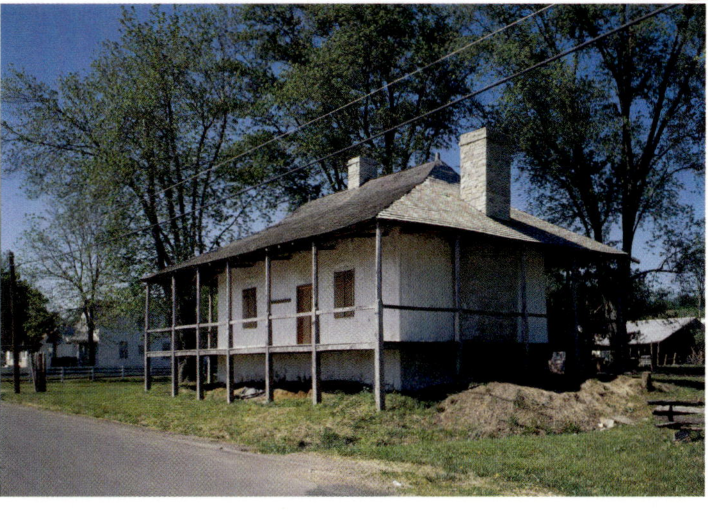

The pyramid shape and extension of the Bequette-Ribault hipped roof can also be seen in the historic Africa House (Figure 2.2) built at about the same time by black slave owner Marie-Thérèse Coincoin (1742–1816). The daughter of enslaved African-born parents, Coincoin (known also as Métoyer) was freed by her owner

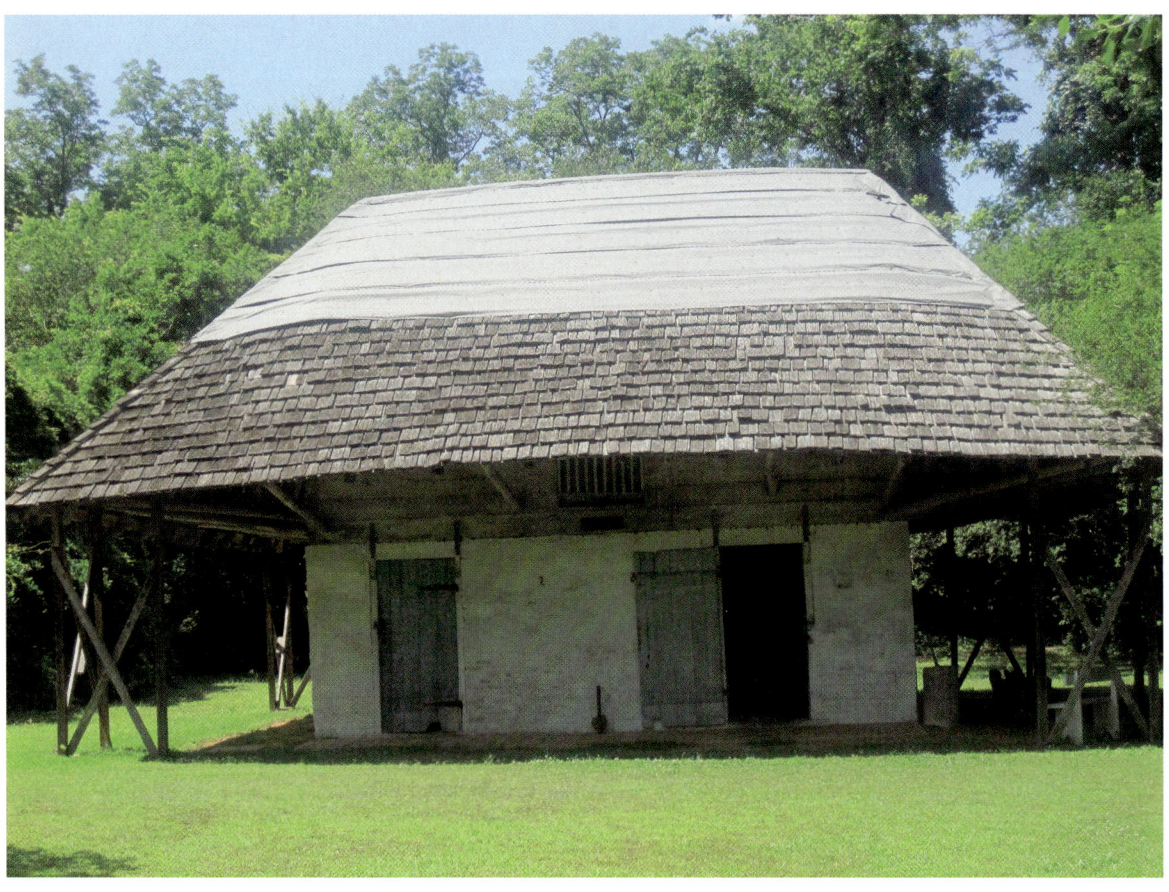

▲ **2.2** *Africa House*, c. 1800. Melrose Plantation, Natchitoches, LA.

Photo: Billy Hathorn, licensed under CC BY-SA 3.0 via Wikimedia Commons.

and paramour, Claude Thomas Pierre Métoyer, in 1778 at the age of 36. Although their affair continued for another decade, the two were never married. During their protracted relationship, Coincoin arranged for Métoyer to free their 10 children as well as her 8 living siblings; he also bequeathed to her 68 acres of land at Isle Breville in Natchitoches Parish, Louisiana. Earning money as a skilled nurse and *médicine* (folk doctor) and later as a tobacco and indigo planter, Coincoin eventually purchased freedom for her three additional elder children from a prior union. Her formidable clan developed into an historical creole Cane River community.

Increasing to 700 acres by the 1790s (and more than100,000 acres by the early 19th century after the bequest of the Métoyer plantation to Marie Thérèse's son Louis), the property was worked by slaves purchased by Coincoin. Although it may seem contradictory, it was accepted practice in the South for freed blacks who could afford to do so, to own slaves of their own. Slave ownership was as much a consequence of economic and class status as it was a racial challenge. In fact, U.S. census records from 1830 indicate that some 3,700 blacks owned as many as 12,000 slaves. Coincoin's slaves built Africa House presumably to her specifications. The structure exhibits elements of both African grassland region architecture and French farmhouse construction—a fusion typical of colonial Louisiana architecture—notably in its wide and steep pyramid (hipped) roof design. Used for storage as well as for the imprisonment of insubordinate slaves, Africa House is constructed of brick and timbers that are chinked with a mixture of animal hair, mud, and moss. It is the only known structure of its particular design in the United States.

African architecture in colonial America often took the form of slave cabins. Although none of the colonial-age cabins are still extant, a number of well-preserved examples from the 19th century exist today. One of the oldest—a rare cabin from the Sea Islands area of South Carolina—is representative of centuries of slave cabin construction (Figure 2.3). Recently donated by the Edisto Island Historic Preservation Society to the Smithsonian Institution's National Museum of African American History and Culture, in 2013 the single-story pine **clapboard** cabin was dismantled at the Point of Pines Plantation on Edisto Island for transport and reconstruction at the museum in Washington, D.C. One of the only surviving such cabins on the plantation, the dwelling appears on an 1851 topographical map and, thus, is dated to the first half of the 19th century.

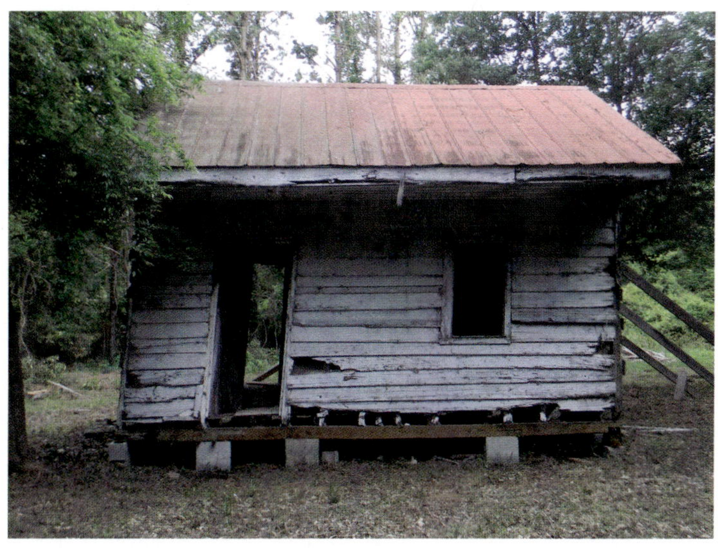

▲ **2.3** *Slave Cabin*, pre-1851. Edisto Island, SC.

Collection of the National Museum of African American History and Culture, Smithsonian Institution, Washington, D.C. Courtesy of the Edisto Island Historic Preservation Society.

The cabin consists of a small living space built on a **tabby foundation** of lime, sand, and crushed oyster shells. It was part of a one-time "street" of 25 such slave homes at Point of Pines. The cabin's most characteristic feature is a deep roof extension that provided shade and protection from the rain for the inhabitants, who performed domestic chores under its eaves. Excavation of the home revealed newspapers stuffed between the pine slats as insulation, a feature that is typical of the **Gullah** tradition (inherited from West Africa) of papering walls and shoes with newsprint. The practice is analogous to the use of a *grigri* (a piece of paper printed with verses from the Qur'an) in Muslim West Africa, particularly Sierra Leone. It was intended to foil evil spirits, who, **Sea Islanders** believed, found it difficult to pass through the printed words. The spare and cramped configuration of the Point of Pines cabin is also a reminder of the brutal conditions under which the thousands of slaves who worked on Edisto Island lived, from its beginnings in 1674 until the outbreak of the Civil War. An octogenarian resident of the plantation site who lived in an identical cabin as late as the 1940s described it (even long after slavery) as "a tough place to live," infested with mosquitos and severely cold during winter nights.

Sculptural Art Forms

Colonial-era African Americas were prolific sculptors who created pewter flatware, clay pipes, earthenware **pipkins**, iron kettles, and untold other useful objects. These skilled artist-craftsmen and craftswomen were of particular value to slave owners because they created items that would otherwise have to be purchased. Their services could also be rented out to the slaveholder's friends, neighbors, and clients who might be in need of specific products. South Carolina colonial governor James Grant noted in 1768, "the Planter has Tradesmen of all kinds in his Gang of Slaves, and 'tis a Rule with them, never to pay Money for what can be made upon their Estates, not a Lock, a Hing [*sic*] or a Nail if they can avoid it."

A common sculptural practice among colonial African Americans was metalwork. Enslaved Africans brought with them to America a 5,000-year-old metallurgical tradition. Bronze casting and ironwork were long established in West and Central Africa, from whence the majority of America's black population emanated. Metal sculptors and blacksmiths represented an honored class in their homelands. The ***cire perdue*** sculptors who serviced Ife and Benin royalty (present-day Nigeria) between 1200 and 1900 were particularly esteemed. Ironworkers contracted by the Edo, Fon, and Yoruba military to equip their armies during the first two centuries of the trans atlantic slave trade were also highly regarded. Blacksmiths were given almost sacred status due to the highly specialized and hazardous nature of their work. They were associated in Yoruba and Bamana cultures with the god of iron and war. In Mande culture, the blacksmith ranked high as a community leader, advisor, and controller of the spiritual energy of metal or *nyama*, from which the society gained its strength and stability.

The status and technical knowledge of the blacksmith was carried forward to colonial America. A late 18th-century wrought-iron figure excavated by anthropologist John Michael Vlach from beneath an African blacksmith's shop in the slave quarters of a plantation in Alexandria, Virginia, showed the technical skill of its unknown maker. The wide-legged and rigidly vertical stance of the figure and its minimalist form implied its sacred origins as a guardian figure and linked it in style with Bamana (Mali) sacred sculpture. African blacksmiths were among the most skilled of all enslaved laborers and, in the Chesapeake area in particular, were allowed to work independently, were given positions of authority, and were sometimes paid for their work.

African metal workers played an integral role in the development of the colonial iron industry. Between 1585, when iron ore was first discovered in the colonies, and the 1770s, North America became the third-largest exporter of iron in the world. The eloquent arabesques of the wrought-iron balconies and gates of Charleston, South Carolina, are reminders of this productive age of American ironwork; and they represent some of the finest existing examples of African-American colonial artistry. Inspired by European imported models, Charleston became a showplace for wrought-iron architectural decoration—much of which was slave made in a city where the black population predominated. A well-preserved example of African-American ironwork can be found at Drayton Hall, near Charleston. Built in 1744 in the Italian **Palladian style**, the structure's central **pedimented** two-story portico and rigid symmetry are counterbalanced by its ironwork details (Figure 2.4).

Drayton Hall is one of the oldest plantation homes in the United States. The surrounding property is also the setting for one of the country's earliest surviving African-American cemeteries—in use before 1790 by the Bowens

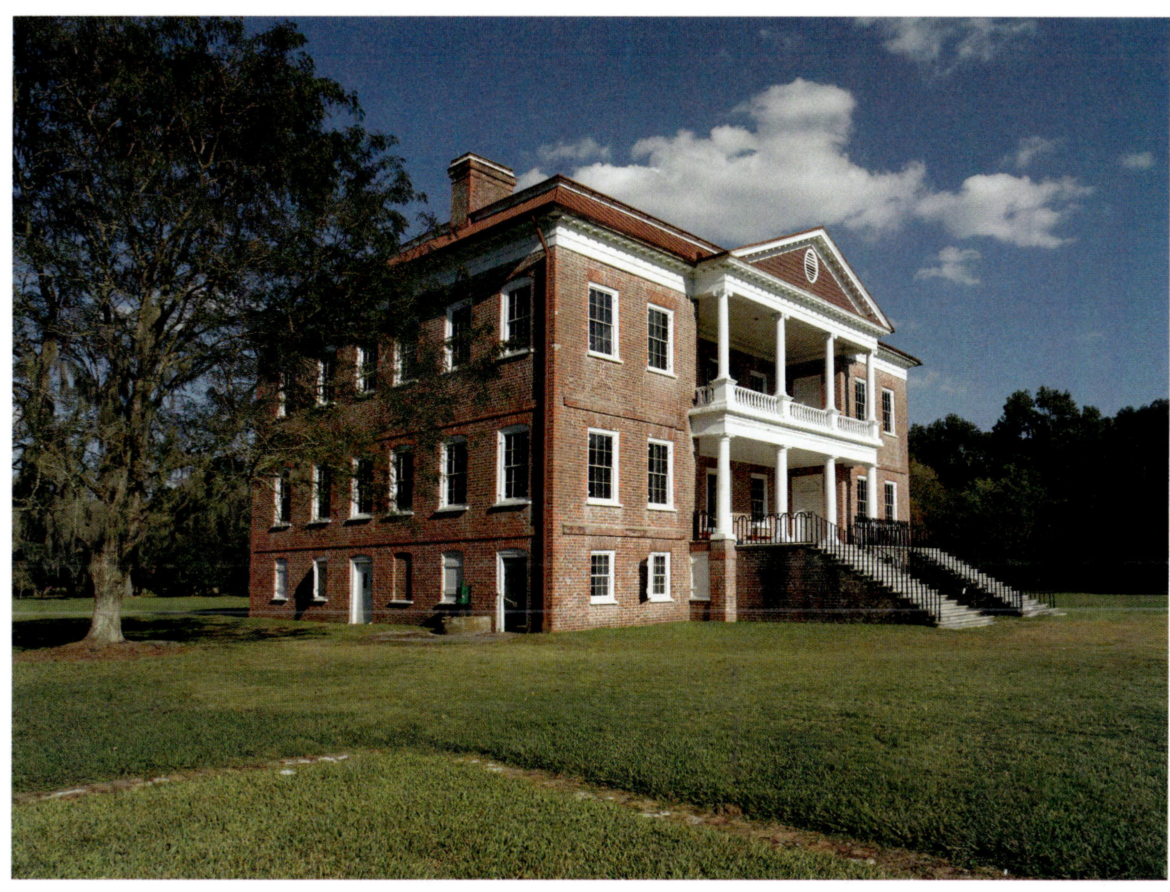

▲ 2.4 *Drayton Hall*, 1744. Charleston, SC.

Carol M. Highsmith Archive, Library of Congress, Prints and Photographs Division.

family (among others), who lived and worked on the plantation for seven generations. Oral tradition indicates that the ancestors of the Bowens family were abducted from Africa to Barbados, where, in the 1670s, they were purchased by Thomas Drayton and transported to South Carolina. Their descendants still resided at Drayton in 1738, when the construction of the house began. The fluid elegance of the wrought iron at Drayton Hall is most evident in the grills of its English-style raised basement (Figure 2.5). This work is typical of grills, railings, gates, and balconies found throughout the old section of Charleston and other southern urban centers such as Savannah and New Orleans. Influenced by English, French, and Spanish models, as well as by African ironwork traditions, African-made wrought iron is among the most stunning features of colonial architecture.

Like ironsmiths, black colonial woodworkers were highly skilled, were often hired out, and were sometimes compensated for their work. They carved and created everything from wood floor planes and spiral staircases for wealthy homes to boats, furniture, and even musical instruments. Carved from wood and gourds, African-American instruments provided a unique outlet for sculptural creativity and for the continuation of African traditions in the Americas. The West African **lute**, for instance, is a direct precursor of the American-made equivalent: the banjo (Figure 2.6). President Thomas Jefferson noted in 1781 that "the instrument proper to [blacks] is the Banjar,

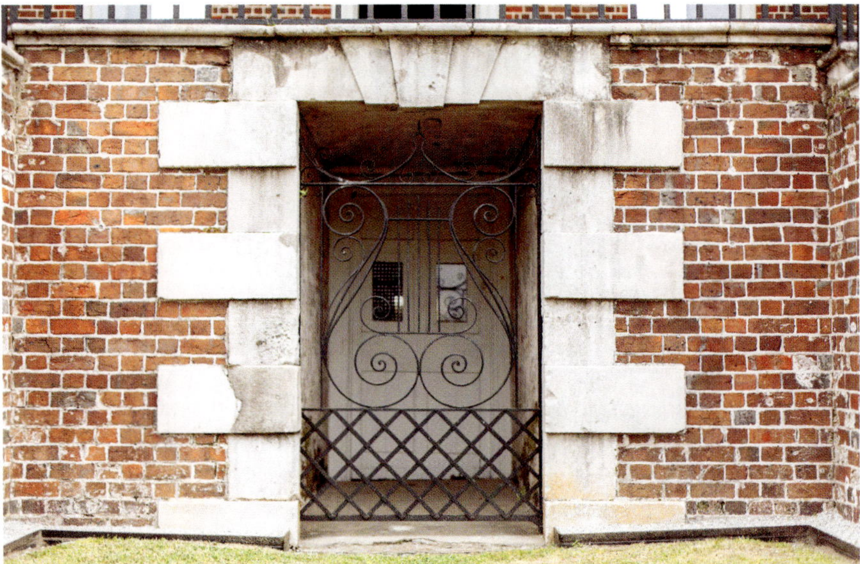

▶ **2.5** *Drayton Hall Grille*, 1744, wrought iron. Charleston, SC.

Photo courtesy of the Drayton Hall Preservation Trust. Photo: John Apsey.

which they brought hither from Africa." Similar references to the African origins of the banjo were made by a number of documented 18th-century observers who compared it to **gourd** lutes stretched with animal skin such as the Jola *akonting* of Gambia; the Mandinka and Wasulu *ngoni* of Sierra Leone, Ivory Coast, Guinea, and Mali; and the *xalam* of Mali and Senegal.

Most like the ***akonting***, the banjo was played during the colonial era in the same manner, with the ball of the thumb and the nail of the index finger. *Akonting* scholar Laemouahuma Daniel Jatta spent a decade tracing the origins of the American banjo to the *akonting*. He found that both instruments had long wooden necks that extended through the gourd body of the instrument and a wooden string bridge that could be removed. Further, the *akonting* and banjo are both **vernacular** instruments—unlike the *ngoni* and the *xalam*, which are played almost exclusively by **griots**, who are traditional African bard-historians who serve the governing classes.

The first recorded use of the banjo in the New World dates to the 1650s in slave communities in Martinique. Over the next few decades, Caribbean slaves who were sold to North America transported with them their

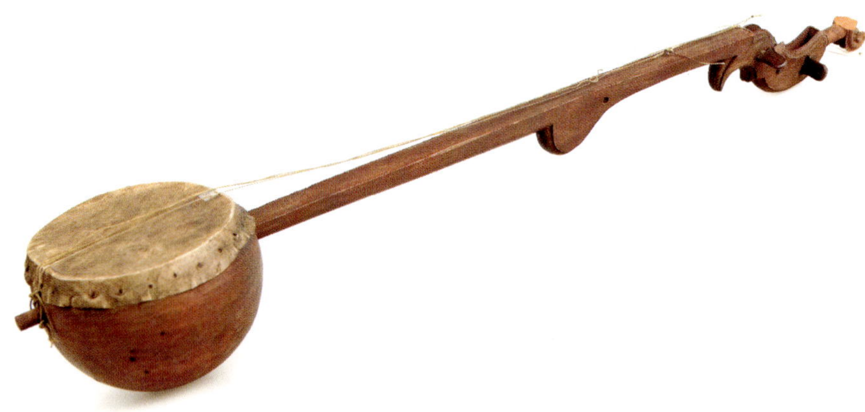

▶ **2.6** *Banjo from Suriname*, before 1777, gourd, wood, sheepskin, iron, 81 × 16 × 31 cm.

Nationaal Museum van Wereldculturen, coll. no. RV-360-5696.

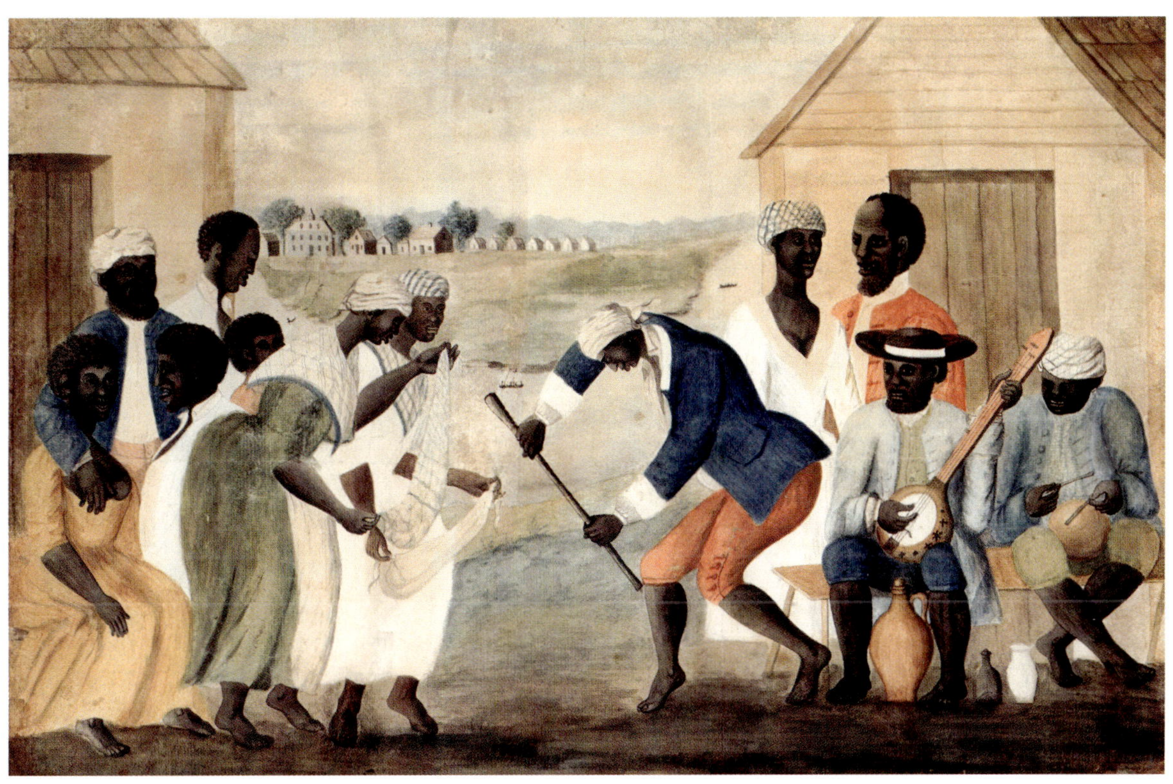

▲ 2.7 John Rose (attributed), *The Old Plantation*, probably 1785–90, watercolor on laid paper, 11¾″ × 18⅞″. Beaufort County, South Carolina.

The Colonial Williamsburg Foundation. Abby Aldrich Rockefeller Folk Art Museum. Gift of Abby Aldrich Rockefeller.

knowledge of the construction and playing of the banjo (or *banza* as it was known in Haiti and Martinique). Slaves were recorded using the instrument in the United States as early as 1749. Forty years later, African-American banjo playing was documented in art by John Rose of South Carolina, whose c. 1785 watercolor painting *The Old Plantation* (Figure 2.7) depicts African Americans, likely from his own plantation, dancing to the music of what appears to be an *akonting*. In the 19th century, the banjo was adopted by Euro-Americans, particularly in the Appalachian mountains of the eastern United States, and was popularized by **blackface minstrels** countrywide. Integral to the evolution of American music from folk to country to bluegrass, the banjo added one or two strings to the three of the *akonting*. Its use became a staple of early African-American culture.

Drums comprise yet another sculptural instrument transferred from Africa to the Americas. Sometimes purchased by, or gifted to, slavers, indigenous African drums made the transatlantic crossing along with the Africans who carved them. During the Middle Passage, drums were played at daily exercise regimens of the enslaved (the exercise was intended to prevent muscle atrophy, because most of the slaves' time was spent in squatting positions below decks). The oldest extant example is an Akan drum in the collection of the British Museum (Figure 2.8). It was fashioned from deerskin, plant fiber, and either *bocote* wood (which is durable, resistant to termites, and native to Sierra Leone, Kenya, Tanzania, Congo, and Angola) or camwood (African sandalwood), a hardwood also found in West Africa.

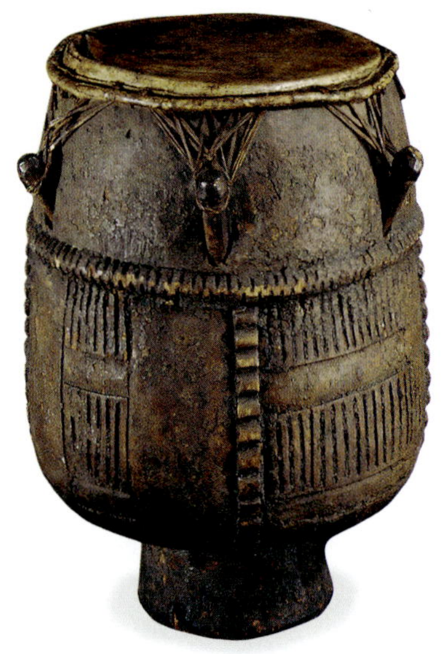

▲ **2.8** *Akan (Ghana) Drum*, 1730–45, wood, deerskin, plant fiber, 16″ × 11″. Virginia. Collection of the British Museum, London.

Discovered in Virginia, the drum was used in America but was made in Ghana by an Akan craftsman around 1700 and later brought to England, following the entire **triangular trade route**. The drum is approximately one foot high and is carved with **incised** striations and raised rows of wood squares that allude to drum rhythms. It sits on a small riser and is peg tuned (the deerskin contracts or expands as the pegs are turned). Its construction and carvings link it directly to the **Rada *boula* drum** used in sacred **Vodou** ceremonies in Haiti. Played with sticks rather than hands, such a drum can also be seen in *The Old Plantation* (Figure 2.7) amid the participants in an African-American wedding ceremony and dance.

One of the most common forms of art produced by colonial American blacks was ceramics. Archeologists working in coastal Virginia, Georgia, Florida, and the Carolinas have unearthed numerous examples of ceramics termed **colonoware**, which were produced by African Americans between the 1500s and the Civil War (Figure 2.9). First codified in the 1960s as a genre of Native-American pottery, later studies indicate that African Americans were the major producers of colonoware in the southern states, particularly as the Native-American population began to decrease. Created for barter at market, for African-derived ceremonial purposes, or as useful domestic objects, colonoware vessels are handformed (rather than **wheel thrown**) from clay coils or slabs. African, Native-American, and European in derivation, colonoware takes the form of bowls, mugs, pitchers, colanders, **porringers**, butter churns, and chafing dishes. It was **burnished** rather than **glazed** and was fired under low heat.

The need in colonial North America for simply made utilitarian pottery was mandated by the British Crown, which prohibited the manufacture in the colonies of high-end ceramics such as porcelain. As a **mercantile economy**, Britain required that raw materials be shipped from America to England, where they would be remade into fine and costly objects to be sold, ironically, back to the colonies. The practice was a circuitous way of taxing colonists. Not only was it illegal for decorative ceramics to be produced in the colonies, but even the production of utilitarian pottery was limited by law. As a result, colonists made their own rudimentary pottery to avoid the expense of importation, and they underreported the amount produced so as to circumvent taxes or prosecution. Those with slave labor, particularly on plantations where a great deal of earthenware was needed, created colonoware in abundance in the 1700s.

▼ **2.9** *Colonoware Bowl*, c. 1700, clay, 6½″ × 9⅞″. Private collection. Wooten and Wooten Auctioneers, Camden, SC.

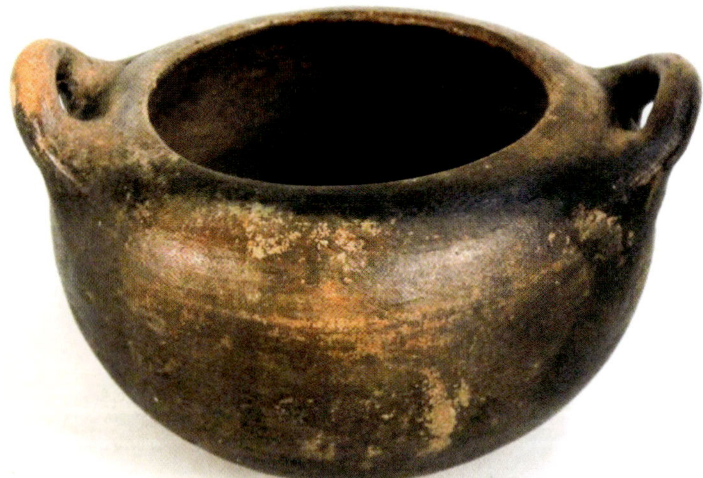

Scholars distinguish slave-made colonoware from the indigenous Catawba or Native-American variety (termed "river burnished") by way of the less highly polished and more austere style of the African version. The latter lacks the scoring and painted decoration common to Catawba-ware. By avoiding embellishments, African-American potters ensured that their colonoware would not be deemed decorative or intended for resale in defiance of the British mandate. Unique to the colonial era, colonoware was no longer produced after the Civil War. Conflicting theories as to why this occurred range from the U.S. secession from Britain, which removed restrictions on pottery manufacture, to a conscious decision on the part of emancipated African Americans to abandon "slave pottery" as a signifier of their bleak past. Because ceramic shortages still existed after Emancipation, the latter explanation carries some weight, but we may never be certain as to why the colonoware tradition came to an end.

FINE ARTS IN THE AGE OF SLAVERY

Understandably, colonial African Americans had limited access to the realm of the professional artist. Because they required an apprenticeship, training in an **academy**, or, at the very least, the free time and access to costly supplies necessary to self-train and produce conventional high art items such as prints, drawings, paintings, and sculpture, professional artists were not likely to emerge from the mostly impoverished and enslaved black sectors of the colonial population. Nevertheless, the history of one such artist—a rare exception—has been documented: the enslaved Bostonian Scipio Moorhead (born c. 1750, fl. 1773), one of the earliest known professional African artists in America. If not for the fact that one of his works was preserved for posterity in a book of **Neoclassical** poetry published in London in 1773 and also produced by an enslaved African American—**Senegambia**-born poet Phillis Wheatley (1753–84)—we would know little, if anything of Scipio Moorhead today (see chapter-opening image).

Wheatley, the author of the book in which Moorhead's art appears, came to the United States on the slave ship *Phillis* (her namesake) when she was seven years old. A precocious child, Wheatley was educated by Mary Wheatley, the daughter of John Wheatley, who purchased the frail West African child in 1760 as a personal servant for his wife. By the time she was a teenager, Wheatley was composing poetry, which the Wheatley family publicized in urban newspapers and gazettes. By the early 1770s, her poetry was being recognized in New England and London, where it came to the attention of evangelical philanthropist Lady Selina Shirley Hastings, Countess of Huntingdon (1707–91). The countess made arrangements for London bookseller Archibald Bell to publish a collection of the young poet's works, and she requested that Wheatley's portrait be included as the frontispiece of the publication.

The painter Scipio Moorhead, Wheatley's Boston neighbor, was commissioned to create the portrait. His original ink drawing, described in the London press at the time as a "fine likeness," was transposed into an **engraving** in England and was included in Wheatley's *Poems on Various Subjects, Religious and Moral*. The Wheatley volume also included a poem dedicated to Moorhead and entitled, "To S. M. a Young African Painter, on

Seeing His Works." The poem describes Moorhead's talent, his ability to inspire through his art, and his (now lost) paintings *Aurora* and *Damon [and Pythias]*. Wheatley's poem reads, in part:

> To show the lab'ring bosom's deep intent,
> And thought in living characters to paint,
> When first thy pencil did those beauties give,
> And breathing figures learnt from thee to live,
> No more to tell of Damon's tender sighs,
> Or rising radiance of Aurora's eyes,
> For nobler themes demand a nobler strain,
> And purer language on th' ethereal plain.
> Cease, gentle muse! the solemn gloom of night
> Now seals the fair creation from my sight.

Although bound in slavery to the Reverend John Moorhead, the Irish pastor of the Church of Presbyterian Strangers and a Wheatley family friend, the reverend gave to Moorhead most of the same rights as a free black. The reverend's wife, Sarah, who was an art educator, trained Moorhead in painting and drawing. Furthermore, a *Boston Newsletter* announcement dated January 7, 1773, advertised his artistic services, describing him as "a negro of extraordinary genius."

Moorhead's portrayal of Wheatley depicts her in profile sitting contemplatively at her writing table. The portrayal reveals Wheatley's unique status as a literate and intellectual woman despite her enslavement; note the book on the table, the pen in her hand, and her pensive pose. Indeed, the depiction negates Wheatley's enslaved status almost entirely. She wears attire typical of free working-class women of the time and place: an attractive colonial day dress, **mob cap**, neckerchief, and apron. Indeed, she too received privileged treatment (including release from domestic service and instruction in Latin and Greek) from the Wheatley family due to both her exceptional literary talents and her fragile health. Despite their evident affection and compassion for Phillis, however, John and Mrs. Wheatley did not emancipate her during their lifetimes but, rather, bequeathed freedom to her in their will.

As the American Revolution approached, the status of African Americans hung in the balance. The rebellion against British taxes and manufacturing limitations was meant to afford colonists prosperity and better control over their own property, and enslaved Africans were considered part of that property; slave labor and products were vital to colonial prosperity. Paradoxically, the American Revolution was rooted in concepts of human equality and freedom, and many Americans began to consider that slavery undermined these values. Thus the Revolution had the potential to both reinforce and undermine the slave system. Furthermore, at the time of the Revolution, tobacco crops—particularly in Virginia, where a vast population of enslaved Africans worked the fields and prepared tobacco for export—began to decline, due to the excessive taxes placed on the colonies for them. With the decline in tobacco production, America's dependence on slaves might have come to an end as well. In fact, immediately following the American Revolution, slavery was on the wane even in the major slaveholding states, where free blacks began to outnumber enslaved blacks.

However, this downturn in slave numbers was not to last. With the invention of the cotton gin (short for "engine"), cotton production increased exponentially, from half a million pounds in 1793 to more than 90 million pounds by the time of the Civil War. Tobacco, rice, and indigo planters throughout the South converted their fields to cotton, thanks to the gin, which drastically reduced the time and labor required to separate seeds from cotton. The immense profitability of postrevolutionary cotton production went hand in hand with an increased demand for slave labor to support the massive industry. As a result, America's black population, by and large, remained enslaved for the next seven decades, but the creative productivity of this group did not diminish. On the contrary, the number of professional artists began to grow. Those working within the cotton industry produced works of art with fabric—namely, quilts—as a continued outlet for their aesthetic sensibilities.

Summary

The earliest works of art and architecture created by Africans in America were limited, for the most part, to the decorative arts—that is, art that had a utilitarian purpose—such as colonoware, metalwork, musical instruments, and architectural design and decoration. Although referred to as folk, naïve, and Outsider Art today, colonial African American artists showed great creativity and skill. Enslaved Africans in America not only created a vast array of necessary objects for the rapidly developing New World but also retained much of their African cultural heritage. Hipped roofs, poteaux-en-terre construction, and broad, shaded galleries are examples of African elements that were preserved in American architecture. The same can be said of instruments such as the *akonting* (the American banjo) and the Rada-style drum. Finally, despite the rigors and restrictions of slavery, African creativity thrived even in the realm of fine arts, as shown by the portrait of Phillis Wheatley by the enslaved Scipio Moorhead.

Key Terms

academy: a formal art school, traditionally government sponsored, where acknowledged master artists set curricula and serve as faculty

akonting: a three-stringed instrument constructed from a hollowed gourd and stretched animal skin, with a wood neck

blackface minstrels: a genre of popular 19th-century entertainers who wore black stage makeup and performed in the guise of a black person; performances were characterized by stereotypical exaggerations and comedic caricature

burnish: to hand or tool polish an object to create a lustrous surface

chinking or *bousillage*: substances used to fill cracks, holes, or spaces between logs in log cabins; substances range from plaster or clay to plant fibers or wood chips *cire perdue*: from the French for "lost wax," a bronze casting process used to create hollow rather than solid sculptures

clapboard: horizontal overlapping wooden boards used as house siding; also known as weatherboard

colonoware: earthenware or clay pottery created during the colonial era along the Atlantic coast of the United States

creole: a term used in the Louisiana Territory beginning in the 17th century to refer to colonists and slaves (as well as their practices and products) who shared a fusion of French, Spanish, African, and Native-American cultural history and ancestry

engraving: a form of printmaking using a metal plate on which an image has been incised with a burin or metal tool; the plate is inked, overlaid with paper, and run through a printing press to create multiple copies of an image

gallery: in architecture, a covered walkway open on one side and often supported by columns

glazed: refers to pottery that is fired after being coated with a lustrous substance (a glaze) that adds shimmer and color to the clay form

gourd: the hollow, dried, and hard shell of certain fruits, such as squash and pumpkin

griot: a West African poet-historian, storyteller, and custodian of oral tradition

Gullah: refers to inhabitants of the coastal islands of South Carolina, Georgia, and northern Florida, whose customs and language fuse English and West African elements; the term traces either to the southwestern African country of Angola, the Gola (Gula) people of Sierra Leone and Liberia, or the indigenous American Guale people who once occupied the Georgia and Carolina coasts

hipped roof: refers to roof construction comprised of two triangular and two trapezoidal sides that slope downward to the walls of the structure, creating a modified pyramid shape

incise: to cut or carve into a surface

lute: any of a variety of wooden stringed instruments with a long, usually fretted neck and a vaulted, hollow, pear-shaped body

mercantile economy: a system in which the government controls foreign trade and encourages product exportation

Middle Passage: journey of slave ships across the Atlantic from West Africa to the Americas

mob cap: a gathered or pleated bonnet that is fringed and usually made of linen or cotton; it was used to cover women's hair in the 18th and 19th centuries

Neoclassical: art and architecture produced in the 18th and 19th century that derives from classical Greece and imperial Rome

Palladian style: a style of architecture inspired by the Renaissance designs of Andrea Palladio, which in turn were derived from the asymmetrical construction of antique Roman buildings

pediment: on a building façade, a triangular area created by and located directly below a pitched roof, and supported by columns

pipkins: small cooking pots

porringers: decorative shallow bowls with one or two handles from which one could either eat or drink poteaux-en-terre (posts-in-earth): a French term that refers to architectural construction wherein the roof is supported by posts that are embedded in the earth

Rada *boula* drum: a peg-tuned, high-pitched drum played with sticks at Haitian-derived Vodou ceremonies in honor of the gods of wisdom, composure, and benevolence

Sea Islanders: inhabitants of a group of islands off the coast of South Carolina, Georgia, and northern Florida

Senegambian: referring to the people and culture of Senegal and Gambia

slave codes: a series of laws enforced beginning in the 17th century that dictated the treatment of African slaves

tabby foundation: an architectural foundation created from a cement-like building material made of lime, sand, water, and seashells

triangular trade route: Atlantic slave trade routes between Africa, the United States, and Europe

vernacular: in art, refers to self-trained artists and to informal or unassuming art and architecture

Vodou (Haiti): a Haitian-based religion derived from religious practices in the Congo and Benin that fuses African beliefs with Christian icons

wheel-thrown earthenware: refers to pottery that is created using a potter's wheel

Questions for Further Study and Discussion

1. Choose a discussion in this chapter of a specific work of art or architecture and identify those portions of the discussion that are formalist in their method of analysis. Do the same for contextual analysis and racial iconography.
2. Why has craft traditionally been considered of lesser value than the high arts of painting and sculpture? Debate the validity, or lack thereof, of valuing crafts as high art.
3. Describe and discuss the differences between traditional African concepts of art as integral to daily, spiritual, and sociopolitical life and Western concepts of art as self-contained, nonutilitarian, and distinct from daily life.
4. Name and describe those features of colonial architecture that can be attributed to African architectural forms.
5. Discuss the reasons why wealthy African Americans owned slaves, and debate whether or not this practice was ethical.
6. Research and discuss the relationship between the neo-African religion of Vodou and Christian Catholicism.
7. Analyze and discuss the symbolism and imagery in Phillis Wheatley's poem "To S. M., a Young African Painter, on Seeing His Works."
8. Research and discuss how and why some slaves, such as Scipio Moorhead and Phillis Wheatley, were given certain privileges associated with free blacks.

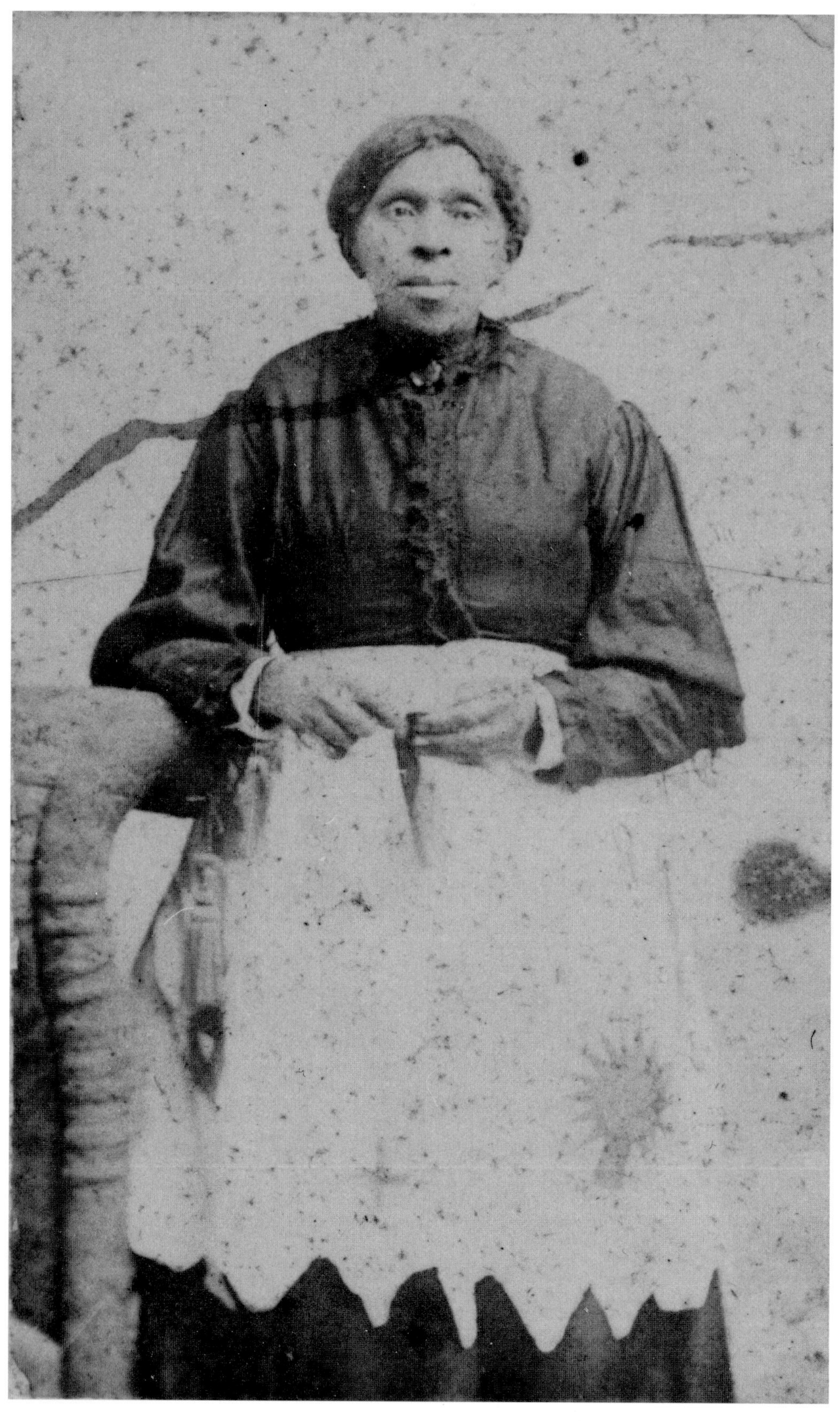

FEDERAL-PERIOD ARCHITECTURE AND DESIGN

3

The Federal era in American architecture and design began immediately following the American Revolution of 1776 and continued full force until the 1830s; however, its influence endured with less intensity from then to the end of the Civil War in the 1860s. As a new country, America strove to associate itself with the great Western civilizations of the past, in both its politics and art. Ancient Greek and Roman motifs were incorporated in varying degrees into many American buildings of the period, structures that came to symbolize the very concept of democracy and the highest ideals of a civilized society.

Despite America's recently won independence from Britain, Britain's influence in architecture and design remained significant in the United States. Silhouettes, proportions, and motifs of British architects and designers were adopted and then altered by their Federal-style counterparts to create a uniquely American genre. Federal-style designers borrowed slender, elegant forms; Grecian vase shapes; and Roman shield, swag, and tassel motifs from British designers, adding girth and robustness while reducing decoration. They adapted to plantation architecture and design the Roman-inspired domes, furniture, and plasterwork and the Grecian columns and pediments popularized by famed Scottish architect and interior and furniture designer Robert Adam (1728–92).

ARCHITECTURE

The Federal style was prompted by newly published archeological studies of the Acropolis in Athens and other historical Greek sites. It was disseminated throughout the United States by way of a how-to book—*The Practical Builder or Workman's General Assistant*—written in 1774 by British carpenter and architect William Pain (c. 1730–90). Another source was 16th-century Venetian architect Andrea Palladio's (1508–80) *Four Books of Architecture*, itself inspired by the Roman architect Vitruvius (c. 75–15 B.C.E.), who detailed classical Greco-Roman building design in his *De Architectura*. Key features of Federal architecture were the incorporation of **Doric** or **Ionic** columns, **porticos**, and pediments along with order and clarity of design. The Palladian style added several other features, including Roman domes, arched windows, and a rigid symmetry that included a centralized primary space with flanking wings.

◀ *Photograph of Harriet Powers*, c. 1900, 2³⁄₁₆″ × 1¼″.

Photo © 2015 Museum of Fine Arts, Boston.

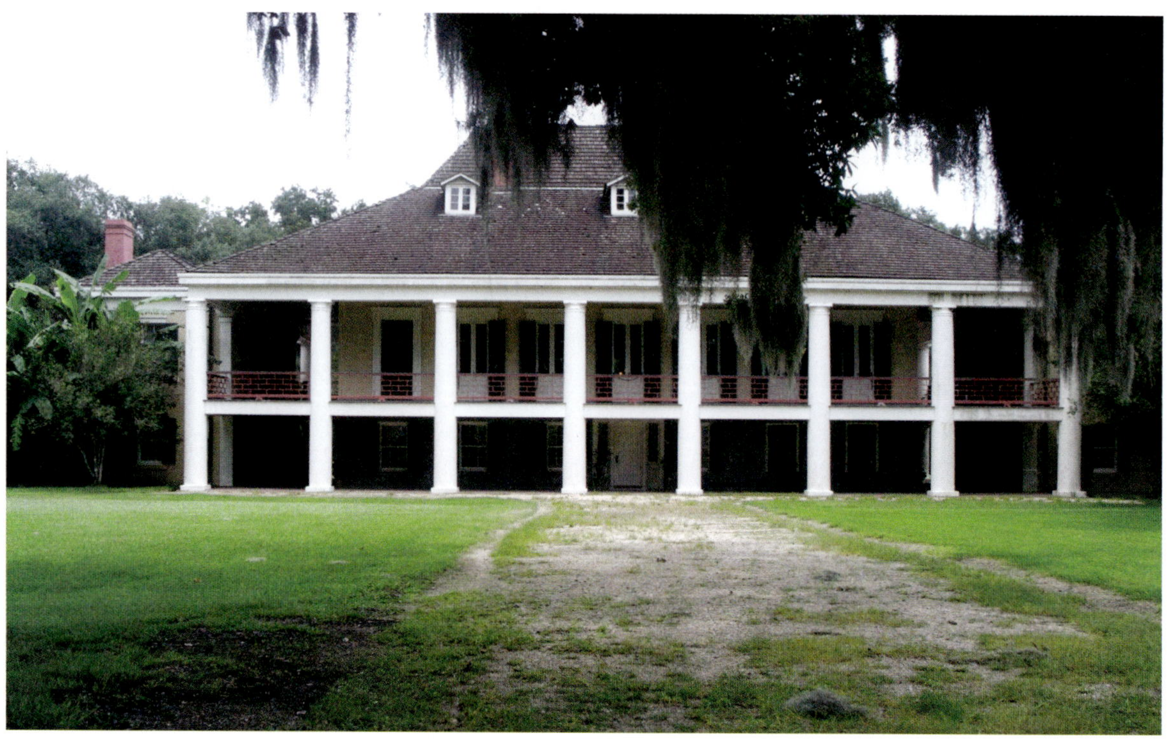

▲ **3.1** Charles Paquet, *Destrehan Manor*, 1790. St. Charles Parish, LA.

Charles Paquet

Showcasing eight Doric columns along its façade, the manor house of the Destrehan plantation in St. Charles Parish, Louisiana (Figure 3.1) was built in 1790 by the free black architect Charles Paquet (fl. 1780s). Architecturally, the Destrehan manor house is a modified example of the European Greek Revival style. Its colossal Doric **colonnade**, which spans two floors, was created using plastered brick to give the illusion of Grecian white marble. The house features an enclosing double-covered portico, French windows, and a sloping hipped roof similar to West African and Afro-Caribbean house designs of the colonial period (see Chapter 2). Constructed of brick and cedar, Destrehan Manor is one of the oldest homes in Louisiana. To facilitate the building project, its owner loaned Paquet a half dozen slaves, who assisted with the construction of the main house and slave quarters. Paquet was paid for his work with one slave (to own), two cows, one hundred bushels each of rice and corn, and one hundred dollars (about $2,000 today)—a poignant statement on the idea of humans as tradable commodities.

Aside from being the site of one of the earliest known American buildings by a professional black architect, Destrehan plantation holds a unique and tragic place in African-American history. It was the location of a trial that resulted in the execution of 18 slaves who participated in the historic 1811 German Coast Uprising, so named because of the significant number of German settlers in the area. The largest slave rebellion in U.S. history, this revolt was carried out by hundreds of slaves from sugar plantations just north of New Orleans. Armed with work tools, the insurgents marched 25 miles along the Mississippi River toward the city, burning five plantations and killing two white men as they went. Although blacks outnumbered whites in Louisiana by five to one, they were no match for the well-armed local militia. Black casualties, including those killed in confrontations with law enforcement and those executed afterward, totaled 95. No slave rebellion of this size was ever attempted again in the United States.

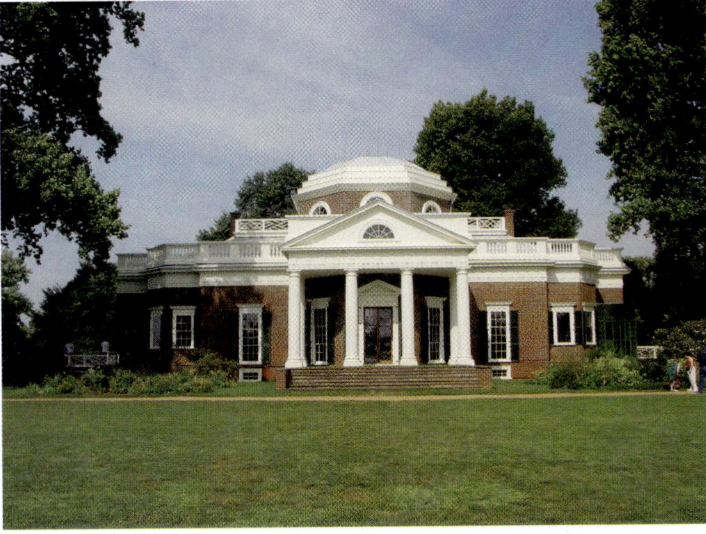

▲ **3.2** Thomas Jefferson, *Monticello*, 1796–1809. Charlottesville, VA.

Carol M. Highsmith Archive, Library of Congress, Prints and Photographs Division.

The one-time home of President Thomas Jefferson—Monticello, in Charlottesville, Virginia—provides another example of slave-built Federalist architecture (Figure 3.2). Although the main house was designed by Jefferson himself and its construction was supervised by a team of professional white builders, the entire wood framework of the house and much of its interior decoration is the work of enslaved Africans. Despite his lifelong public stance against slavery, Jefferson was a slave owner. An abolitionist in theory, Jefferson opposed the unilateral freeing of African-American slaves and advocated instead for gradual abolition and the removal of Africans from American soil.

Jefferson owned 170 slaves, 70 of whom lived at Monticello. This group formed the core of the labor force at the plantation, and one of their key responsibilities was building construction. Initially, the house was designed in the Palladian manner, with a two-story pedimented Doric and Ionic portico separated by an **entablature** of **triglyphs** and **metopes**. However, after spending time in Paris as ambassador to France in the 1780s and observing the construction of the domed Hotel Salm (today's Palace of the Legion of Honor), Jefferson decided to alter his original design. In 1796, he reconfigured the house by replacing the two-story portico with a single-story version, **stepping** the flanking wings, and topping the house with an octagonal dome (different from the typical Palladian-style rounded dome). Monticello consists of 43 rooms, 8 fireplaces, 13 skylights (including an **oculus**), and 11,000 square feet of living space. The massive and protracted project kept generations of enslaved builders, carpenters, **joiners**, brick masons, and other artisans busy for decades, from 1768, when trees were first cleared from the site, to 1809, when the house was finally completed.

WOODWORK

Early Masters

Born at Monticello while the manor house was under construction, John Hemings (1775–c. 1830) was one of the enslaved artisans who helped to build it. Hemings was the literate son of a white woodworker named Joseph Neilson (fl. 1775–79) and Elizabeth (Betty) Hemings (1735–1807),

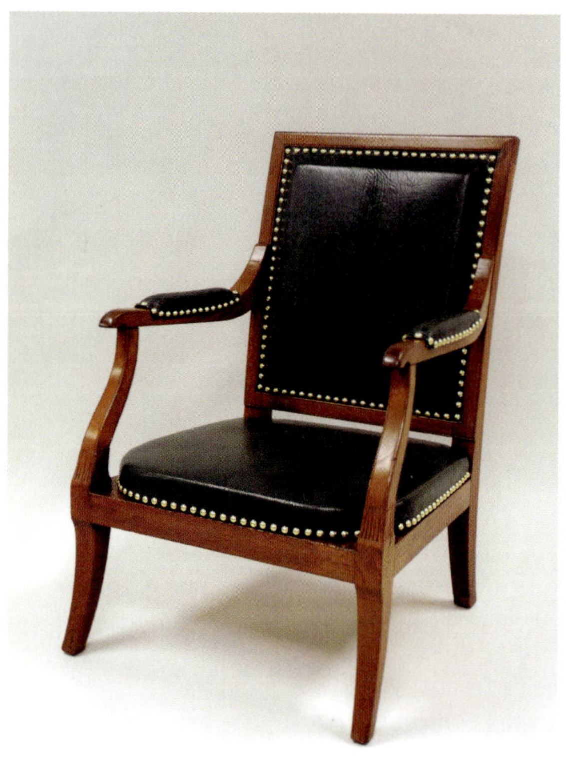

▲ **3.3** *Arm Chair*, attributed to John Hemings, c. 1816, mahogany.

© Thomas Jefferson Foundation at Monticello.

the enslaved biracial mistress of Jefferson's father-in-law, John Wayles (1715–73). Jefferson's wife, Martha Wayles (1748–82), inherited one hundred slaves from her father on his death. Betty Hemings was among this group; she gave birth to her son John not long after coming to Monticello. In 1792, Jefferson hired professional Scottish and Irish woodworkers to train John Hemings as a carpenter and joiner. By 1809, Hemings was lead carpenter at the plantation. A gifted designer, Hemings created elaborate moldings and furniture that were praised by Jefferson in his writings and by plantation overseer Edmund Bacon (1785–1866), who described Hemings as "a first-rate workman."

Hemings's expertise is shown in an 1817 armchair that features a mahogany frame, leather upholstery, nailhead trim, and an elegant curvilinear shape that anticipates Art Nouveau furniture of the latter 19th century (Figure 3.3). John Hemings was freed in 1826 in Jefferson's will. He then apprenticed and trained his nephews Madison (1805–77) and Eston (1808–56)—the sons of Jefferson and his enslaved mistress Sally Hemings (c.1773–1835), who were freed at age 21—as carpenter-joiners, extending the family furniture-making legacy for another generation.

Like John Hemings, Henry Boyd (1802–86) learned the furniture trade as a slave. However, his circumstances were somewhat different in that he began his career as a slave-entrepreneur in Kentucky at age 18, when he was hired out by his owner as a cabinetmaker. Slave-entrepreneurs plied their own trades independently but were required to give the lion's share of their earnings to their owners. By 1826, Boyd had earned enough money to purchase his freedom. He moved north to the bordering state of Ohio, which had abolished slavery in 1802. Boyd worked for 10 years there as a longshoreman and as a house builder for a local contractor. With these earnings, in the 1830s Boyd purchased freedom for the rest of his family and opened his first modest shop in Cincinnati.

Keeping up with the times and with his competitors, Boyd expanded his business in the 1840s, moving to larger quarters at a four-building factory site. He transitioned from handcrafted to mass-produced furniture and from local to regional distribution and specialized in making bed frames. He soon operated one of the most successful bed manufacturing companies in Cincinnati, with a racially integrated workforce of 50 employees, who produced more than 1,000 beds per year. His success was due in large part to his own invention, known as "the Boyd bedstead," which was, in essence, an early version of the modern-day bed frame. Using a **mortise and tenon** construction, the Boyd bed could be easily assembled and taken apart, which made it extremely popular with hotel buyers.

By the mid-1850s, just prior to the Civil War, Boyd opened a showroom at his factory site. Cincinnati trade records indicate that he expanded his furniture offerings at this time to include sophisticated salon pieces in the French Empire style. Unfortunately, Boyd's business was affected by the financial difficulties of the Civil War and by rising anti-black sentiment in Cincinnati; arsonists burned his factory on three separate occasions. After the third fire in 1863, Boyd was unable to obtain insurance and was forced to retire. He remained in his Cincinnati home, however, until his death in 1886. An example of his work survives in a grand **tester bed** made of "curly" walnut with block and turned posts and an unembellished rectangular headboard located in the Golden Lamb Inn in Lebanon, Ohio. It is a fine example of classical American furniture in its simplicity and elegance.

FEDERAL-ERA CRAFTSMEN

Professional black furniture designers flourished throughout the United States during the Federal era. As exponents of the **American Empire style** (an alternate name for the Federal style, applied to furniture), their services were highly prized and well compensated. The style itself was popularized in the United States by **cabinetmaker** Duncan Phyfe (1770s–1854). Specific features of American Empire furniture were a preference for mahogany, a mixture of curving and straight forms, and in some cases decoration including fluting, claw feet, and carved leaf patterns.

▼ **3.4** Célestin Glapion, *Armoire*, c. 1790–1830, Cuban mahogany.

Collections of the Louisiana State Museum. Photo: Jim Zietz / Courtesy of the Historic New Orleans Collection.

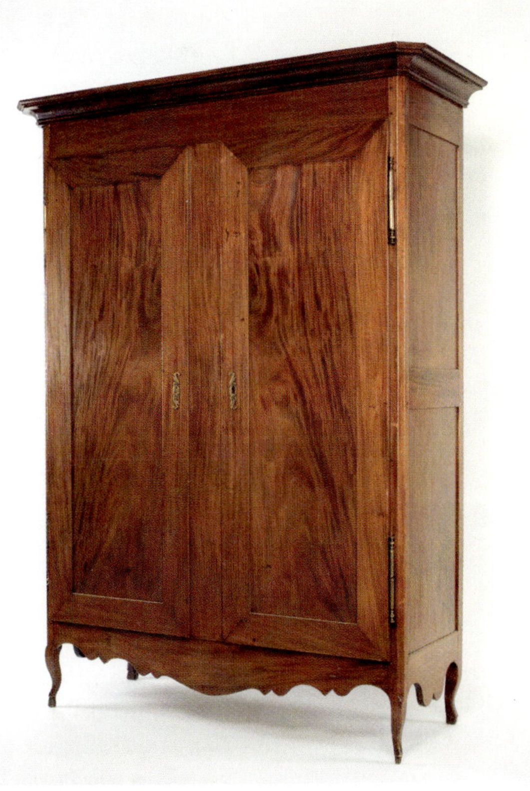

Célestin Glapion (1784?–1826?) and Dutreuil Barjon (c. 1799–after 1854) were prominent black cabinetmakers working in the New Orleans area at the turn of the 19th century. Glapion worked in, among other woods, American black walnut and cypress. He preferred these woods because they did not have to be imported and were, therefore, more cost-effective than mahogany, and because cypress was especially durable and weather resistant. Glapion was also an exceptional joiner who constructed pieces with minimal need for fasteners or binders. In addition to British influences, Glapion incorporated the **Rococo** features of the French Louis XV style, popular in Europe immediately preceding the Greek Revival style. In a mahogany armoire dated c. 1790–1830, Glapion employed *pieds de biche* (literally, "deer hooves"), in which a tiny niche is carved at the base of the armoire's **cabriole legs** to simulate cloven hooves (Figure 3.4). The piece is topped with a **cornice** and features recessed paneled doors and a delicately carved cabriole **apron**. Glapion's cabinetry has been dated as early as 1790, which makes him one of the first professional furniture designers in Louisiana.

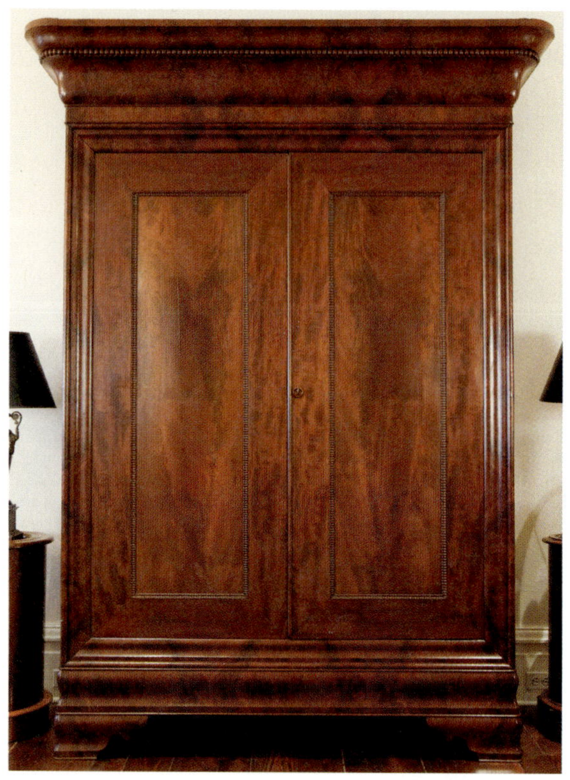

▲ **3.5** Dutreuil Barjon, *Louisiana Armoire*, c. 1840, mahogany wood, 100″ × 73″ × 28″.

The Historic New Orleans Collection, gift of Mr. and Mrs. Robert J. Patrick, acc. no. 2008.0088.

Dutreuil Barjon and his mother—who were members of the *anciens libres*, or enfranchised citizens of Haiti—emigrated to New Orleans in 1813. Barjon would remain there for the next 40 years, working for most of that time as a successful furniture maker. As a teenager, Barjon learned his trade from a master craftsman, the black cabinetmaker Jean Rousseau (fl. 1813–33), who had a shop on Bourbon Street. Not only did Rousseau apprentice Barjon, but he also took on some 30 other black apprentices over 15 years. Within 10 years of his apprenticeship, Barjon had opened his own shop—the Barjon Magasin de Meubles—in the **Vieux Carré**, where he (and later his son and namesake) shared retail space with highly sought-after white cabinetmakers Françoise Siebrecht and Prudent Mallard. Barjon also took on nine apprentices of his own over the course of his career. Specializing in Federal-style furniture design and manufacture, Barjon preferred the sumptuous, undulant shapes of the **French Empire** and **British Regency styles**, although he rejected the overly decorative elements typical of both genres. An example of the artist's preference for American Empire severity can be seen in an immense 1840 armoire that showcases an "ogee," or curved lateral silhouette, on the cornice and plinth, beaded decoration, and bracketed feet (Figure 3.5).

During the 1830s and 1840s, Barjon established himself as one of the finest furniture makers in New Orleans. He not only designed his own pieces but also imported items from Europe and created a business partnership with German-born furniture maker Christophe Voigt to ship furniture from Hamburg and Berlin. However, by 1855, Barjon found himself deeply in debt to his creditors. He was compelled to leave his business in the hands of his son (who had become an expert furniture maker in his own right) and emigrate to France.

Dutreuil Barjon, Jr. (1823–70), was listed in the New Orleans trade directories as a carpenter-joiner by the time he was in his twenties. Even before he took over the business from his father in 1855, he had been managing the shop for nearly a decade. Barjon the younger's work closely reflects the utility and reaction against fussiness of early German **Biedermeier** designs (popular between 1815 and 1848). An example from the Louisiana State Museum, exquisitely handcrafted in mahogany and yellow pine, is a dresser, or *semainière* (seven-drawer chest), from 1856. This was one of the last pieces made at the Barjon shop (Figure 3.6). The younger Barjon kept the business going on his own for more than a decade, until just after the Civil War in 1867, when it folded. Barjon's decline coincided with an overall 50 percent reduction in the number of black furniture makers in Louisiana and, indeed, throughout the South. The cause for this downturn has been attributed to the rising popularity of factory-made furniture, which was less costly than handmade models. A more significant cause, however, was the increased hostility toward free blacks that developed at the time of the Civil War.

CIVIL WAR–ERA CRAFTSMEN

Thomas Day

The black cabinetmaker of the Civil War period about whom historians know the most is Thomas Day (1801–c.1861), who was a member of a highly successful family of black designers. Born in Dinwiddy County, Virginia, to John Day (1766–1832) and Mourning Stewart Day (1766–c.1855), he was descended from a family of longtime free blacks. His mother was the daughter of a slaveholding physician and landowner, Thomas A. Stewart, and his father was a free cabinetmaker and property owner. Thomas and his older brother John Junior (1797–1859) were educated by Quakers and were apprenticed with their father until 1817, when the family moved to the better racial and economic climate of North Carolina. Day the elder conducted business in Warren County, while his sons worked together successfully in Caswell County.

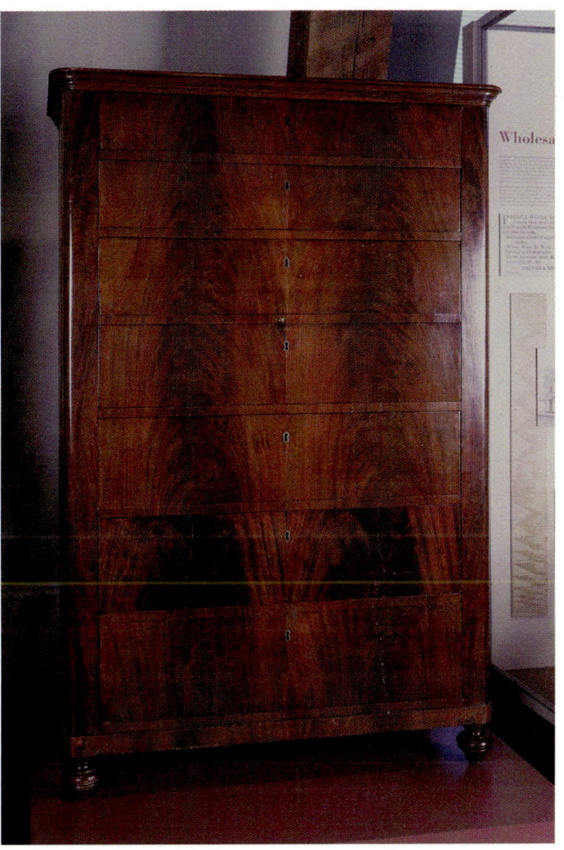

▲ **3.6** Dutreuil Barjon, Jr., *Chest of Drawers, or Semainière*, c. 1855, mahogany, yellow pine, 63¾″ × 20½″ × 41″.

Courtesy of the Collections of the Louisiana State Museum, gift of Friends of the Cabildo.

In 1825, Thomas took over the business from his brother John, who left to pursue a career in the ministry. In 1827, Thomas purchased property on Main Street in the town of Milton, where he opened a modest shop. He advertised his products and services locally, stating that "Thomas Day, Cabinet Maker, . . . wishes to inform his friends and the public that he has on hand, and intends keeping, a handsome supply of Mahogany, Walnut and Stained Furniture, the most fashionable and common Bed Steads. . . . All orders in his line, in Repairing, Varnishing will be thankfully received and punctually attended to."

In 1830, Day married Aquilla Wilson of Halifax County, Virginia, and arranged for her to move to North Carolina by local petition, a process that was necessary to circumvent laws restricting the emigration of free blacks into the state. Permanently settling in Milton, and with the help an integrated workforce of 15 apprentices, over the next 20 years Day developed his business into one of the most successful furniture-manufacturing companies in North Carolina. With the assistance of white and black, free and slave workers, he produced both furniture and architectural **millwork** in a modernized steam-powered factory—one of the first in the state.

In 1848, Day purchased the Union Tavern in Milton and converted it into an expansive dual-purpose shop and home for his family, which by now included his wife; two sons, Devereux (b. 1833) and Thomas Junior (b. 1835); and a daughter, Mary Ann (b. 1835). By 1850, Day's factory had become the largest in the state. His clientele were from the upper classes and included Governor David S. Reid (1813–91), who placed a substantial order for some

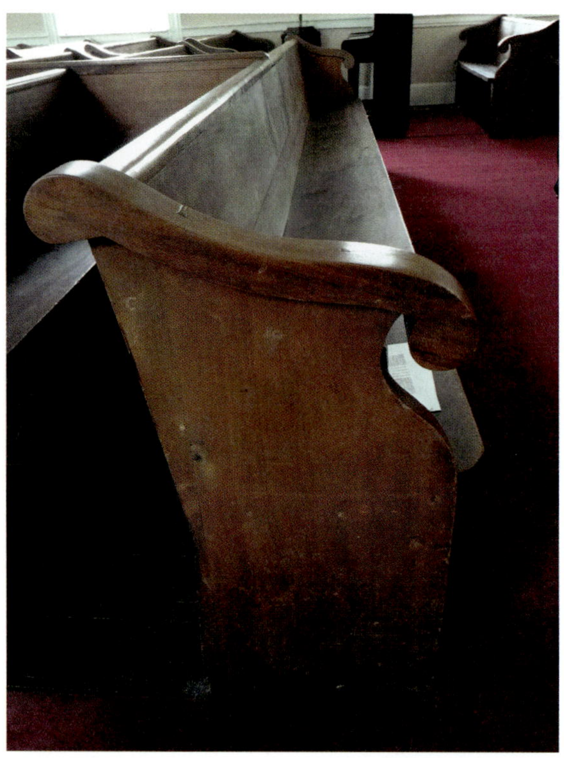

▲ 3.7 Thomas Day, *Pew Benches*, 1837, walnut, approximately 67″ × 33″ × 14″. Milton Presbyterian Church, Caswell County, NC.

Photo: Bob Carlin / Oxford University Press.

45 pieces in 1855. Day's social status and business acumen were reflected in his position as a stockholder in the State Bank of North Carolina. The walnut pews that Day was commissioned to create for the Milton Presbyterian Church are still extant (Figure 3.7) and especially noted for elegantly scrolled forms.

An economic panic in 1857, caused by a reduction in European demand for American goods, affected southern manufacturers, including Day (although its greatest effects were felt in the more industrialized North). Also, faced with steep competition from white furniture makers, Day fell into debt and was forced to sell his real estate holdings. By 1859, he was bankrupt, and he died in 1861. Day's creative legacy has survived, however, in furniture and millwork that are now in private and public collections and homes. His innovative signature designs fuse Greek scroll motifs, curvilinear **fretwork**, and aggressively bold forms, blending American Empire, vernacular, and West African genres.

Day's 1853 variation on the **Gothic Revival** theme (see Chapter 5) in a mahogany bedstead shows his stylistic diversity (Figure 3.8). Framed by four octagonal posts with turned feet and finials, it features two carved inset panels in the reverse ogee footboard and an undulating flow of the side rails. The bed's most distinctive features, however, are three Gothic pointed arches set into a reverse ogee headboard that is crowned by a convex oval and by understated French Rococo details such as scrolls and foliage.

An unconstrained fluidity of form in many of Day's pieces and his frequent incorporation of carved faces and abutting scroll fretwork (as in this headboard) have been linked to West African masks and to the *sankofa* symbol from the Akan (Ghanaian) ***adinkra*** or hieroglyphic system. The *sankofa* glyph is a stylized heart shape that connotes memories and the past (it is also symbolic of the Vodou goddess of love and beauty, Erzulie). Other historians have argued, antithetically, that these same forms derive from European furniture design contexts. Day's furniture likely represents both sides of the African-American equation. In either case, his work exemplifies artistic individuality, ingenuity, and creativity.

Henry Gudgell

Henry Gudgell (1826–95) was a wood sculptor whose walking sticks date to the years immediately following the Civil War. He was born into slavery in Kentucky to a 16-year-old enslaved woman named Rachael. His father is believed to have been Rachael's white owner, Samuel Arbuckle, who moved from Kentucky to Missouri between 1830 and 1832 with his slaves, his daughter Elizabeth Arbuckle Gudgell, and her husband, Jacob Gudgell, Jr. In 1853, Jacob Gudgell's son John sold Henry to his father-in-law, Spencer Hall Gregory, who was a

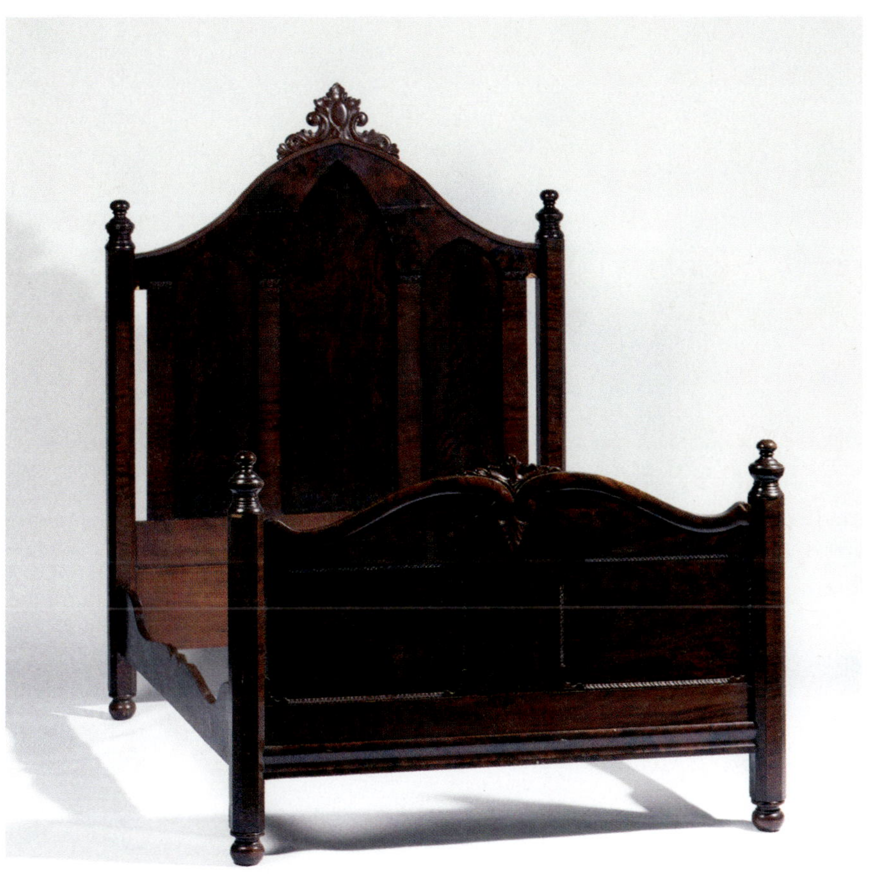

◀ **3.8** Thomas Day, *Bedstead*, 1853–55, mahogany veneer over yellow pine and poplar, 5′4″ × 7′2⅝″.

Photo © North Carolina Museum of History.

wealthy owner of a fleet of merchant ships that traded along the southeastern U.S. coast. By 1861, Henry had been sold again to a Confederate soldier named John Bryan, who sustained a crippling knee injury to his right leg at the Siege of Lexington (Missouri). Henry Gudgell carved a cane for Bryan between 1863 and 1867; Bryan used it until his death in 1899 (Figure 3.9).

Henry Gudgell was trained in a variety of metal and wood "sculptural" trades. He worked as a blacksmith, copper- and silversmith, and a **wheelwright**. His expertise in these areas translated readily to his carved canes. One of only two known surviving Gudgell pieces, Bryan's cane is as much sculpture as utilitarian object and displays the kind of plastic precision and elegance of line often associated with fine metalwork. Spiral grooves adorn the tapered grip, followed by banding and diamond patters. The staff is adorned with a variety of animal and human figures, including a turtle, a lizard, and a clothed man who embraces the shaft as if climbing a tree. This figure appears to hold a tree branch and leaf between its hands.

The cane was ebonized to a dark patina with an iron-and-vinegar mixture, similar to the blackening of sacred reliquary sculpture with palm oil by the Fang people of Gabon. The lower third of the cane is entwined by a snake and has been compared to Bakongo royal scepters, which are also adorned with encircling snakes and nearly identical human and animal figures. The similarity of Gudgell's works to African sculpture has long been a topic of

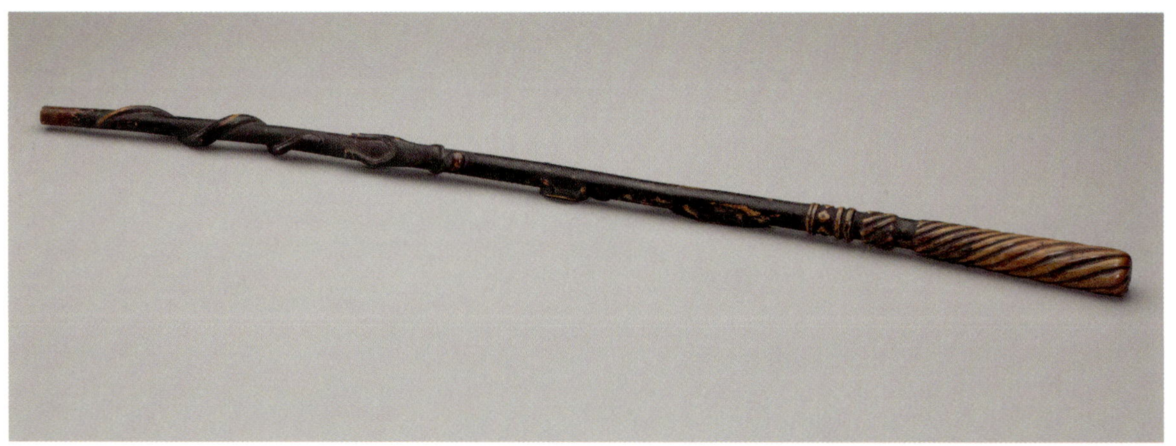

▲ **3.9** Henry Gudgell, *Cane*, c. 1867, ebonized wood, 37″ × 1½″.

Photo: Yale University Art Gallery, Director's Purchase Fund 1968.23.

scholarly speculation. It is not known with any certainty when or how the artist might have been exposed to African-derived sculptural traditions, but it was likely through his wife and other slaves owned by Spencer Hall Gregory, who were brought to Missouri from the North Carolina coast, where African culture thrived.

In 1870, Gudgell purchased 22 acres of land from Gregory's grandson, Spencer Hall Gudgell, and lived there until his death in 1895. His offspring inherited his property and remained there until 1945.

CERAMICS

During the Federal period when manufacturing restrictions placed on the United States by Britain were lifted, it became possible for the ceramics industry to expand beyond the mere production of colonoware (see Chapter 2). This expansion took place most notably in the district of Old Edgefield, South Carolina (today inclusive of Edgefield, Greenwood, McCormick, Saluda, and Aiken Counties). Here, around 1810, inventor Abner Landrum (1785–1859) developed a unique process for making alkaline-glazed, wheel-turned stoneware. Differing from the costly salt-glazed stoneware produced in the North, Landrum's ceramics were, according to 19th-century historian Robert Mills, "stronger, better, and cheaper than any European or American ware of the same kind." At the turn of the 19th century, Landrum had purchased property in Edgefield to create the town of Pottersville, where he set up his first stoneware factory. His brother John Landrum (1765–1846) opened a similar plant in nearby Horse Creek.

The rank and file of Edgefield potters were enslaved workers. So dependent on black ceramicists was the Edgefield potters' trade that, between 1800 and 1820, the enslaved population of the district increased to fully half of the area's residents. Still booming at the onset of the Civil War, 170 Africans were illegally imported to work there as enslaved laborers. These enslaved potters were fully trained in ceramic production, including expertise in the construction, maintenance, and heating of long, tunnel-shaped ovens called **groundhog kilns**; the gathering of clay; the operation of **pugmills**; glaze mixing; shaping clay into vessels on potter's wheels; and **firing** clay into stoneware. Factory

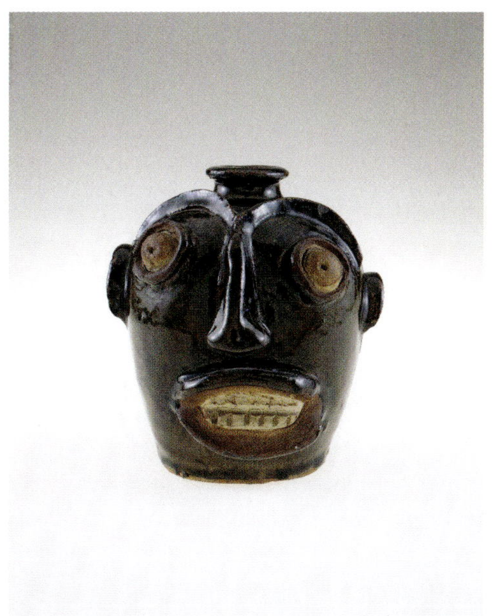

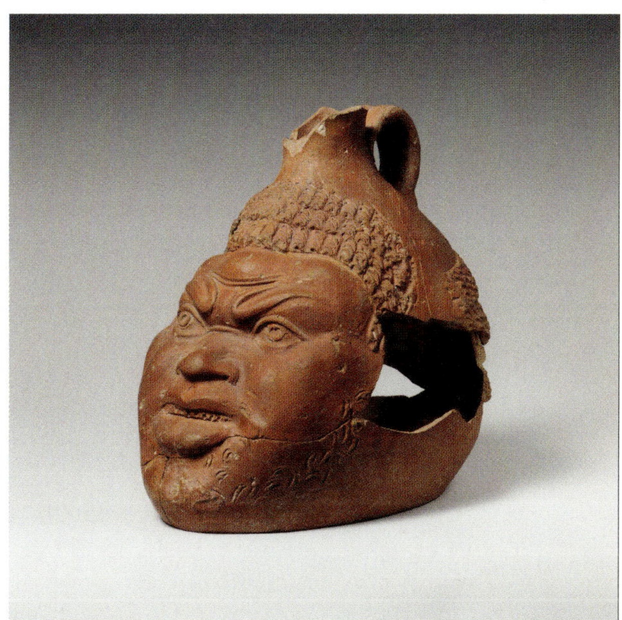

▲ **3.10** Unknown, *Face Vessel*, mid-1800s, Edgefield ceramic, stoneware, coarse, 5⅜″ × 5½″. United States.

National Museum of American History, Kenneth E. Behring Center, the Marcus Benjamin Collection, 150313.

▲ **3.11** Unknown, *Terracotta Jug in the Shape of the Head of an African*, Roman imperial period, 3rd century C.E., terracotta, 7⅛″.

Gift of J. Pierpont Morgan, 1917 (17.194.859). Photo © The Metropolitan Museum of Art. Photo source: Art Resource, NY.

owners were proud of their skilled black potters and advertised their talents in local newspapers as a selling point for their inventory.

Among the most unique forms of pottery produced in Edgefield were Afro-Carolinian face vessels (Figure 3.10). Although found in numerous cultures from Europe to Africa, the face vessels of Edgefield are unique in their appearance and function and in that they were produced by slaves (and later freemen) as personal items, separate and distinct from those made for owners and employers. These vessels are noted for dramatic facial distortions, white kaolin (clay) eyes, and bared or sharpened teeth. The use of white clay in this fashion has been traced to religious practices in Africa, where it was used for facial marking and the enhancement of eyes in Kongo *nkondi* or carved "power" sculptures. Further links to Africa include the distortion and exaggeration of facial features; this technique can be found in African sacred sculpture throughout the western and central continent. Finally, African warriors with sharpened teeth are recorded in Roman terracotta face vessels as far back as the third century (Figure 3.11). Because the origin of the Afro-Carolinian face vessel cannot be fully documented, it is difficult to state with any certainty what precise meaning and purpose these anthropomorphic jugs might have had for their anonymous makers. At the very least, they served as bonafide expressions of their identity and creativity.

"Dave the Potter" (Dave Drake)

One enslaved ceramicist from Edgefield was not anonymous: "Dave the Potter," or Dave Drake (1801–70s). From the 1820s until his emancipation in the 1860s, Dave worked for a series of wealthy planters and businessmen, including Abner Landrum, his nephew Harvey Drake (1796–1832), and John Landrum's son-in-law Lewis J. Miles (1808–68). Dave produced his first known signed work on July 12, 1834, a practice he continued until 1864, by which time he had signed more than 100 pieces. Taking special pride in his creations, Dave is the only known slave potter to have signed his pieces. Along with his signature, he etched rhymed couplets such as the one inscribed on his 1834 jar: "Put every bit and all between— / surely this jar will hold 14." Dave was recognized as a master craftsman by the Landrum family, which might explain why he remained in South Carolina even after his first owner and several of his family members moved to Louisiana. Dave noted their absence on one of his jugs, on which he wrote, "I wonder where is all my relations— / Friendship to all and every nation." It is also believed that Abner Landrum was responsible for Dave's literacy, because Landrum assigned Dave as **typesetter** for the local newspaper he published.

The earliest ceramics produced by Dave and his fellow slave workers were utilitarian vessels used for food storage and preparation. The containers were glazed in gray green or yellow green at the Pottersville factory; in Horse Creek, opaque reddish-brown and translucent brown glazes were used. Both factories produced vessels that were squat and egg shaped in configuration with **ear-lug handles**. The more elongated stoneware containers that were glazed in olive green were produced later in the century (Figure 3.12). Dave's stoneware is remarkable due to its size and holding capacity; the largest piece can hold as much as 40 gallons. Creating vessels of this size required the maker to turn 40 or 50 pounds of clay at the wheel. For this reason, it is assumed that, even with assistance, Dave must have been not only a well-trained ceramicist but an extremely powerful and well-coordinated sculptor of clay. Also extraordinary is the fact that Dave likely made some 40,000 ceramic works throughout his lifetime.

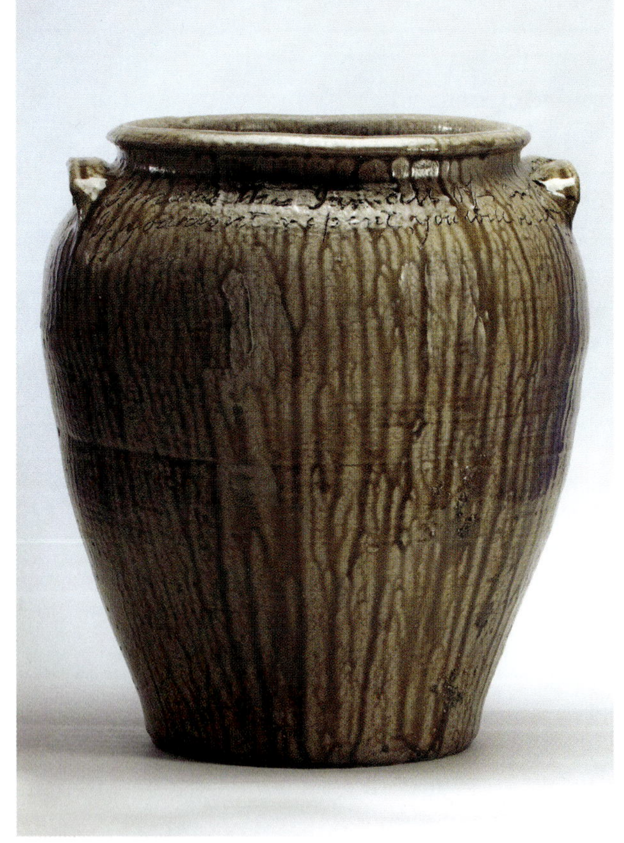

▼ **3.12** Dave Drake, *Jar Made by "Dave,"* 1862, ceramic, stoneware, wheel thrown, 20½" × 18". Lewis Miles Plantation, SC.

National Museum of American History, *Treasure of American History* online exhibition.

Dave's method involved turning the base of the jar first and then applying the shoulder and mouth of the jar individually using the **coil process**. The clay was seamed so expertly that the coils are virtually invisible. Then Dave added the signature Edgefield District watery **slip** glaze, which was made of a mixture of wood ash and lime, rather than the poisonous lead-based glazes used prior to the development of Landrum's method. Lime gave the glaze its unique khaki hue. The fluidity of the glaze created the appearance of color dripping down the side of the container, a look called "slip trailing" that became associated with Edgefield pottery.

About twenty surviving pieces by Dave are inscribed with his original two-line poems on topics such as pottery, work, romance, and religion. A couplet inscribed on an 1858 stoneware storage jar reads, "I made this jar all of cross, / If you don[']t repent you will be lost." The rhyme refers to a biblical passage (Acts 2:14–42) and indicates Dave's Christian devotion. It also suggests a theme of cross bearing indicative of Drake's lifetime as a slave. This particular jar is the last extant one on which Dave inscribed poetry. He dated it May 3, 1862, and signed it with both his own name and the initials of his owner, "L M"—Lewis Miles. Thanks to Dave and so many unnamed others, the Landrum alkaline glazing method quickly found its way to North Carolina, Georgia, Alabama, and even Texas, where the historic Hiram Wilson (1836–1884) Pottery was founded by its namesake (a North Carolina-born ex-slave). It was the first recorded black business in the state of Texas.

Thomas Commeraw

In contrast to Dave Drake and Hiram Wilson, Thomas Commeraw (fl. 1796–1819) was a northerner who lived in New York City. As a free black entrepreneur, Commeraw produced scores of **salt-glazed stoneware** vessels during his career. He maintained a thriving business from 1797 to 1819 in Manhattan's Lower East Side, at Corlear's Hook, an East River shoreline neighborhood halfway between today's Williamsburg and Manhattan bridges. Commeraw's factory was located just north of a neighborhood nicknamed Potter's Hill after the ceramics factories operated there by German émigrés John Remmey (beginning in 1735) and Georg and Wilhelm Crolius (founded in 1718 and 1728, respectively). Remmey and Crolius merged in 1742, and their Potter's Hill business prospered under the management of their descendants until 1849.

The area where the Remmey-Crolius and other private and city-owned ceramics factories were located is significant in that it neighbored the site of the historic African Burial Ground. The potteries drew their labor force from a local population of both free and enslaved African Americans. Commeraw may have learned his trade at the Remmey-Crolius factory before opening his own business, and he might have been a one-time slave of the Crolius family or an actual family member—or both, as suggested by the last will and testament of Wilhelm Crolius, which provided for the manumission of "Tom and wife Venus and their children."

Whatever Commeraw's status before 1796, after this time he operated a successful pottery business as a freeman. Commeraw supplied ceramic vessels in a variety of sizes and shapes to a wealthy interracial clientele of oyster harvesters, church leaders, and abolitionists, for use in the storing and shipping of foodstuffs, preserves, and liquor. Several of his patrons were Dutch and British transatlantic shippers who purchased stoneware in large supply to preserve their merchandise during long voyages. In recent years, Commeraw's stoneware has been unearthed by divers and archeologists in the Hudson River near Lower Manhattan and as far afield as Norway and Guyana.

Commeraw's pottery is often distinctly ovoid in shape and ecru in color (Figure 3.13). It is readily identifiable because he tool-stamped many of his pieces with a **maker's mark**—"Commeraw Stoneware" and the location of his factory, "Corlears Hook." His pottery is similar to that of Remmey

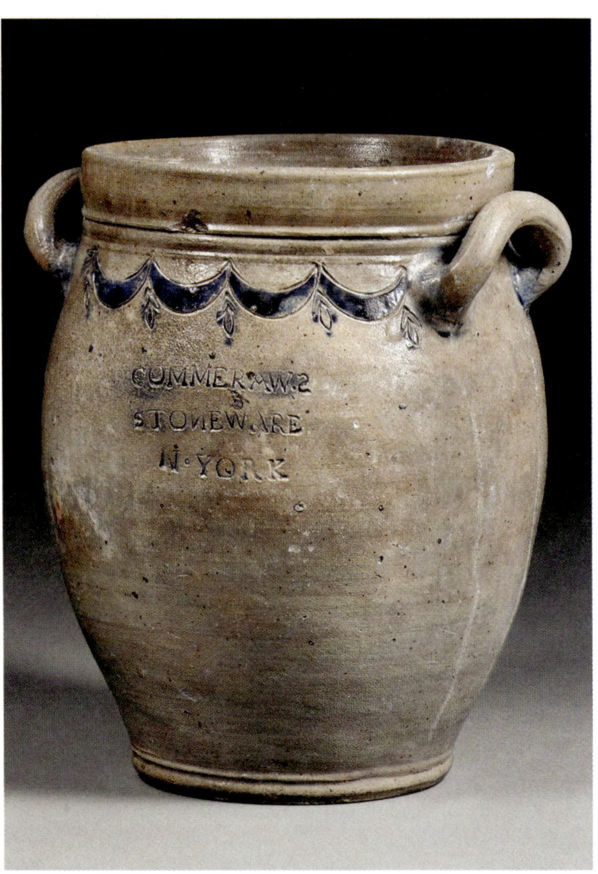

▲ **3.13** Thomas Commeraw, *Stoneware Jar*, c. 1810, ceramic, 11¾″ high.

Courtesy of Skinner, Inc., www.skinnerinc.com.

and Crolius in its color. Its etched blue shells and garland and tassel motifs were popular in the interior and architectural design of the Federal period because of their ancient Roman derivation. The shell decoration also alludes to Commeraw's oyster harvester clients, who needed stoneware to store their highly perishable products. Their oysters were packed in cylindrically shaped jars designed by Commeraw that are similar to modern-day tin cans. Commeraw further decorated his crockpots with stamped images of fruit, spirals, butterflies, birds, and figures, all painted with cobalt-blue slip before firing. He affixed them with open-loop lug handles for transport.

Commeraw operated his pottery business for at least 20 years, during which time he was an active abolitionist and a member of, and Christian cantor in, the African Church in New York. His career in New York came to a close in 1820, when he immigrated to Sierra Leone in West Africa at the request of the American Colonization Society (ACS). He was invited to assist in the establishment of a colony for the repatriation of free black Americans to Africa. The ACS had been founded by whites who opposed slavery but, at the same time, rejected the integration of free blacks into white American society. It was their desire to relocate as many free blacks as possible to Africa. Along with 85 others, Commeraw sailed to Africa that year.

The Sierra Leone colony was established two years later as Christopolis. It was renamed Monrovia in 1824 in honor of President James Monroe (1758–1831), who supported the repatriation project. By 1847, Monrovia had evolved into the independent Republic of Liberia. The settlers' experiences in Sierra Leone were especially difficult due to the harsh topography, the high death rate of the initial colonizers, and personal and political conflicts within the community. The scant records indicate that Commeraw's wife, Ann, died of fever in 1821 and that he and his three children returned to the United States in 1822.

METALWORK

Blacksmithing continued to be a vital industry beyond the lucrative pre–Revolutionary War business of iron ore exporting. President Jefferson's plantation at Monticello featured a fully equipped blacksmith shop beginning in the early 1790s. Enslaved blacksmiths Joe Fossett, "Little George," and Moses supervised a Monticello staff of more than a dozen ironworkers who provided essential services to Jefferson and other local clientele. Their work included horse shoeing, nail making, and the production and maintenance of everything from rifles to farm equipment. The nail-producing business alone earned Jefferson the modern-day equivalent of $24,000 annually by 1796. In addition to Virginia, major ironworks were established in Maine, New York, Pennsylvania, and Massachusetts.

Peter Bentzon

An exemplar of the Pennsylvania metalwork tradition is African-American silversmith Peter Bentzon (c. 1783–after 1850), who was born free in the Virgin Islands. Bentzon was the probable son of Norwegian lawyer Jacob Bentzon and a free black mother. Peter Bentzon is referred to in historic records as a "mustice"—a term that identified his mother as biracial. At eight years of age, Bentzon was sent to Philadelphia to be educated. Later, from 1799 to 1806, he apprenticed as a silversmith, completing his training at age 23. After this time, he regularly traveled between Philadelphia and St. Croix, operating silversmithing businesses in both places. His workshop and home in St. Croix were located in Christiansted, where he lived with his wife, Rachel de la Motta (another mustice, whom he married in 1813), his children, and several slaves. In Philadelphia, he and his family resided in an interracial neighborhood near Market Street.

Bentzon's existing works, of which there are only nine, date from 1815 to 1841. An example from early in his career is an 1817 silver teapot designed with an elegant austerity indicative of much Federal-period decorative art (Figure 3.14). The steeply shallow S-curve of the wood teapot handle is adapted from antique Greco-Roman urns and echoes the gracefully curved spout. The pot is minimally adorned with an acorn-shaped finial and the sweeping initials—"M.C."—of the artist's client. What makes this piece exceptional is the cadenced repetition of horizontal ellipses in the shape of the base, bowl, and lid, creating a look of effortless opulence.

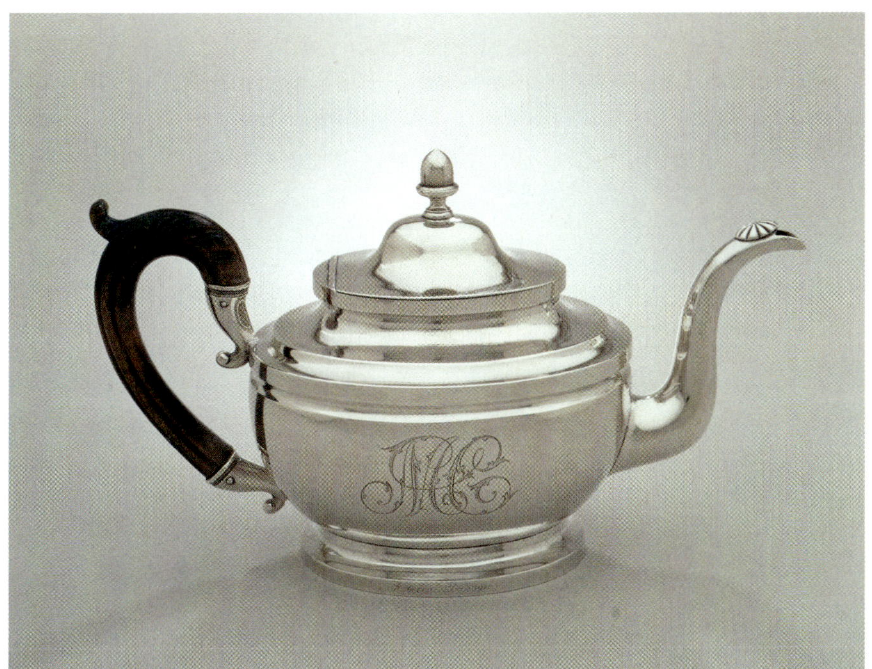

◀ **3.14** Peter Bentzon, *Teapot*, c. 1817, silver and wood, 7″ × 12⅝″ × 6¾″.

Saint Louis Art Museum, Museum Minority Artists Purchase Fund and funds given by the Equal Sweetener Foundation and the Paul and Elissa Cahn Foundation, 41:2001.

Bentzon stamped his pieces with his maker's mark, "P. BENTZON" or "PB," which has made it possible to identify his work. Other black Philadelphia silversmiths, who may or may not have used maker's marks, are listed in city trade directories in 1810 and 1813 and include Henry Bray and Anthony Soweralt. No works by either have been identified, nor have details of their lives been uncovered. Bentzon's later life is obscure. He spent his last years in Philadelphia, where he worked as a silver- and goldsmith, and added to his repertoire jewelry making and repair. Records of him as a "person of color" disappear after 1848, when he is believed to have either passed away or, alternatively, **passed** into white society.

TEXTILE AND CLOTHING DESIGN

Early Quilt Making and Makers

One of the most common forms of African-American art of the 19th century was the quilt. A fusion of African and European techniques, the African-American quilting tradition is a long and vibrant one that has thrived into the 21st century. Quilt production prior to the Federal era was extremely limited due to the manufacturing restrictions imposed by Britain. The preferred quilting design during the 18th century was **broderie perse** (Persian embroidery), which was actually an **appliqué** technique. Broderie perse quilts incorporated cotton floral-print **chintz**, which was carefully cut around the perimeter of each printed floral design and appliquéd onto a larger cloth. Due to their costliness (chintz had to be imported from India) and the labor-intensive appliqué process, quilts of this type were rare. As a result, little physical evidence remains of African-American (or any) broderie perse quilts prior to 1800. One exceptional example from the 1830s is preserved in the Michigan State University Museum collection (Figure 3.15). Made entirely by hand by enslaved women in Pearlington, Mississippi, the quilt is edged in floral and chevron patterns and is decorated throughout with tan, blue, and red floral chintz. It incorporates multiple textile techniques, including quilting, appliqué, and **piecing** and would have been highly prized by its owner.

Historical records clearly indicate that enslaved African women were routinely pressed into service in the textile industry in the eastern and southern United States. After working in the fields throughout the day, enslaved women were required to spin, knit, weave, embroider, dye fabric, make lace, and cut and sew cloth at night. In addition to basic whole-cloth production, African American women made clothing, coverlets, linens, dolls, curtains, purses, and even upholstery for slaveholding families as well as for their own use. Plantation owners harvested raw materials—**hemp**, cotton, and wool—which had to be spun into thread and yarn and then made into cloth. Spindles, spinning wheels, and—later—spinning jennies (invented in 1764 to accommodate multiple spools) were staples on American plantations, as were cloth-making rooms—like minifactories—where the work was done. Slave owners understood the value of skilled textile workers and designers and were known to ask high prices for them at auction.

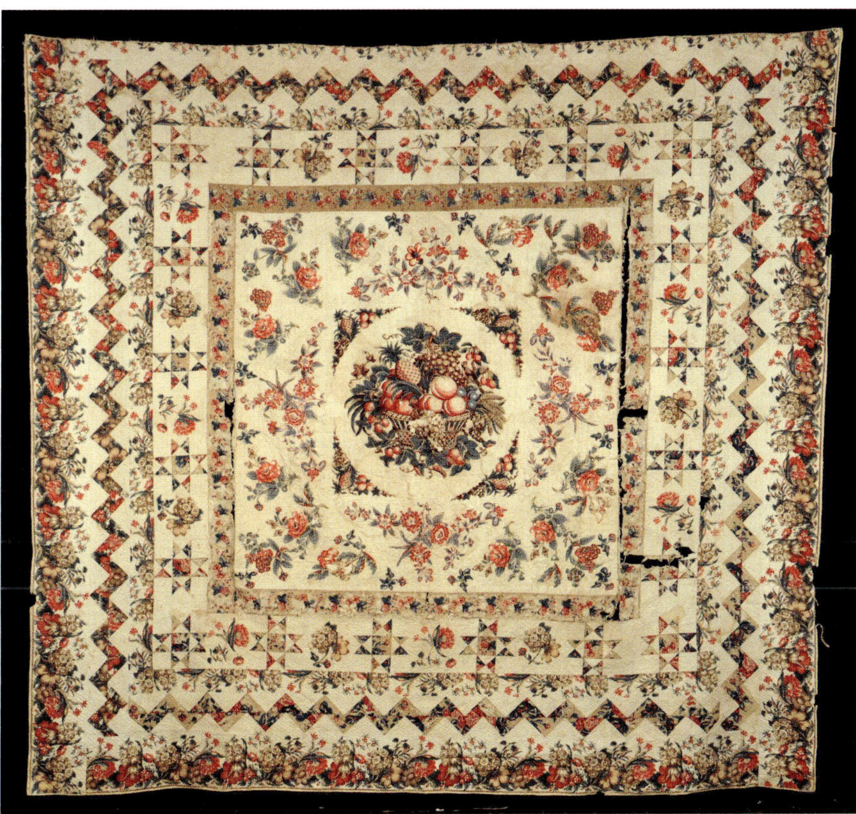

◀ **3.15** Unknown, *Broderie Perse Medallion Quilt*, c. 1830, cotton, 98″ × 92½″. Made in Pearlington, MS.

Courtesy of Michigan State University Museum.

After the Revolutionary War, quilt production boomed in America and a golden age of quilt making began. Free from British ordinances against it, Americans could now create textiles using homegrown raw materials rather than expensive imports. The increase in quilt design and production was also propelled by the invention of the cotton gin in 1793, which vastly facilitated the growth of the cotton industry as well as the institution of slavery (see Chapter 2). The high demand for skilled textile and clothing makers and designers is evident in the routine appearance of advertisements peddling and soliciting the services of enslaved women with these skills.

When made for their own use rather than that of the slave owners, African-American textiles featured more diverse color palettes, asymmetrical patterns, and enigmatic motifs that are traceable to West Africa. Irregular designs were preferred, for example, by the Mande people and their descendants in America due to a long-standing cultural belief that negative energy moved in straight, linear paths and could only be forestalled if those paths were disrupted. Thus, the conventional practice of matching patterns and straight edges in fabric design was substituted in many African-American quilts by mismatched motifs and broken lines. This preference even extended to farm work, where slaves "oftentimes refused to plow in a straight furrow . . . without occasionally deviating to foil the malevolent spirits," as noted by historian Judith Chase.

Another African-derived quilting element found in personal-use slave textiles is the frequent inclusion of inscrutable symbols. African-American quilts from the 19th century incorporate ciphers similar to encryptions found in Nigerian Ekpe cloth (which is stamped with ***nsibidi* signs**) and Yoruban ***adire-eleko*** textiles, as well as in Ghanaian and Ivory Coast fabrics marked with *adinkra* symbols by Akan men. In America, secret symbols such as these took the form of hand- and doll-shaped silhouettes that alluded to protective "mojos" (spellcasting) more commonly seen in neo-African cultures in Haiti and Cuba. The hand shape refers to what Vodou practitioners call *travailler avec deux mains*, or "to work with both hands"—for good and evil. The doll shape is a variation on the theme of protective Kongo power figures, or ***nkondi***.

One controversial hidden-symbol quilt genre from the antebellum years persists today: the Underground Railroad quilt. Based entirely on oral tradition, the Underground Railroad quilt exists only in modern versions. These quilts are said to have been encoded with camouflaged symbols and placed along the Underground Railroad trail between slaveholding states and Canada. The encryptions in these quilts permitted runaway slaves to identify safe houses and provided them with instructions and directions on their journey north.

Since 1990, however, the code theory has been widely debunked by scholars due to the lack of supporting empirical evidence. Others theorists hold fast, believing in the validity of oral tradition as an accurate historical record. Alleged Underground Railroad quilt icons such as bow ties, flying geese, and five-pointed stars are not unique to slave quilts but are common to quilts throughout the United States and Europe. They also have specific African precedents in the ciphers of the Sierra Leonean Poro society and the quilted horse armor of the Hausa of Nigeria (both of which duplicate the bow tie), in cloth that replicates the flying geese design in Ekpe society, and in Egbo secret society works that feature five-pointed stars. Despite these points, staunch contemporary resistance to the non-Western tradition of recording history orally will likely continue to isolate the Underground Railroad quilt theory as questionable, at least from a scholarly vantage point.

Harriet Powers

Harriet Powers (1837–1910) was a slave born near Athens, Georgia. She turned to quilting after Emancipation, when she and her husband, Armstead, purchased their own home. She first gained notoriety when a local artist, Oneita ("Jennie") Virginia Smith, admired one of her quilts at the 1886 Athens Cotton Fair and purchased it five years later for five dollars (Figure 3.16). This example, today housed in the Smithsonian Institution collection, is one of two surviving works by the artist. It was created using a basic block construction of 11 asymmetrical segments, running stitches, and appliqué. The quilt illustrates Adam and Eve in the first two panels, Satan in panel 3, Cain and Abel in panels 4 and 5, Jacob's ladder in panel 6, Christ's baptism and crucifixion in 7 and 8, Judas in the ninth panel, the Last Supper in the tenth, and the Nativity in the last panel. Powers added to each scene crescent, star, and sunburst motifs to reference astrological phenomena and Masonic symbols. These same icons appear in a later Powers quilt that was commissioned by the wives of Atlanta University

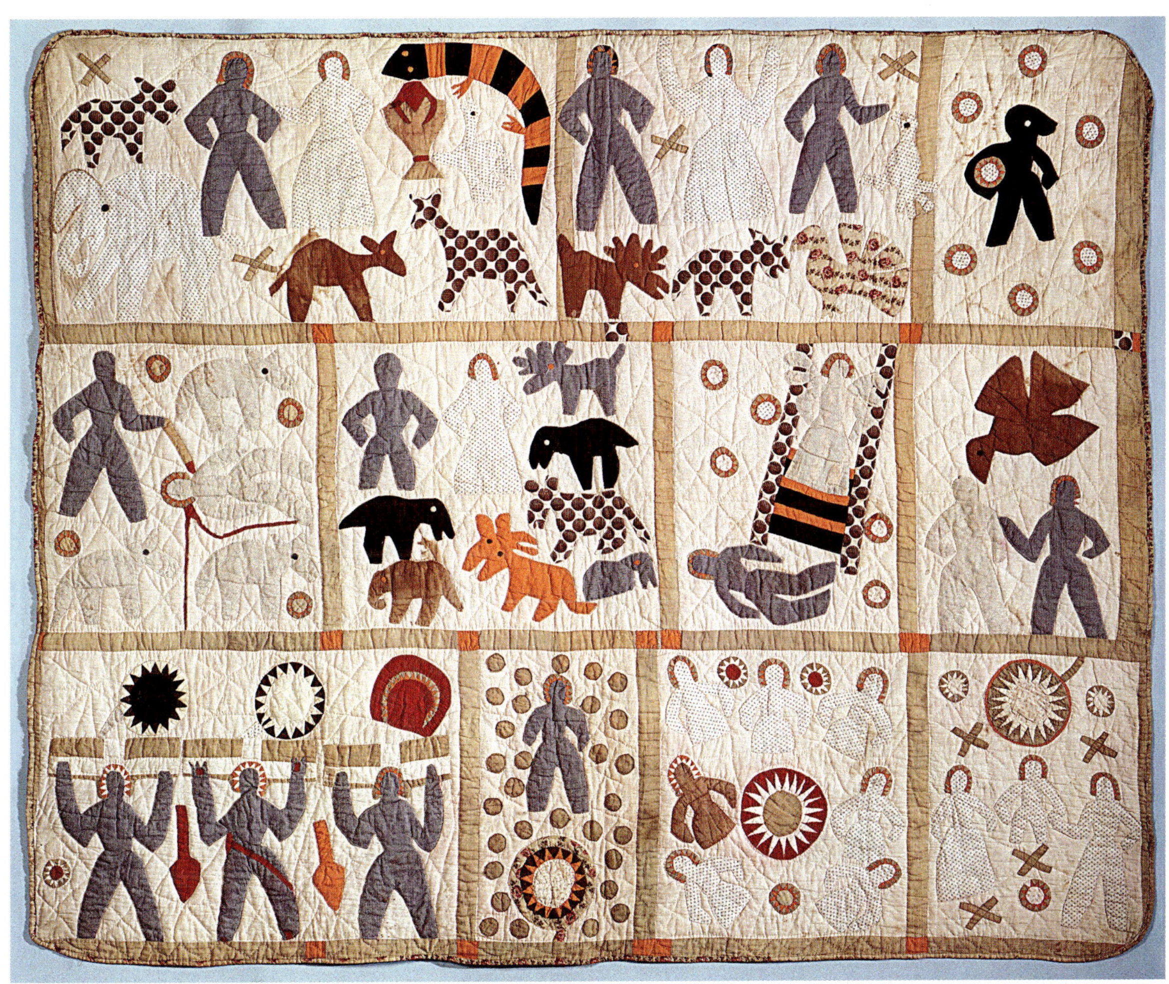

▲ **3.16** Harriet Powers, *Bible Quilt*, 1895–98, fabric: cotton, thread: cotton, filling: cotton (overall materials), 75″ × 89″. Clarke County, GA.

National Museum of American History, Smithsonian Institution.

professors and was completed in 1898. The inclusion of Masonic forms in her textiles alludes to Powers's membership and that of her husband (with whom she had nine children) in a Clarke County Masonic order that aided Underground Railroad activity. Supporting this theory, the only existing photograph of Powers shows her wearing a ceremonial apron decorated with African-informed saw-toothed edges and with the same Masonic symbols found in her quilts (see chapter-opening image). The star emblem on Powers's apron has been identified as the symbol of the Eastern Star Lodge of Women Masons.

Powers's quilts were displayed at the Tennessee Centennial Exposition in Nashville and at the Cotton States and International Expositions in Atlanta at the end of the 1890s. In addition to religious imagery, her second surviving quilt in the collection of the Museum of Fine Arts, Boston, records anecdotal local events and astrological phenomena. Powers's choice of subject matter links her quilt to Yoruba, Fon, Ewe, and Fante textiles, which similarly illustrated the events of a king's reign, meteorological rarities, and other important occurrences. Furthermore, the figural forms in Powers's works duplicate almost exactly those found in Fon and Kongo textiles.

The similarities of West African textiles to those of Powers suggest that she had firsthand knowledge of fabrics from Dahomey (the Republic of Benin). This is entirely possible if we consider that, despite an 1808 U.S. ban on slave importation, Africans were smuggled into Georgia and other coastal states throughout Powers's youth. Because the Fon used regularized cloth templates in their appliqué work, which they passed down from generation to generation unaltered, Powers would have been able to absorb the formulae with relative ease. Powers appreciated her quilts as vital cultural records and expressions of her creativity. In fact, for many years, she was unwilling to part with them, despite repeated offers from potential buyers. Not until she fell on hard times did Powers sell her first quilt to Oneita Smith. Afterward, she called on Smith several times to "visit the darling offspring of her brain."

Elizabeth Hobbs Keckley

Unlike much of the history of antebellum African-American textiles and their makers, the life and work of quilt maker and dressmaker Elizabeth Hobbs Keckley (1818–1907) is well documented by historians and by Keckley, who published her autobiography, *Behind the Scenes: Or 30 Years a Slave and Four Years in the White House*, in 1868. Born into slavery, Keckley was the daughter of an educated slave named Agnes and a slave-holding planter, Colonel Armistead Burwell (1777–1841). Keckley's maiden surname, Hobbs, was taken from her stepfather, George Pleasant Hobbs, a slave from a neighboring plantation who was permitted to marry Agnes but later forced to leave his wife and stepdaughter when his owner moved away. After spending her childhood in Virginia, Keckley was given as a wedding present to Burwell's son Robert, and she was taken by him to Hillsborough, North Carolina. During her four years in Hillsboro, Keckley was repeatedly sexually assaulted by a local merchant and, in 1839, gave birth to a son named George.

Soon after giving birth, Keckley and her son were returned to Virginia to live with a married Burwell daughter, Ann Burwell Garland, who by this time also owned Keckley's mother Agnes. The Garlands moved to St. Louis, Missouri, where Keckley spent the next dozen years learning the seamstress trade and becoming an expert dressmaker. She also met and married her husband, James Keckley, although they lived together only briefly. Aware of the value of her skills, the Garland family hired Keckley out as a slave-entrepreneur. She did business with many middle- and upper-class clients, both black and white. Her position helped to support the Garland family, and by 1852 it also permitted Keckley to save and borrow (from wealthy clients) enough money to purchase her own freedom and that of her son from the Garlands, for $1,200. Keckley's manumission was funded, in part, by wealthy benefactor-clients, and her emancipation became official in November 1855. Highly determined and successful in her business dealings, Keckley repaid all loans within five years. During the same time, she sent her son to Wilberforce University in Ohio, the first private African-American university in the country. (George enlisted in the Union army and was killed in 1861.)

In 1860, Keckley moved to Baltimore, where she briefly taught dressmaking and design to aspiring black seamstresses, before moving on to Washington, D.C. With introductions from her clients in St. Louis, Keckley and her dress designs quickly became popular among the wives of the political elite. In particular, dresses that Keckley designed for Anna Mason Lee, the wife of General Robert E. Lee, and for Mrs. Varina Davis, the wife of Jefferson Davis, greatly increased Keckley's exposure and client base. Her restrained interpretations of French **Victorian** designs—which captured the style's elegant silhouette but rejected excesses of lace and ribbon—became the envy of upscale Washington women, who paid dearly for Keckley's taste and talents. (On one occasion, General Lee gave Keckley $100—more than $2,000 today—simply to purchase fabric trim embellishments to adorn a silk dress that she was to make for his wife.) Most prized were her draping skills and the exceptional fit of her dresses. Working with seamstress assistants, Keckley produced complicated gowns in record time, her speed of execution making her all the more sought after.

One of Keckley's customers, Margaret McLean (the daughter of General Edwin Vose Sumner) was so pleased with her work that she introduced the designer to the newly elected President Abraham Lincoln (1809–65) and his wife, Mary Todd Lincoln (1818–82). Mrs. Lincoln was taken with Keckley's understated Victorian elegance and refined demeanor. She immediately engaged Keckley as a personal ***modiste*** and thereafter referred to her as "My Dear Lizzie." Keckley was responsible for choosing, designing, creating, and maintaining the First Lady's lavish wardrobe. She produced 16 dresses for Mrs. Lincoln in four months and remained on the White House staff as Mary Lincoln's friend and employee for the duration of the Lincoln presidency.

One of the gowns that Keckley designed for Mrs. Lincoln in 1861 (now in the Smithsonian collection) is made of violet velvet with mother-of-pearl buttons and satin piping (Figure 3.17). Keckley designed two separate bodices for the dress, one unadorned for day wear and one with lace sleeves and a lower neckline for evening wear. Its dual purpose helped to counteract Mrs. Lincoln's reputation as an excessive spender, as did its subdued color and simplicity of design, offsetting the sumptuousness of its materials. The strategically placed cream-colored piping was especially figure flattering. Keckley's design was an astute response to the needs of her client and to the social and political environment in which she circulated. The color choice was especially discerning, because purple is traditionally the color of royalty or high office.

▼ **3.17** Elizabeth Keckley, *Mary Lincoln's Dress*, 1861, velvet, satin, lace, 60″ × 48″.

National Museum of American History, Smithsonian Institution, Washington, D.C., bequest of Mrs. Julian James.

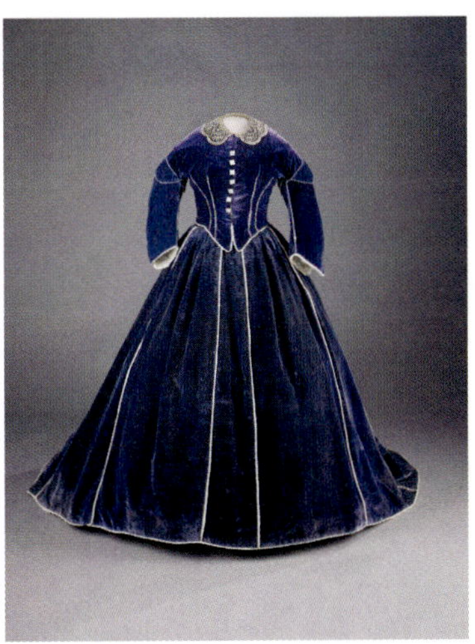

Mrs. Lincoln relocated to Chicago after her husband's assassination but kept in touch with Keckley through letters. In 1868, with the assistance of famed ex-slave and civil rights activist Frederick Douglass (1818–95) and abolitionist James Redpath (1833–91), Keckley published her memoir, which was a national sensation. Describing Mary Lincoln with veracity and a certain empathy, Keckley's book nonetheless exposed aspects of Lincoln family life that they would have preferred be kept private. The book precipitated widespread criticism of the Lincolns and brought to an end the Lincoln-Keckley friendship.

After leaving the White House, Keckley lost most of her affluent clients and faced financial difficulties (earnings from the book were minimal, despite its notoriety). She supported herself by continuing to design dresses and by teaching dressmaking until the 1890s, when Keckley was appointed to a faculty position at her son's alma mater, Wilberforce University. After a few years, however, at nearly 80 years old, Keckley returned to Washington, D.C., and spent the rest of her life as a resident at the National Home for Destitute Colored Women and Children. Artistic evidence of Keckley's extraordinary life, talent, and spirit, such as the Mary Lincoln gowns and a Civil War quilt that she made from the First Lady's dress scraps (Figure 3.18), today hold places of honor in the fabric of American history, as does their maker.

▼ **3.18** Elizabeth Keckley, *Mary Todd Lincoln Quilt*, c. 1861–71, dress scraps, 92½ × 94½″.

The Kent State University Museum, gift of Ross Trump in memory of his mother, Helen Watts Trump.

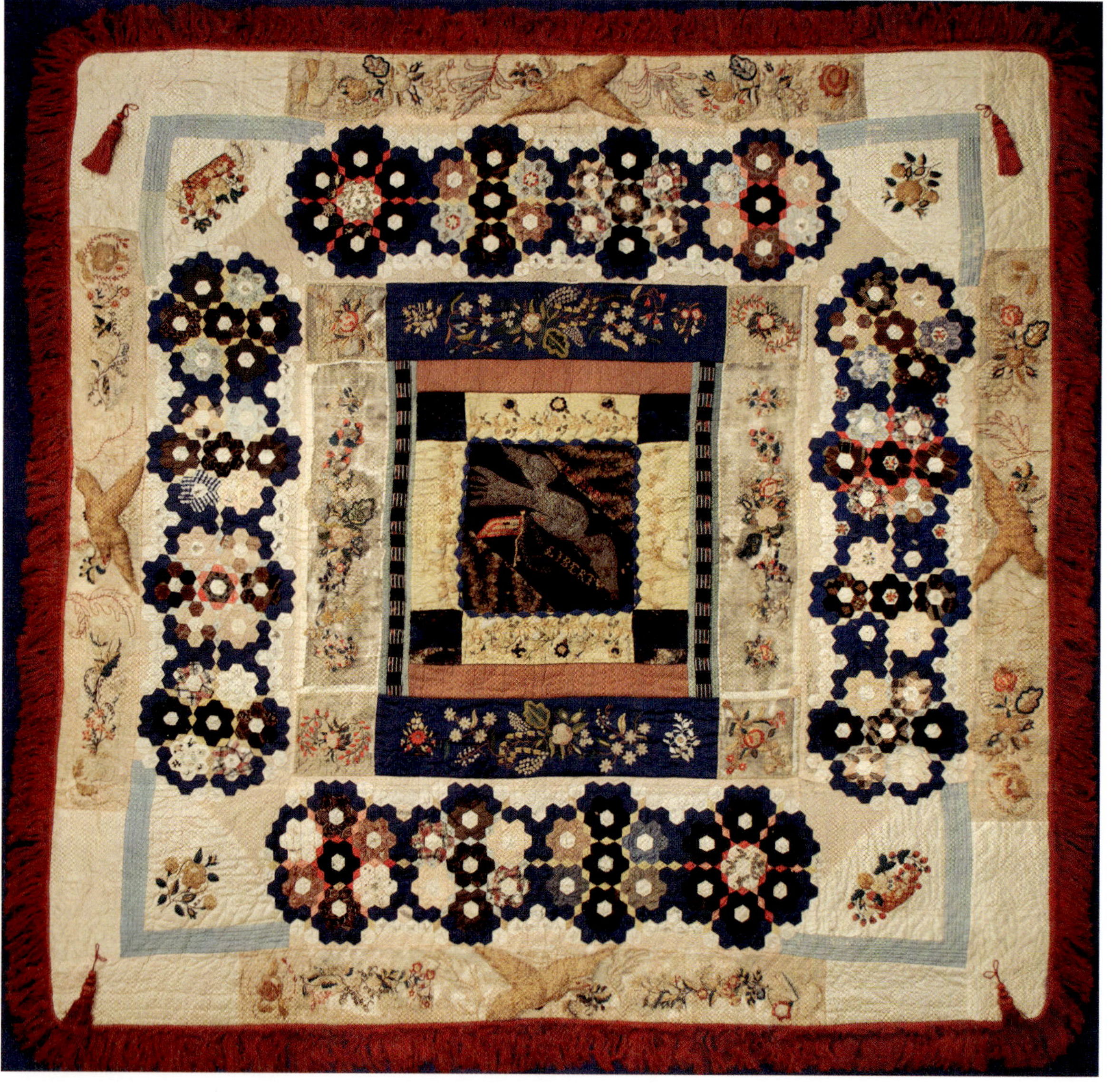

Summary

African Americans of the Federal period forged significant inroads into the fields of art and architecture by combining their creative and technical skills with their business abilities. Both Henry Boyd in furniture and Elizabeth Keckley in fashion design succeeded as entrepreneurs despite their enslaved status. Others merged African and European art-making traditions to create works that were quintessentially African-American. In architecture, West African hipped roofs were coupled with classical Greco-Roman designs, as in Charles Paquet's Destrehan Manor. In producing pottery, Edgefield artisans such as Dave Drake drew from sacred African mask traditions to create useful objects for lucrative sale. African-American quilts such as those created by Harriet Powers combined Fon-derived figures and compositions with European-derived batting and backing. Quilt makers also incorporated encrypted symbols native to Africa into their designs. In architecture, ceramics, metalsmithing, and furniture and textile design, from Monticello to New York, African Americans were asserting their unique brand of creativity into the American artistic landscape.

Key Terms

adinkra: a set of ideographic or conceptual symbols used by the Akan people of Ghana

adire-eleko: a resist-dying process in which designs are hand painted onto cloth with starch paste

American Empire style: Federal-style furniture patterned after the Neoclassical designs created during the reign of the French emperor Napoleon at the turn of the 19th century

appliqué: in needlework, the process of cutting pieces of material and sewing them onto another larger piece

apron: in furniture design, a panel placed at a right angle to the surface or seat of a table or chair that connects to the legs

Biedermeier: an early to mid-19th-century Central European furniture style characterized by functionality, restrained curves and scrolls, and streamlined classical motifs

British Regency style: an early 19th-century furniture style incorporating ancient Egyptian and Greco-Roman decorative elements such as columns, animal legs, lyres, and scrolls

broderie perse: meaning "Persian embroidery," a style of quilt making in which cotton floral-print fabric is cut around the perimeter of each flower and sewn onto a larger cloth

cabinetmaker: a designer and maker of cabinets, shelving, and furniture

cabriole leg: an S-curved furniture leg that derives from ancient China and classical Greece

chintz: polished cotton fabric traditionally made in India and printed with floral designs coil process: rolling clay into long, narrow cylinders; attaching the ends to create a circular coil; and stacking the coils to form a vessel

colonnade: a roof structure supported by evenly spaced columns

cornice: decorative ceiling molding along the top of a building or item of furniture

Doric: a classical Greek architectural order with columns made in multiple sections (drums) with flat, square column tops (capitals) and a decorative roof support (frieze) of alternating carved figures (metopes) and vertical grooves (triglyphs)

ear-lug handle: a crescent- or ear-shaped handle attached to pottery for carrying

entablature: the horizontal area of the façade of a classical building located above the columns and beneath the roof, consisting of a base (architrave), a section of carvings (frieze), and molded top (cornice)

fire; firing: the process of baking clay into pottery, bricks, and other forms

French Empire style: a classical Greek–inspired furniture and fashion design style originating in postrevolutionary France in the early 18th century

fretwork: an openwork ornamental design cut with a narrow, fine-toothed saw (fret saw) into a thin wood panel

Gothic Revival: a design style originating in the 1740s that revived medieval Gothic forms such as spires, pointed arches, and tracery (interlaced openwork derived from Gothic windows)

groundhog kiln: a tunnel-shaped oven often inset into the ground and used to fire alkaline glazed pottery in the 19th century

hemp: a coarse fiber derived from the cannabis plant and used for making cloth

Ionic: a classical Greek architectural order with monolithic columns mounted on a base with scrolled tops (capitals) and a decorative roof support (frieze) of carved figures

joiner: one who cuts and fits wood joints without the need for nails or screws

maker's mark: the stamp of a ceramicist or metalsmith impressed onto pieces to identify the maker

metope: sections of relief sculpture carved on the entablature of a classical Doric temple

millwork: woodwork such as doors and molding, made at a mill

modiste: a French term denoting a fashion designer and stylist

mortise and tenon: a wood joint created with a notch and groove technique

nkondi: a sacred Kongo wood figure sculpture

nsibidi sign: an ideographic or conceptual symbol used by the Ekoi, Efik, and Igbo people of southeastern Nigeria

oculus: a circular window in the center of a domed ceiling

pass; passing: refers to when biracial African Americans self-identify as white due to their Caucasian appearance

piece; piecing: in quilt making, sewing together multiple fabric pieces to create a single large textile

portico: a roofed porch between an exterior building wall and a row of columns pugmill: a device used to grind and mix clay with water to produce a consistent viscous mixture

Rococo: an art and design style that originated in 18th-century France and is noted for its asymmetry, scrolls, floral elements, and elaborate ornamentation

salt-glazed stoneware: ceramics with a high-gloss-textured finish created by adding salt to the firing process

slip: in ceramics, a viscous mixture in which clay particles are suspended in water

stepping: in architecture, a graduated recession of the façade

tester bed: a four-poster canopied bed

triglyph: a three-part vertical groove pattern carved on the entablature of a classical Doric temple

typesetter: one who manually selects and assembles moveable letter forms for a printing press

Victorian: associated with the art, culture, and social attitudes prevalent during the reign of Queen Victoria of England from 1819 to 1901

Vieux Carré: from the French "old square," the term describes the French Quarter, the oldest neighborhood in New Orleans

wheelwright: one who makes and repairs wood or metal wheels and wheeled conveyances

Questions for Further Study and Discussion

1. What are the key visual elements of Federal-style architecture and design? What were their stylistic sources?
2. Discuss the paradox of racial beliefs and practices in the lives of abolitionists such as Thomas Jefferson and the work of the American Colonization Society.
3. What specific elements of the classical Greek Doric order were incorporated into Federal-style architecture?
4. How did the American Revolution affect the production of decorative art and design in the United States?
5. What is the history of the Edgefield pottery industry? What role did African Americans play in it?
6. Design your own maker's mark.
7. Research other important African-American architects who worked in the Federal Period or adopted its style, such as Donum Monford (1771–1838) and Plympton Ross Berry (d. 1917).
8. Research other African-American craftsmen and women of the era, including blacksmith Gabriel Prosser (1775/76–1800) and Solomon Prosser (fl. 1770s), and cabinetmaker Thomas Gross, Jr. (1775–1800).

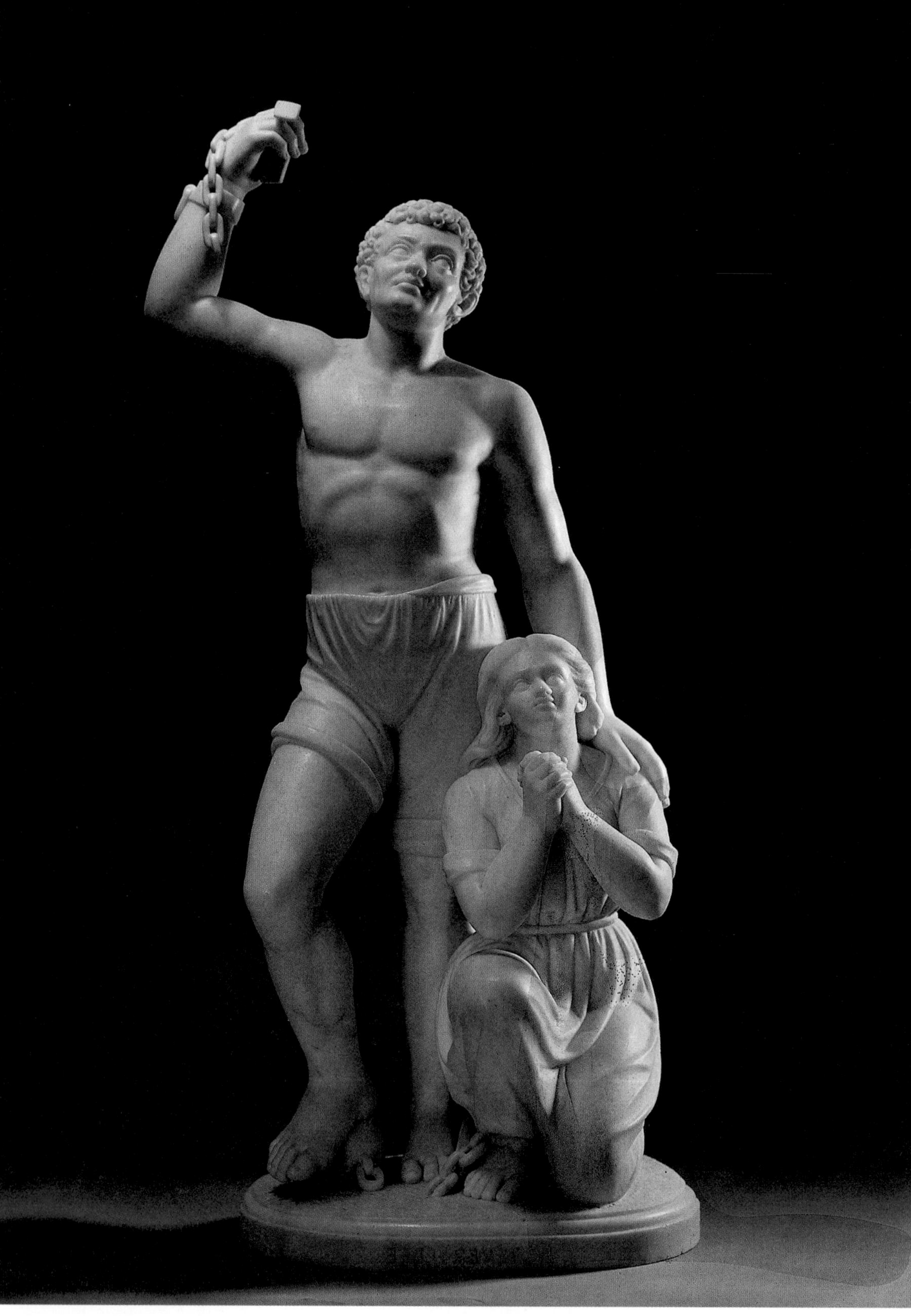

19TH-CENTURY NEOCLASSICISM

4

The corresponding movement to Federal-period architecture and design (see Chapter 3) in the fine arts is Neoclassicism. It was fueled by the highly influential writings of German scholar Johann Joachim Winckelmann (1717–68), which charted the evolution of Greco-Roman art and architecture. His books promoted the **humanist** and **Neoplatonic** concept that the ideal human figure in art should convey "a noble simplicity and sedate grandeur in gesture and expression." Subsequent widespread interest in classical antiquity prompted artists throughout Europe and the United States to create images that embodied Greek humanism as well as the Roman characteristics of logic and **stoicism**. These qualities are evident in the sculptures of African-American artists Edmonia Lewis, Florville Foy, and Eugene Warburg, which were carved in the quintessential Neoclassical medium of marble. Their works incorporate idealized figures based on classical Greco-Roman models. The same can be said of the paintings of Joshua Johnson, Jules Lion, Julien Hudson, and a number of other African-American artists who made significant contributions to American Neoclassicism.

Neoclassical elements of form and style included **planar** and **frontal compositions**, clarity of line and light, symmetry, closed form, smooth surfaces, subdued color palettes, and an emphasis on stable verticals and horizontals. These elements produced well-ordered and restrained portrayals, in direct contrast with the more expressive and active compositions of the earlier Rococo and **Baroque** styles. Iconographically, Neoclassicism tended toward sober, honest, and unsentimental portrayals, as well as allusions to the culturally refined Greco-Roman civilizations. As a new democracy, it was natural for America to document its history and citizens with the same qualities of equable authority and refinement as were associated with ancient Greece and Rome.

SCULPTURE

In 1785, Benjamin Franklin and Thomas Jefferson invited French Neoclassical sculptor Jean-Antoine Houdon (1741–1828) to create portraits of each of them, as well as of George Washington. Houdon was famed for his dedication to visual accuracy, simplicity, and dignity in his marble busts of French aristocrats and intellectuals, making him the perfect choice to immortalize America's founding fathers. The success of these commissions led to an age of American Neoclassicism in sculpture that began in the 1820s. Celebrated American talents followed in the footsteps of Houdon and other French, German, and Italian Neoclassical sculptors by spending time in

◀ Edmonia Lewis, *Forever Free (Morning of Liberty)*, 1867–68, marble, 41¼″ high.

Photo: Howard University Gallery of Art, Washington, D.C.

Rome and Florence. In Italy they were able take advantage of an overabundance of classical art, exceptional marble quarries, and the skill of Italian marble carvers to assist in the completion of their works. Living and working in Italy, American sculptors regularly shipped their works back to the States, where their reputations were greater, for exhibition and sale to patriotic art buyers.

Edmonia Lewis

The first African-American woman sculptor to make the transition to Italy and Neoclassicism, and to achieve international fame, was Edmonia Lewis (1844–c.1911). Born in Greenbush, New York, near Albany, Lewis was the daughter of a Native American (Ojibwe) mother and a Haitian father, whom the artist described as a "gentleman's servant." Her parents died when she still a toddler, after which Lewis was raised by her mother's family, who taught her traditional crafts such as basket-weaving and moccasin embroidery. Her elder brother by twelve years, Samuel Lewis (1832–96), fostered his sister in the home of Captain S. R. Mills and paid for her to enroll in a Baptist and abolitionist-run school, the New York Central School in McGrawville. Samuel supported his sister's education while working as a barber, gold prospector, and commercial real estate investor. He sponsored Lewis's university education, enrolling her in Oberlin College in Ohio when she was fifteen. The historic school was founded in 1833 by Protestant evangelists and was the first interracial and the first coeducational college in the United States. At the time of Lewis's enrollment at Oberlin, one-third of the students there were African-American.

Lewis arrived at Oberlin in 1859, the same year that white abolitionist and Underground Railroad "conductor" John Brown (1800–59) raided the federal arsenal at Harper's Ferry, Virginia. Two of Lewis's fellow Oberlin students, Lewis Sheridan Leary (1835–59) and John Anthony Copeland, Jr. (1834–59), were executed after the failed attack along with Brown and 4 others of the 17-man guerrilla force. Their hanging in December 1859 became a national cause célèbre, fueling fires on both sides of the slavery dilemma. Oberlin faculty openly protested the executions, and Lewis was so struck by these tragic events that, a few years later, she sculpted several likenesses of Brown.

At Oberlin, Lewis received a solid liberal arts education that included study in Neoclassical drawing. Unfortunately, her coursework was disrupted in 1862 when she was falsely accused and arrested for poisoning two of her classmates, Maria Miles and Christina Ennes, with an aphrodisiac known as Spanish fly (cantharidin). After having spent an evening on a sleigh ride with gentlemen friends, the two girls became severely ill and blamed their condition on Lewis, with whom they claimed to have shared a drink of spiced wine earlier that evening. Oberlin locals were "impatient to see Edmonia punished" and promised that "if Oberlin authorities could not handle their colored folk, others would." Oberlin graduate John Mercer Langston (later the dean of the Howard University Law School and the first African-American congressman; 1829–97) defended Lewis at trial. However, before the trial's conclusion, the 18-year-old Lewis was abducted and brutally beaten by assailants who were never identified. After a period of recuperation, Lewis was able to attend her trial, during which Langston argued convincingly that there was no valid physical evidence to convict her, and she was found innocent. Acquittal aside, Lewis faced continued rancor from other students, Oberlin locals, faculty, and board members. Ultimately, she was barred from registering for her last semester and never received her degree.

After the trial, in 1863 Lewis moved to Boston, where she met the influential publisher and abolitionist William Lloyd Garrison (1805–79). He, in turn, introduced her to the self-taught sculptor, poet, and naturalist Edward-Augustus Brackett (1818–1908), with whom Lewis informally apprenticed, learning the tools and techniques of Neoclassical sculpture. Brackett was also an opponent of slavery, and his celebrated patrons included Garrison and poet Henry Wadsworth Longfellow, Senator Charles Sumner, and President William Henry Harrison. Brackett's style was decisively Neoclassical. He sculpted in marble and portrayed his subjects in a forthright manner, often wearing Roman togas, as was the convention. One of his best-known works was a bust of John Brown, which motivated Lewis's own desire to create a similar image. She also created portraits of Brackett's clients Sumner and Garrison.

Within a year of arriving in Boston, Lewis had opened her own studio and was fashioning terracotta and plaster cameos, figurines, and busts of abolitionists and Civil War heroes, including Colonel Robert Gould Shaw (1837–63). Produced and exhibited at the height of the Civil War, Lewis's busts of Brown, Shaw, and other Union protagonists were so popular that they literally sold in the hundreds of copies. Assisted in publicizing and selling her art by her first major patroness, the American abolitionist and social activist Lydia Maria Child (1802–80), Lewis used the proceeds from the sales of her work to travel abroad in the fall of 1865.

Lewis's decision to go abroad came at the urging of Massachusetts-born sculptor Harriet Hosmer (1830–1908), who, although living in Italy at the time, was in Boston in 1864 for an exhibition of her own work. Following Hosmer's advice, Lewis traveled to London, Paris, and Florence (where she met renowned American Neoclassical sculptor Hiram Powers [1805–73]) before settling as a permanent expatriate in Rome in 1866. In Lewis's words, "I was practically driven to Rome, in order to obtain the opportunities for art culture, and to find a social atmosphere where I was not constantly reminded of my color. The land of liberty had no room for a colored sculptor." Lewis delighted in her newfound home, which she described as a "real republic" without racial prejudice.

In Rome, Lewis was greeted by a thriving American expatriate community. Throughout the 19th century, Rome was a hub for American writers such as Nathaniel Hawthorne (1804–64) and Harriet Beecher Stowe (1811–96), as well as for visual artists such as Thomas Ball (1819–1911), Horatio Greenough (1805–52), and William Wetmore Story (1819–95). The circle of American artists there also included a clique of wealthy lesbians, among whom were sculptors Hosmer and her lover Emma Stebbins (1815–52) and the cross-dressing American actress Charlotte S. Cushman (1816–76). These women, like Lewis, chose to live abroad to evade the prejudices against "difference" that plagued the United States. Seeing in her a kindred artistic spirit, Hosmer and Cushman assisted Lewis in finding living quarters and studio space. Cushman was instrumental in bringing the young African-American sculptor to the attention of dealers, critics, and American art-buying travelers on the **Grand Tour**. Lewis quickly established herself as a top-flight sculptor and a member of an elite group of American women expatriate artists.

Writer Henry James (1843–1916) dubbed these women the "marmorean (marble) flock . . . a sisterhood of . . . American lady sculptors." James referred specifically and disparagingly to Lewis's association with the "flock" when he wrote, "One of the sisterhood was a negress, whose colour [*sic*], picturesquely contrasting with that of her plastic material, was the pleading agent of her fame." The juxtaposition of Lewis's dark skin against the gleaming whiteness of her marble sculptures was the only reason James could suggest for her popularity. Mean-spirited characterizations such as these were not uncommon, given that Lewis was both black and a woman at a time when artistic talent was considered almost exclusively the purview of white men. Interested patrons demanded to see Lewis at work in her studio to dispel their doubts that a petite black woman could create monumental sculptures in marble that were comparable to those of her male contemporaries. Lewis routinely admitted guests to her studio to prove just that, wielding chisel and mallet to the amazement of visitors. Ironically, most Neoclassical sculptors did not engage in direct carving, as Lewis did. Instead, they made clay sculptures and hired local craftsmen to transform their visions into stone. Lewis became known at the time as "one of the few sculptors whom no one charge[d] with having assistance in her work. Everyone admits that, whether good or bad, her sculptures are her own," according to 19th-century critic Laura Curtis Bullard.

One of the first statues produced by Lewis in Rome, *Forever Free*, provides an example of what visitors to her studio observed (see chapter-opening image). The subject of the work—two freed slaves—was chosen by the artist in honor of the 1863 Emancipation Proclamation and its freeing of millions of African Americans, whom Lewis described as her "father's people." Originally titled *Morning of Liberty*, *Forever Free* portrays a standing African-American man with his left fist raised, grasping broken chains. His right hand touches the shoulder of a kneeling woman, whose own hands are clasped in a gesture that replicates the one seen in a popular abolitionist emblem of a kneeling slave. *Forever Free* is unique in its fusion of African-American subject matter and Neoclassical elements, such as the **contrapposto** stance of the male figure, the classical drapery of the skirt on the female figure, and the relative passivity of their expressions.

An outstanding feature of this work is its portrayal of black male empowerment: a slave who breaks his own chains and thus participates in his own freedom. Most contemporaneous renderings of this theme depict a kneeling black male (similar to Lewis's female) who is powerless and pleading. And although the kneeling woman is doing precisely that, she, too, departs from virtually all other slave images of the period in her embodiment of

Victorian modesty; note that she is fully, rather than partially, clothed. Because artistic convention dictated that slaves be represented as either nude, seminude, or wearing tattered clothing (to evoke a sense of vulnerability and disenfranchisement), the inclusion of concealing garments in this case functions to empower the kneeling woman and to metaphorically shield her against the many debasements of slavery.

At least two of Lewis's works, including *Forever Free*, were shipped to Boston in 1867 for exhibition. *Forever Free* was hailed by critics for its fluid fusion of Neoclassical restraint and **Romantic-era** passion. Elizabeth Peabody, editor of the *Christian Register*, exclaimed, "Who threw so much emotion into those figures? What well-known sculptor arranged with such artistic grace those speaking forms? Will anyone believe it was the small hands of a small girl that wrought the marble and kindled the life within it? A girl of dusky hue, mixed Indian and African." By the 1870s, Lewis had achieved a level of international fame that brought her commissions, sales, and prestigious showings in the United States and Europe. She won a gold medal at the International Exhibition of the Naples Academy of Arts and Sciences, and she exhibited in the 1876 Philadelphia Centennial and the 1893 World's Columbian Exposition in Chicago.

Throughout the 1860s and 1870s, Lewis regularly returned to the United States to promote the sale of her works and to visit family members. The industrious artist advertised showings of her art in American papers, describing herself as "the young and gifted Colored Sculptor, of ROME, Italy" and charging viewers fees of 15¢–25¢, before selling her sculptures for as much as $6,000 each (approximately $130,000 today). All five of the sculptures that Lewis exhibited in California in 1873 were sold within weeks: of these, three were acquired by Mrs. Sarah L. Knox-Girdrich, an influential suffragette, including a bust of Abraham Lincoln.

In 1875, Lewis created a massive, 3,000-pound statue entitled the *Death of Cleopatra*, which she shipped to the United States for exhibition in the Women's Pavilion of the 1876 Philadelphia Centennial (see the chapter-opening figure in Chapter 1). It was reported that "larger crowds [gathered] around [Lewis's *Cleopatra*] than any other work in the vast collection." *Death of Cleopatra* was so popular that it was included two years later in the Chicago Interstate Industrial Exposition. Lewis's accurate, though evidently unfashionable, portrayal of a dead body shocked audiences, who were both riveted and repulsed by the representation. In his 1878 book *Great American Sculptures*, the president of the Philadelphia Sketch Club, William J. Clark, Jr., described Lewis's *Death of Cleopatra* as "not a beautiful work, but it is a very original and striking one. . . . The effects of death are represented with such skill as to be absolutely repellent. Apart from all questions of taste, however, the striking qualities of the work are undeniable and it could only have been produced by a sculptor of very genuine endowments." Sold to a private collector after its U.S. tour, the whereabouts of *Death of Cleopatra* were unknown until 1972, when it was found abandoned at a Chicago construction site. Restored to its original state, the sculpture now holds an honored place in the Smithsonian Institution collection.

Lewis continued to live in Rome until 1893, when she moved first to Paris and then, in 1901, to London, where she died in 1907. During the last two decades of her life, she sold work less frequently but continued her visits to the United States, exhibiting her works in Syracuse, Cincinnati, Baltimore, and at the 1895 Atlanta World's Fair. Until the end of her life, Lewis continued to receive staunch support from African-American abolitionist Frederick Douglass (whom she had first met at Oberlin during her college years) and a select few loyal clients, including John Patrick Crichton-Stewart, third Marquess of Bute (1847–1900), who was both a patron of the arts and a supporter of women's rights. However, Lewis's career declined with the loss of interest in Neoclassicism (which by 1900 was more than a century old and was considered passé in Europe), and with the rise of antiblack sentiment in the United States during the eras of **post-Reconstruction** and Jim Crow in the 1880s and 1890s.

Florville Foy

Lewis is a singular example of an African-American sculptor who devoted an entire career exclusively to the fine arts. Several others, equally successful, channeled their creativity into the sculpting of marble funerary monuments, which offered a steady income as well as an artistic outlet. A free native of New Orleans, Florville Foy (1819–1903), was one such artist. He was born the son of a free woman of color, Zelie Aubry (d. 1870), and Frenchman Rene Prosper Foy (c. 1790–1854), who immigrated to New Orleans from Haiti. Although they never married, due to antimiscegenation laws, Foy's parents lived together as common-law husband and wife for many years. Rene Foy was a wealthy landowner and a talented and versatile artist, writer, and planter who founded the family stone-carving business that would ultimately bring his son so much success.

Florville was still a teenager, recently returned from study in France, when he took over the family business in 1838 at the time of his father's retirement. One of his first clients was the Neoclassical French architect Jacques Nicolas Bussiere de Pouilly (1804–75), who had arrived in New Orleans in 1833 to design and construct the St. Louis Exchange Hotel in the French Quarter. Foy was hired by de Pouilly to translate the architect's funerary monument designs into stone. The architect was so pleased with Foy's work that he assigned the sculptor many more commissions, helping to establish Foy's reputation as a highly skilled ***marbrier***. After a long and fruitful association, de Pouilly commissioned Foy to design his own funerary monument, located in St. Louis Cemetery.

The creation of elaborate tombs for New Orleans elites required Foy to have command of architecture, **sculpture-in-the-round**, and relief carving. Rescued from the Girod Street Cemetery (which was deconsecrated and disinterred in 1957), Foy's 1838 *Child with a Drum* is an example of the sculpture-in-the-round he created as tomb decoration (Figure 4.1). Depicting a *putto* (plural: *putti*), or male cherub, the motif derives from second-century Roman children's **sarcophagi** (suggesting that the work was part of a child's tomb). Unlike the typically playful poses of *putti* of past eras, however, Foy's figure sits solemn and motionless. The child rests against a

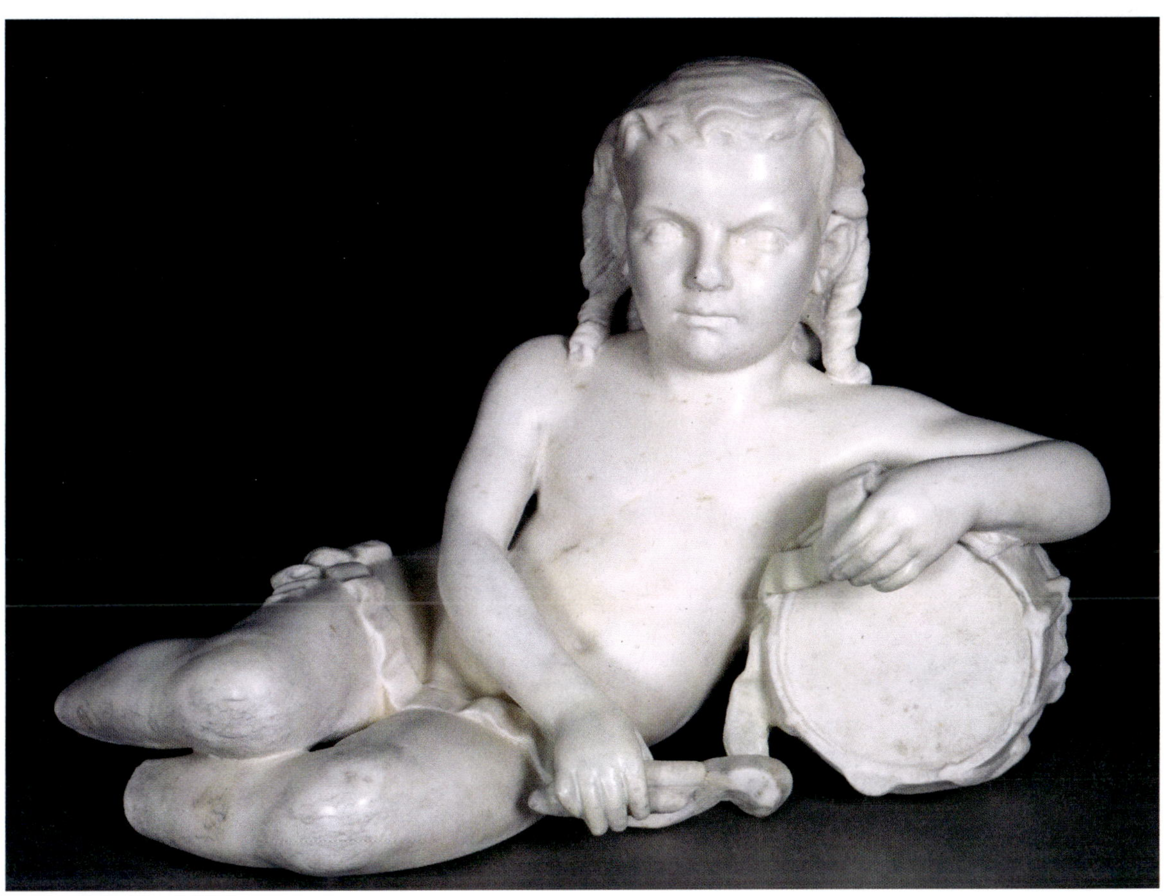

▲ 4.1 Florville Foy, *Child with a Drum*, c. 1838, marble.
Courtesy of the Louisiana State Museum.

drum, but he does not play the instrument; instead, he holds a drumstick inactively in his right hand. Foy's sculpture also deviates from conventional plump *putti* in its slender body, suggesting that it might, in fact, be a portrait of the deceased. Distinctive features, such as the child's deep-set eyes and high forehead, further imply the representation of a particular individual. Understanding that he was creating unique works of "high" art, despite their use as gravestones, Foy often carved his name and the date of creation into his funerary art.

Foy lived and worked in several buildings located conveniently near the St. Louis Cemeteries. He and his staff of eight assistants and a manager produced ready-made and made-to-order items such as gravestones, outdoor seating, decorative sculpture, interment vaults, and large-scale monuments, using expensive imported marble, for which Foy could charge high prices. Foy's Marble Works became one of the most successful businesses of its kind in New Orleans and remained so for more than half a century. The 1882 New Orleans City Trade Directory listed his income that year as more than $20,000 (the present-day equivalent of half a million dollars).

Like his father, Foy had an interracial common-law marriage with Louisa Frances Whittaker, who was white. After 35 years of living together, in 1885, the couple was at last able to marry, because of the temporary suspension of antimiscegenation laws in Louisiana and elsewhere during **Reconstruction**.

At the turn of the 20th century, when Foy was more than 80 years old and no longer able to work, his one-time slave–turned–heir, Jules (d. 1929), took over the business and operated it under the name Jules F. Foy. Foy died in 1907. The unprecedented success and longevity of Foy's career attests to his business acumen and to the quality of his work. Through any number of financial and sociopolitical upheavals—from the economic panic in New Orleans of 1837 when Foy was just beginning to the Civil War, Reconstruction, post-Reconstruction, and Jim Crow eras—Foy continued to cultivate clients and patrons and to create and sell his art.

Daniel and Eugene Warburg

As Foy's work suggests, some of the country's finest funerary monuments were produced in New Orleans. The city's cemeteries were well known for their elaborate aboveground tombs. Because of the city's swampy terrain, underground burial was difficult. As a result, New Orleanians patterned their "cities of the dead" after Paris's Père Lachaise Cemetery, which was consecrated in 1804 and was designed like an actual city, with wide, tree-lined cobblestone "streets," lavish gardens, and thousands of aboveground monuments. Nearly as successful as Foy in this flourishing profession was Daniel Warburg (1836–1911), the son of Daniel Samuel Warburg, Sr. (1789–1860), a Jewish immigrant who came to New Orleans from Hamburg, Germany, in 1821. The artist's mother was a Caribbean slave owned by Daniel Senior, Marie Rose Blondeau (1804–37), who was reportedly the daughter of another Warburg slave named Venus. The elder Warburg was a wealthy merchant and real estate investor who lived with Blondeau for 15 years and had five children with her. By 1830, he had freed Blondeau, but, as was the case with the Foys, he could not lawfully marry her. Nevertheless, they lived essentially as man and wife until Blondeau's death.

Daniel Warburg, Jr., learned the funerary monument trade from his elder brother Eugene, who left New Orleans after running the family business for only a few years, preferring to live abroad. Daniel took over the company when he was just 17 years old and developed it into a prosperous marble-carving enterprise. The company flourished for several decades, until 1871, when financial difficulties required Daniel to dissolve the business and work as a contractor for other, larger companies with whom his modest firm could no longer compete. Despite this turn of events, Daniel continued to sculpt monuments in both marble and granite (which had replaced marble as the preferred carving stone by the end of the 19th century) until his death in 1911.

Daniel's art can be found in several New Orleans cemeteries and includes etched plaques, tombstones, and Roman-inspired columns embellished with elegant scrolling, floral bouquets, and vine garlands. A massive Daniel Warburg monument commissioned by the Holcombe-Aiken family rises high above the Metairie Cemetery in New Orleans (Figure 4.2). Derived from antique and Neoclassical models such as the Column of Trajan in Rome (113 C.E.) and the Place Vendôme Column in Paris (1810), Warburg's design incorporates a pillar set on a rectangular base and topped by a square capital. Rather than statues of a conquering hero, as on the classical models,

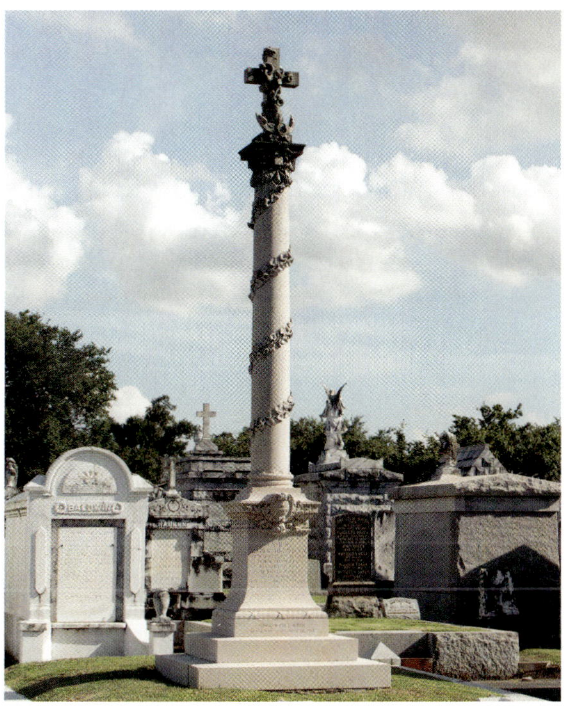

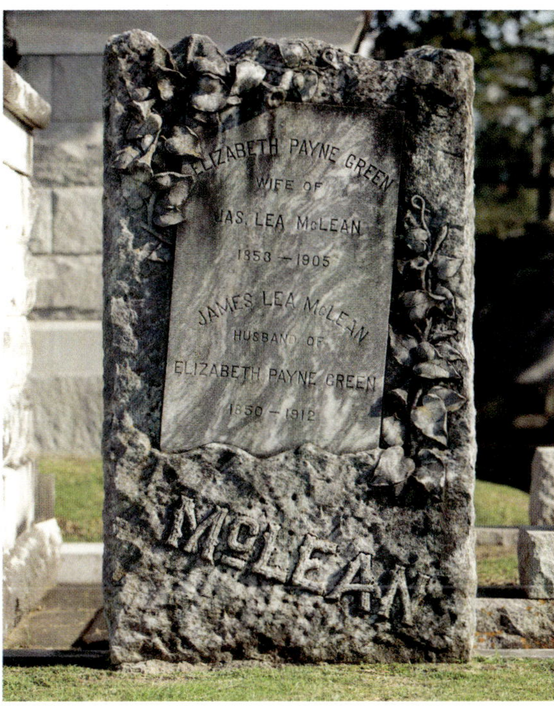

▲ **4.2** Daniel Warburg, *Holcomb-Aiken Family Monument*, c. 1904, marble, approximately 30′ high. Metairie Cemetery, New Orleans, LA.

Photo © 2015 Tina Freeman.

▲ **4.3** Daniel Warburg, *McLean Tomb Monument*, 1905, granite, approximately 10′ high. Metairie Cemetery, New Orleans, LA.

Photo © 2015 Tina Freeman.

the Holcombe-Aiken monument is crowned by a crucifix and an anchor, to memorialize the death of Ensign Hugh K. Aiken, a naval engineer who died in an explosion on the U.S.S. *North Carolina* in 1906. Warburg adapted the spiraling element of the two earlier monuments, replacing scenes of battle with a morning glory vine, a motif common to Victorian-era headstones. An especially short-lived flower that withers and reblooms repeatedly within a given season, the morning glory symbolized life, death, and rebirth. The Holcomb-Aiken column attests to the artist's exceptional skill as a sculptor in the many organic forms and undulating linear elements that decorate the monument and defy the rigidity of the stone. The base of the sculpture boasts an oval pendant framed by scrolling and foliage, similar to that found in Federal-period furniture design (see Figure 3.8). A similar connection can be seen between the garland-and-tassel detail at the top of the column and a motif seen in Federal-period ceramics (see Figure 3.13).

Like Foy and Lewis, Daniel Warburg worked within the Neoclassical genre until the turn of the 20th century, long after the style had declined in Europe. Even in the United States, Neoclassicism had been all but replaced by more expressive styles such as Romanticism and **Symbolism**. At ease with both past and present art movements, Daniel Warburg produced tombs that suggest his awareness of changing tastes and artistic evolution. His McLean family monument, also at Metairie Cemetery, combines a smooth surface and a scrolled parchment motif, which were typical of Neoclassicism, with an encasement of seemingly unfinished roughhewn stone (Figure 4.3). This juxtaposition of smooth and rough surfaces calls to mind the work of French artist Auguste Rodin (1840–1917), who was considered one of the latter 19th century's most innovative sculptors. Warburg's grasp of avant-garde trends can also be seen in the asymmetrical composition and the use of Art Nouveau typography on the tombstone, which exemplifies the artist's creativity perhaps more than any other of his works.

Daniel's brother, Eugene Warburg (c. 1825–59), began as a tomb carver but spent most of his career as a fine arts sculptor. He was the oldest son of Blondeau and Daniel Senior, and the only one of their children to be born a slave, which seems to have made him especially sensitive to racial slights throughout his life and which may have influenced his decision to leave America. When Warburg the elder emancipated his wife, Blondeau, he also freed his four-year-old son, Eugene. Because their mother was now free, the subsequent Warburg children, including Daniel, were born free. Although Eugene may have smarted from the sting of his slave birth, he was nonetheless treated well by his father, who—with the assistance of a friend and lawyer, the French revolutionary Pierre Soulé (1801–70)—arranged for Eugene's education and apprenticeship. Soulé, who was named Eugene's godfather, also organized fine arts study for Eugene with French-born Neoclassical sculptor Philippe Garbeille (c. 1818–53), who himself had studied in Rome with the prominent Danish Neoclassicist Bertel Thorwaldsen (1770–1840) before migrating to New Orleans in 1841.

Following his education, in the late 1840s Eugene opened a marble-carving shop with his brother, Daniel, serving as his apprentice. Simultaneously, Eugene pursued a career as a fine arts sculptor, exhibiting for sale in 1850 a now-lost statue of the Greek hero Ganymede. It was praised by the *New Orleans Bee*, which described it as an "exquisite specimen of sculpture . . . by a young Creole of our city [which] reflects infinite credit upon the taste and talent of our townsmen." At the time, the sculpture was assigned an estimated value of $500 (about $15,000 today) and was sold by raffle at the showing.

▼ **4.4** Eugene Warburg, *John Young Mason*, 1855, marble, 23″ × 15″ × 10″.
Photo © Virginia Historical Society.

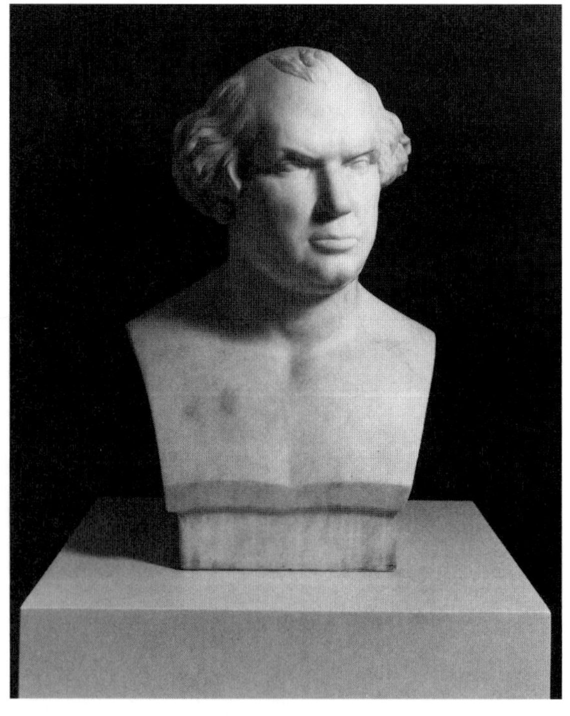

Commissions received by Eugene while still in New Orleans included a design for a new marble floor for the St. Louis Cathedral and several now-lost figure sculptures. Using proceeds from sales and commissions and a small inheritance left to him by his mother, Eugene sailed for Europe in 1852, armed with a letter of introduction from Soulé. Eugene spent a number of years traveling and working in France, Belgium, England, and Italy. He spent four years at his first stop, Paris, studying with Neoclassical sculptor Francois Jouffroy (1806–82) at the prestigious **École des Beaux-Arts**. In Paris, Eugene was honored with four entries in the juried Paris Salon of 1855, alongside such French masters as Courbet, Gérome, and Delacroix. One of Eugene's entries was a portrait of the U.S. minister to France, John Young Mason (1799–1859), who was a colleague of the artist's godfather, Soulé (Figure 4.4). The honesty of the portrayal and the severity of Mason's expression link the work, stylistically, to the ancient Roman portrait tradition, rather than to the idealism of classical Greek sculpture.

In 1856, at the end of his stay in Paris, Eugene traveled to London, where he gained an introduction to, and sculpture commission from, Harriet Sutherland-Leveson-Gower (1806–68), a dedicated abolitionist and the Duchess of Sutherland. Eugene remained in London for one year in order to complete **bas-relief** sculptures of episodes from Harriet Beecher Stowe's anti-slavery novel *Uncle Tom's Cabin*. The next year, he traveled to Italy. Both the Duchess of Sutherland and Stowe, whom the artist had also met in London, provided Warburg with letters of introduction that gained him entrée into artistic circles in Florence.

After a brief stay in Florence, Warburg joined the American expatriate community in Rome, settling there with his wife, Emilie Louise Ernestine Warburg (1844–1905), whom he evidently met abroad. Birth records indicate that Emilie was born on February 6, 1844, in Hamburg, Germany, to the Warburg family and, thus, was likely a family relation of the artist. Eugene remained in Rome until his premature death from an unnamed illness in early 1859. Despite his expatriate status, the *New Orleans Bee* lamented the loss of the American and acknowledged his artistic gifts in his obituary, which read, in part, "Eugène Warburg would incontestably have taken an eminent place in the pleiad [distinguished group] of those American artists who strive to add one more ray to the lustre [*sic*] of their land. It is a loss for America; a cause of mourning for New Orleans; an emptiness in the arts."

TWO-DIMENSIONAL ART

In 1785, one of the first major Neoclassical paintings—*Oath of the Horatii*—was commissioned by the king of France and exhibited at the **Paris Salon**. Created by the leader of the French Neoclassical painting movement, court artist Jacques-Louis David (1748–1825), the work portrayed a military family of three brothers and their father calmly pledging to fight to the death in a battle against their enemies. The setting is an unadorned and stark stone chamber with Roman arches and Doric columns. David's work replaced the ostentatious French Rococo painting style and its pretentious iconography with the more sober and monumental Neoclassical genre and sparked the Neoclassical painting movement. Like sculpture, Neoclassical painting eschewed ornament, decoration, and emotion and embraced sober and unemotional portrayals.

Joshua Johnson

The first known professional black portraitist of any genre was Baltimore painter Joshua Johnson (sometimes spelled Johnston; c. 1763–c. 1827). His affinity with Neoclassicism was as much intuitive as it was calculated, because he was self-trained and likely absorbed the style through observation of the works of other artists. Johnson was born to an enslaved mother—known only by the name of her owner, William Wheeler, Sr. (1694–1767)—and a white father, George Johnson. The elder Johnson purchased his son from Wheeler for £25 (about $6,500 today) while his son was still an infant. The bill of sale promised freedom to the child on completion of an apprenticeship with a local blacksmith or at age 21, whichever came first. In 1782, when Joshua Johnson was about 19 years old, his father honored his promise by formally acknowledging paternity of his "mulatto" child and securing his son's freedom.

During the ten years following his emancipation, Joshua Johnson taught himself the art of portrait painting and by the mid-1790s had begun advertising his skills as a **limner**. Colonel John Moale, the judge who signed Johnson's manumission order years earlier, became one of his first clients when the artist painted a portrait of Moale's wife and granddaughter in 1798. For the next 20 years, Johnson, twice married and the father of several children, supported himself and his family working almost exclusively as a painter.

As a limner, Johnson was one of a thriving group of postrevolutionary portrait painters and **miniaturists** who traveled from city to city documenting the faces of Americans. In general, limners were self-taught, and their style was less sophisticated than that of trained artists. This naïveté, however, did not affect their popularity. On the contrary, many Americans preferred folk artists because they associated their academically trained counterparts with the same British aristocracy from which America had so recently won its freedom. Indeed, scholars have argued that the naïveté of some American portrait painters was deliberately contrived to appeal to an American audience that proudly identified with the "common man."

Johnson's painting style falls into the latter category. His sitters are posed awkwardly, but in a way that cleverly directs the eye to a particular area of the composition or to a significant pictorial detail. His portrayals are impassive, and his compositions powerful in their simplicity, aligning him with Neoclassicism—as does his ability to capture distinguished and honest likenesses of his subjects. Common features of Johnson's portraits are minimal **modeling**, oval faces, tapered lips, and rigid poses that create a sense of poise and dignity. Another Johnson signature trait is the application of translucent layers of **oil glaze** to achieve delicate skin and fabric tones. All of these elements are evident in his c.1805 portrait *Grace Allison McCurdy and Her Daughters, Mary Jane and Letitia Grace*, which portrays this Frederick County, Maryland socialite, the wife of a wealthy businessman (Figure 4.5). Johnson's composition poses Mrs. McCurdy seated on a dark divan beside her two standing daughters.

One of Johnson's best-known paintings, though untitled, has been identified as a portrait of Rev. Daniel Coker (1780–1846) (Figure 4.6). Coker was a noteworthy abolitionist who cofounded the African Methodist Episcopal (AME) Church in Philadelphia in 1816. In 1820, en route to Sierra Leone to establish a colony for freed slaves that would eventually become the country of Liberia, Coker also founded the West African Methodist Church. Although painted when Coker was only a 25-year-old minister, Johnson's portrait seems to portend the reverend's illustrious future. A three-quarter oval composition, the painting represents Coker with composure, wearing gentlemanly attire, including a black frock coat, a white collared shirt, vest, and ascot. His face is subtly modeled and captures an expression of concern and empathy that seems to have marked Coker's personality.

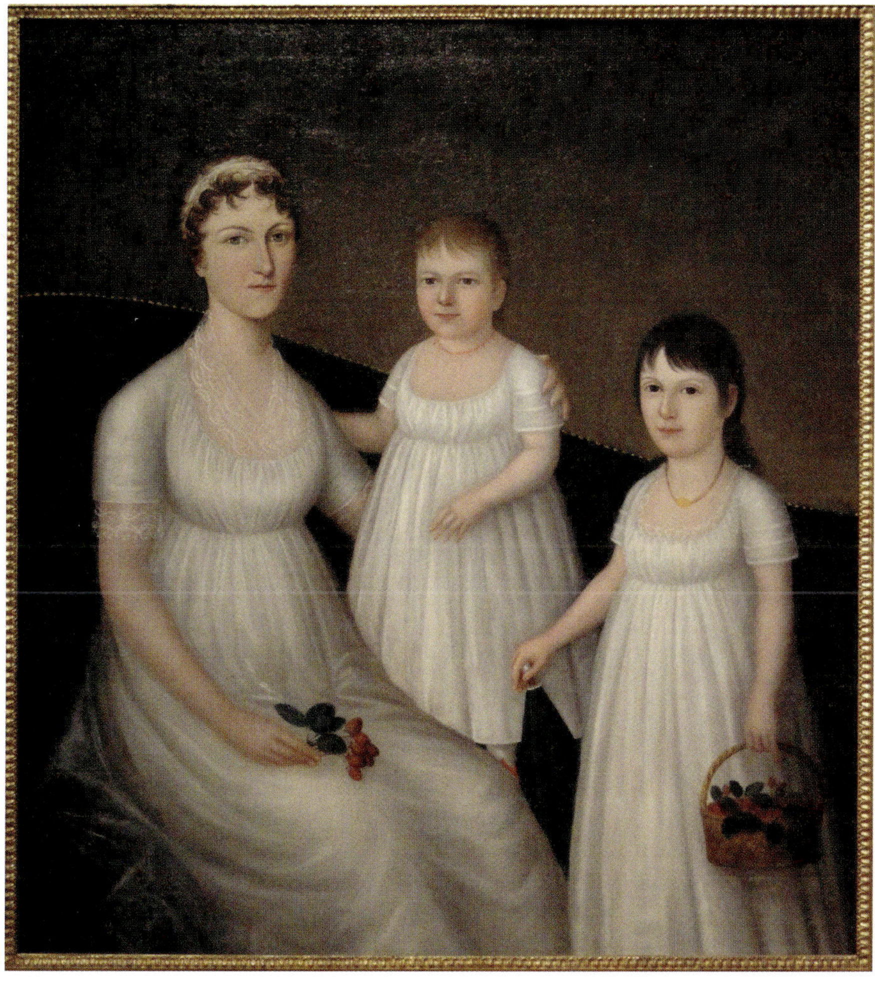

◀ **4.5** Joshua Johnson, *Grace Allison McCurdy & Her Daughters, Mary Jane & Letitia Grace*, c. 1806, oil on canvas, 43⅝″ × 38⅞″.

Collection of the Corcoran Gallery of Art, Washington, D.C. Museum purchase through the gifts of William Wilson Corcoran, Elizabeth Donner Norment, Francis Biddle, Erich Cohn, Hardinge Scholle, and the William A. Clark Fund. Photo available under the Creative Commons CC0 1.0 Universal Public Domain Dedication.

Johnson painted more than 80 portraits of prominent Maryland and Virginia residents before records of his activities cease in 1827. His paintings provide valuable historic and artistic records of the age. His standing as the first professional African-American painter situates him at the beginning of a long road that would soon be taken by many more black artists.

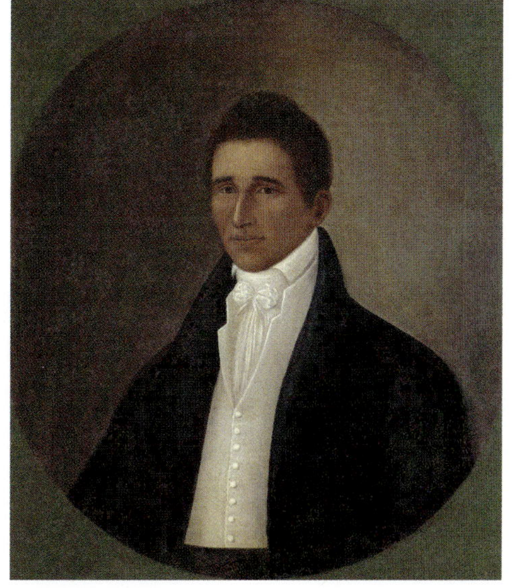

▼ **4.6** Joshua Johnson, *Portrait of a Gentleman*, 1805–10, oil on canvas, 22.8″ × 26.7″.

Produced courtesy of the American Museum in Britain (Bath, U.K.).

William Simpson

Painter William Simpson's (1818–72) work shares many stylistic similarities with Johnson's portraits, including dark, unadorned backgrounds and sober portrayals. Exhibiting exceptional drawing skills as a youth in Buffalo, New York, Simpson was apprenticed early to English-born and French-trained Neoclassical portraitist Matthew Henry Wilson (1814–92). Although Wilson maintained a permanent home in Brooklyn, New York, Wilson and his wife, Mary Kemp, traveled extensively, often spending years in other cities. In the 1850s, they found themselves in Buffalo, where they met Simpson and employed him

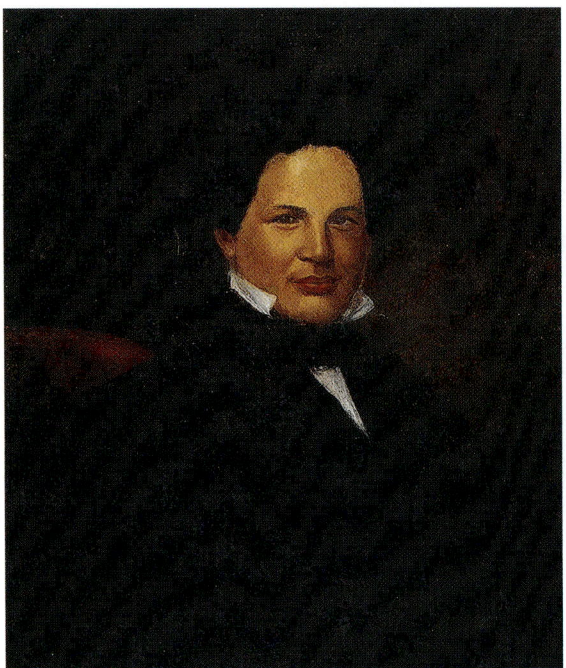

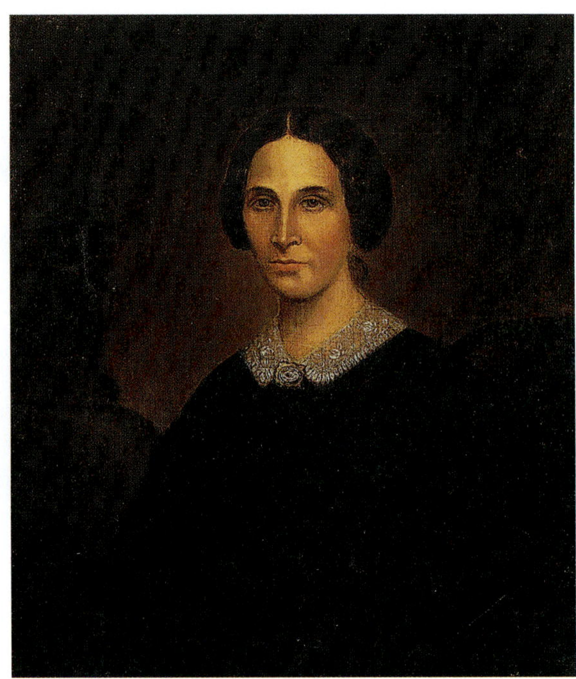

▲ **4.7** William Simpson, *Bishop Jermain W. Loguen*, 1854, oil on canvas, 35″ × 30″.
Collection of the Howard University Art Gallery, Washington, D.C.

▲ **4.8** William Simpson, *Caroline E. Storum Loguen*, 1854, oil on canvas, 35″ × 30″.
Collection of the Howard University Art Gallery, Washington, D.C.

first as a delivery boy and then, after realizing his potential, as an artist's assistant. In 1854, Simpson moved with the Wilsons to Massachusetts. Wilson settled his family in the whaling town of New Bedford, while establishing an art studio with Simpson there. Simpson's artistic career and skill developed with surprising speed. In August 1855, the distinguished black journalist and author William Cooper Nell (1816–74) reported that Simpson's portraits were "remarkable in fidelity and finish," and that the artist had already completed several portrayals of renowned Bostonians, including Senator Charles Sumner.

Simpson's 1854 pendant portraits of the bishop of the New York AME Church, Jermain Wesley Loguen (1813–72), and his wife, Caroline E. Storum Loguen (1817–67), are excellent examples of his work (Figures 4.7 and 4.8). Loguen (née Logue) escaped slavery in Tennessee via the Underground Railroad to Canada in 1834. He eventually settled in upstate New York, where, in 1840, he married and settled in Syracuse. The Loguens served as "stationmasters" of the Underground Railroad in that city for more than a decade, helping an estimated 1,500 fugitives to freedom. Bishop Loguen was an active and outspoken abolitionist whose 1859 autobiography, *The Rev. J. W. Loguen, as a Slave and as a Freeman, a Narrative of Real Life*, served as an important antislavery document. Simpson's paintings of the couple present distinguished likenesses. Mrs. Loguen is seated somberly in front of a faintly articulated Greek vase, a model of Victorian restraint and severity in a black dress and lace collar. Reverend Loguen is portrayed more sympathetically, with a barely perceptible smile, a probing gaze, and a demeanor that exudes gentility and intelligence. The warm skin tones and highlighted areas on his forehead and cheekbones link the depiction to Romantic painting trends (see Chapter 5), while the pose, smooth painting surfaces, and understated emotional expressiveness are indicative of Neoclassicism. Simpson accommodated the "look" of Neoclassical portraiture by understating the ethnic features of the subjects, as Edmonia Lewis did in the female figure in *Forever Free*. Nevertheless, this pairing is one of several rare instances of black subjects rendered within the formal context of Neoclassical portraiture.

Throughout much of the 1860s, Simpson appeared in Boston city directories as a professional portrait painter, completing many single and family portraits for clients in Canada, Liberia, and Haiti as well as throughout the United States. His reputation was such that William Wells Brown (1814–84)—a fugitive from slavery and Underground Railroad activist, as well as a novelist and playwright—included Simpson in an 1863 collection of more than 50 biographies of the most influential Africans in the West, *The Black Man: His Antecedents, His Genius and His Achievements*. Comparing his paintings to both Baroque and **Renaissance** masters, Brown identified Simpson as a **colorist** in the manner of Titian and praised his painterly precision. Brown was also struck by the Neoplatonic ability of Simpson's portrayals to evoke a spiritual and emotional response in the viewer. Interestingly, Brown described Simpson as being "of small figure, unmixed in blood, [with] a rather mild and womanly countenance, firm and resolute eye, gentlemanly in appearance, and intelligent in conversation."

Julien Hudson

An equally gifted painter, Julien Hudson (1811–44) was born free in New Orleans to John Thomas Hudson, a British merchant, and Desirée Marcos, an affluent woman of color who was described in census records as a quadroon—someone with one-quarter African blood. Hudson would thus have been considered black based on the one-drop rule, which dictated that anyone with so much as a single drop of African blood was indeed black by racial designation. In 1826, at age 15, Hudson apprenticed for six months with Italian Neoclassical miniaturist Antonio Meucci (fl. 1818–37), who was a theater scene painter and world-traveled limner. Meucci had come to New Orleans from Rome in 1818 with his wife, Nina (fl. 1818–27), also a painter. Hudson's work shared their Neoclassical style, as exemplified in an 1839 self-portrait (Figure 4.9). Hudson used a fine-hair brush to articulate the details of hair and fabric down to the smallest detail. This attention to intricacies is likely the result of his miniaturist training, which would have required him to paint on a very small scale. Hudson also adopted the ***trompe l'oeil*** oval frame from the miniaturist tradition. On the other hand, his use of subtle color blending to create the skin tones

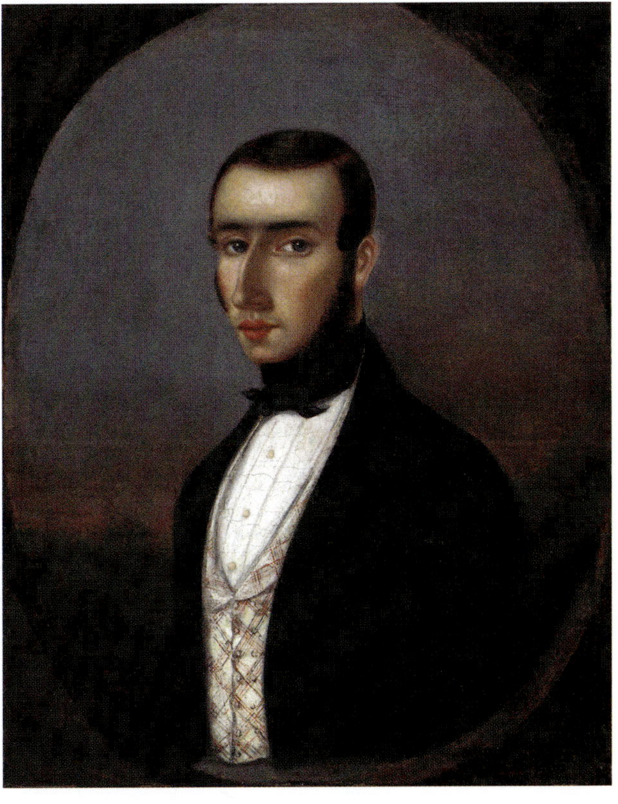

▼ 4.9 Julien Hudson, *Portrait of a Man (Self-Portrait)*, 1839, oil on canvas, 8¾″ × 7″.
Courtesy of the Collections of the Louisiana State Museum.

and his sophisticated modeling link Hudson with the more monumental portrait tradition.

Although not described as such by the artist, the work is presumed to be a self-portrait due to the age and appearance of the sitter as well as his fixed sidelong glance, a common feature of self-portraiture, wherein an artist must move his eyes back and forth continuously between a mirror and the canvas. Hudson depicts himself with unflinching Neoclassical veracity, with a slightly receding hairline; large, almond-shaped blue-gray eyes; a prominent Roman nose; and a full mouth. The elements of academic training evident in this painting reflect fine arts study abroad, which Hudson was able to pursue in 1829 after receiving an inheritance from his grandmother, Françoise Leclerc, of three slaves and more than $100 (about $2,000 today). Hudson made several trips to Paris in 1831, 1835, and 1837. There he studied with Neoclassical Prix de Rome winner Alexandre-Denis Abel de Pujol (1785–1861), who was a portrait and mural painter as well as a one-time student of Jacques-Louis David. It is likely that Hudson learned the art of self-portraiture from Pujol, whose own uncompromising 1806 self-portrait is in the Musée de Beaux-Arts in Valenciennes, France.

As early as 1831, Hudson began to advertise his services as a miniaturist who had undergone a "complete course of study with Meucci" and had "lately returned from Paris." By this time, Hudson had opened a studio in his home, servicing wealthy creole clientele such as Jean Michel Fortier III (d. 1836) (Figure 4.10). Fortier was the son of Colonel Jean Michel Fortier II (1750–1819), who led free black troops in the 1815 Battle of New Orleans, the last battle of the War of 1812. Fortier's stern expression and severe attire are emphasized by the artist's use of a Baroque **palette**, and suggest the sitter's affinity with the republican virtues of stoicism and self-discipline. Fortier's tie pin has been identified as **Masonic** in origin due to his membership in that fraternity of merchants and property holders. The sheet music held in his hand suggests his cultured social status and musical avocation. Fortier had an interesting history (although it was hardly atypical of 19th-century New Orleanians) in that he lived in "concubinage" with a wealthy free woman of color, Margarete Henriette Milon (d. 1838), for some 30 years and had several mixed-race children with her. Hudson may have been commissioned by the Fortier children to create this portrait as a posthumous memento, because Fortier died three years prior to its completion.

▼ **4.10** Julien Hudson, *Jean Michel Fortier III*, 1839, oil on canvas, 30″ × 25″.

Courtesy of the Collections of the Louisiana State Museum, gift of Marguerite Fortier.

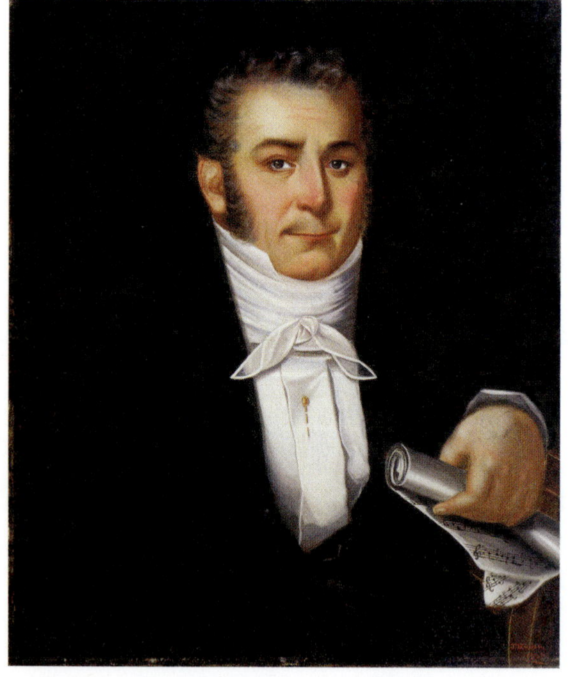

In 1840, Hudson apprenticed at least one known student who went on to become an accomplished artist, George David Coulon (1822–1904). Coulon migrated to New Orleans from France with his family at the age of ten. After studying with Hudson, Coulon worked as a successful portrait and landscape painter in New Orleans for half a century. Because Hudson died young, at age 33, and because little more is known about his life or death, Coulon's success provides evidence, beyond Hudson's paintings, of his abilities as an artist and teacher.

African-American Women Artists and Friendship Albums

African-American men who chose to become professional artists had to overcome a broad spectrum of financial, racial, and social obstacles. As numerous as these were, they were outnumbered by the impediments faced by women. The 19th century offered few opportunities for women to forge careers as artists, largely limiting their vocations to teaching and domestic work. Despite the social strictures imposed on them, however, some women cultivated highly developed skills in the fine arts. Young women from upper-class families were often taught to draw and paint as part of a proper Victorian education. In the case of African-American women, a select few from the black aristocracy preserved evidence of their exceptional artistic gifts in unique documents known as friendship albums. These albums were crosses between graduation yearbooks and scrapbooks and included original and transcribed poetry, dedications, commentary, paintings, and drawings. These ***album amicorum*** were traditionally kept by students and scholars, sometimes for many years. The first known such documents date to mid-16th-century Germany. The practice of keeping ***Stammbücher***, as the Germans called them, was popular in Europe for several centuries and by the 19th century had become almost exclusively the purview of women. At this time, friendship albums made their way to the United States along with German immigrants who settled primarily in New York and Pennsylvania.

One of only a rare few African-American friendship albums from the 19th century that remains intact is that of Philadelphia abolitionist and intellectual Amy Matilda Cassey (1809–56). She maintained her album as a personal treasure and record of her life for more than 20 years, beginning in 1833. The book contains original and transliterated poetry and essays on abolition, religion, literature, horticulture, and issues of race, femininity, and existentialism. Also included are paintings of flora by multiple contributors, including Cassey and members of her wealthy circle, such as abolitionists Frederick Douglass and William Lloyd Garrison; the leader of the Philadelphia Underground Railroad, Robert Purvis; African-American artist Patrick Reason; and members of the influential Philadelphia Female Antislavery Society (which Cassey cofounded in 1833), among others.

Cassey's album consists of 76 pages bound in a gilt-embossed Moroccan (goatskin) cover and includes 10 drawings in ink, graphite, watercolor, and gouache—the first known signed paintings by African-American women. Cassey introduces the album with a preface, excerpted below, which provides a sense of its significance as a personal, intellectual, creative, and collaborative project:

> Reader! Within these folds you'll find
> Effusions various as the wind
> From numerous prolific brains,
> In sorrowful and merry strains.
> This little book, in prose or rhyme

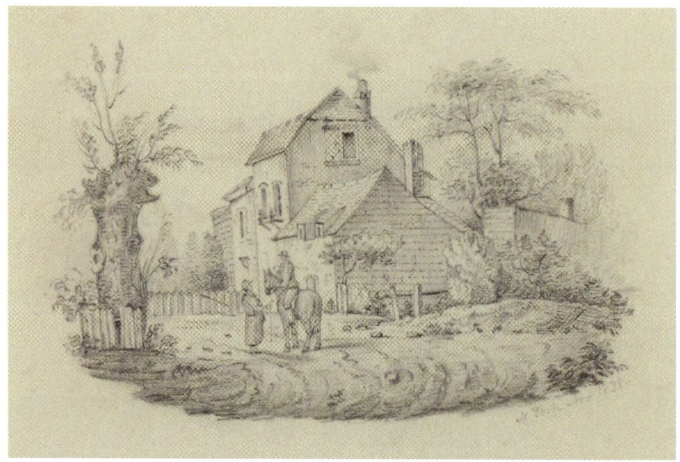

▲ **4.11** Amy Matilda Cassey, *Residential New York Street*, 1838, graphite, 11″ × 9″ (page size).

The Library Company of Philadelphia.

> Is meant to cheat old father time . . . .
> 'Tis hoped, in gratitude alone,
> You'll add a tribute of your own.

Cassey's words invite readers to enjoy the contents of her album and to contribute to it, encouraging unrestricted participation in any chosen format of the highest creative and intellectual caliber. Most prophetic is her pronouncement that the book was meant to cheat time, which indeed it has by preserving art, poetry, and ideas that would otherwise have been lost.

Among the artwork in Cassey's album is a meticulous graphite drawing of a house and garden entitled *N. York Ave* (1839, page 49) attributed to Cassey (Figure 4.11). Landscape, architecture, and animal and human figures have been executed with remarkable fidelity, indicative of Cassey's artistic skill. Several watercolor paintings also grace the album's pages, including still-life floral arrangements (page 14) by Female Anti-Slavery Society cofounders Margaretta Forten (1806–75) and Sarah Mapps Douglass (1806–82). Douglass was an African-American artist, educator, abolitionist, Quaker, and advocate of women's literacy. The only child of well-to-do and politically engaged parents, she received an exceptional education including private tutoring throughout her youth. She began her teaching career in the 1830s, when she opened the first African-American girls' high school in the country in her hometown of Philadelphia. Over the next quarter century, until her marriage to Episcopal minister William Douglass in 1855, she taught at, established, and supervised several highly successful educational institutions for African Americans, one of which ultimately became Cheney State University. Douglass was also the first African-American student to attend the Female Medical College of Pennsylvania in the 1850s.

Douglass contributed paintings to several extant friendship albums, including Cassey's. On page 24 of the Cassey album, Douglass's delicate rendering of a pink camellia and indigo forget-me-not nosegay is accompanied by an original poem that compares women to flowers and laments that both are "dying beneath neglect" (Figure 4.12). The sentiment is a clear indication of Douglass's dedication to the education and civic and social betterment of women. The artist's choice of flowers is also significant. The forget-me-nots are a reminder to Cassey to remember Douglass's friendship by way of her painted gift. Douglass's pink camellia, on the other hand, symbolizes longing in Victorian iconography and refers back to the lament of the artist's prose.

Douglass advertised her art for sale in local newspapers as early as the 1840s. She was evidently encouraged to do so by her milliner mother, Grace Bustill Douglass (1782–1842)—herself an educator—and her artist brother Robert Douglass, Jr. (1808–87), who operated a sign-painting businesses out of the family home. Robert was an art teacher who had studied painting

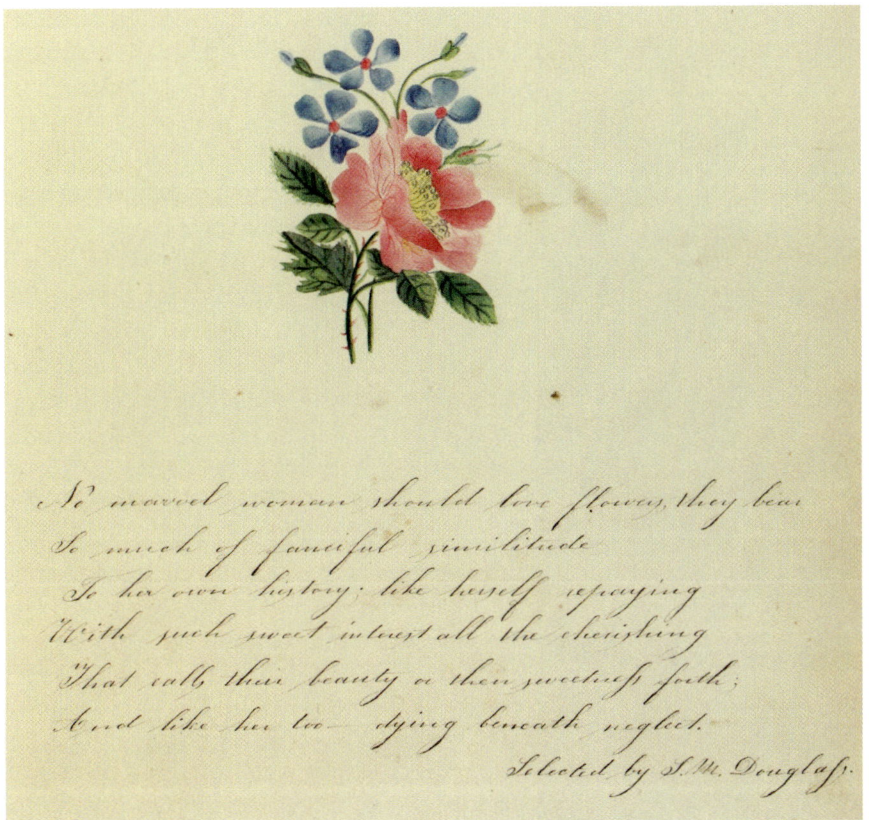

◀ **4.12** Sarah Mapps Douglass, *Untitled [No Marvel Women Should Love Flowers]*, c. 1833, watercolor and gouache on paper, 11″ × 9″ (page size).

The Library Company of Philadelphia.

with presidential portraitist Thomas Sully (1783–1872). Other artist-members of the family include Sarah's cousin, David Bustill Bowser, who created publicity engravings and battle flag designs for the black Civil War regimens (see Chapter 5). These artists represent only a few members of the Douglass clan, which was one of 19th-century America's most influential black families. Its ranks included not only prominent artists but also abolitionists, businesspeople, educators, writers, and athletes, many of whom were responsible for significant social change for African Americans through both their activism and example.

Jules Lion

Another New Orleans artist, Jules Lion (c. 1809–66), was a portrait painter as well as a photographer and **printmaker**. His portrait clients included artist John James Audubon (1785–1851)—himself a son of Haiti and of a mixed-race family—and statesmen Andrew Jackson (1767–1845) and Zachary Taylor (1784–1850). Before relocating from his birthplace, Paris, to New Orleans in 1837, Lion was among the first American artists of any race to have **lithographs** included in the exclusive juried academic salon exhibits. His prints were also featured in the 1833 Paris Exposition, where he was awarded an honorable mention (the youngest artist to have ever received such an award for a lithograph). Once in the United States, Lion was considered something of an artist-celebrity, due to his French birth and salon acknowledgments, and success came quickly to him. A New Orleans journalist

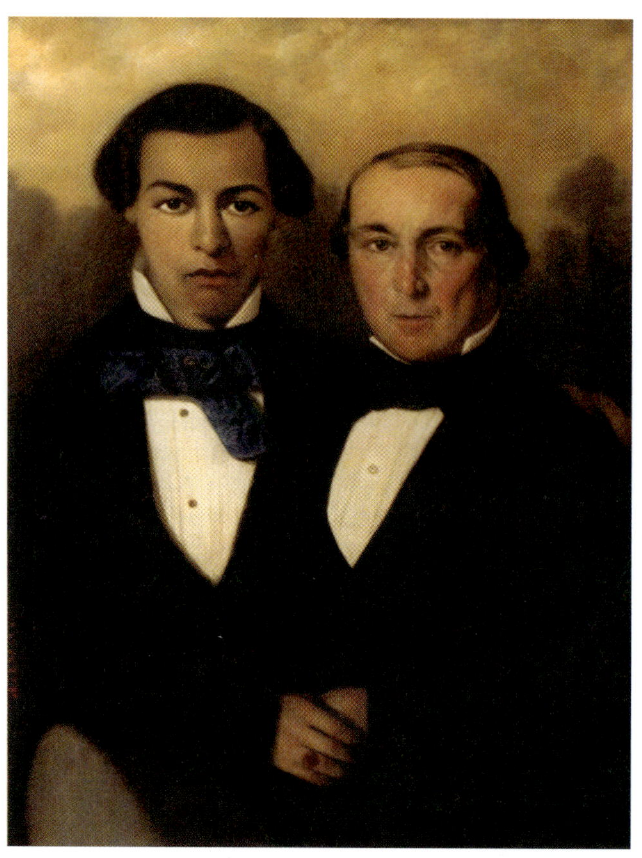

▲ **4.13** Jules Lion, *Asher Moses Nathan and Son (Achille)*, c. 1845, pastel on paper, 26″ × 36″.

Collection of Ann and Jack O. Brittain, Sr., and children. Photo: John Sepulvedo.

described Lion as "a young French gentleman, after saying which we need not add that he is pleasing, courteous, and polite." Although he was identified as a "free man of color" in city directories, Lion was most often referred to in contemporary newspaper articles and reviews as, simply, a Frenchman.

Lion's 1845 pastel portrait *Asher Moses Nathan and Son (Achille)* (Figure 4.13) is an example of the exceptional draftsmanship that so impressed the Paris Salon jury. Father and son are portrayed with Neoclassical solemnity, shown in frontal poses, holding hands, and gazing directly at the viewer. Elegantly dressed in dark suits and cravats offset by crisp white shirts, their social status is evident (note the jeweled ring on the finger of Achille). Expert modeling delineates the faces and fabric textures; the clarity of line of the figures is balanced by a hazy, arbored background. What is most striking about this duo is that the two are not of the same race. Though such a portrayal would have been scandalous to many in the United States at the time, the overwhelmingly biracial makeup of New Orleans and the liberal social attitudes of its many French residents allowed for such a portrait to be painted and displayed, albeit in the privacy of the Nathan home.

Asher Moses Nathan (1785–1863) was a Dutch-Jewish immigrant who came to the United States from Amsterdam around 1800. He operated a successful brokerage firm in New Orleans and by the time of his death had become the equivalent of a present-day millionaire. Although married, Nathan and his wife did not have children. However, in 1836, he purchased a house on Burgundy Street—today the Sun Oak House Museum and Gardens—and redesigned it in the Greek revival style for his black mistress, Marie Emma Manos, with whom he had two children, Catherine and Achille. Indicative of Nathan's wealth and affection for his black family, the house was lavishly designed with 36 rooms and 6,000 square feet of living space. As a further expression of his attachment to them, after the death of his wife in 1853, Nathan legally adopted his African-American children. In an ironic twist, when Nathan himself died in 1863, his mistress married Jules Lion, who was godfather to Catherine and Achille and who had fathered his own child with Manos in 1862, Celine O. Lion. Even more curious is the fact that Achille Nathan shares his name with Lion's brother, Achille Lion, a dentist who followed Lion from Paris to New Orleans. Although there is no empirical evidence indicating that the Lions and Nathans were related by blood, this possibility cannot be ruled out.

Lion also worked as a lithographer for the *New Orleans Bee* (*L'Abeille de la Nouvelle-Orléans*), a French-language newspaper founded by Haitian immigrant François Delaup and known as "the least racist of the city's newspapers." In 1837, the *Bee* began to offer portrait studio services to local clientele for representations "of distinguished men and cherished friends," and Lion secured a position on their staff. During a return visit to Paris in 1839, Lion familiarized himself with the cutting-edge art of the daguerreotype. Invented by Louis-Jacques-Mandé Daguerre (1787–1851), the daguerreotype was one of the first photographic forms. The daguerreotype reproduced reverse images on silver-coated copper plates. After creating a sensation at the 1839 Paris Salon, it rapidly replaced painted miniatures as the preferred form of visual self-documentation. On his return to New Orleans, Lion opened a photo studio—one of the first ever in the United States—in the French Quarter, where he documented the local citizenry, in life and in death, by creating photographic images of living clients and **memento mori** of the deceased.

For the next several years, Lion worked and exhibited successfully as a photographer. In 1840 he treated the city of New Orleans to its first-ever fine arts photography exhibit, a showing of his architectural still lifes that was mounted at the St. Charles Museum, which opened to rave reviews. In the late 1840s, facing financial difficulties, Lion attempted to shore up his income by founding an art school; however, the venture was short-lived and ended later that same year. By the 1850s, Lion's reputation was waning. While continuing his activities as a portraitist, Lion created narrative lithographs for Confederate sheet music and taught drawing at Louisiana College. Lion died in January 1866. His descendants still reside in New Orleans.

Patrick Henry Reason

Patrick Henry Reason (née Patrick Rison, 1816–98) was a printmaker and an active abolitionist. The son of Caribbean émigrés, Reason was born and raised in New York City. He was educated at the New York African Free School, an institution for African-American children founded in 1787 by America's first chief justice, John Jay (1745–1829); Secretary of State Alexander Hamilton (1755–1804); and other members of the New York Manumission Society. Reason's artistic talents became evident as a child, when in 1830, at age 13, he created a painstaking drawing of the school building, which was engraved for use as the frontispiece of a book on its history.

Beginning in 1833, Reason spent four years learning the printmaking trade as an apprentice in lithography and engraving in the studio of English illustrator Stephen Henry Gimber (1806–62), who had arrived in the United States a few years before, in 1828. When Reason's apprenticeship was completed, he opened his own studio and became a widely published engraver of portraits and illustrations. He advertised his services as a portraitist, draftsman, engraver, and landscape artist in the African-American weekly newspaper the *Colored American*. In 1839, the newspaper reported on a lecture given by Reason in which he expressed his belief in the value of the fine arts as an edifying pursuit. The artist said: "The Fine Arts are contrived to give pleasure to the eye and ear, which have in themselves a natural aptitude to draw us from the immoderate gratification of corporeal pleasures, and sensual appetites." This Neoplatonic concept—that art has the capacity to elevate the human mind beyond the physical to a more transcendental state—echoes Greek, Gothic, and Renaissance beliefs in the spiritual nature of art. Reason also addressed the value of intelligent art criticism over mere art appreciation, explaining that "those who, having a clear conception of what is . . . beautiful in painting, receive from [it] true permanent intellectual pleasure." Decisive in his opinions about artists and critics, Reason concluded (in French), "Grand Dieu delivré nous de ses amateurs sans amours, et de ses connoisseurs sans connoissance [*sic*]" ("Great God, deliver us from these amateurs without love, and from these judges without knowledge").

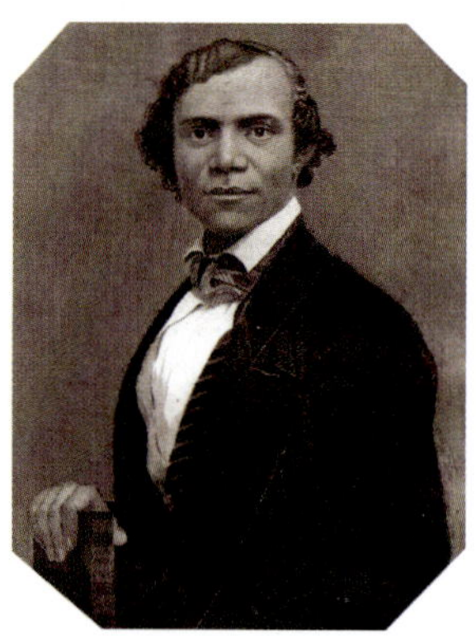

▲ **4.14** Patrick Reason, *Henry Bibb, 1848*, engraving. Frontispiece of *Narrative of the Life and Adventures of Henry Bibb, an American Slave, Written by Himself* (New York: H. Bibb, 1849).

Reason received many commissions throughout his career, from prestigious publications such as *Harper's Bazaar* and *Harper's Weekly*, from abolitionist leaders and other influential Americans, and from the government. In 1840, he completed a copper engraving of renowned African-American abolitionist, author, and escaped slave, Henry Bibb (1815–54) (Figure 4.14). Bibb escaped from Kentucky to Detroit in June 1838, at which time his owner, Daniel Lane, posted a $50 reward for his capture. In the 1840s, Bibb began his work as an abolitionist, lecturing on the evils of slavery. By 1849, he had published his autobiography, in which Reason's engraving of the abolitionist appears as the frontispiece. The artist portrays Bibb face-frontal, with his torso in three-quarter view. He is dressed formally, and his hand is resting on a book—presumably his autobiography—as an allusion to Bibb's literacy. The precision of Reason's draftsmanship and the direct, intense gaze of the subject create a riveting and honest portrayal of a dynamic man. The Fugitive Slave Act of 1850 made Bibb's continued residency in the United States dangerous, so he was forced to flee to Ontario, Canada. There he was joined by three of his six brothers, also escaped slaves. He founded Canada's first black newspaper, *Voices of the Fugitive*, and he became a leader of Ontario's thriving black community.

Reason dedicated his artistic talents to documenting significant Americans, especially those who were working to end slavery. Once the Civil War ended, however, Reason's abolitionist client base disappeared. In 1869, he relocated to Cleveland, Ohio, with his wife, an Englishwoman named Esther Cunningham (1835–1920), whom he had married in 1862. Within three years of the move, Reason landed a position with the jewelry firm of Sylvester Hogan. He spent his later years as an engraver and designer there.

Summary

During the Neoclassical era, African-American artists were more closely aligned with their Euro-American counterparts than they had been previously. Their sculpture and painting were representative of the Neoclassical genre in austerity and stoicism. That being said, the subject matter of artists such as Edmonia Lewis and Patrick Reason suggests an ongoing concern for the condition of blacks in America. Similarly, the portraits of

Simpson, Johnson, Hudson, and Lion—which represent rare examples of African Americans portrayed with dignity and equanimity—contributed in their own way to the struggle for racial parity. Although sculptors such as Foy and the Warburgs earned their livings creating funerary monuments, and women artists such as Cassey and Douglass were limited to expressing their creativity in friendship albums, others were able to achieve success as recognized painters and sculptors for the first time in African-American history.

Key Terms

album amicorum: from the Latin, refers to a friendship album or autograph book

Baroque period: in visual art, a 17th-century European style marked by dramatic content and lighting contrasts, exaggerated movement, monumental themes, and ornamentation

bas-relief: meaning "low relief," refers to sculpture that projects only slightly from a background surface

colorist: an artist who emphasizes color over line or who employs a vibrant color palette

contrapposto: from the Italian for "counter pose," the term refers to the Classical Greek sculptural tradition of posing a standing figure with one knee bent and the figure's weight supported by the opposing leg

École des Beaux Arts: a prestigious French school of fine arts first established in 1648, where many of France's greatest artists were trained

frontal composition: an image in which figures and objects are forward facing

Grand Tour: an extended cultural tour of continental Europe considered vital to the education of wealthy young Americans and Europeans from the 17th to the 19th centuries

humanist: refers to a belief in the supremacy of human achievement over spiritual or religious concerns

limner: an 18th- and 19th-century itinerant or traveling portrait painter

lithograph: an image created by first writing or drawing with a wax-based crayon on a flat limestone and then inking the stone and running it through a printing press to produce multiple paper copies

marbrier: one who carves or sculpts in marble

Masonic: referring to Freemasons, an international fraternal organization originally founded by stonemasons in the Middle Ages

memento mori: an image intended as a reminder of death

miniaturist: an artist who paints on a very small scale

modeling: in two-dimensional art, shading forms to give the illusion of three-dimensionality; in sculpture, shaping forms

Neoplatonic: based on the philosophy of third-century Greek philosopher Plotinus, which suggests that the visible world is an illusory manifestation of a more transcendent reality

oil glaze: a thin, transparent layer of oil paint applied to opaque painted surfaces to create subtle color or luster effects

palette: colors used by an artist in a specific composition; the portable surface on which an artist mixes paint
Paris Salon: in the 18th and 19th centuries, the official art exhibit of the French Fine Arts Academy (École des Beaux-Arts) and the Société des Artistes Français
planar composition: in two-dimensional art, that which is parallel to the picture surface
post-Reconstruction era: a period in southern U.S. history from 1877 to the turn of the 20th century, marked by legalized segregation and racial violence against and systematic disenfranchisement of African Americans
printmaker: one who creates images for reproduction using a printing press
Reconstruction: a period in U.S. history from the end of the Civil War to 1877 when Confederate states were readmitted to the Union under northern military supervision, and African-American men were politically enfranchised by the Thirteenth, Fourteenth, and Fifteenth Amendments to the Constitution
Renaissance: a period in 15th- and 16th-century Europe marked by a revival of classical Greco-Roman culture, intellectual achievement, scientific advancement, and transatlantic exploration
Romantic era: a 19th-century visual arts period noted for emotional and imaginative subject matter and an interest in the grandeur of nature
sarcophagi: plural of sarcophagus; a stone coffin decorated with relief sculpture and inscriptions
sculpture-in-the-round: freestanding sculpture that is meant to be seen from many angles
Stammbücher: from the German word for "albums," refers to friendship albums or autograph books
stoicism: accepting the misfortunes of life without complaint, based on an ancient Roman philosophy
Symbolism: a late 19th-century literary and visual art movement in the United States and Europe noted for macabre and decadent themes and veiled meanings
trompe l'oeil: French for "trick the eye," refers to the practice of painting images that appear identical to actual objects

Questions for Further Study and Discussion

1. What formal and iconographic elements characterize Neoclassicism?
2. What was the one-drop rule? How did this rule benefit and/or damage the careers of such artists as Julien Hudson, Daniel Warburg, Eugene Warburg, and others of mixed race?
3. Describe the technique of lithography. What were its uses?
4. What effect did the invention of photography have on the miniaturist tradition?

5. What are the similarities and differences between lithography and engraving?
6. Why was Edmonia Lewis able to succeed as a professional artist when so many American women did not? Include in your discussion finances, mentorship, the political milieu, and the artist's social status and personality.
7. Edmonia Lewis and Eugene Warburg chose fine art sculpture as a career; Florville Foy and Daniel Warburg chose funerary monuments rather than fine art sculptures. If given a choice, which would you choose and why? Consider holding a class debate of this topic.

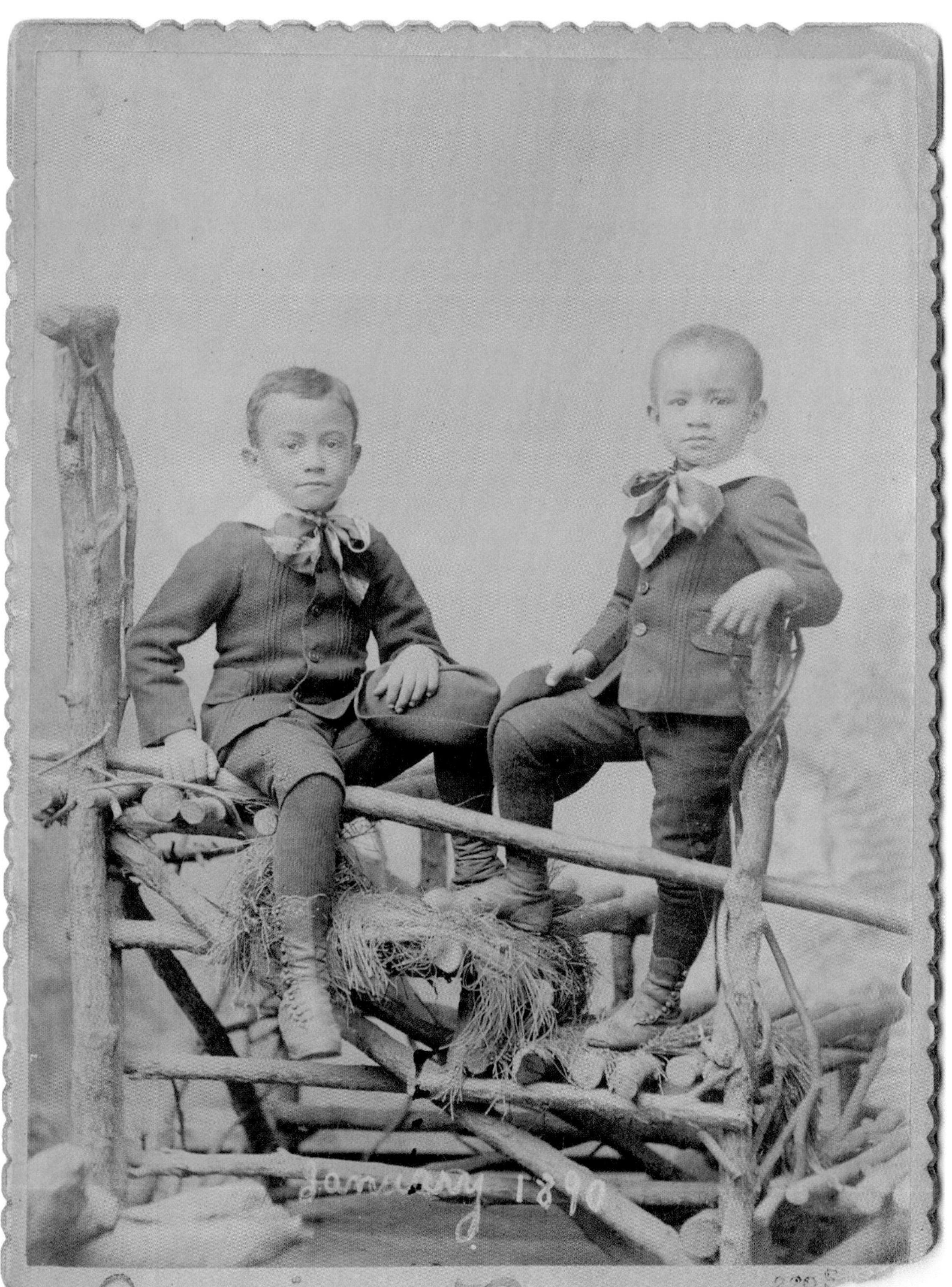
January 1890
Goodridge Bros

ROMANTICISM TO IMPRESSIONISM IN THE 19TH CENTURY

5

Romanticism, a 19th-century trend in art and architecture, chronologically overlapped with Neoclassicism but promoted a very different aesthetic outlook. Romantic art tended to be intuitive rather than rational, subjective rather than objective, and passionate rather than unemotional. Proponents of Romantic painting preferred the strokes of the paintbrush to remain visible, rejecting the smooth, glassy surfaces of earlier painting. The result was a much more active painting surface. Intense contrasts of light and dark (**chiaroscuro**) were also employed to facilitate drama. Forms were merged with one another and with the background, rather than being individually articulated, resulting in unified compositions with emotive power. A number of African-American figurative artists, such as Henry Tanner and David Bustill Bowser, were inspired by Romanticism's emotional and spiritual approach to content. They found in Romanticism a welcome counterpoint to the stoic coldness of Neoclassicism and an approach that was more in tune with the volatility of post-Reconstruction America and with their own religious sensibilities.

Landscapes (often of exotic, medieval, or imagined locales) were especially popular in the Romantic age because of their ability to inspire awe of nature's beauty, indomitability, and ferociousness (in terms of natural disasters such as fires or floods) and as an indicator of God's presence on earth. Taking advantage of the expansive American countryside, from New England to the Ohio River valley and the Northwest Coast, African-American painters such as Edward Mitchell Bannister, Grafton Tyler Brown, and Robert S. Duncanson created dramatic landscape vistas.

THE LANDSCAPE TRADITION

Robert S. Duncanson

Robert S. Duncanson (1821–72) was an internationally acclaimed landscape painter whose scenes of ancient ruins and grand natural vistas were applauded for their emotive power and painterly precision. His work fused the smooth Neoclassical surface with dramatic Romantic scenery. Duncanson was born in Fayette, New York, to a free black family of carpenters and house painters. After moving to Monroe, Michigan, as a teenager, Duncanson began advertising his own services as a house painter, but his true aspiration was to become a fine artist. At age 20, he became a limner and traveled between Monroe, Cincinnati, and Detroit painting portraits and still lifes. During his time as an itinerant painter, Duncanson honed his skills by

◀ William and Wallace Goodridge, [*William O., Jr. and John Goodridge*], c. 1895, cabinet card, 6.5″ × 4.3″ (image size).

Goodbridge Brothers collection, Local History and Genealogy Department, Public Libraries of Saginaw, GB243.

copying the works of other artists that he found in books. In particular, he was inspired by the scrupulous drawings of Mayan pyramids and ruins, Nicaraguan and Salvadorian volcanoes, and Central American mountain ranges and cave structures reproduced in an 1839 travel journal entitled *Incidents of Travel in Central America*. It greatly influenced Duncanson's decision to become a landscape painter of Romantic scenes.

Duncanson painted his first landscapes in 1848 after viewing **Hudson River School** painter Thomas Cole's (1801–48) *The Voyage of Life: Childhood*, which had been recently purchased by a Cincinnati collector. The Hudson River School was a group of 19th-century Romantic landscape painters whose subject matter centered on grand pastoral visions of the Hudson River Valley and the nearby Adirondack and Catskill Mountains. The Cole painting, which symbolized birth and early life, depicted a diminutive haloed girl in a golden canoe, emerging from a dark cave onto a lush mountain lake set within a vast landscape. Its influence can be seen in many Duncanson landscapes. Duncanson's transition from limner to landscape painter also coincided with an 1848 commission for a painting of Lake Superior that he received from a wealthy abolitionist and Methodist minister named Rev. Charles Avery (1784–1858). Pleased with this painting, Avery rewarded the artist by giving him access to his circle of abolitionist art patrons.

Included among Duncanson's illustrious clientele was Charlotte Cushman, who, in turn, introduced Duncanson's work to the Duchess of Sutherland (both women were also patrons of Edmonia Lewis; see Chapter 4). Another important Duncanson benefactor was Cincinnati vintner Nicholas Longworth (1783–1863), who was one of the wealthiest men in the United States at the time. In 1850, Longworth invited Duncanson to paint eight landscape murals in the entryway of his Federal-style mansion, known then as Belmont (today the Taft Museum of Art) (Figure 5.1). Bordered in *trompe l'oeil* Rococo frames, the murals depict idyllic pastoral panoramas scattered with rustic figures and cottages, gothic structures, streams, and lakes. Expertly rendered and enveloped in Duncanson's signature hazy, dreamlike aura, the murals portray a world that stands in stark contrast to Cincinnati's new industrialized landscape. Indeed, the Romantic Movement as a whole was a reaction against the Industrial Revolution and an expression of longing for a simpler, more agrarian time. The largest extant antebellum murals in the country, Duncanson's Belmont suite gave him unprecedented exposure to Cincinnati's high society and greatly increased his reputation and client base.

During the summers from 1850 to 1852, Duncanson made sketching trips with friend and fellow landscape artist William Sonntag (1822–1900), who had studied at the Cincinnati Academy of Fine Arts. Sonntag was also a proponent of the Hudson River School, although he and Duncanson preferred to explore the scenery of the rural Ohio River valley rather than that of New York State. Duncanson and Sonntag sketched **en plein air** (outdoors) extensively, creating a body of preliminary works that served as resources for finished paintings that they completed later in their studios. The duo had abutting studio spaces in a commercial building. Although Sonntag was the

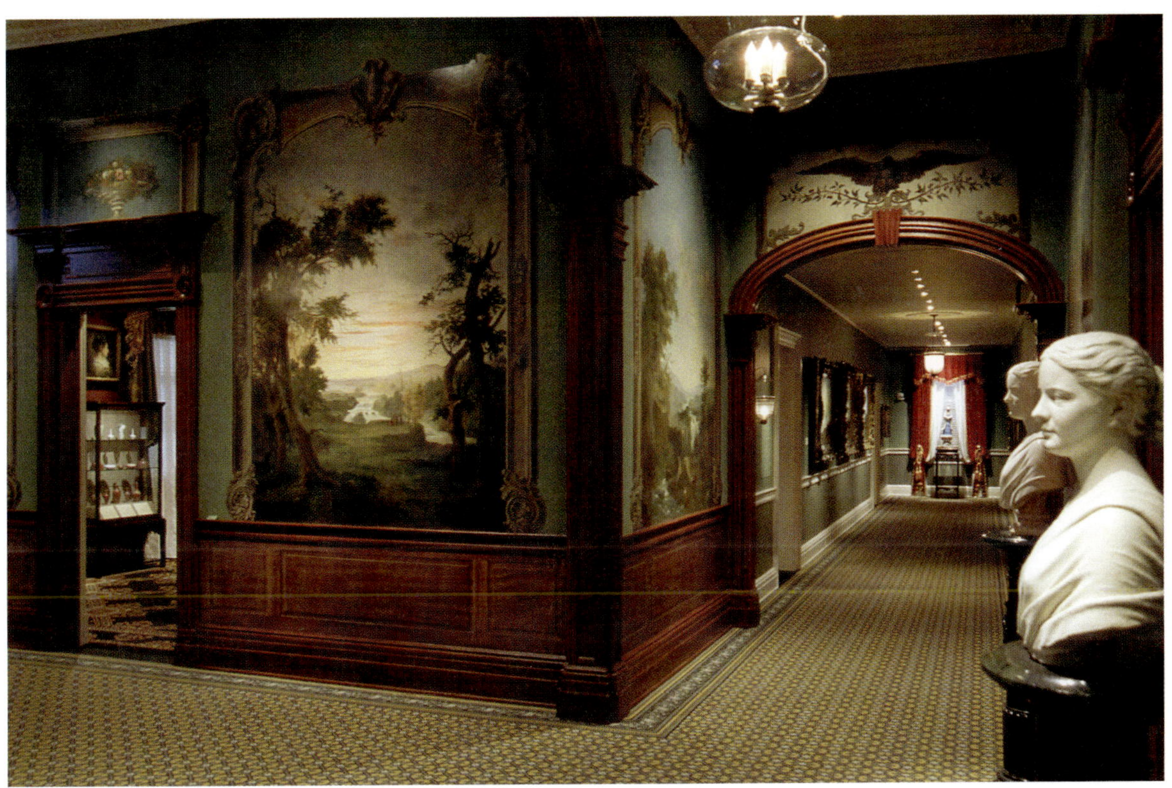

▲ **5.1** Robert S. Duncanson, *Landscape Murals*, oil on plaster, 30⅞″ × 59¼–110¼″ × 86¼″.

The Belmont (now Taft Museum of Art). Photo courtesy of the Taft Museum of Art, Cincinnati. Photographer: Tony Walsh.

senior artist, Duncanson rapidly matched his skills and became as much an inspiration for Sonntag as vice versa.

With financial assistance from Longworth, Duncanson made a lengthy Grand Tour of Europe, again accompanied by Sonntag, from April 1853 to June of the following year. The tour included London, Paris, and Florence (where the artists met Hiram Powers; see Chapter 4). Duncanson made copious sketches of the Italian countryside and architectural ruins, which he transformed into finished paintings after his return to Ohio. He also saw the work of Europe's most esteemed landscape painters, in particular the Baroque artist Claude Lorrain (1600–82). In his own art, Duncanson reified Lorrain's fantasy landscapes of classical ruins into decisively Romantic visions that eliminated or minimized human presence and activity. His tour abroad greatly influenced the artist's growth: he wrote in 1854 that his travels "shed new light over my path." He observed that viewing the works of other artists "enabled me to judge my own talent," proclaiming "I do not feel discouraged."

Back in Cincinnati, Duncanson supplemented his income by hand-coloring black-and-white photographs for the prominent African-American photographer James Ball and assisted Ball in the creation of a monumental antislavery **panorama** (see the discussion of Ball later in this chapter). Duncanson also completed a series of portrait commissions of noted abolitionists, including a full-length rendering of Longworth in 1858. But Duncanson's landscapes gained him the most attention and praise. His dreamlike visions of ancient Pompeii, Arcadia, the Yucatan, and India and his sublime, mist-infused scenes of the American wilderness and Scottish countryside catapulted him, according to an 1861 review in the *Daily Cincinnati Gazette*, to the status of "the best landscape artist in the West."

Duncanson's paintings based on literary subjects—such as Harriet Beecher Stowe's *Uncle Tom's Cabin* and Alfred, Lord Tennyson's (1809–92) *The Lotus Eaters*, which inspired Duncanson's 1861 painting *The Land of the Lotus Eaters* (Figure 5.2)—were especially popular. After a May 1861 exhibit of this work at Pike's Opera House in Cincinnati, the *Cincinnati Daily Enquirer* applauded the painting's "lifelike fidelity" and extraordinary detail, calling the work a "masterpiece." The opera house showing was followed by another in Toronto in November of that same year and yet another in Montreal's Notman Gallery. Duncanson moved to Montreal for a year in 1863, where he befriended the Scottish photographer William Notman (1826–91), who owned the gallery/photo studio that exhibited this work.

Duncanson's stimuli for *The Land of the Lotus Eaters* derived not only from the British poet laureate Tennyson's poem but also from Hudson River School painter Frederic Church's (1826–1900) South American landscape, *Heart of the Andes* (1859), which was shown at Pike's Opera House in November 1860, a few months before Duncanson completed his work. Duncanson's painting is a tropical interpretation of Church's, incorporating warmer tones, a more unified palette and composition, and lush, equatorial vegetation within a visionary setting.

With assistance from Notman, in 1864 Duncanson sailed for the U.K. for a showing of *The Lotus Eaters* and other works in Glasgow, Dublin (1865), and London (1866). When, thanks to an introduction from Notman,

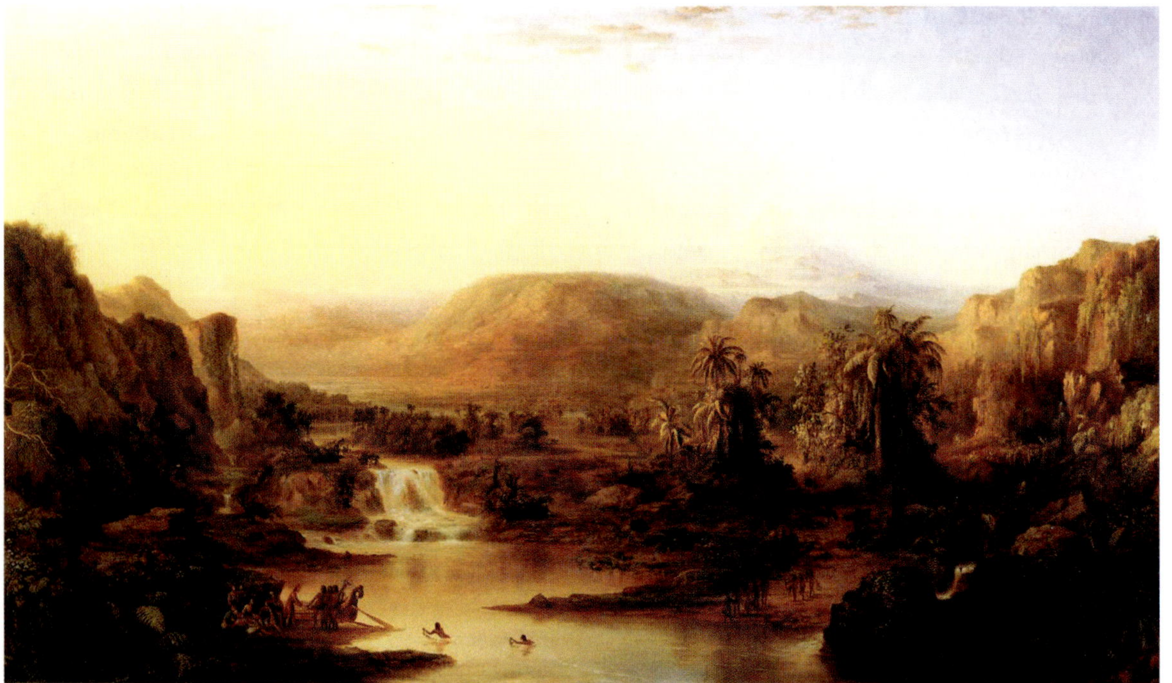

▼ **5.2** Robert S. Duncanson, *Land of the Lotus Eaters*, 1861, oil on canvas, 52¾ × 88⅝″.
Swedish Royal Collection, Stockholm.

Duncanson presented the painting to Tennyson himself at the poet's home on the Isle of Wight, according to an 1864 report, Tennyson described the painting as "a land in which one lives to wander and linger." The following year, the *Cincinnati Weekly Gazette* expressed amazement at the colorblind nature of Duncanson's European acquaintances: "Think of a Negro sitting at the table of Mr. and Mrs. Alfred Tennyson, Lord and Lady of the Manor, and Mirror of Aristocracy[!]"

In 1866, Duncanson returned to Ohio, where he enjoyed a successful painting career as one of the most respected American artists of his time. He made one last trip abroad to Scotland in 1870–71, but by this time his health was failing. Suffering from dementia (possibly from paint lead poisoning), Duncanson passed away in a sanitarium at the age of 51. His objective as a painter—to express deep human emotion through art—was quintessentially Romantic, as confirmed by a motto that he kept posted on the wall of his studio: "True art is the development of the sentiments and principles of the human soul—natural objects being the medium of illustration."

Grafton Tyler Brown

Working on the West Coast, Grafton Tyler Brown (1841–1918) depicted the panoramic vistas of California and the Pacific Northwest. A native of Harrisburg, Pennsylvania, Brown worked as a janitor in a print shop when he was 14 and learned the printmaking trade by observing lithographers at work. In his late teens, during the Gold Rush, he traveled to California, where he taught himself how to draw from nature by rendering scenes of the life around him. He experienced one of his first successes in 1861, when the prominent New York printing firm of Currier and Ives accepted the 20-year-old Brown's romanticized rendering of mountain miners—*Goldmining in California*—for reproduction as a **chromolithograph** in their popular suite of prints. This print became so popular that it is still widely available for purchase today.

That same year, Brown was hired by the respected lithography team of Emil Dresel (1819–69) and Charles Conrad Kuchel (1820–65), as both an artist and lithographer, creating all manner of drawings for translation into prints. His first major assignment was an elaborate rendering of Virginia City, Nevada (the legendary silver-mining boom town), which incorporated both an aerial view of the town and detailed drawings of the façades of its buildings (Figure 5.3).

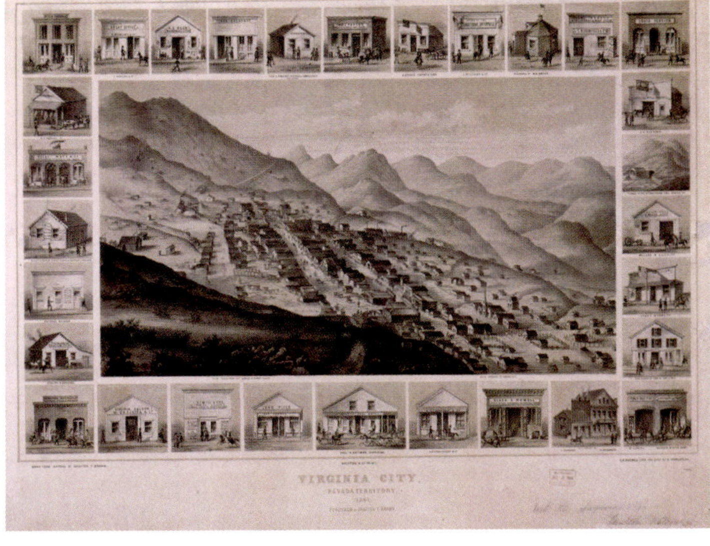

▼ **5.3** Grafton Tyler Brown, *Virginia City, Nevada Territory, Drawn from Nature by Grafton T. Brown*, 1861, lithograph, 41″ × 30″.

The Library of Congress, Prints and Photographs Division LC-USZ62-77569 to LC-USZ62-77582.

Considered by collectors today to be one of the rarest and most coveted of visual records of the town, Brown's Virginia City view was published in at least three versions in 1861 and again in a larger format and with slight variations in 1864. Especially significant is Brown's rendering of thirty façades of the town's major businesses and structures, from the livery stable to the fire- and courthouses and to the clothing and tobacco stores. Among these is the *Territorial Newspaper* office, where *Huckleberry Finn* and *Tom Sawyer* author Mark Twain (Samuel Clemens, 1835–1910) was working as a reporter at the time.

In 1867, after Kuchel's death, Brown (now 27) purchased Dresel and Kuchel's business and established the firm anew in the name of G. T. Brown and Company. He joined a growing number of African-American printing companies fueled by the black press, which had begun producing newspapers in the late 1820s. In addition to maps and topographical drawings, Brown's company illustrated and printed paper money, stock certificates, labels, and public notices for California and Nevada Territory companies. After more than a dozen successful years, Brown sold his company and began traveling, sketching, and painting the grand outdoor vistas of the Northwest. He settled briefly in Victoria, Canada, where he opened a studio and advertised himself, for the first time, as a landscape painter. He completed nearly two dozen paintings of the Victoria area that were exhibited in a one-person show in 1883 in the newly constructed offices of Victoria's *Daily Colonist* newspaper. Brown's display opened to positive reviews posted—not surprisingly—in the *Daily Colonist*.

Later in 1883, Brown returned to the United States, where he painted the scenery of Oregon, California's Yosemite National Park, Mt. Rainier National Park in Washington State, and Yellowstone National Park. His awe-inspiring watercolor and oil paintings of the virgin wilderness included panoramic depictions of mountain ranges, geysers, waterfalls, and other natural phenomena. *Mt. Tacoma at Sunset from Lake Washington* represents the mature artist's style (Figure 5.4). Depicted is the distant snowcapped

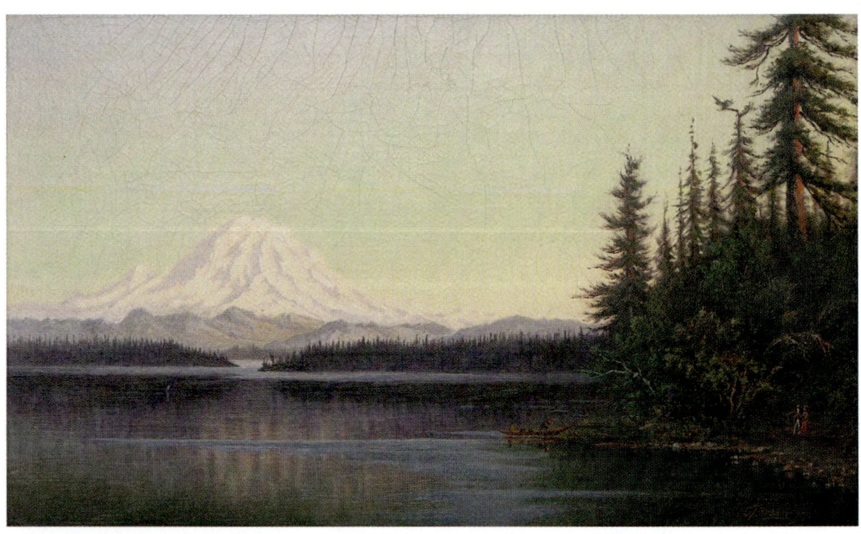

▶ **5.4** Grafton Tyler Brown, *Mount Tacoma at Sunset from Lake Washington*, W.T., 1884, oil on canvas, 15⅝″ × 25⅝″.

Washington State Historical Society / Art Resource, NY.

peak of Mt. Tacoma framed on the right by an outcropping of pine and ash trees. The peak is separated from the foreground by the placid, glassy surface of Lake Washington. The compositional arrangement suggests that the viewer is standing on the lake's shore (as the artist likely was), and pulls the viewer into the scene. Romantic in theme, the artist's use of a fine brush and controlled brushwork is anything but Romantic and allies him with the measured Neoclassical rendering style found in Duncanson's otherwise Romantic pictures.

In 1892, Brown settled in Minnesota, where he remained for the rest of his life. He worked as a cartographer, draftsman, and civil engineer for the U.S. Army Corps of Engineers until 1897 and then for the City of St. Paul, intermittently, from 1900 to 1916. He died in 1918 after a protracted illness. His obituary described him simply as an engineer and city employee. Until recently, no paintings by Brown from his later career in Minnesota were known to the public. However, a snowy mountain scene signed and dated 1898 by the artist was unearthed for sale at auction in 2013, indicating that Brown continued to paint grand landscapes into the 20th century.

Edward Mitchell Bannister

New England landscape painter Edward Mitchell Bannister (1828–1901) preferred active brushwork and painterly surfaces over the glass-like finishes of Duncanson and Brown. His approach to painting shared much in common with English Romantic painter John Constable (1776–1837) and with the en plein air landscape tradition of the **Barbizon School**, named after the town, about 100 miles south of Paris, where its practitioners lived and worked. Bannister was born in the seaside town of Saint Andrews in New Brunswick, Canada, which boasted a small black population. Bannister and his younger brother William (b. 1830) attended the village school and were considered by the townspeople to be "smart and athletic." Young "Ed" had a knack for creating "clever pictures" in the words of a local journalist. It was assumed, even then, that he would become "a great artist."

In 1846, Bannister left home to work as a cook on a sailing vessel. After four years at sea, he settled in Boston, where he earned a living as a barber working for the Madame Carteaux men's haircare and wig-making chain. In 1857, he married his 37-year-old employer (Bannister was 29), an African-American and Narragansett Indian businesswoman named Christiana Babcock Carteaux (1822–1903). Mrs. Bannister's income supported her husband's interest in the fine arts, which allowed him to retire from barbering in 1860. Bannister opened a combination painting and photography business in the same building as the studio of Edmonia Lewis (see Chapter 4). He found clients from among his wife's philanthropic abolitionist circle. Mrs. Bannister was an active abolitionist and acquainted with such important antislavery figures as William Lloyd Garrison. Within a few years, Bannister had earned a respectable reputation as a painter and was included in William Wells Brown's 1862 book *The Black Man, His Antecedents, His Genius, and His Achievements* along with William Simpson (see Chapter 4).

Offended by an article published in the *New York Herald* in 1867 that asserted that "the Negro seems to have an appreciation for art while being manifestly unable to produce it," Bannister determined to prove this allegation untrue. He immediately began taking evening classes in the fine arts at the Lowell Institute to improve his painting skills. He studied there under English-American artist and physician William Rimmer (1816–79). After completing his studies, in 1869 Bannister moved with his wife to Providence, Rhode Island. His first Providence studio was small, but by 1874, Bannister's career was flourishing, and he had relocated to improved quarters that would remain his workspace for the next 25 years. The artist made regular sketching excursions to the Narragansett coast about 30 miles south of Providence and became a yearly participant in the Boston Art Club's annual exhibits.

Throughout the 1870s, Bannister exhibited and sold his paintings and won a number of prizes in both Providence and Boston. In 1876, he learned that his submission of a landscape entitled *Under the Oaks* to the Philadelphia Centennial had won first prize. In an interview for the *New York Tribune,* he recounted the circumstances under which he accepted the award:

> *I hurried to the committee rooms to make sure that the report [of my award] was true. There was a great crowd there ahead of me. As I jostled among them; many resented my presence; some actually commenting within my hearing in a most petulant manner, "What is that colored person in here for?" and similar discourteous remarks. The official in charge . . . was very insolent. . . . He demanded in the most exasperating tone of voice, "Well, what do you want here anyway? Speak lively." I responded, "I want to inquire concerning #54 [Under the Oaks]. Is it a prize winner?" "What's that to you?" Controlling myself, I said deliberately. ". . . I painted the picture." An explosion could not have made a more marked impression. Without hesitation he apologized, and soon everyone in the room was bowing and scraping to me.*

When it was learned by the jury that Bannister was African-American, there was some discussion of a revocation of his prize. Participating white artists, however, objected strenuously and demanded that Bannister receive his award.

The whereabouts of *Under the Oaks* is unknown today, but an existing graphite study indicates its close resemblance to Bannister's extant *Tree Landscape* of 1877 (Figure 5.5). The later painting is representative of much of Bannister's imagery in its painterly surface, bucolic scenery, use of thick **impasto**, and subdued verdant and umber tones. Nature is depicted as unmanicured, unrestrained, and untouched by civilization. Two cows graze quietly in the background, at one with their surroundings. The sky is cloud-filled and gray, suggesting an impending rainstorm and the powerful forces of nature. The natural elements are metaphors for the volatility and uncertainty of the human condition. Considered the artist's magnum opus, *Under the Oaks* sold to Boston art collector John Duff (d. 1918) for $1,500 (more than $30,000 today).

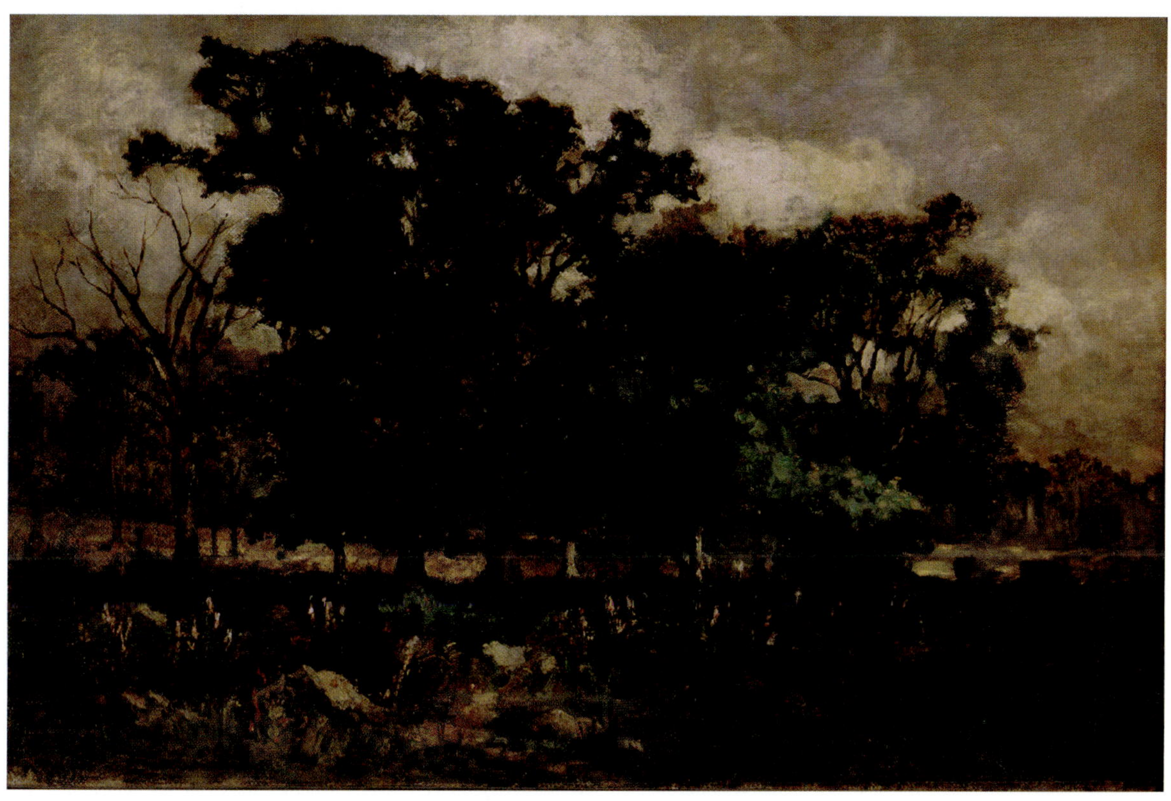

▲ 5.5 Edward Mitchell Bannister, *Tree Landscape*, 1877, oil on canvas, 20″ × 30″.
Photo: Smithsonian American Art Museum, Washington, D.C. / Art Resource, NY.

Bannister's works of the 1880s and 1890s display reduced impasto, staccato brushwork, and a vibrant palette, indicative of his late-career affinity with **Impressionism**. Led by French artist Claude Monet (1840–1926) in the 1870s and 1880s, Impressionist artists strove to capture the mercurial nature of visual reality as perceived by the human eye. Bannister's exposure to the style may have come in 1886, when 300 paintings by French Barbizon and Impressionist artists were exhibited in New York by Parisian art dealer Paul Durand-Ruel (1831–1922). This pivotal show received national attention and sparked widespread interest in Impressionism in the United States. Bannister's *Apple Trees in a Meadow*, painted about 1890, is an example of his Impressionist-inspired work (Figure 5.6). Whereas the lower half of the painting exhibits the artist's signature dark palette of browns and greens, the entire upper portion, including the blossoms of the apple tree and the sky beyond, utilize the lightened palette and abbreviated, energetic brushstrokes of Impressionism.

In 1880, Bannister became a founding member of the Providence Art Club, today one of the oldest art clubs in the United States. The club is located near the First Baptist Church, where Bannister was attending when he suffered a fatal heart attack and died in 1901. A memorial exhibit of more than 100 of his paintings was held at the Art Club to honor Bannister, who was, and is, considered one of Providence's most beloved and respected residents.

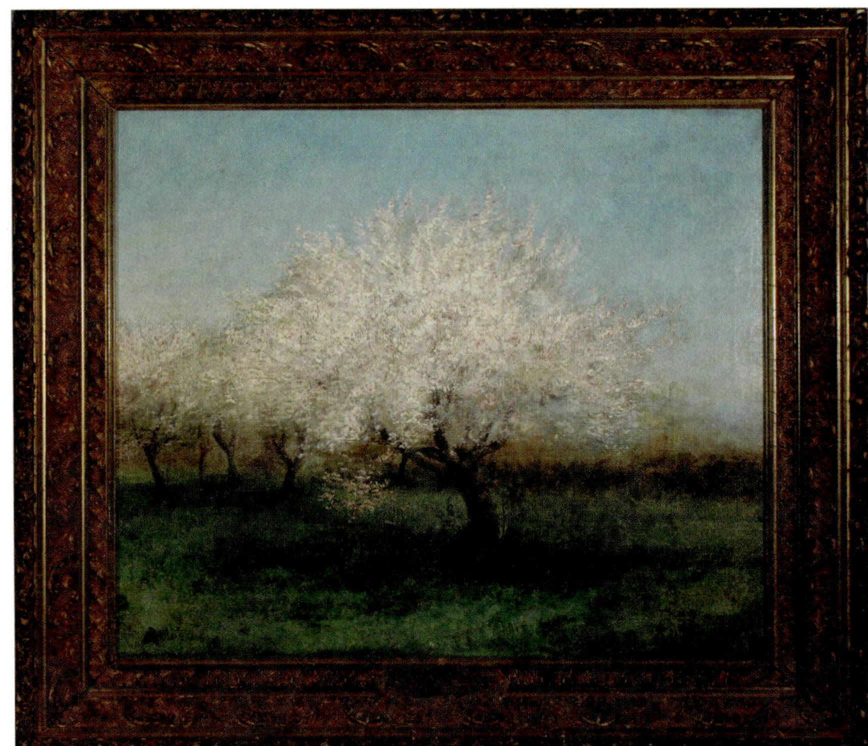

▶ **5.6** Edward Mitchell Bannister, *Apple Trees in a Meadow*, c. 1890, oil on canvas, 20″ × 24″.

High Museum of Art, Atlanta, purchased with funds from the Jean and Glenn Verrill Foundation and the American Art Acquisition Fund.

PORTRAITURE AND FIGURATIVE ART

David Bustill Bowser

David Bustill Bowser (1820–1900) was a student of Robert Douglass (see Chapter 4) and a gifted painter. Bowser won first prizes for his marine and landscape pictures, displayed at the Colored American Institute's exhibits in Philadelphia in 1851 and 1852. Better known as a portrait painter, Bowser completed several important commissions, including a likeness of John Brown, begun when the abolitionist visited Bowser's family home just prior to his execution (Figure 5.7). In its painterly execution and emotional content and in the mercurial nature of Brown's expression, Bowser's portrayal is a model of Romantic portraiture. Most effective in invoking a dark mood is the shadow cast over Brown's left eye, which seems to foretell his demise. In fact, the entire left side of the sitter's face appears disengaged from the right side. The right side of Brown's face is dark, sorrowful, and appears to gaze into an unknown future, while the left side presents an intense and direct gaze and the furrowed brow of a man of intellect and determination. This schizophrenic portrayal may be due, in part, to the fact that Bower completed the portrait posthumously, without the benefit of a live sitter. Just as likely, he knowingly captured Brown's determination to end slavery by violence in contrast with his distress at what he seemed to know, prophetically, would come to pass in the near future—a bloody civil war that would nearly destroy the Union.

Nelson A. Primus

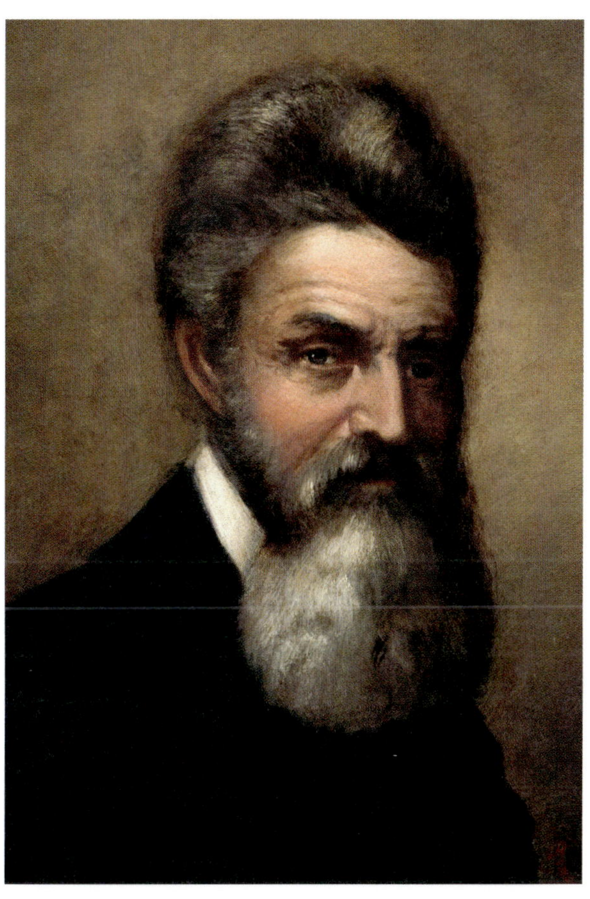

▲ 5.7 David Bustill Bowser, *John Brown*, 1865, oil on canvas, 28″ × 20¾″ × 5″.

Courtesy of the Philadelphia History Museum at the Atwater Kent, the Historical Society of the Pennsylvania Collection.

Nelson A. Primus (1842–1916) was a native of Connecticut, born to a well-to-do Hartford family that was among the most respected of its black residents. As a child, Nelson apprenticed with folk artist and carriage maker George Francis (1790–1893). A precocious talent, in 1851 (at age nine) and again in 1859 Primus won two awards for drawing at the Hartford County Fair. He later trained with professional still-life, portrait, and Romantic landscape painter Elizabeth Gilbert Jerome (1824–1910).

In 1865, Primus remarked determinedly, "I am bound to be an artist, if there is any such thing." To that end, he moved to Boston with his wife Amoretta (whom he had married the previous year) and newborn daughter, Leila. He worked at a variety of odd jobs—waiter, bookseller, and house and carriage painter—while also pursuing his aspirations to be a fine artist. Primus met several practicing artists who rented space in the Boston Studio Building, including Edward Bannister. Despite giving Primus creative advice, Bannister told Primus that he had poor taste in art and showed little interest, in Primus's view, in introducing his protégé to potential clients. Primus was able to find very few buyers for his paintings, mostly selling them with the assistance of his family and friends in Hartford. He longed to travel to Europe to further his studies, believing that this would boost his reputation and sales, but he could not afford the cost of passage.

Primus led a difficult life during his first decade in Boston. His daughter was sickly and spent much of her time in the care of the artist's parents in Connecticut (she died of tuberculosis at age 28), and his wife died after the stillbirth of their second child in 1876. Despite personal tragedy, Primus persevered in his chosen vocation, advertising his services as a portraitist and a painter of "carriages, fancy signs, and ornamental work." By the 1880s, he had completed several portraits of society notables, including abolitionist Wendell Phillips, Boston mayor Hugh O'Brien (1827–95), bank president and politician Nehemiah Gibson (1816–82) and his family, and the co-owner of New York's luxury Astor House Hotel, F. J. Allen (whose portrait received critical praise in the local press).

In the late 1880s, Primus moved to San Francisco but found little professional success there. He earned his living primarily working as a store clerk and as an artist's model at the San Francisco Art Institute (then the Mary Hopkins Institute of Art). He lived in modest boarding houses, including one in San Francisco's Chinatown, where he found the Asian population welcoming. While living in Chinatown, Primus painted at least two versions of *The Fortune Teller*, based on a photograph (Figure 5.8). Rendered in the

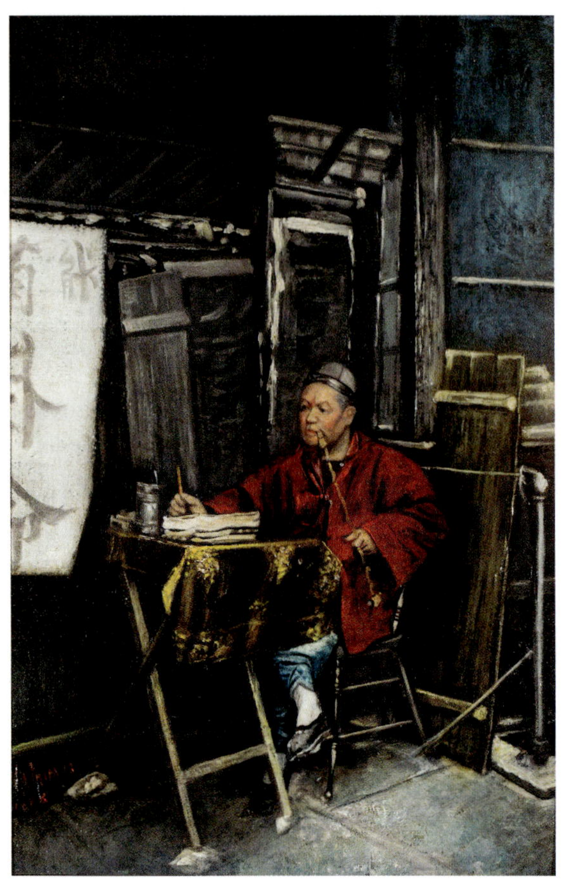

▲ **5.8** Nelson A. Primus, *The Fortune Teller*, 1898, oil on board, 12.5″ × 8.5″.
Walter O. Evans Collection of African American Art, Savannah College of Art & Design (SCAD) Museum of Art.

Realist style of renowned American painter Thomas Eakins (1844–1916), the work depicts a Chinese man smoking a pipe as he practices his calligraphy at a **drafting table**. The subject takes its cue from the Realist tradition of depictions of the everyday life of the working class. Rendered with painterly confidence, the composition is substantively more complex than the artist's earlier portraits. Multiple **planar** elements—windowpanes, shutters, rice paper sign, flooring—fluidly intersect and overlap and serve as a muted backdrop for the shimmering gold of the silk table cover and the man's red jacket. Primus's skill as a portraitist is evident in the subtle articulation of brown and rose skin tones, and in the look of concentration on the fortune teller's face.

A number of Primus's paintings were lost in the infamous 1906 San Francisco fire. Primus nevertheless continued painting in the evenings and working at other labors during the day. The artist received periodic portrait commissions from friends and employers until his death from tuberculosis—the same illness that had killed his daughter 20 years earlier.

Henry O. Tanner

Henry O. Tanner (1859–1937) combined elements of Romantic and Realist subject matter that ranged from moving spiritual subjects to equally touching **genre** scenes. He also embraced the active brushwork of Romanticism and Impressionism. Tanner was an expatriate who lived much of his life in France. His permanent presence abroad, coupled with his stellar reputation, lured many other African-American artists to France to meet this international master painter whose beginnings were as modest as their own.

Tanner was the eldest son of college-educated parents: Sarah Miller Tanner (1840–1914), a former slave, and Benjamin Tucker Tanner (1835–1923), who was an African Methodist Episcopal (AME) minister and later bishop. Greatly involved with the antislavery movement, Tanner's parents christened their son Henry Ossawa after Ossawatomie, Kansas, the "Free State" town that John Brown and a small band of abolitionist guerillas defended against some 300 proslavers, who ultimately burned the settlement to the ground.

Although born in Pittsburgh, Tanner was raised in Washington, D.C., and Maryland before his family finally settled in Philadelphia in 1868, where the elder Tanner took a position as editor of the AME journal. Soon after the move to Philadelphia, a 13-year-old Tanner observed an artist working en plein air in Fairmount Park and immediately informed his father that he wished to become a painter. Tanner completed his first painting—an Atlantic City harbor scene—four years later, at age 17, while on holiday with his family. In 1879, Tanner became the first African American to enroll in the

Pennsylvania Academy of Fine Arts. There, he was greatly influenced by the Realist subject matter of Thomas Eakins. Tanner studied with Eakins until 1882, and the two remained friends for many years; Eakins painted Tanner's portrait in 1900. Toward the end of his tenure at the Pennsylvania Academy, in 1885, Tanner painted another Atlantic City picture, *Sand Dunes at Sunset*, that in 1995—more than a century later—became the first painting by an African American to enter the White House art collection.

In 1889, Tanner moved to Atlanta, Georgia, where he opened a photography studio but was unable to earn a steady income. Instead, he took a position as an art professor at Clark College, an historically black college known today as Clark-Atlanta University, which was founded in 1869 by the Methodist Freedman's Aid Society. While at Clark, Tanner made sketching excursions to the Georgia countryside, completing a suite of Barbizon– and Hudson River–style paintings. His stay in Georgia was brief, however. The racial restrictions imposed on African Americans by recently passed segregation laws made life in the South unpalatable for Tanner. After three years, he mounted a studio exhibition of his Georgia paintings and sold the entire collection to Bishop Joseph Crane Hartzell (1842–1929), a Methodist missionary and assistant secretary of the Freedmen's Aid Society. This money allowed Tanner to travel to Paris in 1891, where he took classes at the Académie Julian with **orientalist** Jean Joseph Benjamin-Constant (1845–1902) and academic painter Jean-Paul Laurens (1838–1921). Tanner also spent time painting in rural Brittany during the summers, where he was exposed to the experiments of the Impressionists.

In 1893, Tanner returned temporarily to the United States, where he participated in the celebrated 1893 World's Columbian Exposition in Chicago, delivering an academic paper on African-American art at the exposition's Congress on Africa. The fair celebrated the 400th anniversary of Christopher Columbus's landing in the Americas and showcased the latest in American industrial and technological advancements. Attended by more than 26 million people in six months, the fair was housed in eight massive **Beaux Arts** pavilions (referred to as the "White City") on a nearly 700-acre site on the shores of Lake Michigan. The influence of the fair's architecture alone was unparalleled and can be seen in the buildings of black architect Julian Abele (discussed later in this chapter).

Despite its grand purpose of showcasing America's advances in a wide array of areas, the fair did little to promote the advancements of African Americans. Instead it included crude mock African "villages" that portrayed people of African descent as uncivilized. Booker T. Washington joined a group of protestors who published a pamphlet that decried the misrepresentation and exclusion of people of color by the fair committee. Organizers responded by approving the "Colored American Day," during which—adding insult to injury—black visitors were offered free watermelon. Booker T. Washington, Paul Laurence Dunbar, Tanner, and others presented talks on black culture and social concerns throughout the day, but their efforts were seen by many blacks as a weak response, at best, to the fair's inequities. (Blacks had also been refused employment during the construction phase of the fair.)

Sensitized to escalating racism in America, Tanner made a number of paintings of African-American subjects during his stay in the States. In his autobiographical writings (penned in the third person), Tanner explained the importance of African-American themes:

> *Since his return from Europe he has painted many Negro subjects; he feels drawn to such subjects . . . because of a desire to represent the serious and pathetic side of life among them; and it is his thought . . . he who has most sympathy with his subject will obtain the best results. To his mind, many of the artists who have represented Negro life have only [shown] the comic, the ludicrous side of it and have lacked sympathy with and affection for the warm big heart within such a rough exterior.*

Tanner refers here to the growing number of both pop culture and fine arts imagery that portrayed blacks as "shuffling darkies," "pickaninnies," "bug-eyed minstrels," and other such Jim Crow stereotypes. As an African American himself, Tanner felt most suited to portray blacks with honesty and empathy.

Among Tanner's finest "Negro subjects" from this period are *The Banjo Lesson* (1893) and *The Thankful Poor* (1894; Figure 5.9). The latter work expresses the artist's identification with Christianity and with the struggles of African Americans. A black elder and a child are depicted, hands folded in prayer over a modest meal in a spare setting. Using a muted palette similar to that of Realist painters such as his teacher Eakins, Tanner created a scene of quiet reverence and familial dignity, directly contradicting racial stereotypes. *The Thankful Poor* is monumental in that it lends great significance to a humble domestic scene. The artist achieves this effect in part

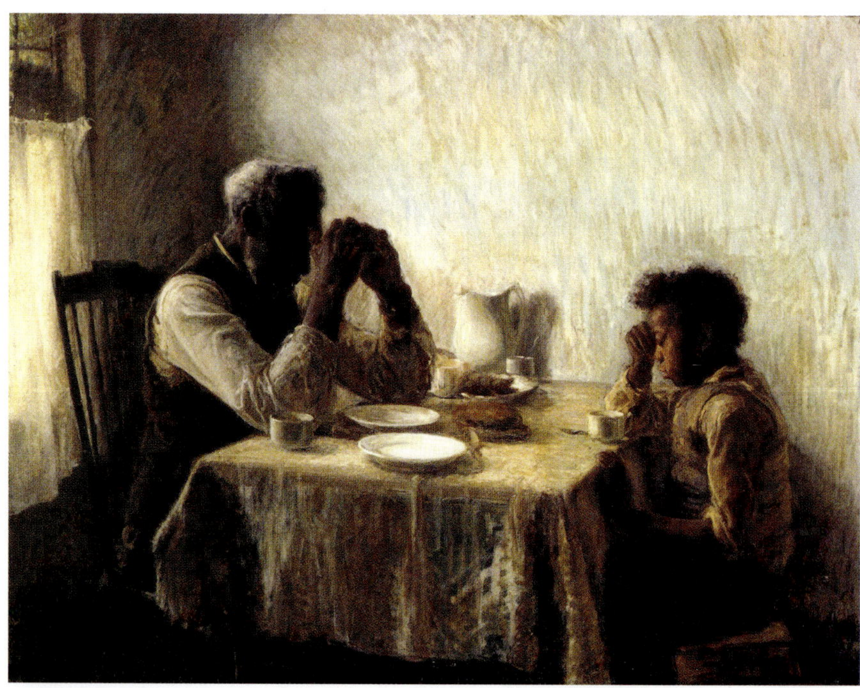

▶ **5.9** Henry O. Tanner, *The Thankful Poor*, 1894, oil on canvas, 35½ × 44¼″. Private collection.

through the use of symbolic lighting. Cool white and dark shadows envelope the older figure, alluding to his proximity to the end of life, while the boy is bathed in a golden glow, and his shirt is a warm tan rather than pale white, symbolizing the vibrant life he has yet to live. Although one would not usually refer to a nearly monochromatic work such as this one as colorist, it is evident in the variegated shades of white—from warm to cool on the wall and clothing and from pale gossamer in the curtains to the starched stiffness of the tablecloth—that Tanner was a master of color, which his later, more overtly colorist works bear out.

In 1895, Tanner returned to France, and, almost immediately, one of his paintings was accepted at the Paris Salon. Tanner described that it was hung so high on the wall of the Salon (as was the case with almost all works by newcomers) that he had to "break his neck" to see it. Despite the poor placement of the painting, inclusion in the Salon was a coup. The following year, Tanner began to fuse working-class subject matter with religious motifs, which were more popular with the French Salon jury. Soon, biblically themed pictures became his hallmark. In 1896 his *Daniel in the Lion's Den* was accepted by the Salon jury and was awarded an honorable mention. The next year, his *Resurrection of Lazarus* received the Salon bronze medal and won widespread critical acclaim. As was customary with prize-winning Salon entries, Tanner's pictures were acquired by the French government for its Luxembourg Museum collection (today the Musée d'Orsay). These triumphs, which were reported in the *New York Times*, launched Tanner's career in earnest.

Department store magnate and religious art patron Lewis Rodman Wanamaker (1863–1928) was living and working in Paris at the time of the 1896 Salon. He met Tanner through his corporate partner, Robert C. Ogden (1836–1913), who had purchased Tanner's *Banjo Lesson* for Hampton Institute (now University) in Virginia, where Ogden was a trustee. On viewing Tanner's *Resurrection of Lazarus*, which included a turbaned African observer of Christ's miracle, Wanamaker decided to fully fund Tanner on a cultural tour of the Holy Land. In two trips taken between January 1897 and March 1898, Tanner visited the Middle East and North Africa, returning to Paris by way of Naples, Rome, Pisa, Florence, and Venice. (Tanner made additional trips to Algiers in 1908 and Morocco in 1912.) Wanamaker remained Tanner's loyal friend and patron until the retailer's death in 1928.

In 1897, after his initial excursion to the Holy Land, Tanner once again traveled to the United States, stopping in Philadelphia and Kansas City (where his parents had moved). At the time of his return to Paris the following year, he met his future wife, San Francisco–born Jessie Macauley Olssen (1873–1925). The couple married in 1899 and spent much of their time in Étaples, a thriving expatriate art community near Normandy that consisted mainly of American, Canadian, Australian, and British residents. The two were avid travelers, regularly touring Europe and the United States. In 1903, when their son Jesse was born, the Tanners were residing in New York City. At this point, Tanner began to develop his own palette, which incorporated his now-characteristic "Tanner blues": shimmering and saturated indigo and turquoise shades. Works such as *The Three Marys* (1910; Figure 5.10)

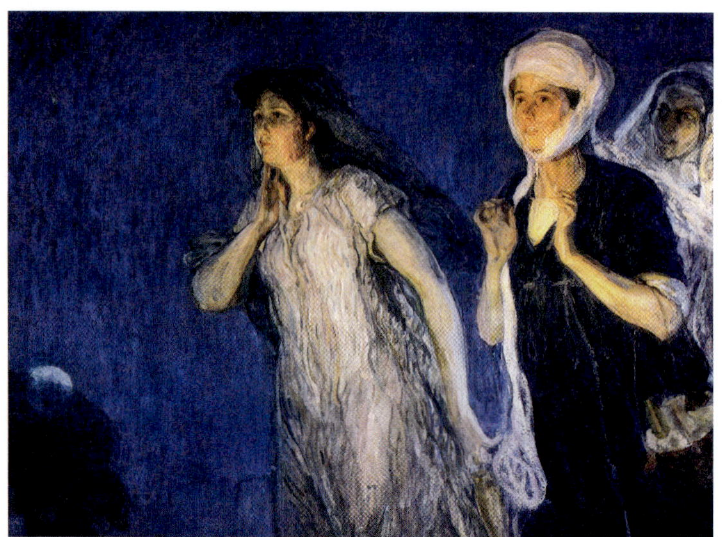

▲ **5.10** Henry O. Tanner, *The Three Marys*, 1910, oil on canvas, 42″ × 50″.
Collection of the Carl Van Vechten Gallery at Fisk University, Nashville.

reveal his ability to work within a specific color range while maintaining variety and dynamism of hue, brushwork, and lighting effects. Also evident is Tanner's skill with textures, particularly in the rendering of the diaphanous elements of fabric, and his understanding of composition. Note that the negative space to the left in *The Three Marys* creates a sense of urgency in the figures, who rush toward their destination with evident determination.

By this time, American and European art historians and critics were taking regular note of Tanner's activities. Tanner's fusion of Realism, Impressionism, and spiritual subject matter won him medals at the 1900 Paris Exposition, the 1901 Pan-American Exposition in Buffalo, the 1904 St. Louis Exposition, and the Paris Salon of 1906. His alma mater, the Pennsylvania Academy, invited him to serve on their annual exhibit selection jury in Paris in 1906 and 1907, and he was honored with a one-man show at the American Art Galleries in New York in May 1909. That same year, Tanner's autobiography, *The Story of an Artist's Life*, was published in two issues of the American lifestyle monthly magazine *World's Work*.

Tanner maintained a successful career for the rest of his life, becoming in 1923 an honorary chevalier of the Order of the Legion of Honor, France's highest honor. He was also the first African American to become an academician of the National Academy of Design. Despite his expatriate status, Tanner greatly influenced the artists of the Harlem Renaissance of the 1920s and 1930s (see Chapter 6), who strove to counter racist stereotypes just as Tanner had done. Tanner died at home in his beloved adopted city of Paris in 1937.

Annie E. Anderson Walker

Annie E. Anderson Walker (1855–1929) was born and raised in Flatbush, Brooklyn, in New York City. After the Civil War, when Anderson was in her twenties, she became a teacher in the Deep South, where millions of newly freed African Americans were legally permitted to attend school for the first time. Anderson taught in Florida and Alabama, where, in 1875, she met and married a lawyer and politician named Thomas Walker (1850–1935), who had been born into slavery near Selma. At this time in post-Reconstruction Alabama, the Ku Klux Klan and other right-wing forces had wrested political power from the moderate Republican Party. Blacks were being arrested, ejected from the state, and, in some instances, shot and killed on sight. Walker and Anderson were forced to leave Alabama. The couple spent three years in Arkansas from 1879 to 1881 before moving permanently to Washington, D.C., where Walker became a lawyer and Anderson became an artist.

During the early 1890s, Anderson worked with private art tutors to prepare a portfolio for submission to the Corcoran Gallery School of Art, which had officially opened in Washington in 1890. Her portfolio earned her a coveted place as a student there, but her acceptance was reversed when her racial identity was discovered. A school official explained to her that "the trustees have directed me not to admit colored people. If we had known you were colored, the committee would not have examined your work." Frederick Douglass, who was acquainted with the Walkers through their NAACP and Equal Rights Association work, wrote a letter of protest to the Corcoran in 1891, requesting that they "reconsider this exclusion and admit Mrs. Walker . . . and thus remove a hardship, and redress a grievous wrong imposed upon a person guilty of no crime, and . . . in every way qualified to compete with others in the refining and ennobling study of art." The Corcoran's board was unmoved.

Walker trained her sights instead on enrollment at the Women's Art School of the equally prestigious Cooper Union in her hometown of New York City. Founded by abolitionist Peter Cooper in 1859, Cooper Union was one of the first American higher education institutions to accept women, and one of very few that admitted blacks and whites alike. As a tuition-free school, Cooper Union was highly competitive and only accepted students who showed the greatest degree of promise. Anderson spent the next several years at Cooper Union studying with distinguished American Impressionist John Henry Twachtman (1853–1902) and with Thomas Eakins, who taught anatomy at Cooper. After graduating in 1895, Anderson traveled to Europe for a protracted Grand Tour, during which she visited artists, galleries, and museums in Italy, Switzerland, England, and France.

In Paris, Anderson spent time furthering her artistic education at the Académie Julian. The school catered to foreigners and women, the latter of whom were not permitted to enroll in the more established and historic French Fine Arts Academy—the École des Beaux-Arts—until 1898. Anderson's pastel portrait of a woman entitled *La Parisienne* was exhibited at the celebrated Paris Salon in May 1896 along with Tanner's award-winning *Lion's Den*. Walker's style ranged from the Realism of Eakins to the Impressionism of Twachtman. Her *Study of a Man in 16th Century Dress* is an example of the latter (Figure 5.11). The modeling of the figure with color rather than ***grisaille*** and the active brushwork are evidence of a mature Impressionist style. In the handling of the sitter's beard, right hand, and ruffled collar, Anderson's expert brush and sense of color subtleties distinguish among these forms—so similar in

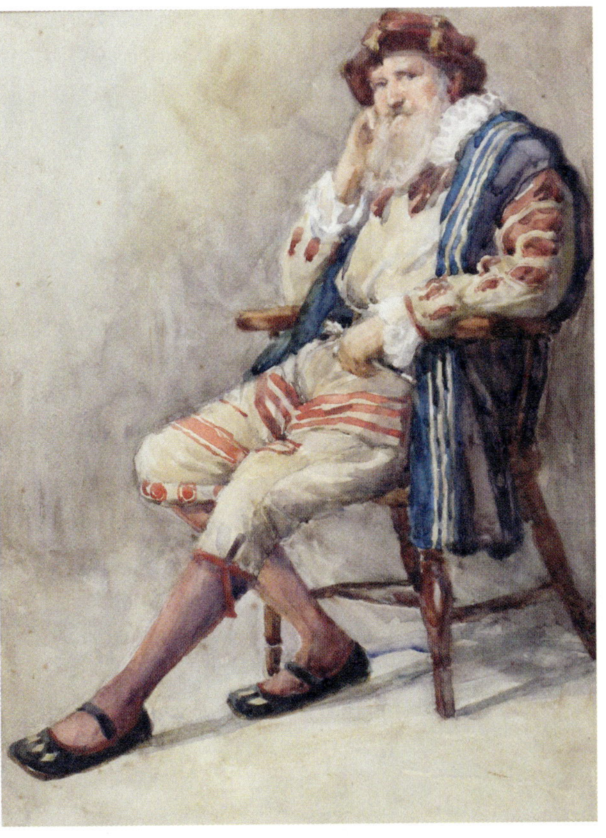

▼ **5.11** Annie E. Anderson Walker, *Study of a Man in 16th Century Dress*, c. 1803–07, watercolor, 13½ × 10¼″.

Photo by permission of Woolley & Wallis Salisbury Salerooms.

tone—with a few expert strokes. Also evident is Anderson's highly evolved understanding of the human anatomy, thanks to Eakins's insistence on permitting women to study the nude figure (a policy which prompted his dismissal from the Pennsylvania Academy).

At the turn of the century, Anderson contracted tuberculosis but recovered fully after a course of treatment. After regaining her health, she continued to paint and to teach art from her home, but her Paris success was the highlight of her professional career.

Photography

Photography as a field grew exponentially after its appearance on the world stage in 1839. In addition to formal portraiture, by midcentury photography had become an ideal vehicle for documenting dramatic and monumental subjects, particularly newsworthy people, places, and events, from public executions to floods and fires. Portrait photographers sought to create images that would engage viewers with maximum effectiveness. They achieved this through their choice of subject matter, the use of theatrical lighting contrasts to create a sense of drama, active and open compositions, and the employment of rustic or otherwise natural settings that humanized their subjects and lent their images a sense of reality.

James Presley Ball, Sr.

James Presley Ball, Sr. (1825–1904), created both formal and informal portraits with technical skill and creative insight. He was born in Franklin County, Virginia, and later resided in Cincinnati, Ohio. At about age 20, Ball met another, lesser-known African-American photographer, John B. Bailey, who taught the young Ball the art of daguerreotyping. In the mid-1840s, shortly after apprenticing with Bailey, Ball set up his own daguerreotype studio in Cincinnati; but the business quickly foundered. He became instead an itinerant photographer traveling among Ohio, Richmond, and Pittsburgh, offering his services as a portrait photographer, in the same way that limners had offered their services as portrait painters.

After several years of travel, in 1849 Ball returned to Cincinnati and rented a large studio, which he dubbed "Ball's Great Daguerrian [*sic*] Gallery of the West" (and which today is a landmark Cincinnati historic site). The lavishly decorated shop consisted of four rooms, including a grand 40- by 20-foot-long portrait gallery. Between 1849 and 1853, the gallery became one of the most well-known photo studios in the country and was compared to the New York studio of famed Lincoln and Civil War photographer Matthew Brady (1822–96). Ball employed his brother Thomas, who managed the studio; his brother-in-law Alexander Thomas; and a staff of nine assistants, including Robert Duncanson, whose landscape paintings were exhibited in Ball's gallery.

In 1855 Ball hired Duncanson and a team of artists to create a massive 7,200-square-foot abolitionist panorama on canvas. The mural was dramatically and descriptively titled *Ball's Splendid Mammoth Pictorial Tour of the United States Comprising Views of the African Slave Trade; of Northern and Southern Cities; of Cotton and Sugar Plantations; of the Mississippi, Ohio, and Susquehanna*

Rivers, Niagara Falls &C. (Etc.). For a small entry fee, the mural was exhibited twice daily over a period of several weeks at multiple national venues, including Ball's Cincinnati studio and the Boston Armory. It was an unequivocal success with antebellum viewers, who visited the exhibition by the thousands.

Like the panorama, Ball's daguerreotypes were perceived as works of art in an age when many resisted the idea that a mechanical device could produce high art. To expand his reputation and expertise, in 1856 Ball spent six months in Europe, hoping to establish studios there, although these efforts produced no tangible outcomes. While in England, Ball reportedly photographed English writer Charles Dickens (1812–70) and Queen Victoria (1819–1901); however, these portraits have not been located. Nevertheless, Ball's popularity and reputation as a portrait photographer remained strong in the United States. Throughout the 1860s, Ball's prestige enticed luminary sitters to his studios, including Frederick Douglass, General Ulysses S. Grant's mother and sister, Swedish opera star Jenny Lind (1820–87), and circus producer and entertainer P. T. Barnum (1810–91).

Ball remained active during the Civil War, earning additional income by photographing Union soldiers. In November of 1864, Ball married Fannie Cage, shortly after divorcing his first wife, Virginia (who was the mother of James Junior, born in 1854). In the 1870s, the Ball family left Cincinnati and moved several times, eventually settling in Minneapolis, Minnesota. There, Ball served as the official photographer for the 25th anniversary of the Emancipation Proclamation. By 1887, his son had joined him in the business, and the family had moved again to Helena, Montana. In addition to working as a documentary and portrait photographer, Ball became a political activist and civic leader.

During his time in Montana, Ball created a suite of disturbing photographs of the ex-slave William Biggerstaff, who was hanged for murder in 1896 (Figure 5.12). On June 8, 1895, Biggerstaff had a violent quarrel with Montana's black boxing champion, Dick Johnson, over Biggerstaff's white mistress. Biggerstaff killed Johnson during the struggle, and, although he

▼ **5.12** James Presley Ball (J.P. Ball and Son), *Studio Portrait of William Biggerstaff; Hanging of Biggerstaff; William Biggerstaff Lying in Coffin*, 1896, albumen prints. Helena, MT.

Montana Historical Society Research Center, 957-610; 957-611; 957-613.

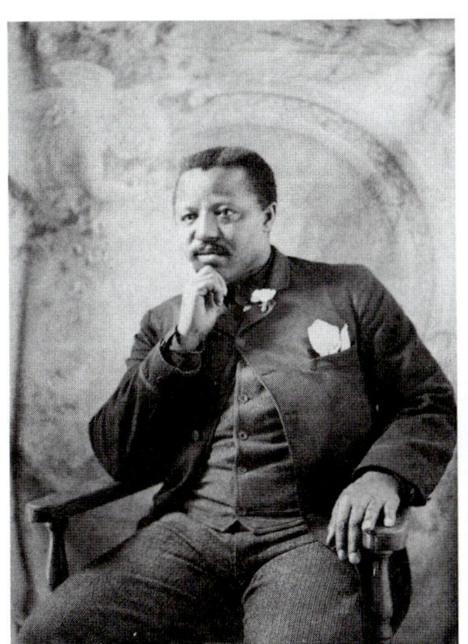

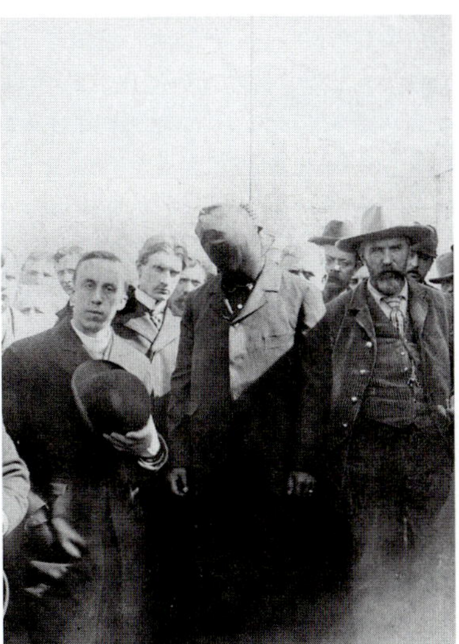

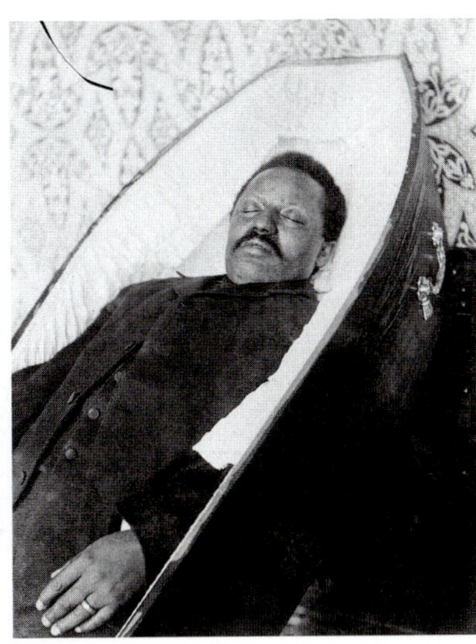

claimed that Johnson's death was accidental, Biggerstaff was convicted and hanged in 1896. Ball documented the last weeks of Biggerstaff's life in three images—a formal portrait, a photograph of him hanging from the gallows, and a final image of Biggerstaff in his coffin.

In the portrait, Biggerstaff is formally dressed in a three-piece suit with a pocket square. Biggerstaff sits relaxed and thoughtful in a high-backed chair with his hand on his chin. Behind him, a faux backdrop of a putto and flowers softens the representation and, in its pallor, offsets Biggerstaff's dark skin. The curved back of the chair crowns his head and suggests both a throne and a halo.

The second photograph in the **triptych** captures Biggerstaff, now dead, hanging from the gallows and, disturbingly, wearing the same jacket he wore in the earlier portrait. Over his head is a customary fabric sack that renders him both anonymous and cruelly objectified. The body is surrounded by a crowd of Helena residents, including sheriff Henry Jurgens and the local reverend, Victor Day, who each gaze unsympathetically at the camera (the reverend, in fact, strikes a pose). The element of spectacle in this photograph reflects how hangings were experienced by the public at this time, as gruesome displays. Scholars have compared this image to the photographs of Jim Crow–era lynchings that were so common in the 1890s. However, this image differs in that the deceased's race (and any concomitant racist overtones) is hidden by the head covering. Also, Biggerstaff's execution is the result of a trial and is a black-on-black killing rather than the result of a white lynch mob.

Ball's third photo in the suite presents the viewer with Biggerstaff's deceased body in a coffin, which is angled upward, so that Biggerstaff seems to be reclining in sleep rather than being laid to rest. The strong diagonal thrust of the composition creates movement rather than stillness and alludes to an active "passing" from life to death. Ball was part of the crusade to prove Biggerstaff's innocence, which explains his interest in the subject and the humanity with which it is infused. Ball had also been the victim of a violent physical attack by his first wife, Virginia, over another woman (possibly his second wife, Fannie) and may have empathized deeply with Biggerstaff's circumstances.

Ball's Montana studio was as successful as his Cincinnati businesses had been and attracted hundreds of clients. Following a dozen-year period in Montana, in 1900 the Ball family moved to Seattle, Washington. By 1902, however, Ball was suffering from severe rheumatoid arthritis and relocated a final time to Honolulu for the sake of his health. He died there in 1904. A large body of his work has been preserved in the Ball and Thomas Photograph Collection in the library at the Cincinnati Museum Center.

Augustus Washington

Photographer Augustus Washington (1820–75) was a native of Trenton, New Jersey. As a young man from a well-to-do family, at age 23 he enrolled in New Hampshire's Dartmouth College, where he learned the photography trade. A year later, in 1844, he moved to Hartford, Connecticut, where he became a local school headmaster. Simultaneously, he opened a photo studio and advertised his services as a portrait photographer in the *Charter*

Oak—an abolitionist newspaper—and in the Hartford City Directory. His advertised prices were high for the time—$10–$50 per portrait ($300–$1,500 today)—but evidently not too high for Connecticut's elite citizenry who served as his client base. Over the next decade, Washington's studio became one of the most established and successful in Hartford.

An example of the kind of work that made Washington's reputation is his 1846–47 portrait of John Brown. In this dramatic portrayal—the earliest known of Brown—the abolitionist stands in a frontal pose with his right hand raised (Figure 5.13). He pledges his fealty to what appears to be the flag of his unrealized Subterranean Pass-Way (a 1,000-mile extension of the Underground Railroad into the Deep South). Because Brown had not yet begun his career as a militant abolitionist, it is likely that the standard was retouched by Washington at a later date. The crisp outlines of Brown's head and shoulders and the compositional contrasts of light and dark share much in common with Matthew Brady's famed images of Abraham Lincoln. Unlike most of the Brady portraits, however, Washington's photo allows for no shadowing of the sitter's eyes, which stare with piercing clarity at the viewer. Also, Washington uses a nearly all-black background, against which Brown's face and shirt gleam in their whiteness. The image fully captures the intensity and determination that marked Brown's character.

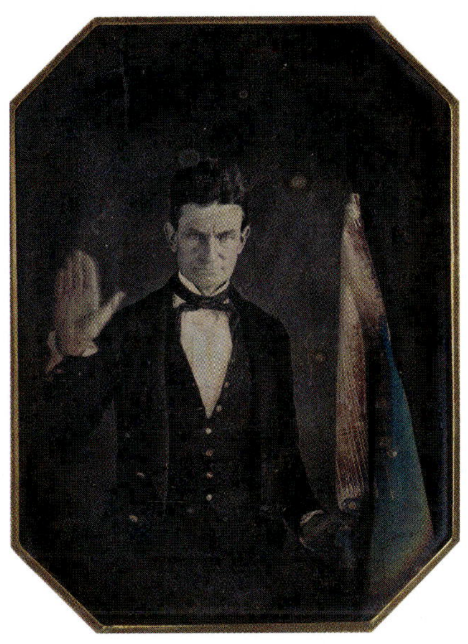

▼ **5.13** Augustus Washington, *John Brown, 1800–1859, Abolitionist*, 1847, daguerreotype, 3¼″ × 4¼″.

Purchased with major acquisition funds and with funds donated by Betty Adler Schermer in honor of her great-grandfather, August M. Bondi. National Portrait Gallery, Smithsonian Institution / Art Resource, NY.

In March 1853, after ten years in business in Hartford, Washington decided to close his studio and move to Liberia. He did not anticipate a positive future for blacks in America and viewed Liberia as the only real hope for African Americans to escape oppression. The artist briefly furthered his photography career after his move to Africa, creating portraits of the citizens of Liberia and later Senegal, Gambia, and Sierra Leone. He also apparently tried his hand at landscape painting. By 1858, Washington had put photography behind him to become a merchant and plantation owner. For the remainder of his life, he operated a 1,000-acre sugarcane plantation on the St. Paul River near Monrovia. He also owned and edited a local newspaper—the *New Era*—and served as both a Liberian congressman and senator before his death.

Glenalvin, Wallace, and William Goodridge

Glenalvin Goodridge (1829–67) of York, Pennsylvania, founded his photography concern in 1847. Fifteen years later, his much younger brothers, Wallace Goodridge (1840–1922) and William O. Goodridge (1846–90), opened another Goodridge studio in Saginaw, Michigan, which thrived until the early 1920s. The Goodridges specialized in portraiture, outdoor urban and rural scenes, civic events such as parades, and views of cataclysmic natural disasters. The three artists were sons of William C. Goodridge (1806–73), a slave from Baltimore, and Evalina Wallace Goodridge (1803?–51). In the decades before the Civil War, the Goodridge parents operated a combination barbershop, bathhouse, sundry store, and loan establishment in York. For a time, they were among the wealthiest African-American families in the area. The Goodridges' office building on Centre Square housed Glenalvin's photo studio on its highest floor, which featured a skylight that provided excellent natural light for taking pictures. Glenalvin advertised it as his "Skylight Gallery."

The first of the Goodridge brothers to enter the field, Glenalvin began his career in photography at age 18, creating daguerreotypes, **ambrotypes** (photos on glass), and **stereographs** (double images that, when viewed through a special viewer, created a three-dimensional effect). Glenalvin obtained exclusive rights to the ambrotype process in York County in 1855 and 1856. He also offered gilded photo cases, hand coloring, and low prices and quickly gained a significant client base. The *York Gazette* described his award-winning ambrotypes and stereographs, which were considered the cutting-edge technology in the medium, as "the very perfection of the art" and exceptionally lifelike.

In 1861, Glenalvin opened a second studio in partnership with his much younger brother Wallace. In his new "American Photographic Gallery," Glenalvin added the more affordable paper photographs to his repertoire and expanded his operations into a second studio in nearby Columbia. Glenalvin, however, experienced a disastrous setback in 1862, when he was convicted of raping a white woman and sentenced to five years in prison. His father obtained counsel and a plea for clemency was submitted to the governor. Supported by the charge of "unsatisfactory evidence" and contradictory testimony and by the fact that Glenalvin's health was failing, he was granted a pardon. The decree required that Glenalvin leave the state, however. In 1865, he followed his sister Mary and brothers to Saginaw, Michigan, where they had moved in 1863 at the time of Mary's marriage. Glenalvin died in Saginaw three years later of tuberculosis, which he contracted while in prison.

Wallace and William Goodridge were able to extend their brother's legacy, and by 1864 they had opened another photo studio on the top floor of a brand-new three-story office block in Saginaw. They took advantage of its skylights to illuminate their sittings, as Glenalvin had done in his York studio. William and Wallace advertised that they had the largest skylight studio in the state. The *Saginaw Daily Enterprise* described their gallery as a "photographic palace." William and Wallace specialized in portraits, which they produced using the **tintype** process (images on a tin plate). Their portraits of children were especially popular, as both brothers seemed to have a gift for posing and costuming youngsters in the manner of adults and eliciting from them romantically wistful expressions. For their full-length compositions, they created a popular studio prop referred to as the "rustic steps" (a detached stair made of tree branches), which gave their portraits a romantic aura when coupled with a *trompe l'oeil* backdrop of flora (see chapter-opening image).

The Goodridge brothers were vital community builders among Saginaw's African-American population. They cofounded the Colored Debating Society in 1866, which deliberated such topics as the need for education for freed African Americans. William led a community orchestra. Wallace organized the fifth anniversary celebration of the Emancipation in 1869 and later became an officer of the Eastern Star Masons.

William passed away in 1900, and Wallace continued to run the business on his own. He ventured into new territory, including moving pictures, medical X-rays, and camera-free **photogram** techniques. He licensed the firm's photos of historic Michigan to national picture postcard distributors and sold his own souvenir postcards at the 1893 World's Columbian Exposition in Chicago. Wallace also continued the family tradition of social activism. In 1900, he organized a committee for "the betterment of the black race." In 1915, he accepted an appointment from Michigan's governor as an African-American delegate to the Lincoln Jubilee and Celebration of the Half-Century Anniversary of Negro Freedom in Chicago. Seven years later Wallace passed away, at age 82. Only then did the Goodridge studio, which had been in business in one form or another for 75 years, close its doors.

ARCHITECTURE OF THE GILDED AGE

The Gilded Age in the United States spanned a period from Reconstruction to the early 20th century. The era was marked by economic growth, increased industrialization, technological advancements, escalating immigration, and social change. It also sparked increased urban building nationwide. Beginning in Chicago in the 1880s, American architect Louis Sullivan (1856–1924) popularized the first skyscrapers (at ten stories) and the use of **steel-frame construction**. Stylistically, the period was eclectic, comprising modern trends, a resurgence of classical building forms, and a revival of medieval models. The latter trend was felt in Romantic architecture that incorporated asymmetrical design and **undressed stone**. The genre borrowed from cathedral and castle structures.

Calvin Thomas Stowe Brent

Given the rapid growth of African-American congregations after Emancipation, it is not surprising that a number of prominent black architects made their reputations in church design; one such individual was architect Calvin Thomas Stowe Brent (1854–99). Constructed in Washington, D.C., in the 1880s and 1890s, Brent's buildings fused the roughhewn stone façades of 11th-century **Romanesque** structures with the pointed arch designs of the 12th-century Gothic style. Brent was one of the only practicing African-American architects in the city at the end of the 19th century. At about age 20, the young Brent apprenticed with architect Thomas M. Plowman (fl. 1852–79); within two years, Brent's name was listed as a professional architect in the city directory. The next year, in 1876, Brent designed and built his first major project, the English Gothic–style Saint Luke's Episcopal Church (Figure 5.14), which he designed to the specifications of the church rector, Rev. Alexander Crummel (1819–98).

Located at 15th and Church Streets NW, in Washington, D.C., the building serves as a primer in **Neo-Gothic** construction. Saint Luke's features asymmetrically arranged blue stones quarried on the Potomac River. The façade is supported by stone **buttresses** and features pointed Gothic arches in the doors and stained glass windows. The stone **tracery** of the main east façade window encases five **lancets** below and a **quatrefoil** and two

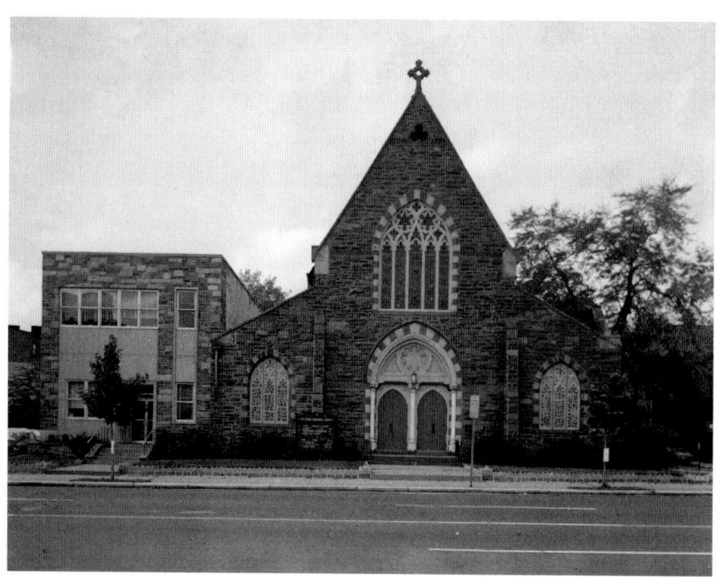

▲ **5.14** Calvin Thomas Stowe Brent, *St. Luke's Episcopal Church at 1514 15th Street, NW in Washington, D.C.*, 1880. Library of Congress, Prints and Photographs Division, HABS DC,WASH,231—1.

rose windows above. The door jambs and **trumeaux** are cut from limestone and crowned with foliated capitals. In the **tympanum** above the door, Brent placed a carved roundel. Especially unique to the structure is Brent's incorporation of a definitive Neo-Gothic "exotic" element: the alternating red and white **voussoirs** that frame the doors and windows, which derive from medieval Islamic mosque architecture.

During Brent's prolific career, which spanned more than 20 years, he was the architect of record for more than 6 churches and 80 homes. A number of his domestic structures still stand today, including a group of nine brick row houses in Washington, D.C., that are listed on the National Register of Historic Places. Brent's obituary, published in the *Colored American* in December 1899, mourned the loss to the architecture community of this pioneer, calling him "a man of exceptional ability and untiring industry. In business life it was his distinction to adorn a calling—that of Architecture—which has hitherto been chosen by few men of color anywhere; and his demise . . . creates a void in this constantly growing department of industry." That void was filled, in part, by one of Brent's seven children, John Edmonson Brent (1889–1962), who also became an architect. A 1907 graduate of Tuskegee Institute and the Drexel Institute School of Architecture (1912), John Brent is best known for his design of the Michigan Avenue YMCA in Buffalo, New York, built in 1922 in the modern industrial style of Sullivan.

John Anderson and Arthur Edward Lankford

Washington, D.C.–area architect John Anderson Lankford (1874–1946) designed some 200 domestic and public buildings nationwide. Born on a Missouri farm, Lankford received much of his education in the South and Midwest between 1889 and 1908, including study at the Tuskegee Institute, where he took courses in mechanical engineering in 1895–96. In 1897, he received his first instruction in architecture from a correspondence school based in Scranton and later completed three master of science degrees. During this period, Lankford worked as a chief engineer and master mechanic at several companies to support his educational pursuits and served on the faculty of four colleges. One of Lankford's students, Charlotte Josephine Upshaw (1876–1973), became his wife in 1901. A year later, the couple settled in Washington, D.C., where Lankford was commissioned to design and construct offices for the United Order of True Reformers, an African-American fraternal order of which he was a member. By 1904, Lankford was advertising his architectural services and reporting earnings of half a million dollars over two and a half years. The following year his younger brother, Arthur Edward Lankford (1879–1908), joined the firm. Arthur studied mechanics at Tuskegee and architecture with the same international correspondence school in Scranton as his brother. Arthur assisted his brother in various construction, architecture, and mechanical engineering work until his death from tuberculosis in 1908.

In 1907, the elder Lankford won second-prize honors for his submission of a design for the African American Pavilion of the Jamestown (Virginia) Tercentennial Exposition. The expo celebrated the city's 300th year and was attended by such luminaries as Mark Twain, Booker T. Washington, and President Theodore Roosevelt. The "Negro" pavilion was reported to be the most successful of all the fair's exhibits, visited by as many as 12,000 people daily. Lankford was appointed supervising architect of the project, along with fellow Tuskegee-ite William Sidney Pittman (1875–1958), whose Beaux Arts design for the pavilion had won first prize. Following this coup, Lankford was appointed global supervisor of architecture for the AME church. In this capacity, he designed nearly 20 AME church buildings in Arkansas, D.C., Florida, Michigan, Virginia, Indiana, Maryland, North and South Carolina, Georgia, and Cape Town, South Africa. He also designed the Baltimore YMCA in 1915.

In 1916, Lankford documented his accomplishments in a 30-page book entitled *Lankford's Artistic Churches and Other Designs*, which was released in a second edition in 1924. In the years between the two editions, Lankford spent two years studying law and passed the D.C. bar in 1921. He received his architect's license from the state of Virginia the following year (the year that state began issuing such licenses), the first African American to do so. Lankford also became licensed to practice architecture in D.C. two years later, which was the first year the district issued such licenses. Commissioned after a fire destroyed the prior church structure, a fine example of Lankford's style is the Big Bethel AME Church in Atlanta's historic Sweet Auburn District (Figure 5.15). Lankford's design is marked by round Romanesque arches and two façade towers of differing configurations: one square with a pointed, octagonal spire and the other rounded with castle turrets.

▼ **5.15** John Anderson Lankford, *Big Bethel AME Church, 220 Auburn Ave., Atlanta, GA*, 1924.

Library of Congress, Prints and Photographs Division, HABS GA,61-ATLA,1C-14.

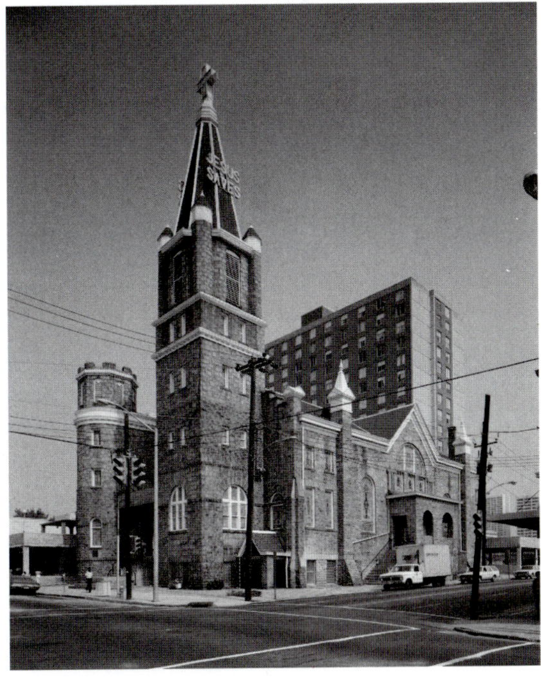

George Washington Foster, Jr.

George Washington Foster, Jr. (1866–1923), was one of the first black architects to obtain a license in the state of New Jersey (in 1908), and he secured another in New York in 1916. He was born in Newark to Isabella Davis Foster (a purported descendant of Confederate president Jefferson Davis, 1807/8–89) and her husband, George Foster, Sr. The family moved to New York City when George Junior was 14 years old, and soon thereafter he enrolled at Cooper Union to study design. By 1888, Foster was employed by the architectural firm of Henry J. Hardenbergh (1847–1918), designers of the first iterations of

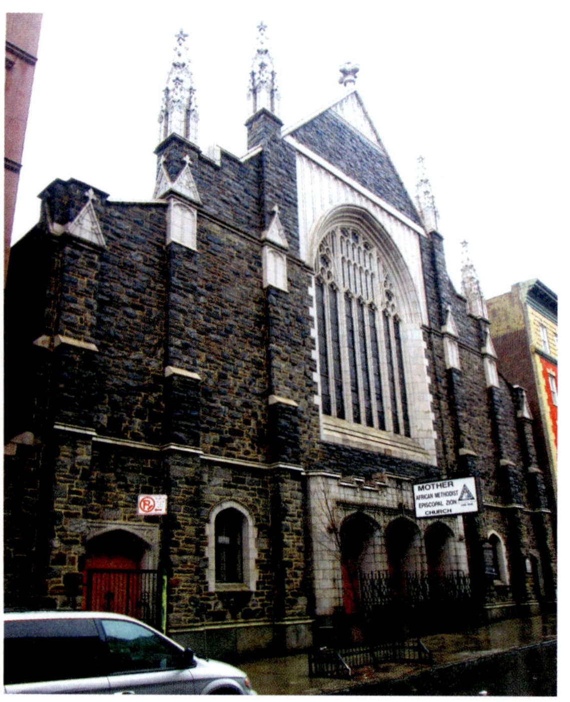

▲ **5.16** George Washington Foster, Jr., *Mother AME Zion Church, New York City*, 1925. 140–148 W. 137th Street, New York, NY.

Photo: Beyond My Ken, licensed under Creative Commons Deed 3.0.

New York's Waldorf and Astoria hotels in 1893 and 1897, respectively, the landmark Dakota apartments (1884), and the Plaza hotel (1907).

Between 1908 and 1914, Foster was one-half of the African-American architectural firm of Tandy & Foster in New York City. Specializing in church and residential architecture, he and Vertner Woodson Tandy (see Chapter 6) received a notable commission to design St. Philip's Protestant Episcopal Church, which was completed in 1911. Located in West Harlem, St. Philip's was the first Harlem church to be designed by black architects. The building became a New York City designated landmark in 1993 and was added to the National Register of Historic Places in 2008.

Equally ambitious are the projects that Foster completed after the dissolution of his partnership with Tandy in 1914. One of Foster's most important commissions was the Gothic Revival–style Mother AME Zion (Mother Zion) Church, also in Harlem (Figure 5.16). Foster conceived a uniquely expressive Neo-Gothic building of stone and terracotta. Its **gabled** façade is supported by six **pinnacled** buttresses and constructed of unevenly laid gray **ashlar stones**. The triple central **portico** is trimmed in **crenelated** terracotta and crowned with a massive arched window. The window's stained glass is set into ornamental tracery and framed in alternating terracotta blocks. Above the window, and at the gable peak, are blind lancets flanked by four ornate spires. The building also boasts double **transepts**. Mother Zion, on 137th Street in Harlem, is New York's oldest black congregation and its church is a designated historic site.

In 1916, Foster formed a new partnership—Tillack & Foster—with offices in downtown Manhattan. The architectural and construction team designed a Sunday school for the First Congregational Church in River Edge, New Jersey, in 1917. In the few years before his passing, Foster worked in conjunction with the construction firm of Lawlor and Hayes, also in River Edge.

Julian Francis Abele

Julian Francis Abele (1881–1950) was one of the most significant African-American architects of the early 20th century, responsible for the design of such noteworthy buildings as Harvard University's Widener Library (1915); Philadelphia's Museum of Art (1919), Stock Exchange (1912), and Free Library (1927); the New York *Evening Post* building (1925); and the Duke University campus (1924–47). Abele was an exponent of both the Neo-Gothic and the Beaux Arts styles of architecture. Beaux Arts building design comprised an updated version of the Baroque and Rococo forms of the 17th and 18th centuries and allowed for a creative approach to architecture as a form of fine art. Abele's career in this style spanned over 40 years, during which he was senior and supervising architect for the respected Philadelphia firm of Horace Trumbauer (1868–1938) and was responsible for the design and construction of some 200 structures.

Abele was born to a large and well-respected Philadelphia family. He received initial education at the Quaker-sponsored Philadelphia Institute for Colored Youth (ICY; today Cheyney University), graduating in 1897 as a mathematics valedictorian. His commencement speech was entitled, "The Role of Art in Negro Life." The following year, Abele became the first African American to earn a certificate in architectural design from the Pennsylvania Museum School, where he attended evening classes, and won the Graff Prize for Architectural Design.

Certificate in hand, Abele enrolled in the University of Pennsylvania School of Architecture. A gifted talent and an intellectual, Abele won no less than five first-prize architectural awards while at the University of Pennsylvania. He was president of the university's Architectural Society during his senior year, and, in 1902, he graduated with a BS in architecture. Determined to have the best-possible expertise in his field, Abele pursued further study at the Pennsylvania Academy, where he earned a certificate of completion in architectural design in 1903. By the time his formal education was complete, Abele was adept not only in architecture but also in watercolor painting, stone and metal plate printing, furniture design and fabrication, and wood and metal sculpture.

Following his studies at the academy, Abele traveled for more than two years in Europe, studying historic architecture firsthand and, reportedly, taking classes at the Sorbonne and the École des Beaux Arts in Paris. After his return, he landed what would become a lifelong position at Trumbauer, and by 1908 he was the firm's managing architect. One of Abele's first and most significant assignments was the design of the central branch of the Philadelphia Free Library (Figure 5.17). Abele unveiled his vision for the library in 1911, although financial issues stalled the building's completion until 1927. When it finally opened, the library building was considered one of the most beautiful and technologically advanced in the country due to its fireproof steel framework, granite base, and Indiana limestone **elevation**.

Abele based the building's exterior on that of the Hôtel de Crillon in Paris, which was constructed in the 18th century by King Louis XV's chief architect, Ange-Jacques Gabriel (1698–1782). Massive in size, the 100-foot-high Free Library occupies an entire square block. The exterior is composed of a **rusticated** ground floor punctured by full-height arched windows and doors and a double-height second-story façade set behind a gallery of colossal limestone Corinthian columns on the north and south sides. The gallery is flanked by pedimented porticos adorned with limestone relief sculptures of **allegorical** figures, and Corinthian half columns and pilasters rim the east and west upper elevations. Additional exterior decoration includes swags, niches, and **cartouches**. This grand Beaux Arts edifice is today considered one of Philadelphia's most important historic sites.

Abele fully conceived, or was the major contributor to, literally hundreds of designs for his firm, but he was required by prevailing racial antipathies to remain in the shadow of his white employer. In Abele's words, the "lines

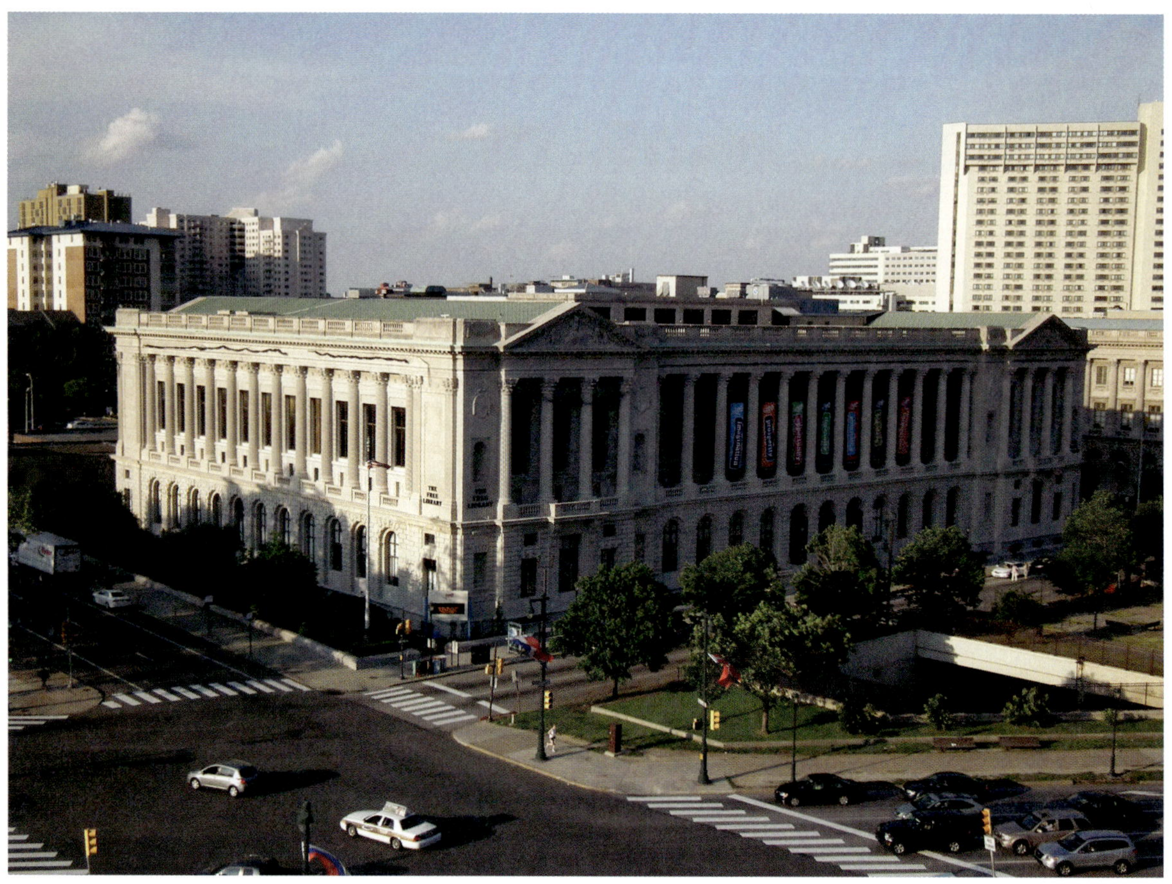

▲ **5.17** Julian Francis Abele, *Philadelphia Free Library Central Branch*, 1911–27.

Photo: Nanoman657, licensed under Creative Commons Deed 3.0.

are all Mr. Trumbauer's, but the shadows are all mine." Although those closest to the firm readily acknowledged Abele's supervision of its designs and his status as Trumbauer's invaluable right hand, senior architect, and second-highest-paid officer at the firm, all designs were signed by the owner, Trumbauer, until after his 1938 death, when Abele was free to take formal credit for his work. At Trumbauer's death, Abele took over the company in partnership with William O. Frank (1887–1968), who had been with Trumbauer since 1908. The partners changed the name to the "Office of Horace Trumbauer," and Abele continued to cohead the firm until his death. Abele's son, Julian Abele, Jr. (b. 1927), and his nephew, Julian Abele Cook (1904–86), both pursued architecture (the latter designed the Howard University Carnegie Library and Clark Hall in the 1930s), as did several of his later descendants.

BLACK VERNACULAR ARCHITECTURE

Not all African-American architecture of the Gilded Age was the work of trained designers. Black vernacular architecture in the form of the "shotgun" house became widespread after the Civil War and predominated in many black neighborhoods through the 1920s (Figure 5.18). The nickname, which first appeared in a 1903 advertisement in the *Atlanta Journal*

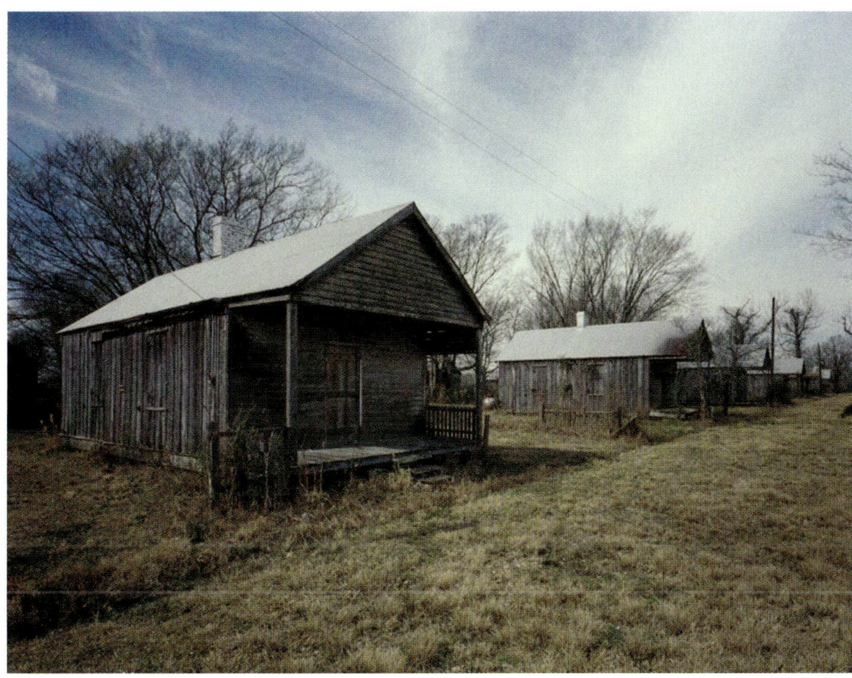

◀ 5.18 Anonymous, *Workers' Shotgun Houses, Laurel Valley Sugar Plantation, Rte 308, Thibodaux, Lafourche Parish, LA,* 1904–20.

Photo courtesy of the Historical American Engineering Record Collection, Prints and Photographs Division of the Library of Congress, HAER LA,29-THIB, 1J—6.

Constitution, is widely believed to derive from the configuration of the house: a narrow rectangular building with rooms constructed in a single straight line like railroad cars, such that (theoretically) a gunshot might travel through the entire house, from the front to back doors, without hitting a wall. However, historians have also argued that the name evolved from the Dahomean word for "gathering place": *to-gun*. The origins of the shotgun house can be traced to Haiti, where the homes of rural blacks replicated those of their predecessors, the **Arawak**-speaking Taino pre-Colombians. Because virtually all of the indigenous Haitians were wiped out by the Spanish by the early 16th century, enslaved blacks who were transported to Haiti from Dahomey to replace them as laborers carried on this domestic building tradition.

In the 1830s, the design was transferred to Louisiana, where many Haitians emigrated after the Haitian Revolution. Over the course of the 19th century, the shotgun house spread to a dozen states from Florida to the West Coast. Usually made of wood, no more than 12 feet wide, and raised off the ground by several feet, the shotgun house was the southern companion to the brick row house of the urban North. The narrow design of both met a growing demand for inexpensive and compact domestic architecture in ever more crowded cities. The design was especially popular as housing for factory workers. Often with a front porch set near the street, shotgun houses included two or three main rooms: a living room, followed by a bedroom and then a kitchen. Bathrooms, when included, were small and situated within, or adjoining, the bedroom or kitchen. More elaborate variations included the "double shotgun," or two houses connected by a hallway, and the "camel back," which featured a partial rear second story accessed by stairs. With a wraparound porch on three sides, "north shore"

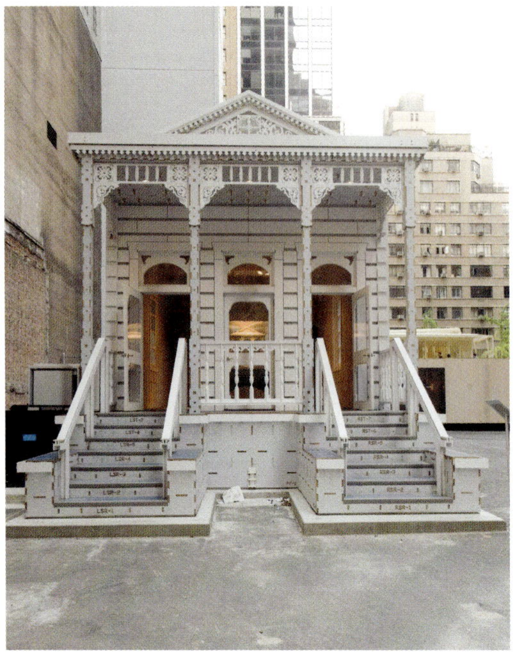

▲ **5.19** Larry Sass, *Digitally Fabricated Housing for New Orleans (Exterior)*, 2008, plastic and plywood, 16′4″ wide × 38′2″ long × 20′ high. Installation view of the Museum of Modern Art exhibition *Home Delivery: Fabricating the Modern Dwelling*. © Larry Sass. Photo: Suzie Ball.

versions were initially designed as vacation homes for Louisiana's upper class.

Few shotgun houses were built after the 1920s, but a number have been refurbished and preserved as historic records of African-American culture. Indeed, the style has lately attracted widespread attention among art historians thanks to an exhibition of prefabricated domestic architecture at New York's Museum of Modern Art entitled *Home Delivery*. For this temporary outdoor show, MIT professor and architect Larry Sass (b. 1964) used CAD (computer-aided design) technology to plan and construct a prefabricated shotgun house "for Post-Katrina New Orleans" based on original models still standing in that city (Figure 5.19). Sass's full-scale "Digitally Fabricated House for New Orleans" included such traditional features as a crenelated gable above the porch, triple façade doors to maximize airflow, a raised foundation, and split front steps.

Summary

The Romantic impulse, with its emphases on drama and spirituality, influenced many African-American artists working in architecture, landscape, figure painting, and photography. Figurative art tended toward religious, somber, and contemplative scenes. Images of nature were embraced as an expression of God's presence on earth and as a way of documenting the beauty of America, paradoxically at a time when so many blacks were struggling with the vicissitudes of post-Reconstruction life. For some black artists such as Duncanson, Tanner, and Walker, Europe presented a welcome refuge from racial strife at home and a place where their talents could be appreciated irrespective of their race. Others such as Primus and Brown found the West Coast more welcoming to blacks than either the South or East. Still others, such as Abele and Bannister, were spurred by racism to the heights of personal achievement. The determination and successes of these artists set the stage for one of the most prolific African-American art movements in history: the Harlem Renaissance.

Key Terms

allegory; allegorical: a narrative or image that symbolizes an idea or concept—such as freedom, victory, or justice—or that has a moral or political meaning

ambrotypes: negative photographs on glass that, when placed on a black background, appear to be a positive image

Arawak: an indigenous people of the Caribbean who occupied the present-day locations of Haiti, the Dominican Republic, Cuba, Jamaica, Puerto Rico and the Cayman Islands before the arrival of Columbus; also refers to their language

ashlar stone: a building façade stone that has been squared and smoothed to fit snugly with adjoining stones

Barbizon School: 19th-century French landscape painters, including Théodore Rousseau, Charles Daubigny, and Jean-François Millet, who painted outdoors, directly from nature, in the town of Barbizon on the edge of the Fontainebleau forest, 30 miles southeast of Paris

Beaux Arts: A style of 19th-century architecture that took its name from the Paris École des Beaux Arts (School of Fine Arts) and is marked by dramatic visual statements, oversized proportions, and ornate sculptural decoration that enhance an otherwise classical framework

buttresses: an architectural reinforcement built against or projecting from a wall as support for the weight of the roof

cartouche: in architecture, a decorative oval form, often embellished with scrolls, that frames a symbol, letters, or a secondary design

chiaroscuro: the use of strong contrasts of light and dark to create the illusion of three-dimensional form on a two-dimensional surface

chromolithograph: a color image printed from a series of stone-plate drawings; a color lithographic print

crenelate: to notch the top of a wall structure in the manner of medieval castle battlements

drafting table: a slanted desk for creating drawings, technical sketches, or diagrams

elevation: a front or side view of an architectural structure from base to roof

en plein air: the French term for "outdoors" (literally, "in the open air")

gabled: a pitched roof comprised of two slanted sides and forming a pyramid shape

genre: artistic portrayals of scenes from everyday life; also, a type or style of artistic representation

grisaille: from the French word for "gray," describes painting in black, white, and gray tones only

Hudson River School: a group of 19th-century Romantic painters, including Thomas Cole, Frederick Edwin Church, and Asher B. Durand, who painted the Hudson River valley landscape

impasto: the thick or heavy application of paint

Impressionism: a style of painting that emerged in France around 1870 and is noted for a chromatic palette and short brushstrokes to depict the changing effects of light and atmospheric conditions on a given scene

lancet: in architecture, a tall and narrow Gothic-style window with a pointed arch at its apex

Neo-Gothic: a synonym for Gothic Revival, a design style originating in the 1740s that revived medieval Gothic forms such as spires, pointed arches, and tracery (interlaced openwork derived from Gothic windows)

orientalist: refers to a 19th-century European interest in North African, Middle Eastern, and Asian motifs panorama: a large-scale work of art that depicts an epic scene such as a vast landscape, cityscape, or complex historical event, often designed in a long, horizontal format that could be mounted and viewed in the round

photogram: a photograph made without the use of a camera by blocking out areas on the surface of light sensitive paper (or other photographic surface, such as metal) and exposing it to light

pinnacled: refers to an architectural tower, spire, or buttress that is crowned with a vertical, pointed form in the shape of a narrow pyramid or cone

planar: describes a two-dimensional composition or elements of its design that are rendered parallel to the picture surface

portico: a covered porch set between an exterior building wall and a row of outer columns

quatrefoil: a four-leafed clover design made up of overlapping circles

Romanesque style: a style of medieval architecture characterized by rough-hewn stones and rounded arches

rose window: a circular window found in church architecture

rusticate: in architecture, to decorate with large stones that feature rough surfaces and wide, deeply set joints

steel-frame construction: building design utilizing vertical steel columns and horizontal beams as a grid-shaped understructure to which the floor and walls are attached

stereograph: a double photograph of the same image meant to be viewed through a stereoscope or two-lens optical viewer to create a three-dimensional effect

tintype: a fast-developing positive photograph exposed on a thin iron sheet

tracery: carved ornamental stonework that encases the stained glass in a Gothic church window

transept: in church architecture, a rectangular section of a building that intersects its main space

triptych: a work of art that is divided into three components

trumeau: in church architecture, a central column, often decoratively carved, that separates double doors and supports a lintel or overhead crossbeam

tympanum: in church architecture, an arched decorative area above a door

undressed stone: stone that has not been cut or sanded to a desired shape or surface texture

voussoirs: in architecture, stone or masonry wedges used to create an arch

Questions for Further Study and Discussion

1. Name and describe three formal elements of Romantic landscape painting.
2. Compare and contrast the two Bannister paintings in this chapter: the earlier Romantic painting and the later Impressionist painting.

Identify the characteristics that associate each with its respective style.

3. Most 19th-century African-American artists chose to paint landscapes or religious subjects rather than African-American subjects. Why do you think this was so? Debate whether or not these artists should have devoted their art to black themes.
4. Compare both the painted and photographic portraits of John Brown illustrated in this chapter by Bowser and Washington. Debate whether and why (or why not) the photograph is as expressive as the painting and deserving of high art status.
5. Identify the following elements on Calvin Brent's St. Luke's Episcopal Church: buttress, tracery, lancet, quatrefoil, rose window, trumeau, tympanum, and voussoirs.
6. What is a shotgun house, and what is its significance in African-American culture?
7. Research other African-American Romantic and Impressionist landscape painters such as Charles Ethan Porter (c. 1847–1923) and William A. Harper (1873–1910). How does their work compare with the artists studied in this chapter?
8. Research other African-American photographers such as Harry Shepherd (1856–c. 1905?), George O. Brown (1852–1910), and Daniel Freeman (1868–1920s?). How does their work compare with the photographers studied in this chapter?

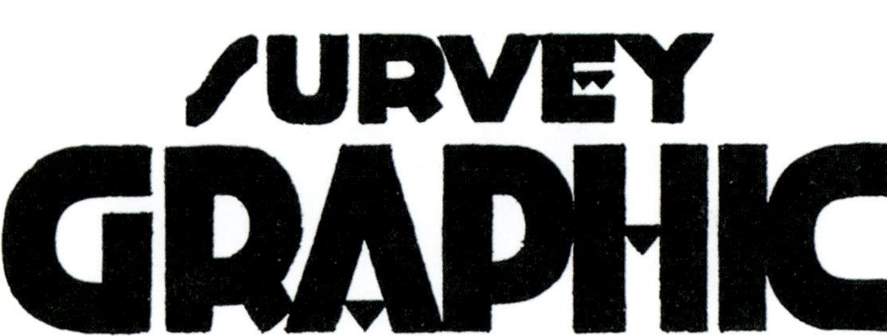

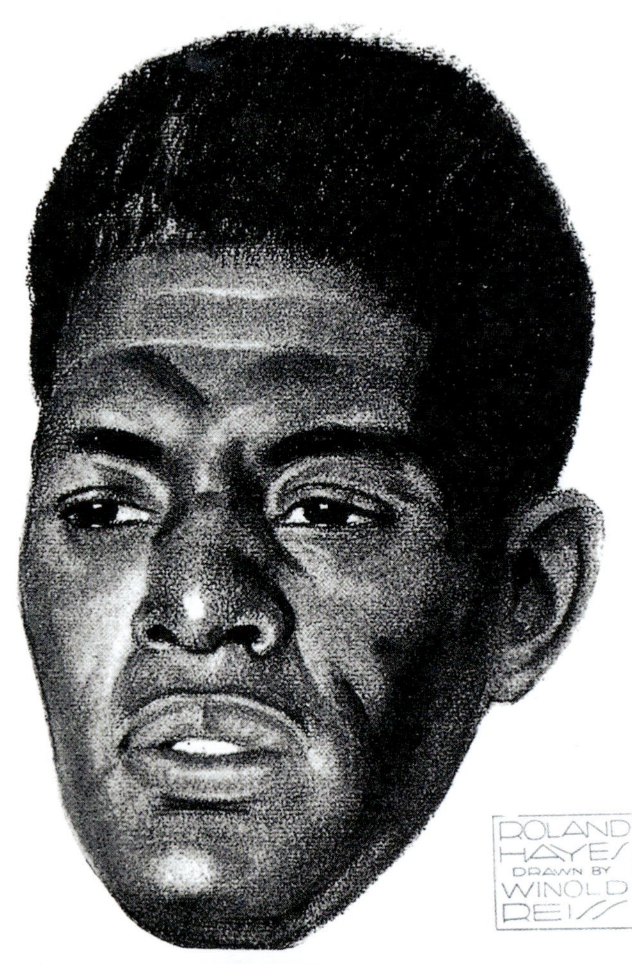

HARLEM
MECCA OF THE NEW NEGRO

MARCH 1925

MODERNISM AND THE HARLEM RENAISSANCE

6

For a brief moment in the 1920s and 1930s, Harlem was the nexus of an artistic movement the effects of which were felt across the country and around the world. The Harlem Renaissance was one of the first truly international art movements to take root on American soil. Involving music, dance, theater, literature, and the visual arts, this was an unprecedented period of cultural activity among African Americans. For the first time in history, the interests of dealers, patrons, critics, and curators were sparked by African-American art across racial lines and on a grand scale.

This new interest in black art was inspired by a series of landmark art shows in New York. In 1919, when an exhibit of the paintings of Henry Tanner (see Chapter 5) was mounted at the upscale Knoedler Gallery in New York City, it drew widespread attention to black artistic genius. The Tanner show was followed in 1921 by an exhibition of African-American painting and sculpture at Harlem's 135th Street branch of the New York Public Library (today's Schomburg Center for Research in Black Culture). This show became an annual event and set the stage for the ascendency of African-American visual arts.

THE MAKING OF HARLEM

The Great Migration

Although famous today as a culturally rich black neighborhood, at the time of the 1921 Schomburg exhibit Harlem was a mostly white enclave. Beginning in the 1920s, however, blacks began to move there from Midtown and downtown Manhattan, pushed north by an influx of Irish and Italian immigrants. Over a period of ten years, 90,000 blacks moved into Harlem and 120,000 whites moved out. The African Americans who moved to Harlem included not only Manhattanites but migrating southerners who came north to escape Jim Crow violence and discrimination. Known as the **Great Migration**, this mass exodus comprised more than 1.5 million African Americans who moved to northern cities from the rural South between 1910 and 1930.

"Harlem: Mecca of the New Negro"

Among Harlem's new disparate population of blacks, an estimated 10 percent were members of the cultural elite. Dubbed the "Talented Tenth," these movers and shakers comprised not only artists but also scholars and political activists. They made their presence known in the March 1925 issue of

◀ Winold Reiss, *Drawing of Roland Hayes*, cover of *Survey Graphic*, March 1925.
Private collection.

the literary journal *Survey Graphic*, with the cover headline, "Harlem: Mecca of the New Negro" (see chapter-opening image). The magazine was edited by the Harvard-educated African-American philosopher Alain Locke (1885–1954), who sought the "spiritual emancipation" of African Americans through visual art. A primary arbiter of the Harlem Renaissance, Locke believed that the fine arts were a potent vehicle for reconfiguring the image and identity of blacks in America, an identity bogged down by degrading Jim Crow stereotypes.

Locke outlined his strategy in his essay "The Art of the Ancestors," in which he urged black artists to take pride in their African artistic heritage rather than looking to European models for inspiration. He pointed out that traditional African sculptures had served as inspiration for European Modernists for nearly two decades. It seemed logical to Locke that African sculpture should be as inspirational to African-American artists. In response to Locke's call to action, African-American artists embraced figural abstraction based on African sculptural models. They also began to use African-inspired subject matter in their art.

The publication of the Harlem issue of *Survey Graphic* had an immediate and profound impact. In two weeks, it sold an unprecedented 40,000 copies to mostly white subscribers and became the manifesto of the era. The persuasive power of the journal drew widespread attention to the activities of Harlem culture and attracted artists and aficionados to Harlem from all over the globe. Its irresistible allure was best captured by the words of African-American painter Aaron Douglas, who, after reading the journal, determined to leave his home in Kansas City for New York, remarking, "I've got to go, even if I have to sweep floors for a living."

SUPPORTING THE RENAISSANCE: ART PATRONS

Private and Institutional Patronage

Whereas the producers of Harlem Renaissance art and culture were black, its consumers were, by and large, white, which resulted in a problematic tug of war between the races. As patrons of black culture, whites had immense control over the form and content of black creativity. African-American artists felt pressured to draw their creative inspiration from African sculpture, as Locke (himself sponsored by white philanthropy) had suggested. Scholar and social activist W. E. B. Du Bois made a similar argument in a 1915 essay published in the **NAACP** magazine *Crisis*, urging black artists to combat racial stereotypes by portraying blacks in only the noblest light.

On the other hand, there was direct pressure from white art consumers who preferred fantasy images of black **primitivism**: naïve, childlike characters that were untainted by Western civilization and its moral codes. One of the most influential patrons was Charlotte Osgood Mason (1854–1946), who lent financial support to black artists and literati such as Locke, Aaron Douglas, authors Langston Hughes (1902–1967), and author/anthropologist Zora Neale Hurston (1891–1960) to the tune of what would today amount to more than one million dollars. In return, Osgood expected the recipients of her benevolence to promote black primitivism in their work.

Unwilling to accommodate Osgood's desire for primitivist stereotypes in their writing and art, Douglas, Hurston, and Hughes eventually broke ties with her. Hughes accused Locke—who was considered Mason's "chief advisor on all things Negro"—of knowingly cultivating artists who would work within her iconographic parameters, while criticizing those who did not. Indeed, Locke condemned Henry Tanner for abandoning black themes and adhering "brilliantly but futilely, [to] a lapsing French style."

The most significant institutional support for the Harlem Renaissance artists came from the Harmon Foundation. Beginning in 1926, the foundation offered cash prizes of up to $400 to African Americans for achievement in science, business, education, race relations, religious service, and the arts. Between 1927 and 1935, the Harmon Foundation mounted a series of annual traveling art exhibitions to introduce African-American art to audiences in some 50 cities.

African-American artists clamored to be included in the Harmon shows and juried competitions which promised widespread exposure for their work. They understood implicitly that the five-member (four whites and one black) Harmon jury, which included Locke, would favor works of art that espoused the Osgood style of black form and content. As a result of the foundation's preferences, many artists who would otherwise have painted landscapes, religious motifs, marine pictures, and floral still lifes chose instead to create portraits and genre scenes of blacks or, at the very least, to include some visual reference to Africa in their compositions. Those who were drawn to Modernist abstraction were careful to present their avant-garde techniques in a naïf manner, so as not to seem overtly sophisticated.

The philanthropic Rosenwald Fund was another significant institutional patron, although it did not aggressively urge or require its awardees to address ethnic themes. From 1928 until its dissolution in 1948, thanks in great part to Locke's influence, the fund awarded yearlong grants to hundreds of African-American artists, writers, and scholars.

Black Patronage

Although the majority of Harlem Renaissance arts philanthropy came from whites, black patronage also played a significant role. Support came from the "Negro chapters" of the YMCA, which served as venues for Harmon exhibitions and other showings of African-American art. Historically black colleges and universities (HBCUs) collected and exhibited the works of African-American artists. Well-to-do black members of the Talented Tenth similarly supported black artists. Among these was bibliophile and scholar Arthur (Arturo) Schomburg (1874–1938) and cosmetics tycoon A'lelia Walker (1885–1931).

Schomburg migrated to New York from Puerto Rico in 1891. He was a collector of objets d'art and literature by and about Africans in the diaspora. In 1911, he cofounded the Negro Society for Historical Research to support black scholars. In 1926, Schomburg's collection of art, rare books, and historical memorabilia was purchased by the New York Public Library. This acquisition formed the core of Harlem's Schomburg Center for Research in Black Culture, which remains an important research institution today.

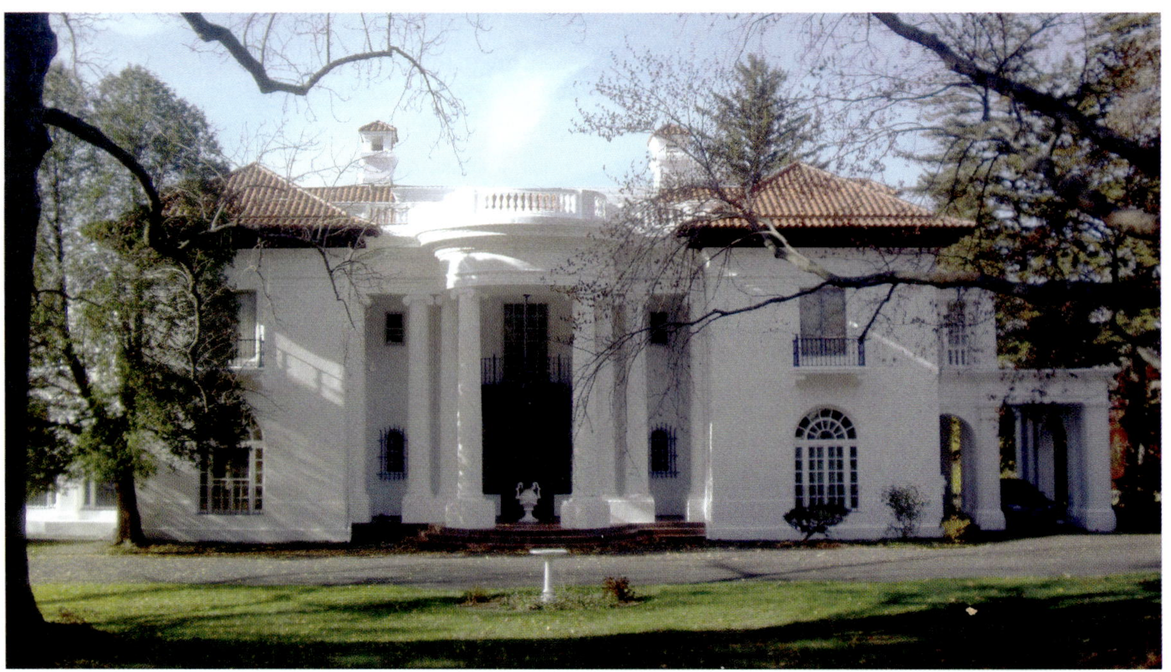

▲ **6.1** Vertner Woodson Tandy, *Villa Lewaro*, 1918. Irvington-on-Hudson, NY.

Photo: Dmadeo, cropped by Beyond My Ken, licensed under Creative Commons Deed 3.0.

A'lelia Walker was an avid collector of African-American art and a supporter of musicians and visual artists. She was heir to the fortune of her mother, Madame C. J. Walker (née Sarah Breedlove; 1867–1919), who made her money selling black haircare and beauty products. In 1917, Mme. Walker moved to Irvington-on-Hudson in New York's affluent Westchester County. She hired New York State's first licensed African-American architect, Vertner Woodson Tandy (1885–1914), to design a Neoclassical residence for her in the **Italianate style**, spending an estimated $250,000 on her manor home (Figure 6.1).

The one-time partner of George Washington Foster (Chapter 5), Tandy was born in Lexington, Kentucky, to Emma Brice Tandy and brick mason and builder Henry Tandy (1854–1918), who constructed the Fayette County courthouse in 1898. Influenced by his father's profession, after graduating from the Tuskegee Institute in 1902, Tandy the younger received his architectural degree in 1907 from Cornell University. A member of the Elks and founding member of the influential black fraternity Alpha Phi Alpha, he was well connected among the black elite and designed prolifically, especially in the area of domestic architecture.

C. J. Walker occupied the home that Tandy designed for just more than a year, before high blood pressure led to her death. However, her daughter A'lelia continued to live in the mansion throughout the 1920s. She counted among her circle New York's wealthiest and most celebrated residents.

In addition to her Westchester country home, A'lelia owned a four-story brick and limestone townhouse on 136th Street in Harlem, which was also designed by Tandy in the **Georgian Revival** style. Walker initially approached African-American artist Aaron Douglas (discussed later in this chapter) to create **fresco** murals for the townhouse but ultimately awarded the commission to Viennese **Art Deco** designer Paul T. Frankel (1886–1958). Frankel bedecked the Harlem residence with gilded wall coverings and with framed excerpts from poetry by Langston Hughes and Countee Cullen (1903–1946). Walker dubbed a floor in her townhouse "the Dark Tower" after Cullen's poem "From the Dark Tower." She hosted **cultural salons** there for artists, writers, musicians, activists, and elite guests. "Dark Tower" salons featured poetry readings, musical performances, and stimulating cultural and intellectual exchanges and were held until the fall of 1928.

SCULPTURE

Some of the earliest proponents of the Harlem Renaissance were talented women sculptors. At least two of these artists anticipated the movement's focus on African-American history, culture, and social progress by several years: Philadelphia-born sculptors Meta Vaux Warrick Fuller and May Howard Jackson.

Meta Vaux Warrick Fuller

Meta Fuller (1877–1968) is credited with creating the first sculpture to consciously embrace what would become Harlem Renaissance aesthetic philosophy. She was the youngest child of William H. Warrick and Emma Jones Warrick, who operated a barbershop, hair salon, and wig-making business. Among the elder Mrs. Warrick's clients was Mary Vaux (1830–95), the wife of Pennsylvania senator and later Philadelphia mayor Richard Vaux (1816–95), whose last name she gave to her daughter as a middle name. Fuller was first introduced to fine arts by her artist-sister Blanche, ten years her senior, who encouraged her to develop her drawing skills.

In the early 1890s, Fuller began formal training by enrolling in weekend classes at Philadelphia's Public Industrial Art School, founded in 1880 by progressive educators Charles Godfrey Leland (1824–1903) and J. Liberty Tadd (1863–1917). Tadd emphasized creative self-expression in the school's curriculum. When she was 16, one of Fuller's wood sculptures was included in the school's exhibit at the 1893 World's Columbian Exposition in Chicago. This led to a scholarship for Fuller to attend the Pennsylvania Museum School for the Industrial Arts (today the Philadelphia College of Art) from 1884 to 1888. As a condition of her scholarship, Fuller was required to create a work of art for the school's collection. She made a 37-figure **bas-relief** sculpture entitled *The Procession of the Arts and Crafts*, a Romanesque-inspired piece. In addition, she won two senior-year awards, one of which was for a metal sculpture entitled *Crucifixion of Christ in Anguish*.

In October 1899, Fuller went to Europe for further study, traveling to London, where she spent a month with family friends before going on to Paris for a three-year stay. On arrival in Paris, Fuller was told that she could not register at the boarding house that she had reserved—the American Girls' Art Club—because blacks were not permitted. Fellow Philadelphian Henry Tanner, who was a family friend, arranged for alternate accommodations for her in a modest hotel. By way of apology, the club's director arranged for Fuller to meet **American Renaissance** sculptor Augustus Saint-Gaudens

(1848–1907), who befriended her and advised the young artist to work with a live model. Fuller actively pursued this study in the summer of 1900.

During her first year in Paris, Fuller attended lectures at the École des Beaux-Art. From 1900 to 1902, she took classes at the progressive Paris atelier, the Académie Colarossi. In 1901, a fellow Colarossi student introduced Fuller to France's premiere modern sculptor, Auguste Rodin (1840–1917), who visited Fuller's studio. Rodin told her, "My child, you are a sculptor—you have a sense of form!" Rodin encouraged her to explore the depths of human feeling in her work and arranged private showings of her sculptures for members of his circle.

Fuller returned to the United States in October 1902. Back in Philadelphia, she re-enrolled at the Pennsylvania Museum School to study ceramics with master ceramicist Leon Volkmar (1879–1959). Within a year, she had received the school's Battles Ceramics Prize for an elegantly formed four-handled urn. Fuller opened a studio that year and began taking private lessons with portrait sculptor Charles Grafly (1862–1929). In 1906, her work was included in the Pennsylvania Academy's annual exhibit, and she would continue to show in its annuals into the 1920s. Fuller's career took another leap forward when, in 1907, she was invited to design a suite of historical **dioramas** for the Jamestown Tercentennial African American Pavilion (see Chapter 5). Fuller's work portrayed 150 figures and detailed the history of African Americans since their arrival in Jamestown in 1619. It received a gold medal and made Fuller the first African American to be awarded a federal government commission in the fine arts.

▼ **6.2** Meta Warrick Fuller, *Emancipation Proclamation, Harriet Tubman Park, South End, Boston, MA*, 1913, painted plaster (cast in bronze in 2000), 85″ × 42″ × 41″.

Collection of the Museum of the National Center of Afro-American Artists and the Museum of Afro-American History.

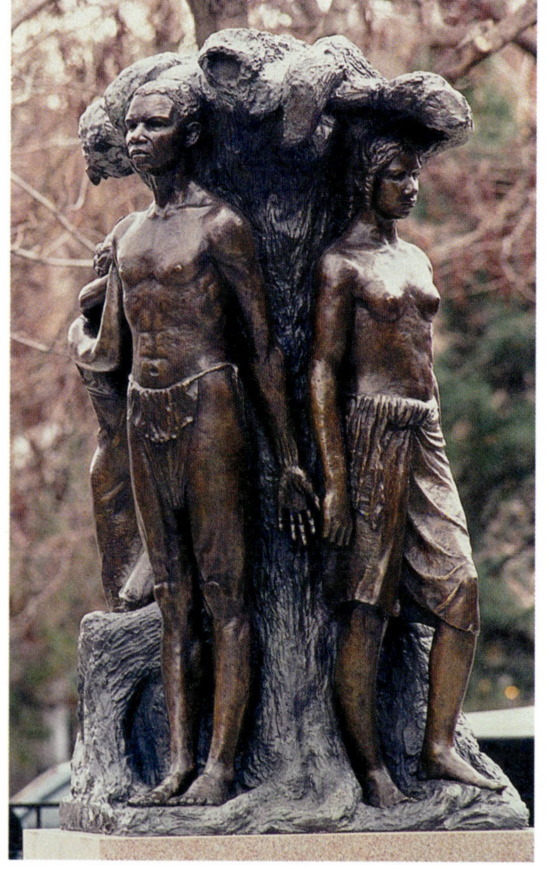

In 1909, Fuller married Liberian neuropathologist and psychiatrist Dr. Solomon Fuller (1872–1953) and moved with him to Massachusetts. A year later, a fire destroyed the Philadelphia warehouse where her Paris works were stored, and, tragically, most of her early pieces were lost. Over the next decade, Fuller bore and raised three children while continuing her art career. She also became interested in **Pan-African** politics, which influenced her work.

Fuller first turned to black subject matter when Du Bois (whom she had met in Paris while he was organizing the African-American pavilion at the 1900 Paris Exposition) commissioned her to create a sculpture for the celebration of the 50th anniversary of the Emancipation Proclamation to be held in New York. In response, Fuller created her 1913 allegorical sculpture *Emancipation Proclamation* (Figure 6.2). Fuller wrote in 1916 about this work: "The Negro has been emancipated from slavery but not the curse of race hatred and prejudice. . . . It was not Lincoln alone who wrote the Emancipation but the humane side of the nation." She further described the sculpture as a depiction of "Humanity weeping over her suddenly freed children, who, beneath the gnarled fingers of Fate, step forth into the world, unafraid." The central element of the work—the "gnarled" tree—is a veiled metaphor for the cruelties of fate and points to the artist's affinity with the bleak themes of **Symbolist** art. Fuller's figures, on the other hand, are more optimistic in their iconography: while one appears fully downtrodden and stooping over, the next is proud and standing upright, and a third courageously steps forward.

In 1929, Fuller designed and supervised the building of a larger workspace on the shore of a 36-acre lake near her home. The expanded space allowed Fuller to sculpt, teach, and flourish professionally. In the early 1930s, she was awarded a place on the Harmon Foundation jury, which only allotted one seat annually to a nonwhite juror. Fuller's Afrocentric and politically centered sculptures are among the first quintessentially Harlem Renaissance works of art on record.

May Howard Jackson

May Howard Jackson (1877–1931) anticipated the Harlem Renaissance by even more years than Fuller, having already begun, at the close of the 19th century, to sculpt ennobling portrayals of African Americans. In 1899, she created a nude bust of a solemn black man that, in its honest and sympathetic treatment of African physical features, anticipated the artist's career-long dedication to elevating portrayals of blacks (Figure 6.3).

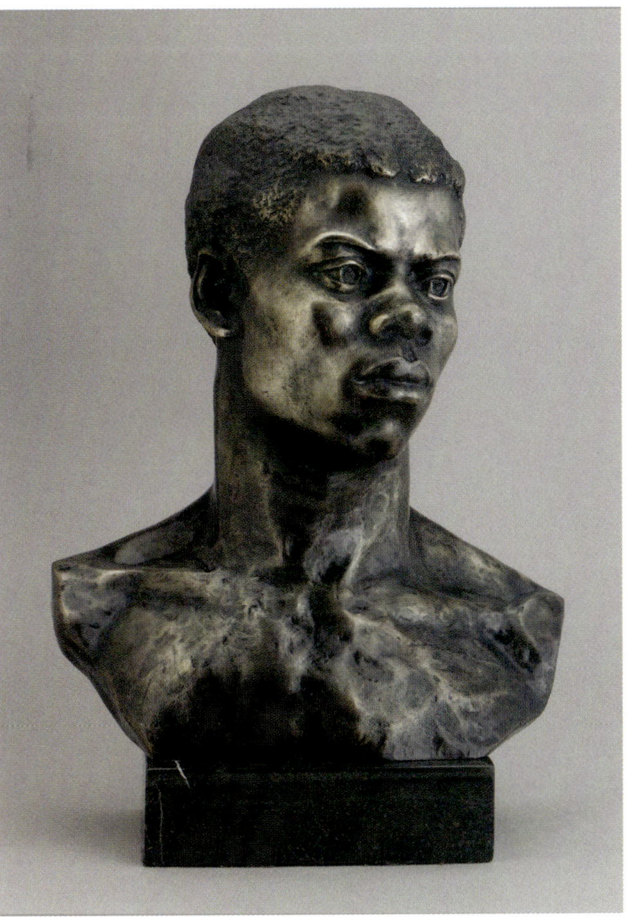

▼ **6.3** May Howard Jackson, *Portrait Bust of an African (a.k.a. Head of a Slave Boy; Negro Youth)*, 1899–1900, bronze, 21″ × 12¾″.

The Kinsey African American Art and History Collection.

Although born the same year and in the same city and educated at the same schools as Meta Fuller, Jackson's path as an artist was very different. Most importantly, she rejected the Grand Tour experience, despite an invitation from Fuller's parents (who were family friends) to accompany their daughter abroad. Jackson remarked pointedly that she "did not think it necessary to go to Europe to further her education." This decision would haunt her all-too-short career, which came to an end at the height of the Harlem Renaissance.

Jackson was the daughter of affluent parents, Floarda and Sallie Howard, who enrolled her in Tadd's Industrial Art School. She next attended the Pennsylvania Museum School and, in 1895, won a scholarship to the Pennsylvania Academy—a full 10 years before Fuller—making her the first African-American woman to attend it. She studied under renowned Impressionist William Merritt Chase (1849–1916) and sculptors Charles Grafly (1862–1929) and John Joseph Boyle (1852–1917). At the academy, Jackson took advantage of classes that featured live nude models, a privilege that was finally afforded to women there a decade after the dismissal of Thomas Eakins for allowing the practice.

Four years after receiving her degree, Jackson married educator William T. S. Jackson and moved with him to Washington, D.C., in 1902. He served as principal of the first African-American public high school in the country, Dunbar High School; the school is today the home of Jackson's 1919 bronze bust of its namesake, African-American poet Paul Laurence Dunbar (1872–1906). The sculpture exemplifies virtually all of Jackson's distinguished portrayals in its emphasis on black beauty, elegant naturalism, and introspective expression. Jackson established a sculpture studio in D.C. and mentored her husband's nephew, Sargent Claude Johnson (discussed later in this chapter), who would become an important Harlem Renaissance sculptor in his own right. In 1919, she announced the opening of a Harlem studio, stating in a printed announcement that she would "be in her studio daily from 2:00 to 4:00 P.M. and . . . will take pleasure in receiving visitors and in discussing her work with them." Jackson joined the Howard University faculty from 1922 to 1924, and in 1928, three years before her death, she won a Harmon Foundation bronze award.

Despite her many successes and honors, Jackson sold few works during her lifetime. This embittered her, as did her experiences of bigotry within the art world. On one occasion, the Washington Society of Fine Arts reversed their acceptance of her application for membership when they learned that she was African-American. She was also criticized for her lack of continental training, and for the conventional nature of her portraiture, which lacked the Modernist and Rodin-inspired edginess of Fuller's work. In her obituary in *Crisis*, Du Bois commented about the difficulties that she faced, stating that Jackson was "at once bitter and fierce with energy, cynical of praise and above all at odds with life and people. . . . With her sensitive soul, she needed encouragement and . . . delicate appreciation. Instead of this, she ran into the shadows of the Color Line."

Sargent Claude Johnson

Jackson's nephew, Sargent Claude Johnson (1887–1967), lived with her in D.C. after his mother's death in 1902; his father had predeceased her by five years. Jackson's influence on his art can be seen in the element of idealized black beauty that their work shares. Born in Boston, Johnson moved to Massachusetts after his stay with Jackson in D.C. and attended Worcester Art School. In 1915, he moved again to San Francisco to study at the A. W. Best School, run by the husband-and-wife **Neo-Impressionist** art team of Alice (1870–1926) and Arthur Best (1859–1935).

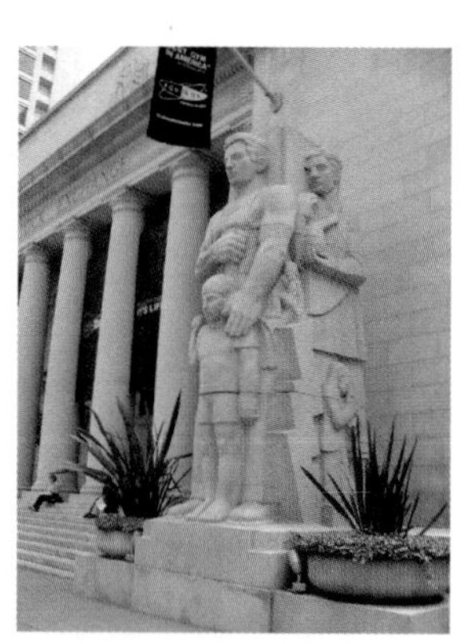

▲ **6.4** Ralph Stackpole, *Industry*, 1931–32, granite, 21′ high.

Photo: Binksternet, public domain license, Wikimedia Commons.

From 1919 to 1923, Johnson studied at the California School of Fine Arts (now the San Francisco Art Institute), and for two years, he took classes with one of the city's foremost sculptors, Ralph Stackpole (1885–1973). Johnson's reductive Modernist style of sculpture shows Stackpole's influence. Johnson's *Forever Free* (Figure 6.5) has much in common with Stackpole's 14-ton granite sculpture *Industry* (Figure 6.4), particularly in its representation of a fully in-the-round adult figure protecting, with enlarged hands, relief carvings of children. However, Johnson's vision presents a black matriarch shielding nude black children, and it is decidedly more reductive and organically formed than Stackpole's Art Deco portrayal.

Johnson showed in the first Harmon exhibition in 1926. Within two years he had won the foundation's Otto Kahn First Prize for a terracotta bust of a black child, while his aunt took second place. (Her nephew's rapid rise to success that eclipsed her own achievements may have added to Jackson's feelings of professional disappointment.) The foundation also included him in a 1935 three-man show with Malvin Gray Johnson and Richmond Barthé (discussed later in this chapter). He created an 18- by 24-foot redwood relief organ screen for Berkeley's California School for the Deaf and Blind in 1937 and several pieces for Stackpole's Court of Pacifica pavilion at the 1938 Golden Gate International Expo. The artist's later career was marked by immersion in Mexican culture and indigenous Mesoamerican art, to which Stackpole had introduced him. The formal simplicity and elegance of Mexican sculpture continued to inspire him until his death.

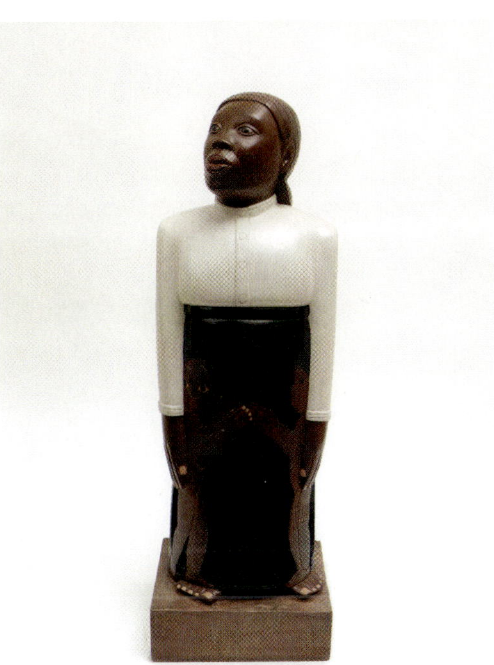

▲ **6.5** Sargent Johnson, *Forever Free*, 1933, sculpture, wood and paint, 36″ × 11½″ × 9½″.

San Francisco Museum of Modern Art, gift of Mrs. E. D. Lederman. © Estate of Sargent Johnson. Photo: Don Ross.

Nancy Elizabeth Prophet

Unlike Johnson, the life and career of sculptor Nancy Elizabeth Prophet (1890–1960) was marked by cycles of affluence and fiscal distress, compelling her, at times, to work as a maid in order to support herself. When asked on a Harmon Foundation application to list her academic record, Prophet named her alma mater as "the College of Serious Thought . . . situated in the campus of Poverty and Ambition." Prophet grew up in Rhode Island and studied fine arts at the Rhode Island School of Design from 1913 to 1918. Shortly after completing her degree, she was invited to participate in a postgraduate exhibit but was cautioned not to attend the whites-only opening reception. By way of protest, Prophet refused to participate in the show at all. Attracted by the New York art scene, she moved there after graduation and befriended artist Gertrude Vanderbilt Whitney (1875–1942), a member of New York's cultural elite and founder of the Whitney Museum of American Art. Whitney and Prophet shared a studio, and Whitney helped to finance Prophet's first trip to Europe in 1922, where the latter remained for 10 years.

In Paris, Prophet studied at the École des Beaux Arts. Within two years, she was exhibiting works in the Paris Salons, where she showed consistently over the next decade. Her sculptures earned kudos from the French critics, who described them as "vigorous and energetic" and as "conceived in a . . . supple, assured style." The rugged surfaces and forceful modeling of *Negro Head*, which won the Otto Kahn Prize from the Harmon Foundation, exemplify the dynamism and confidence of Prophet's chisel (Figure 6.6). Carved in wood, the sculpture highlights the forceful gouges made by the artist's hand. The piercing gaze, flaring nostrils, and ample lips of the sculpted head foreground the beauty and nobility of the black male.

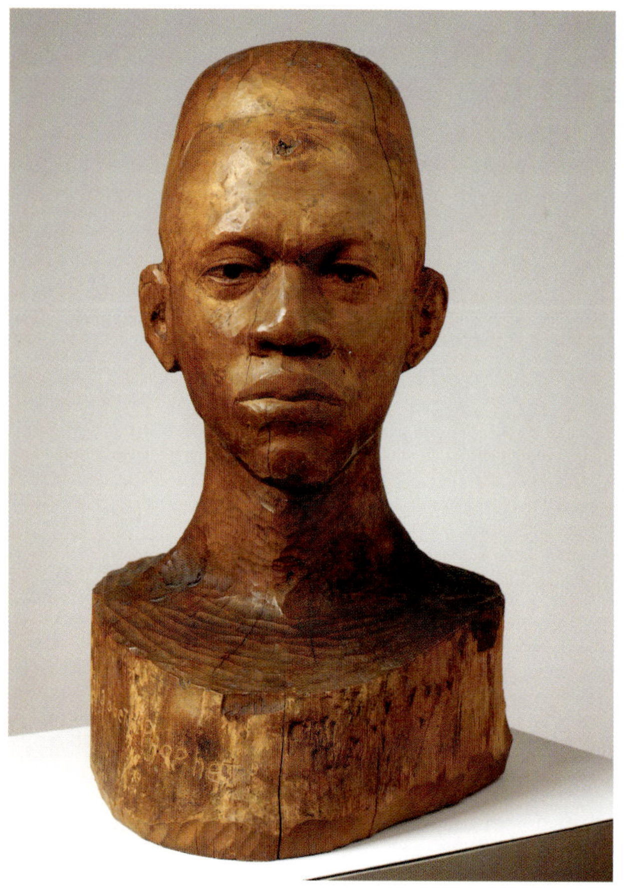

▲ **6.6** Nancy Elizabeth Prophet, *Negro Head*, before 1928, wood, 20½″ × 11″ × 14″.

Museum of Art, Rhode Island School of Design, Providence.

While in France, Prophet received an invitation to teach sculpture at Spelman College. She accepted the position and returned permanently to the United States in 1934. She expanded the art curriculum established by artist Hale Woodruff (see Chapter 7) to include her own expertise in sculpture and art history. As the decade progressed, so did Prophet's career. Prophet became one of the first African-American artists to enter the Whitney collection, when the museum purchased her bust of an African entitled *Congolaise*.

By the early 1940s, however, Prophet's career began to wane, due in part to the loss of private patrons resulting from the Great Depression and to the rise in interest in abstract art. In 1944, she returned to Providence, finding the social restrictions of the segregated South too taxing. After several failed attempts to rekindle her reputation in the Northeast, including one last exhibit at the Providence Public Library, Prophet came full circle and was forced once again to accept work as a housekeeper. The reduced state of her finances resulted in the loss of many of her works, which were either destroyed or left to deteriorate outdoors because she lacked the funds to store them. Until her death from a heart attack in 1960, Prophet lived an impoverished and isolated life.

Richmond Barthé

Sculptor Richmond Barthé (1901–89) was born in Bay St. Louis, Mississippi. As a young man, he taught himself drawing by copying illustrations from newspapers and magazines. At age 14, he was hired as a summer babysitter by Mr. and Mrs. Harry Pond, a wealthy New Orleans couple who were vacationing in Mississippi along the Gulf of Mexico. At the end of the summer, they invited Barthé to New Orleans with them as a live-in domestic. The Pond family was especially fond of Barthé, and, aware of his artistic talents, they presented him with a gift of his first set of oil paints. Over the next 10 years, Barthé trained himself as a painter.

After donating a religious picture to a fair at his local church, Barthé came to the attention of a Catholic priest, Father Harry F. Kane, who raised funds to pay for the artist's first year of study at the Art Institute of Chicago. Barthé attended classes at night and worked days as a busboy. At the institute, he studied with Czech artist Albin Polasek (1879–1965), whose nude figure sculptures greatly influenced Barthé's own style. Barthé also studied outside of class with African-American painter Archibald Motley (discussed later in this chapter), who had graduated from the institute in 1918. A year before completing the institute program, two of Barthé's sculpted busts were chosen for inclusion in the 1927 *Negro in Art Week* exhibit organized by the Chicago Woman's Club. The show was attended by Alain Locke, who encouraged Barthé to come to New York. After graduation, in February 1929, Barthé did so. He worked with intensity, completing more than two dozen figure sculptures that year. He immersed himself in the Harlem Renaissance milieu and counted among his inner circle Langston Hughes, actress Rose McClendon (1884–1936), and actor-painter Richard Bruce Nugent (1906–86).

Consisting almost entirely of Rodinesque male nudes and prepossessing busts of black men and women, his sculptures appealed to a wide audience of art buyers, who were attracted to their supple, dance-like movements; corporeal beauty; and tenor of spirituality. His *Féral Benga* exemplifies these qualities (Figure 6.7). The sculpture is modeled after the Senegalese exotic dancer François "Féral" Benga (1906–57), whom Barthé saw perform at the Folies Bergère in Paris in 1934. The work captures the sensuous movements of the dancer's performance. His gleaming dark skin is realized in the dark **patina** and high polish of the sculpture's surface. Using open form and faultless serpentine balance, Barthé exalts the male nude as the embodiment of both Renaissance humanism and Baroque spiritualism. As he explained: "All my life I have been interested in trying to capture the spiritual quality I see and feel in people, and I feel that the human figure as God made it, is the best means of expressing this spirit in man." To best imbue his sculptures with transcendent humanism, Barthé spent many hours studying body movements at the Martha Graham Center of Contemporary Dance. The fluidity of Graham's signature style of modern dance found plastic form in Barthé works.

▼ **6.7** James Richmond Barthé, *Féral Benga*, 1935, bronze, cast, 18¾″ × 7″ × 4⅜″.

Museum of Fine Arts, Boston, William Francis Warden Fund and American Decorative Arts Deaccessioning Fund, 2007. Photo © 2016 Museum of Fine Arts Boston.

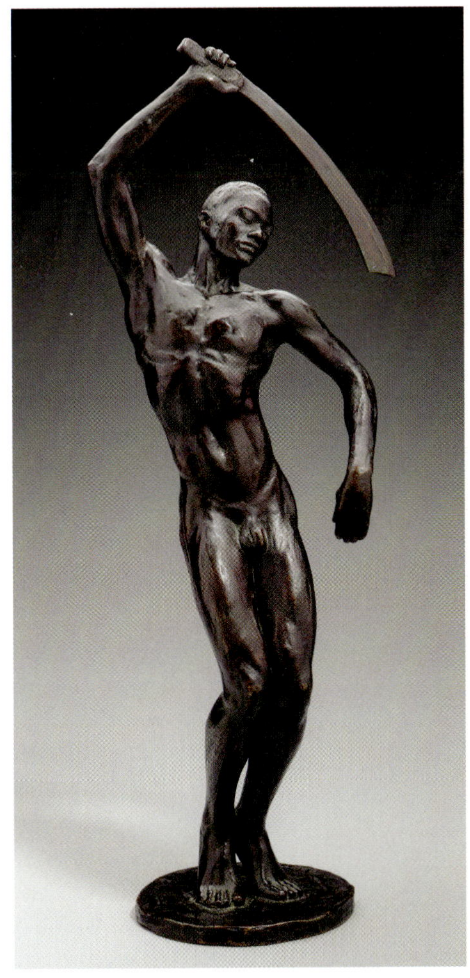

Barthé's public commissions included two works for the Harlem River Housing Project that were completed in 1937 and 1938: a monumental sculpture of African-American folk hero John Henry and an 80-foot Art Deco bas-relief **frieze** on the themes of dance and the exodus of African Americans into a "magical" all-black heaven (based on *The Green Pastures*, a Broadway play by Marc Connelly). The garden apartment complex was designed by a team of six architects, one of whom was African-American: John Louis Wilson, Jr. (1899–89). Barthé capped the decade with a showing of art at the 1939 New York World's Fair with fellow members of the Sculptor's Guild, of which he was an instrumental cofounder.

The 1940s were equally fruitful. Barthé won consecutive Guggenheim Fellowships in 1940 and 1941. He exhibited in the Metropolitan Museum's *Artists for Victory* show, after which the museum acquired Barthé's *Boxer* in 1943. In 1949, Barthé was commissioned to create two public monuments of Haitian Revolutionary leaders Toussaint Louverture and Jean-Jacques Dessalines for the Haitian city of Port-au-Prince.

At the end of the 1940s, Barthé left his thriving career and the fast-paced atmosphere of New York behind for the more laid-back atmosphere of Jamaica in the Caribbean. He spent 20 successful years there as an artist and minor celebrity. However, the rise of gang violence following Jamaica's independence from Britain in 1962 compelled Barthé to leave Jamaica for Europe, where he lived for five years in Switzerland, Spain, and Italy. In the early 1970s, he returned to the United States and settled in Pasadena, California. By this time, however, Barthé's notoriety had all but evaporated, and he fell on hard times. While facing dire financial difficulties, Barthé met Hollywood actor James Garner (1928–2014), who quietly supported Barthé for the remainder of his life.

PAINTING

In Locke's *Survey Graphic* essay, he referred specifically to the influence of African abstraction and motifs on the early evolution of 20th-century European Modernism, particularly the abstracted and distorted forms of **Fauvism**, **Expressionism**, and **Cubism**. The first major African-American art exhibit to highlight the influence of African aesthetics on modern art was *The Negro in Art*, a show organized in 1927 by the Chicago Women's Club and the Chicago Art Institute. Its catalog—which featured an Art Deco cover replete with a monumental depiction of an Egyptian pharaoh—stated that the exhibit was mounted "in the belief that a knowledge of the accomplishment of the Negro in the various forms of art would improve relations between the races." The exhibition paired original African sculpture with art by 19th-century and early 20th-century artists Edmonia Lewis, William A. Harper (1873–1910), Edward Mitchell Bannister, and Henry Tanner, as well as Harlem Renaissance sculptors Meta Fuller and Barthé and painters William Edouard Scott, Aaron Douglas (discussed later in this chapter), and others. Although these artists did not share a specific formal style, they had in common a self-conscious awareness of the growing visibility of African and African-American art and culture on the global stage. They hoped to make their mark on the American art scene through creative excellence, social commentary, and cutting-edge Modernism.

William Edouard Scott

Famed for his murals, William Edouard Scott (1884–1964) was a pioneer of early Modernist painting in America. His style incorporated elements of Impressionism, **Post-Impressionism**, and Expressionism, while focusing almost exclusively on black genre subjects. Born in Indianapolis, Scott's high school boasted an art department headed by Otto Stark (1859–1926), a well-known Impressionist of the Indiana **Hoosier group**. Scott received further instruction on weekends at the John Herron Art Institute (today the Indianapolis Art Museum). At the age of 20, he moved to Illinois to study at the Chicago Art Institute from 1904 to 1908. He supported himself by painting murals in local churches and by working as an illustrator for popular magazines.

After graduation, in 1909 Scott traveled to Italy, Holland, and France for two years. He studied at the Académie Julian in Paris. He also spent time in

Étaples with Tanner, coming under the elder artist's influence while residing in his home. While living there, Scott befriended another Tanner acolyte, Hale Woodruff (see Chapter 7). The trio spent many hours discussing art, race, and life as they worked side by side in Tanner's studio. Scott's first trip abroad was capped in 1911 with a showing of his work in a nearby beach resort.

Back in the United States, in the winter of 1911 Scott exhibited three of his paintings with the Society of Western Artists, a group of midwestern Impressionists. Scott sold most of the works he had created while in France and was able to travel abroad again in 1912 and 1913, where he continued to work with Tanner. During this period abroad, Scott's work was included in the Paris Salon, and one of his Salon pictures, *La pauvre voisine* (*The Poor Neighbor*), was purchased by the Argentine government. Meanwhile, back in Indianapolis, more than 20 of Scott's paintings—including *Rainy Day, Etaples*, which was purchased for the Herron Institute in 1918—were exhibited at a solo show organized in Otto Stark's studio. Another Étaples street scene, *La Misère*, was reproduced in the catalog of the 1913 Paris Salon and won first prize at the Indiana State Fair.

Scott found his way back to the States in April 1914 on the eve of the First World War. He set up a studio in Chicago, where his European cachet lent much to his reputation and to the demand for his work, particularly for large-scale murals. In the first year after Scott's arrival in Chicago, he completed 20 mural commissions. He also spent several months during 1915 at Tuskegee Institute, where he met African-American scientist George Washington Carver (1864–1943) and Tuskegee president and ex-slave Booker T. Washington (1856–1915). That year, Scott completed the first of many portraits of them and other historical African-American figures. He also created paintings that documented southern black life, especially the living conditions and daily lives of the most impoverished.

In 1927, the Harmon Foundation awarded Scott a gold medal for distinguished career achievement. A few years later, he won a grant from the Rosenwald Foundation that funded his trip to Haiti in 1931, where he completed a suite of more than 140 paintings and drawings of Haitian landscapes, fishing boats, peasants, historical monuments, and market scenes (the latter subject occupied him for the remainder of his career). Scott's work took on more vibrant tones in response to the colorful environment and intense tropical light of Haiti. *Night Turtle Fishing* exemplifies his work of this period (Figure 6.8). Compared favorably by historians to celebrated American seascape painter Winslow

▼ **6.8** William Edouard Scott, *Night Turtle Fishing in Haiti*, 1931, oil on canvas, 39½″ × 29¼″.

Courtesy of Clark Atlanta University Art Collection.

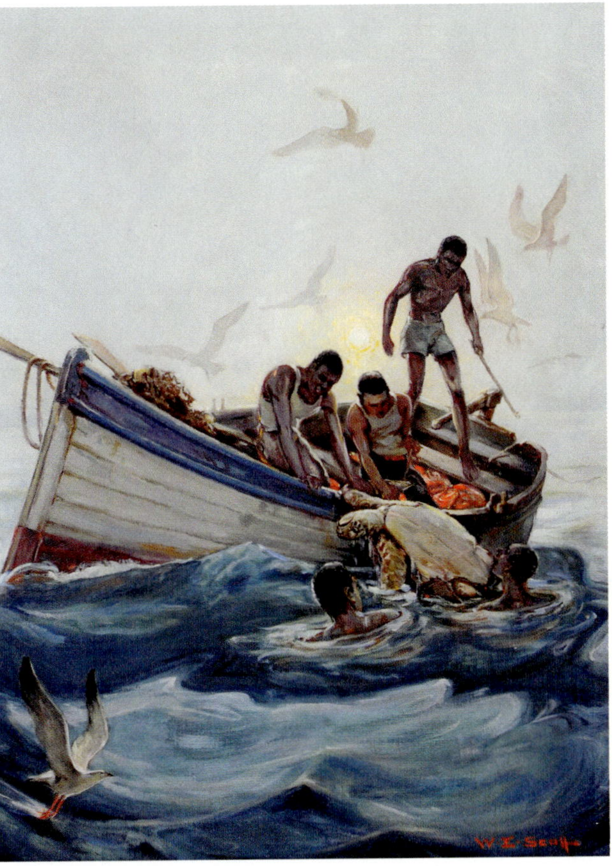

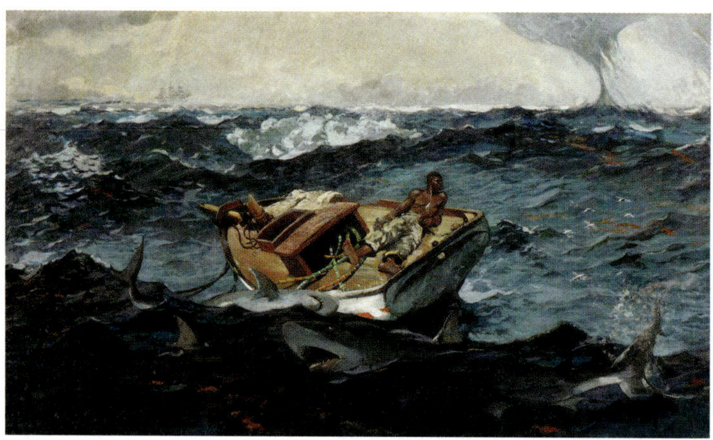

▲ **6.9** Winslow Homer, *The Gulf Stream*, 1899, oil on canvas, 28⅛″ × 49⅛″. Catherine Lorillard Wolfe Collection, Wolfe Fund, 1906 (06.1234). Photo © The Metropolitan Museum of Art. Photo source: Art Resource, NY.

Homer's (1836–1910) 1899 *The Gulf Stream* (Figure 6.9), Scott's picture does, indeed, share with it certain elements of subject matter (black men at sea) and formal treatment (a sure-handed, weighty handling of the water). Portraying industrious Haitian fishermen at work hoisting turtles from the water, Scott's rendering diverges from Homer's depiction of an idle black man, adrift and oar-less in a roiling, shark-infested ocean. Scott's image suggests self-empowerment, whereas Homer's, impotence. Intended or not, Homer's depiction sustained stereotypes of the lackadaisical black man, helpless or unwilling to improve his condition. In the Realist tradition, Scott allows the honesty of his portrayal to speak for itself. Scott's painterly talents are further revealed in his light-infused and gossamer handling of the sky, sun, and seagulls.

At the end of a 14-month stay in Haiti, Scott was honored in 1931 with a government-sponsored solo showing of his paintings in Haiti's capital of Port-au-Prince. It was especially well received, attracting some 300 visitors a day. Interest in the exhibition dovetailed with Haiti's burgeoning **Indigenist Movement**, a literary and visual arts movement parallel to the Harlem Renaissance that promoted the unique culture of Haiti's working class rather than its elite. So pleased was Haiti's president, Sténio Vincent (1874–1959), with Scott's works that he purchased a dozen of the artist's paintings for his private collection and awarded Scott the country's highest honor.

After his Haiti experience, Scott returned to mural painting. His first major work was a series for the 1933 Chicago World's Fair. In 1936, he completed an ambitious **secco** mural entitled *Mind Body Spirit* for the Wabash YMCA in the Bronzeville area of Chicago. In all, during his lifetime Scott completed more than 75 murals that depict positive aspects of African-American culture. These murals are installed in public buildings in half a dozen states from New York to Arizona. The majority of his murals were done in the straightforward **Social Realist** style that had become popular by the late 1930s (see Chapter 7).

In the 1940s, Scott returned to France, where he created a number of sketches of African-American soldiers there. Scott made a final trip abroad in 1955, this time to Mexico City, where he produced oil sketches of the Mexican people, which he planned to develop into a formal series. Unfortunately, Scott was diagnosed with diabetes while in Mexico and, after a lengthy period of illness, succumbed to the disease.

Palmer Hayden

More than most other African-American artists, Palmer Hayden's (1890–1973) work was shaped by the expectations of the Harmon Foundation. He catered to the wealthy white patrons of the Harlem Renaissance in a way that far exceeded the lengths to which other Harlem artists were willing to go. Virginian by birth, Hayden spent most of his life in New York City, where he moved after spending 10 years in the armed services. On his discharge in 1920, he studied art at Cooper Union, Columbia University, and at the Boothbay Commonwealth Art Colony in Maine, where he developed a gift for marine pictures. His works in this vein were exhibited in the annual shows of the New York Society of Independent Artists in 1925 and 1926. To support himself, Hayden worked as a laborer at various jobs.

In 1926, an impressionistic marine painting by Hayden won the Harmon Foundation's first-ever art prize. Hayden used the money to travel to Paris, where he lived, studied, and exhibited for five years, from 1927 to 1932. During his years in France, Hayden studied privately with École des Beaux Arts instructor Clivette Lefevre. He painted marine pictures, traveling to the coastal fishing village of Concarneau and other cities in Brittany, where he met Tanner and Woodruff. He also socialized with other Harlem Renaissance artists, thinkers, and writers, including Locke and Countee Cullen, who were in France at the time. In addition to marine pictures, Hayden painted Cubist-inspired domestic and street scenes of blacks as well as depictions of African-American folklore, which became a staple of his oeuvre for the remainder of his career.

There were troubling elements about Hayden's portrayals of blacks. They often incorporated exaggerated facial features such as enlarged lips and bulging eyes—elements that were criticized by African-American artist and critic James Porter (1935–2005) as satirical and degrading (Figure 6.10). The appearance of this imagery in Hayden's work coincided with his newly acquired role as the face of the Harmon Foundation, which marketed him in press releases, films, and catalogs as a self-taught naïf, despite his Modernist techniques and professional training. The influence of the Harmon Foundation and other white art patrons on Hayden's painting was believed to mark the downfall of his credibility as a serious painter. Hayden's use of stereotypes foreshadows that of 21st-century artists such as Robert Colescott, Michael Ray Charles, and Kara Walker (see Chapter 13). Their works, too, are collected and lauded by white museum curators, historians, and critics, even as they are viewed with skepticism by some black scholars and artists for their perpetuation of caustic stereotypes.

Hayden made one final trip to Paris in 1936, otherwise remaining in New York for the next 25 years as a fixture on the New York art scene. Despite his critics, Hayden continued to paint and to exhibit until his death at age 88.

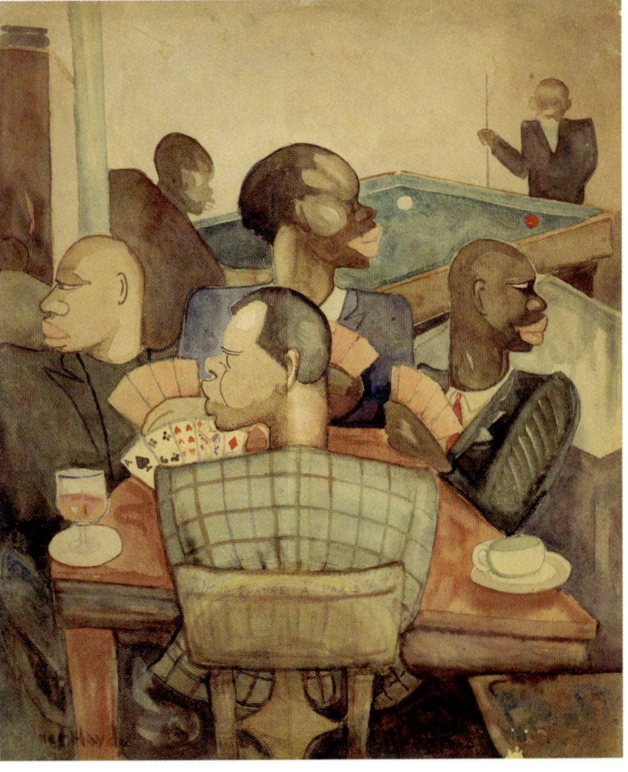

▼ **6.10** Palmer Hayden, *Nous Quatre à Paris (We Four in Paris)*, c. 1930, watercolor and pencil on paper, 21¾″ × 18⅛″.

Purchase, Joseph Hazen Foundation Inc. Gift, 1975. Photo © the Metropolitan Museum of Art. Photo source: Art Resource, NY.

Archibald Motley, Jr.

Archibald Motley, Jr. (1891–1981), achieved fame in 1927 when his work was featured in a Newark Museum of Art show of living American artists. Motley's delicately rendered portrait of an elderly woman, seated with her sewing beside a lace-covered table, was voted by visitors the most popular work in the show. Motley was a New Orleans native whose family moved to Chicago in 1894 during the early wave of the Great Migration. Motley received his art training at the Art Institute of Chicago. He graduated in 1918 and spent the next year studying with prominent **Ashcan School** painter George Bellows (1882–1925). After graduation, from 1918 to 1925, Motley worked as a Pullman porter to support himself. During this period, he married a daughter of German immigrants named Edith Granzo (1895–1948), whose family disowned her for marrying a black man.

After several years working as a porter, Motley's success at the 1927 Newark Museum show propelled his career forward. He was best known for his *Octoroon* series—paintings of near-white-skinned women of mixed race—a subject of great interest to Motley due to the prominence of mixed-race families in his New Orleans birthplace. In 1928, Motley won the Harmon Award for a discerning portrait of an elderly black woman entitled

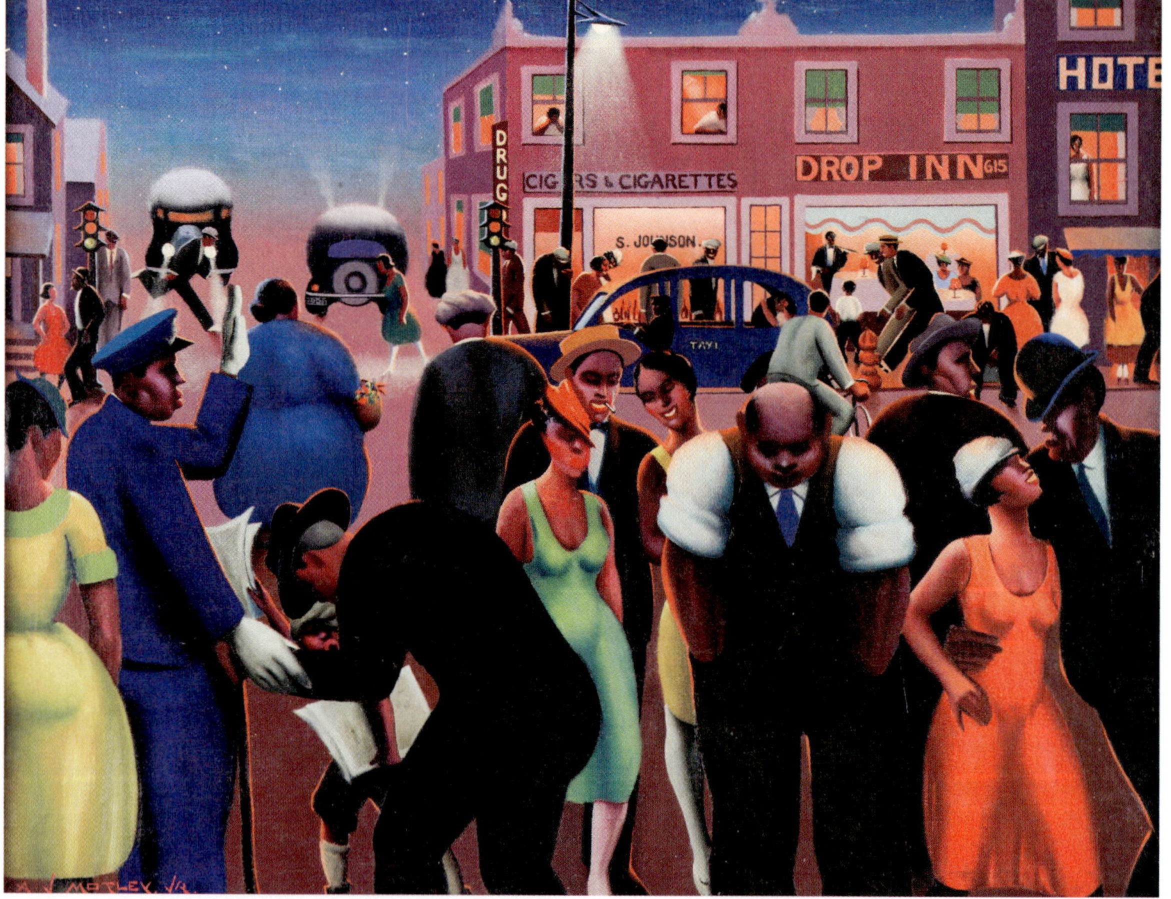

▼ **6.11** Archibald Motley, *Black Belt*, 1934, oil on canvas, 33″ × 40½″.

Courtesy of the Chicago History Museum. Photo © Valerie Gerrard Browne.

The Old Snuff Dipper. However, by this time, his penchant for realistic portraits of black women was replaced by a more stylized and Modernist vision. In his newer paintings, Motley generalized figures and faces, simplified forms, and subordinated details in favor of mood-invoking ambience (Figure 6.11). He was able to capture the emotional as well as visual impressions of each of his chosen scenes, bringing to life crowded Harlem nightclubs or nocturnal city streets. He achieved this feat through the use of vibrant colors, diffuse lighting, overlapping shapes, unique angles of vision, and expert handling of space.

In 1929, Motley received a Guggenheim Foundation Fellowship to study in Paris for a year. After his return to Chicago, from 1933 to 1936, Motley painted murals on African-American history for schools and post offices sponsored by the WPA (see Chapter 7). He was also appointed visiting professor at Howard University in 1933. However, despite his contributions to African-American art, he was largely ignored after the rise of abstract art in the 1940s, until, in 1980, a year before his death, he was awarded an honorary PhD by the Chicago Art Institute.

Malvin Gray Johnson

Malvin Gray Johnson (1896–1934) was born in Greensboro, North Carolina, and received his first art lessons from his sister Maggie. In 1912, at age 16, he came to New York with his family as part of the Great Migration and within four years was admitted to the National Academy of Design (NAD). Shortly after beginning his studies there, Johnson was drafted into the armed forces. In the mid-1920s, he returned to New York and resumed his studies at NAD. In 1925, concurrently with his NAD classes, he exhibited his Modernist harbor scene *Along the Harlem River* with the Society of Independent Artists. After graduating in 1928, his work was included in that year's Harmon exhibition, and, a year later, his entry, a nocturnal southern prayer scene, won the foundation's Otto H. Kahn Prize.

Johnson's 1934 *Self-Portrait* reveals the artist's preference for minimalist shapes and a restrained palette of dark blues and browns (Figure 6.12). It also demonstrates several Cubist traits, including flattened forms, a distorted perspective, and a handling of negative space as solid matter. Also evident is a **Cézannesque** tilting of objects toward the picture plane. *Self-Portrait* is a painting-within-a-painting; the artist's 1932 *Negro Masks* is integrated into it as a completed painting hanging on the wall of his studio. The similarity between one of the painted masks and Johnson's own portrait links him symbolically to his African past.

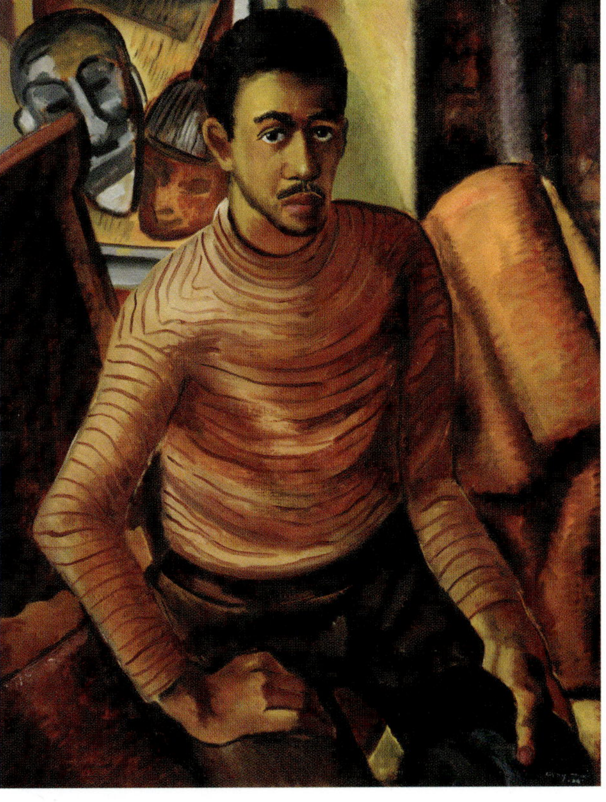

▼ **6.12** Malvin Gray Johnson, *Self-Portrait*, 1934, oil on canvas, 38¼″ × 30″.

Collection of the Smithsonian American Art Museum, gift of the Harmon Foundation. Photo: Smithsonian American Art Museum, Washington, D.C. / Art Resource, NY.

In 1933, Johnson began a mural sequence on the topic of black achievement. He worked out his initial ideas for the design with 1933 Harmon Prize winner Earle W. Richardson (1912–35), who was his collaborator and lover. Eight panels featured narratives about the accomplishments of blacks in the arts and military services, along with portraits of historic personalities such as Frederick Douglass, Haitian revolutionary Toussaint Louverture (1743–1803), Underground Railroad "conductor" Harriet Tubman (1820–1913), rebel slave Nat Turner (1800–31), and **Amarna** pharaoh Akhenaten. However, Johnson died unexpectedly in the fall of 1934 of heart failure at age 38. Richardson continued to map out the complex mural sequence but committed suicide less than a year later.

Aaron Douglas

Aaron Douglas (1898–1979) is the artist most closely identified with the Harlem Renaissance. He followed Locke's belief that African-American art should incorporate African motifs as well as Du Bois's call for depictions of the New Negro in the most ennobling manner possible. Following undergraduate fine arts study at the University of Nebraska, Douglas taught briefly in Kansas City before coming to New York in 1925, where he met Winold Reiss (1886–1953), a German-born artist who was art editor of the March 1925 issue of *Survey Graphic*. Reiss mentored Douglas and encouraged him to incorporate African abstraction into his work. Douglas quickly developed a unique method of painting that combined accessible narrative imagery with a complex compositional substructure of geometric abstraction. His stylized representations of African-American life and history greatly appealed to Harlem patrons and literati. In 1927, he illustrated NAACP cofounder James Weldon Johnson's (1871–1938) collection of poems *God's Trombones*. That same year, the Barnes Foundation awarded Douglas a fellowship to study its famed collection of African and modern art in Merion, Pennsylvania. This experience and a one-year stay in Paris from 1931 to 1932 exposed Douglas to a variety of African art objects as well as to European Modernism.

Douglas painted his most memorable works in mural format, comprising a synthesis of the monochromatic palette of **Analytic Cubism** and the ***papier collé*** quality of **Synthetic Cubism**. In 1929, Douglas was commissioned by Fisk University to create a suite of murals for its Cravath Library. The series chronicles black history from slavery to the modern age and visually narrates the value of an education in the arts and sciences. Douglas was assisted in the project by portrait painter Edwin A. Harleston (1882–1931), whose 1930 portrait of Douglas recorded the artist standing, palette in hand, in front of one of his murals. Douglas's most famous mural sequence, *Aspects of Negro Life*, was produced under the auspices of the federal government's WPA art program (see Chapter 7). It was installed at the Schomburg Center in Harlem in 1934, where it remains today. The large-scale oil compositions present a chronological record of four critical moments in African-American history. The first panel, *African Backgrounds*, portrays African dancers, musicians, and sacred objects prior to the African slave trade. The second, *From Slavery to Reconstruction*, illustrates enslaved workers behind a screen of cotton plants, men breaking their chains, and a figure

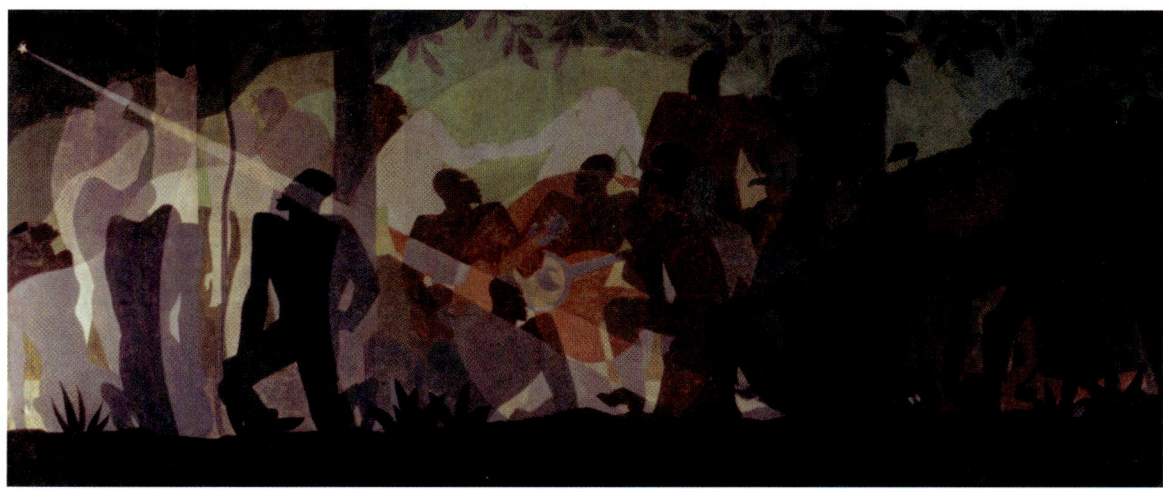

▲ **6.13** Aaron Douglas, *Aspects of Negro Life: An Idyll of the Deep South*, 1934, oil on canvas, 5′ × 11′7″.

The Art and Artifacts Division of the Schomburg Center for Research in Black Culture of the New York Public Library, Astor, Lenox, and Tilden Foundations.

holding up a copy of the Emancipation Proclamation in the shadow of the Capitol Building. *An Idyll of the Deep South* depicts a time just after Reconstruction, during the age of Jim Crow, when legal segregation and rampant lynching marred African-American life (Figure 6.13). This panel includes a group of farmworkers and banjo players amid stylized flora. The seemingly idyllic existence of those portrayed is overshadowed by a harsh reality: the specter of the dangling feet of a lynched body hanging from a tree, which occupies the upper-left quadrant of the mural. Below the scene of death, a man kneels in silent prayer. The final panel, *Song of the Towers*, portrays a businessman and a saxophone player (metaphors for the black creative spirit) overcome by emotional anguish within a towering industrial setting. Crisscrossed with sinister and shadowy forms that haunt the figures, the composition is a requiem for the working man.

Douglas's inimitable fusion of disparate elements—abstraction and figuration, Africanism and Modernism, and social and historical narrative—within the context of his signature lyrical, translucent, and nearly monochromatic palette had wide appeal. The clarity of his imagery and its dignified black subject matter made Douglas one of the most popular artists of the period. One year after the completion of *Aspects of Negro Life*, Douglas was elected president of the Harlem Artists Guild, through which he fought for better opportunities for black artists.

William H. Johnson

William H. Johnson (1901–70) was a prolific artist who painted hundreds of works over his 40-year career. Johnson came to New York from South Carolina in 1918. He supported himself as a cook, dockworker, and porter, while taking classes at the National Academy of Design from 1921 to 1925 with en plein air painter Charles Webster Hawthorne (1872–1930) and Symbolist Charles Louis Hinton (1859–1950). Johnson spent summers during this period studying at Hawthorne's school in Provincetown, Massachusetts. Johnson was an exceptional draughtsman. His still lifes and figure studies of the 1920s show a keen understanding of form and color and evoke the loose brushwork and spatial analyses of the Impressionists and Post-Impressionists.

After working briefly with Ashcan School artist George B. Luks (1867–1933), Johnson relocated to the Montparnasse section of Paris in 1926. During his first year, Johnson traveled to Étaples to meet Tanner while also immersing himself in the Paris art scene. By the end of the year, Johnson had completed a suite of paintings—mainly landscapes—for a solo exhibition in Paris. In 1927, Johnson moved to Cagnes-dur-Mer in the South of France, where he met his future wife, Danish textile artist Holcha Krake (1885–1944), and was exposed to German Expressionism by her brother-in-law, artist Christoph Voll (1837–1939). Johnson's portraits and landscapes from this period reveal the influence of the German and French Expressionists and show evidence of a broad-based understanding of European Modernism.

After a well-reviewed solo exhibit in Nice in the winter of 1928–29, Johnson returned to New York and entered his work in the Harmon Foundation annual show, receiving a gold medal award for painting. The next years were spent abroad, from 1930 to 1936, during which time Johnson traveled with his wife throughout France, Norway, Denmark, Sweden, Germany, and Tunisia. He continued to paint prolifically and to exhibit in the Harmon shows as well as in group, solo, and two-person exhibits (with Holcha).

In 1938, Johnson returned to New York and took a position as an instructor at the Harlem Community Art Center (see Chapter 7), where he remained until 1942. At about this time, his eclectic Modernism and non-racial subject matter gave way to more deliberately ethnic themes and to the flat, colorful forms of Synthetic Cubism. He painted African-American religious subjects and genre scenes of Harlem couples, street musicians, and farmworkers. These works show a keen understanding of color and form and an undeniable gift for complex design. Johnson's *Going to Church* (Figure 6.14) is an example of his mature style. The interlocking vertical and horizontal elements of the composition fit together like a mosaic. A vivid and varied palette is judiciously offset by areas of black and white. The elongated, cylindrical necks and bodies of the figures derive directly from Mali sculptural forms of the Bamana and Dogon people. Johnson's rigorous handling of formal elements along with the stoic simplicity of his theme—both Christian and pastoral—made this and many similar works popular favorites.

Throughout the early 1940s, Johnson was featured in dozens of exhibits in the United States, Europe, and Africa. Like many other leading African-American artists, he was included in Locke's 1940 *Art of the American Negro: 1851–1940* show at the American Negro Exposition in Chicago. However, 1944 marked a turning point in Johnson's career. His wife died that year from breast cancer, after which, in 1946 he moved to her native Denmark. Sadly, by this time Johnson had developed a form of dementia brought on by long-term untreated neurosyphilis. In 1947, while traveling in Norway, he had a mental breakdown and, after a return voyage home, was admitted to New York's Islip State Mental Hospital. Johnson remained there for the next 23 years, creating very little art, until his death from pancreatitis.

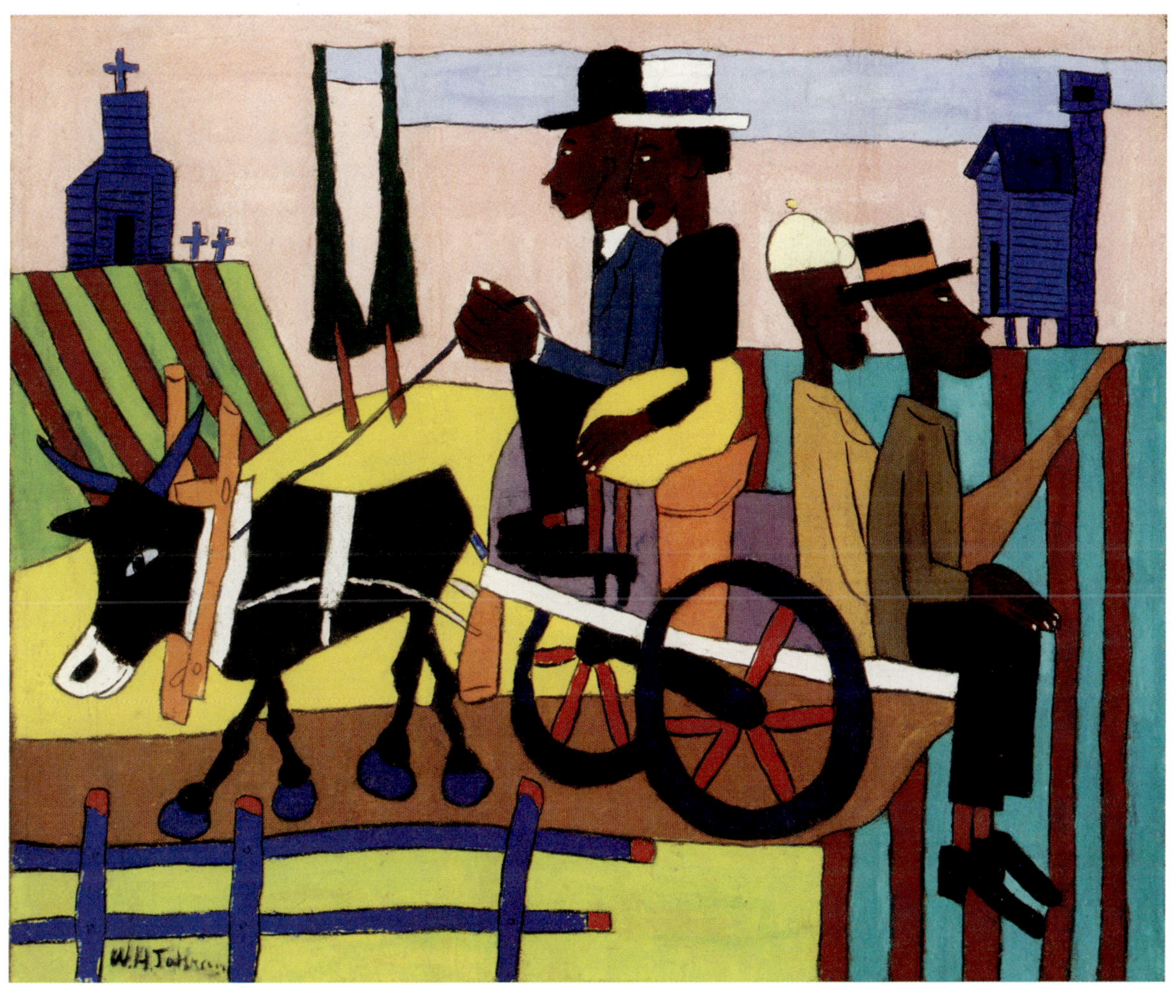

▲ **6.14** William H. Johnson, *Going to Church*, c. 1940–41, oil on burlap, 38⅛″ × 45⅜″.
Smithsonian American Art Museum, Washington, D.C. / Art Resource, NY.

A year after his passing, the Smithsonian Institution, which had acquired more than 1,000 of his paintings from the Harmon Foundation, held the first-ever retrospective of Johnson's art. The show went on to tour Europe and Africa, reviving Johnson's international acclaim and inspiring a whole new generation of admirers.

Lois Mailou Jones

Lois Mailou Jones (1905–98) began her career as a designer and, initially, had little interest in black themes. Once exposed to Locke and the Harlem Renaissance, however, she, too, focused on black subjects using Modernist techniques. Jones grew up in Boston and, in 1919, enrolled in the High School of Practical Arts there. She also took afternoon and weekend classes in drawing at the Boston Museum and worked as an assistant to costume designer and Rhode Island School of Design professor Grace Ripley. Ripley introduced Jones to African costumes and masks, a motif that would surface later in her art. During the summers, the Jones family vacationed at Martha's Vineyard, where Jones met sculptor Meta Fuller. Fuller encouraged her to travel abroad, explaining to her the importance of international study to a successful art career. Years later, Jones would remember this conversation and begin spending time each year in Paris and Haiti.

After her high school graduation, Jones won a four-year scholarship to attend the Boston Museum School. She majored in design and studied with the Art Nouveau graphic designer Henry Hunt Clark (1875–1962). After college, Jones received a private scholarship to spend a postgraduate year at the Designers Art School in Boston. By 1928, she had earned three diplomas and certificates and had become an accomplished textile designer.

Jones's textiles tended toward an intense Fauvist palette and **Art Nouveau** floral motifs. Sharing certain pattern elements in common with the style of the celebrated Wiener Werkstätte (Vienna Workshops) textiles, Jones's designs were bolder in both form and color and had great appeal for U.S. fabric manufacturers. Jones quickly began to sell her textile designs to prominent New York fabric houses. As a textile designer, however, Jones realized that she would never achieve the notoriety of an accomplished fine artist, because it was not the practice of fabric manufacturers to give credit to the artist who designed their fabrics. She noted, "That bothered me because I was doing all this work but not getting any recognition. And I realized I would have to think seriously about changing my profession if I were to be known by name."

In the fall of 1928, Jones made her first step toward changing her career when she became the founding chair of art at the Palmer Memorial Institute in Sedalia, North Carolina, a private black high school and junior college. While at Palmer, Jones invited Howard University Art Department chair James Herring to lecture. Impressed with Jones's program, Herring invited her to join the Howard University faculty. Jones accepted the position in 1930 and taught design at the **HBCU** for the next 50 years.

During the 1930s, Jones immersed herself in the New Negro Movement. She met Langston Hughes, Countee Cullen, Aaron Douglas, and her Howard University colleague Alain Locke, who was by now chairing the University's philosophy department. Under the influence of Locke and the Harmon Foundation, Jones began focusing on African and African-American subject matter, alternating these interests with her more personal interests in landscape, abstract design, and the human figure. In an interview shortly before her death in 1998, Jones confirmed that much of the art she produced for the Harmon exhibits was designed especially to appeal to the foundation's conceptual program:

> *[When I first studied art] I wasn't thinking . . . of any particular racial boundary—you know, limit. . . . But . . . the Harmon exhibits did sort of change you into working in the direction of black art because, to interest the people in Harlem . . . the black subject would be popular.*

Jones's *Les Fétiches* (1938) strikes a balance between black subject matter and Cubist form (Figure 6.15). The painting is a **kinetic** and dynamic composition of overlapping shapes and is one of the artist's most abstract works. Depicted within a framework of Analytic Cubism are Dan, Yaure, and Baule masks from the Ivory Coast and a striped ***kifwebe*** headdress from the

Congo. A nearly monochromatic palette, an emphasis on planar surfaces, and flattened forms indicate Jones's understanding of the relationship between Cubism and African sculpture, which she studied firsthand in Paris in 1937 while she was there on sabbatical leave from Howard.

While in Paris, in addition to Cubist abstraction, Jones painted en plein air Impressionist pictures along the Seine. She met and was mentored by Symbolist painter Émile Bernard (1868–1941) and studied at the Académie Julian. Jones's Paris works alternated between academic portraits and figures and lively Impressionist street scenes and still lifes. She painted so prolifically that by the end of her sabbatical year she had completed more than 40 pictures. When she returned the United States, Jones held a solo exhibit in Boston of her Paris street scenes, figures, and portraits. The exhibition was well received by critics, who declared her paintings to be "imbued with the qualities the Impressionists sought to achieve through painting with broad strokes [and] summary patches of color, which catch the effect of sunlight upon surfaces."

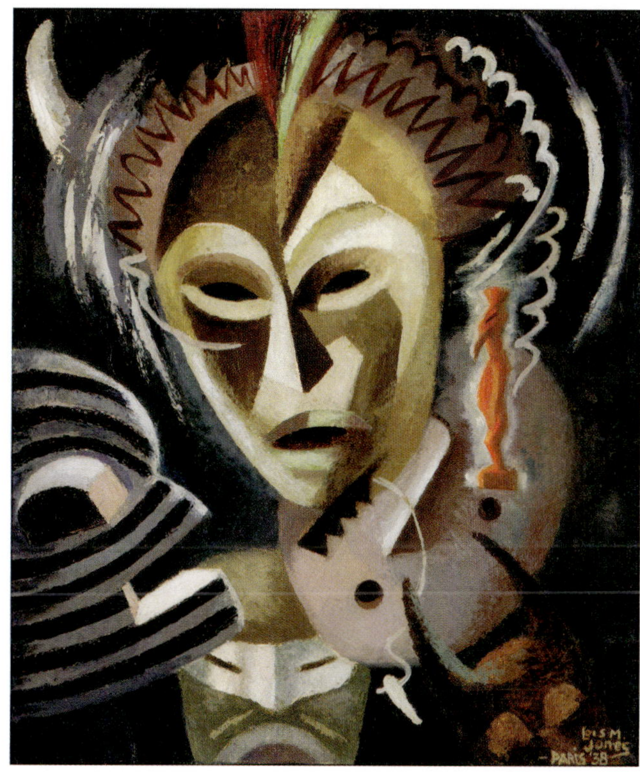

▲ **6.15** Lois Mailou Jones, *Les Fétiches*, 1938, oil on canvas, 25½″ × 21¼″.

Museum purchase made possible by N. H. Green, R. Harlam, and F. Musgrave. Photo: Smithsonian American Art Museum, Washington, D.C. / Art Resource, NY.

Jones won dozens of painting and design prizes during the 1930s and 1940s and exhibited prolifically in cities nationwide. She also continued to spend summers in France. In 1952, *Loïs Mailou Jones Peintures, 1937–1951*—one of the earliest monographs on an African-American artist—was published in Paris. In 1953, after marrying Haitian graphic designer Louis Vergniaud Pierre-Noël (d. 1982), Jones began spending time in Haiti. She taught at the Centre d'Art in Port-au-Prince and depicted Haitian genre and Vodou subjects in her art. African, Haitian, and African-American themes were integral to Jones's work throughout her 70-year career. Yet, despite her dedication to black subject matter, by the end of her life Jones admitted that she was "tired of being considered only as a black painter. I'm an American painter who happens to be black," she insisted. Like many black artists, Jones did not want her creativity to be confined to an exclusively racial experience.

PHOTOGRAPHY AND PRINTMAKING

James Van Der Zee

Photographer and musician James Van Der Zee (1886–1983) is considered the most significant photographer of the Harlem Renaissance. Between 1916 and 1945, he chronicled the private and public life of Harlem. As the official photographer for the Universal Negro Improvement Association (UNIA), he documented its Pan-Africanist founder Marcus Garvey (1887–1940) and his militia-style entourage. Van Der Zee also photographed important public occasions such as parades, assemblies, and orations.

Van Der Zee was born and raised in Lenox, Massachusetts. His parents, John and Susan E. Egberts Van Der Zee, earned a living running a bakery and laundry business and working as domestic and restaurant servers to provide for their six children. The Van Der Zee siblings were educated in local schools and were encouraged to study music and visual arts. James was an accomplished violinist and pianist by the time he reached his teens.

In the late 1890s, Van Der Zee earned a camera as wages for selling women's sachet bags door to door. With it, he took his first pictures, and his 80-year career as a photographer began. By 1900, when Van Der Zee was 14, he dropped out of school to work as a hotel waiter, while continuing over the next four years to teach himself the art of picture taking. In 1905, at age 19, Van Der Zee and his brother Walter moved to Harlem, where their father had already relocated to take a position on the kitchen staff of a Manhattan bank. Van Der Zee worked as a waiter and elevator operator in New York, where he met and married a seamstress named Kate Brown in 1907 and then traveled to Virginia to spend time with his in-laws.

In Virginia, Van Der Zee taught music and worked as a portrait photographer privately and as an events photographer for Hampton Institute. Although the Van Der Zees had planned on a lengthy stay in Virginia, they felt especially constricted by the state's segregation laws, and, by 1908, they were back in Harlem. Van Der Zee earned his living as a musician with the Wanamaker department store band and in the band of black jazz composer Fletcher Henderson (1897–1952), who later wrote numerous swing hits for Benny Goodman. In 1910, the Hahne & Company department store in Newark, New Jersey, hired him as a photographer for $5 a week. A year later, Newark portrait photographer Charles Gertz hired him as a darkroom assistant and then asked him to work as a portrait photographer. Van Der Zee offered Gertz's clients near-instantaneous photos (rare for the time), charging only 25 cents for three photos "finished while you wait."

Within a year, Van Der Zee established his own photo business in his sister Jennie's Harlem home, where she operated the Toussaint Conservatory of Art and Music. From 1912 to 1915, Van Der Zee taught music and took photographs, establishing his reputation as one of Harlem's premiere photographers. In 1916, Van Der Zee and his wife separated. They'd had a trying marriage, marred by the death of their second child, Emile, in infancy in 1908, and by arguments over Van Der Zee's business, which provided only minimally for his family. Two years later, Van Der Zee married a German-American telephone operator named Gaynella Katz Greenlee (1891–1976), who supported his photography work. Greenlee identified herself as a very fair-skinned person of African descent, to avoid any anti-miscegenation backlash. Together the two launched the Guarantee Photo Studio on the ground floor of a brownstone in a prime location next door to the Schomburg Center.

By 1928, Van Der Zee had established himself as Harlem's most sought-after photographer and could boast the area's most celebrated residents as his clients. He photographed his sitters in carefully orchestrated Victorian *tableaux vivants*, or studio sets, so as to present his sitters in the best possible light, using an array of props, from costumes to elaborately hand-painted (by Van Der Zee) backdrops. He shrewdly posed his clients, in his words, "according to their type and personality," making certain that each image portrayed the subjects as members of the wealthy elite (whether or not they actually were). In this way, Van Der Zee heeded Locke's directive to "reveal the beauty which prejudice and caricature have overlaid" by representing African Americans in the most urbane manner possible. Following his studio sessions, Van Der Zee would retouch, overprint, or hand-paint his photographs to achieve a variety of special effects and to make each portrait unique to a given client and occasion.

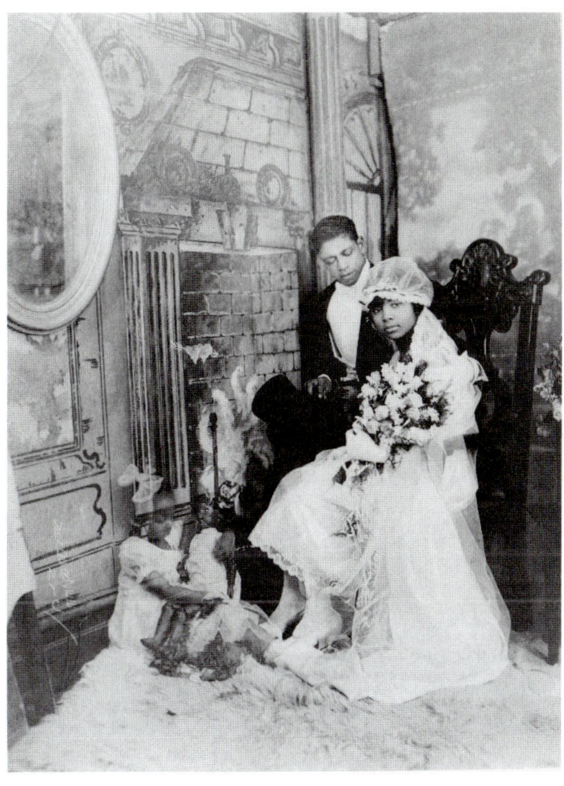

▲ **6.16** James Van Der Zee, *Future Expectations (Wedding Day)*, 1926, gelatin silver print.

Library of Congress, Prints and Photographs Division, LC-USZ62-112472. Reproduced by permission of the artist's estate.

In his 1926 studio portrait *Future Expectations (Wedding Day)*, Van Der Zee captured the image of a newlywed couple (Figure 6.16). The groom is elegantly attired in a tuxedo and holds his top hat in his hand while gazing lovingly at his wife. The bride is seated in a throne-like, elaborately carved Victorian chair. Her eyes directly engage the camera lens as she presents a vision in gossamer white tulle. Everywhere around the couple is evidence of Van Der Zee's hand-painted theatrical settings, from a faux fireplace complete with flames to fluted columns and bucolic outdoor scenery. In order to suggest the couple's happy and fruitful future, Van Der Zee double-exposed the photograph with a ghosted image of their as-yet-unconceived daughter, who sits, beribboned, at their feet holding a large black doll. The overall effect is contemplative, quiet, self-contained, and sophisticated, all hallmark Van Der Zee features.

Van Der Zee's popularity ebbed after the 1940s, as was the case with so many Harlem artists. For the next 20 years, his studio struggled financially, and he and Gaynella barely subsisted on their income. Their troubles, which reached a crisis point in the 1960s, were due in part to Harlem's economic decline, and to the fact that, by this time, most people owned their own cameras. As a result, the Van Der Zees were evicted from their studio space in the late 1960s. Fortuitously for the near-destitute couple, at just this moment a Metropolitan Museum curatorial consultant, African-American photographer Reginald McGhee, happened on Van Der Zee's Harlem storefront and "rediscovered" his work. Dozens of the artist's now-historic prints were subsequently included in the pivotal and controversial *Harlem on My Mind* exhibit (see Chapter 10), which launched Van Der Zee into the spotlight once again. He renewed work as a celebrity portrait photographer for the likes of prizefighter Muhammad Ali, actor Ossie Davis, and Neo-Expressionist artist Jean-Michel Basquiat (Chapter 13). On the day of his death, Van Der Zee missed a ceremony at Howard University, which awarded him an honorary PhD. Since his passing, the artist's reputation has continued to grow. Van Der Zee's photographs, now in collections around the world, have permanently preserved Harlem's cultural legacy.

James Latimer Allen

Another key Harlem photographer, James Latimer Allen (1907–77), was a native New Yorker. He received early formal training in the fine arts in 1923, when, at age 16, he accepted a four-year apprenticeship with a family-owned printing company, Stone-Van Dresser, where Harlem Renaissance artist Richard Nugent also apprenticed. Bolstered by his teenage exposure to the arts, in 1927 Allen opened a photo studio catering to Harlem literati as a portrait and figure photographer. That year he took his first self-portraits and was featured in his first show—*Independent Exhibition of Younger Negro Artists*, in Harlem. Other participants in the show included Motley, Nugent, and Aaron Douglas. Allen also submitted his first photographs to the Harmon competition in 1927. Although his work was not initially accepted, he persisted and won an honorable mention in 1929 and two Harmon Commission on Race Relations prizes for photographic work in 1931 and 1933. Allen operated his photography business at several West Harlem locations until 1944. During these years, he worked as an instructor at the Harlem Community Art Center (see Chapter 7) and photographed the center's classes and events. He also served as staff photographer for the Harmon Foundation, photographing works of art, artists, and exhibits. His images were featured on literally dozens of covers of *Crisis*, *Opportunity: A Journal of Negro Life*, and the black literary magazine *The Messenger*. Allen's pictures also appeared in Claude McKay's book *Harlem: Negro Metropolis*, published in 1940.

In the 1940s, Allen enlisted in the army. He was assigned to develop film for the Office of Strategic Services in Washington, D.C., where he married and decided to remain after World War II. For the rest of his life, Allen worked as a government civil servant, giving up his photographic career, evidently, to please his wife. Nevertheless, his contribution to the Harlem Renaissance, though little known today, was greatly appreciated at the time. Locke wrote of Allen: "Through the medium of the camera and with Negro subjects, [Allen] is seeking to achieve beauty. So few photographers know how to capture with the lens, the shades and tone of the Negro skin colors . . . and none make of it an art."

Unlike Van Der Zee, Allen's portraits comprised spare settings without elaborate props, relying instead on subtle indicators, such as an artist's smock or camera, to suggest the sitter's character. Allen photographed his subjects from compelling vantage points and steep angles to reveal the complexity of each personality. Figures and faces were captured against unadorned, softly focused backgrounds of mid-tones, within a shallow and intimate space reflective of 20th-century modernity rather than the 19th-century Victorianism preferred by Van Der Zee. Allen's portrait of African-American printmaker James Lesesne Wells (1902–1993) is an ideal exemplar. Shot on an angle, the composition counterbalances the artist's head, cropped in the upper-right corner, with a **Bakuba** flask from the Congo, held in Wells's hands and examined with quiet contemplation (Figure 6.17). Its multilayered iconography suggests the Lockean importance of African sculpture to the Harlem

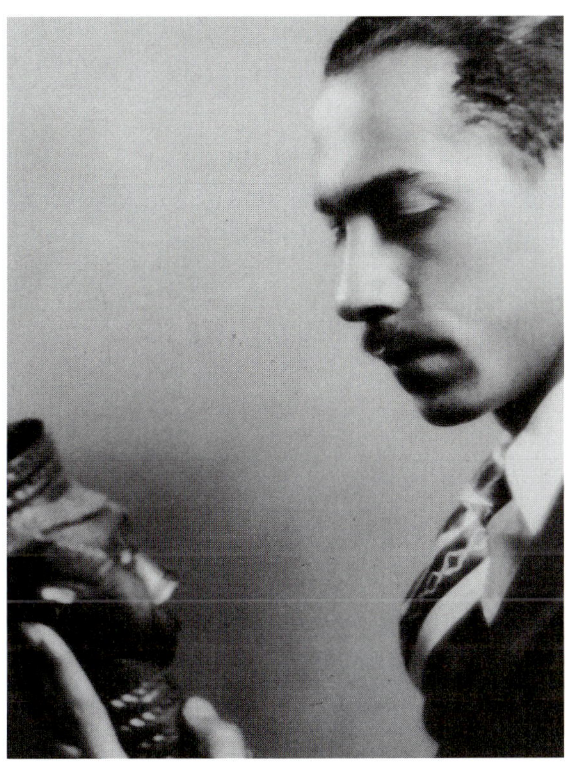

▲ **6.17** James Latimer Allen, *Portrait of James Lesesne Wells*, c. 1930, gelatin silver print, sepia toned, 8¾″ × 6″.

Alain Locke Papers / Moorland-Spingarn Research Center, Howard University.

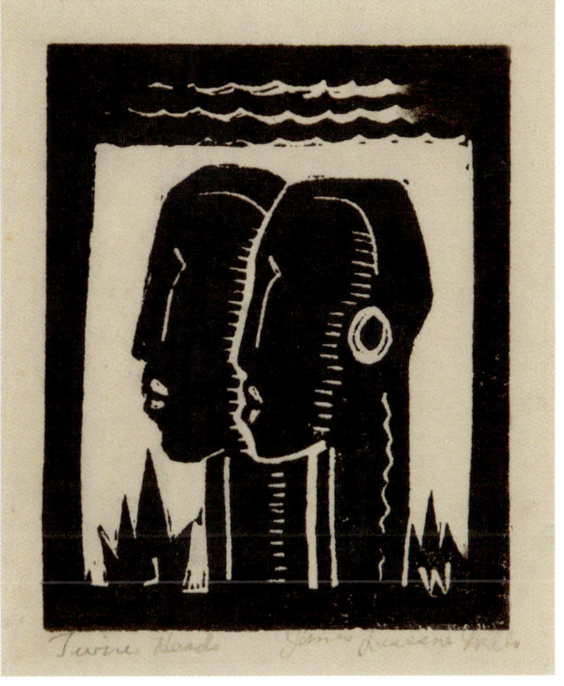

▲ **6.18** James Lesesne Wells, *Twin Heads*, c. 1929, woodcut on thin laid Japan paper, 3¾″ × 3″ (block), 6 9/16″ × 6 3/8″ (sheet).

Harvard Art Museums / Fogg Museum, Jakob Rosenberg Fund, George R. Nutter Fund, Gray Collection of Engraving Fund, and Margaret Fisher Fund, 2007.72. Photo: Imaging Department © President and Fellows of Harvard College.

Renaissance artist, the cerebral nature of the New Negro, and a dialogue between 20th-century African Americans and their cultural past.

James Lesesne Wells

Allen's portrait of James Lesesne Wells reveals much about the sitter's own aesthetics, which routinely incorporated African sculptural forms. Wells's 1930 **woodcut** *Twin Heads* offers a typical example (Figure 6.18). Boldly carved and flatly inked, the print features distinctly African silhouettes with elongated necks similar to Dogon statuary from Mali. An elegantly minimalist and abstract shorthand suggests water and flora as well as the facial features of the two heads. Wells was a visionary printmaker whose art incorporated elements of African sculpture and of German woodcut traditions. In particular, he drew from the art of Renaissance master printmaker Albrecht Durer (1471–1528) as well as from the 20th-century German Expressionists. Although primarily known for his **linoleum** and **woodblock prints**, Wells was a lifelong art educator, painter, and photographer as well.

Born in Atlanta, Georgia, Wells moved to Jacksonville, Florida, with his family as a child. In 1918, Wells graduated from Florida Normal and Industrial Institute (Florida Memorial University today), which was also the alma mater of James Weldon Johnson. He moved north to New York in 1919 to study at the National Academy of Design with Impressionist painter George Laurence Nelson (née Hirschberg; 1887–1978). Following his NAD training, Wells enrolled at Lincoln University in Pennsylvania from 1922 to 1924 and later completed his degree at Columbia University Teacher's College.

In 1929, Wells was invited by Austrian art critic and print dealer Israel Ben Neumann (1887–1961) to exhibit in an "international Modernists" show at Neumann's New York gallery alongside renowned European Modernists such as Wassily Kandinsky (1866–1944), Max Beckmann (1884–1950), Paul Klee (1879–1940), and Georges Rouault (1871–1958). That same year, Wells joined the faculty of Howard University's Art Department, where he taught sculpture and printmaking for the next 40 years, retiring in 1968. In 1931, Wells exhibited nine images of religious and African sculptural motifs in the Harmon show and won a gold award for his *Flight into Egypt*. In 1933, he won the foundation's George E. Haynes Prize for best black-and-white artwork.

During the summers, when not teaching at Howard, Wells supervised an art workshop in Harlem, mentoring young African-American artists such as Charles Alston and Georgette Seabrooke Powell (see Chapter 7), Jacob Lawrence (Chapter 8), and Palmer Hayden. In the 1940s, Wells studied for a sabbatical year in Paris at the avant-garde print workshop Atelier 17 with Abstract Expressionist Stanley William Hayter (1901–88), one of the 20th century's most noteworthy experimental printmakers. During his later career, Wells continued to teach and became active in the Civil Rights Movement and the NAACP.

King Daniel Ganaway

Working out of Chicago rather than New York, King Daniel Ganaway (1882–1944) photographed industrial Chicago within the context of Modernist abstraction. Born in Murfreesboro near Chattanooga, after migrating north to Chicago, in 1914 the artist began working as a photographer while supporting himself as a butler for a wealthy Lake Shore Drive family, and while teaching himself photography. His most celebrated photograph, *The Spirit of Transportation*, depicts the 20th Century Limited train pulling into Chicago in the winter of 1918. The artist wanted to capture the essence of urban industrialization within a shadowy context of diffused beams of natural light, dark silhouettes, and nebulous clouds of smoke (Figure 6.19). This stark and somber photograph took two years to orchestrate. The artist was even questioned by police for lurking in the station on so many occasions. Ganaway remarked to the police, "Did you ever see anything more beautiful than the way the light falls on the smoke?" A true abstractionist, Ganaway saw "designs in everything. . . . As I am riding on a streetcar, I am constantly watching the changing lights and shadows along the streets. Using the car as a frame, I compose pictures."

Described by the *Chicago Tribune* as a "masterpiece of light and shadow," *The Spirit of Transportation* first appeared in a 1921 issue of the *Chicago Defender* and quickly gained national attention for its austere beauty. Against strong competition from the country's most acclaimed photographers, including Edward Weston, Man Ray, and Paul Strand, Ganaway's photo won

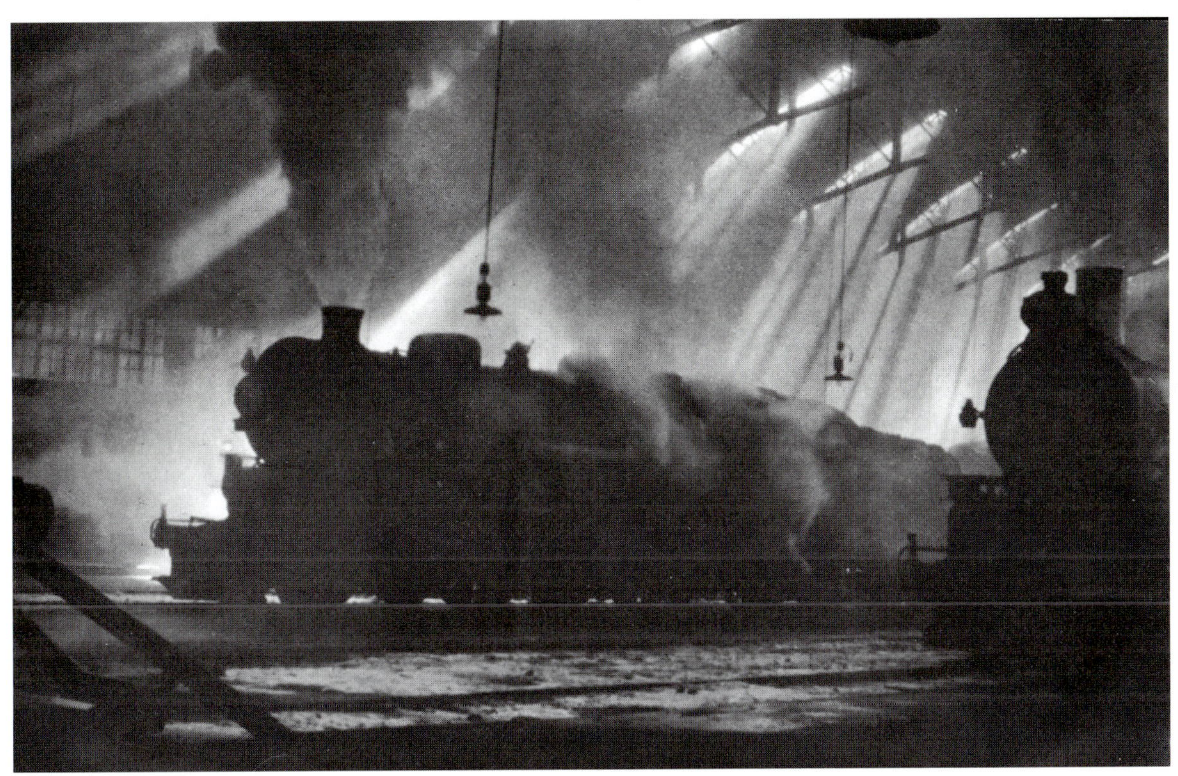

▲ **6.19** King Daniel Ganaway, *The Spirit of Transportation*, 1918.

The Estate of King Daniel Ganaway. Photo courtesy of the California State Railroad Museum.

the top prize in a national photo competition sponsored by Wanamaker's department store. Ganaway's notoriety led to a flood of freelance assignments with local newspapers and *National Geographic* magazine, among many others. He documented the ever-evolving face of Chicago's metropolitan terrain: from its marketplaces to its steel mills, lakefront, and skyline. Allen preferred cold, wintry, or rainy outdoor shots that evoked a blend of gloom and spirituality.

In 1925, Ganaway was hired by black millionaire businessman Anthony Overton (1865–1947) as the staff photographer for Overton's newly founded newspaper, the *Chicago Bee*. After sustaining himself for 10 years as a butler, Ganaway was at last able to resign from his domestic service position and earn a living exclusively as a photographer. Throughout the Harlem Renaissance, his photos were exhibited at the Chicago Art Institute, in traveling Harmon Foundation shows, and at the 1933–34 Chicago World's Fair.

Like Allen, Ganaway abandoned professional photography after the waning of the Harlem Renaissance. Ganaway turned to a life in the church. He taught for the Unity Movement, at one of their Chicago centers, and taught Bible Study at the Greater Bethel AME Church on Chicago's South Side where he was a member. By the time of his death from a cerebral hemorrhage in the mid-1940s, he was virtually unknown as a photographer but clearly beloved by his students—his headstone reads, "King Daniel Ganaway, Our Beloved Bible Teacher." The vast majority of Ganaway's photographs and negatives have never been found, an ill-fated finale to the life of a man who was once described by the editor of *Fort Dearborn Magazine* as "the greatest photographer I ever knew."

Other African-American Photographers

The early 20th century gave rise to a great many talented African-American photographers, whose images of historic black personalities have become an integral part of black visual culture. Twin photographers Morgan and Marvin Smith (1910–1993 and 1910–2003, respectively) worked together documenting Harlem's celebrities from the 1930s to the 1950s (see Figure 7.7). Washington, D.C.–based photographer Addison Scurlock (1883–1964) was the official staff photographer for Howard University and for the black elite of the nation's capital. A group of photographers associated with the Tuskegee Institute have had distinguished careers as well. Working in New York and Cleveland, C. M. (Cornelius Marion) Battey (1873–1927) chaired the Photography Department at Tuskegee, where he took now-historic photos of Du Bois, John Mercer Langston, Frederick Douglass, Paul Laurence Dunbar, and Booker T. Washington. Prentice Herman Polk (1898–1984) joined the Tuskegee faculty after studying with Battey and took portraits of Langston Hughes and Zora Neale Hurston, as well as a series of images of ex-slaves. Battey's students Ellie Lee Weems (1901–1983) and Elise Forest Harleston (1891–1970) carved out their careers in Georgia and South Carolina, respectively, the latter alongside her painter-husband Edwin Harleston; and Hooks Brothers Studio founded in 1907 by Robert B. and Henry A. Hooks, Sr., which, as one of oldest black businesses in Memphis, was still in operation until 1979.

New Orleans photographer Villard Paddio (1894?–1947) is best known for his images of jazz musicians, including visual records of the young Louis Armstrong and his family. Herbert Collins (fl. 1890–1920) photographed Boston's African-American community; Perry A. Keith (fl. 1900–10), Paul Poole (1866–1955?), and Andrew T. Kelly (1890?–1965) did the same in Atlanta. One of the earliest successful black women photographers, Florestine Perrault Collins (1895–1987), owned and operated a photo studio in New Orleans, where she sometimes "passed" for white to secure new clients. Traveling portrait and funerary photographer Richard S. Roberts (1881–1936) worked out of Columbia, South Carolina, until the mid-1930s. Richard Aloysius Twine (1896–1974) was from St. Augustine, Florida, and documented the middle-class African-American citizens of that city. Allen Edward Cole (1893–1970) photographed Cleveland's black citizens for the *Call and Post* newspaper for more than four decades beginning in the 1920s. William Edward "Eddie" Elcha (1885–1939) photographed Harlem's nightlife, theater performances, and jazz musicians for the *Saturday Evening Post*, the *Philadelphia Evening Post*, and the *New York Morning Telegraph*.

Summary

The Harlem Renaissance marked a significant turning point in African-American art. Black artists responded to Locke's call to adopt an African-inspired aesthetic and to Du Bois's call for lofty subject matter that would "uplift the race." European Modernism, itself inspired by the abstract forms of African sculpture, was embraced by African American artists, who, consequently, represented some of the most avant-garde artists in the United States. Women artists, previously marginalized, became major players at this time, thriving alongside their male counterparts. Finally, the artists of the Renaissance grappled with the pressures of patronage, which required them to walk a fine line between their personal aesthetics and the expectations of white patrons who insisted on black subject matter and folksy execution.

Key Terms

Amarna: refers to art produced during the 14th century B.C.E. under the direction of the Eighteenth Dynasty Egyptian pharaoh Akhenaten and his wife Nefertiti

American Renaissance: in visual art and architecture, the period from 1876 to 1917, when American artists associated themselves with the achievements of the 15th-century Italian Renaissance masters

Analytic Cubism: the first stage of Cubist painting, from 1909 to 1912, characterized by a monochromatic palette and highly abstracted compositions

Art Deco: an architecture and design style of the 1920s and 1930s characterized by geometric motifs

Art Nouveau: a late 19th-century French architecture and design movement characterized by floral and vine motifs and curving linear forms

Ashcan School: an art movement characterized by scenes of urban poverty and the working class

Bakuba: refers to people of the Kasai River region in the Democratic Republic of the Congo

bas-relief: also known as low relief, a sculpture composed of figures that project only slightly from a flat surface

Cézannesque: in the style of French Post-Impressionist founder Paul Cézanne (1839–1906)

Cubism: an early 20th-century European abstract art movement practiced most notably by Pablo Picasso and Georges Braque that depicted objects and space from multiple vantage points at once

cultural salon: an event at which artists, intellectuals, and literati gather to discuss issues of culture

diorama: a scenic representation composed of three-dimensional figures and a two-dimensional background

Expressionism: an early 20th-century European art movement characterized by distorted figural forms, vivid colors, and emotive content

Fauvism: an early 20th-century French art movement characterized by vivid and clashing colors

fresco: a painting made with powdered pigment on wet plaster

frieze: an extended horizontal relief sculpture or painting usually situated high on a wall

Georgian Revival: an early 19th century style of architecture that incorporates the Greek architectural orders

Great Migration: the migration of more than 1.5 million African Americans from the rural South to the urban North, chiefly between 1910 and 1930

HBCU: acronym for Historically Black Colleges and Universities

Hoosier group: late 19th- and early 20th-century Indiana Impressionist artists

Indigenist Movement: a Haitian literary and visual arts movement from the late 1920s to the mid-1940s during which artists focused on uplifting portrayals of the Haitian poor rather than on the elite

Italianate style: a style of Neoclassical architecture popular in the second half of the 19th century characterized by a similarity to Italian Renaissance villas

kifwebe: the Songye (Democratic Republic of the Congo) word for a mask representing spirits who support social order

kinetic: in art, refers to moving sculptures

linoleum print: a printed image created by carving an image into a linoleum sheet and then inking it, overlaying it with paper, and running it through a printing press

NAACP: the National Association for the Advancement of Colored People; a civil rights organization founded in 1909

Neo-Impressionism: a painting style of the 1880s wherein compositions were created using small touches from the tip of a paintbrush to create a mosaic effect; sometimes referred to as pointillism

Pan-African: refers to a philosophy that promotes international collaboration among people of African descent

papier collé: paper collage

patina: the surface color or appearance of a sculpture

Post-Impressionism: a French painting movement of the 1880s and 1890s dedicated to improving on Impressionism by adding geometric structure, arbitrary color, and emotional content

primitivism: a style of art that mimics the art of children or of untrained artists

secco: a fresco mural technique in which egg and water are added to powdered pigment before it is applied to the wet plaster wall

Social Realism: a style of art popularized in 1930s and characterized by figurative representations that extol the working class or promote a socialist agenda

Symbolist: a literary and visual art movement of late 19th-century Europe characterized by veiled symbols, mythology, fantasy, and macabre subject matter

Synthetic Cubism: the second phase of Cubism, practiced after 1912, which incorporated elements of collage and flatly painted areas of color

woodblock print: see woodcut

woodcut: a print created by carving an image into a block of wood and then inking the block, overlaying it with paper, and running it through a printing press

Questions for Further Study and Discussion

1. Research one of the photographers mentioned in the section at the end of the chapter, "Other African-American Photographers."
2. What was the Haitian Indigenist Movement? What role did it play in the art of this period?
3. What was the Great Migration and what circumstance prompted it? How did it impact the creation of African-American art?
4. Read, summarize, and critically review one or more essays in the March 1925 issue of *Survey Graphic* magazine. Why was this essay so important to the artists of the time?
5. Discuss the pros and cons of white patronage of Harlem Renaissance artists.
6. What was the significance of the Harmon Foundation to the Harlem Renaissance?
7. Palmer Hayden was criticized for his caricatured portrayals of black people, which catered to white patrons. Debate whether or not an African-American artist has an obligation to depict only positive black imagery.
8. Research others of the period, such as artists Allan Freelon (1895–1960), Laura Wheeler Waring (1887–1948), Richard Bruce Nugent (1906–1986), Edward Harleston (1882–1964), John Wesley Hardrick (1891–1968), James Porter (1935–2005), and architect John Louis Wilson, Jr. (1899–1989). How does their work compare with that of the artists studied in this chapter?
9. Research the career of philosopher Alain Locke.

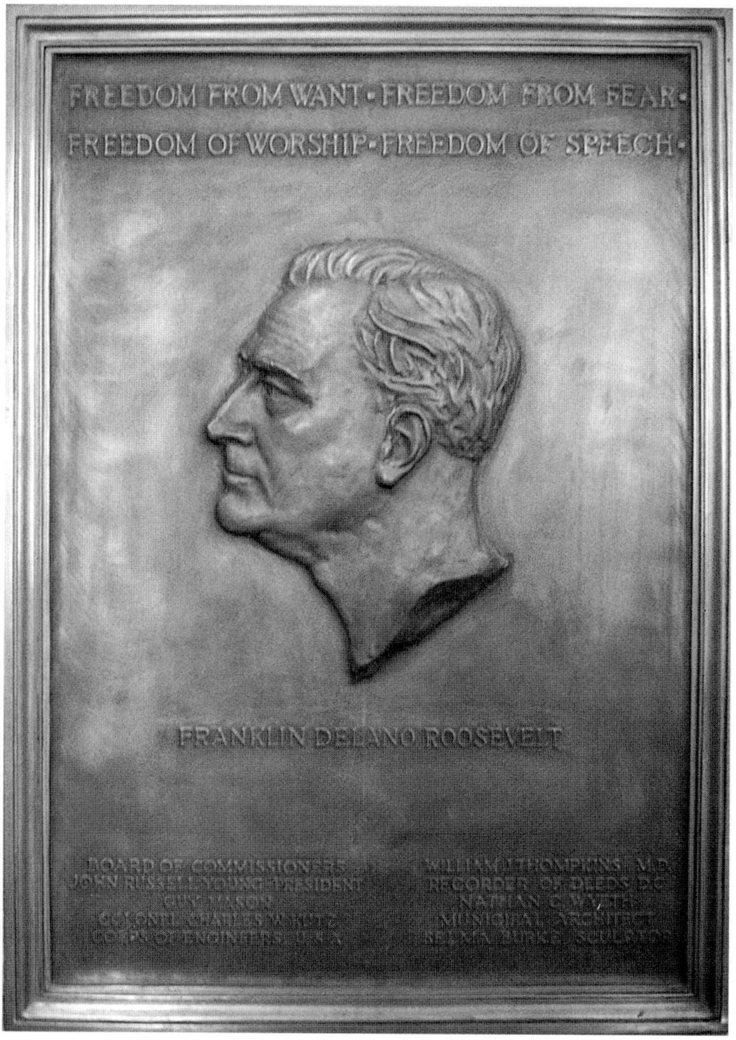

FREEDOM FROM WANT • FREEDOM FROM FEAR •
FREEDOM OF WORSHIP • FREEDOM OF SPEECH •

FRANKLIN DELANO ROOSEVELT

SOCIAL REALISM

7

Social Realism chronologically overlapped the latter years of the Harlem Renaissance and remained a popular artistic genre into the 1940s. Whereas private Harlem Renaissance patrons preferred black subject matter and eclectic styles of art, the major patron of Social Realism—the U.S. government—favored **illusionistic** imagery and sociopolitical content. The shift from private to public patronage in the 1930s was a direct response to the Great Depression. Brought on by the 1929 Stock Market Crash, the Depression signified a slow death for the Harlem Renaissance. More than ten thousand banks failed, and many bank depositors lost their life savings. Unemployment rose from 3 percent to 25 percent nationwide; the rate was double that in the African-American community. Many artists' careers suffered or ended completely by the 1940s.

Those artists who survived the Depression did so in large part thanks to President Franklin D. Roosevelt's (1882–1945) New Deal. A sweeping, government-sponsored financial recovery program, the New Deal comprised a dozen major bailout and welfare programs, including the Works Progress Administration (WPA), which employed millions of citizens in road construction, park maintenance, building projects, and educational programs. Progressive in its outreach, the WPA also hired musicians, writers, actors, and, significantly, visual artists through its Federal Art Project.

THE WPA FEDERAL ART PROJECT

After several attempts to establish programs to support unemployed workers, in 1935 President Roosevelt created the WPA. Its support of the arts extended to the Federal Music Project (FMP), the Federal Theatre Project (FTP), and the Federal Writer's Project (FWP) and, most significantly for visual artists, to the Federal Art Project (FAP). Art produced under these programs was expected to serve the community or specific governmental agendas, such as the promotion of the President's New Deal programs, American history, and the working class.

Under the directorship of curator and arts administrator Holger Cahill (1887–1960), the FAP employed painters, sculptors, graphic designers, and art teachers. It funded 100 community art centers in 22 states. Among these were several key centers in black communities, including Cleveland (Karamu House), Detroit (Heritage House), Chicago (South Side Community Art Center), and New York (Harlem Art Workshop and Harlem Community Art Center). Between 1935 and 1943, the FAP supplied some 10,000 artists with

◀ Selma Burke, *Franklin Delano Roosevelt*, 1945, bronze, 3′6″ × 2′6″. Recorder of Deeds Building, Washington, D.C.

Photo © Lisa Farrington.

salaries, training, and supplies. During the eight years of its existence, the WPA spent $85 million in support of the arts and refocused sponsorship away from private patrons toward the public sphere. It also introduced incalculable numbers of Americans to the fine arts and permanently mainstreamed fine arts into American culture. More importantly, the WPA rescued hundreds of African-American artists from destitution, largely due to its mandate against discrimination. An estimated 15 percent of the WPA artists were African-American, which was higher than the percentage of the African-American population in the country at the time.

SOCIAL REALIST MURALS

Public murals were especially favored by the WPA-FAP because they had the capacity to engage large numbers of viewers while also beautifying public buildings. The form and content of WPA murals were greatly influenced by the Social Realist artists of Mexico, who had come of age in the 1920s, after the Mexican revolution. Known as *los tres grandes* (the three greats), Jose Clements Orozco (1883–1949), Diego Rivera (1886–1957), and David Alfaro Siqueiros (1896–1974) were among the most significant of these artists. During the 1930s, all three were commissioned to paint the walls of a number of American buildings, including the San Francisco Stock Exchange, the Detroit and San Francisco Art Institutes, the New School for Social Research, and New York's Rockefeller Center (where Rivera's mural was destroyed almost as soon as it was completed due to its perceived communist content). Rivera and Orozco frequented Harlem and mentored African-American artists there. The stylistic approach of the Mexican muralists took the form of figurative monumentality: imagery that portrayed the working class as heroic; depicted revolutionary political history as epic; and promoted gender, racial, and economic equality.

Charles Alston and the Harlem Hospital Murals

After languishing in a state of disrepair for decades, in 2012, as part of a $325 million building project, a series of WPA-FAP murals were restored and unveiled in Harlem Hospital's new patient pavilion, dubbed the Mural Building (Figure 7.1). Commissioned in 1936 by the FAP, the Harlem Hospital murals were the first major WPA mural project assigned to an African-American artists' collective. Now the central feature of the Hospital Center, the installation has recently been augmented to include a 12,000-square-foot glass façade on which sections of the original murals have been digitally etched and backlit for dramatic visual effect. Visible from Lenox and 136th Streets, where the hospital stands across from the Schomburg Center, the murals are an historic record of the achievements of African-American WPA-FAP artists.

Seven senior artists and half a dozen assistants were employed to complete this multipart mural project. Under the direction of Charles Alston (1907–77), participating artists included Elba Lightfoot (1910–89), Sara Murrell (fl. 1930s), Selma Day (fl. 1933–51), Georgette Seabrooke Powell (discussed later in this chapter), Vertis Hayes (discussed later in this chapter), and

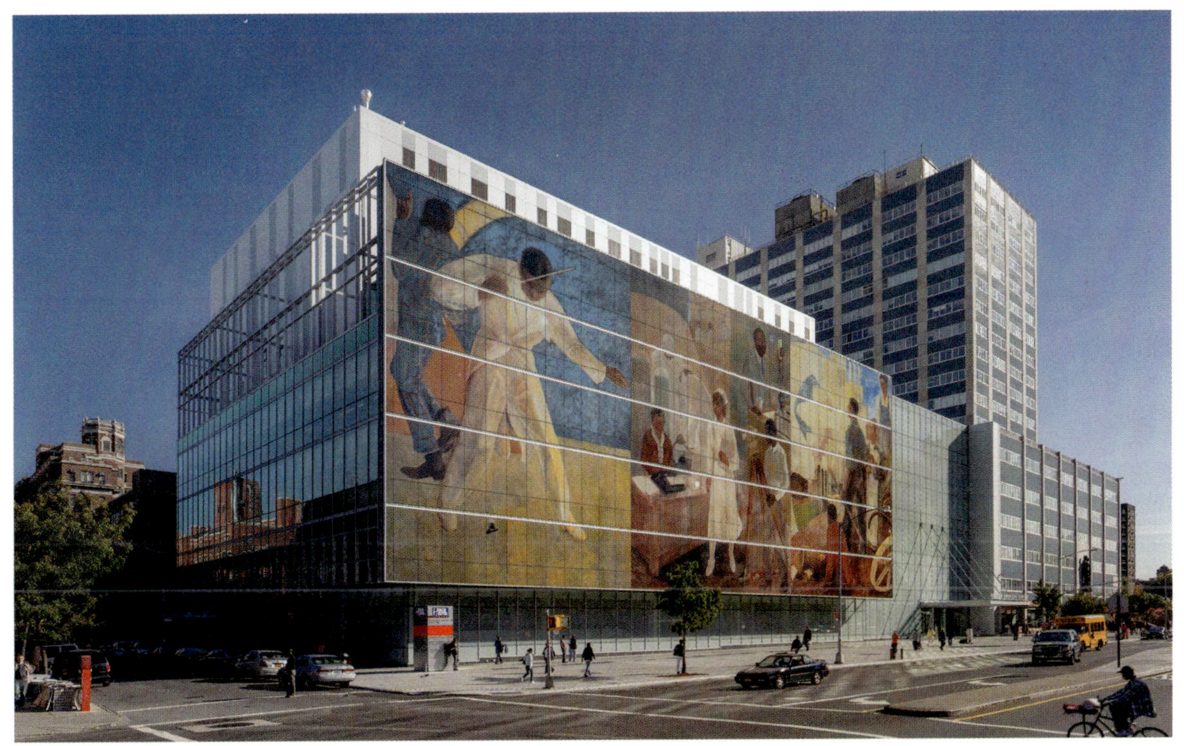

▲ 7.1 Vertis Hayes murals and HOK Global Design glass façade, *The Pursuit of Happiness*, original mural 1937, glass façade 2012, 12,000 sq. ft. glass façade based on original oil on canvas murals, original murals: 8 panels, 735 sq. ft. Building design by HOK Vertis Hayes murals.

Photo © Paul Warchol, courtesy of HOK.

Sicilian fresco painter Alfred Crimi (1900–94). They were ably assisted by apprentice artists Jacob Lawrence, Gwendolyn Knight (who later married Lawrence; see Chapter 8), Beauford Delaney (see Chapter 9), Louis O. Vaughn (1910–37), and photographer Morgan Smith (see Chapter 6), among others. Cooperative efforts and the participation of women seen in the Harlem Hospital mural project were characteristic of the Social Realist Movement. This Harlem assignment was Alston's first mural commission. Nevertheless, his educational credentials—a BFA and MA from Columbia University—and his familiarity with the murals of Aaron Douglas (see Chapter 6) and the work of the Mexican Muralists (in particular, Rivera, whom Alston had met while Rivera was painting the Rockefeller Center mural in 1934) made him an ideal candidate to administer the hospital project.

Alston grew up in Charlotte, North Carolina, with an older brother, Wendell, who was a neophyte artist and Alston's first inspiration to pursue the arts. Alston's father, Rev. Primus Alston, was a respected social activist who died in 1910 when the artist was three years old. His mother, Anna, remarried in 1913 to Harry Bearden, the father of artist Romare Bearden (see Chapter 8). Not only would the stepbrothers share a lifelong passion for art, but they would both become significant 20th-century African-American artists.

In 1915, the Alston-Bearden family moved to Harlem. Alston showed artistic talent as early as his elementary school years and served as art editor of his high school newspaper. He also took weekend classes at the National Academy of Design (NAD). He earned a bachelor's degree in fine arts at Columbia University and, in 1931, a master's degree in education at Columbia's Teachers College. After college, Alston rented space in a popular artists'

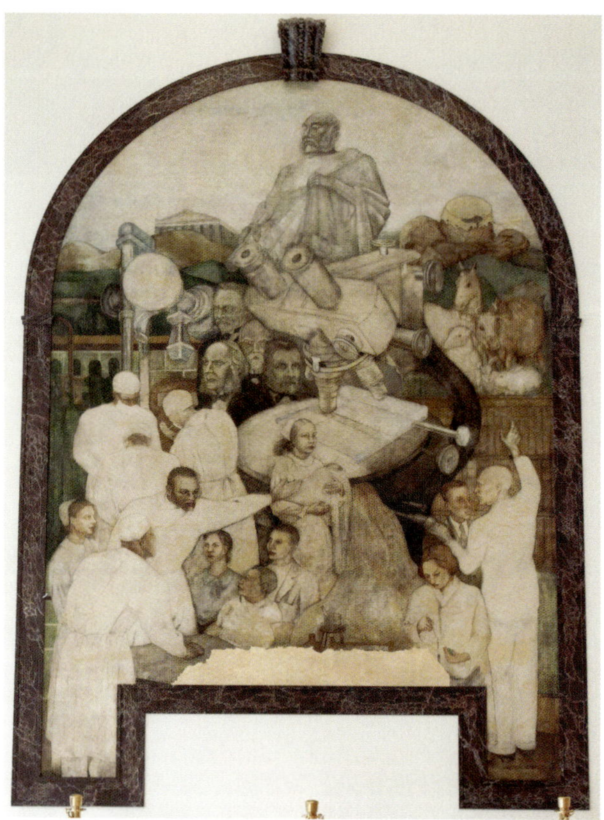

▲ **7.2** Charles Alston, *Modern Medicine*, 1936, oil on canvas, 17′ × 6′.

Collection of Harlem Hospital Center of the New York City Health and Hospitals Corporation. Photo: Meredith Keffer / Oxford University Press.

studio building at 306 West 141st Street, where he and artists Henry Bannarn (1910–65) and Augusta Savage (discussed later in this chapter) managed the Harlem Art Workshop. One of the workshop's students there was Jacob Lawrence, who, at age 19, became Alston's apprentice on the Harlem Hospital murals, and who would soon become one of the most well-known African-American artists of the 20th century.

Alston's personal contribution to the Harlem mural sequence included two paintings on the history of black medicine from traditional African healers to modern doctors and surgeons. Flanking the entrance to the hospital's women's pavilion, the first mural is entitled *Magic in Medicine* and features a Fang (Gabon) **reliquary sculpture** towering over portrayals of homeopathic and missionary healers. The second panel, *Modern Medicine*, includes a racially integrated group of scientists, doctors, and nurses in several visually dynamic vignettes (Figure 7.2). Presiding over the composition is a classical Greek temple and a soaring image of Hippocrates (c. 460–c. 370 B.C.E.), the ancient Greek "father of Western medicine," clad in Grecian robes and presented as a classical marble sculpture. Below Hippocrates, several portrait busts of men of modern science and medicine are positioned near an oversized microscope. Additional vignettes include doctors conferring in a library setting, a woman scientist conducting research in a laboratory, a black doctor overseeing a medical team, and surgeons at work in an operating room. In a self-referential gesture, Alston incorporated a portrait of a Harlem hospital surgical intern, Myra A. Logan (1908–77), as a neonatal nurse. She would soon become the artist's wife and, in 1943, the first woman to perform open-heart surgery. Also depicted is Harlem Hospital's first black physician, Dr. Louis T. Wright (1891–1952), who helped to support the mural project.

Other murals at the hospital include a series of eight panels that depicted the transition by blacks from life in Africa to slavery in the southern United States and the evolution of African Americans from rural southern farmworkers to northern urbanites during the Great Migration. Among these is included the 1937 *Pursuit of Happiness*, by Vertis Hayes (1911–2000) (Figure 7.1). Hayes's colorful panels, which now grace the expansive façade of the new Harlem Hospital, pay homage to African Americans in all walks of professional life, with depictions of a college graduate, an office worker, a preacher, an engineer, an athlete, a mother and child, medical professionals, laborers, artists, dancers, and musicians.

Hayes learned the art of mural making in 1934 and 1935 from French-born painter Louis Henri Jean Charlot (1898–1979), a protégé of Rivera who lived in Mexico in the 1920s. Charlot also worked for the FAP in New York in 1934, when he oversaw the creation of Rivera-esque murals at Straubenmuller Textile High School in Chelsea (today's Bayard Rustin Educational Complex). Hayes contributed to the Straubenmuller project a panel entitled *Decoration*. Hayes also painted a (no longer extant) mural for the lobby of what is today Parsons School of Design. A key mural that has survived the years is Hayes's narrative of the achievements of George Washington Carver (1942), which is installed at the social science building of Jackson State University in Mississippi.

Hayes came to New York from Atlanta, Georgia, during the 1930s but spent much of his career in the South and West. For a decade after completion of the Harlem Hospital project, he exhibited widely and taught art at Lemoyne College (now Lemoyne-Owen), an HBCU in Memphis, Tennessee. He spearheaded an FAP art center and gallery there and became its director in 1938. By 1947, Hayes had developed the center into a full-fledged art department that he chaired. From 1947 to 1952, Hayes directed a private art school—the Hayes Academy of Art—and he offered art training to veterans at the local VA hospital. In 1952, after his marriage to Florence T. Alexandrowicz and the birth of his son and namesake (b. 1950), the artist moved to California, where he remained for the rest of his life. He taught art at Cal State and Immaculate Heart College in Los Angeles. In 1969, he became a founding member of the Black Academy of Arts and Letters, and in 1971, he received an honorary doctorate from the Boston Art Institute.

Georgette Seabrooke Powell's (1916–2011) Harlem Hospital mural, *Recreation in Harlem* (presently being restored), visually narrated the day-to-day activities of Harlem's citizens (Figure 7.3). A native of Charleston, South Carolina, Seabrooke Powell migrated to New York in 1920 and subsequently worked on mural projects at both Harlem Hospital and Queens General Hospital. Nearly 20 feet in length, *Recreation in Harlem* depicts several groups: a choir performing in a small amphitheater; two women conversing through an open apartment window; a domestic scene including four women, an infant, and a child; a couple dancing; a reveler; a postman; and two children wrestling. At the time of the Harlem Hospital project, Seabrooke Powell was an art student at Cooper Union, where she had just won the school's painting prize for her depiction of a lively church service. She later studied theater design at Fordham University, the influence of which can be seen in the stage-like construction of *Recreation in Harlem*.

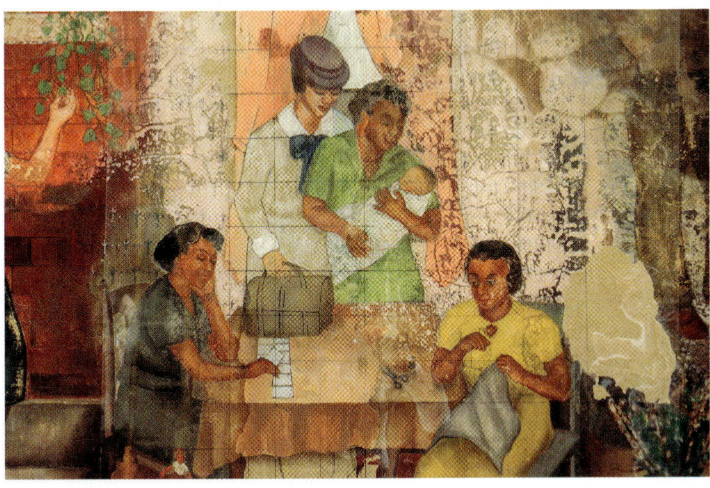

▼ **7.3** Georgette Seabrooke Powell, with project assistance provided by Louis Vaughn and Beauford Delaney, *Recreation in Harlem* (detail), 1936, oil, 5′ × 19.5′.

The Harlem Hospital Center of the New York City Health and Hospitals Corporation. Photo: Karsten Moran / The New York Times / Redux.

Because so much of the content of the Harlem murals was dedicated to black subject matter, the work was controversial at the time. Despite the fact that the FAP approved the preliminary sketches submitted by Alston and his colleagues, hospital officials rejected four of the mural **cartoons** for their overt African and African-American foci. They expressed concerns that their institution would become known as a "colored hospital." In response, an interracial protest against the hospital's censorship was launched by the Harlem Artists Guild, chaired at the time by Aaron Douglas, and by the Artists Union. Public pickets were launched by white and black protestors, and several articles on the controversy appeared in the local press. Under public pressure, the hospital was compelled to reverse its decision. Thanks to the collective efforts of the Artists Union and the Harlem Artists Guild, the Harlem Hospital murals were soon hailed as among the finest produced in New York during the 1930s. The Museum of Modern Art included preparatory sketches for the murals in its 1936 exhibit *New Horizons in American Art*.

Alston continued his own outstanding career after the completion of the Harlem commission. From 1938 to 1940, supported by a grant from the Rosenwald Fund, Alston toured the southern United States with the Farm Security Administration (FSA) to document farmworkers and the rural poor in photographs, which served as resources for the artist's long-running *Family Series* of paintings of the black working class. Alston also worked as an illustrator for mainstream magazines such as *Fortune* and the *New Yorker*, as a portrait sketch artist for the Office of War Information (which published his drawings in hundreds of national black newspapers), and as a record album cover designer for Duke Ellington and others. Alston completed additional murals between 1949 and 1964 for the American Museum of Natural History, several New York City schools, and the New York family courthouse in the Bronx. In collaboration with artist Hale Woodruff, Alston likewise painted *The Negro in California History* for the Golden State Mutual Company (see Figure 7.4).

Hale Woodruff and the Golden State Mutual Murals

Hale Aspacio Woodruff (1900–80) is best known for his murals, painted in a distinctive **American Regionalist** style. He was born in 1900 in Cairo, Illinois, to Augusta and George Woodruff. Following his father's death when

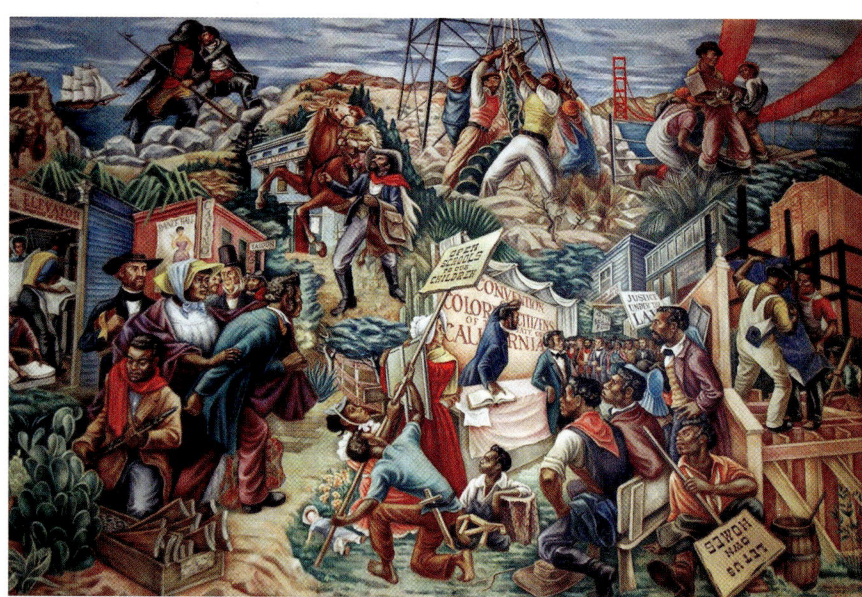

▶ **7.4** Hale Woodruff, *The Negro in California History: Settlement and Development Panel 2*, 1949, oil on canvas, 9′3¼″ × 16′5″. Installed at the Golden State Mutual Life Insurance Company building, Los Angeles, CA.

he was a child, Woodruff moved with his mother to Nashville, Tennessee. At Nashville's Pearl High School, Woodruff was a cartoonist for the school newspaper; he also illustrated menus for a restaurant where he worked. After high school, Woodruff traveled to Indianapolis in search of a better-paying job. He worked for two years as a porter and maintenance man at local hotels and restaurants, at the YMCA where he lived, and as a freelance illustrator for the *Indianapolis Freeman* newspaper to raise the money to enroll at the Herron Art Institute in 1920.

At Herron, Woodruff studied with Hoosier Impressionist William Forsyth (1854–1935), met William E. Scott (see Chapter 6), and learned about his travels in France and of Henry Tanner's life there (see Chapter 5). Woodruff longed to follow the paths of Tanner and Scott to Europe, but financial hardship temporarily prevented this. By 1924, Woodruff had depleted his savings and had to leave Herron. However, learning of the Harmon competitions, he submitted five paintings in 1926 and won a second-prize bronze medal for his landscapes and figure paintings. Woodruff's work was also included in the 1927 Hoosier exhibit in Chicago. Among Woodruff's patrons were German art and book dealer Herman P. Lieber (1873–1939), who exhibited Woodruff's paintings to help him raise money, and wealthy banker and philanthropist Otto H. Kahn (1867–1934), who learned of Woodruff's talent from his connections with the local NAACP.

By 1927, Woodruff had accumulated enough money to travel to Paris. There he met Paris's "Negro Colony" of African-American literati and entertainers, including McKay, Cullen, Locke, Hayden, and Savage. He also traveled to Étaples to meet Tanner, who reviewed his portfolio and advised him on how to improve his work. Woodruff studied at the Académie Scandinave and at the Académie Moderne, which was run by Cubist painters Fernand Léger (1881–1955) and Amedee Ozenfant (1886–1966). For a year from 1928 to 1929, the *Indianapolis Star* printed articles and accompanying illustrations by Woodruff chronicling his experiences in France. Woodruff won another Harmon Award in 1929.

In 1931, Woodruff joined the faculty at Atlanta University (today Clark-Atlanta) and taught there for 15 years. He established the university's art program and became one of the first African-American fine arts professors in Georgia. He also founded the Atlanta University Art Annuals (1942–70), which essentially replaced the Harmon exhibits (which were discontinued in 1933) as the premier exhibition venue for African-American artists. In addition, he taught and mentored young African-American artists such as Wilmer Jennings (1910–90), who, after graduating from college in Atlanta, created woodcuts for the WPA in Rhode Island and became a well-established jewelry maker.

In the 1930s, Woodruff's style shifted from Post-Impressionism to Social Realism and "American scene painting," or Regionalism. A form of Social Realism, Regionalism similarly embodied an interest in the everyday American experience. However, where Social Realism focused on political themes and the celebration of the working class, often in an urban or industrial setting, Regionalist subject matter tended toward scenes of rural and small-town America, without explicit sociopolitical commentary. Unlike most

Regionalists, however, Woodruff's 1930s paintings and woodcuts of bleak and unbridled Georgia landscapes, African-American migrant workers, cotton farmers, "Negro cabins," rural housing developments, and scenes of southern lynchings carried with them a distinctive tone of social criticism. In 1935, Woodruff participated in a show at Arthur Newton Galleries in New York on the subject of lynching. Through this exhibit he came into contact with Regionalist painter Thomas Hart Benton (1889–1975) and Ashcan School artist Reginald Marsh (1898–1954), who exhibited with him, shoring up his interests in both rural and gritty urban subject matter.

Woodruff shared the goals of the Mexican Muralists: to make art accessible to the public, outside of the rarefied museum environment to which so few had access at the time; and to communicate the achievements and history of minorities and the poor through art. In particular, Woodruff admired the work of Rivera, with whom he studied fresco painting in Mexico in 1936. After his return, Woodruff completed several major mural projects between 1938 and 1952, including the 1949 *Negro in California History* for the Golden State Mutual Life Insurance Company in Los Angeles (Figure 7.4). The mural consists of two panels: *Exploration and Colonization* by Alston and *Settlement and Development* by Woodruff. Together, they portray an epic account of the state's evolution from the 16th to 20th centuries that teems with dramatic and colorful figures acting out the history of California. Woodruff's panoramic vision depicts African Americans as the rank and file of a labor force that greatly contributed to the modernization of the state by constructing its great bridges, buildings, and towers. He interposes within this motif the racial oppression that black Californians faced while performing this work.

In 2009, the home of the Alston-Woodruff murals, the Golden State Mutual Company building in Los Angeles, was forced to close its doors. At the time, there was concern that state regulators would compel the sale of the murals to settle the company's debts (the Smithsonian briefly offered to purchase them), but a public outcry that removal of the murals would be tantamount to their destruction (because they were designed as **site-specific** pieces) resulted in the 2011 decision to leave the paintings in situ. That same year, the murals and the building were officially declared Historic-Cultural monuments by the Los Angeles City Council.

AVANT-GARDE ARCHITECTURE

The Golden State Mutual building itself is as historically significant as the murals. It was designed by African-American architect Paul R. Williams (1894–1980) in 1949 (Figure 7.5). Striking in its modern simplicity, cubic clarity, lack of decoration, and emphasis on verticals and horizontals, the structure epitomizes the **International Style** of architecture from which its forms derive. Although a number of talented African-American architects, such as Howard University leading light Albert Cassell (1895–1969), were also active during this period, Williams stands out as a vanguard of cutting-edge Modernism. He was commissioned to design the building by the

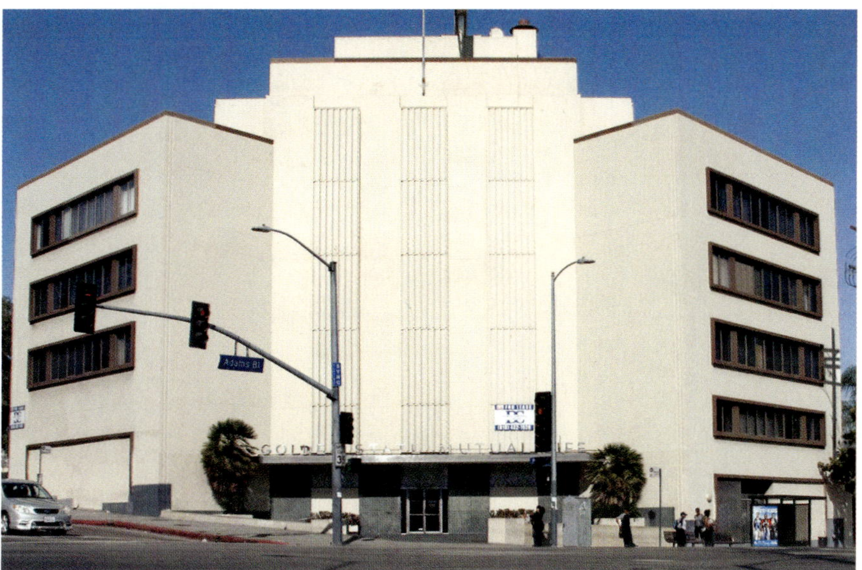

◀ **7.5** Paul R. Williams, *Golden State Mutual Life Insurance Building*, 1949. West Adams Boulevard, Los Angeles, CA.

Photo: Downtowngal, licensed under the Creative Commons Attribution-Share Alike 3.0 Unported License.

founding owners of the company, which was then the largest black-owned business in the West. The entire building project was conceived as an opportunity to employ African Americans in all aspects of the design and construction and in the insurance business itself. At a time when African Americans were routinely denied insurance policies, Golden State filled this need, insuring tens of thousands of minority citizens and employing hundreds.

In addition to serving as the building's architect, Williams sat on a three-person committee that chose the subject matter of the murals and selected Alston and Woodruff to render them. An ideal choice for the building project, Williams became the first certified African American architect in the state of California in 1921 and, two years later, the first African American member of the AIA (American Institute of Architects). His Los Angeles area designs alone include such landmark buildings as the Hollywood and South Central YMCAs (1925–27), several UCLA campus buildings (1926–58), Chasen's Restaurant (1936), the LA County Courthouse (1958), the Polo Lounge at the Beverly Hills Hotel (1959), and the futuristic LAX "Theme" Building (with William Pereira, Charles Luckman, and Welton Becket, in 1961). Globally, Williams's projects reach as far at the UN building in Paris (1953) and hotels, hospitals, and country clubs in Columbia and Ecuador (1945–55).

A domestic architect as well, Williams designed more than 2,000 private homes for a client list that reads like a Hollywood who's who. In the 1920s and 1930s especially, many of those who hired Williams did so based solely on the buildings and homes he had already designed; they were more than a little surprised when they actually met the architect and found him to be an African American. Although some potential clients rejected Williams after meeting him, many were too impressed by his designs to do so. Their commissions carried the architect through the difficult years of the Depression.

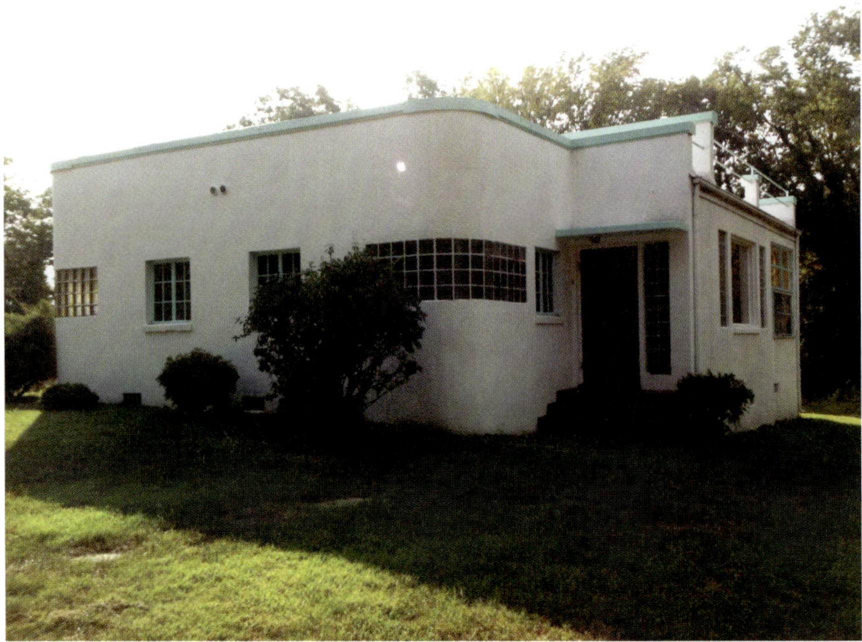

▶ **7.6** Amaza Lee Meredith, architect, *Azurest South*, 1939. 2900 Boisseau Street, Ettrick, VA.

Photographed for Cinnamon Traveler Heritage Trust by © Grace Lynis Dubinson 2010. Reproduced with the permission of the photographer.

During World War II, Williams served as a navy architect and designed bases in Long Beach, San Diego, and Los Alamitos. He documented his modern home designs in two books, *The Small House of Tomorrow* (1945) and *New Homes for Today* (1957). His forte was adapting traditional motifs within a modern context.

Also in the 1930s, a little-known domestic structure dubbed "Azurest South" was designed by Virginia native Amaza Lee Meredith (1895–1984). One of a rare few women architects working at the time, Meredith designed and built Azurest South near the campus of Virginia Normal and Industrial Institute (today Virginia State College) in the style of the German **Bauhaus** (Figure 7.6). Founded by Walter Gropius (1883–1969), the Bauhaus thrived in Weimar, Dessau, and Berlin from 1919 to 1933, when the Nazis permanently closed the school. Afterward, in 1937, Gropius relocated to the United States to teach at Harvard. Meredith's Azurest South, with its flat roof, glass brick windows, and lack of exterior decoration, is closely aligned with the Bauhaus belief that "form follows function." It shares its key features with Gropius's own Bauhaus home that he built in Lincoln, Massachusetts, in 1937.

Meredith grew up in Virginia and graduated valedictorian from Virginia Normal in 1922, after which she obtained advanced degrees at Columbia. She returned to her alma mater in 1935 to found the art department there, which she headed for the next quarter century. She designed Azurest South for herself and her life partner, Dr. Edna Meade Colson, who was director of education at the school. Meredith designed a number of other homes, including one in the modernist Prairie style of American architect Frank Lloyd Wright (1867–1959) for the historic black community of Azurest in Sag Harbor, New York. An enclave in East Hampton, Azurest was founded by Meredith and a group of her wealthy family and friends in 1947. Although not as prolific as numerous other black architects practicing in the 1930s, Meredith is distinguished as one of very few, along with Williams, who dispensed with past architectural styles and created truly modern architecture. Azurest South is today on the National Register of Historic Places and is considered among one of the most avant-garde domestic structures of its time.

AUGUSTA SAVAGE, THE HARLEM ART CENTERS, AND THE HARLEM ARTISTS GUILD

Sculptor Augusta Savage (1892–1962) was one of the most politically influential artists of the 1930s. She was born the seventh of fourteen children to Cornelia (a laundress) and Edward Fells (a cabinetmaker, fisherman, and farmworker) in Green Cove Springs, Florida. She began sculpting clay figures from a young age, despite the initial resistance of her father. At age 15, while attending high school, she married John T. Moore and, the following year, gave birth to her only child, Irene Connie Moore. When her first husband died soon after the birth of their child, in 1915 Savage married a second time to carpenter James Savage. Throughout this period, Savage continued to sculpt small figures of animals and she persuaded former West Palm Beach mayor George Graham Currie to let her display her sculptures at the local county fair. Her efforts won her a blue ribbon and a $25 prize for most original exhibit, and she earned $150 selling her pieces to fair visitors.

Believing in her potential, Currie commissioned a portrait of himself from Savage, and the two became friends and confidants. Currie encouraged Savage to move to New York to further her career, and he gave her a letter of introduction to Solon H. Borglum (1868–1922), a sculptor of American West themes who headed the School of American Sculpture there. After studying briefly at Florida A&M University (then Tallahassee State Normal School), Savage divorced her second husband and moved to Harlem in 1921. She was able to enroll at Cooper Union thanks to Borglum, who taught part-time there.

At Cooper, Savage studied modeling with American architectural sculptor George T. Brewster (1862–1943). She also frequented the Schomburg Center in Harlem to hear lectures and to give her own poetry readings. Soon thereafter, the library commissioned Savage to sculpt a portrait of W. E. B. Du Bois for its collection (now lost). Savage was subsequently commissioned to do portraits of other prominent Harlemites, including, most notably, Marcus Garvey. The multitalented Savage also published her poetry in Garvey's newspaper, *Negro World*. Through her association with Garvey, Savage met her third and last husband, UNIA secretary general Robert Poston (1891–1924). Sadly, he died of pneumonia just five months later while on a return trip from Liberia. Savage never again married.

In 1923, Savage applied for one of a hundred French government scholarships for American women to study at the Fontainebleau School of Fine Arts near Paris. As part of her application, she had to obtain commitments from patrons to underwrite any additional travel expenses not covered by the $500 award for summer study. However, her application was rejected because it was determined that the presence of a woman "of the Negro race" in the school would be "disagreeable" to white students. Incensed, Savage wrote a flurry of letters to the committee and the press, asking, "How am I to compete with other American artists if I am not to be given the same opportunity?" Despite an outpouring of protests, including written pleas from Du Bois and a month-long series of articles on the controversy in New York's newspapers, the Fontainebleau committee would not be dissuaded. Angered by the decision, American sculptor Hermon Atkins MacNeil (1866–1947) gave the artist private lessons in his studio. Savage was also able to study with Onorio Ruotolo (1888–1966), director of Manhattan's Leonardo da Vinci Art School, which catered to working immigrants.

Six years passed before Savage was finally able to travel abroad. These were difficult years for the artist, who, in addition to the loss of her third husband, was obliged to house and support her parents after her father's incapacitation from a crippling stroke. She also had to accommodate six more family members in her three-room apartment after the family's Florida home was destroyed by a hurricane. Tragedy struck a third time in 1928, when the artist's father burned to death in a fire. Savage went to work as a laundress to pay for his funeral and to support her family. She was so taxed by her obligations that she had to turn down a 1926 travel grant from the Italian American Society to study at the Royal Academy in Rome (secured with the help of Du Bois). Savage finally made the trip to Europe in 1929 with the support of a $1,500 Rosenwald Fellowship and $300 in private funds received from her numerous supporters.

Savage carried with her to Paris letters of introduction to black expatriates such as McKay, Prophet, and Tanner. She also became acquainted with Countee Cullen, Hale Woodruff, Palmer Hayden, and Aaron Douglas. Savage studied sculpture with Felix Benneteau-Desgrois (1879–1963) at the Académie de la Grand Chaumière, and privately with Salon sculptor Charles Despiau (1874–1946). She produced attenuated figure sculptures as well as allegorical nudes. Savage remained in Paris for a second year thanks to a renewal of her Rosenwald Fellowship and a Carnegie Foundation grant that she used to travel to other regions of France as well as to Belgium and Germany.

Savage returned to New York in 1932, where she continued to sculpt portrait busts of noted African Americans such as James Weldon Johnson, Frederick Douglass, and composer W. C. Handy (1873–1958). In 1932, she established her own Studio of Arts and Crafts in response to the desperate need for art education for African-American youth. The following year, with WPA funds, Savage expanded the studio's offerings and, in collaboration with Harmon Foundation director Mary Beattie Brady and Alston, Bannarn, and Seabrooke Powell, opened the Harlem Art Workshop. Its first home was in the Schomburg Center, but, quickly outgrowing the space, soon the workshop moved to a townhouse at 306 West 141st Street and was established as an affiliate of the State University of New York (SUNY). Known affectionately as "306," the location became an artistic hub where African-American artists and writers (including Richard Wright, Countee Cullen, and Ralph Ellison) gathered to discuss the pressing issues of the day. As an acknowledgment of her accomplishments, in 1934 Savage became the first African-American member of the National Association of Women Painters and Sculptors.

Three years later, with an infusion of additional funds from the WPA-FAP, Savage opened the Harlem Community Art Center in a loft space on 125th Street and Lenox Avenue. The center provided art instruction to some 1,500 students and employed dozens of African Americans. As its assistant director and then its first WPA director, from 1937 to 1939 Savage helped to train a new generation of leading black artists, including Ernest Crichlow (discussed later in this chapter), William Artis (1914–77), Jacob Lawrence (see Chapter 8), and Norman Lewis (see Chapter 9). Prior to the founding of the center, the vast majority of New York's art centers and galleries were located in Midtown Manhattan and catered to white artists. Vertis Hayes observed at the time that there "are more Negro artists living in New York than any other city, yet most of the art galleries exclude work done by Negroes. . . . [The Harlem Art Center] has become an active force filling a long neglected need in Harlem [and] stands as a tribute to the Federal Art Project."

Soon after assuming its directorship, Savage was offered a professional commission by the organizers of the New York World's Fair to create the sculpture *The Harp (Lift Every Voice and Sing)*. The sculpture was named for the well-known black national anthem, written in 1899 by James Weldon Johnson and scored by his musician brother John Rosamond Johnson (1873–1954). Savage created a monumental "harp" composed of twelve traditionally modeled heads of black choir singers mounted atop fluted columns that stood in for conventional bodies. These ten figures formed the strings of the harp, while an elongated arm and open hand formed the soundboard. The completion of this large sculptural project was documented by Harlem photography team Morgan and Marvin Smith (see Chapter 6), who photographed Savage as she worked (Figure 7.7). It received the fair's silver medal and widespread press attention, and it was displayed throughout the fair's run in the courtyard of the Contemporary Arts Pavilion. Unfortunately, at the close of the fair, Savage did not have the funds to cast or to store the 16-foot plaster sculpture, which was subsequently bulldozed when the fair was demolished. To make matters worse, Savage discovered that, because she had become privately employed (even though only temporarily), she no longer qualified for her WPA-FAP position, and her employment with the Harlem Community Arts Center was terminated.

Savage launched a commercial gallery venture in 1939: the Harlem-based Salon of Contemporary Negro Art, which was the first African-American sales gallery in the country. In addition to Savage's own work, the Salon exhibited the art of Fuller, Barthé, Lois Jones, Artis, Wells, Selma Burke (discussed later in this chapter), and Beauford Delaney (see Chapter 9). Sadly, Savage's hopes for the gallery were never realized. Sales were poor, and the space was closed within a few months. The WPA ceased operations entirely in 1943, and President Roosevelt passed away in 1945, marking the end of FAP sponsorship of the arts and the decline of Social Realism. Minority artists found fewer and fewer outlets and support for their endeavors. By 1945, Savage had retired to a farm in New York's Catskill Mountains, where she worked for more than two decades as a summer camp art instructor and part-time farmworker until her death from cancer. Although

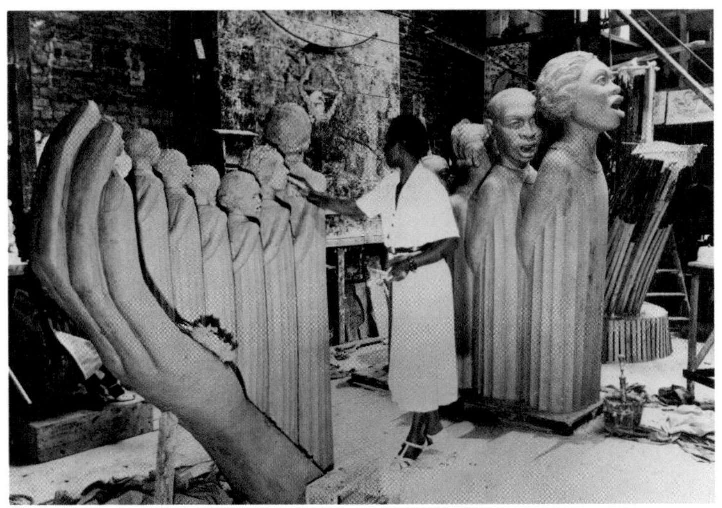

▲ 7.7 Morgan and Marvin Smith, *Augusta Savage with the Harp: Lift Every Voice and Sing*, 1939, gelatin silver print.

Morgan and Marvin Smith Photograph Collection, Photographs and Prints Division, Schomburg Center for Research in Black Culture, the New York Public Library, Astor, Lenox, and Tilden Foundations.

Savage was all but forgotten during her later life, today her contributions to African-American art are much revered.

Selma Hortense Burke

Selma Hortense Burke (1900–95) was an acolyte of Augusta Savage, drawn to the New York art community in the 1930s from Philadelphia. An exhibitor at Savage's Salon of Contemporary Negro Art in 1940, Burke would achieve national fame five years later for her 1945 relief portrait of President Roosevelt.

Burke was born in Mooresville, North Carolina. The local school district had only a single school for African Americans, a poorly maintained one-room structure. In order to secure the best possible education for her daughter, Mrs. Burke sent Selma to the National Training School for Women and Girls—a private college prep school in Washington, D.C. After a year away from home, Burke returned to Mooresville and, from age 14 to 18, traveled nearly 50 miles each day in order to receive a high school education in Winston-Salem, the nearest town that accepted black high school students.

After graduation, Burke studied nursing in various colleges, getting her degree from Women's Medical College (now Drexel College of Medicine) in Philadelphia. By the end of the 1920s, she was a registered nurse with certification as an anesthesiologist. In 1929 Burke was recommended by the president of Women's Medical College to be a private nurse for an heiress of the Otis Elevator dynasty who lived in Cooperstown. According to journalist Thomas Sieg, Burke's benefactress was "affectionate, generous, and very rich. By the time her employer died four years later in 1933, Miss Burke had a fantastic wardrobe, had become a regular at the Metropolitan Opera and Carnegie Hall and had an acquaintance with royalty and a nest egg." Not only had Burke been exposed to New York's most privileged social and cultural circles, but the salary she earned had allowed her to save enough money to realize a long-deferred dream to become a sculptor.

In 1935, Burke moved to New York to pursue her dream. She found work as an artist's model at Sarah Lawrence College and studied sculpture at the Harlem Community Art Center. She also joined the Harlem Artists Guild and by 1936 had won a Rosenwald Foundation award. The following year, Burke received a full scholarship to Columbia University, where she met classmate Margot Einstein, daughter of Albert. The Einsteins had a special regard for African-American art and artists and provided invaluable support and encouragement to Burke. At the end of her first year at Columbia, Burke was awarded one of only five honorable mentions, for a portrait bust featured in a juried exhibition of more than 150 art students.

In 1938, Burke took a hiatus from Columbia to study in Europe. She spent a year in Italy, France, Germany, and Austria. She studied with French sculptor Aristide Maillol (1861–1944) and Viennese ceramicist Michael Powolny (1871–1954), who had helped to launch the celebrated **Vienna Secession** in 1897. When Burke returned to New York, she began exhibiting almost immediately in Manhattan galleries, including Edith Halpert's famed Downtown Gallery on 51st Street. Her coexhibitors at Halpert's included Tanner, Savage, Barthé, Alston, May Howard Jackson, and Sargent Johnson, among others. Halpert was representative of an ever-growing set of white art dealers who, during the politically liberal years of the 1930s, promoted the careers of African-American artists. Burke's sculptures were singled out by the press as some of the best at Halpert's gallery. In 1941, Burke completed her studies at Columbia, earning her MFA degree. She also taught at the Harlem Community Art Center until its closing.

In 1944, Burke learned of a national competition sponsored by the D.C. Board of Commissioners to create a profile portrait of President Roosevelt. From a large pool of competitors, she was chosen along with a dozen other artists (four of whom were African-American) as a finalist. From this group, Burke's submission was chosen as the winning entry. President Roosevelt sat for Burke at the White House on two occasions in 1944 (see chapter-opening image). Her portrait was cast in bronze in 1945 and was unveiled just after the president's death.

Burke's portrait is almost identical to—with barely perceptible differences—U.S. Mint engraver John R. Sinnock's 1946 profile of the president made for the casting of the dime, which many scholars believe was patterned after Burke's prize-winning sculpture. The most evident distinctions between the two are the jutting chin and steeply sloping forehead and nose in Burke's composition, which she believed gave the president "that wonderful look of going forward."

Before Burke's bronze portrait was displayed, Eleanor Roosevelt visited Burke's studio to approve the final image. The First Lady endorsed the sculpture, but not without comment. She was uncomfortable with Burke's decision to portray the president as younger than his sixty-plus years. To this the artist replied:

> *I have not done it for today, but for tomorrow and tomorrow. Five hundred years from now America and all the world will want to look at our president, not as he was for the few months before he died, but as we saw him for most of the time he was with us—strong, so full of life. . . . I did not realize then that tomorrow would come so soon and he would be gone.*

That year, Burke was given a solo exhibit of eighteen of her sculptures at the famed Modernage Gallery on East 34th Street. The centerpiece of the exhibit was Burke's profile of Roosevelt, which was unveiled in New York before it was installed in Washington. In his review of the New York show, *New York Times* art critic Allen Jewell lavished praise on Burke's portrait busts, calling them "eloquent," "sensitively carved," "vital and honest," and "emotional and deeply sincere." Jewell's comments on the Roosevelt profile were equally favorable: "[Burke] has striven to present him [FDR] at the height of his powers . . . as she feels the future should think of him. And her task has been accomplished with marked success."

Like Savage, Burke was dedicated as much to educating young artists as to producing art. She opened the Selma Burke School of Sculpture in Greenwich Village in January 1946. The atelier offered beginner and advanced sculpture classes. Within a year, Burke had raised enough money to offer $500 tuition scholarships to worthy students, who were chosen based on merit by a jury that included, among others, sculptor Barthé. Unfortunately, Burke lost her space to a real estate development project in 1947 and decided to leave New York. In 1948, she married the prominent architect and politician Herman Kobbe (1885–1966), whose socialist concerns for better public housing dovetailed with Burke's own sensibilities. The couple relocated to Bucks County, Pennsylvania, near the art community of New Hope. There Burke began to experiment with a more expressive and abstract style that boasted robust elemental forms and textured surfaces.

For the remainder of her life, Burke continued to receive commissions and to enjoy a long and prolific career. Highlights include appointment to the Pennsylvania Council on the Arts in the 1960s; the founding of the Selma Burke Art Center in Pittsburgh, which she directed from 1972 to 1981; and the launching of the Bucks County Sculpture Show, which still thrives today as an annual art festival. Burke also taught at Haverford, Swarthmore, and several other institutions throughout Pennsylvania. In 1979, the Women's Caucus for Art chose Burke to receive their Lifetime Achievement Award, presented to the artist by President Jimmy Carter. When Burke died, she was 95 years old and working on a federal commission to sculpt civil rights activist Rosa Parks.

THE CHICAGO ARTS AND CRAFTS GUILD, ARTISTS UNION, AND SOUTH SIDE COMMUNITY ART CENTER

In 1932, a group of teenaged African-American artists came together to form the Chicago Arts and Crafts Guild. Initially founded by sign painter William McGill, the group was joined by 26-year-old college student George E. Neal (1906–38), who, by 1934, had become its unofficial guiding light. Although Neal died young of tuberculosis only a few years later, he nurtured a remarkable cadre of fledgling artists who would soon join the ranks of the country's most respected fine artists. Among these were 14-year-old Charles White (discussed later in this chapter), 16-year-old Eldzier Cortor (see Chapter 8), 17-year-old Margaret Burroughs (discussed later in this chapter), and 18-year-old Charles Sebree (1914–85). On Saturdays, the guild met at Neal's coach house, which the group renovated into an art studio.

Neal, who was a student at the School of the Art Institute of Chicago (SAIC), offered up his free time to teach the group what he was learning there, in particular, painting techniques. He led the teenagers on sketching excursions and gallery visits. They organized "pay parties" and other events to raise money to further their artistic pursuits, which included mounting exhibits at the YMCA, Hull House, and South Side Settlement House, and in churches and storefronts. Their fundraising efforts expanded to provide art prizes for juried shows and modest scholarships that subsidized a dozen guild members' enrollment at SAIC. The guild came to an abrupt end when a fire destroyed their studio and dozens of artworks that were housed there, but their activities were rescued by the founding of the WPA-FAP South Side Community Art Center (SSCAC) in 1938.

The SSCAC's formation was spearheaded by gallery owner and FAP staffer Peter Pollock (1909–78), who was among the first Chicago dealers to exhibit black art, along with other local businessmen and leaders. Members of the guild were also central to the founding of the SSCAC. Members Motley, Cortor, White, Burroughs, Bernard Goss (1913–66), who married Burroughs in 1939, William Carter (1909–96), and Joseph Kersey (1908–82) were all in attendance at its first meeting held in the fall of 1939. The state's FAP director, George Thorpe, pledged funds to pay for renovating and staffing a site for the center in an unoccupied palatial home on Michigan Avenue. The mansion was up for sale at a bargain price because the neighborhood was transitioning from white to black (as had Harlem in the 1920s). The building was renovated in the Bauhaus style by German designer Hin Bredendieck (1904–95) and Chicagoan Nathan Lerner (1913–99) of the city's New Bauhaus Institute.

Interest in the SSCAC was bolstered by the 1940 *Art of the American Negro: 1851–1940* exhibit organized by Locke, which exposed Chicagoans to African-American visual art on a grand scale. Locke, First Lady Eleanor Roosevelt, and jazz singer and Hollywood actress Ethel Waters (1896–1977) were in attendance at the 1941 dedication of the SSCAC; and the ceremonies were broadcast on national radio. The SSCAC served, in part, as an exhibition space for African-American art. One of its first major shows featured Barthé's sculptures. It also offered art classes, meeting spaces, and theatre, music, and dance performances. Just two years later, however, in 1943, when the FAP was dissolved, the SSCAC faced the threat of closing. With the help of appeals in the *Chicago Defender* and *Tribune*, as well as from funds raised at the Annual Artists and Models Ball (held at the Chicago Savoy Ballroom), the SSCAC not only survived the end of FAP funding but also continues to operate today. Over the course of nearly a century, the SSCAC has provided support to some of the country's best-known American artists, both black and white. Among these are famed photographer Gordon Parks (see Chapter 8), sculptor and printmaker Elizabeth Catlett (see Chapter 8), Social Realist artist Ben Shahn (1898–1969), jazz singer Nat King Cole, and black author Richard Wright.

Margaret Burroughs

A founding member of SSCAC, Margaret Burroughs (1915–2010) was its driving force for 30 years. Known for her **linocut** portraits and genre scenes of African Americans, Burroughs was a native of Louisiana. She migrated to Chicago with her family in 1920 to become an accomplished artist, teacher, and children's book author. While a member of the guild, Burroughs attended Englewood High School and then went on to Chicago Teachers College, receiving her degree in 1937.

Burroughs best articulated the SSCAC's socialist goals and philosophy when she wrote in 1941:

> *We believed that the purpose of art was to record the times. As young black artists, we looked around and recorded in our various media what we saw. It was not from our imagination that we painted slums and ghettos, or sad hollow-eyed black men, women and children. They were the people around us. We were part of them. They were us.*

Burroughs's Marxist take on the role of art to record truth, the use of realism to do so, and the role of artists as members and defenders of the proletariat became the manifesto of the SSCAC. On seeing the works of Burroughs at the center in 1941, Gordon Parks described them accurately as "grim paintings of the jobless and oppressed which had forsaken the pink ladies of Manet and Renoir [and] the . . . landscapes of Monet hanging at the Art Institute just a few miles north on Michigan Avenue."

Burroughs went on to earn BA and MA degrees in art education from the SAIC in 1946 and 1948. She put her teaching credentials to use at DuSable High School from 1947 to 1969, and subsequently as a professor at Kennedy-King Community and Elmhurst Colleges. Tireless and prolific in her endeavors, Burroughs founded the DuSable Museum of African American History in 1961, which gestated in her Bronzeville home, and she served as its president for 10 years. The DuSable Museum is now located in Chicago's Washington Park and boasts a collection of some 15,000 historical artifacts and works of art by and about African Americans, one of the largest such collections in the country. From 1986 until the year of her death, Burroughs served as Chicago park district commissioner, supervising art and culture events in Chicago's parks for 25 years.

▼ **7.8** Charles White, *There Were No Crops This Year*, 1940, graphite on paper, 28¾″ × 19¼″ (original image). Catalog cover for the Exhibition of the Art of the American Negro, assembled by the American Negro Exposition.

Chicago Public Library.

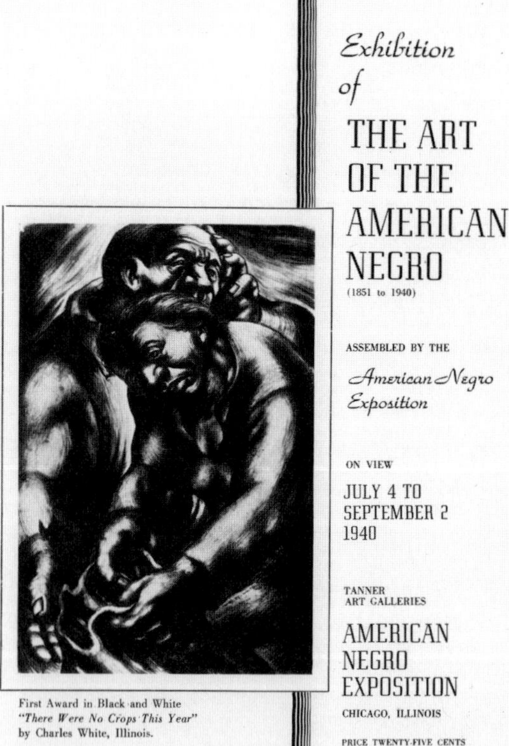

Exhibition of THE ART OF THE AMERICAN NEGRO (1851 to 1940)

ASSEMBLED BY THE American Negro Exposition

ON VIEW JULY 4 TO SEPTEMBER 2 1940

TANNER ART GALLERIES

AMERICAN NEGRO EXPOSITION

CHICAGO, ILLINOIS

PRICE TWENTY-FIVE CENTS

First Award in Black and White "There Were No Crops This Year" by Charles White, Illinois.

Charles White

The art of Charles White (1918–79) ideally exemplifies the visual works of the SSCAC. His graphite drawing of 1940, *There Were No Crops This Year*, fills the page with two pitiable farmworkers holding an empty grain sack (Figure 7.8). The work's title as well as the expressions and gestures of the figures tell a bitter tale of destitution within a powerful formal context of narrative minimalism. White's use of dramatic chiaroscuro features an overabundance of shadow rather than light and sets the disconsolate stage. Yet the apparent poverty, hunger, and distress of the couple are offset by their immensely proportioned heads, hands, and limbs, as well as by their powerful musculature, hallmarks of White's imagery, which infuses these otherwise downtrodden figures with sublime grandeur.

White was one of the leading lights of the guild and the SSCAC. He and Margaret Burroughs met at

Englewood High School, and they remained friends and collaborators for many years. A native of Chicago, White was a politically active and exceptionally gifted artist from his youth. As a teenager, he worked as a sign painter when he was not in school. He also socialized with an older circle of New Negro university students who made up the literary arm of the **Black Chicago Renaissance**. Among them were dancer-anthropologist Katherine Dunham, who was then attending the University of Chicago Graduate School; WPA-FWP poet Gwendolyn Brooks; award-winning FWP and South Side Writers Group author Margaret Walker; and South Side Writers Group founder and FWP author Richard Wright. Exposed to the intellectual rigor and political engagement of this group, White was greatly swayed by their **Weltanschauung**, as the iconography of his work would soon reveal.

In 1934, White won a scholarship to study at the Chicago Academy of Fine Arts, a graphic design and applied art complement to the SAIC, founded in 1902 by artist-educator Carl Werntz. Unbeknownst to White, the school was segregated, and his award was rescinded when he arrived to formally enroll. Two years later, White suffered a similar experience when his hard-won scholarship to the newly opened Frederic Mizen Academy of Art, founded that year by the renowned illustrator of the same name, was also revoked. Undaunted, White applied directly to the SAIC, which awarded him a full scholarship, and White's career began. Taking classes virtually around the clock, White completed the two-year program in a single year. Immediately thereafter, in 1939, he began working for the FAP as a muralist. His exposure to Mexico's *los tres grandes* at the SAIC greatly influenced his monumental style. Several years later White would travel to Mexico with his wife, artist Elizabeth Catlett, to meet the legendary Rivera and Siqueiros, about whom he observed: "I saw artists working to create an art about and for the people. This has been the strongest influence in my whole approach."

After completing a 1939 mural of black leaders for Howard University, in 1940 White received a commission to paint *A History of the Negro Press* for display in the 1940 *Art of the American Negro* exhibit at the American Negro Expo, the catalog cover of which featured his *There Were No Crops*. Although the painting is now lost, vintage photos of *A History of the Negro Press* record the similarity of its figures to those depicted in *There Were No Crops*. Depicting historic black press editors such as John Brown Russwurm (1799–1851) of the *Freedom's Journal*, published in the 1820s; Timothy Thomas Fortune (1856–1928), editor of *New York Age* and the UNIA's *Negro World*; and Frederick Douglass, who founded the antislavery newspaper *North Star* in the 1840s, White's mural won the Chicago Expo's first prize for art. Despite his earlier predilection for African-inspired Modernism rather than Social Realism, Locke praised White's work as a testament to the "sober realism" of African-American existence during the Depression.

In 1941, White married Catlett, an equally prolific artist who was studying at the SAIC during a summer break from her teaching position at Dillard University in New Orleans. They returned to Dillard and taught briefly before relocating to New York in 1942. In New York, White was represented by ACA (American Contemporary Art) Galleries, which was cofounded in 1932 by author and art dealer Herman Baron, and by Artists Union leader

Stuart Davis. ACA Galleries actively sought out artists with a social agenda and was among the first commercial galleries to regularly exhibit African-American art. After the 1940s, White exhibited in group and solo shows at more than a hundred venues and won many awards, including Rosenwald and Whitney Museum Fellowships and appointments to the Black Academy of Arts and Letters and the National Academy of Design.

White's later career was spent as a professor at Otis Art Institute (Otis College of Art and Design) in Los Angeles, where he began teaching in 1965. At about this time, White began working on his *Wanted Poster* series, a group of sepia paintings and lithographs based on original antebellum slave auction and runaway broadsides. White eloquently summarized his artistic philosophy in a January 1940 *Opportunity* magazine interview, when he stated, "Paint is the only weapon I have with which to fight what I resent. If I could write, I would write about it. If I could talk, I would talk about it. Since I paint, I must paint about it."

PRINTMAKING

The WPA-FAP oversaw graphic arts departments that included poster divisions and fine arts printmaking workshops. Understood as egalitarian media, prints, like murals, were popular Social Realist art forms due to their ability to be produced in multiple—hence low-cost—copies, making them readily available to a large numbers of people. This feature differentiated reproducible media from painting, which was seen as rarefied and unique, costly, and inaccessible to all but the wealthy art collector. More than two dozen African-American artists produced prints under the auspices of the WPA-FAP. Among the most notable were Alston, Catlett, Crichlow, Burroughs, Jennings, Woodruff, Sargent Johnson, William H. Johnson, Norman Lewis, Dox Thrash (discussed later in this chapter), Robert Blackburn (discussed later in this chapter), and Hughie Lee-Smith (see Chapter 8). FAP printmakers used conventional media such as woodblock, lithography, etching, and **aquatint**, but they also invented new techniques; in particular, they augmented etching, color lithography, and **silkscreen** (**serigraph**) printing by using unconventional tools such as sandpaper and cutting blades on the printing surface to create new textures and effects, and they invented the black-and-white **carborundum mezzotint**.

Dox Thrash and the Philadelphia Fine Prints Workshop

One of the FAP's most innovative printmakers was Dox Thrash (1893–1965). Born in rural Georgia and raised there until age 15, Thrash drew a lifetime of subject matter from the sharecroppers, cotton farmers, washerwomen, fishermen, itinerant entertainers, and "Negro cabins" of his youth. He had only a few years of elementary education before going to work full time at age 10. Nevertheless, he was certain of his career path as an artist, even in childhood, and began studying by way of a correspondence course at age 14. Thrash left home the following year and worked odd jobs as he made his way slowly north with the Great Migration. In 1911, Thrash arrived in Chicago determined to study art formally. For a time, he could only afford the mail-order courses, but by 1914 he had enrolled in evening classes at the SAIC, supporting himself as an elevator operator.

From 1917 to 1919 and again in the early 1920s (after a two-year tour in the army), Thrash studied commercial and decorative art and painting at the SAIC. He also studied privately with William Edouard Scott. Restless, in the mid-twenties he traveled east, first to Boston and then to Connecticut, New York, and finally Philadelphia, working odd jobs as he went. Settling in Philadelphia, Thrash obtained a position as a graphic artist at a print shop, designing ads, invitations, and announcements for local businesses and events. While at the print shop, Thrash became interested in the printmaking process itself and decided to join the Graphic Sketch Club (now the Samuel S. Fleisher Art Memorial) to study print media as well as illustration and painting. He studied with Earl Horter (1881–1940), whose expertise included etching, aquatint, advertising art, and painting.

By 1931 Thrash had mastered a variety of printing techniques and had secured his first exhibit at the YMCA in southwestern Philadelphia. The next few years saw multiple group and solo exhibits of Thrash's art. A second 1933 solo show at the YMCA gained praise from the *Philadelphia Tribune*, which cited Thrash as one of Philadelphia's most talented artists whose imagery was imbued with "realistic power."

In 1937, Thrash took a position at the newly founded Philadelphia Fine Prints Workshop, which was supervised by statewide WPA-FAP director Mary Florence Curran (1885–1976). Thrash began making prints for display at local schools, libraries, civic buildings, and other public venues. To showcase the posters and prints made at the workshop, an exhibition was held in the fall of 1937. On display were several Thrash prints created using the new carborundum mezzotint technique. Thrash had developed the process using carborundum (a gritty silicon and carbon compound), which he ground into a copper plate before inking it. The result was a print with subtle gradations of light and dark and a grainy surface texture that looked more like a charcoal drawing than a print. Among Thrash's cohorts at the Fine Prints Workshop were Hubert (Hugh) Mesibov (b. 1916) and Michael J. Gallagher (1895–1965), who collaborated with Thrash to evolve his innovation into what has since become known as carborundum mezzotint. (The trio later developed a carborundum etching process as well.) All three artists exhibited examples of the new technique in 1938 at FAP shows mounted in Philadelphia and Washington. Thrash's work was widely displayed through the mid-1940s and gained even more widespread attention when his images were featured in Alain Locke's pivotal 1940 book *The Negro in Art* and James Porter's equally significant 1943 book *Modern Negro Art*.

Thrash's subject matter was devoted mainly to African-American workers, female nudes, and portraits. He also produced a number of farm landscape, farm building, and wharf scenes. The artist's 1940 carborundum mezzotint *Grinding* depicts an African-American knife grinder intently pressing a long, curved blade to a grindstone—an image that is both a literal and metaphoric reference to this hard labor (Figure 7.9). The worker's large hands and muscular forearms, as well as his clothing, identify him with the proletariat and suggest the innate power and dignity of ordinary labor. The artist's choice of

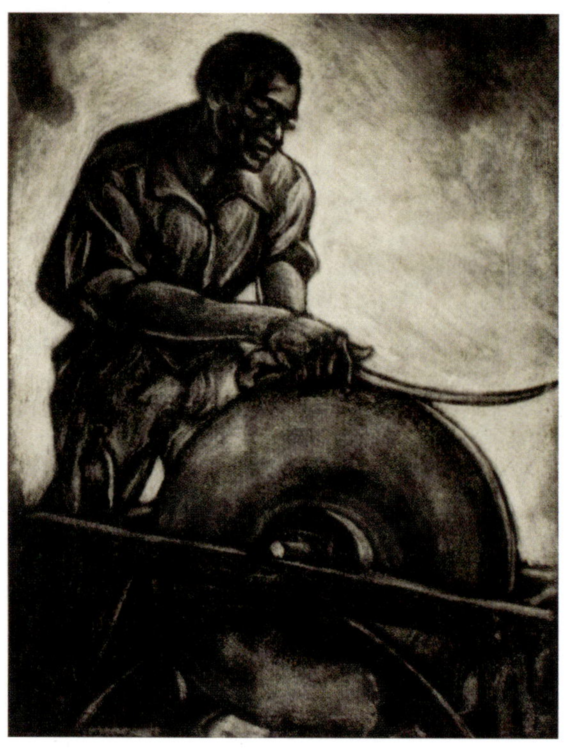

▲ **7.9** Dox Thrash, *Grinding (Grinder)*, c. 1940, carborundum mezzotint, 9⅞″ × 7⅜″ (plate), 12⅝″ × 9⅞″ (sheet).

Philadelphia Museum of Art: gift of James D. Crawford and Judith N. Dean, 1996. Photo and digital image © Philadelphia Museum of Art.

a worm's-eye view situates the viewer below the figure and, thus, monumentalizes both the man and his exertions. The carborundum mezzotint technique allowed Thrash to produce deep, rich shades of black and gray. Perhaps more than any other print medium, the carborundum process lent itself to the representation of black skin.

Thrash's African-American colleagues at the Philadelphia Fine Prints Workshop included Claude Clark, Sr. (1915–2001), a 1939 graduate of the Philadelphia Museum School of Industrial Art. Clark was devoted to images of southern black themes and of the common man. Other black members of the Philadelphia workshop included Humbert Lincoln Howard (1906–90), who was a student of James Porter at Howard University and at the Pennsylvania Academy of Fine Arts before joining the workshop, and Raymond Steth (née Ryles; 1917–97), who worked alongside Thrash and Gallagher at the Philadelphia Fine Prints Workshop, assisting in the development of a color carborundum process.

The Printmaking Legacy of Riva Helfond

As an instructor at the Harlem Community Art Center from 1936 to 1941, and later a professor at New York University, the Brooklyn-born daughter of Jewish parents, Riva Helfond (1910–2002) encouraged many budding artists to explore printmaking. Included among her Harlem students were Bearden and Jacob Lawrence (see Chapter 8), Robert Blackburn, Claude Clark, and Ernest Crichlow (all three discussed later in this chapter), and the West Indian-born Ronald Joseph (1910–1992). Helfond studied at the Art Students League and was versed in virtually all print media. Her images of coal miners, in particular, show the influence of the Social Realist Movement. *Out of the Pit* depicts miners, their faces black with coal dust, claustrophobically pressed against the picture plane and each other (Figure 7.10). The astutely composed image makes the two men appear trapped in a bleak and crushing environment, condemned to a life of mind-numbing toil. Even the lights on their hardhats are dimmed by coal dust.

Over the course of her 60-year career, Helfond witnessed several of her Harlem workshop students develop into significant players on the art world stage. Among these was Robert "Bob" Blackburn (1920–2003), who was a teenager when he studied printmaking with Helfond. He was also one of the youngest participants in the activities of the 306 atelier. Like Savage and Burroughs, Blackburn's most profound contribution was his nurturing of younger artists through the establishment in 1948 of one of the most esteemed print workshops in the world: the Robert Blackburn Printmaking Workshop (RBPMW). With the assistance of his Art Students League instructor Will Barnett (1911–2012), Blackburn founded and supervised a printmaking establishment that nurtured generations of printmakers. Under the auspices of the Elizabeth Foundation for the Arts, the workshop

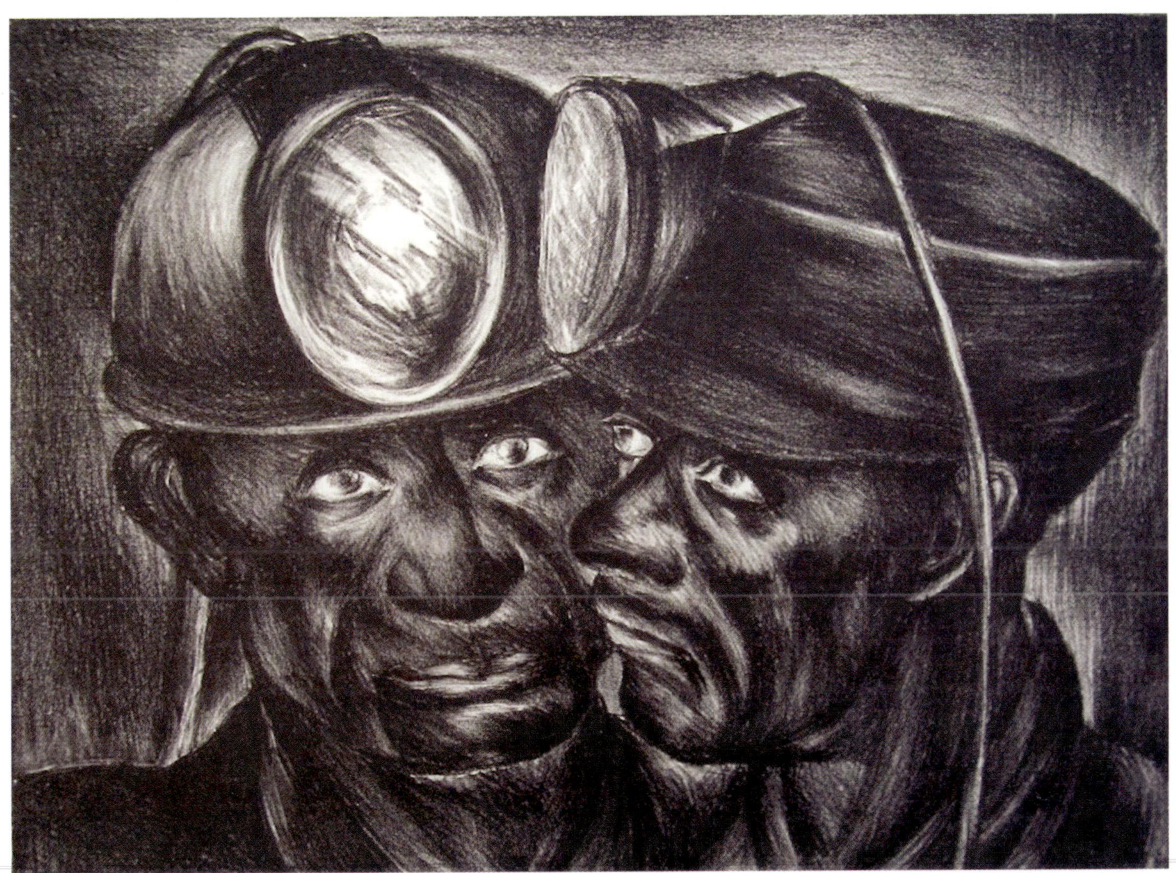

▲ **7.10** Riva Helfond, *Out of the Pit*, 1935, Teller 19, lithograph, 11″ × 14″.

Courtesy of the Estate of the Artist and the Susan Teller Gallery, New York, NY.

continues today to host master printers; provide artists with studio space, presses, and equipment; mount exhibitions; encourage innovation; and offer fellowships and classes to an international community of thousands of students and artists. In turn, Blackburn alums have expanded the workshop's legacy to similar programs in South America, Australia, and Africa.

Blackburn is known as much for his teaching and mentorship as for his abstract, multi-stone color lithographs. He was designated a master printer by the National Academy of Design in 1949 and became the first master printer to work for Universal Limited Art Editions (ULAE). Established in 1957, ULAE hired Blackburn to produce print editions for such A-list artists as Helen Frankenthaler (1928–2011), Jasper Johns (b. 1930), Robert Rauschenberg (1925–2008), and Larry Rivers (1923–2002). Blackburn also held teaching positions at many universities including Columbia University, where he served on the faculty from 1970 to 1990. In 1992, Blackburn won the coveted MacArthur Foundation Genius Award and was given the College Art Association's Lifetime Achievement Award shortly before his death.

Another Helfond student, Ernest Crichlow (1914–2005), was born in Brooklyn to a large immigrant family originally from Barbados. He began formal art study when he was awarded a scholarship to attend New York's School of Commercial Illustrating and Advertising Art. From there he went on to New York University and the Art Students League. In addition, he attended Helfond's workshop at the Harlem Community Art Center—which sponsored

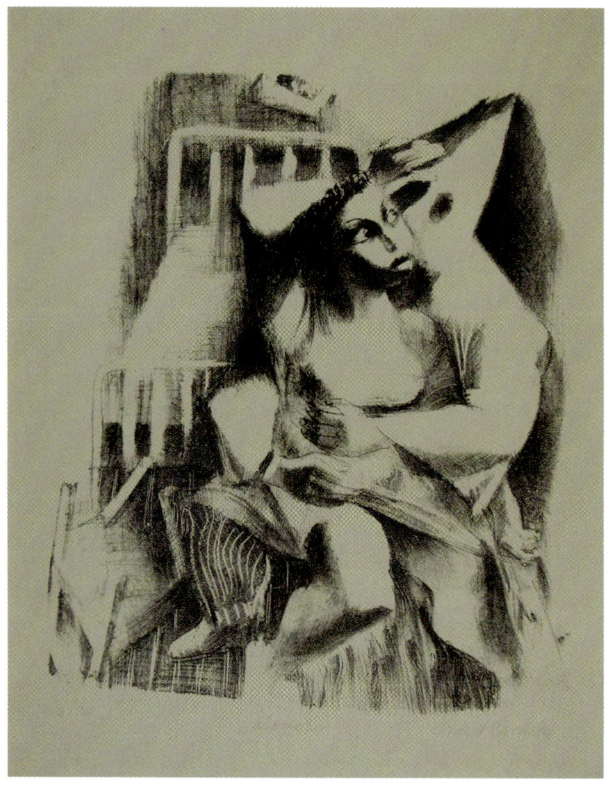

▲ **7.11** Ernest T. Crichlow, *Lovers*, 1938, lithograph, 22 1/8″ × 15 1/8″ (lithograph sheet), 14″ × 11½″ (image). Davis Museum at Wellesley College, Wellesley, MA. Museum purchase, the Nancy Gray Sherrill, Class of 1954, Acquisition Fund 2002.27.

his first exhibitions in 1938 and 1939—and worked for the FAP. One of Crichlow's best-known works from this period is a lithograph entitled *Lovers* (1938; Figure 7.11).

Lovers is a disquieting portrayal of a black woman in the grip of a Ku Klux Klan figure. The couple is situated in a threadbare bedroom, where an overturned chair and lopsided wall painting bear witness to their violent struggle. He grips her from behind as she struggles in his arms, a compelling depiction of a Freudian anal rape—that is, not an actual rape but, as the artist has asserted, a metaphor for a union of "lovers" that can bear no fruit. It is an assault by one who is empowered (though cryptically so, because he hides his identity) on one who is not. The artist explained in a 2003 National Public Radio interview that he envisioned the woman (symbolic of all blacks) successfully fighting off her attacker (an incarnation of bigotry and oppression), although this outcome is unclear in the actual image.

Crichlow's style in later years evolved from realism to an updated form of Synthetic Cubism that featured saturated hues and flattened forms. In addition to prints, Crichlow painted murals, illustrated books, and taught at several universities and his alma mater, the Art Students League.

Printmakers at Karamu House in Cleveland

Initially a settlement house founded in 1915, Cleveland's FAP-funded Karamu House took its name from the Swahili word for "banquet" or "joyful gathering." Karamu House boasted among its members and supporters such noteworthy Harlem Renaissance literati as Katherine Dunham, Langston Hughes, Zora Neale Hurston, and James Weldon Johnson. While working with the Cleveland branch of the NAACP, Johnson had approached Karamu House directors Russell and Rowena Jelliffe (1891–1980 and 1892–1992, respectively) to establish a visual arts program for black youth. Already the home of a black theatre troupe, the Gilpin Players (named for the acclaimed 1920s black actor Charles Sydney Gilpin), in 1919 Karamu House instituted its first art classes. More than a decade later, in 1933, with an infusion of WPA-FAP funds, Karamu House hired printmaker Richard R. Beatty (1899–1961) to create a full-fledged art curriculum.

Trained in lithography at Carnegie Institute in Pittsburgh and at the Chicago Art Institute, Beatty had worked in the Print Department of the Cleveland Museum of Art in 1925. In 1929, he was hired by Korner & Wood Booksellers, a famed Cleveland institution since the turn of the century and a favorite haunt of local artists and writers. Beatty provided classes at Karamu House in printmaking, ceramics, painting, and drawing. Some of the first artists to enroll were Charles Sallee, Jr. (1911–2006), Elmer W. Brown (1907–71), and William E. Smith (1913–97), who, after studying with Beatty for several years, formed Karamu Artists Incorporated, a dynamic group of self-promoting artists. The fraternity mounted its first art show in 1942 in conjunction with the Cleveland Museum of Art. The show opened at Associated American Artists Gallery in New York with Eleanor Roosevelt in attendance and also traveled to Temple University. Karamu artists also exhibited yearly at the "May Shows" of the Cleveland Museum of Art, with which Karamu House maintained a close relationship.

William E. Smith learned the art of linocut under Beatty's tutelage and developed a style of extreme contrasts of black and white articulated without modeling; and Sallee was Karamu's first Gilpin Award winner (a scholarship offered to Karamu students to study art at John Huntington Polytechnic Institute and the Cleveland Institute of Art). While affiliated with Karamu House from 1935 to 1941, Sallee made aquatints, etchings, and FAP-funded murals for schools, hospitals, and housing projects throughout the Cleveland area.

Elmer W. Brown made his way to Karamu House in 1929 after spending time on a Michigan state prison chain gang for illegally hitching a ride on a freight train. At Karamu, Brown met the Jelliffes, who allowed him to board on-site in exchange for doing odd jobs, making costumes and sets, and performing in plays. Brown studied with Beatty and developed into a gifted artist, excelling as a printmaker. Brown's linocut *Numbers Pulling* was conceived in the Ashcan School mode of hard-bitten urban scenes (Figure 7.12). It represents a black numbers runner wearing a newsboy cap. He observes impassively as the hands of gamers reach into his bag of numbered chips. Ingeniously composed, the print frame is filled to overflowing with the face of the numbers runner and cropped hands reaching in from beyond the picture space. The artist's resolute **hatching** into the linoleum plate energizes the design, as do the stark contrasts of black and white, presenting to the viewer a telling tableau of Depression-era life.

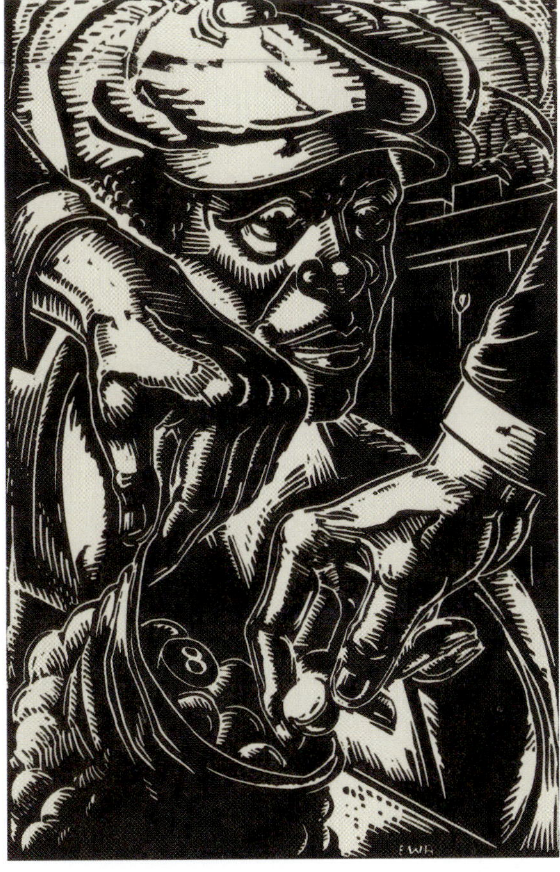

▼ **7.12** Elmer W. Brown, *Numbers Pulling*, 1938–41, linoleum cut, edition 2/50, 9½″ × 6″.

Cincinnati Art Museum, Ohio / Museum purchase: art acquisition by Minority Artists Fund, Millard F. Rogers, Jr. Gift of Art Fund, the Albert P. Strietmann Collection / Bridgeman Images.

Brown's Karamu training led to inclusion in the May Shows and to a position with the WPA mural division, for which he completed murals at the Valleyview Housing Project in Cleveland's Tremont neighborhood (today installed at the Cleveland State University Student Center). A versatile artist with a command of illustration, painting, printmaking, and design, Brown exhibited with Karamu Artists Inc. in New York, Atlanta, and Philadelphia. In 1953, Brown was the first black person to be hired as a full-time artist by the newly integrated American Greetings Corporation. He remained on their art staff until his death.

Summary

The age of Social Realism was prompted by political and economic changes in the United States, specifically the Great Depression. Figurative art that extolled the working class and minority achievement while promoting various government agendas took precedence over Modernism. The WPA supported the creation of murals and prints as forms of art that could be easily accessed by the general public. Community achievement embodied in WPA-FAP workshops was emphasized, as was racial and gender equality. After the death of FDR and the demise of the WPA, however, the atmosphere of egalitarianism that had thrived in the 1930s and early 1940s ended, along with the careers of many African-American artists.

By the 1950s Abstract Expressionism had replaced Social Realism as the preeminent style in American art. Championed by Jackson Pollock and the New York School of abstractionists, the movement lured a generation of artists away from sociopolitical and realist depictions of the working class, toward more erudite and abstruse imagery. Those who did not embrace the new abstraction struggled to find a place in the art world at midcentury. African Americans whose artistic capabilities had been celebrated during the 1930s lost their footing in the art world. The opportunities afforded to African Americans during the Depression were fleeting. In the words of art historians Norma Broude and Mary Garrard, "The narrow window of opportunity [for women and minorities] that had briefly opened during the economic hard times of the 1930s quickly snapped shut again in the forties with the emergence of . . . the Abstract Expressionist Movement."

Despite the short-lived existence of the WPA-FAP, its centers, workshops, and programs launched the careers of many artists, most of whom did not remain Social Realists. Many of them made significant forays into abstract painting. Others made their greatest impact as Surrealists, or political artists of the Black Arts Movement. The WPA-FAP was responsible either directly or indirectly for the artistic education and professional development of thousands of artists, a significant number of whom were African-American. Without this far-reaching government program, many of these artists might not be known today.

Key Terms

American Regionalist style: a painting style of the 1930s that focused on themes of American rural life

aquatint: a form of printmaking using acid and rosin (solid resin) on a metal plate to create a subtly toned image for transfer to paper using ink and a printing press

Bauhaus: a German school of modern architecture and design active from 1919 to 1933 and headed by Walter Gropius

Black Chicago Renaissance: an interdisciplinary arts movement of the 1930s and 1940s akin to the Harlem Renaissance

carborundum mezzotint: a form of printmaking using a gritty silicone carbon compound ground into a metal plate to create an image of subtle tones for transfer to paper using ink and a printing press
cartoon: a preliminary sketch for a mural or other painted composition
hatching: creating tonal gradations in a drawing or print using multiple lines either parallel to one another or crisscrossed (crosshatching)
illusionistic: refers to art that aims to replicate visual reality
International Style: a style of modern architecture formulated in the United States and Europe in the 1920s and 1930s and characterized by rectilinear forms, glass façades, and a lack of exterior ornamentation
linocut: a print created by cutting an image or design into a flat sheet of linoleum for transfer to paper using ink and a printing press
reliquary sculpture: a sculpture that adorns a container of human remains such as bones, teeth, hair, and so on
silkscreen (serigraph): a printmaking technique wherein an image is painted onto a mesh fabric using water-diluted glue and then ink is pushed through the nonglued areas onto paper or another surface using a squeegee
site-specific: refers to a work of art designed for a specific physical space
Vienna Secession: a group of Viennese artists led by Gustav Klimt who rejected the traditional art styles of the Association of Austrian Artists by resigning from the group in 1897
Weltanschauung: a philosophy or worldview

Questions for Further Study and Discussion

1. Define and discuss the form and content of Social Realism.
2. What circumstances motivated the 1930s interest in Social Realist motifs in art?
3. What caused the shift from private to government art patronage in the 1930s?
4. What was the WPA-FAP? What influence did it have on artists and their subject matter?
5. Discuss the function and purpose of the many community art centers sponsored by the WPA-FAP. How did they encourage African Americans to become artists?
6. Why did the WPA-FAP value mural painting and printmaking?
7. Who were *los tres grandes* and what was their significance to the Social Realist Movement?
8. Why did so many Social Realist artists have difficulty sustaining their careers after the 1940s?
9. Research artists of this period not discussed at length in this chapter, such as Allan Rohan Crite (1910–2007), Joseph Delaney (1904–91), Wilmer Jennings (1910–1990), Beulah Ecton Woodard (1895–1955), William Artis (1919–1977), Charles Sebree (1914–1985), Humbert Lincoln Howard (1906–1990), Raymond Steth (1917–1997), Ronald Joseph (1910–1992), William E. Smith (1913–1997), Charles Sallee (1911–2006) and architect Albert Cassell, Sr. (1915–2001).

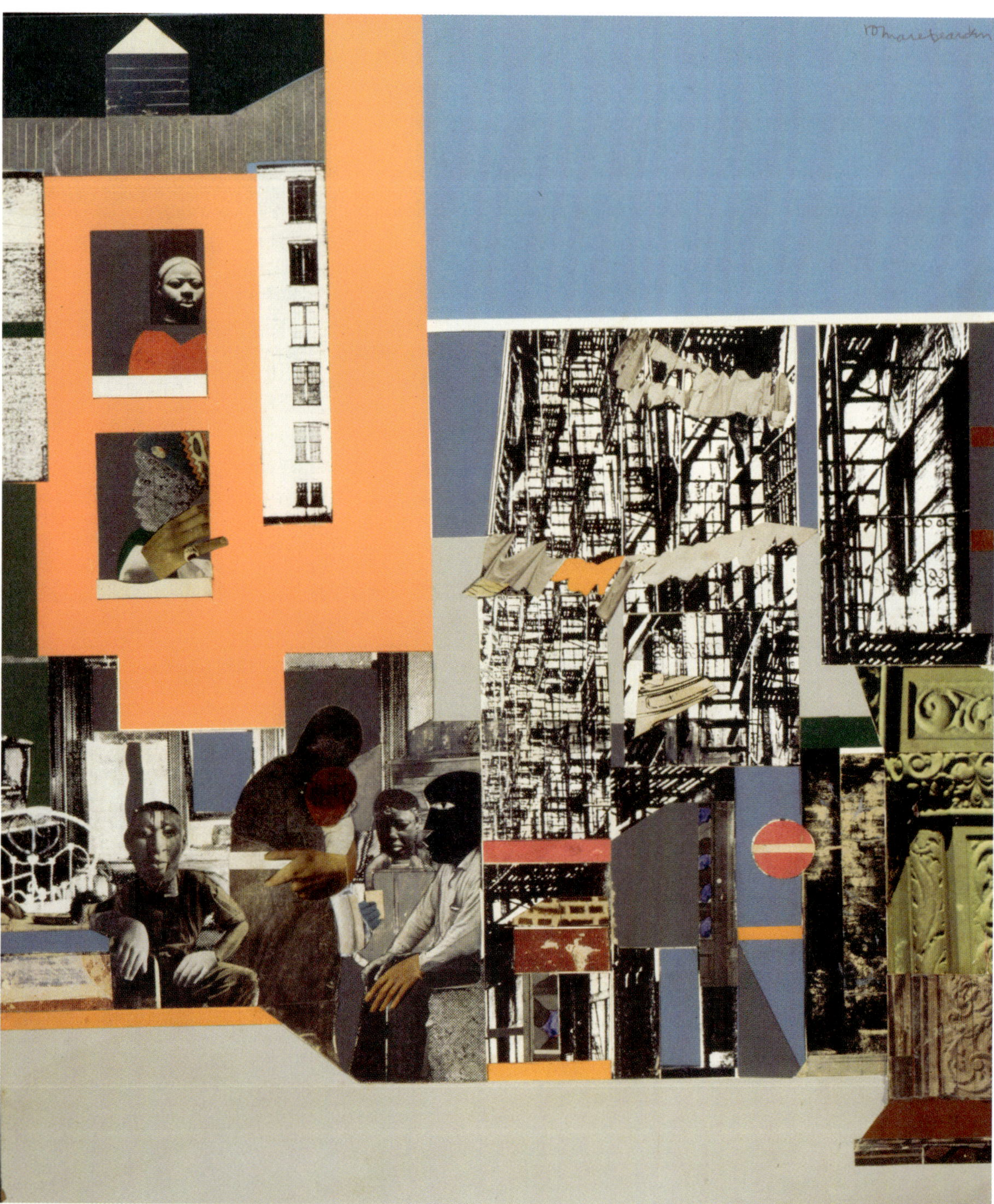

MID-20TH-CENTURY TRANSITIONS AND SURREALISM

8

By the mid-20th century, Social Realism had come into direct conflict with a renewed interest in abstract art, which in the 1940s was hailed by critics for its implicit denunciation of social agendas and of accessible narrative. National interest in art shifted from the iconography of the worker and the communal achievements of art centers and collaborative mural projects to more personal motifs and solitary accomplishment. Printmaking—which had flourished during the Depression years—was devalued because it could be readily reproduced. On the other hand, easel painting was reasserted as the most valued form of art because it was a rarefied expression of artistic genius. This change also mirrored a shift in American socioeconomics from the socialism of the Depression years to the capitalism of the war years, during which the country regained economic stability. This tug of war between collectivist and individual endeavors, political and personal iconography, and figurative and abstract art resulted in an eclectic midcentury mix of genres.

FIGURATION VERSUS ABSTRACTION: A NATIONAL DEBATE

The tension between figurative and abstract art was publicized in a canonical debate between two of the 20th century's most influential art theorists: Walter Benjamin (1892–1940) and Clement Greenberg (1909–94). In 1936, Benjamin, a **Marxist** critic, published the essay "The Work of Art in an Age of Mechanical Reproducibility." Benjamin contended that, with the onset of film, photographic, and mechanical print production, art became available (in reproduction) to so many people that it lost its status as the embodiment of creative genius and cultural rarity. Mechanical reproduction allowed for millions of images of an original artwork to be disseminated. At the same time, mass dispersal stripped the original artwork of its uniqueness—democratizing it, so to speak. Benjamin applauded the potential for art to abandon its highbrow aura—once nurtured only in the exclusive atmosphere of museums and in the homes of wealthy collectors—and to make itself accessible to the proletariat.

Benjamin's argument was countered in 1939 by Clement Greenberg, who was a champion of abstract art. Greenberg argued in his essay "Avant-Garde and Kitsch" that art should be neither figurative nor easily comprehended, because these characteristics were essentially lowbrow and reduced art to simple storytelling. He referred to figurative art styles such as Social Realism as "**kitsch**," a word that has since come to mean "tacky" and "inauthentic." Greenberg believed that art had to be **avant-garde**, original, and centered on

◀ Romare Bearden, *Black Manhattan*, 1969, collage on board, 25½″ × 21¼″.

process and materials—that is, form—rather than narrative content or iconography. Greenberg also argued that artists who created art for the establishment (i.e., the government or private patrons with a given agenda) rather than for themselves would invariably produce work that is clichéd. Hence, abstraction became associated with individual freedom and Social Realism with communist collectivism.

The debate between Benjamin and Greenberg mirrored sweeping changes in the political climate of the United States that began in 1940s and peaked after World War II. Conservative elements took control of Congress in 1940, and President Roosevelt's New Deal came under attack as "wasteful, propagandistic, and filled with Communists." The WPA-FAP was especially targeted, because of its collectivist and socialist reputation. By 1943, the WPA had lost popular support, and those associated with its programs became suspect as "un-American," an accusation that anticipated the indictments of the **McCarthy era** and the **Cold War**.

The Cold War between the United States and the Soviet Union commenced after World War II, as the two nations contended for imperial control of the globe. By the early 1950s, growing anticommunist sentiment culminated in the formation of the House Un-American Activities Committee (HUAC). Spearheaded by Senator Joseph R. McCarthy (1908–57), the HUAC targeted political progressives who were, or had been, affiliated with the Communist Party and with the WPA. The HUAC maintained blacklists: rosters of citizens of all races who were suspected, with and without substantiation, of harboring communist sympathies. It succeeded in destroying or impeding the careers of many Americans. If one's name appeared on a blacklist, one's career, job, and even friends could be lost. As a result of the HUAC's hearings (which were televised nationwide), an atmosphere of acute suspicion and paranoia prevailed in the United States for nearly a decade.

African-American artists, whether or not they had been associated with the Communist Party or the WPA, were viewed with skepticism, as was the Social Realist art that so many black artists had embraced. The proletariat themes of WPA murals and prints became synonymous with communist concepts of collective labor and social parity. Artists of color—who, in the past, had routinely been consigned to the fringe of the art world—found themselves even further displaced. They were barred access to art dealers and galleries, particularly if they continued to produce figurative rather than abstract art. Many found the climate in the United States untenable and opted to relocate permanently to either Europe or Mexico. Many expatriates favored Mexico because of its lively socialist art scene. As Romare Bearden and historian Harry Henderson stated, "No one knows exactly how many of these [expatriate] artists there are, but their absence represents a cultural loss to the United States."

THE LEGACY OF SOCIAL REALISM

Elizabeth Catlett

Sculptor, painter, and printmaker Elizabeth Catlett (1915–2012) was one such loss to American culture. Best known for her political prints and her commanding abstract sculptures of women, Catlett's large body of work, spanning nearly a century, is difficult to quantify. She was part of the Social Realist printmaking scene at the South Side Community Art Center in Chicago in the 1930s (see Chapter 7), and of a similar movement in Mexico in the 1940s. In the 1950s, she became a target of the HUAC because of her staunch support of labor unions and her association with communist institutions. In the 1960s and 1970s, she created a persuasive suite of prints and sculptures in support of the Civil Rights and Black Liberation Movements; and she became one of the leaders of the Black Arts Movement (see Chapter 10). A political and creative powerhouse, Catlett could rightly be identified with Social Realism, abstraction, the Black Arts Movement, or the Women's Art Movement, all of which are embodied in her artwork.

Catlett was born in Washington, D.C., and was encouraged to develop her artistic talent by her family and teachers. As a teenager living in the nation's capital, Catlett was as much an activist as she was an artist. While in high school, she participated in a rally in front of the Supreme Court building, during which she and other demonstrators wore nooses around their necks to draw Congressional support for antilynching legislation.

As a Howard University student in the early 1930s, Catlett joined the National Student League, an antifascist and pacifist group. Catlett also came into contact with key Harlem Renaissance figures who served on Howard's faculty. She studied African art with James Herring, printmaking with James Wells, design with Lois Jones, and painting with James Porter. Although she did not meet Alain Locke during her college years, Catlett was very much aware of his aesthetic doctrine and had read his important 1925 essay, "The Legacy of the Ancestral Arts." These influential role models shaped Catlett's own aesthetic outlook as well as the development of her early career. Porter and Wells, for example, arranged for a PWAP (an early iteration of the WPA) assignment for Catlett to design a mural on the subject of Harlem.

Catlett's Howard professors also exposed her to the art of Mexican painter and illustrator Miguel Covarrubias (1904–57). Covarrubias lived in New York during the Harlem Renaissance and created celebrity caricatures for the *New Yorker* magazine as well as book illustrations for Langston Hughes, Zora Neale Hurston, and others. Catlett was most impressed with his bitingly witty—if not very flattering—caricatures of celebrities that were wildly popular. She borrowed from his stylistic approach a synthesis of the figurative and the abstract that marked Art Deco–era caricature in general. This exposure to the art of Mexico would also fuel in Catlett a lifelong admiration for the country.

Catlett graduated from Howard University in 1935 and began teaching in the Durham, North Carolina, public school system. She campaigned to raise the salaries of African-American teachers, who were paid only half as much as their white colleagues, but she soon tired of the long hours and low pay. Catlett resigned from her teaching position and enrolled in the graduate art program at the State University of Iowa, where she trained in a variety of sculptural and painting media. Her painting professor was Regionalist and WPA artist Grant Wood (1891–1948), who encouraged Catlett to strive for technical precision in her work and to derive her subject matter from her own experiences. Just before graduation, Catlett was informed that she would be receiving an MA rather than an MFA degree on the pretext that she had not completed enough studio courses (although this was not the case). As Catlett understood it, the real reason for the degree substitution was to prevent a black woman from becoming the first person to receive an MFA from Iowa, ahead of one of Catlett's own instructors, who was also vying for the degree. However, Wood convinced the university to grant Catlett the MFA degree she had earned.

In 1940, Catlett was hired to chair the art department at Dillard University in New Orleans, an HBCU chartered in 1930, where she taught art history, drawing, painting, and printmaking. However, she came into direct conflict with the university administration when she attempted to organize drawing classes with nude models, which they prevented. She also protested when her students were refused admittance to the Delgado Museum, which was located in a segregated park. Eventually, a special arrangement was made for her students to visit on a day when the museum was closed to the public. When several Dillard students were arrested for tampering with public segregation signage, Catlett arranged for the students' release from jail, which also angered the Dillard Board of Trustees. Finally, when the Dillard board mandated that faculty had to teach during the summer session without a salary increase, Catlett resigned. She had only been at Dillard for two years.

Although Catlett faced challenges in her teaching career, she had no difficulty in her career as an artist. Her work was included in Alain Locke's 1940 Chicago American Negro Exposition, where she won a first prize in sculpture for a limestone work of a mother and child. Catlett spent the summer of 1941 in Chicago with friend and fellow artist Margaret Taylor Burroughs studying sculpture at the Chicago Art Institute and lithography at the Southside Community Art Center. Catlett met Charles White there and married him later that year. During their brief marriage, the couple shared an interest in Social Realism and portrayals of the black proletariat. In the spring of 1942, they moved to New York, where Catlett was exposed to the Cubist forms of Russian-born sculptor Ossip Zadkine (1890–1967), with whom she studied privately. Catlett's figurative style began to transform into a fusion of Cubism and African figural austerity. In addition to developing her sculptural technique, Catlett studied lithography at the Art Students League

Catlett supported herself by teaching at Harlem's progressive George Washington Carver Community School, which was administered by socialists who sought to provide educational opportunities to the black poor. The Carver School was supervised by writer Gwendolyn Bennett (1902–81), onetime president of the Harlem Artists Guild and the director of the Harlem Community Art Center after Savage. Other sponsors of the Carver School included Rev. Adam Clayton Powell, Sr. (1865–1953), and Benjamin Davis, Jr. (1903–64), who was associated with the National Central Committee of the Communist Party. Catlett designed posters, raised funds, and taught an assortment of classes, from sculpture to dressmaking, for the school.

In 1945 and 1946, Catlett was awarded a Rosenwald Fellowship to produce a series of works on the subject of black women. She traveled to Mexico, where she immersed herself in the public art movement there and met Rivera and Siqueiros. Catlett was sympathetic to their ***mexicanidad* style**, which fused elements of indigenous Central American art with Spanish artistic traditions. Catlett also allied herself with the Taller de Gráfica Popular (People's Print Workshop; TGP), which produced graphic design for antifascist, popular, and labor coalitions. Catlett was one of the first women to join the Taller, and she would remain an affiliate for more than two decades.

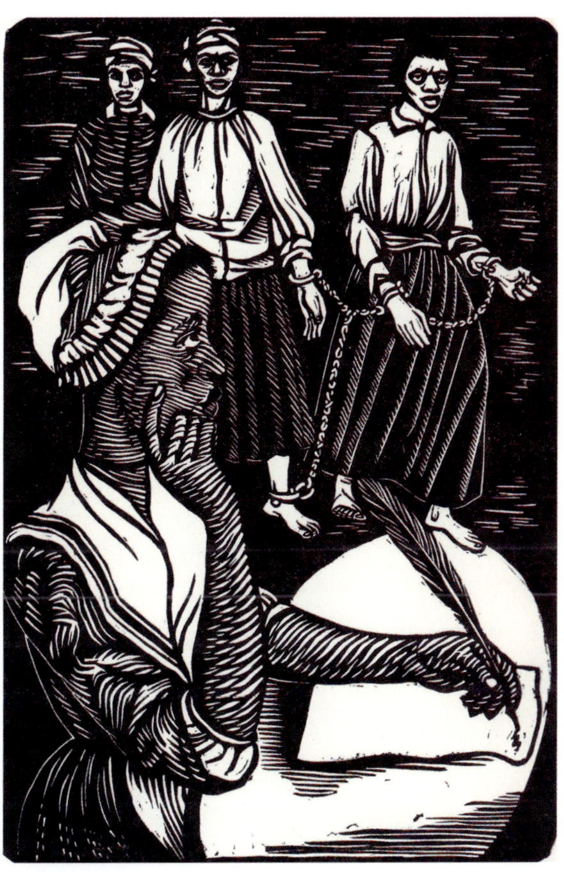

▲ 8.1 Elizabeth Catlett, *In Phillis Wheatley I Proved Intellectual Equality in the Midst of Slavery*, from *The Negro Woman* series, 1946–47, linocut, 9″ × 5.75″.

Catlett met TGP member Francisco (Pancho) Mora (1922–2002), and, in 1946, after divorcing Charles White, she moved to Mexico and married Mora, with whom she had three sons. The couple remained together as spouses and creative colleagues for more than half a century. Under the sway of the Mexican aesthetic and in the supportive atmosphere of the Taller, Catlett completed her Rosenwald Fund assignment: a series of 15 linocuts entitled *The Negro Woman*. The print suite paid homage to the achievements of African-American women, from anonymous field hands and servants to specific heroines such as Sojourner Truth, Harriet Tubman, and Phillis Wheatley (Figure 8.1). The Wheatley print was deliberately patterned after Scipio Moorhead's 1773 drawing of the black poet (Chapter 2 chapter-opening image). Catlett created multiple images of Wheatley in a variety of media over several decades, from the 1940s to the 1960s. Indicative of her stylistic and material fluidity, Catlett produced a bronze figurative sculpture of Wheatley in the same pose, now in the collection of the Cincinnati Art Museum. She also made several abstract sculptures entitled *Pensive Figure* (see Figure 8.2 for one example) in both bronze and cedar, which radiate the same mood of intellectualism as the more figurative versions. Inspired by multiple aesthetic wellsprings, Catlett imbued *Pensive Figure* with the austerity of Modernist abstraction and pre-Columbian sculptural form.

In the 1950s, Catlett became a target of the HUAC as a result of her earlier associations with the WPA and the Carver School, as well as her membership in the TGP. Coincident with the rise of abstract art in the United States, the Mexican predilection for Social Realism also began to wane. Younger Mexican artists allied themselves with what they saw as the loftier aims of **art-for-art's-sake** rather than art for the people. The Mexican muralists lost ground to their "ideological nemesis," apolitical painter Rufino Tamayo (1899–1991). Tamayo revived easel painting as the preeminent medium for Mexican art. His painting style seamlessly merged influences

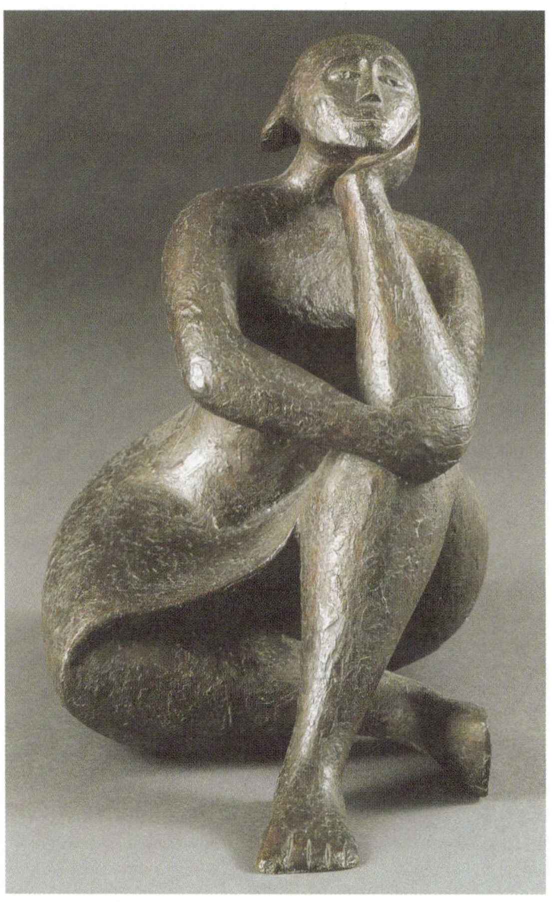

▲ **8.2** Elizabeth Catlett, *Pensive Figure*, 1968, bronze, 18″ × 12″ × 17″.

Art © Catlett Mora Family Trust / licensed by VAGA, New York, NY. Image: Sheldon Museum of Art, University of Nebraska—Lincoln, Anna R. and Frank M. Hall Charitable Trust, H-3113. Photo © Sheldon Museum of Art.

from Cubism, Mexican folk art, and pre-Hispanic sources, making him a Modernist paradigm for young artists. Abstraction soon predominated in Mexico just as it did in the United States.

Due to its commitment to left-wing politics and to the tenets of Social Realism, the TGP was designated a communist front organization by the HUAC, and its members were barred from entry into the United States. Catlett, who was a U.S. citizen, was ordered in 1955 to submit a written declaration of her political affiliations and to name other alleged Communist Party affiliates. She refused and was arrested as a "foreign agitator" by Mexican authorities in collusion with the HUAC. In protest, she made the radical decision to renounce her American citizenship on her release from prison. In 1962, she became a citizen of Mexico, at which time the U.S. government promptly declared her an "undesirable alien" and for the next ten years prohibited her from returning to America.

Despite this setback, Catlett thrived professionally in Mexico. In 1958, she was appointed the first woman to head the department of sculpture at the Universidad Nacional Autónoma in Mexico City. She remained on the faculty there for the next 15 years. While in exile in Mexico, Catlett produced dozens of prints in support of the Civil Rights and Black Power Movements in the United States (see Chapter 10). Finally, in 1971, she was permitted to return to the United States after officials from the Studio Museum in Harlem (who were mounting a major Catlett retrospective) lobbied the State Department to grant her a visa.

Catlett remained active and prolific for the remainder of her life. Splitting her time between Cuernavaca and New York's Battery Park City, where she maintained a pied-à-terre, Catlett became an icon of African-American political art and received many honors and awards. Well into her nineties, Catlett was still creating monumental public artworks such as her 15-foot-tall bronze sculpture honoring black writer Ralph Ellison's *Invisible Man*, installed in New York's Riverside Park in 2003, and her 13-foot-tall bronze sculpture of jazz great Mahalia Jackson, installed in 2010 in Louis Armstrong Park in New Orleans.

Ellis Wilson

Ellis Wilson's (1899–1977) now-iconic 1950s painting *Funeral Procession* was viewed by millions of Americans thanks to its appearance on the top-rated TV series *The Cosby Show*, about the black upper-middle-class Huxtable family (Figure 8.3). The show aired for eight years, from 1984 to 1992, and for seven of those years Ellis's *Funeral Procession* hung proudly over the Huxtable mantel.

While still a boy, Ellis Wilson worked as a custodian in a dress shop. When the proprietor of the store discovered Wilson's talent for drawing, he asked him to draw images on the store window to attract customers, which Ellis did from 1912 to 1915. Ellis was educated in Kentucky's segregated school system in Mayfield and then studied education and agriculture for two years at Kentucky Normal and Industrial Institute (now Kentucky State University). However, his desire to study art led him in 1919 to Chicago; there he enrolled in the School of the Art Institute, where he learned conventional drawing and painting techniques. He also joined the Chicago Art League, which had held annual exhibits at the institute beginning in 1880. After graduating from the institute in 1923, Wilson worked as a graphic designer for the next five years. Unable to earn a reliable living in Chicago, however, he decided to move to New York in 1928, where he would remain for the rest of his life.

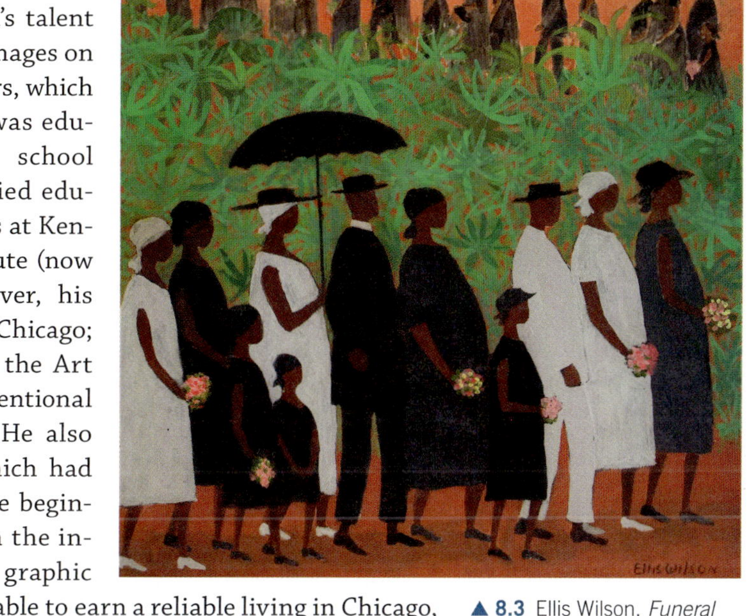

▲ **8.3** Ellis Wilson, *Funeral Procession*, c. 1950s, oil on composite board, 30.5″ × 29.25″.

Aaron Douglas Collection, Amistad Research Center, Tulane University, New Orleans, LA.

In New York in the 1930s, Wilson studied privately with the Ashcan School artist Xavier Barille (1891–1981), who worked for the WPA and ran his own boutique art school. Wilson joined the Harlem Artists Guild, participated in the Harmon Foundation exhibits (winning an honorable mention in 1933), and worked for the WPA-FAP as a painter of topographic views of New York City.

Wilson's early works reflected Social Realist form and content. By the 1940s and 1950s, however, he had developed his signature painting style, which featured the compressed space and flat forms of Synthetic Cubism. His *Funeral Procession* portrays a cortège of mourners, in two rows, winding up a verdant hillside. The vibrant organic forms of the tropical flora contrast with the plain clothing of the procession, and with the rigidity of their profiles and the flatness of their bodies, which appear like paper cutouts. Carefully composed, Willis's semiabstract design plays the lush, sunlit atmosphere of the tropics—the embodiment of life at its most fertile—against the solemnity of the event and the theme of death.

In 1944, Wilson won a Guggenheim award and used the funds to travel throughout the American South, including the Georgia Sea Islands, where Eldzier Cortor was also painting at the time (discussed later in this chapter). Between 1944 and 1948, Wilson created and exhibited images, painted with empathy and dignity, of American blacks in rural settings—including farmworkers, market vendors, town scenes, farm animals, and fishermen—maintaining ties with Social Realist content, if not form.

Wilson's 1952 painting of a fisherwoman won a $3,000 prize at the second annual Terry National Art Exhibition in Coral Gables, Florida. He used the prize money to spend two years in Haiti (to which the artist later made three additional prolonged visits). On his return to New York in 1954, Wilson's Haitian paintings were featured at New York's Contemporary Art Gallery in a show titled *Impressions of Haiti*. The critics were most impressed by Wilson's rich palette and minimalist forms. They also remarked on the artist's ability to imbue ordinary people with heroism and dignity. After a second showing of his Haitian pictures at the same venue in 1960, Wilson's success ebbed abruptly resulting from the popularity of nonrepresentational painting and the rise of conceptual art. He worked for the next several years as a security guard and docent at New York's Riverside Museum.

Wilson exhibited twice more during his lifetime. In 1971, Fisk University in Nashville mounted a retrospective, and the North Carolina Museum of Art included him in a group show. Impoverished at the end of his life, Wilson died eight years before *The Cosby Show* drew so much attention to his work. Wilson is buried in a pauper's grave in New York, whereabouts unknown. However, after being featured on *The Cosby Show*, there was renewed interest in him. In 2000, the University of Mississippi Museum mounted a well-received traveling retrospective of the artist's work.

Romare Bearden

Like that of Wilson and Catlett, the art of Romare Bearden (1911–88) fluctuates from illusionism to abstraction and covers a wide range of media, from painting to collage. Bearden began his career in the socially engaged decade of the 1930s. He was a multitalented artist with professional success in visual art, musical composition, art and world history, and classical literature.

Although Bearden was born in Charlotte, North Carolina, he lived as a youth in Pittsburgh and Harlem at the end of the Renaissance. While attending college in New York in the early 1930s, Bearden exhibited at the Harlem YMCA, Savage's Harlem Art Workshop, and the 306 salon. By 1941, he was living in rented studio space in the heart of Harlem on 125th Street. Although he left Harlem for downtown Manhattan in 1956, his memories of Harlem would continue to inform his work for decades. Bearden also drew on his childhood in Charlotte and Pittsburgh, and on such eclectic historical sources as Dutch Baroque and early Renaissance painting, Cubism, Fauvism, African sculpture, Byzantine mosaics, Japanese ***ukiyo-e*** woodblock prints, traditional Chinese landscapes, and jazz and popular music. Bearden worked in oil and watercolor, **collage**, **photomontage**, and prints. In addition, he designed costumes and sets for the Alvin Ailey American Dance Theater Company, among other groups.

During the 1930s, Bearden studied at Lincoln University, Boston University, and New York University (NYU), receiving a BS-degree education from NYU in 1935. During this period, he also published his own editorials and essays on art, society, and politics and was an active member of the Harlem Artists Guild. From 1935 to 1937, Bearden studied at the Art Students League with German **Neue Sachlichkeit** artist George Grosz (1893–1959), who specialized in political caricature. Bearden also worked as an editorial cartoonist for the *Baltimore Afro-American*, the *Crisis*, the *Saturday Evening Post*, and *Colliers*. His steadiest income, however, came from a 30-year career (with occasional breaks to travel and serve in the armed forces) with the New York City Department of Social Services, which lasted until his retirement in 1969.

A consummate colorist, even Bearden's figurative works of the early 1940s on Social Realist subjects, such as *Factory Workers* (Figure 8.4), were vibrantly painted—a formal element that remained consistent throughout his career. *Factory Workers* was produced for the June 1942 issue of *Fortune* magazine to accompany an essay on the detrimental effects of racial segregation on America. The Social Realist style of Bearden's depiction ideally suited the subject matter, as did its predominantly red, white, and blue palette, symbolizing America. Occupying the foreground space are three black men in suit jackets and caps. In the distance Bearden rendered the smokestacks of a steel mill, where the three men were refused work due to their race.

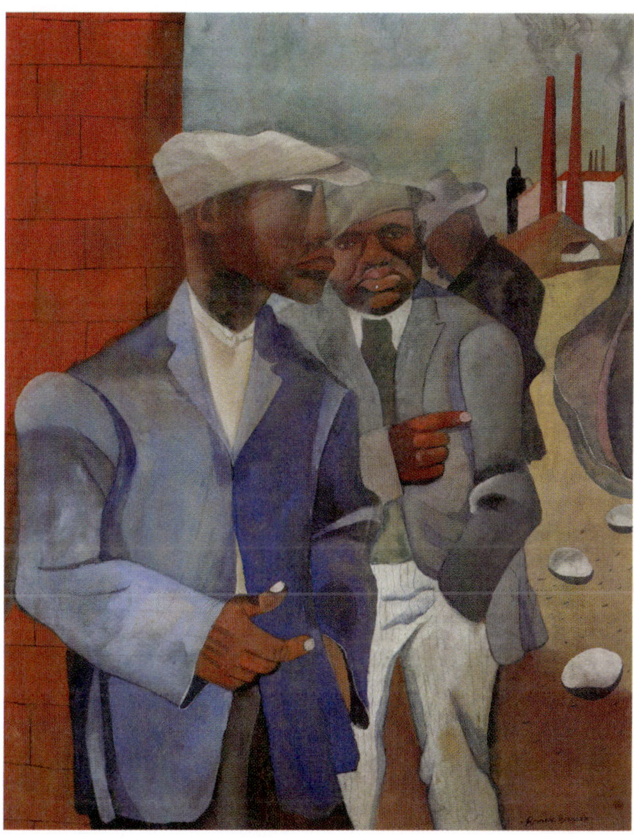

▲ **8.4** Romare Bearden, *Factory Workers*, 1942, gouache and casein on paper, 37.25″ × 28.5″.

Art © Romare Bearden Foundation / licensed by VAGA, New York, NY. Image: Minneapolis Institute of Arts, MN / the John R. Van Derlip Fund / Bridgeman Images.

After serving in the U.S. Army, stationed in Harlem during World War II, Bearden traveled on the GI Bill for seven months in 1950 to Nice, Florence, Rome, Venice, and Paris. He studied philosophy at the Sorbonne in Paris and took classes in French language and Buddhism. Bearden's exposure to abstraction in Europe and a harsh critique published in the *New York Times* that lambasted Bearden's earlier Social Realist art prompted him to turn to abstraction. By the second half of the 1940s and continuing throughout the 1950s, Bearden abandoned the overt figuration of works like *Factory Workers*, replacing it with a Cubist lexicon that approximated the look of stained glass. Thematically, during this period Bearden tended toward biblical, Homeric, and jazz themes.

By the 1960s, however, Bearden had developed his signature style of abstract collage and photomontage, for which he is best known. His cut-and-pasted paper compositions offer flat, abstracted scenes of African-American spiritual practices, mood-invoking Harlem street scenes, depictions of jazz clubs and southern American interiors, and organically composed portrayals of African-American domestic and familial life. Bearden's acclaimed collage *Black Manhattan* is a classic representation of the artist's formal approach (see chapter-opening image). Again utilizing a suggestive red, white, and blue palette, Bearden constructed a composition evocative of the early 20th-century **De Stijl** paintings of Dutch artist Piet Mondrian (1872–1944) in both its palette and block construction. Flat areas of color for blue sky and red tenements are interspersed with photo cutouts of brownstones and fire escapes, African sculptural faces, collaged profiles framed by windows, architectural decoration, and interior elements that evoke the energy and vitality of urban life.

Bearden is also well known for cofounding the civil rights artists group Spiral, which mounted a single show of works by member artists in monochromatic shades of gray, black, and white intended to signify the racial struggle between blacks and whites in America. Although Spiral existed for only a few short years, it set an example for other politically engaged artists' collectives to follow (see Chapter 10). During the course of his career, Bearden helped to found the Studio Museum in Harlem, New York's Cinque Gallery with Norman Lewis (see Chapter 9) and Ernest Crichlow, and the Black Academy of Arts and Letters. Among Bearden's most important contributions to African-American art are his two books (written with collaborator Harry Henderson), *Six Black Masters of American Art* (1972) and *A History of African American Artists: From 1792 to the Present* (1993). In 1987, a year before the artist's death, President Reagan presented Bearden with the National Medal of Arts.

Jacob Lawrence

Jacob Lawrence (1917–2000) likewise bridged the gap between Social Realism and abstraction. Born in Atlantic City, in 1930, at age 13, he moved with his mother to Harlem. He began studying art with Charles Alston while he was still a teenager, and he took classes at the Harlem Community Art Center. By 1937, he had enrolled in a two-year program at the American Artists School, a socialist institution. In 1937, Lawrence assisted Alston on the Harlem Hospital murals (see Chapter 7), and in 1938 he joined the easel division of the WPA-FAP. Lawrence was interested in documenting black history through painting. After research at the Schomburg Center, he created several memorable narrative suites on Haitian revolutionary leader Toussaint Louverture, Underground Railroad heroine Harriet Tubman, and escaped slave and abolitionist Frederick Douglass.

In 1940, Lawrence won a Rosenwald Fund award that enabled him to rent a studio on 125th Street in Harlem, in the same building as Bearden. At this time, Lawrence began work on his most celebrated series of paintings, the *Migration of the Negro* (Figure 8.5). Using tempera paint on wood panels and a Synthetic Cubist formal language similar to that of Aaron Douglas and Ellis Wilson, Lawrence chronicled the ongoing migration of vast numbers of African Americans from the rural South to the urban North. Lawrence's future wife and fellow artist, Gwendolyn Knight (discussed later in this chapter), assisted on the project by **gessoing** the panels and helping Lawrence to select key historical moments for inclusion in the epic series. Lawrence completed 60 scenes, which reveal his consummate understanding of color harmonies and contrasts and his inimitable flair for compositional balance.

Grounded in the Social Realist philosophy of art for the people (despite the abstracted forms), the panels are accompanied by protracted descriptive titles such as "The Negroes were given free passage on the railroads which was paid back by Northern industry. It was an agreement that the people brought North on these railroads were to pay back their passage after they had received jobs." The purpose of the titles was to teach workaday viewers the history of the Great Migration. In this series, Lawrence

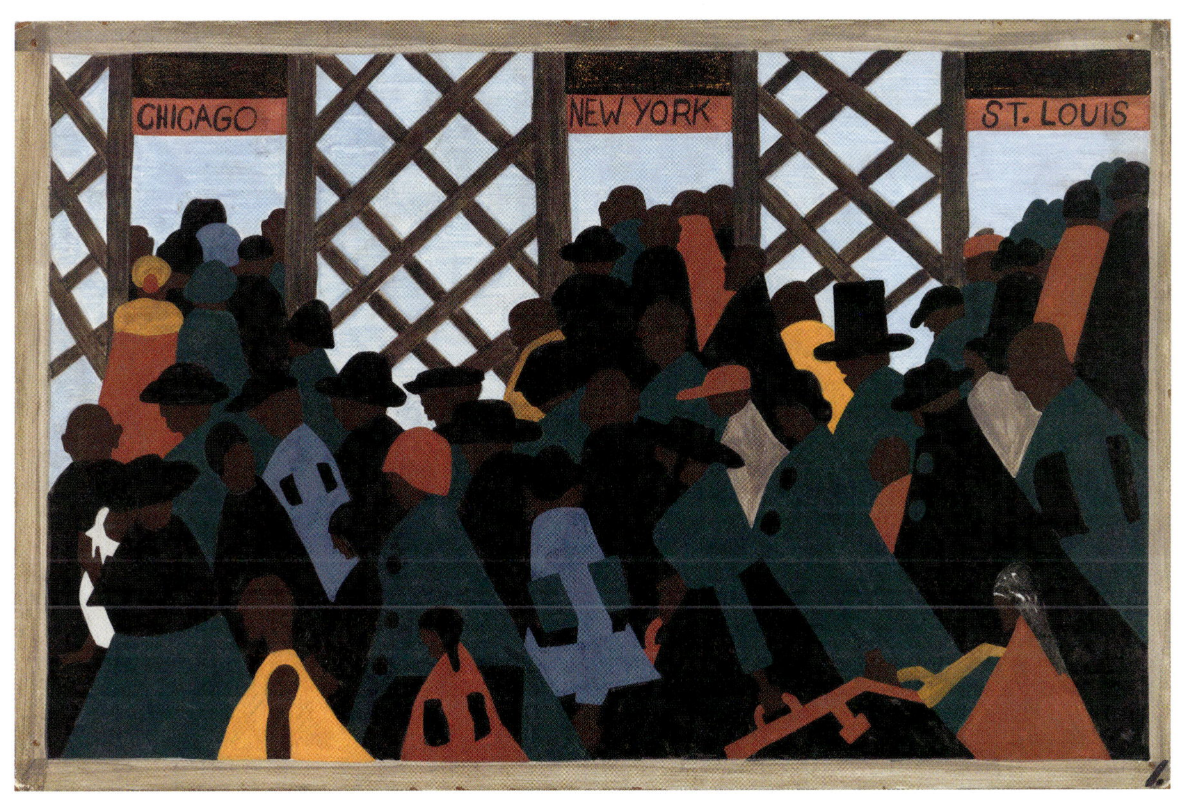

addressed a range of critical concerns. Among these were the role of women workers in society, poverty, hunger, the rigors of travel for black migrants, race riots, lynchings, the struggle for adequate education, discrimination in the workplace, overcrowded urban tenements, tuberculosis epidemics, and voting rights.

▲ **8.5** Jacob Lawrence, the *Migration* series, panel no. 1: *During World War I there was a great migration north by southern African Americans*, 1940–41, casein tempera on hardboard, 12″ × 18″.

The Phillips Collection, Washington, D.C. © 2015 the Jacob and Gwendolyn Knight Lawrence Foundation, Seattle, WA / Artists Rights Society (ARS), New York, NY.

Art dealer Edith Halpert mounted an exhibit of the series in the Downtown Gallery in 1941. (She continued to represent and show Lawrence's work until 1953.) The 1941 show brought unprecedented attention to the young Lawrence, including color reproductions of six of the works in *Fortune Magazine* and a national touring show of the suite. The *Migration* series impressed art world arbiters to such an extent that it became the object of a bidding war between the Phillips Collection in Washington, D.C., and New York's Museum of Modern Art (MoMA). Today, the odd-numbered panels reside in the Philips Collection and the even-numbered panels belong to the MoMA (although all of the 60 panels are periodically exhibited together).

Lawrence's celebrity led to regular showings at the Whitney Museum, among numerous other prestigious art venues. Throughout the 1940s, Lawrence provided illustrations for various magazines as well as for Langston Hughes's *One Way Ticket*, published in 1949. He also secured a series of teaching positions during the 1940s and 1950s, beginning in 1946 with an appointment from one-time Bauhaus artist Joseph Albers (1888–1976) to the faculty of Black Mountain College in North Carolina. This led to a position at Brooklyn's Pratt Institute, where he taught for 15 years, from the mid-1950s until the early 1970s, and at several other schools.

Eventually, in 1971, Lawrence was appointed to a full-time tenured faculty position at the University of Washington in Seattle, where he and his wife settled permanently.

Lawrence worked tirelessly in Seattle. In response to ever-growing commissions, he painted murals for institutions such as the University of Washington and Howard University and created a 72-foot mosaic mural entitled *New York in Transit* for the Times Square subway station in New York City. His major awards include the National Medal of Arts, the NAACP Spingarn Medal, membership in the American Academy of Arts and Letters, and 18 honorary doctorates.

Gwendolyn Knight Lawrence

Lawrence's wife, Barbadian émigré Gwendolyn Knight Lawrence (1913–2005), settled first in St. Louis and then, in 1926, at the onset of the Renaissance, in Harlem. From 1926 to 1931, the teenager came under the influence of the intense creative energy of the Harlem Renaissance. In 1931, she enrolled at Howard University, where she studied design with Lois Jones, painting with James Porter, and printmaking with James Wells. When, in 1933, the financial difficulties of the Depression made it impossible for Knight to pay her university expenses, she returned to Harlem to study at the Harlem Community Art Center, where she met Lawrence, who was also a student there.

▼ **8.6** Gwendolyn Knight Lawrence, *Portrait of a Girl*, 1940, oil on canvas, 15″ × 14″.

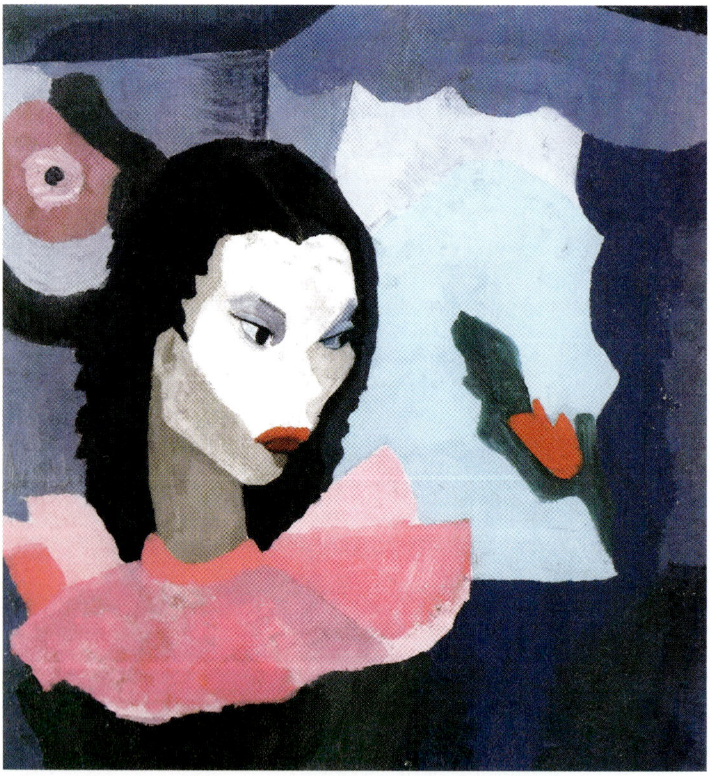

Knight's art ranged from portraits to landscapes to iconic mother-and-child portrayals. Equally eclectic were her artistic influences, which were at once abstract and figurative, Fauvist and Expressionist. In addition to paintings, Knight's work included lithographs, serigraphs, silkscreens, etchings, and aquatints. Knight painted in the lyrical style of Marie Laurencin (1883–1956), a French artist of the Cubist circle. Knight transfigured Laurencin's style, however, with dynamic silhouettes and a commanding palette. Although her works were often described in feminine terms such as "light" and "airy," a discerning eye will recognize the intense introspection of many of Knight's works, achieved with an exquisitely subtle use of line and unmodulated zones of color. These qualities are evident in Knight's *Portrait of a Girl*, from the 1940s, which utilizes sharp facial angles, saturated color, and an intense sitter's gaze to emote depth of feeling and a sense of isolation (Figure 8.6).

Suggested in the right background of *Portrait of a Girl* is the pale blue silhouette of a horse's head, which, like the girl, is shown in a three-quarter view with a red swipe of the brush at its mouth. The horse motif and its allusions to dance-inspired movements stemming from the artist's avocation as a dancer, would become a recurring theme in Knight's art toward the end of her career, suggesting its self-referential iconography. As a devotee of the German Expressionists, Knight may have borrowed the motif from Der Blaue Reiter (the Blue Riders) group member Franz Marc (1880–1916), who painted the signature *Large Blue Horses* in 1911 as an expression of the profoundly transcendent and spiritual nature of art. As a **Jungian archetype**, the horse image has the potential to symbolize everything from personal freedom (the "unbridled") to physical grace, endurance, and strength. Knight's late-career horses, darkly rendered in blacks and grays, denote speed, agility, strength, steadfastness, mystery, and unknown destinations, as if they are metaphors for the artist herself. In Knight's own words, "Once I set that stage [for a work of art], it happens that some other spiritual, psychological things come into it." The self-referential nature of the artist's use of the horse motif, and of *Portrait of a Girl* specifically, may also be inferred from the resemblance of the sitter to the artist at the time she painted the work.

For a decade during the 1950s, Knight worked as an archivist for Condé Nast, publisher of dozens of popular magazines. Knight began exhibiting in the 1960s at the Forum Gallery in New York, noted for its stable of top-flight artists working in many different styles, including Bearden's teacher George Grosz, Matisse, Picasso, Ernst Ludwig Kirchner, Alexander Calder, Reginald Marsh, Ben Shahn, Jacob Lawrence, Charles White, and Ernest Crichlow. In 1976, Knight was honored with a major solo exhibit at the Seattle Art Museum sponsored by the Seattle chapter of the Links, Inc., now a 70-year-old exclusive, not-for-profit coalition composed mainly of professional black women who support cultural, educational, and civic causes. Many other awards and exhibits followed until her death, a few short years after her husband's passing.

John Biggers

Though too young to be directly associated with Social Realism, John Biggers (1934–2000) embodies its legacy more than most artists of his generation. Biggers shares with the Social Realist Movement an appreciation of the mural as a form of egalitarian public art. He was directly influenced by Charles White and Elizabeth Catlett, whom he met while the former was completing a mural commission for Hampton University. Biggers enrolled at Hampton in 1941 and studied under Viennese art educator Viktor Lowenfeld (1903–60). (Lowenfeld also arranged for the White mural commission.) Of particular interest to Lowenfeld was the relationship between art and psychology and the ability of art to express various aspects of the human condition. Lowenfeld shared his theories with both White and Biggers, which he outlined in his 1947 book, *Creative and Mental Growth*.

Biggers created his first major mural, *Dying Soldier*, as a college freshman, and Lowenfeld included it in a landmark exhibit entitled *Young Negro Art* which he curated for New York's Museum of Modern Art in 1943. Biggers's graphic depiction of a bloody battlefield and a dying soldier caught in a barbwire fence with the flesh of his chest torn away drew harsh criticism from the press, which, if nothing else, attested to the work's visual efficacy. Prophetically, Biggers was drafted into the navy that year and had to suspend his studies at Hampton. The experience drove Biggers into a severe depression, resulting in his medical discharge. By 1946, Biggers had resumed his art education and followed Lowenfeld to Pennsylvania State University, where his mentor had moved to develop an art education program. By 1948, Biggers had completed both BA and MA degrees.

In 1949, Biggers was hired to develop the art department at Texas Southern University, which he chaired for the next 34 years. Soon after his arrival, in the early 1950s, both the Houston and Dallas Museums of Fine Arts exhibited and then purchased his paintings for their collections (although Biggers was not permitted to attend either opening reception because of the segregation laws enforced in the state). While working at Texas Southern, Biggers simultaneously pursued a PhD under Lowenfeld at Penn State. A 1952 commission he received from the YWCA in Houston's African American Third Ward formed the core of his doctoral thesis. Proletariat, revolutionary, cultural, and historical in scope, *The Contribution of the Negro Woman to American Life and Education* depicts African-American women as mothers, teachers, nurses, doctors, revolutionary leaders, farmers, quilt makers, and lynching victims. In his dissertation, Biggers explained his choice of motif: "The [YWCA] building . . . offers a place for study, work, play, relaxation and communion for the Negro girls and women of Houston. Thus the writer's choice of subject matter for a mural grew naturally out of a folk need . . . such that occupants could . . . relate the subject matter to . . . their own personal experience." This statement underscores Biggers's belief in art as an implement of service to the "folk" community.

In 1957, with support from a UNESCO Fellowship, Biggers toured West Africa for six months. Biggers recorded his experiences in Africa and of "the washerwomen, farming women, fishermen, lumber workers, market women, mothers, fathers, and children" he met there (Figure 8.7). The trip resulted in Biggers's acclaimed 1962 book *Ananse: The Web of Life in Africa*, a collection

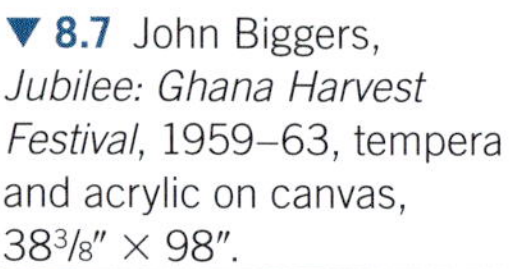

▼ **8.7** John Biggers, *Jubilee: Ghana Harvest Festival*, 1959–63, tempera and acrylic on canvas, $38\frac{3}{8}'' \times 98''$.

Art © John T. Biggers Estate / licensed by VAGA, New York, NY; Museum of Fine Arts, Houston, TX / museum purchase funded by Duke Energy / Bridgeman Images.

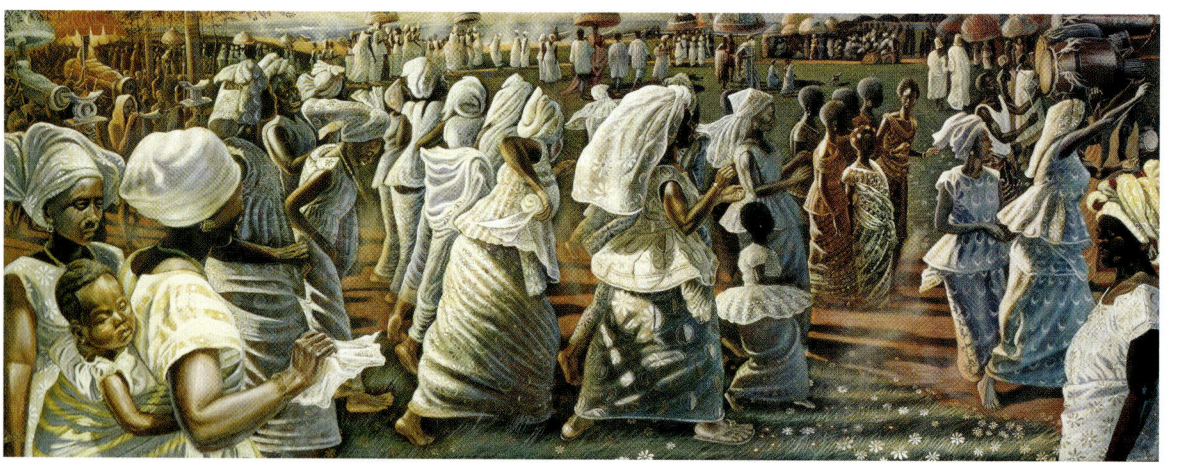

of nearly 90 drawings. The book's title pays homage to a powerful Ghanaian "trickster" god and griot whose cleverness, indomitability, and cultural role has been compared to that of the folkloric African-American storyteller Uncle Remus and one of his most beloved animal characters, Br'er (Brother) Rabbit.

Although Biggers retired from teaching in 1983, he continued as a prolific muralist for another 15 years. His public works are located in parks and buildings and on university campuses across the country, including *Sharecroppers* at the University of Pennsylvania (1947), the Adair Park Mural of shotgun houses in Houston (1982), and four African-inspired allegorical murals installed at Hampton University.

SURREALISM

Surrealism began as a literary art movement, founded in the mid-1920s by French poet André Breton (1896–1966), but it quickly expanded to include visual artists. The term "surreal," which means "beyond reality," was coined by French poet, filmmaker, and critic Guillaume Apollinaire (1880–1918) and was adopted by Breton when he wrote the *Surrealist Manifesto* in 1924. Breton promoted art that consisted of "pure psychic **automatism** by which . . . one expresses the true function of thought, dictated in the absence of all control exerted by reason, and outside all aesthetic or moral preoccupations." Breton believed in the artist's right to create without concern for moral judgments, censorship, or sociopolitical concerns—a concept known as **aestheticism**. Breton also advocated "pure psychic automatism," or free association that is created by the subconscious rather than the logical mind. Breton's ideas were applied to drawing and painting wherein the artist would allow his hand to move freely over a canvas or paper surface, without attempting to "compose" an image.

The Surrealist art movement was related to, and inspired by, the writings of psychoanalyst Sigmund Freud (1856–1939). Freud's analyses of dreams and the subconscious (in particular his 1900 *Interpretation of Dreams*) brought international attention to the power of the subconscious mind to affect outward human behavior. Both Freud and Breton believed that dreams were actualizations of the mind's subconscious activity and were, therefore, worthy of examination and interpretation. For visual artists, this meant that dreams could and should be externalized as paintings. Such images might include **anamorphs** (hidden images), elements of the intuitive and spontaneous, themes of fantasy and imagination, and irrational narrative—all characteristics that one finds in dreams. With certain exceptions, Surrealist artists avoided abstraction. Their paintings are stylistically "realistic" or representational, while at the same time iconographically dreamlike and profoundly psychological. By the 1930s in Europe and the 1940s in the United States, Surrealism had amassed a significant following of practitioners and admirers, including African-Americans who engaged the activities and philosophies of the Surrealists to varying degrees—mostly in paintings that evoked the quality of dreams.

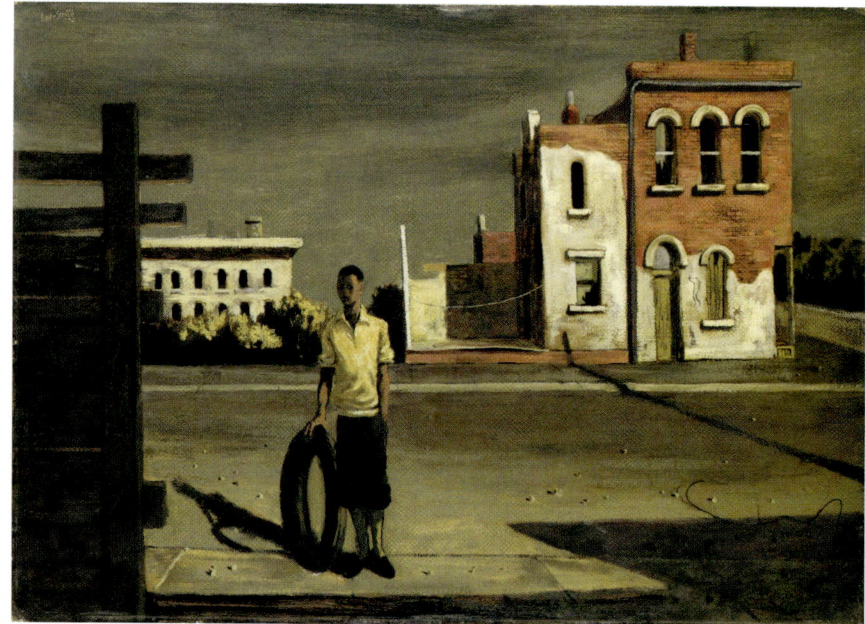

▶ **8.8** Hughie Lee-Smith, *Boy with a Tire*, 1952, oil on panel, 25″ × 18¼″.

Art © Estate of Hughie Lee-Smith / licensed by VAGA, New York, NY. Photo: Detroit Institute of Arts / Bridgeman Images.

▼ **8.9** Giorgio de Chirico, *Mystery and Melancholy of a Street*, 1914, oil on canvas, 33½″ × 27″.

© 2015 Artists Rights Society (ARS), New York, NY / SIAE, Rome. Photo: Private collection / De Agostini Picture Library / G. Nimatallah / Bridgeman Images.

Hughie Lee-Smith

The African-American artist whose work most closely epitomized Surrealism was Hughie Lee-Smith (1915–99). His paintings are based on real and imagined visual paradoxes and are intended to express his inner feelings about the outer world. Lee-Smith's paintings call to mind the work of Surrealist Giorgio de Chirico (1888–1978), including the use of desolate architectonic environments, long cast shadows, and isolated figures. Indeed, Lee-Smith's 1952 *Boy with a Tire* shows similarities to de Chirico's 1914 *Mystery and Melancholy of a Street*, which also depicts a solitary child with a hoop in an abandoned architectural setting (Figures 8.8 and 8.9). However, Lee-Smith's adherence to Social Realist content within the Surrealist style marks his work as significantly different from the earlier artist.

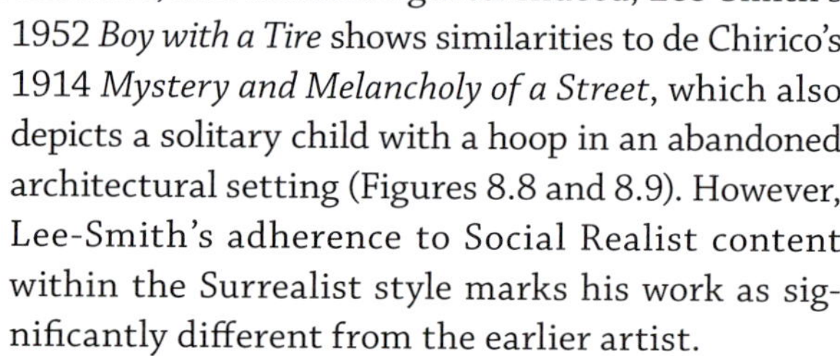

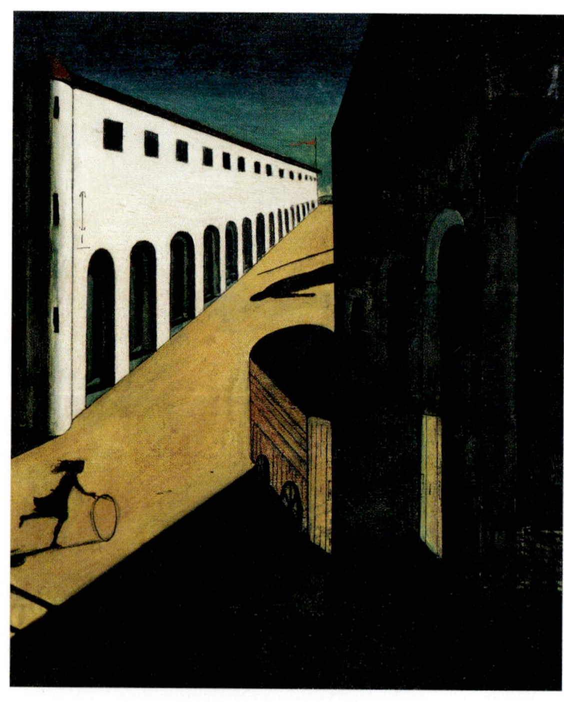

Lee-Smith was born in Florida but spent his childhood years in Atlanta with his grandmother, where he was fascinated by the local circuses and carnivals that routinely set up camp near his home. His recollections of fairgrounds, Pierrots, balloons, carousels, and colorful flags and costumes would inform his paintings throughout his life. After joining his mother in Cleveland at age 10, Lee-Smith began taking drawing classes at the Cleveland Museum of Art, continuing to study there through his teen years. He was captivated by the Symbolist-style works of New England–born painter Albert Pinkham Ryder (1847–1917). The haunting and nightmarish quality of Ryder's apparitions would

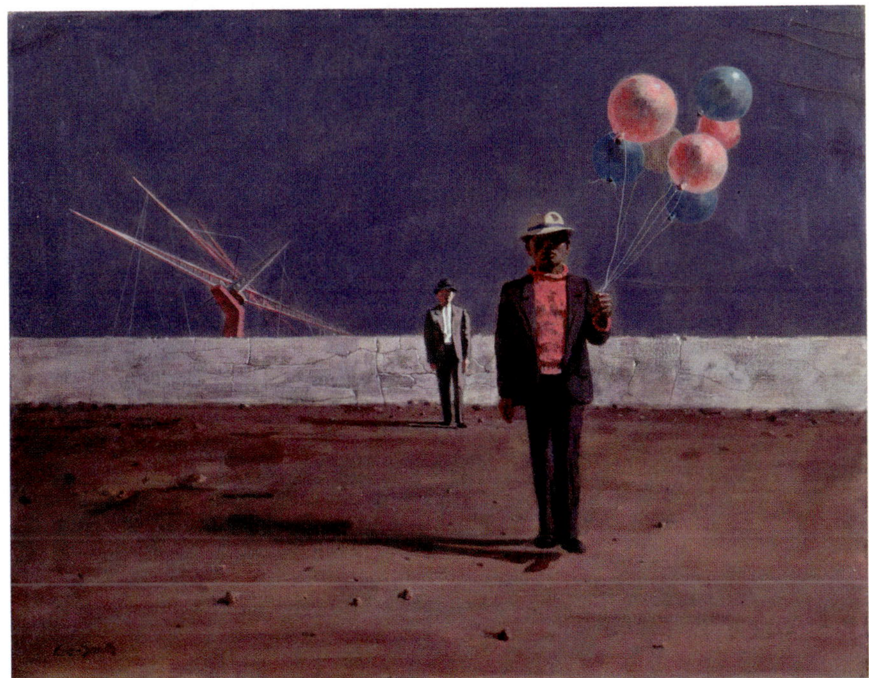

◀ **8.10** Hughie Lee-Smith, *Man with Balloons*, 1960, oil on canvas, 36″ × 46″.

Art © Estate of Hughie Lee-Smith / licensed by VAGA, New York, NY. Private collection; courtesy of Michael Rosenfeld Gallery LLC, New York, NY.

permeate Lee-Smith's mature work with the same profundity as would carnival scenes. Yet, despite their diametrically opposed natures, Lee-Smith was able to seamlessly synthesize the cheerlessness of Ryder's imagery with bright and joyous carnival colors and motifs. The result was a singular style and body of work that set him apart from his contemporaries (Figure 8.10).

After he graduated from high school in 1934, *Scholastic* magazine awarded Lee-Smith a one-year scholarship to attend the Detroit Society of Arts and Crafts. When he received the Karamu House Gilpin Players Award the following year, Lee-Smith enrolled in classes at Huntington Polytechnic and in a degree program at the Cleveland Institute of Art. He also taught classes at Karamu House and was one of the cofounders, in 1935, of the Karamu House Artist Association (see Chapter 7).

In 1938, Lee-Smith graduated with awards for his prints and drawings from the Cleveland Museum School. He joined the WPA-FAP program as a painter and lithographer, working in the Social Realist style on themes of patriotism and social politics. In 1944, the artist entered the armed services and was stationed for 19 months at the Great Lakes Naval Station just north of Chicago. He was assigned to paint three large-scale works on "the history of the Negro in the United States Navy." In addition to his work at the Naval Station, Lee-Smith became associated with Chicago's South Side Community Art Center, where he befriended Eldzier Cortor (discussed later in this chapter), Charles White, Archibald Motley, Jr., and Charles Sebree. By 1953, Lee-Smith had completed a BS degree in art education at Detroit's Wayne State University, which made it possible for him to obtain a number of teaching positions.

By midcentury, Lee-Smith had abandoned Social Realist aesthetics and turned to Surrealism. A more apt description of his style, however, might be "social Surrealism," because his subject matter often alluded to poverty and racial oppression within the framework of Surrealism, as is evident in *Boy with a Tire*. Lee-Smith moved to New York in 1958 to nurture his growing reputation and secured representation with prominent New York art dealer Janet Nessler. Over the next decade, the artist developed a solid patron base and exhibition record. In 1967, he was elected as a full member to the National Academy of Art and Design, the second African American, after Tanner, to join this venerated institution. From 1969 to 1971, Lee-Smith joined the faculty of Howard University. Returning to New York in 1972, he spent the next 15 years, until 1987, teaching at New York's Art Students League. Lee-Smith moved to New Mexico for his health late in life and died of cancer in 1999.

Eldzier Cortor

Painter and master printmaker Eldzier Cortor (1916–2015) devoted his career to paintings of alluring, lithe, and mysterious black women in either surreal settings or **Dada** collage that emphasized visual implausibility and disjuncture. Cortor described his women as being symbolic of the timeless and enduring spirit of African culture. He was influenced formally by the dark patina and attenuated forms of African sculpture that he saw on display at Chicago's Field Museum and by his extensive research on Africans in the diaspora, particularly those in the American South and the Caribbean.

Cortor came to Chicago from Virginia with his family when he was an infant. The family eventually settled on Chicago's South Side, where Cortor attended high school with Charles White, Charles Sebree, and Margaret Burroughs. By the mid-1930s, Cortor had earned a fine arts degree from the Chicago Art Institute and had also studied with the director of the New Bauhaus, László Moholy-Nagy (1895–1946), who had taught at the Bauhaus in Germany. From 1938 to 1943, Cortor worked in the WPA-FAP easel painting division documenting poverty on Chicago's South Side. In 1944 and 1945, he was awarded Rosenwald Fund grants to study and paint Gullah people and culture in the Sea Islands of Georgia, the Carolinas, and the nearby coastal low country. The Gullah were of special interest to Cortor because of their retention of African cultural practices, including elements of language, teaching techniques, cuisine, folk tales, agricultural methods, and crafts.

▼ **8.11** Eldzier Cortor, *The Couple*, c. 1948, oil on Masonite, 28″ × 22″.

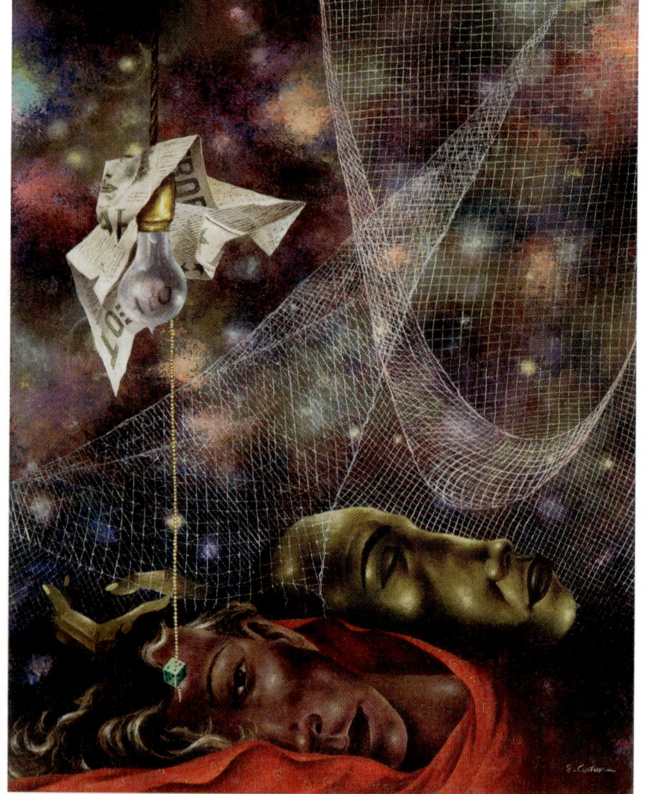

For two years, Cortor immersed himself in Gullah life and, for the remainder of his artistic career, immortalized their distinctive beauty and grace. His 1948 *The Couple* is a typical example of his Gullah-inspired portraits set within the context of Surrealism (Figure 8.11).

Two faces positioned horizontally occupy the lower portion of the composition, as if lying in bed. The woman looks serenely at the viewer. One eye is obscured by a red serape and lock of hair, and her skin glows with tones of mahogany and dark berries. The male face is in profile behind hers. His eyes are closed as if in sleep, and his skin gleams like polished bronze. Gossamer mosquito netting hangs above them, suggesting their interconnectedness or perhaps their ensnarement within each other's lives and within a dream. The dream world is actualized by the starlit night sky that serves as the painting's background. A bare bulb with a newspaper shade hangs above them. This motif alludes to Gullah practices of blocking negative energy with newsprint (see Chapter 2), to the makeshift nature of poor black homes, and to the physical world lurking just beyond the subconscious field of the dream. Finally, at the end of the bulb's pull chain hangs a single die, signifying chance. Perhaps the metallic skin and black lips of the male figure are indicators that he is dead rather than sleeping, and that the woman's luck in love has run out. Iconographic complexity is pervasive in Cortor's art, as are color subtleties and harmonies and an abiding sense of tranquility.

Cortor's paintings of the Gullah people brought him to national attention in 1946, when *Life* magazine reproduced one of his sensuous female nudes; four years later, the magazine proclaimed Cortor one of the best emerging painters in the country. In 1949, Cortor was awarded a Guggenheim Fellowship that allowed him to deepen his knowledge of neo-African culture by traveling to Jamaica, Cuba, and Haiti, where he settled for two years. In Haiti, Cortor taught at the Centre d'Art in Port-au-Prince, where both Lois Jones and William E. Scott also taught.

After his Caribbean sojourn, Cortor spent much of the 1950s in exile in Mexico to escape the oppressive McCarthy era. There he devoted himself to developing his talents as a lithographer before returning to the United States in the 1960s and settling in New York. Over the next several decades his career thrived, and his art was featured in several major exhibitions. *Black Spirit: Works on Paper by Eldzier Cortor* opened at the Indiana University Art Museum in 2006, in celebration of the artist's ninetieth birthday. In 2014, the San Antonio Museum of Art reconfigured a 2002 Cortor installation, *Eldzier Cortor: Master Printmaker*, which included surrealist paintings and prints by the artist, who was 98 years old at the time.

Rose Ransier Piper

Rose Ransier Piper (née Sams; 1917–2005) created paintings that combined abstraction and surrealism. A New York City–born textile designer and painter, Piper studied at Art Students League from 1943 to 1946 with Czech-born Abstract Expressionist painter Vaclav Vytlacil (1892–1984) and Japanese-American surrealist Yasuo Kuniyoshi (1895–1953). She won a Rosenwald Fund grant in 1946 that she used to travel throughout the southern United States studying black folklore and the musical tradition of the blues. The outcome of her research was a solo exhibit in 1947 entitled *Blues and Negro Folk Songs* mounted at New York's RoKo Gallery, which had been established the year before to showcase emerging local artists.

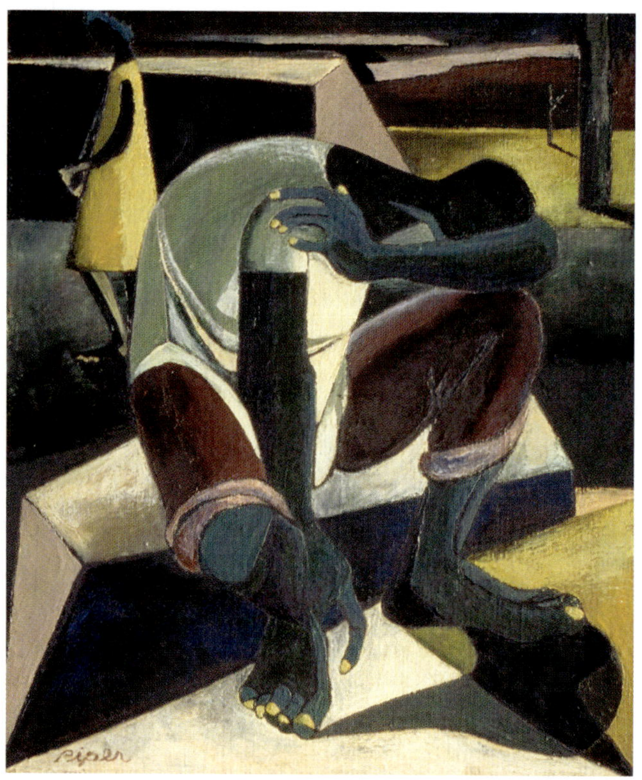

▲ 8.12 Rose Piper, *Grievin' Hearted*, 1948, oil on canvas, 36″ × 30″.

Collection of Clark Atlanta University Art Collection.

Piper next traveled to Paris to study at the École des Beaux-Arts from 1947 to 1948, where she developed her painting skills and was exposed to modern art. The 1948 Atlanta Annual featured her painting *Grievin' Hearted*, which won the Annual's highest honor (Figure 8.12). The painting brings to life "Grievin' Hearted Blues," recorded in 1927 by blues great Ma Rainey (1886–1939).

Piper's image features a gloomy and desolate Surrealist landscape typical of Lee-Smith, de Chirico, and Salvador Dali (1904–89). The work depicts two abstracted figures separated by physical and psychological space. The woman stands in the background and exhibits the same stony, pyramidal shape as the concrete blocks that dominate the composition, suggesting her cold hardness, despite her bowed head. A seated man in undergarments looms larger in the foreground, literally and metaphorically stripped bare by the anguish of amorous rejection. His face (and presumably his tears) is hidden by his arm, and his body wilts with sorrow—a telling foil to the woman's rigidity. Piper, not surprisingly, chose a palette of blues to set the lamentable mood of the painting, which echoes Ma Rainey's lyric: "My heart is grieving. I've been refused / I got those grievin' hearted blues." According to Piper, abstract forms were equally as important as color as sources of emotive power. She believed that abstraction could provoke "the powerful passions and anguished recollections of the black experience. The abstraction of the human figure arises out of a single moment of heightened expression. The attenuated form suggests the essence of longing."

Facing an economic crisis due to the simultaneous illnesses of her parents and husband, Piper was forced to abandon her career as a painter. To earn a more steady income that would support her family, Piper went into business as the owner of an upscale greeting card company—Ransier Studio Cards—which she operated from 1949 to 1953. She followed this venture with a career as an award-winning textile designer, which she practiced for more than two decades, until 1975. During these years, Piper created silk fabric designs for several leading textile manufacturers. In 1975, Piper retired from her career in textiles and by 1978, at age 61, had returned at long last to painting and drawing. Within a decade, she had secured her second solo show—her first in 40 years—held in 1989 in New York. The iconography of Piper's works of her later career picked up where her midcentury art had left off. Her imagery was based on the lyrics of black music. Formally, however, Piper's style had transformed from figurative abstraction to an intensely chromatic and illustrative **magic realism**.

Minnie Evans

Minnie Evans (1892–1987) was born and lived in the Gullah territory of coastal North Carolina. Evans attended school until the sixth grade, after which she went to work as a "sounder," hawking shellfish for sale in North Carolina's Wrightsville Sound area. At age 16, she married and relocated to the Pembroke Park Estate near Wilmington, North Carolina. Owned by the wealthy financier Pembroke Jones and his wife Sarah, the more-than-2,000-acre country estate supported an extensive workforce. Evans was employed there as a maid and lived there with her husband and three sons for 30 years. In 1948, the Jones descendants sold a 67-acre portion of the estate known as Airlie Gardens—a lush botanical garden and arboretum that welcomed public visitors (and is today a public park)—to another wealthy couple, Albert and Bertha Corbett, who employed Evans as its gatekeeper. At this time, inspired by the natural beauty of Airlie, Evans became a full-fledged artist (although she had begun making geometric line drawings as early as 1935).

Initially, Evans worked with wax crayons, colored pencil, and ink on paper, later transitioning to large-scale oil, watercolor, and tempera paintings and collage. Evans's artistic style has often been described as dreamlike and visionary rather than Surrealist, but these designations are more indicative of her status as a self-taught artist. Actually, her "visions"—which came to her in the early morning hours after awakening from a dream state—align well with Surrealist imagery. In these moments of first awakening, Evans recorded her dreams as art. According to Evans, she never planned her drawings but, rather, just "let them happen"—embodying the Surrealist practice of automatism. The result of her creative musings were intricately constructed, symmetrically composed, kaleidoscopic compositions that, literally and figuratively, bloomed with color. Embedded in many of Evans's floral designs are faces, disembodied eyes, and smiling mouths, which signify God's omnipresence in the artist's Elysium (Figure 8.13).

Evans sold her drawings to Arlie Gardens visitors, which brought her local attention and led, in 1961, to the artist's first formal exhibition at the Little Gallery (today the Cameron Art Museum) in Wilmington. The following year, Evans came to the attention of photographer and art dealer Nina Howell Starr (1903–2000), and her career took a more professional direction. After a visit to New York City on the occasion of a 1966 showing of her work, Evans was inspired by the large-scale paintings she observed at the Metropolitan Museum of Art. Subsequently, she began to work in large format, and her designs became more complex. Other influences include the Pembroke Jones collection of Chinese and Persian carpets and their Asian and European porcelain and flatware patterns. Evans's influences are so complex that scholars have noted sources for them as disparate as the Buddhist, Yoruba, and Jaina religions, and Indian, African, and Jungian philosophy.

A 1969 *Newsweek* review of Evans's solo show at Art Image Gallery in New York brought national fame to the artist. Subsequently, in 1972, the Smithsonian's National Museum of American Art purchased one of her works for its permanent collection. The next year, following an exhibit of Evans's art at the Studio Museum in Harlem, the internationally renowned French **Art Brut** artist Jean Dubuffet (1901–85) purchased several Evans

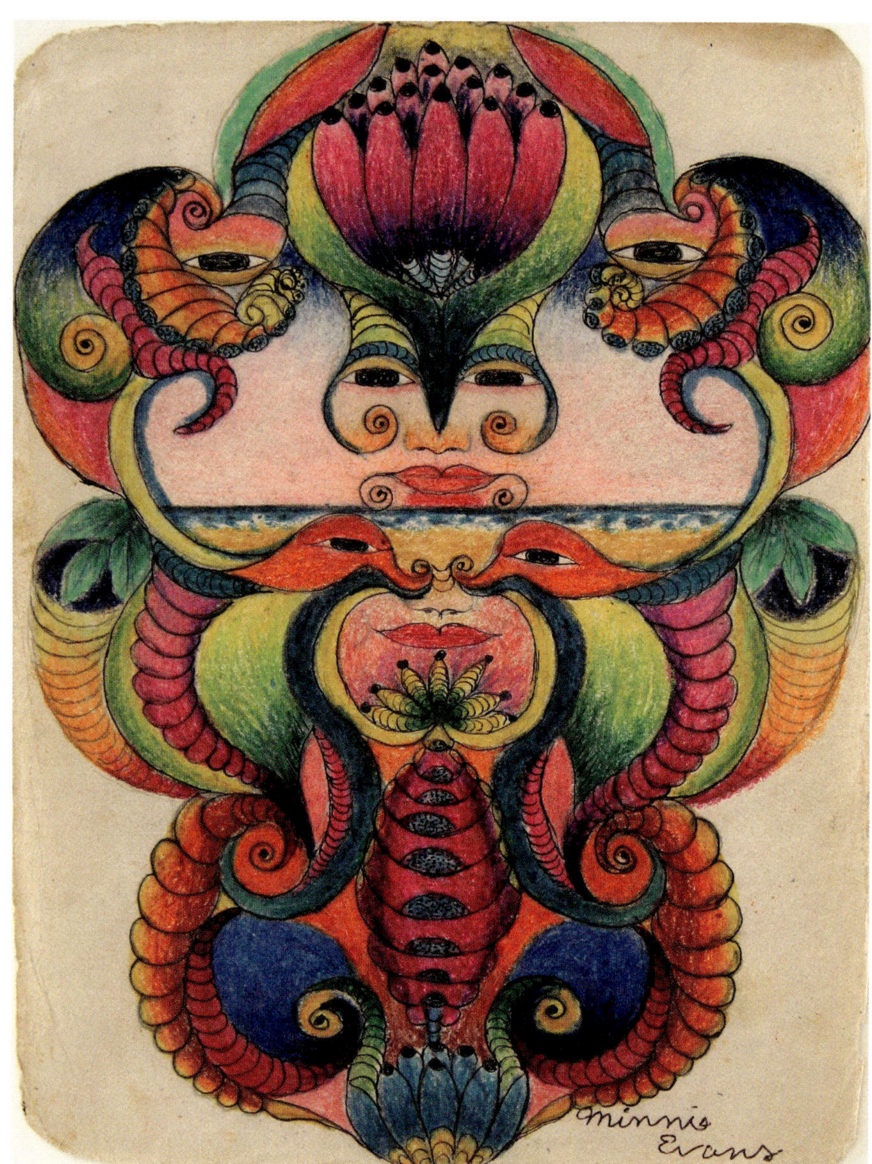

▶ **8.13** Minnie Evans, *Untitled (Faces with Rising Sun)*, c. 1960, colored crayon, ink, pencil on paper, 11.5″ × 8.25″.

Collection of the Luise Ross Gallery, New York, NY.

drawings for his personal collection. These successes led to Evans's 1974 retirement from her job at Airlie Gardens and to a major 1975 show at New York's Whitney Museum of American Art. A year before her death, in 1986, Evans was the subject of a retrospective at the North Carolina Museum of Art. Since then, Evans has become a legendary figure in the art world; her work is collected and exhibited in the United States and abroad by literally hundreds of galleries, museums, and private collectors.

ART BRUT AND SELF-TAUGHT ARTISTS

The term "Art Brut," or "raw art," was coined in 1945 by Dubuffet to describe the work of artists like Evans who practiced without the benefit of formal arts education. Dubuffet was especially interested in art made by children and those with mental disabilities. He described Art Brut as art created in solitude, untainted by artistic convention, and derived from authentic creative impulses—art that was pure and "raw" rather than pretentious and over-intellectualized. Dubuffet's description sounds very much like Breton's definition of Surrealism. In fact, in 1948 Dubuffet and Breton together founded the Compagnie (now Collection) de l'Art Brut, which is today a museum in Lausanne, Switzerland. Artists such as Evans who acquired their expertise without the benefit of sanctioned academic instruction have been persistently included in this group of **Outsider artists**—the term used in the United States for those who practice Art Brut—and are routinely segregated from the arena of "high" art. Terms such as "primitive," "naïve," "folk," "visionary," and "vernacular" have been most commonly used to categorize these artists. As descriptors of the art makers rather than their art, these terms are inherently inaccurate. Evans, for example, was a Surrealist who happened to lack formal education.

A reason for the popularity of self-taught artists between the 1930s and 1950s was due, in part, to the widely publicized 1938 national traveling exhibition *Masters of Popular Painting*, which was launched by New York's Museum of Modern Art and which tagged its participating artists "modern primitives." Despite this categorization, the style of these artists, like the styles of their academically trained counterparts, ranged from Gestural Abstraction to reductive Minimalism and from illusory to realistic.

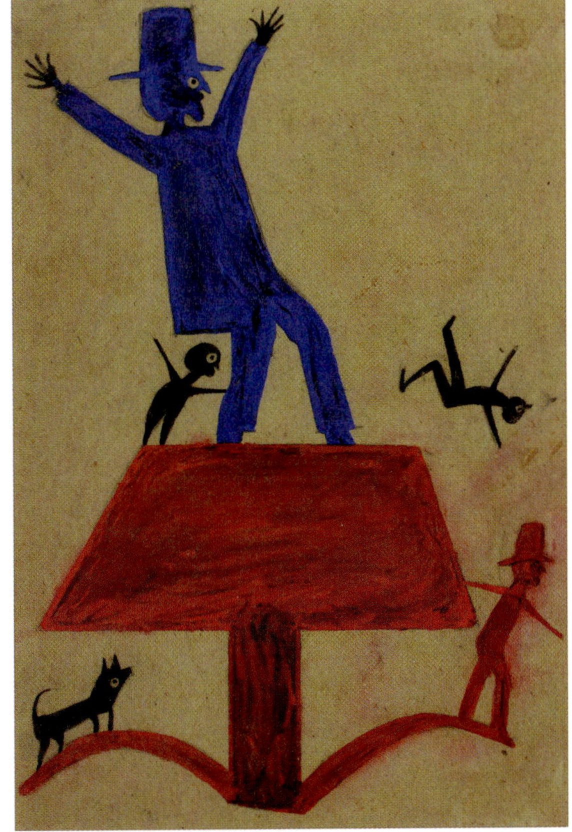

▼ **8.14** Bill Traylor, *Untitled [Blue Man on Red Object]*, c. 1939–42, poster paint and pencil on cardboard, 11¾″ × 7¾″.

High Museum of Art, Atlanta, Georgia. Purchased with funds from Mrs. Lindsey Hopkins, Jr., Edith G. and Philip A. Rhodes, and the Members Guild, 1982.93.

Bill (William) Traylor

The art of former slave and lifelong farmworker Bill (William) Traylor (1854–1949) is routinely categorized as Outsider Art, even though it is essentially Modernist in the unmodulated flatness of his forms and palette and in his lack of interest in anatomical exactitude (Figure 8.14). Born in the 19th century, Traylor was nearly 90 years old when he became an artist, and he died a short decade later. After emancipation, Traylor remained on the Alabama cotton plantation of George Hartwell Traylor (1801–81), where he had been born and from whom he took his last name. After the deaths of his wife and his employers, in 1935, at age 82, he moved to nearby Montgomery. By this time crippled with rheumatism, Traylor was homeless and unable to work. He slept in the storeroom of a local business at night and sat on the sidewalks of Monroe Avenue during the day. To pass the time, he sketched geometric compositions and abstract figures on discarded cardboard.

Traylor hawked his art to passersby with minor success until, in June 1939, painter and educator Charles Shannon (1915–96) happened by his Monroe

Avenue perch. Shannon began to buy Traylor's art and provide him with paints and other art supplies. The following year, in 1940, Shannon organized a solo exhibit for Traylor—*Bill Traylor: People's Artist*—at Montgomery's New South Gallery, founded by Shannon and fellow artists in 1938. The short-lived but influential school and gallery specialized in exhibiting Social Realist art and in supporting artists across class and race boundaries. It was an ideal venue for the impoverished Traylor, whose images of farm animals, farm workers, and blue-collar Alabamans suited the gallery's agenda. The gallery's goal to feature artists irrespective of social or economic status or access to fine arts education was farsighted given that, even today, these distinctions continue to separate self-trained artists from the so-called avant-garde.

Positive reviews of Traylor's New South exhibit led to a second show in New York in 1942. However, few of his works sold to anyone other than Shannon, and Traylor continued to struggle financially. After the New York show, Traylor lived with different relatives around the country, from 1942 to 1947, finally returning to Montgomery for the last year of his life, still drawing at age 95. Traylor's art was not again exhibited until 1979, when New York's Oosterom Gallery mounted *Bill Traylor 1854–1974, Works on Paper*, borrowing many of the works from Shannon. The exhibit returned Traylor to national attention. Three dozen Traylor pieces were featured at the Corcoran Gallery in its 1982 show *Black Folk Art in America, 1930–1980*. Serious critical discussion of Traylor's art followed, and he soon became the subject of exhibitions at major museums, as well as university and commercial galleries in the United States and Europe.

William Edmondson

Stone sculptor William Edmondson (1874–1951) was the child of ex-slaves and farmworkers. Like Traylor, he did not become an artist until late in life. A native of Tennessee, Edmondson spent a lifetime at labor-intensive blue-collar jobs as a sewer worker, farmworker, and railroad worker and as a stonemason in the Nashville area. At age 57, he began to sculpt in limestone. Edmondson claimed he had spiritual inspiration for his art making, which he described as miraculous and directed by Christ. His earliest works were, indeed, religious in that they were funerary monuments created for what is today Nashville's Greenwood West Cemetery. Later, Edmondson expanded his repertoire to include secular art that comprised human and animal figures, garden statues, and portraits of historic Americans such as Eleanor Roosevelt and controversial black prizefighter Jack Johnson (1878–1946). Edmondson obtained his materials locally and at low or no cost—limestone was abundant in Tennessee—and used recycled railroad spikes for chisels. Over time, Edmondson's work became well known to locals, who would contribute limestone to his creative cause.

By 1935, four years after creating his first sculpture, the artist had amassed a large collection of objects. He displayed them in his yard, where he also nurtured a vegetable and fruit tree garden that served as a source of income. At about this time, Edmondson came to the notice of poet and playwright Sidney Hirsch (1883–1962), who taught in the art department of Peabody College (now Vanderbilt University) near Edmondson's home. Edmondson was also embraced by wealthy local patrons Elizabeth and Alfred Starr. The Starrs introduced photographers Louise Dahl-Wolfe (1895–1989) of *Harper's Bazaar* fame and Edward Weston to Edmondson's work. Over the next several years, both took many photographs of the artist at work and of his sculptures. After Dahl-Wolfe showed her photographs of Edmondson's sculptures to curators at the Museum of Modern Art, a 1937 one-man show was organized. Edmondson became the first African-American artist so honored. (Jacob Lawrence was the second, in 1938.)

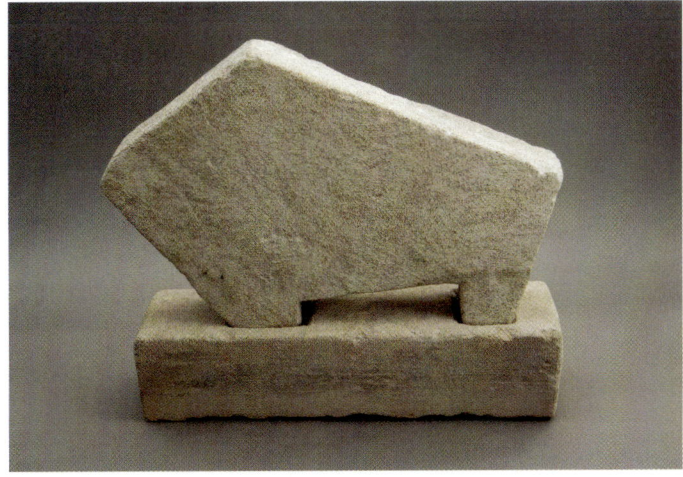

▲ **8.15** William Edmonson, *Critter*, c. 1940, limestone, 21″ × 15″ × 6″.

Collection of Cheekwood Botanical Garden and Museum of Art, gift of the 1993 Collector's Group with matching funds through the bequest of Anita Bevill McMichael Stallworth.

Edmondson was included the following year in the historic 1938 MoMA retrospective *Three Centuries of American Art*, which traveled to Paris in 1939. Two years later, Edmondson was showcased in a second solo exhibit at the Nashville Art Gallery. During this period, he was employed by the WPA-FAP, which helped to subsidize his art making and living expenses. By the end of the 1940s, after sculpting for 17 years, Edmondson was too weak and infirm to practice the arduous task of stone carving. At the time of his death a few years later, Edmondson was honored with an exhibit at the Nashville Artists Guild.

Edmondson's *Critter*, from about 1940, is a masterpiece of formal economy that, with decisive angles, planes, and shapes, articulates the form of a buffalo with minimalist profundity (Figure 8.15). In its incorporation of a rectangular base as an integral part of the sculpture, and in its use of polygonal geometric forms to articulate the shape of a buffalo, *Critter* is the embodiment of Cubist structure as well as of the De Stijl philosophy of expressing, through art, the intrinsic geometric order that lies beneath the variegated surfaces of figures and objects.

Clementine Hunter

Funeral Procession by Louisiana artist Clementine Hunter (1886–1988) (Figure 8.16) offers an instructive comparison to Ellis Wilson's depiction of the same subject (Figure 8.3). The two pictures share a palette of oranges and earth tones and the use of black and white, the narrative of an African-American funeral procession, unarticulated black faces in profile, and orthogonal directional elements. Yet, despite so many shared qualities, the two images could not be more different. Ellis's unmodulated Synthetic Cubist abstraction contrasts with Hunter's painterly style, which has more in common with the German Expressionists. Intensified colors, figural distortion, and hierarchic proportions in Hunter's image identify the important characters and create a joyful rather than somber mood. Her approach derives from the "second line" in a typical Louisiana creole funeral, which celebrates the deceased's life rather than mourning his or her death.

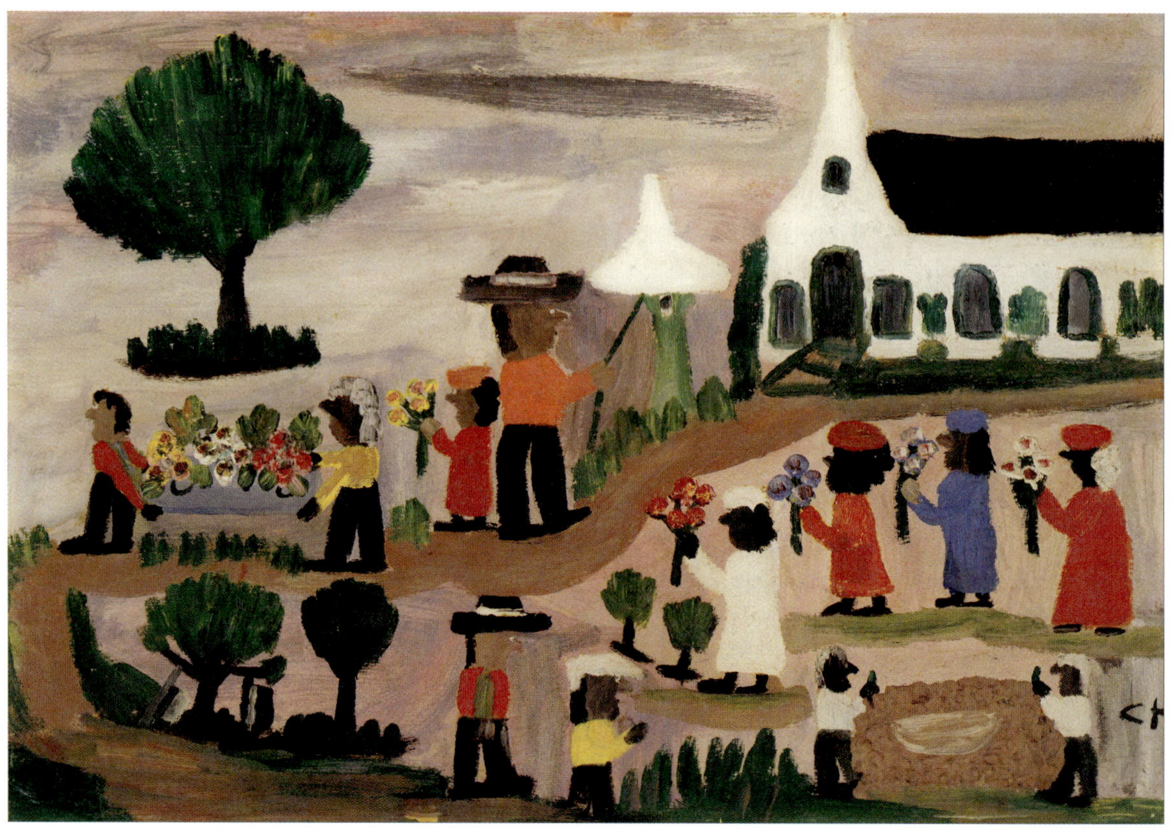

▲ **8.16** Clementine Hunter, *Funeral Procession*, 1950, oil on board, 13″ × 18″.
The Walter O. Evans Collection at the SCAD Museum of Art.

Hunter lived for most of her life on the Melrose (Yucca) Plantation in Cane River, Louisiana. The plantation was originally owned in the 1790s by the Métoyers, one of the wealthiest black families in America (see Chapter 2). The plantation was purchased in 1898 by the family of John and Carmelita ("Cammie") Henry. For much of the 20th century, until the Henrys sold Melrose in 1970, Hunter worked there as a field hand and lived in a small cottage on the grounds.

When Hunter reached middle age, she was reassigned to full-time domestic service as a laundress, maid, nanny, seamstress, and cook. Her creativity found its first real outlets in the making of dolls, clothing, and quilts for the Henry children. She also wove baskets, made lace curtains, and devised recipes for family meals that, years later, became the subject of the venerable *Melrose Plantation Cookbook*, coauthored by Hunter and Melrose curator François Mignon. In the 1940s, the Melrose Plantation became something of an artists' colony, frequented by writers such as Alice B. Toklas and William Faulkner, as well as by visual artists. Exposed to this creative element, and having access to art materials left behind by visiting painters, at about age 50 Hunter began to experiment with palette and brush.

Hunter's works first came to the attention of the public in 1946, when Mignon, who had befriended the artist a decade earlier, arranged for an informal showing of her paintings in a drugstore window. Mignon quickly became one of Hunter's champions and remained so until his death in 1980.

He gave Hunter art supplies and financial support and published dozens of articles on her work in his Cane River Memo, a column that he wrote for the *Natchitoches Enterprise*. Hunter painted prolifically, completing thousands of works in her lifetime. Another Hunter patron, writer James Register, left a position at Oklahoma University in the 1940s to move to Natchitoches, having become enthralled by the artist and her Louisiana community. He aided Hunter in successfully applying for a Rosenwald Fellowship and worked to educate the art world about the artist and her oeuvre.

Believers in the alleged "purity" of vernacular art took exception to the presence of these advocates in the artist's life—even though their devotion to Hunter was instrumental to her success—on the grounds that such self-ordained agents took advantage of their less-than-sophisticated artist-wards. This, however, mistakenly assumes a certain naïveté on the part of vernacular artists who have agreed to work with the dealer or patron; and it overlooks the conflicting opinion that the acquisition of patrons and dealers by more trained artists adds to, rather than detracts from, their credibility. Whatever their motives, Hunter's supporters were influential in securing an exhibition of the artist's paintings at the New Orleans Arts and Crafts Show in 1949. A few years later, in the mid-1950s, the Delgado Museum (now the New Orleans Museum of Art) chose Hunter for its first one-person exhibition of the works of an African-American artist. A second show was mounted by Northwestern State College in Natchitoches, which was then a segregated institution. Hunter was permitted to view her paintings on display at Northwestern, but only after special arrangements could be made to bring her into the university's gallery when no white visitors were present.

Mignon hoped to make the Melrose Plantation a permanent setting for Hunter's work. In 1954, Mignon suggested to the artist that she create a mural for installation on the second-floor walls of Africa House (Figure 2.2), the one-time storage and slave interment facility on the plantation. For the commission, Hunter designed a nine-panel opus (and additional smaller connecting panels). The subject of the mural was Hunter's favorite one: Louisiana life. Working from master cartoons (sketches), Hunter, at age 68, designed what has been termed "the most colorful room in the Old South." The mural segments depict a plan of the Cane River area, cotton fields, farmworkers, animals, folkloric narratives, washerwomen, pecan tree harvesters, and religious and secular events such as revival meetings, funeral processions, and honky-tonk patrons drinking, fighting, and gambling.

Horace Pippin, Jr.

Even a cursory glance at the art of Horace Pippin, Jr. (1888–1946) reveals an economy of form and interlocking shapes as well as an intelligible narrative that shares much in common with the style of Jacob Lawrence. In his deceptively straightforward views of war, biblical and historical themes, portraits, landscapes, and still lifes, Pippin encoded racial, political, and personal content while masking a keen understanding of design principles and painterly

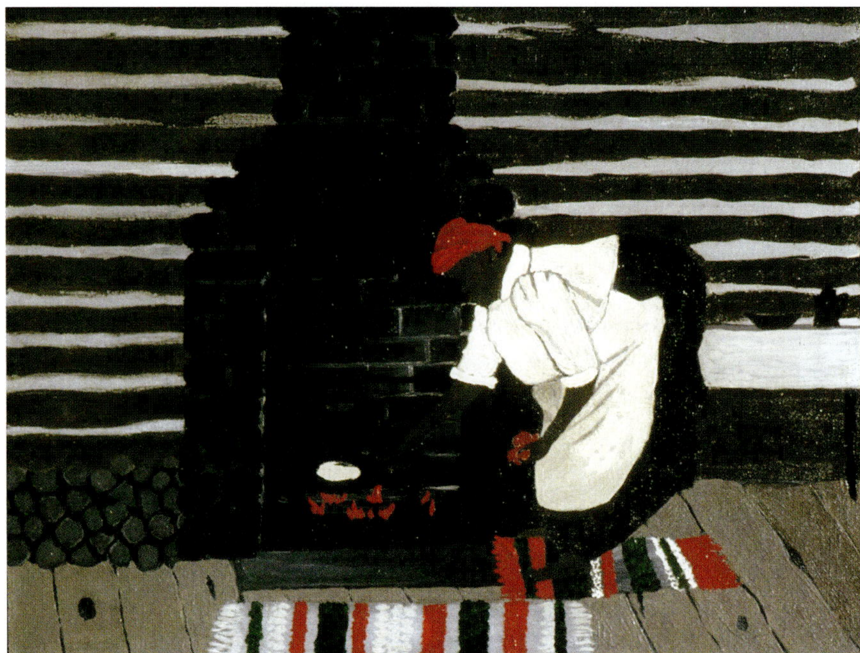

▶ **8.17** Horace Pippin, *The Hoe Cake*, c. 1946, oil on canvas, 14″ × 18″.

Collection of the New Jersey State Museum, Purchase FA1986.13. Reproduced with permission.

techniques. *The Hoe Cake*, from about 1946, is a fitting example (Figure 8.17). A partly imagined and partly remembered scene from his late 19th-century childhood in Goshen, New York (where he lived until age three), *The Hoe Cake* portrays Pippin's mother, Harriett Johnson Pippin, cooking over an open fireplace. Beyond the broad, rough brushstrokes and simply conceived palette lies an intricate pattern of vertical, horizontal, and oblique lines that encase the bending figure in her sparse surroundings. The scarf, crisp white shirt, and apron she wears lend dignity to the image of a poor, hard-working, African-American homemaker. The heavy, dark weight of the fireplace is perfectly balanced by the fulsome mass of the figure. Strategically placed (and a recurring motif in Pippin's interiors) are the small, brightly colored carpets, which anchor the composition while enlivening its otherwise somber setting.

Pippin and his mother moved to West Chester, Pennsylvania, when he was three years old. He began drawing at age ten after receiving colored pencils, paint, and brushes in the mail from an art supply company as an award for an art contest that he had entered. At age 14, Pippin left school to become a porter at the hotel where his mother, no longer healthy enough to work, had previously been employed as a maid. Pippin took additional jobs as a farmworker, coal miner, and ironworker until his mother died in 1911, at which point he relocated to Paterson, New Jersey. There, he worked a series of labor-intensive jobs, including furniture crater. After six years in New Jersey, Pippin enlisted in the army in 1917.

Pippin was stationed in France, where black soldiers were permitted to fight alongside white French troops (this was not permitted in the then-segregated American armed forces). A member of the famed Harlem Hell Fighters, Pippin fought with the 369th Regimen against German soldiers in the Meuse-Argon offensive in northeastern France. One of several black soldiers to receive the French Croix de Guerre (War Cross) for heroism in battle, Pippin was discharged in 1919 with a partially paralyzed right arm and returned to West Chester. He married a widow and mother named Jennie Giles the following year. Despite economic and physical obstacles, Pippin continued to create art. His injury required him to improvise, and he began to draw with a hot poker on wood surfaces, a technique known as **pyrogravure**. Eventually, and with painstaking effort, he was able to work with palette and brush by supporting his wounded limb with his left hand. The process was arduous and slow. It took Pippin three years, from 1928 to 1931, to complete his first oil painting—a narrative about his traumatic memories of war. More paintings followed as he gained dexterity.

During the 1930s, Pippin began to exhibit his paintings and pyrogravures in shop windows in West Chester. As a result, he came to the notice of renowned illustrator N. C. Wyeth (1882–1945), whose family lived a few miles away in Chadds Ford. Wyeth and West Chester Art Association president Christian Brinton (1870–1942) became Pippin's advocates. Brinton arranged for the inclusion of Pippin's work in the West Chester Art Association exhibit held in 1937. The following year, Pippin's work was included in the national touring exhibit *Masters of Popular Painting*, which debuted in the spring of 1938 at the Museum of Modern Art in New York. Organized by WPA-FAP director Holger Cahill in conjunction with museum curators, the show featured 13 American and 9 European artists, including Bill Traylor and French self-taught painter Henri Rousseau (1844–1910).

Pippin's work quickly gained nationwide popularity, and by 1939 he was being represented by the newly founded Robert Carlen Galleries in Philadelphia, which specialized in folk art. In late 1939, Albert C. Barnes invited Pippin to lecture at the Barnes Foundation in Merion, Pennsylvania, and to enroll in art classes there. However, Pippin found art instruction tedious and rarely attended classes. Over the next several years, despite (or perhaps because of) his lack of interest in academic training, Pippin painted some of his finest works of the American scene, particularly the Brandywine River Valley. He also portrayed epic narratives of American history, including the legend of John Brown and the life of Abraham Lincoln. During the 1940s, his art appeared in popular magazines such as *Time*, *Newsweek*, *Life*, and *Vogue* and in dozens of exhibits. He died in 1946. After nearly a century, Pippin's art continues to have far-reaching appeal.

PHOTOGRAPHY

There were many black photographers working professionally at midcentury; among the best were Gordon Parks, Roy DeCarava, and Charles (Chuck) Stewart.

Gordon Parks

Gordon Parks (1912–2006) was an award-winning filmmaker and photographer whose early career was supported by the Southside Community Art Center in Chicago. In 1941, the year of the center's inauguration, Parks was given a one-man show of his photographs, and he remained a friend of the

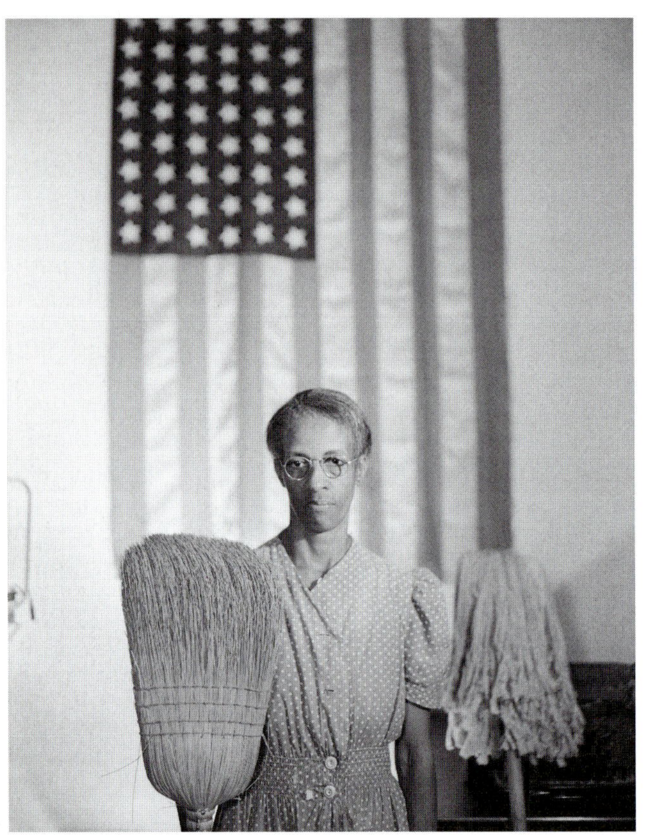

▲ **8.18** Gordon Parks, *American Gothic*, 1942, gelatin silver print, 4″ × 5″.

Washington, D.C. Library of Congress, Prints and Photographs Division, FSA / OWI Collection, LC-USF34-013407-C.

center for many years. Born on a farm in Kansas, Parks lived on his own from age 17, when the Depression began. He traveled by freight train from city to city earning a living working odd jobs. After a chance meeting with Marva Louis, the wife of world heavyweight champion boxer Joe Louis (1914–81), he settled in Chicago in 1940. Parks was able to parlay his acquaintance with the Louis family into a photography business, specializing in portraits of society women and fashion models.

In the early 1940s, Parks received a Rosenwald Fund award and secured a position with the Farm Security Administration (FSA), which was headed by photographer Roy E. Stryker (1893–1975), an early Parks mentor. During his FSA tenure, Parks created one of his most classic images, *American Gothic* (Figure 8.18)—an ironic commentary on the acclaimed 1930 Regionalist painting of the same name by Grant Wood. Wood's representation of a stoic farmer and his daughter epitomizes the Protestant work ethic of the rural American family. Standing before their white clapboard house, the couple's rigid columnar poses, lean physiques, and placement on either side of a gothic window in the gable of their home recall Gothic statuary and allude to religious morality.

Parks's photograph, by contrast, poses a single black woman (a government-employed cleaning woman named Ella Watson) in front of an American flag. Like the figures in the Wood painting, she wears simple work clothes—a house dress—and is slender and rigidly posed. However, unlike the male figure in Wood's painting, holding a pitchfork (which identifies him, and not his daughter, as the worker), Parks's protagonist is a two-fisted female laborer with a broom in one hand and a mop in the other. She is also defined (and confined) by the indoor setting and her attendance to someone else's property, rather than, like Wood's figures, standing in the open air in front of their own home. Parks's deft allusion juxtaposes divergent types of American workers—white and black, male and female, sovereign and subordinate, unbounded and confined, rural and urban, and together and alone—and is a telling statement about racial inequality and segregation in 1940s America.

After the dismantling of the FSA in 1942, Parks moved to New York, where he became a freelance photographer for *Vogue* magazine. He also worked with Stryker (who had moved to Standard Oil Company) documenting industrial workers and sites. During Parks's tenure chronicling gang activity in Harlem in 1948, his poignant profile of 17-year-old Harlem "Midtowners" gang leader Leonard "Red" Jackson (1931–2010) smoking a cigarette and staring solemnly out of a tenement window won Parks widespread attention and a **photo essay** in *Life* magazine (Figure 8.19). *Life* hired Parks as a staff photographer, making him the first African American to hold this position. After a 22-year career with *Life*, Parks went on to make a film for Warner Brothers based on his autobiographical novel, *The Learning Tree*, in 1969. He also directed two *Shaft* films in the 1970s and made a cameo appearance in the 2000 remake starring Samuel L. Jackson. A cofounder of *Essence* magazine, Parks was awarded the NAACP Spingarn Medal in 1972 and earned numerous honorary doctorates for his contributions to photography, filmmaking, and literature.

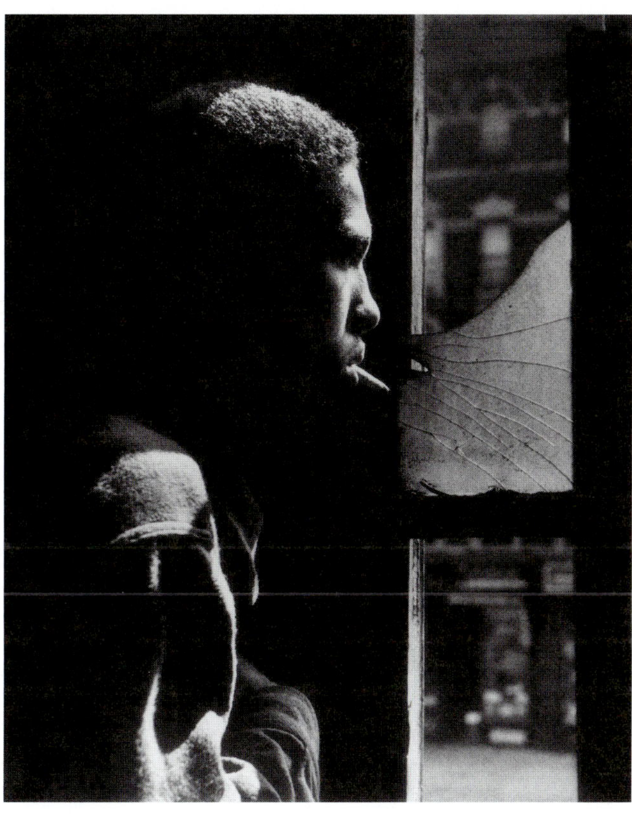

▲ **8.19** Gordon Parks, *Red Jackson, Harlem Gang Leader*, 1949, gelatin silver print.

University of Kanas Spencer Museum of Art. Museum purchase, state funds. © The Gordon Parks Foundation.

Roy DeCarava

Roy DeCarava (1919–2009) was a child of Harlem who spent a 60-year career interpreting the city and its people in photographs. During his youth, he studied fine arts at Cooper Union from 1938 to 1940 (and later taught there from 1969 to 1972) and at the Harlem Community Art Center from 1940 to 1942. He also worked for the WPA-FAP painting government signage. DeCarava served briefly in the army in 1942–43 as a topographer, but his experiences of prejudice in the segregated military and his abhorrence of violence led to a medical discharge. Back home in 1944, DeCarava studied printmaking with Catlett and White at the George Washington Carver Community School and earned a living as a freelance graphic designer. In 1946, his practice of taking photos for later conversion into paintings and prints sparked an interest in photography that led rapidly to the achievement of several career milestones in the subsequent decade.

In 1950, DeCarava planned a project to portray the people and places of his own neighborhood that were familiar to him, with the deliberate intention to avoid a sociological approach and instead photograph the community, in his own words, "as subjects worthy of art." When the MoMA director of photography, Edward Steichen, saw DeCarava's work at a 1950 show at New York's Forty-Fourth Street Gallery, he purchased several photos for the MoMA collection. This coup led to DeCarava's inclusion in MoMA's 1955 historic and internationally traveling exhibit *The Family of Man*. DeCarava also won a Guggenheim Fellowship in 1952 to take a series of intimate and introspective images, which resulted in an insider's portrait of Harlem rather than merely a document. A number of these images were included in a collaborative book by DeCarava and Langston Hughes published later that year and entitled *The Sweet Flypaper of Life*. The book featured Hughes's prose and poetry and DeCarava's portrayals of black New Yorkers.

DeCarava always photographed with available light, rejecting the effect of a flash, as unwanted artifice. Thus his images often appear deeply contoured with many subtle gray tones and they are replete with natural shadows that heighten the visual experience. Indeed, he called this effect in his silver gelatin photography an "infinite tonal scale of grey." The technique allowed him to avoid harsh contrasts and to rely instead on his preferred palette of subtle and radiant shades of deep grays. Furthermore, many of his photographs require direct visual inspection of the original silver gelatin print, since reproductions can only suggest the luminosity he characteristically achieved in the original. Even in his photographs that were composed more deliberately of contrasting light and dark elements, there is important visual detailing in the shadows. His subject matter ranged widely over the course of a long career—always including the human element—from images of clotheslines hung between tenement buildings to close-up portraits of unwary sitters lost in thought and summertime scenes of Harlem children drenching themselves with abandon in a fireplug geyser.

From *The Sweet Flypaper of Life*, DeCarava's 1949 *Graduation, New York* portrays a young girl in a full-length white gown treading with extreme care (so as not to dirty her hem) along a litter-strewn Harlem street (Figure 8.20). Shot from a distance, the composition is diagonally split by light and shadow.

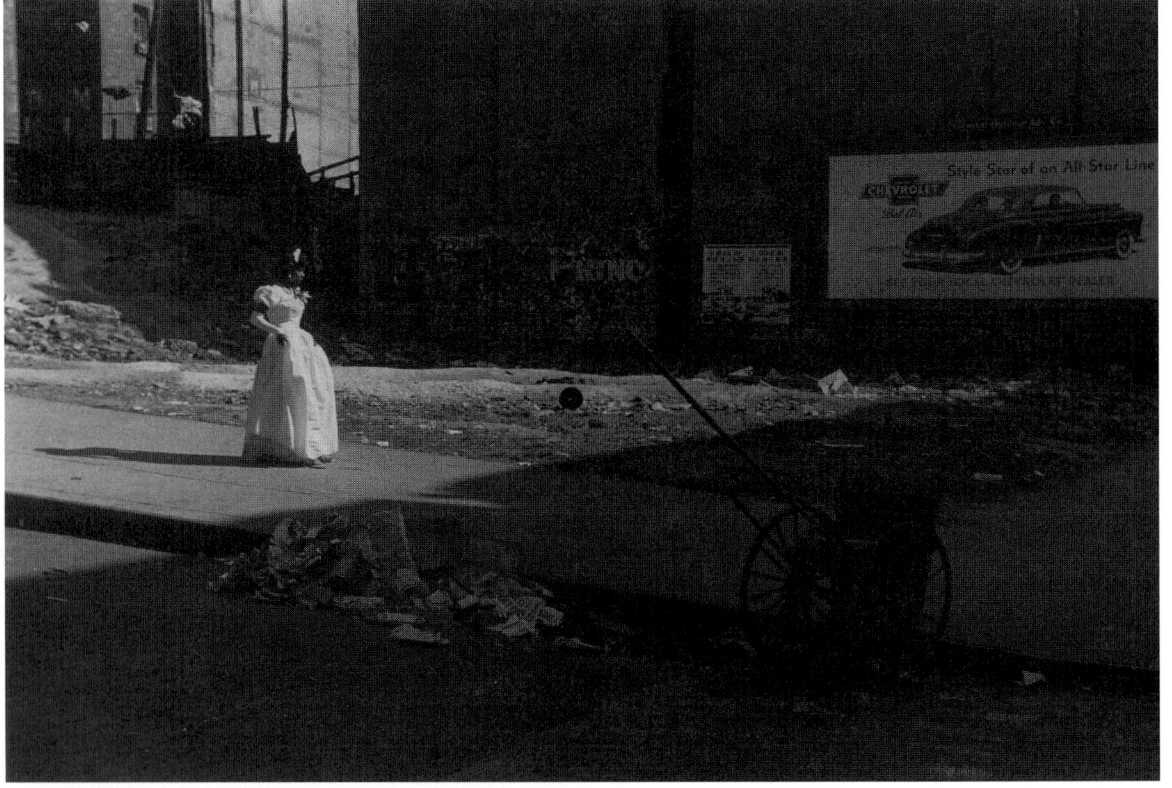

▼ **8.20** Roy DeCarava, *Graduation, New York*, 1949 (printed 1982), gelatin silver print, 10⅞″ × 14″ (sheet).

Graduation by Roy DeCarava © 2015 Sherry Turner DeCarava.

Bright sunlight in the upper-left quadrant causes the dress to gleam in its whiteness and signifies the girl's purity and innocence. Shadow occupies much of the right side of the picture, enveloping and obscuring the trash and the wheelchair that doubles as a pushcart, toward which the girl gingerly moves. The image is at once a dynamic geometric composition and an authentic representation of the contradictory nature of poverty-ridden urban neighborhoods and the often irreproachable people who fill them. *Graduation* symbolizes a young girl's rite of passage and is a testament to DeCarava's enduring artistic objective to render metaphors as well as pictures.

In addition to his artistic work, beginning in 1958, DeCarava worked as a freelance photographer for magazines including *Time*, *Life*, *Fortune*, *Newsweek*, and later in the 1960s, *Sports Illustrated*. He was discouraged, however, by the lack of black photographers assigned to full-time positions with these magazines. As chair of the Committee to End Discrimination Against Black Photographers (a chapter of the American Society of Magazine Photographers), DeCarava engaged in a political protest against *Life* magazine for racial discrimination. As *Life*'s only full-time black photographer, Gordon Parks dissociated himself from the group's efforts, which resulted in an ideological rift between the two men.

Dedicated to aiding emerging photographers, from 1963 to 1966, DeCarava served as founding director of the Kamoinge (a Bantu word meaning "communal work") Workshop, which lent support, supplies, and show and workspace to young black photographers. DeCarava experienced his first museum success at the end of the 1960s with a solo exhibit in 1969 at the Studio Museum in Harlem. In 1975, he was appointed to the full-time faculty of Hunter College, where he taught for the next 30 years and was named distinguished professor by the City University of New York.

DeCarava's career came full circle in 1996, when a traveling retrospective of 200 of his photographs was organized by MoMA (his second MoMA retrospective). The show was accompanied by a catalog with an introductory essay by his partner, art historian Sherry Turner DeCarava. In 1998, DeCarava won the Master of Photography Award from the International Center of Photography; and in 2001, a long-awaited book—*the sound i saw*, hand made by the artist decades earlier and representing an expansive body of his work on jazz musicians—was published. It exists as an outstanding summation of his extensive contributions to artistic photography. In addition to numerous honorary doctorates received during his lifetime, he notably received the National Arts Club Master of Arts Award and, in 2007, the National Medal of Arts awarded by the National Endowment of the Arts and presented to the artist by the president.

Charles (Chuck) Stewart

Charles (Chuck) Stewart (b. 1927) photographed jazz, R & B, pop, and rock musicians for more than 3,000 album covers and numerous publications, beginning in the mid-1950s. Among his subjects were Louis Armstrong, Ray

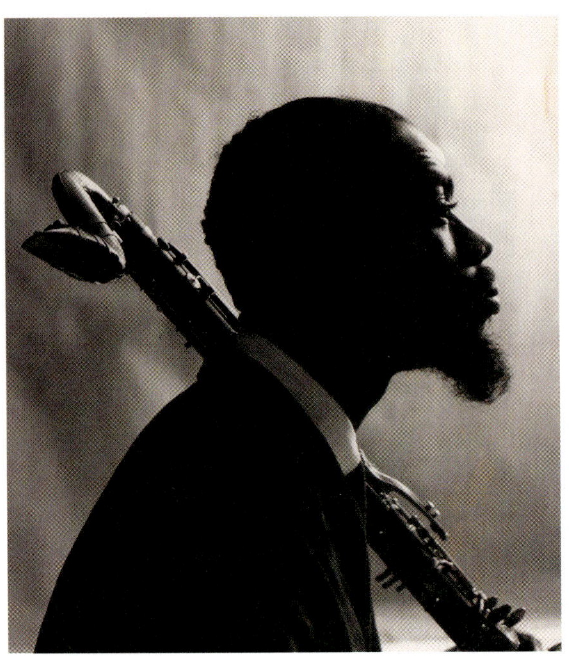

▲ **8.21** Charles Stewart, *Eric Dolphy*, 1964, gelatin silver print, 17¼″ × 13³/₈″.
© Chuck Stewart.

Charles, John Coltrane, Miles Davis, Ella Fitzgerald, Judy Garland, Quincy Jones, Max Roach, Sonny Rollins, Frank Sinatra, Sarah Vaughan, Dinah Washington, and Led Zeppelin. In addition to his album covers, Stewart's publicity photos of musical icons appeared in dozens of print publications. Born in Texas, Stewart was raised in Tucson, Arizona, where he and his family moved soon after his birth. He took his first celebrity photos—of Marian Anderson (on tour in Tucson)—when he was 13 years old and sold copies for $2 each. In high school, he worked as photographer for the school yearbook, and he majored in photography at Ohio University. After graduating in 1949, Stewart served as a combat photographer in the U.S. Army.

After his discharge from the army, Stewart reconnected with a college buddy named Herman Leonard (1923–2010), who would go on to become one of the most renowned jazz photographers in the country. As Leonard's collaborator, Stewart was given entrée into the New York music scene that served as Leonard's client base. Stewart became an oft-tapped photographer for the major New York record labels, including Impulse, Mercury, Reprise, and Verve records. When Leonard relocated first to Asia and then Paris in 1956, Stewart took over his New York business and spent the next half century as one of the country's most sought-after jazz photographers.

Stewart is best known for deceptively casual portraits of musicians both in the studio and in concert, which present the subjects in the best possible light, literally and figuratively. Often capturing his sitters unaware and, thus, in unaffected postures, Stewart's behind-the-scenes images became his trademark. Adroitly conceived, Stewart's 1964 portrait of avant-garde wind instrumentalist Eric Dolphy (1928–64) was created the year of the musician's death from diabetes (Figure 8.21). Stewart portrays Dolphy as the flesh-and-blood reflection of the clarinet he holds. Employing an X-shaped design, Stewart balances Dolphy's slender frame against the backward tilt of his instrument. The mouthpiece of the clarinet is almost the exact shape and size of the musician's beard. The quiet, moody image of Dolphy lost in thought is heightened by Stewart's use of softly focused light and shadow.

In 1985, Stewart published a collection of his works in a book entitled *Jazz Files*, coauthored with African-American playwright and educator Paul Carter Harrison (b. 1936). Throughout the 1980s and 1990s, Stewart's works were exhibited widely. More recently, in 2008, he was awarded the Milt Hinton Award for Excellence in Jazz Photography, and his contributions to American visual culture were acknowledged in two solo exhibits hosted by Jazz at Lincoln Center in 2008–09 and by the Bergen Performing Arts Center in Englewood, New Jersey in 2010.

Summary

The mid-20th-century was a time of shifting aesthetic sensibilities, from Social Realism to abstraction. African-American artists were under pressure from the anticommunist movement and prevailing art trends to abandon socialist art and activities. Some, such as Catlett and Cortor, created art in exile in Mexico. Others transitioned from figuration to abstraction to maintain professional viability. Still others explored the apolitical art of Surrealism. Most—including black photographers—however, continued to express their black heritage, history, and culture thematically, even as they explored new formal methods. Seemingly disengaged from the politics of the era, nonacademic artists were a creative force to be reckoned with at the time. Their art was as visually compelling and compositionally erudite as their art school–trained contemporaries.

Key Terms

aestheticism: a philosophy that advocates that the arts should not be judged by political, social, or moral standards, but by artistic ones only

anamorph: an extremely distorted image whose form is revealed only by viewing it from a specific angle

Art Brut: art created outside of the institutions and traditions of the academic art world

art-for-art's-sake: a philosophy that asserts that art should be created for the sake of its appearance alone and should not be required to serve any other purpose

automatism: the creation of art through subconscious rather than deliberate action

avant-garde: French for "look ahead," refers in art to those who are innovative or cutting-edge

Cold War: political tension and antagonism between the United States and the USSR beginning in 1945 and ending in the early 1990s

collage: art made from torn or cut pieces of paper or fabric glued or otherwise attached to a flat surface

Dada: a literary and visual art movement founded in Zurich in 1916 and based on expressions of irrationality, accident, and nihilism as a reaction against the supposed rational reasoning that had sparked World War I

De Stijl: a Dutch art movement founded by Piet Mondrian and Theo van Doesburg in 1917 characterized by the use of rectangular forms, primary colors, and black and white

gesso: a white plaster mixture used to prepare a surface for paint application

Jungian archetypes: refers to universal symbols or mental images common to humankind and first postulated by Carl Jung in his 1953 book *The Archetypes and the Collective Unconscious*

kitsch: low-quality art with mass appeal

magic realism: fantasy or dream images rendered in a scrupulously realistic manner

Marxism: a theory based on the 1949 *Communist Manifesto* by Karl Marx and Friedrich Engels that advocates the establishment of a classless society through proletariat revolution

McCarthy era: a period characterized by political and economic persecution of American socialists and communists from the mid-1940s until 1960

mexicanidad style: a nationalistic art style that embraced Mexico's pre- and post-Columbian art, culture, and history

Neue Sachlichkeit: a term that means "new objectivity" and refers to figurative art produced in the 1920s that critiqued German society and politics and that rejected abstraction and Expressionism for Realism as indicative of a "return to order" in the wake of World War I

Outsider Art: art created outside of the institutions and traditions of the academic art world

photo essay: a series of photographs that, collectively, express a single narrative or viewpoint

photomontage: a work of art composed of multiple cut or torn photographs

pyrogravure: a French term referring to art made by drawing with a metal poker or similar heated instrument on wood or leather

ukiyo-e: meaning "floating world," a Japanese term that refers to colored woodblock prints of landscapes, kabuki theater, domesticity, courtesans, and entertainment created between 1660 and 1868

Questions for Further Study and Discussion

1. Discuss the relationship between art and politics at midcentury with regard to Social Realism and abstraction.
2. What group in Mexico paralleled the WPA-FAP graphic arts division, and how did it do so?
3. Debate the pros and cons of art-for-art's-sake versus art for the people.
4. What are the characteristics of Surrealist art?
5. What field of medicine and which medical theorist most influenced the Surrealist Movement? Research and discuss this influence.
6. Create a Surrealist drawing or poem using automatism. Analyze its meaning.
7. Discuss why self-taught artists are often segregated from mainstream art. Why does this segregation persist?
8. Discuss the differences and similarities between self-taught artists and their advocates and academic artists and their dealers.

9. Research other artists of this period, such as sculptor Ulysses Davis (1914–90), James Hampton (1909–64), Sister Gertrude Morgan (1900–80), David Butler (1898–1997), Joseph Yoakum (1889–1972), Elijah Pierce (1892–1984); ironsmith Philip Simmons (1912–2009); and photographers such as Charles "Teenie" Harris (1908–98), Robert H. McNeil (1917–?), Gilbert Dwoyid Olmstead (1914–85), and Richard Saunders (1922–87).

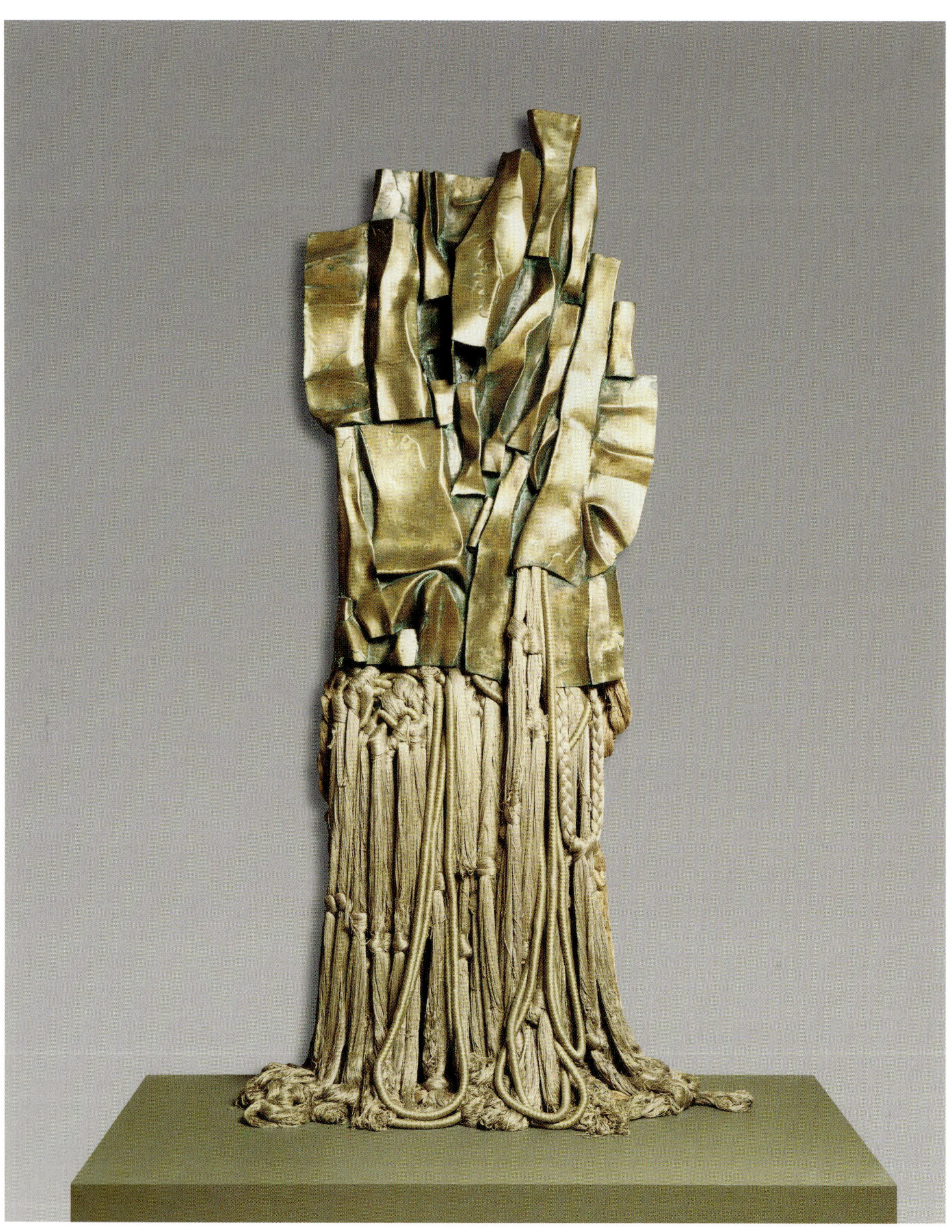

ABSTRACT EXPRESSIONISM

9

The term "Abstract Expressionism" was coined in 1946 by *New Yorker* art critic Robert Coates (1897–1993) to describe the **nonobjective** paintings of German-born artist Hans Hofmann (1880–1966). The trend became a major artistic movement that flourished over two decades. The first wave of Abstract Expressionism took root in New York City. Known as the New York School, its practitioners included American artists Norman Lewis, Hale Woodruff, Beauford Delaney, Jackson Pollock, Helen Frankenthaler (1928–2011), Lee Krasner (1908–84), and Robert Motherwell (1915–91) and European émigrés Mark Rothko (1903–70) and Willem de Kooning (1904–97), among others.

Abstract Expressionist art encompassed a wide variety of styles from nonobjective art that did not feature any recognizable forms to **figurative expressionism**, which, like much of modern art, distorted forms from the natural world to varying degrees. A prominent and early strain of the movement was known as **Action painting** or **Gestural Abstraction**. It emphasized vigorous paint application as a record of the physical actions and gestures of the painter. This approach was slowly supplanted by **Color Field painting** or **Post-Painterly Abstraction**. Color Field painting involved a rejection of the painterly or textured surfaces of Action Painting and replaced it with large, soft-edged areas of chromatic pigment. In the 1960s, **Hard-Edge painting** developed as an offshoot of the Color Field approach but with straight edges and sharp silhouettes. The formal elements of art—such as line, color, shape, balance, pattern, and texture—became the subject. Story and narrative, though sometimes present, were secondary to the artistic process.

Many African Americans took part in the movement, but just as many went against its grain by maintaining a strong connection to the storytelling aspects of art and to its ability to make political statements. This trend was due, in large part, to the intensely political nature of African-American life at the time. Simultaneously with the rise of Abstract Expressionism in the 1950s and 1960s, African Americans were engaged in the Civil Rights Movement, a nationwide struggle for racial equality (see Chapter 10). As such, excluding politics from their art was antithetical to the realities of their existence. Many could not.

◀ Barbara Chase-Riboud, *Malcolm X #3*, 1969, polished bronze, rayon, and cotton, 8′6½″ × 3′1″ × 2′8″.

Philadelphia Museum of Art: 125th Anniversary Acquisition. Purchased with funds raised in honor of the 125th anniversary of the museum and in celebration of African-American art, 2001. Photo and digital image © Philadelphia Museum of Art.

ACTION PAINTING/GESTURAL ABSTRACTION

Beauford Delaney

Tennessee-born Beauford Delaney (1901–79) was one of the first African-American exponents of Abstract Expressionism. Born at the turn of the century, he painted his first "commissioned" picture at age 14 when his after-school employer invited him to paint a seascape. The result so impressed Delaney's newly found patron that he showed the work to noted Knoxville portraitist Lloyd Branson (1854–1925), who immediately hired Delaney as his studio assistant. Branson gave Delaney his first art lessons in pastel drawing and in oil and watercolor painting. In 1923, armed with a small stipend and letters of introduction from Branson, Delaney left Knoxville for Boston to continue his artistic training at the Massachusetts College of Art. Over the next six years Delaney took classes there and at the Copley Society, the Lowell Institute (where Edward Mitchell Bannister had studied in the 1860s), and the South Boston School of Art, which provided low-cost and free art classes for South Boston residents.

From Boston, Delaney moved to New York at the height of the Harlem Renaissance in 1929. Delaney enrolled in classes at the Art Students League, studying with Ashcan School artist John Sloan (1871–1951) and Thomas Hart Benton. He worked on the Harlem Hospital murals with Charles Alston, and he immersed himself in the vibrant Harlem culture. Delaney spent time at the 306 salon and joined the Harlem Artists Guild. After he had lived in the city for less than a year, his paintings came to the attention of the Whitney Studio Gallery (now the Whitney Museum), which opened in 1930. Delaney was invited to exhibit and won a first prize award for his paintings. Needing a job, Delaney was given a staff position at the Whitney Gallery. On the heels of this success, he was honored with his first solo show, held at the Schomburg Center.

After several years at the Whitney, Delaney resigned from his gallery position to spend all his time painting. He earned a reputation as an exceptional abstract portrait painter; Du Bois, Duke Ellington, Alfred Stieglitz (1864–1946), Georgia O'Keefe (1887–1986), surrealist author Henry James (1891–1980), and caricaturist Al Hirschfeld (1903–2003) were among his friends and sitters. In addition to portraits, Delaney painted New York interior and street scenes.

Stylistically, Delaney's worked comprised a Fauvist color palette, impasto, and expressive brushwork. These early career works were exhibited in 1938 in a solo show at the 8th Street Playhouse in Greenwich Village. Another one-man exhibit followed three years later at Vendome Gallery in Midtown, where Ellis Wilson (see Chapter 8) had been similarly honored a few years earlier. Delaney's show received critical praise from both the *New York Times* and *Art Digest*.

Subsequent years were more difficult for the artist, who was victim to a violent gay bashing in 1942 and suffered from depression and financial deprivation. In 1945, author Henry Miller (1891–1980) published a "chapbook" (a small, cheaply printed pamphlet) on Delaney. Despite Miller's somewhat skewed description of Delaney as an erratic and psychologically troubled artistic visionary, the essay gave Delaney the cachet of a local celebrity. By the late 1940s, Delaney was exhibiting routinely again in group and solo shows at Roko Gallery and the Artist's Gallery. His paintings by this time had become more abstract and painterly than those of the 1930s. His notoriety earned Delaney a fellowship in 1950 to the famed Yaddo literary and visual artists' retreat in Saratoga Springs, New York.

One of Delaney's close friends was famed African-American author James Baldwin (1924–1987). When Baldwin moved permanently to Paris in 1950 to escape the racial and sexual oppression that he suffered as a black gay man in the United States, Delaney (who faced similar discrimination) decided to follow his lead. Intending to stay for only a short visit, Delaney traveled to Paris in 1953 and remained there until his death 25 years later, never returning to New York. Delaney lived in the artistic area of Montparnasse on the Left Bank, where he found himself part of the thriving expatriate community of African-American artists. He reacquainted himself with Baldwin, who is believed to have been his lover, at least for a time, and immediately began painting and showing his work. The writer remained a loyal friend and supporter of Delaney's for 30 years, traveling with him throughout France, Venice, and Istanbul, and caring for him as his psychological state deteriorated over time.

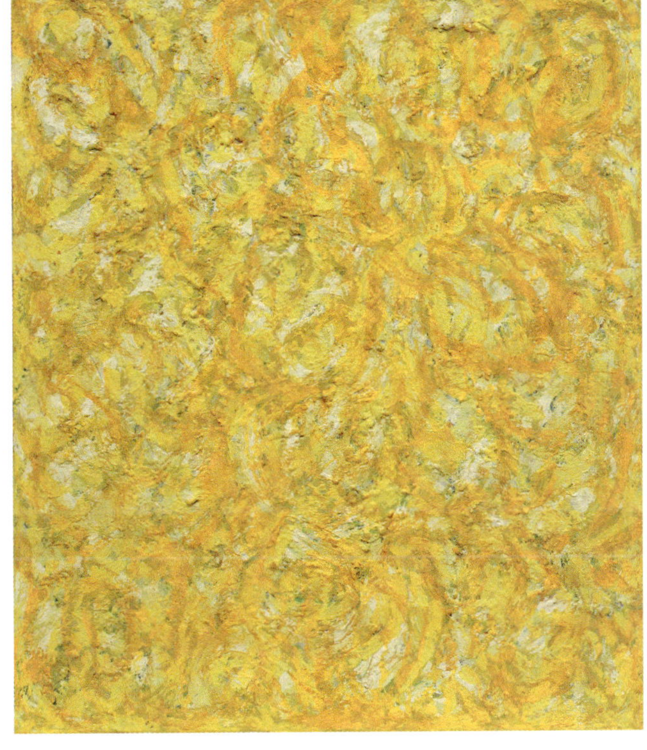

▲ **9.1** Beauford Delaney, *Untitled*, c. 1958, oil on canvas, 30″ × 25″.

Estate of Beauford Delaney, by permission of Derek L. Spratley, Esquire, Court-Appointed Administrator. Photo courtesy of Michael Rosenfeld Gallery LLC, New York, NY.

During the 1950s, Delaney's abstract picture style developed into full-blown nonfigurative expression. His glowing, light-filled, and chromatic compositions were laid down in all-over patterns with intensely active brushwork (Figure 9.1). The 1960s saw solo shows of Delaney's paintings in Paris as well as in other locations, most notably in a group show of African-American art at Fairleigh Dickinson University in New Jersey. In 1968, Delaney received a grant from the National Council of the Arts that helped to fund a return trip home to visit his family in Knoxville. In 1969, his first retrospective was held at the American Cultural Center in Paris. The center was founded by a Delaney patron and friend, gallerist Darthea Speyer (1930–2010), who mounted multiple showings of Delaney's paintings in Paris.

Despite his many exhibits and creative productivity, Delaney sold few works and often had to rely on the financial support of friends. He succumbed to increasing bouts of depression and psychotic episodes. In 1961, while traveling in Greece, Delaney was hospitalized after suffering from auditory hallucinations. The artist attempted suicide on more than one occasion, and he also suffered from failing liver and kidneys, likely due to alcoholism. In 1962, Delaney was released from the hospital. A friend and wealthy winery owner, Madame Bernard du Closel, paid the artist's rent and subsequently purchased an apartment for him in Montparnasse. She supported him until 1975, when Delaney lost the mental capacity to care for himself. Baldwin arranged for Delaney's admission to St. Anne's Hospital for the Insane, where he died four years later. He was tragically unaware of the blockbuster 1978 retrospective held in his honor at the Studio Museum in Harlem.

Norman Lewis

A few years younger than Delaney, Harlem-born Norman Lewis (1909–79) had a very different career trajectory. At age 20, Lewis joined the crew of a sailing vessel and spent two years at sea traveling throughout South America and the Caribbean. On his return, between 1933 and 1939, Lewis took classes at Augusta Savage's Studio of Arts and Crafts and taught under the auspices of the FAP at the Harlem Community Art Center. He also attended the 306 salons, joined the Artists Union, and became a founding member of the Harlem Artists Guild. Lewis augmented his art training at Columbia University and at the John Reed Club, a Marxist-run art school. Lewis's moving painting of a Depression-era itinerant man won honorable mention in 1933 at a Metropolitan Museum of Art juried exhibit. During this period, Lewis worked in the Social Realist style and portrayed images of poverty and deprivation.

By the late 1930s, Lewis was exhibiting his art at local venues such as the Harlem YWCA and at national museums, including the Baltimore Museum of Art's 1939 *Contemporary Negro Art* show. He was also included in Alain Locke's historic *Art of the American Negro* exhibit mounted in Chicago, and in his 1945 traveling exhibition, *The Negro Artist Comes of Age*. The following year, Lewis secured representation with dealer Marian Willard (1904–85). As a member of the Museum of Modern Art's board, Willard was widely respected in the art world. She mounted Lewis's first solo show in 1949 and, over the next 15 years, exhibited Lewis's paintings in five additional solo and group shows.

In 1948, Robert Motherwell, Mark Rothko, William Baziotes (1912–63), and David Hare (1917–92) founded the Subjects of the Artist School at 35 East Eighth Street in Greenwich Village, which quickly evolved into the famed "Studio 35." The studio featured lectures on art by its members and by others of the avant-garde art elite, including artists Franz Kline (1910–62), Willem and Elaine de Kooning (1904–97 and 1918–89), Barnett Newman (1905–70), and art critic Harold Rosenberg (1906–78). Lewis was the only African-American member of this group. Short-lived, Studio 35 led to the formation of The Club in 1949, which embraced both visual artists and poets. The Club met regularly over the next 13 years to discuss issues of art and aesthetics. Lewis and Hale Woodruff were both members and were greatly inspired by the group's meetings, lectures, and readings, as well as by the art of its constituents.

Partly as a result of his association with the Studio 35 circle, Lewis was included in the Museum of Modern Art's 1951 show *Abstract Painting and Sculpture in America*. The show was a major survey organized by internationally renowned curator Andrew Carnduff Ritchie (1907–78). Lewis's work was included in a section of the show titled "Expressionist Biomorphic," which the curator explained as inclusive of irregular forms, calligraphic brushwork, and elements of the emotive and symbolic. Ritchie's description ideally characterized Lewis's style, evident in the artist's painting *Phantasy II* (Figure 9.2). Consisting of a variegated palette of **complimentary contrasts** such as reds, greens, blues, and yellows, *Phantasy II* combines broad

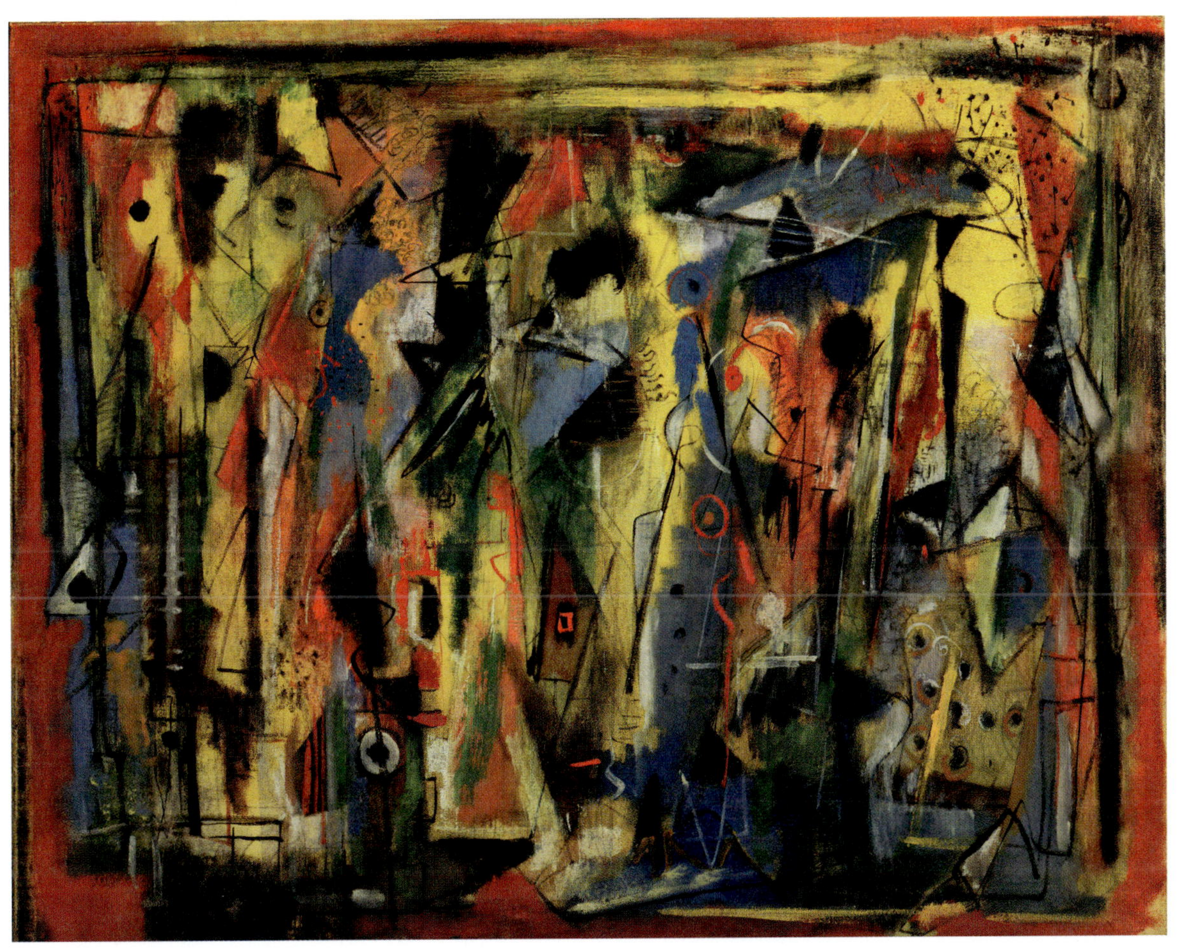

▲ **9.2** Norman Lewis, *Phantasy II, September 23, 1946*, oil on canvas, 28⅛″ × 35⅞″.

brushstrokes with dynamic black calligraphic lines. The asymmetrical balance of colors, textures, and linear and spatial elements in *Phantasy II* has been likened by critics to the syncopation of jazz music and the cacophonous nature of life in the city.

By this time, Lewis had completely dispensed with Social Realism and had fully adopted an Abstract Expressionist approach. He gave his new works non-narrative titles such as *Composition* and *Untitled* in the manner of Wassily Kandinsky's nonobjective pictures. Kandinsky's canonical 1911 essay "Über das Geistige in der Kunst: Insbesondere in der Malerei" ("Concerning the Spiritual in Art: Especially in Painting") described the ability of nonobjective imagery to spark transcendence and greatly influenced Lewis's art. Despite rejecting social topics in his painting, Lewis was politically engaged personally. He had taught in the 1940s with Catlett at the socialist Carver School and at the Thomas Jefferson School of Social Science, where the curriculum required faculty to emphasize social issues in all classes.

After the rise of the Civil Rights Movement, Lewis joined with Bearden and others in 1963 to cofound Spiral, an artists' group that addressed African-American political concerns as they related to art (see Chapter 10). Beginning in 1965, he taught for six years at Harlem Youth in Action (HARYOU-ACT). It offered educational and social services to low-income youths and engaged in outspoken social protests to draw attention to inner-city poverty. With Bearden and Crichlow, he cofounded Cinque Gallery to support emerging minority artists. During the years of the Black Arts Movement in the late 1960s and early 1970s, Lewis joined in protests against the Whitney and Metropolitan Museums for their exclusionary curatorial practices.

In the years just prior to his death, Lewis's star rose considerably. He was elected to the American Academy of Arts and Letters and received grants and fellowships from the National Endowment for the Arts (NEA), and from the Mark Rothko and Guggenheim Foundations. Teaching and painting until the last, Lewis spent much of the 1970s as an instructor at the Art Students League. He capped his career in 1976 with the completion of an untitled abstract mural at the historic (and oldest) New York public school, Boys and Girls High School in Brooklyn (where Crichlow also completed a mural the same year). Lewis's final mural used a limited palette of blues, black, and white and lively geometric forms to express the joys of youth—a final commitment to his belief in the power of abstract art to communicate feelings and ideas.

Alma Thomas

Synthesizing elements of both gestural abstraction and color field painting, the career of nonobjective painter Alma Thomas (1891–1978) unfurled at the very end of her life, prior to which she had been a teacher and an academic painter for 60 years. In 1972, at the age of 81, Thomas became the first African-American woman to be given a solo exhibit at the Whitney Museum. When critics viewed her large, nonfigurative, and radiant canvases, the reaction was overwhelmingly positive. Later that year, the Corcoran Gallery in Washington, D.C., mounted a major retrospective.

A consummate colorist, Thomas was affiliated with the **Washington Color School**—a group of color field and hard-edge artists including Gene Davis (1920–85), Kenneth Noland (1924–2010), and Morris Louis (1912–62). Unlike these abstractionists, however, Thomas relied on brushwork and gesture to infuse her paintings with energy. Yet, distinct from action painters, she applied her staccato brushstrokes with methodical control. She counted nature as her greatest inspiration, deriving her subject matter from flowers, landscapes, and space exploration, which especially enthralled her. In her *Wind and Crepe Myrtle Concerto* (Figure 9.3), the artist's love of nature in bloom mingles with the concept of musical harmonies, expressed through color and movement. The painting's color scheme of luxuriant pinks brushed over vaporous clouds of yellow, blue, and green is Impressionism reinvented. One can almost distinguish the poplar trees and French countryside of Monet's visions in Thomas's own nonobjective design.

Thomas was a lifelong Washingtonian and friend of Lois Jones (see Chapter 6), with whom she worked and exhibited in the "Little Paris Studio," a salon (located in Washington) that Jones organized for her artist-colleagues. Thomas first came to D.C. from Columbus, Georgia, when she was 15. In the nation's capital, she had access to the kind of education that was denied her in segregated Columbus. In 1924, she became the first student to graduate from Howard University's newly founded art department. Ten years later,

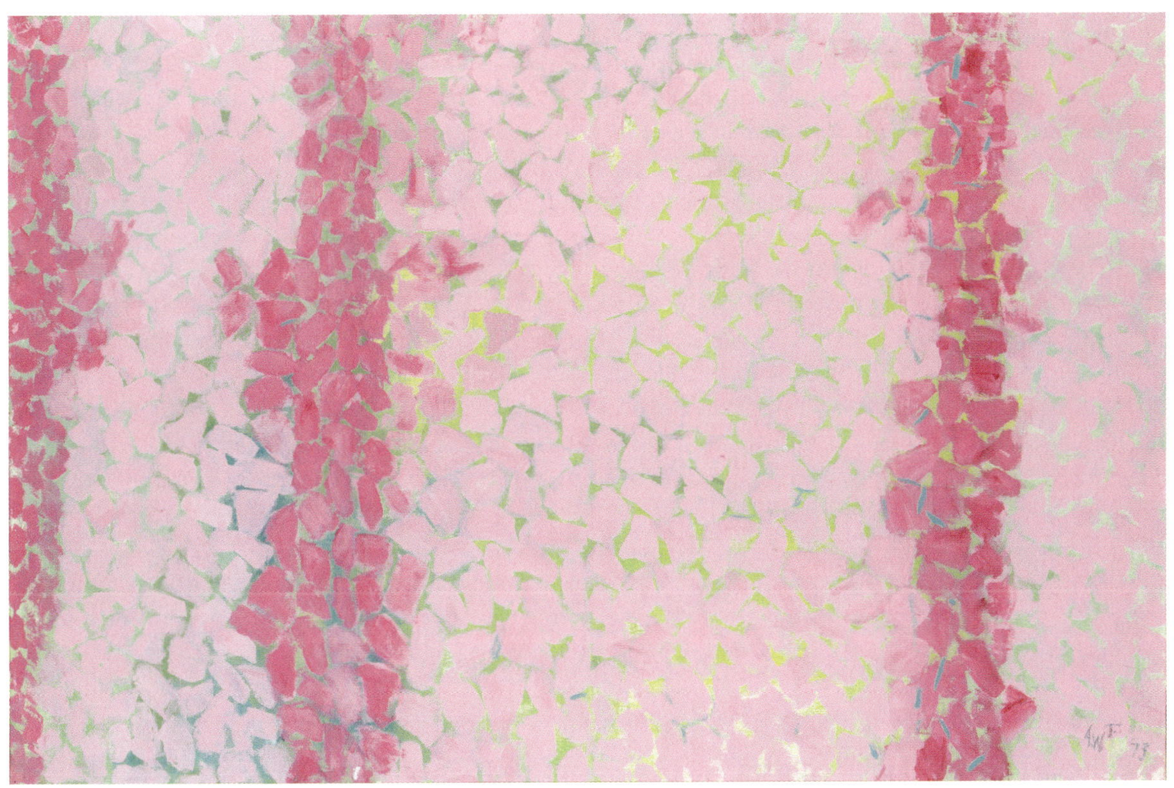

▲ 9.3 Alma Woodsey Thomas, *Wind and Crepe Myrtle Concerto*, 1973, acrylic on canvas, 35″ × 52″.

Photo: Smithsonian American Art Museum, Washington, D.C. / Art Resource, NY.

Thomas earned a master's degree in education from Columbia University and spent the next 35 years as an educator at D.C.'s Shaw Junior High School. During her years as a teacher, Thomas worked to refine her painting skills. Most influential was a period of study in the 1950s at American University with nonfigurative colorists Jacob Kainen (1909–2001) and Robert Franklin Gates (1906–82) and Cézanne-inspired painter Ben L. Summerford (b. 1924), some of whose abstract techniques Thomas embraced in her own art.

During this period, Thomas joined the celebrated Washington Workshop Center for the Arts, where Kainen also taught. Established in the mid-1940s by Color Field painter Leon Berkowitz (1911–87) and his wife, poet Ida Fox (1913–79), for 10 years the center was an art, music, theater, and dance center that inspired artists across disciplines to create and study. Thomas and the workshop's other artists would later form the core of the Washington Color School.

In 1966, James Porter, who was then director of the Howard University Art Department and gallery, curated a Thomas retrospective to honor her status as the department's first graduate. In preparation for the exhibit, Thomas painted a series of compositions that revealed how completely she had assimilated Abstract Expressionism. Thomas succinctly described these works as "geometric abstractions composed of mosaic-like patterns of vivid color rhythmically arranged in concentric circles or parallel lines." These distinctive parallel vertical lines came to be known as "Alma stripes." Thomas's long and prolific life incredibly spanned post-Reconstruction, the Harlem Renaissance, the Depression, and the civil and women's rights eras. Asked shortly before her death why she declined to respond through her art to the polemically charged eras in which she lived, she answered: "Through color I have sought to concentrate on beauty and happiness, rather than on man's inhumanity to man." Thomas wished her art to stand independent of time and place, and it seems her wish has been granted.

COLOR FIELD PAINTING

Sam Gilliam

Color Field artist Sam Gilliam (b. 1933) spent his youth in Mississippi and Kentucky and took his first art classes in junior high school. He attended the University of Louisville and studied painting with Abstract Expressionist Ulfert Wilke (1907–87). Gilliam completed his BFA in 1955 and then spent two years in the armed services, stationed in Japan. After his 1958 discharge, he returned to the University of Louisville to complete an MFA, which he obtained in 1961. Just as the Washington Color School was evolving, Gilliam relocated to Washington, D.C., where he met Thomas and the group's other artists. He remained a Washingtonian for the rest of his life.

Among several methods used by Color Field artists, Gilliam chose **staining**—pouring rather than brushing paint onto the canvas. Gilliam not only forsook the paintbrush but went a step further and abandoned the

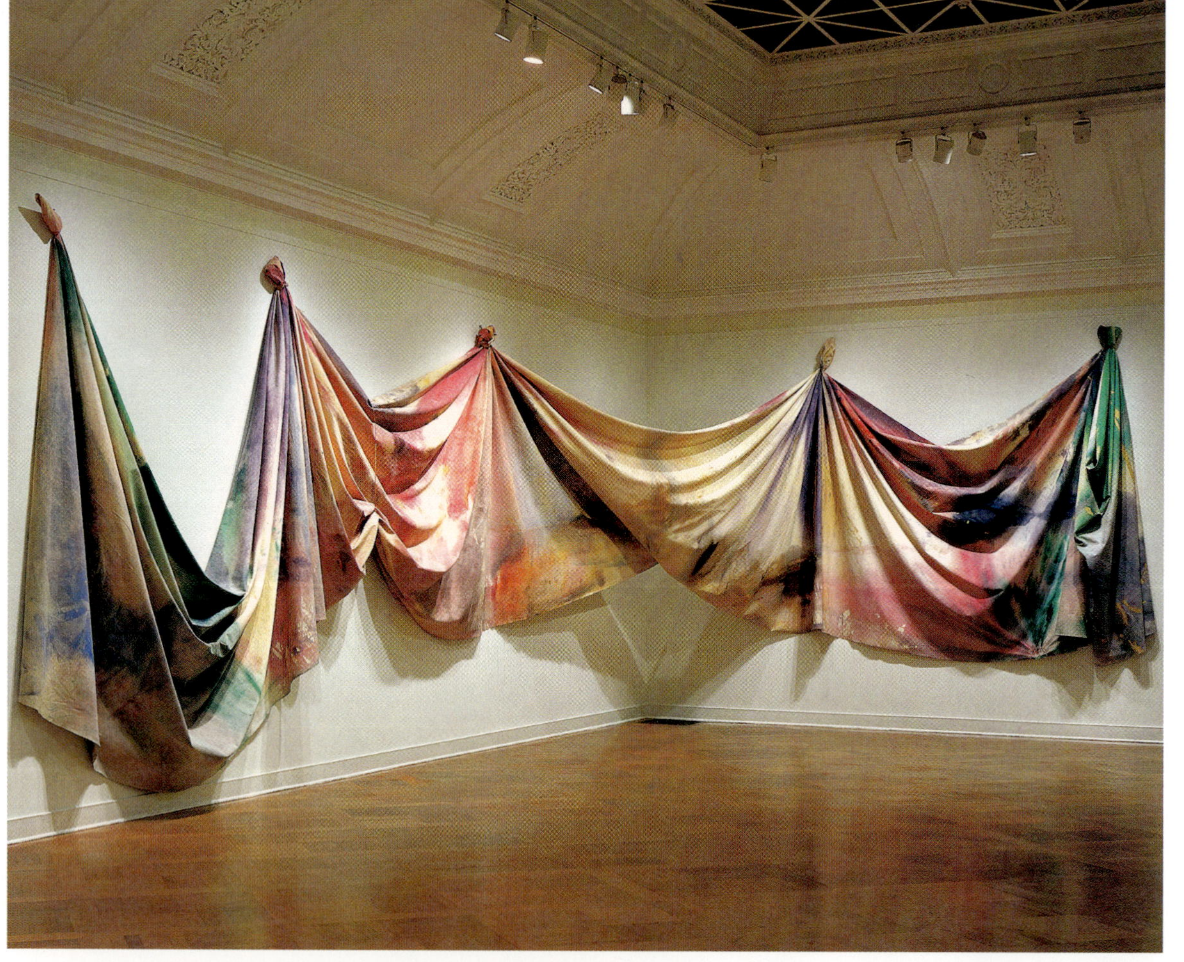

▼ **9.4** Sam Gilliam, *Light Depth*, 1969, acrylic on canvas, 120″ × 900″ flat.

© Sam Gilliam. Courtesy of David Kordansky Gallery, Los Angeles, CA.

canvas stretcher, preferring to fold his unstretched canvases so that the wet paint from one area would stain its other sections. The result was a diaphanous layering of multiple colors on a malleable object—the canvas—that Gilliam could shape, reshape, hang from an armature, or pin to a wall (Figure 9.4). His method, termed "draping," transformed the two-dimensional canvas into a three-dimensional object similar to a soft sculpture.

Within a few short years of his arrival in D.C., Gilliam was participating in group and solo exhibits at key venues nationwide. Washington's Phillips Collection featured his work in a major one-man show in 1967. Gilliam won an NEA grant the year of his Phillips Collection exhibit and again on three other occasions in the 1970s and 1980s, which helped to fund the next creative phase of the artist's development. Gilliam reconnected with stretched canvases in 1970. However, instead of traditional rectangular stretchers, he devised beveled-edged, multisided, and multipart canvas frames and painting surfaces. He also intensified and clarified his color palette. The dynamic and innovative results, which blurred the boundaries between painting and sculpture, were acknowledged as early as 1971 by a Guggenheim Foundation award and an exhibit that year at the Museum of Modern Art in New York.

Over time, Gilliam incorporated collage, **assemblage**, and pieced quilting techniques into his material repertoire, influencing an entire generation of young multimedia artists. His career boasts more than 20 one-man shows, more than 30 public commissions, and representation in the permanent collections of nearly 60 museums in the United States and abroad. The recipient of seven honorary PhDs, Gilliam is a staunch believer in the educational process and dedicated 30 years of his life to teaching. He retired from the profession in 1989 but continues to make art in his Washington studio.

Richard Mayhew

Richard Mayhew (b. 1924) creates highly abstracted and Expressionist landscapes that have the look of Color Field staining but are, in fact, created with the brush. His light-infused and chromatic palette and his organic gossamer forms have been described as both mystical and spiritual in their evocation of land, sky, water, and trees. Although widely identified as a landscape artist (he is certainly inspired by landscape), Mayhew's pictures share much in common with the color field works of Rothko that suggest sky, earth, and horizon but do not depict them in any definitive way. Composed of organic cloudlike shapes (rather than Rothko's rectilinear forms), Mayhew's pictures similarly evoke rather than portray landscape. According to the artist, his so-called landscapes are abstract and freeform, spiritual and spatial—the essence of the soul on canvas. He said: "To work with figures would be very limiting because that would identify a particular place and situation. The paintings look like landscapes but that is not necessarily my preoccupation in painting." To emphasize this fact, Mayhew often chooses abstract titles for his pictures, such as *Spiritual Space*, or musical designations such as *Vibrato* or *Sonata in G Major*. A one-time jazz singer himself, many of Mayhew's paintings are inspired by the music of Miles Davis and Duke Ellington, rather than by nature.

Mayhew was born to parents of Shinnecock, Cherokee, and African descent. He grew up in the Long Island village of Amityville, about 40 miles east of New York City and 50 miles west of the Shinnecock Reservation. Mayhew's connection to the natural environment was inspired by his Native American grandmother, Sarah Steele Mayhew. She taught him that nature must be respected, and that humans are an integral part of, rather than separate from, the larger natural world. Paintings with titles such as *Chippewa* and *Kiowa* (both from 1974) paid homage to this heritage and philosophy throughout the artist's career. His connection to nature was reinforced artistically when, after observing en plein air artists from New York City who painted land- and seascapes on Long Island during the summer season, the then 14-year-old Mayhew borrowed paints and brushes from his father's house- and sign-painting business and created his first pictures. After befriending the visiting landscape artists, Mayhew began to paint side by side with them each summer. Throughout this period, his high school years, Mayhew visited New York City's galleries and museums, in particular the Metropolitan Museum, where he was especially drawn to the Hudson River School. By the time Mayhew graduated from high school, he had chosen his career.

Encouraged by one of the painters he had met in Amityville, James Wilson Peale, Mayhew moved into New York City in 1945 at age 21. He earned money as a medical illustrator working with Peale. Mayhew built on Peale's tutelage by spending time at the New York Academy of Medicine on 103rd Street in East Harlem, where he studied drawings of human anatomy. To support himself, he worked a variety of creative jobs, as a product designer, children's book illustrator, jazz singer, and actor. From 1953 to 1957, he studied at the Brooklyn Museum Art School, Pratt Institute, and the Art Students League. Among his teachers were major innovators in nonobjective and Expressionist art—Hans Hofmann and Max Beckmann, respectively—as well as abstract landscape artists Reuben Tam (1916–91) and Edwin Dickinson (1891–1978). Mayhew also pursued a course of study in art history at Columbia University from 1957 to 1959.

During the 1950s, Mayhew became acquainted with the Cedar Bar crowd, where the Abstract Expressionists socialized. Exposure to their art and theories intensified his interest in transforming nature into mood-invoking abstractions. He began to exhibit at prominent New York venues. In 1958, Mayhew won a residency at the famed MacDowell Artists' Colony in New Hampshire. After completing his fellowship, Mayhew spent a year in 1959 at the Academy of Fine Arts in Florence, Italy, with funds from a Whitney fellowship. Returning to the United States in 1960, Mayhew received several major grants that supported his art making and allowed him to make additional trips to museums abroad between 1960 and 1962. Mayhew was especially drawn to the French Impressionist landscape painters, whose brushwork, color, and light experiments he analyzed in depth.

Within a year after returning to New York in 1962, Mayhew had received a Louis Comfort Tiffany Foundation grant. By this time, the Civil Rights Movement was in full swing, and Mayhew partnered with Romare Bearden to help found the civil rights artists group Spiral (see Chapter 10). He also participated in the late 1960s protests organized by the Black Emergency Cultural Coalition (BECC) against the Whitney Museum for racial discrimination.

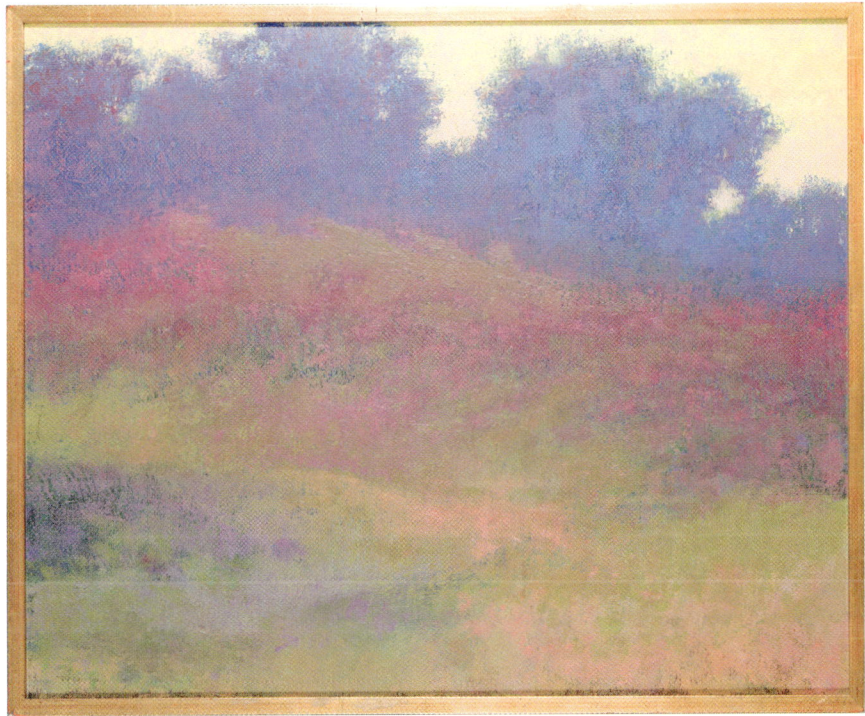

◀ 9.5 Richard Mayhew, *Coyote*, 2008, oil on canvas, 29″ × 35″.

Image Courtesy of N'Namdi Contemporary, Miami.

During these tumultuous years, Mayhew began to layer pigments so that echoes of the initial coats showed through the overlays. The results were softer and more nuanced than his earlier works.

Throughout the 1960s, 1970s, and beyond, Mayhew's art continued to secure him awards and inclusion in significant exhibits, a highlight of which was a major 1978 retrospective at the Studio Museum. He also had a prolific teaching career, which culminated in 1977 with a full-time faculty position at Penn State, where he taught for 15 years. In the early 1980s, Mayhew relocated permanently to Santa Cruz, California, and was as inspired by the natural surroundings there as by those of the East Coast. Paintings from his *Santa Cruz* series, for example, reveal the artist's signature use of a jeweled palette to create gossamer and amorphous abstractions derived from nature (Figure 9.5).

HARD-EDGE PAINTING

Related to the **Minimalist** movement in sculpture, hard-edge painting was characterized by the use of geometric forms, flat surfaces, precise outlines, and large, flat areas of brightly painted color. The style aimed to eliminate the overt expressiveness and emotionality of Abstract Expressionism, so that the artist's gestures were obscured, if not eliminated. An outgrowth of the early 20th-century geometric art of the Bauhaus, De Stijl, and **Suprematism** styles, Hard-Edge painting embodied the Bauhaus precept that less is more—that is, the fewer elements of form contained in a work of art, the more powerful it will be. Hard-Edge art was popularized in the United States by Frank Stella (b. 1936), whose Hard-Edge and Minimalist "black pictures" (paintings in black) were first exhibited at the Museum of Modern Art in 1959.

Al Loving

When the geometric paintings of Detroit-born Al Loving (1935–2005) were unveiled to the art world in a groundbreaking exhibit at the Whitney Museum in 1969, the artist seemed to have appeared from nowhere. In fact, he had walked a long and dedicated road to that moment. Loving was initially encouraged to become an artist by his father, Al Loving, Sr., who was an educator. At his dad's suggestion, at age 12 the younger Loving made copies of landscape paintings. Loving attended Detroit's only magnet high school at the time—Cash Tech—where he painted sets for the theater program. After graduation in 1954, he enrolled at Wayne State University. Loving's education was interrupted for a year in the mid-1950s, when he moved to India, where his father, on leave from his position as a dean at the University of Michigan, had taken a teaching position.

After the family's return from abroad, Loving enrolled at Flint Junior College and completed his undergraduate education at the University of Illinois at Urbana, earning a BFA in 1963, followed by an MFA at the University of Michigan, in 1965. At Michigan, Loving studied with Albert Mullen (1921–83), an Abstract Expressionist who had trained with Hans Hofmann and French Modernist Fernand Léger. A proponent of the compositions of Hofmann and Albers based on the square, Mullen shared this idea with Loving, who was profoundly swayed by geometric abstraction. The influence would inform Loving's art for the next decade and would lead to his trademark style of intensely colored, multidimensional cubes, triangles, and hexagons.

▼ **9.6** Al Loving, *Multiple of 8, #3,* 1974, acrylic on canvas, 35″ × 35″.
Courtesy of Garth Greenan Gallery, New York, NY.

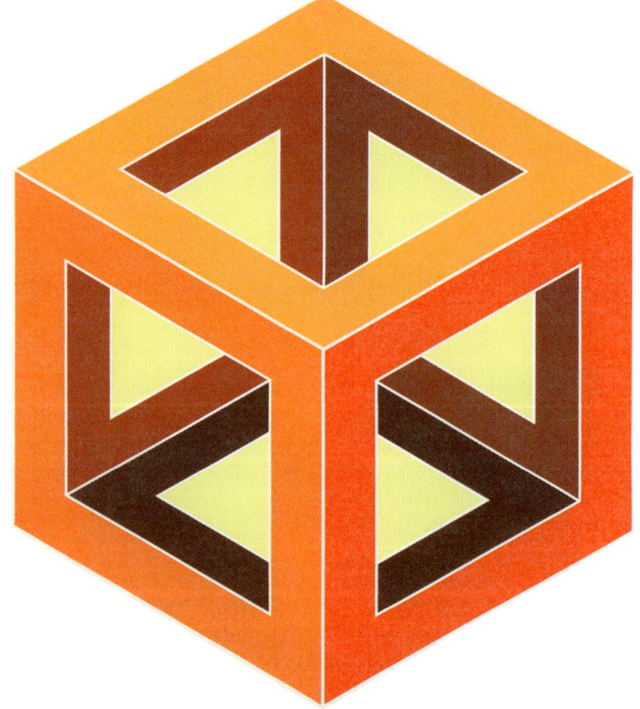

Multiple of 8 is typical of Loving's best-known works (Figure 9.6). A hexagonal form of vivid colors is painted on a shaped canvas. Its electric hues are balanced by more earthen red-orange tones in the inner areas. The result is a binary composition that is static and changeable, solid and hollow. Loving's painting can be traced to the iconic 1915 *Black Square* by Suprematist Kasimir Malevich (1879–1935), which embodied the Russian artist's intellectual inquiries into metaphysical dimensions and transcendental states. However, Loving improves on Malevich's conception by adding the optical illusion of a square as it might actually be seen in four dimensions—with many sides visible simultaneously.

Multiples of 8 was created a few years after the artist's four-year tenure on the faculty of Eastern Michigan University, when, in 1968, he moved to New York City to further his art career. Within a year, Loving had landed a one-man show at the Whitney Museum that brought his geometric paintings to national attention. Loving's purely formal pictures that blurred the boundaries between Abstract Expressionism, Minimalism, and **Op Art** were instantly in high demand with collectors, dealers, and museums. By the end of the decade, he had won five NEA fellowships and, later in the 1980s, a Guggenheim award.

Not one to rest on his laurels, Loving soon felt pigeonholed as the artist who painted cubes. As a result, in the latter 1970s he began to experiment with new and innovative media, in particular cut, torn, and sewn fabric **constructions** and **installations** that transformed entire gallery spaces into works of art. By the 1980s and 1990s, Loving was creating multimedia and three-dimensional collages and using an ever more vivid palette. In 1988, he joined the full-time faculty of City College (part of the City University of New York [CUNY]) in Harlem, where he remained until 1996. The Metropolitan Transit Authority (MTA) commissioned Loving in 2001 to complete a prismatic and panoramic stained glass window installation and wall mosaic entitled *Brooklyn, New Morning* at the Broadway/East New York subway station. This would be his last major work. Loving died of lung cancer four years later, at age 69.

William T. Williams

Nonobjective painter and printmaker William T. Williams (b. 1942) was born in North Carolina but was raised from age four in the New York City borough of Queens. When he was 14 Williams enrolled in one of the city's elite public art schools: the High School for Industrial Arts (today the High School of Art and Design). Williams completed a BFA with honors at Pratt Institute in 1966, and two years later he received an MFA degree from Yale's School of Art and Architecture.

Back in New York in 1968, Williams settled in Soho and, a year later, curated the Studio Museum's *X to the 4th Power* exhibit with abstractionists Sam Gilliam and Melvin Edwards (discussed later in this chapter). His first one-man show in 1971 at Reese Palley Gallery was a great success; the entire collection of his Hard-Edge abstractions sold out to enthusiastic collectors. In addition to his paintings, Williams produced prints at Bob Blackburn's printmaking workshop beginning in 1975 and over the next two decades produced nearly 20 print suites in collaboration with the master printmaker.

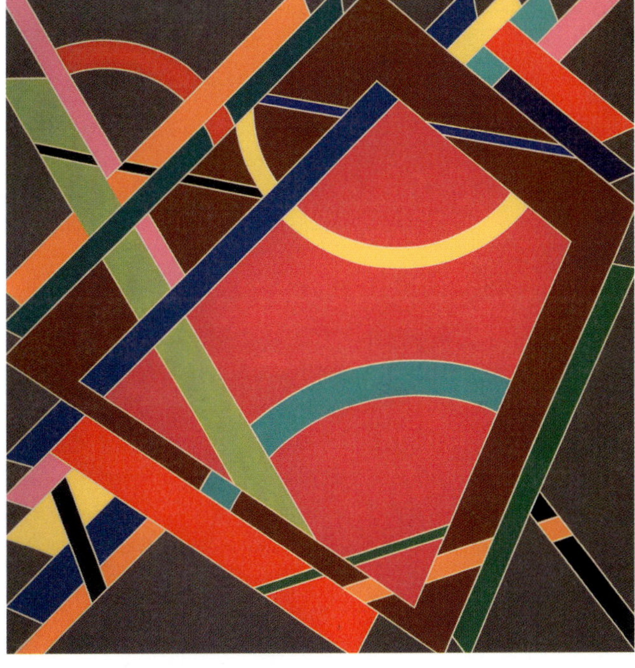

▼ 9.7 William T. Williams, *Elbert Jackson L.A.M.F. Part II*, 1969, synthetic polymer paint and metallic paint on can, 9′7¼″ × 9′1⅞″.

Williams's paintings often display overlapping trapezoid and diamond-shaped forms. Vibrantly colored and delineated by thin white outlines, the forms create the illusion of movement through a multidimensional space (Figure 9.7). Standing apart from the planar Minimalist paintings of such artists as Frank Stella, Williams's paintings embody a commanding spatial dynamism which one critic described, diametrically, as both violent and intensely positive in form and substance. Not unlike the abstract syncopations of jazz music,

Williams's paintings depict multiple planes that shift and glide across and between one another in shapes that repeat like echoes. The artist's works are life affirming expressions of his history and experiences—memories of, and homages to, family, friends, childhood, travels, Harlem, North Carolina, jazz musicians, and nature's diversity—distilled into epigrammatic visual statements that signify each painting's iconographic impetus.

Williams's paintings are grand in scale (as much as 10 feet square) and have tremendous physical impact on the viewer. Beginning in 1971, he added to his formal repertoire undulating calligraphic elements and concentric circles. His works after 1973 became even more painterly and color and form transitions are more subtle. After a visit to Africa in 1977 to participate in FESTAC (the second World Festival of Black Art and African Culture) in Lagos, Nigeria, Williams was inspired by shifting colors and repeating forms in nature, as well as by the earth-tones patterns of African textiles, which he experienced as dynamic rather than static elements. Subsequently, he created a series of earth-tones paintings using expressive brushwork painted over an architectonic understructure. In these and similar pictures, Williams incorporated pearlescence to create a shimmering, light-filled effect.

An historic moment for Williams (and for African-American art history) occurred in 1986, when the widely used college textbook *Janson's History of Art* included Williams as the first-ever African-American artist to be featured therein. A Guggenheim Fellowship followed in 1987, as well as a four-person show at the Smithsonian Institution with Gilliam, figurative colorist Keith Anthony Morrison (b. 1942), and multimedia artist Martha Jackson-Jarvis (see Chapter 12). Williams has continued to receive major awards and honors, including an NEA grant in 1994, the North Carolina Governors Award for Fine Arts in 2006, and the Detroit Institute of Art Alain Locke Award in 2011.

FIGURATIVE EXPRESSIONISM

Robert (Bob) L. Thompson

Robert (Bob) L. Thompson (1937–66) was one of a number of Abstract Expressionists who maintained a connection to the figural in their work. Thompson grew up the son of middle-class Kentucky business owners in Louisville. In the mid-1950s, he moved to Boston to live with his sister and to attend Boston University as a premed student. Quickly losing interest in medicine, Thompson returned to Kentucky to enroll in the art program at the University of Louisville, where, like Gilliam, he studied with Ulfert Wilke. During a summer break in 1958, Thompson visited Provincetown, Massachusetts, one of the country's oldest continually active art colonies. It was also a summer haven for many Abstract Expressionists, including Pollock, Krasner, Frankenthaler, Hofmann, Motherwell, Rothko, and Franz Kline (1910–62), as well as Pop artist Red Grooms (b. 1937) and African-American figurative expressionist Emilio Cruz (1938–2004).

The painting style of the Provincetown figurative expressionists had much in common with Post-Impressionism and Symbolism, including veiled metaphors and intense colors, abstract figures, and painterly brushwork designed to evoke emotions. In Provincetown, Thompson incorporated these elements into his own art, and his contact with so many New York School artists convinced him to leave Kentucky for New York. Over the next several years Thompson developed his signature style: a distinct fusion of coarsely rendered and distorted figures, rich impasto, and brilliant colors.

Thompson chose known masterpieces from past eras as subject matter for his own painting, appropriating and reinterpreting the original compositions. His sources included the works of Renaissance artists Cranach, Masaccio, Piero, and Titian, Baroque painter Poussin, Rococo artist Boucher, and the nude bather themes of Cézanne. Thompson drastically altered the look of the earlier works by distorting forms, applying **arbitrary color**, and updating the iconography. Thompson's singular interpretations of old masterworks using figurative expressionism distinguished him from his Provincetown compeers.

Living in relative poverty in New York City in 1959, Thompson, Grooms, and New York School painter Jay Milder (b. 1934) founded a gallery in Red Grooms's Lower East Side studio. Initially dubbed the City Gallery, it was renamed the Delancey Street Museum in honor of its address. Hardly a museum, it served as an exhibition space for the three artists' works. Thompson's art was featured there in a one-man show curated by Grooms in February and March 1960. This bit of savvy self-promotion led to a two-man Thompson and Milder show at a more legitimate and prestigious Madison Avenue gallery. The following year, Thompson received a grant from the Walter Gutman Foundation, which he used to finance study in Europe.

Thompson spent most of his first year abroad in Paris, where he studied the Louvre collection, observing and sketching the paintings of the European masters who provided his subject matter. Thompson remained abroad for two more years, moving to Ibiza, Spain, after winning a Whitney Foundation Fellowship. He returned to New York in 1963, where he immediately secured a one-man exhibit of his Europe pictures at the Martha Jackson Gallery. Attendance was overwhelming, as was the critical response to his work.

Thompson's European suite of paintings featured a chromatic and emotive palette, carefully structured compositions, and a synthesis of imagined and appropriated motifs. His 1964 *Triumph of Bacchus* engages a classical Greco-Roman theme of the god of wine and sexual abandon—Bacchus (or Dionysus in Greek)—who is often presented in art returning in "triumph" from some unnamed orgiastic fest (Figure 9.8). Thompson borrowed the seated pose of his Bacchus (a bright yellow figure in the center of the composition) from Poussin's 1636 painting of the same name (Figure 9.9). However, Thompson exchanged Poussin's golden chariot for a large, green, flightless bird. In contrast to the advancing thrust of the bacchanalians, the bird stands quite still on one leg (as certain species of birds do when they sleep) and cannot carry the central character forward.

The bird can be viewed as an anchoring element designed to stabilize the otherwise highly active composition, or it may be interpreted symbolically as a commentary on the artist's life. One interpretation might be that Thompson's Bacchus represents the artist himself triumphant in the art world, surrounded by revelers who honor him. Bacchus, who in Thompson's

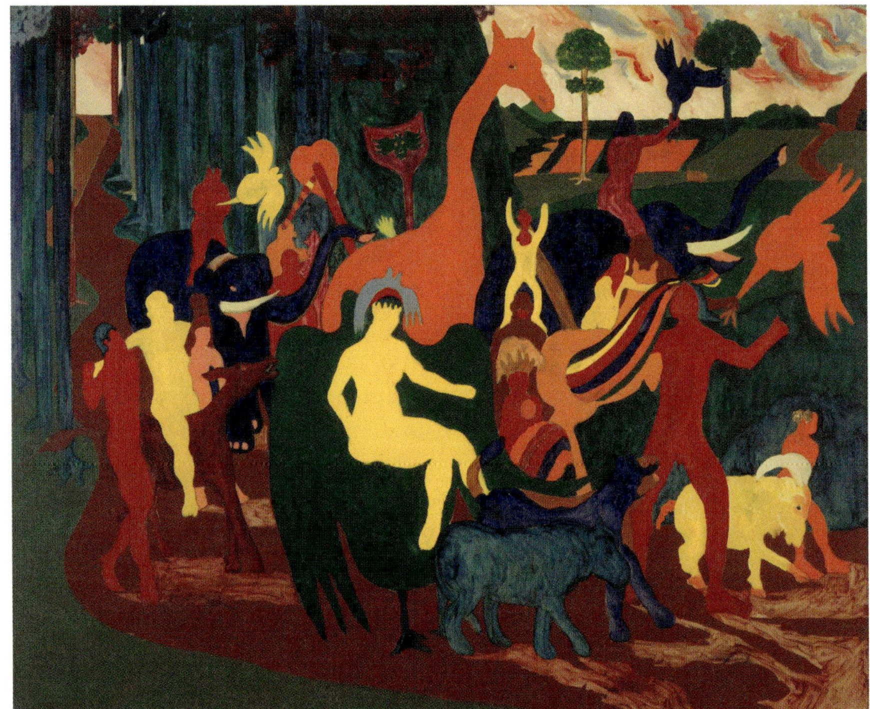

▶ **9.8** Bob Thompson, *Triumph of Bacchus*, 1964, oil on canvas, 60¼″ × 72⅛″.
Whitney Museum of American Art, New York; purchase with funds from the Painting and Sculpture Committee and Lauder Foundation, Leonard and Evelyn Lauder Fund. © Estate of Bob Thompson; courtesy of the Michael Rosenfeld Gallery LLC, New York, NY.

▼ **9.9** Nicolas Poussin, *Triumph of Bacchus*, 1635–36, oil on canvas, 50.4″ × 59.4″.
Collection of the Nelson-Atkins Museum of Art, Kansas City, MO. Purchase: William Rockhill Nelson Trust. Digital image: Google Cultural Institute.

picture wears a pale blue crown, was the youngest of the Greek gods and the last to enter Olympus, paralleling the artist's quick rise to fame, being only 27 at the time, and suddenly finding himself the darling of the art world. However, a psychoanalytic analysis might interpret the artist as crippled by a bird that cannot fly, a possible reference to the artist's depression from which he suffered most of his life. The one-legged bird may also refer to the artist's crippling addiction to heroin.

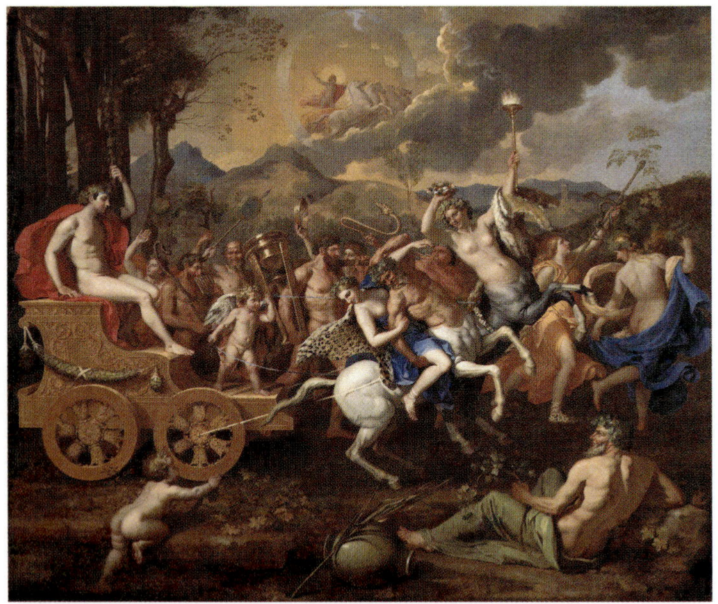

True to legend, Poussin's Bacchus wears a laurel crown, carries a phallic staff known as a thyrsus, and is surrounded by satyrs, centaurs, and maenads (frenzied female beauties). The god's entourage carries (and topples) vats of wine, grape vines, cymbals, and thyrus staffs as they dance with abandon under Apollo, god of the sun, whose chariot careens across the sky. Thompson's painted retinue also consists of human and animal revelers, but his animals are greater in number and prominence. Thompson included goats, rams, deer, birds, and African specimens such as a giraffe and elephants straddled by human riders. The S-shape of the giraffe's neck is echoed in the trunks of the elephants, underscoring the psychosexual symbolism of the painting.

In the summer of 1965, Thompson decided to take a break from the city and return to Provincetown with his wife, Carol Penda Thompson, whom he had met in Provincetown in 1958. There he completed a number of new paintings and drawings. He also befriended jazz singer Nina Simone and painted an homage to her (similarly inspired by a Poussin composition). In November, Thompson traveled to Rome to continue his study of the great Renaissance artists. The following March, he was hospitalized for emergency gall bladder surgery. Instead of taking time to recuperate afterward, as advised by his doctors, Thompson continued his manic lifestyle, which included an intense schedule of painting and heroin abuse. He died in Rome two months later, in May 1966, from a heroin overdose fueled by the recent surgery, which had weakened his body. He was 28 years old. During his tragically short career, Thompson produced more than 1,000 paintings.

Betty Blayton

Betty Blayton (b. 1937) was born in segregated Virginia, the daughter of a doctor and a college-educated mother who was a member of Delta Sigma Theta—the exclusive black sorority founded on the Howard University campus in 1913. As a child she attended a private boarding school for African-American children, Palmer Memorial Institute in North Carolina, whose art department Lois Jones had developed in the late 1920s. From Palmer, Blayton made her way to Syracuse University, where she completed a BFA in painting and illustration in 1959. Arriving in New York City after graduation, Blayton took classes in children's education at City College and in fine arts at the Art Students League. Beginning in 1964, she spent six years studying at the Brooklyn Museum School with Japanese abstract sculptor Minoru Niizuma (1930–98). However, Blayton found the physical demands and space requirements of sculpture a deterrent to her work and refocused her attention on painting.

Known for her colorful abstract **tondos** of the 1970s and 1980s, Blayton embraced figurative expression as early as 1959. By the mid-1960s, she had developed a fluid method of paint application that made her oil paintings appear more like watercolors. In her early works, figures were recognizable, although they bordered on the nonobjective, appearing ethereal as a result of blurred contours and translucent paint application. By the end of the 1970s and into the 1980s, however, much of the artist's work could be described as fully nonobjective, with figures appearing as mere echoes within otherwise nonrepresentational compositions designed to communicate states of mind, moods, and concepts through color, shape, and line (Figure 9.10). Critics described Blayton's particular style of painting as delicately hued and Zen-like. A superb colorist, Blayton's palette gained in vibrancy and intensity in later years; her forms, although still organic, grew more concrete and sharply defined.

As interested in advocating for art and artists as she was in making art, in 1965 Blayton became a founding member of the Studio Museum. Three years later, she founded the Children's Art Carnival, which continues to offer arts education and activities to Harlem youths. Initially founded in

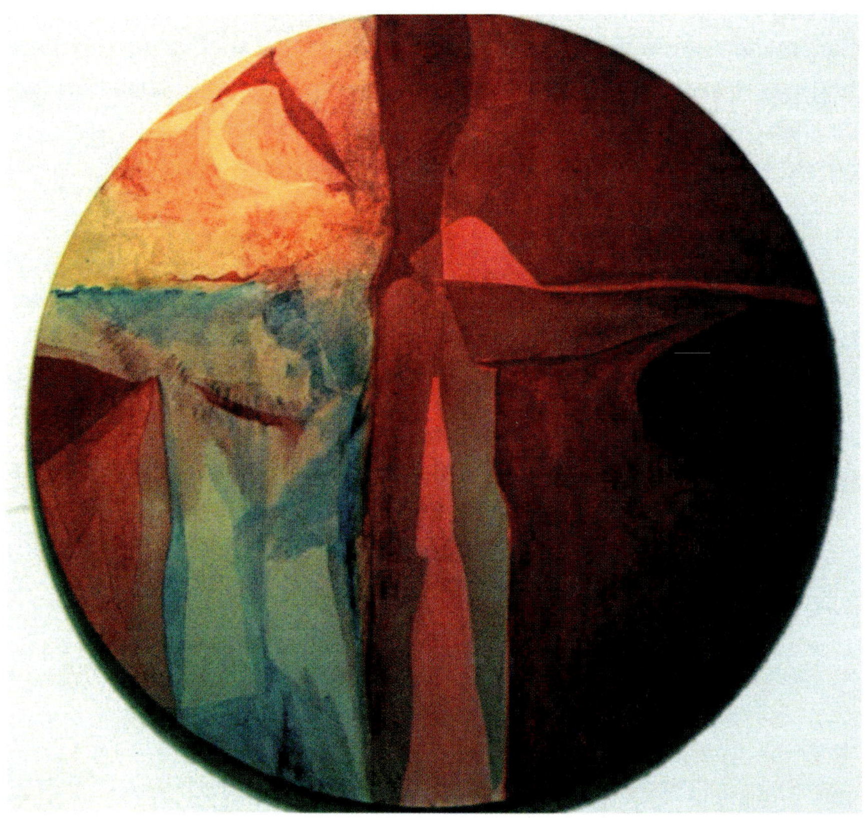

▶ **9.10** Betty Blayton, *Reaching for Center*, 1970, oil and mixed media on canvas, 58½″ diameter.

Courtesy of the artist.

conjunction with MoMA as a community outreach effort, the carnival's mission is to engender creativity, communication, learning, and life skills through art. From 1969 until 2004, Blayton served the program in various capacities. She has been honored with several awards for her creative and educational work, including, in 2005, the distinguished Lifetime Achievement Award from the Woman's Caucus for the Arts.

SCULPTURE

Sculptors also fell under the spell of Abstract Expressionism. Like painters, their formal approaches ran the gamut from figurative expression to geometric sculpture. Initiated in the 1930s and 1940s by one of America's foremost 20th-century sculptors, David Smith (1906–65), Abstract Expressionist sculpture gained widespread favor during the 1950s.

Harold Cousins

One of the first African-American exponents of abstract sculpture was expatriate Harold Cousins (1916–92), whose metal and mixed-media sculptures broke new ground. Raised in Washington, D.C., Cousins first began carving in soap as a teenager. After serving in World War II, he worked for the postal service by day and took classes in sculpture at night at Howard University, where he was greatly influenced by Alain Locke's appreciation for African sculpture and its abstracted forms.

In 1947, Cousins completed an associate's degree at Howard and, the following year, used his GI Bill stipend to relocate to New York and to enroll at the Art Students League. He studied figurative Modernism and Social Realist styles there with Lithuanian-born sculptor William Zorach (1887–1966), printmaker Will Barnett, and painter Reginald Marsh (1898–1954). At the league Cousins also met fellow student and sculptor Peggy Thomas, who would later become his wife. Cousins did not remain long in the city, however. In 1949, he moved with his wife to Paris to study with sculptor Ossip Zadkine, who had taught Catlett earlier in the decade. Under Zadkine's mentorship, Cousins created figurative sculptures with bold and simplified forms that centered on subjects from Greek mythology and other academic themes.

In Paris, Cousins regularly visited the Musée de l'Homme, where he was particularly impressed by Kongo "power figures." These sacred objects included male figures sculpted in wood and embedded with metal shards and nails. Cousins's own works began to display similar use of unconventional media. He experimented with welding to join incongruous metal forms together, and he created multimedia sculptures with wood, wire, rope, scrap metal, and other **found objects**. As he moved rapidly beyond his conventional training, his work became increasingly abstract. This evolution was fueled by the highly tactile metal sculptures of Cubist Julio González (1876–1942), whose daughter, a friend of Cousins's, gave the artist access to her father's work.

In the early 1950s, Cousins exhibited his abstractions in Paris at several key salons. He became an integral member of the Paris Tachisme, or French Abstract Expressionist, avant-garde. He had his first one-man show at Amsterdam's Kunzthall Hamel, a gallery that catered to American artists. For his solo debut, Cousins created a suite of wood, metal, and terracotta masks inspired by African forms and Cubist abstraction.

By the mid-1950s, Cousins had earned an international reputation and was invited to show at the prestigious Galerie Raymond Creuze in 1954–55. For one of three Creuze shows—a solo show in 1955—Cousins designed a nonobjective "forest" of welded horizontal and vertical steel rods and hammered metal plates, which filled the gallery. This critically acclaimed installation triggered a series of related pieces, referred to by the artist as *plaiton*: a fusion of the English word "plate" and the French word for brass, *laiton*. The *plaiton* incorporated rectangular metal sheets mounted on wire-thin supports. (Figure 9.11). Carefully constructed orchestrations of negative and positive space, Cousins's abstractions have the quality of three-dimensional drawing in space and bear comparison to the steel and cast-iron sculptures of David Smith.

The Creuze exhibit led to a veritable barrage of international showings during the second half of the 1950s and into the 1960s, including Documenta II—the now-legendary biennale held in Kassel, Germany. In the late 1960s, Cousins moved to Belgium with his wife, who worked for NATO. Continuing to sculpt and to exhibit, by the mid-1970s Cousins's 30-year career was acknowledged with a retrospective at the newly opened Cultural Center of Woluwe-St-Pierre, near Brussels. Since his death in 1992, Cousins has been rediscovered by American historians, critics, and collectors as one of the first internationally renowned African-American abstract sculptors.

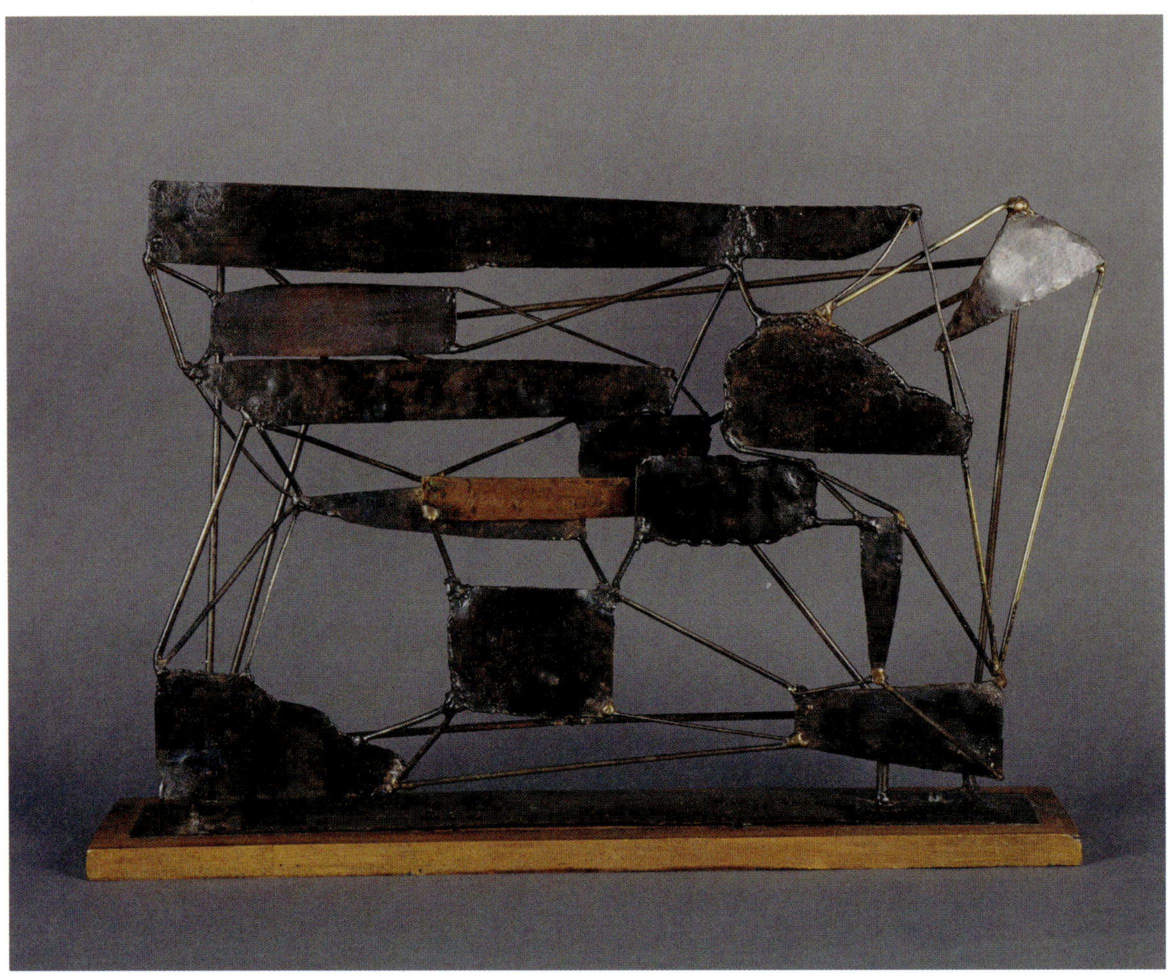

▲ **9.11** Harold Cousins, *Abstract Composition 2*, 1952, welded steel, brass, copper, 13″ × 19½″ × 4″.

Courtesy of the Estate of Harold Cousins and Michael Rosenfeld Gallery LLC, New York, NY.

Richard Hunt

In 2014, South Side Chicago sculptor Richard Hunt (b. 1935) was awarded the James A. Porter Colloquium Prize by Howard University for his prolific body of work, which shares much in common with the art of Cousins. Both often preferred the direct rather than cast-metal process. Both shared an affinity with the metal sculpture of Julio González and David Smith in their openwork approach to form. The works of both incorporate found objects into their designs. Distinctly dissimilar is Hunt's often anthropomorphic approach to form that calls to mind living creatures such as birds and insects.

Hunt began sculpting at 13, when his parents enrolled him in special classes for teens at the Art Institute of Chicago (SAIC). His mother, a librarian, encouraged him to visit the Field Museum, where Hunt was most drawn to African metalwork. He completed a BA in education at the SAIC in 1957. It was there that he first saw the works of Julio González, in a 20th-century sculpture exhibit mounted at the institute. Inspired by González, Hunt studied welded metal sculpture, working with steel, aluminum, copper, and bronze. He quickly developed his own stylistic approach and began winning awards even before graduation. In 1956, Hunt won the first of three Logan Medals given by the institute, for a work entitled *Arachne*, a welded-steel anthropomorphic sculpture that resembled an oddly deformed insect and typified Hunt's early work. Its originality greatly impressed the institute jury, one of whom arranged for the Museum of Modern Art to acquire the sculpture the following year. One work from this period, *Extending Horizontal Form*, exemplifies the artist's early signature style (Figure 9.12). A dense central steel core forms the nucleus of an anthropomorphic sculpture that extends outward into the surrounding space as if propelling itself forward on attenuated limbs.

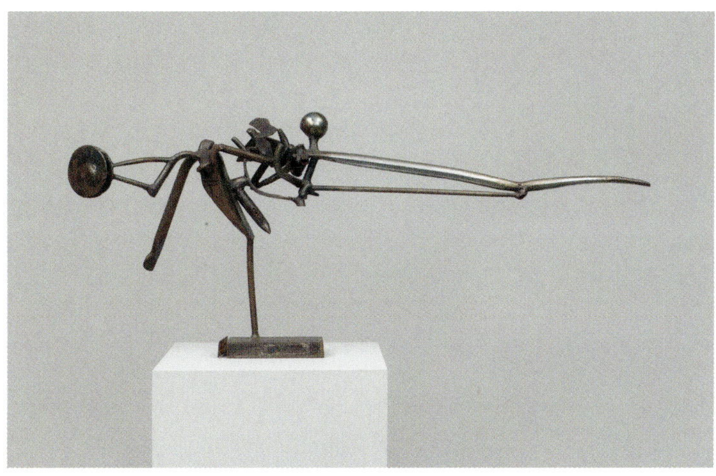

▲ **9.12** Richard Hunt, *Extending Horizontal Form*, 1958. Steel, 23 15/16″ × 56 1/2″ × 11 3/8″. (60.8 × 143.5 × 28.9 cm.) Whitney Museum of American Art, New York; purchase, with funds from the Friends of the Whitney Museum of American Art 58.53

An SAIC travel grant funded Hunt's first trip abroad. From 1957 to 1958, he visited art museums and galleries in England, France, Italy, and Spain. This stay was followed by two years in the military, and one year each teaching at SAIC and the University of Illinois. During this period, Hunt secured New York dealer representation with the Alan Gallery (later Landau-Alan), where he was featured in three solo shows between 1958 and 1963.

After moving to New York in 1961, Hunt's career soared throughout the 1960s. He won a Guggenheim Fellowship in 1962–63, followed by a 1965 Ford Foundation Tamarind Fellowship. Yale University and the California Institute of the Arts (CalArts) each awarded Hunt an artist's residency in 1964, and he has since held similar posts almost yearly at dozens of universities. By 1967, Hunt was the focus of a retrospective at the Milwaukee Art Center, but his most significant coup came in 1971, when, resulting from a focused protest campaign by black artists to draw attention to their marginalization by MoMA, the museum mounted a major 50-sculpture Hunt retrospective (and a simultaneous one-man show of Bearden's work). A similar Hunt retrospective was hosted that year by SAIC.

By the time of the MoMA and Chicago retrospectives, Hunt's style had transformed into a "hybrid" approach (the artist's term) that featured bolder, broader, and heavier shapes than his earlier work. In the latter 1970s and 1980s, Hunt built on this trend, developing a style that has been described by historians as baroque due to the artist's use of sumptuous, curvilinear forms. In every phase of his art, Hunt's aim was to fuse natural forms and industrial materials. His work linked the natural, organic world and the high-tech, hard-edged urban world, a strained relationship that exemplifies modern human existence and represents one of its basic dichotomies. In addition to producing small- and medium-size sculptures of six feet or less, throughout his career Hunt has received public commissions for large-scale pieces in welded aluminum, bronze, and Corten and stainless steel. Approximately 60 of his public works are installed at locales nationwide. These works span the artist's creative range, from curvilinear to angular and from hybrid to monolithic. Hunt was founding president of the Chicago Sculpture Society from 1982 to 1988 and is a member of the both the American Academy of Arts and Letters and the National Academy of Design. In 2009,

Chicago's International Sculpture Center honored Hunt with a Lifetime Achievement Award for his overwhelming contributions to the arts.

Melvin (Mel) Eugene Edwards, Jr.

Sculptor, painter, and printmaker Melvin (Mel) Eugene Edwards, Jr. (b. 1937) is a Texas native, born in Houston. He first became aware of abstract art in high school in Dallas, where an art teacher introduced him to the genre, setting the course of his artistic career. At age 18, Edwards moved to Los Angeles to live with relatives, serve in the naval reserve, and study art. He enrolled in the art program at the University of Southern California (USC) in 1957 and studied with Hungarian artist Francis de Erdely (1904–59). Edwards was drawn to abstraction. He believed that nonfigurative art had just as much capacity to communicate powerful narrative as did representational imagery. He developed his own style, combing steel welding and found metal assemblage. Edwards's work was exhibited in major museums while he was still a university student—including the Los Angeles County Museum of Art in 1960 and the La Jolla Museum of Art in 1962. These works were informed by the politics of the Civil Rights Movement. In 1962, members of the Los Angeles Police Department beat and shot to death Nation of Islam secretary Ronald Stokes in a confrontation at a mosque and reportedly shot into an unarmed crowd of worshippers who had come to Stokes's aid after hearing gunfire. The incident prompted a federal investigation. It was this particular event that inspired Edwards to begin a lifelong series of welded-steel relief sculptures entitled *Lynch Fragments*.

The first of these nonobjective works, *Some Bright Morning*, was created in 1963. It is a circular wheel rim shape embellished with bolts, sharp protruding knife blades, and a hammer and mallet (Figure 9.13). The insinuation of brutality is evident. A chain is suspended from the sculpture's irregularly shaped central steel core, a reference to enslavement and lynching. The artist has continued to add to this series of more than 200 sculptures—all consistent in scale (about one foot square) and format (metal relief)—for half a century. According to Edwards, *The Lynch Fragments* is the nucleus of his oeuvre: a continuing thread that chronicles his personal and creative evolution. The popular series has been the subject of several one-person exhibits at major museums.

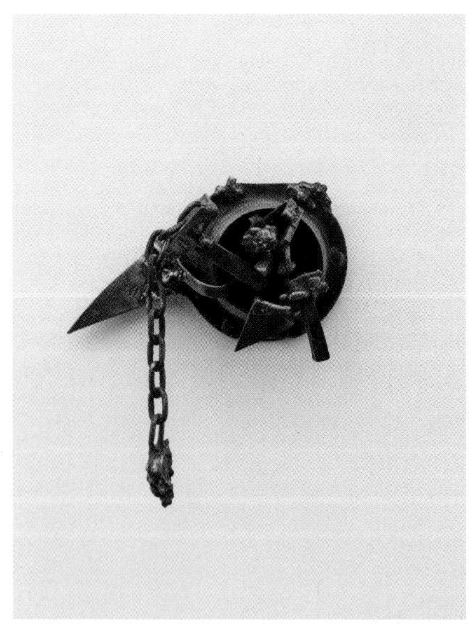

▼ **9.13** Melvin Edwards, *Some Bright Morning*, 1963, welded steel, 14.5″ × 9.3″ × 5″.

Courtesy of Alexander Gray Associates, New York; Stephen Friedman Gallery, London. © Melvin Edwards 2015 / Artist Rights Society (ARS), New York.

In addition to welded steel, his sculpture incorporates chains, tools, tin pots, knives, scissors, engine parts, railroad spikes, and nails. In his estimation (and to his creative eye), any object has the potential to become art. Once transformed by Edwards, an object's original use recedes into the abstracted form of the overall sculpture, but its physical tension remains. Edwards's works have been likened to those of Abstract Expressionist John Chamberlain (1927–2011), who used old car parts to create art, and to early works by David Smith. However, the tenor of potential violence embedded in Edwards's works distinguishes them from that of both of his peers.

A year before graduating from USC, Edwards won a Whitney Fellowship, and he landed a teaching position at San Bernardino

Valley College. Edwards's first solo show took place at the Santa Barbara Museum of Art in 1965, also before he received his BFA. For the remainder of the 1960s, Edwards exhibited at a dozen or more West Coast galleries and museums. In 1966, he relocated to New York, where he rented a studio in Brooklyn. The following year, the Walker Art Center in Milwaukee mounted a one-man outdoor exhibit of Edwards's large-scale sculptures. In 1969, Edwards's work was featured in the historic *X to the 4th Power* show at the Studio Museum. His reputation, already formidable, skyrocketed when the Whitney Museum selected Edwards for a one-man show in their Projects Gallery in 1970; that same year, he was awarded a NEA Fellowship. This early New York period was especially productive for Edwards. He and his life partner, poet Jayne Cortez (1934–2012), whom he married in 1975, collaborated on half a dozen books of poetry published between 1971 and 1991, for which Edwards provided the illustrations. In 1972, Edwards joined the faculty at Rutgers University's Mason Gross School of Creative and Performing Arts, where he taught for the next 30 years.

In 1973, Edwards made the first of many trips to Africa, spending the summer in Nigeria and Ghana. A few years later he returned to participate in FESTAC 1977 in Nigeria. Edwards used a Fulbright Fellowship in 1988 (renewed in 1989) to fund a third African visit, to Zimbabwe. From then on, Edwards split his time between Africa and the United States, teaching and exhibiting in Ghana, Nigeria, Zimbabwe, Egypt, Ethiopia, Morocco, Kenya, and Senegal, where he maintains a second home in Dakar. Informed by his connection to the continent, Edwards's iconography often includes references to African theology and its practices on both sides of the Atlantic, particularly in Brazil, where Yoruba culture continues to flourish; in Cuba, where Santeria is practiced; and in the United States, where Vodou and Santeria communities abound.

Though less known for his prints, Edwards became a member of Blackburn Printmaking Workshop in 1973 and has created prints throughout his career. Edwards also produced numerous welded-steel public sculptures during this period for many sites nationwide, including a number of housing projects. The latter venues have been a conscious choice for Edwards, who believes in the socialist ideal of bringing art to the working class.

The 2012 Hammer Museum show *Now Dig This* (a survey of black Los Angeles artists from 1960 to 1980) exposed Edwards to a new and younger audience. He was invited to replicate his large, barbed wire, netlike construction *Pyramid Up and Down Pyramid* (originally exhibited at both the Studio and Whitney Museums in 1969 and 1970, respectively) for the avant-garde fair Art Basel, in 2012. Edwards's star continues to rise. He was included in the 2014 Brooklyn Museum blockbuster *Witness: Art and Civil Rights in the Sixties*, and was honored with solo shows at both the Chicago Cultural Center and the Museum of Contemporary Art Chicago.

Barbara Chase-Riboud

Artist and author Barbara Chase-Riboud (b. 1939) is an American expatriate who has pursued widely divergent careers. She earned a BFA from Temple University's Tyler School of Art in 1957. After graduating, the artist embarked on a tour of Europe under the auspices of a Whitney Fellowship. She spent much of her time abroad engaged in postgraduate study at the American Academy in Rome and began a lifelong career in **direct wax casting** at a local bronze foundry. While abroad, Chase-Riboud traveled to Turkey, Greece, and Egypt, where she spent three months and found "the blast of Egyptian culture . . . irresistible; the sheer magnificence of it; the elegance and perfection, the timelessness, the depth."

Chase-Riboud returned to the United States in 1958, where she enrolled at Yale University as the only African-American woman at its School of Design and Architecture. She studied under Bauhaus devotee and nonobjective painter Josef Albers, International Style architect Philip Johnson (1906–2005), and Louis Kahn (1901–74), one of the most influential architects of the 20th century. After receiving her master's degree from Yale in 1960, Chase-Riboud moved permanently to Europe, where her career flourished in both France and Italy. In 1961, while working in Paris as an art director for the *New York Times*, Chase-Riboud met and married photographer Marc Riboud, a member of the famed Magnum Photos cooperative. The two traveled extensively during the 1960s, to Morocco, Spain, the Soviet Union, and the People's Republic of China. Chase-Riboud was the first American woman since the Cultural Revolution to be invited to China, to meet communist leaders Chou En-lai and Mao Tse-Tung. During these years, her sculptures expressed the artist's existentialist proclivities as well as reflecting the influence of Swiss artist Alberto Giacometti (1901–66), whose decaying surface textures Chase-Riboud restyled into a distinctive visual language of her own.

In 1969, Chase-Riboud traveled to Algeria to attend the Pan-African festival. She met several of the American leaders of the Black Panther Party there, including Eldridge and Kathleen Cleaver and Huey Newton. Her involvement with the struggle for black liberation, although indirect, was nevertheless genuinely experienced, as she explains: "I found myself with all the freedom fighters and liberation groups, the Algerians, the South Africans, the Black Panthers from America. . . . Though I didn't know it at the time, my own [aesthetic] transformation was part of the historical transformation of the blacks that began in the '60s." This transformation manifested itself in the artist's signature style, evident in her *Malcolm X* series, which debuted at galleries nationwide beginning in 1970. The series comprises a collection of polished bronze sculptures that incorporate black and gold patinas and silk, wool, or cotton cords (see chapter-opening image).

In the series, Chase-Riboud distilled many aesthetic stimuli into a matchless blend of intuitive and rigorously ordered elements, constructed with the detailed attention of an architect. Creased and cumbersome metal "heads" cast from folded wax sheets are balanced by "skirts" of handmade rope that simultaneously hang from and appear to support the upper tiers. In fact, the fiber skirts hide metal armatures that support the sculpture. Chase-Riboud draws on indigenous African headdresses that, although often referred to as masks in the West, are, in fact, designed to mount on top of the head and shoulders. In Mali, for example, the wearer of the Chi Wara (Tyi Wara) antelope headdress camouflages his body with raffia fibers to create an entire costume that obscures the performer entirely. The result is a heavy wooden head resting on a soft fiber skirt that hides the actual (in this case human) support. Ever mindful of the yin and yang—contradictory forces that, according to Chinese philosophy, exist in all things—Chase-Riboud contrasts within a given work hard and soft, dull and polished, and, within the series, light and dark and ponderous and tenuous forms. She also transposes obverse ideals so that the yin, or female, fleeciness of the fibers becomes the yang, or masculine, strength that buttresses the weight of the sculpture.

A Yale classmate, Fulbright Fellow and fiber artist Sheila Hicks (b. 1934), first suggested that Chase-Riboud use woven cords in her work. A second motivation was the art of Warsaw sculptor Magdalena Abakanowicz (b. 1930), especially her burlap figures and fiber installations. A third inspiration emerged from an extensive tour of Africa that Chase-Riboud made in the 1970s. In Senegal, Mali, Ghana, and Sierra Leone, Chase-Riboud observed the widespread use of raffia, hemp, feathers, and other fibrous materials in local art. She also had the rare opportunity to see African sculptures in situ, and to come to understand these objects as part of the "interplay of sculpture, costume, dance, and dream" that composes African devotional customs. As a result of this experience, Chase-Riboud began to see her own art as endowed with spiritual energy, approximating the transcendent élan of African sacred icons.

The *Malcolm X* series brought Chase-Riboud significant recognition both in the United States and abroad. The series served as an esoteric rather than literal celebration of the life of the black Muslim leader. As exhibitions of her work were mounted throughout the country, Chase-Riboud turned her attentions to her second career: writing. In 1974, she published a collection of poems, *From Memphis to Peking*, which was edited by the distinguished author Toni Morrison (b. 1931). In 1979, Jacqueline Kennedy-Onassis (1929–94), Chase-Riboud's friend and supporter, edited the artist's best-selling book *Sally Hemings*, which plotted the life of President Thomas Jefferson's slave and lifelong mistress. She wrote subsequent volumes over the next two decades, including *Validé*, *The President's Daughter*, and *Echo of Lions* (a chronicle of the Amistad slave mutiny).

After divorcing her first husband in 1981, Chase-Riboud married gallerist, archeologist, and publisher Sergio Tossi. The Metropolitan Museum acquired Chase-Riboud's *All That Rises Must Converge*, a monumental adaptation of the *Malcolm X* archetype that measures nearly 10 feet in height. The 1990s brought to the artist an ambitious government commission, *Africa Rising* (1998). The 20-foot-tall bronze **Nike figure** is located in the lobby of the Ted Weiss Federal Building at 290 Broadway in New York City. *Africa Rising* shares this space with Houston Conwill's *The New Ring Shout* (see Chapter 12) and with Clyde Lynds's (b. 1936) stone relief *America Song*. These works commemorate the once-forgotten gravesite of lower Manhattan's 18th-century African population, whose remains were discovered in 1991 during excavations for the building.

As yet unrealized, Chase-Riboud's sculptural monument *Middle Passage* is envisioned as a memorial to the 11 million Africans who died on slave ships during the passage from Africa to the New World. Presently extant only in mock-ups, the monument in its final form is intended to soar to 60 feet and to consist of two monolithic steles from which an immense spool of golden chain would be suspended. The pillars, which will symbolically join East and West with 11 million links of chain, will be inscribed with the names of African cities from which enslaved prisoners were taken. In a proposal sent to President Clinton in 1994, Chase-Riboud suggested that the U.S. government sponsor the project, noting that no monument existed anywhere in the world to the memory of the African deportees of the triangular trade route between Africa, America, and Europe. The artist's letter was accompanied by a detailed plan that advocated a site for the monument on Theodore Roosevelt Island in the Potomac River (near the Lincoln and Jefferson Memorials in Washington, D.C.). No government sponsorship was forthcoming, and the sculpture remains unrealized.

Summary

African-American artists practiced all forms of Abstract Expressionism, including Action, Color Field, and Hard-Edge painting and figurative abstraction. Their art included vibrant color and a variety of innovative approaches and experimental techniques, such as staining, taping, draped canvases, direct welding, and wax casting. Although the Civil Rights Movement was in full swing at the time, most of these artists preferred to dedicate their aesthetic energies to art-for-art's-sake and creative experimentation rather than to social narrative or protest. That being said, sculptors such as Chase-Riboud and Edwards infused their abstract work with allusions to the struggle for racial equality without compromising their nonobjective explorations.

Key Terms

Action Painting or Gestural Abstraction: a form of paint application that results in an abstract visual record of the artist's gestures or actions during the painting process

arbitrary color: color that is chosen for visual, symbolic, or emotional effect rather than for visual accuracy

assemblage: a work of art created by assembling preexisting objects

Color Field painting or Post-Painterly Abstraction: a painting composed of large areas of color in which individual brushstrokes are deemphasized

complimentary contrasts: colors on opposite sides of the color wheel that intensify each other

constructions: works of art constructed of preexisting objects and differing from assemblage in their larger format

direct wax casting: sculpture created from a wax form that is covered with clay and baked, so that the wax melts away, leaving a clay mold from which a metal sculpture can be cast

figurative expressionism: art characterized by a vivid, nonliteral palette and by distorted figures and forms

found objects: preexisting non-art objects used to create works of art

Hard-Edge painting: a painting style characterized by clearly defined geometric shapes and often vibrant color installation: a form of art composed of multiple components and installed in a large interior or outdoor space

Minimalism: monochromatic painting and sculpture characterized by simple geometric forms, industrial materials, and lack of evidence of the artist's subjective input

Nike figure: refers to the ancient Greek allegorical female figure of victory

nonobjective: refers to art that does not depict any known or recognizable object

Op Art: abstract or non-representational art designed to create an optical illusion such as movement, popularized in the 1960s

staining: a method of painting an unprimed (ungessoed or raw) canvas so that large areas of paint seep into the material of the canvas

Suprematism: a Russian art movement founded by Kasimir Malevich in 1915 that used simple geometric forms and a red, black, and white palette to express and invoke transcendence and the unknown

tondo: a circular-format painting

Washington Color School: 1950s and 1960s non-representational art movement centered in Washington, D.C. and defined by bold colors and geometric forms

Questions for Further Study and Discussion

1. What is the difference between abstract and nonobjective (or nonfigurative) art?
2. What is meant by "form as content"?
3. Discuss how some Abstract Expressionist artists engaged in the Civil Rights Movement.
4. Read and summarize Kandinsky's theories on the power and value of nonobjective art, discussed in his 1912 treatise "On the Spiritual in Art."
5. Debate which art is more expressive: figurative or nonfigurative art.
6. What innovations were made to conventional painting on stretched canvas during the Abstract Expressionist era? Which artists initiated or adopted these innovations?
7. Choose an emotion, mood, or state of mind and create a nonrepresentational drawing or painting that expresses it. Explain in a written manifesto how and why the formal elements (lines, shapes, colors, textures, composition, etc.) of your artwork communicate your intended emotion, mood, or state of mind.
8. Debate whether or not found object art—a work of art created from discarded non-art objects—should be valued as high art.
9. Several other African-American artists were key participants in the Abstract Expressionist Movement, including Edward (Ed) Clark (b. 1936), Emilio Antonio Cruz (1938–2004), David Driskell (b. 1932), Herbert Gentry (1919–2003), and Felrath Hines (1919–93). How does their work compare with the artists studied in this chapter?

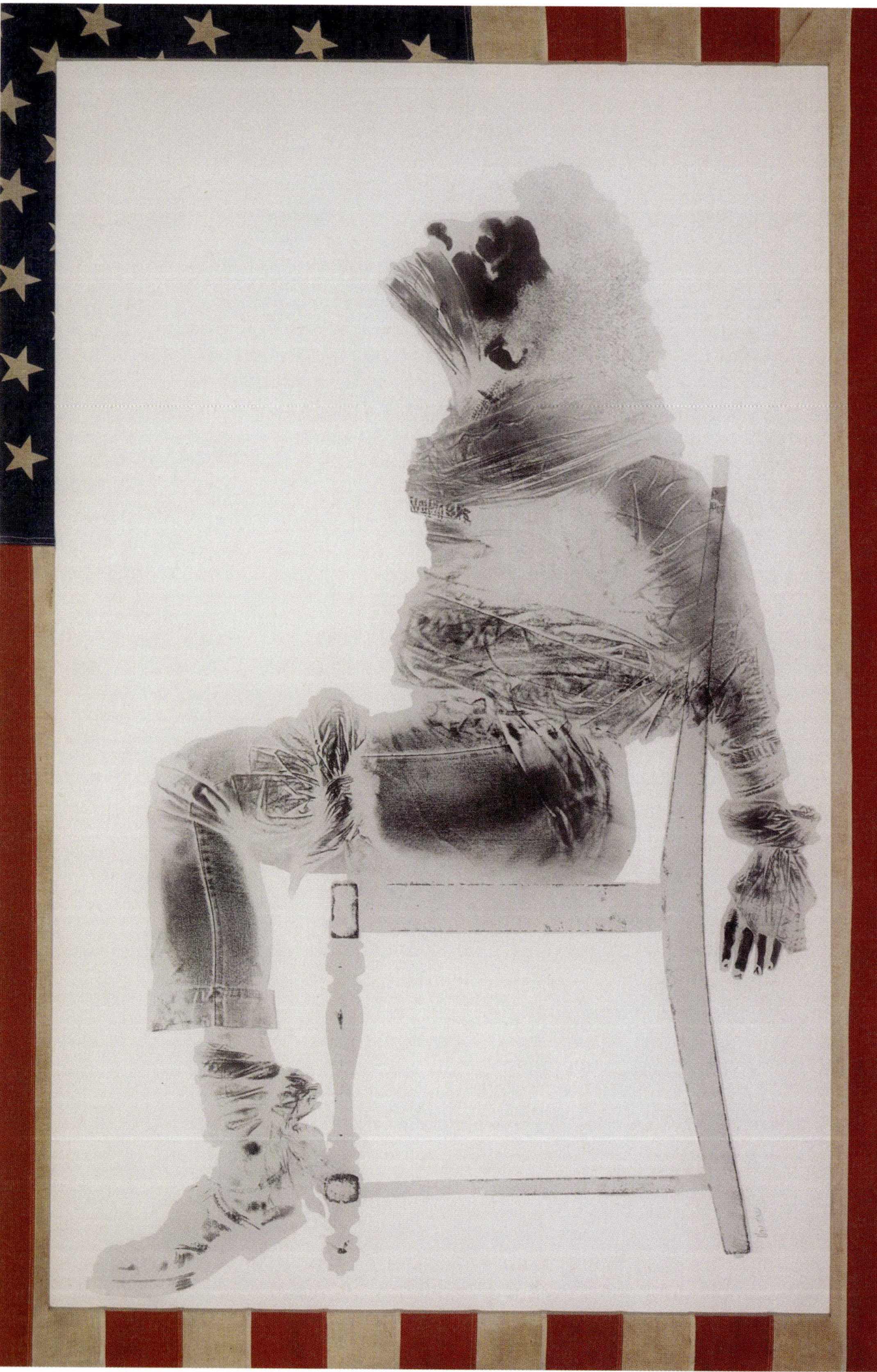

POP AND AGITPROP: THE BLACK ARTS MOVEMENT

10

Whereas Abstract Expressionist artists did not directly address political issues in their work, members of the Black Arts Movement made it central to their aesthetic mission. Influenced by a virtual maelstrom of civil unrest and sweeping changes in racial attitudes, many African-American artists felt compelled to create political art. Over two decades, beginning in the mid-1950s, African-American artists witnessed (and participated in) a systematic campaign to end racism. Central to the struggle for racial equality was the Southern Christian Leadership Conference (SCLC), founded in 1957 and led by Dr. Martin Luther King, Jr., and others. The SCLC staged dozens of protests and demonstrations against racial injustice. Also leading the charge against minority oppression was the NAACP's Legal Defense Fund. Masterminded by the soon-to-be Supreme Court justice Thurgood Marshall (1909–93), this legal team successfully argued the historic 1954 case *Brown vs. the Board of Education of Topeka*, in which the Supreme Court ruled that public school segregation was unconstitutional. In 1956, following the arrest of Rosa Parks (1913–2005) for refusing to give up her seat to a white passenger on an Alabama bus, segregation in public transportation was declared unlawful. In 1957, the first significant civil rights legislation since 1875 was passed, protecting voter rights. Large voter registration campaigns strengthened the African-American political voice.

The civil rights victories made by African Americans in the 1950s were answered by some whites with fierce antagonism. In 1957, African-American students in Little Rock, Arkansas, while attempting to register at a newly integrated high school, were met by irate white citizens and state troopers who blocked their entry into the school building. Not until President Dwight D. Eisenhower sent federal troops to the scene were the students permitted to attend classes. Reports of murders and lynchings, which had subsided almost completely by 1952, once again escalated. One of the most heinous racial crimes took place in Mississippi in 1955: 14-year-old Emmet Till, after being accused of whistling at a young white woman named Carol Bryant, was abducted, viciously beaten, and shot to death by Bryant's husband and brother-in-law. Despite admitting that they had kidnapped Till (and later detailing the murder in a popular magazine), the two were acquitted by an all-white jury. The Till murder sent shock waves through the African-American community and marked the beginning of years of civil unrest.

The struggle for civil rights reached a fever pitch between 1961 and 1965, when the Congress of Racial Equality (CORE) organized a series of well-publicized, interracial freedom rides designed to integrate bus routes

◀ David Hammons, *Injustice Case*, 1970, body print (margarine and powdered pigments) and American flag, 63″ × 40 ½″ (sheet).

Los Angeles County Museum of Art. Digital image © 2015 Museum Associates / LACMA / Jack Tilton Gallery.

in the South. Participants were firebombed, battered, and arrested; freedom rider James Chaney along with two of his white companions, Michael Schwerner and Andrew Goodman, were murdered by the Ku Klux Klan. In 1963, NAACP field secretary Medgar Evers was assassinated by a white separatist in Jackson, Mississippi. In 1965, Malcolm X was assassinated in the Audubon Ballroom in Harlem. Finally, in 1968, Martin Luther King, Jr., was shot to death in Memphis, Tennessee.

Although by 1965 President Lyndon Johnson had signed the Civil Rights Bill and the Voting Rights Act into law, many African Americans felt that these gains were too little, too late. In the face of such vehement and violent resistance to change by white extremists, young blacks especially saw nonviolent protest as ineffectual. In 1966, Stokely Carmichael, spokesman for the Student Non-Violent Coordinating Committee (SNCC), began advocating militant civil rights and black power. That year, the Black Panther Party was founded in Oakland, California, to combat police brutality. An ever-increasing militancy began to transform the Civil Rights Movement, accompanied by a resurgence of African pride. African-derived clothing and hairstyles became fashionable, and the slogan "black is beautiful," first popularized by Marcus Garvey in the 1920s, was resurrected. By the mid-1960s, the Civil Rights Movement had yielded to the more radical Black Power Movement. The nonviolent, integrationist movement epitomized by Martin Luther King was replaced by militant **black nationalism**, personified by Malcolm X and the Black Panthers.

Black artists were grappling with just how to address the racial unrest and momentous events that marked the age. Despite her exile in Mexico, Elizabeth Catlett was one of the leaders of the Black Arts Movement (see Chapter 8). In 1961, she addressed the third annual meeting of the National Conference of Negro Artists. Her widely influential speech, "The Negro People and American Art at Mid-Century," reaffirmed her allegiance to African Americans and to their art. She urged artists of color to spurn the inherently racist and exclusionary network of American museums and galleries and to organize their own all-black exhibits. She also issued a directive to black artists to create art that would "express . . . racial identity, communicate with the black community, and participate in struggles for social, political, and economic equality." Catlett's moving speech sparked a surge of politically engaged art. Black artists nationwide began to organize their own shows rather than depending on the whims of white-run institutions and galleries that preferred at the time to promote abstract rather than political art. As a result, numerous black arts groups were formed, one of the most historic of which was Spiral.

SPIRAL AND THE CIVIL RIGHTS MOVEMENT

Spiral was a cooperative of black artists founded by Romare Bearden, Norman Lewis, Charles Alston, Hale Woodruff, Ernest Crichlow, Felrath Hines (1913–93), Richard Mayhew, James Yeargans (1908–72), Alvin Hollingsworth (1928–2000), Reginald Gammon, and Merton Simpson (1928–2013). The name Spiral was chosen by Woodruff; it referred to the spiral of Archimedes, a third-century B.C.E. Greek mathematician who conceived of an abstract vortex that remained in perpetual motion. One of several catalysts for Spiral's founding was the 1963 March on Washington at which Martin Luther King, Jr. delivered his historic "I Have a Dream" speech. The first Spiral meeting took place in Bearden's Greenwich Village studio. The group set as its goal establishing the African-American artist's place in the struggle for racial equality.

In May 1965, the group mounted its first and only exhibit, titled *Black and White* to signify the ongoing racial struggle; works in the show were limited to a black-and-white palette. Although the exhibit was well attended, Spiral was plagued by internal philosophical conflicts. A number of its members advocated a centralized, formal philosophy so that their works would share a certain "look" or style. Others preferred to express their social engagement without losing their individual artistic identities. Some felt strongly that the group should be racially integrated, whereas others advocated black exclusivity. Members wrangled over everything from aesthetic standards to the dangers of ghettoization that could result from all-black art shows. These differences caused Spiral to disband after only two years. Despite the brief life of the group, however, Spiral inspired the formation of many similar groups.

A number of Spiral artists chose not to overtly express their engagement with civil rights in their art, as is evident in Bearden's works of the 1960s, such as *Black Manhattan*, which depicts Harlem in a relatively apolitical manner (Chapter 8 chapter-opening figure). The same can be said for the abstractions of Lewis (Figure 9.2), Mayhew (Figure 9.5), Felrath Hines (1913–93), and Woodruff, whose early Social Realist style had given way to an abstract idiom. Others embraced the new Pop Art Movement. This movement borrowed from such sources as commercial printing, typography, magazine images, cartoons, and comic books. Mainstream Pop artists such as Andy Warhol (1928–87) and Roy Lichtenstein (1923–97), despite the intensely political climate in the country at the time, tended to avoid politics (although not completely). Black artists who capitalized on Pop Art techniques, however, often reconfigured them to suit political ends.

Reginald Gammon

Philadelphia-born painter and printmaker Reginald Gammon (1921–2005) was a member of Spiral and was interested in a wide range of motifs derived from African-American history and culture. Gammon began his career at the Philadelphia Museum School, where he studied painting and drawing from 1941 to 1944. His training was interrupted when he was drafted into the U.S. Navy for two years and stationed in Guam. After his tour of duty, Gammon returned briefly to Philadelphia, but by the end of the 1940s he had moved to New York, where he would spend the next two decades. Gammon worked for the post office and as a freelance commercial artist during the day, which left his evenings free for painting. In the 1950s he met Bearden, who invited him to join Spiral.

Gammon created his iconic *Freedom Now* for the Spiral *Black and White* show using a black-and-white palette, as required of all participating artists (Figure 10.1). *Freedom Now* presents a throng of protest marchers, shouting and holding placards. Although not chromatic, as was the Pop Art trend, the image is rendered in precisely the kind of unmodulated flatness typical of the genre and of newsprint. The work's didactic message pulls no punches, but, that being said, the composition is cunningly constructed. The multiplicity of shapes in the lower half is balanced by open areas above. There is

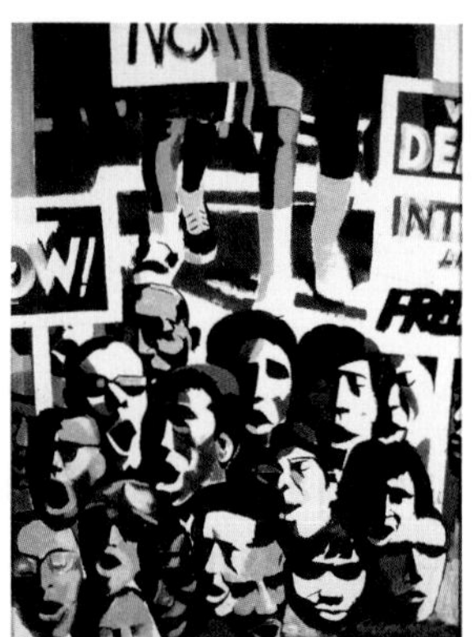

▲ 10.1 Reginald Gammon, *Freedom Now*, 1963, acrylic on board, 40″ × 30″.

Collection of the National Afro-American Museum and Cultural Center in Wilberforce, OH. Art © Estate of Reginald Gammon / licensed by VAGA, New York, NY. Photo courtesy of Estate of Reginald Gammon, Russell H. Jackson, Trustee.

also an underlying pyramidal structure that anchors the composition, formed by the mass of protestors' heads and reinforced by the three placards. The design and clarity of the work call to mind similarly structured paintings in Lawrence's *Migration* series (Figure 8.5).

Gammon followed the Spiral exhibit with two solo shows at the Acts of Art Gallery. His works of the 1960s included paintings of Martin Luther King and the Scottsboro Boys. Near the end of the 1960s, Gammon organized a youth art academy in which he partnered Harlem schoolchildren with black artists in studio workshops. The success of the program prompted Spiral artist Lee-Smith to suggest to officials at Western Michigan University (WMU) that Gammon organize a similar academy for their students. Launched in 1970 and initially designed as a 10-day workshop, the popularity of Gammon's workshop resulted in a semester-long extension of the academy at WMU. Gammon soon joined the faculty there, serving for more than 20 years.

Gammon's paintings of the 1970s and 1980s incorporated more expressive brushwork and a chromatic palette. His portraits included historical black figures such as Paul Robeson, Henry Tanner, Du Bois, and Frederick Douglass, as well as a series of paintings he dubbed *Voices in Harlem*, portraying jazz, blues, and gospel singers. He experimented with new media by incorporating fabric, natural fibers, rope, and other materials into his paintings and began to work frequently in pastel. Gammon also created a suite of fabric "paintings" of Gullah women and black matriarchs, a body of prints and paintings on the subject of tattooing, and numerous portraits of family and friends.

Gammon retired from WMU as a full professor in 1991 and moved to Albuquerque, New Mexico. There, he created a series of large-scale autobiographical pictures and continued his jazz series. In 1996, Gammon cofounded the city's New Grounds Print Workshop and Gallery, where he was an active participant until his death.

Raymond Saunders

Spiral artist Raymond Saunders (b. 1934) grew up in Pittsburgh. As a teenager, he studied at the Carnegie Institute of Technology from 1950 to 1952. Between 1953 and 1957, Saunders took art classes at both the Barnes Foundation and the Pennsylvania Academy of Fine Arts. After serving in the army for two years, in 1960 he completed his BFA at Carnegie before relocating to California to earn an MFA in 1961. In 1964, Saunders won a Ford Foundation award and a two-year Prix de Rome Fellowship for study and exhibit in Italy and North Africa. His travels in Africa inspired a series of paintings entitled *Africa* in which the artist integrated images of its people with abstract patterns based on African textiles.

Back in the States in 1967, Saunders wrote an historic essay entitled "Black Is a Color" that argued that race was extraneous to art and that black artists should neither be required nor expected to create art exclusively about race-related concerns. Going against the grain of many of his contemporaries, Saunders argued that racial iconography was restrictive to an artist's creativity:

> *Some angry artists are using their art as political tools, instead of vehicles of free expression. An artist who is always harping upon resistance,*

> *discrimination, opposition, besides being a drag, eventually plays right into the hands of the politicians he claims to despise—and is held there, unwittingly (and witlessly) reviving slavery in another form. For the artist, this is aesthetic atrophy.*

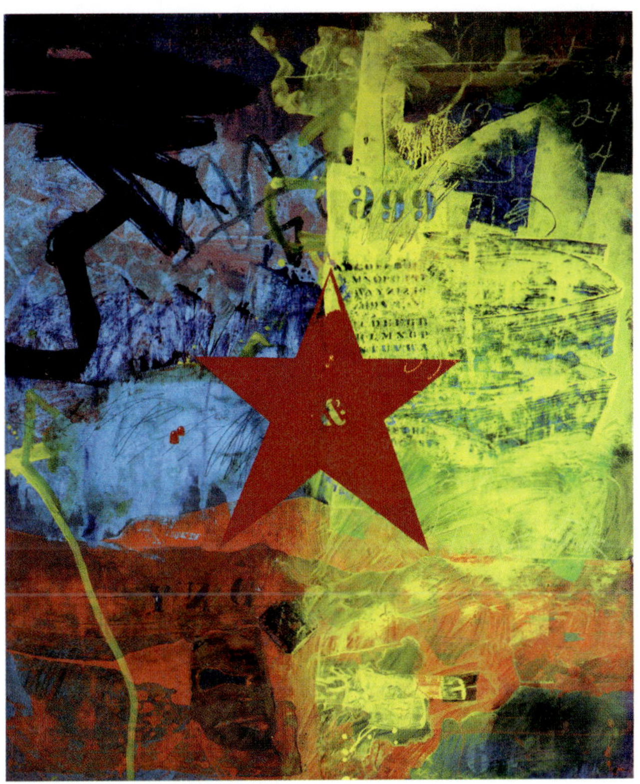

▲ **10.2** Raymond Saunders, *Red Star*, 1970, oil, metallic paint, collage (paper, fabric tape), canvas, 55⅞″ × 45¾″ × 1¼″.

© Raymond Saunders, courtesy of Lora Schlesinger Gallery.

Despite these strong sentiments, Saunders periodically chose racial subject matter, such as in a well-known portrait of black prize fighter Jack Johnson—which confirms the artist's stance that racially motivated art, although not essential, is not off limits either.

Typical of Saunders's work of this period is the 1970 collaged painting *Red Star* (Figure 10.2). The artist's technique of using highly textured brushstrokes is rooted in Abstract Expressionism. Like a number of Pop artists, however, he added to this substructure stenciled letters, popular symbols such as the star, and nontraditional materials including fabric and tape. He also scratched numbers and other symbols directly onto the canvas, adding an element of graffiti. Repeated words such as "race" and "stock" and numbers such as "2–24" etched by the artist onto the canvas suggest an enigmatic iconography that is surely personal and likely political, despite the artist's apolitical posture. The red star evokes references to the American, Chinese, and Russian flags; to the Russian military (whose official newspaper is called the *Red Star*); and to communist ideology. It may even refer to the war in Vietnam, which was ongoing at the time and was the target of widespread protest. The artist may or may not have had any such conscious iconographic agendas. In fact, he stated in a 1994 interview that an artist sometimes doesn't know, consciously, what he or she is creating.

At the base of the picture just left of center, the artist's signature is scratched vertically into the painted surface along a yellow diagonal brushstroke. It is situated very near the masklike face of a black man, scowling and partially obscured by dripped and splattered paint. Taking the face and the signature together, these symbols suggest the artist's displeasure—with what, we cannot be certain, but it is safe to say the scowl is directed at some aspect of the painting's iconography. Still today a highly influential work of art, *Red Star* was recently chosen as the theme of the 2012 Cosmo Couture fashion show and fundraiser, wherein local designers created garments that appropriated elements from Saunders's image, such as **graffiti**-style text, intense colors, and dynamic textures.

In the 1960s and 1970s, five solo shows of Saunders's work were mounted. In 1976 and 1977, he received Guggenheim and NEA Fellowships. Another coup was his inclusion in the celebrated print portfolio *America: The Third Century*, with famed Pop artists Lichtenstein, Robert Rauschenberg, James Rosenquist (b. 1933), and Edward Ruscha (b. 1937). A boon year for Saunders came in 1984, when he received a second NEA grant, a commission from the Los Angeles Summer Olympics committee to design one of its posters, and an assignment to design the book cover and theatre poster for David Mamet's Pulitzer Prize–winning play, *Glenngary, Glenn Ross*. After teaching for a number of years at California State University in East Bay, in 1987, Saunders left to join the faculty at his alma mater, the California College of Arts and Crafts, where he continues to teach painting and drawing.

THE BLACK ARTS MOVEMENT

The art of Gammon and Saunders underscores the dichotomy that marked much black art of the period. Gammon saw art as an appropriate vehicle through which to critique society, whereas Saunders saw protest art as potentially limiting to the artist. By the late 1960s, when the Black Arts Movement reached its apex, a significant percentage of black artists sided with Gammon. The Black Arts Movement was a direct answer to Catlett's call for a "black aesthetic" that would address the concerns and sensibilities of black rather than white Americans. It was rooted in African rather than European artistic traditions, rejected Abstract Expressionism as a "white" art form, and denounced dependency on the mainstream art world.

The Black Arts Movement was formalized on a global scale through the organization of FESTAC, first in Dakar, Senegal, in 1966 and then in Lagos, Nigeria, in 1977. In addition, museums dedicated to black art were established across the country. Among these were the Studio Museum in Harlem, the International Afro-American Museum in Detroit, the Anacostia Museum of Culture and History in Washington, D.C., the Museum of African American Art in Los Angeles, and the Afro-American Historical and Cultural Museum in Philadelphia. Black-owned galleries were founded as well, including Kenkeleba House, Just Above Midtown (JAM) and Cinque Galleries (the latter founded by former Spiral members), the Weusi-Nyumba Ya Sanaa (Swahili for "people's house of art"), and Acts of Art Gallery.

Museum Protests

Black art venues were vital to the Black Arts Movement, which railed against the exclusionary practices of most American art museums. When the Whitney Museum mounted its 1968 show *The 1930s: Painting and Sculpture in America* without including a single black artist, outraged minority artists and curators responded by organizing *Invisible Americans: Black Artists of the 1930s* a few months later at the Studio Museum. Their curatorship showcased the Harlem Renaissance and WPA artists that the Whitney Museum show had excluded. Meanwhile, the Whitney show was picketed by members of the soon-to-be-formed Black Emergency Cultural Council (BECC) and the Art Workers Coalition (AWC).

In the spring of 1969, the BECC met with Whitney administrators to demand that the museum regularly show and purchase black art, include more black artists in its annuals and biennials, and involve black curators in its exhibit planning. When the Whitney Museum assigned a white curator to organize its 1971 *Contemporary Black Artists in America* show, the BECC held a now-historic "rebuttal" show at Acts of Art Gallery. More than a dozen artists chosen for the Whitney exhibit made the bold move to withdraw their works as a show of solidarity and submitted them to Acts of Art.

The BECC also picketed the MoMA memorial exhibit dedicated to Martin Luther King, Jr., which similarly lacked black artist representation. The most memorable BECC protest occurred, however, in reaction to the controversial 1969 Metropolitan Museum show *Harlem on My Mind*. Although it included the images of long-forgotten Harlem Renaissance photographer James Van Der Zee, it did not include any painting or sculpture by past or present Harlem artists. Without engaging the Harlem community, museum curators had decided that photographs of Harlemites would compose the show's only content. This approach seemed demeaning to the black artistic community, who felt snubbed. It was also perceived as incredibly high-handed that white curators were assigned to represent such an historic black neighborhood.

At the center of the *Harlem on My Mind* debate was Allon Schoener, director of both the museum's Exhibition Committee and the New York State Council on the Arts. In response to widely publicized art protests regarding the show (including complaint letters, demonstrations, news articles, and face-to-face meetings), Schoener opened a dialogue with artist Benny Andrews (discussed later in this chapter) and Harlem Cultural Council director Edward Taylor. When the show proceeded as originally planned, however, Andrews and Taylor quickly realized that they were to have neither decision-making power nor any meaningful influence over Schoener's curatorial decisions. Frustrated, Andrews called on fellow artists to form the BECC. Among those who heeded his call were Brooklyn Museum curator Henry Ghent (b. 1926) and artists Vivian Browne (1929–93), Cliff Joseph (discussed later in this chapter), Bearden, Gammon, Hines, Lewis, Saunders, DeCarava (who was invited, but refused, to exhibit in the Met show), and white portrait painter Alice Neel (1909–84), among others.

The BECC met in Andrew's studio and, as their first order of business, organized a protest campaign against the Metropolitan. Demonstrators arrived on the steps of the museum on January 9, 1969, carrying signs that denounced the Harlem show. Placards read, "Harlem on Whose Mind?," "Visit the Metropolitan Museum of Photography," "That's White of Hoving," and "Sold Out by Massa Hoving" (Thomas Hoving was then the Met's director). The group was greeted by barricades and a line of police but was permitted to picket peacefully. The BECC protestors called for visitors to boycott the Met, but their widely publicized activities served to increase rather than reduce the number of visitors to the Harlem exhibit. Some 10,000 viewers lined up to see the show on its first day. The entire affair was immortalized in Gammon's 1969 photomontage entitled, appropriately, *Harlem on My Mind*, in which a photo of Jack Johnson, arms folded like an Egyptian sentinel, is superimposed over a shot of the Metropolitan Museum façade (Figure 10.3).

▼ **10.3** Reginald Gammon, *Harlem on My Mind*, 1969, silver gelatin print, 10″ × 13″.

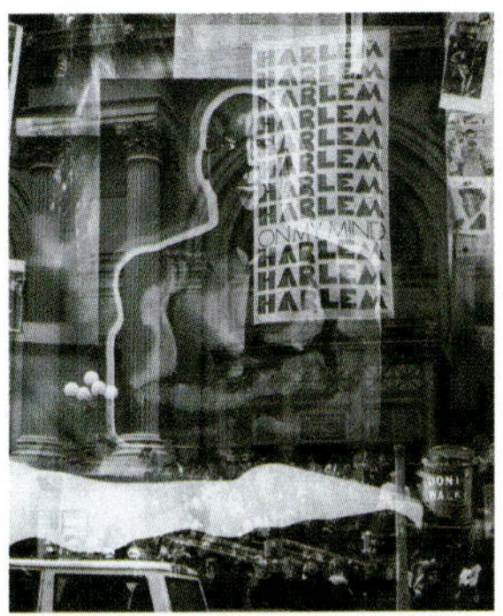

The BECC's strategic protests, which continued through 1971, led to more than half a dozen shows of African-American art at the Whitney Museum between 1970 and 1975. Furthermore, their activities breathed life into a growing community of black arts activists and helped to propel the Black Arts Movement forward. Faith Ringgold (see Chapter 11) and Tom Lloyd (1921–96) founded the United Black Artists' Committee (UBAC) in 1969 and mounted a campaign against the MoMA to protest its limited representation of minority artists. The UBAC demanded that a separate wing be established for artists of color, a curator be appointed to supervise the acquisition of works by minority artists, and a series of exhibitions of art by African Americans be implemented.

UBAC's actions, which consisted of an extensive letter-writing and publicity campaign as well as on-site demonstrations, were an unqualified success. Within a year, the MoMA agreed to revamp the museum's procurement guidelines and to schedule exhibits of the works of Bearden and Hunt. Within a short span of years, the art world had been persuaded to sit up and take notice of black art for the first time since the Harlem Renaissance. Although historically not nearly as well known as Spiral, the efforts of the BECC and UBAC had far-reaching repercussions, prompting black art exhibits at museums, universities, and **alternative spaces** across the country.

Benny Andrews

Notwithstanding his commitment to arts activism, BECC founder Benny Andrews (1930–2006) remarked in 1975, "I don't really think that art does that much in terms of social change." Although he considered himself an artist of "the people" and created imagery that advocated for human rights and portrayed what he termed "the folks"—prison inmates, janitors, working women, and so on—Andrews ultimately saw art making as distinct from political activism. Art, he believed, was by nature a personal expression of an artist's individuality and aesthetics. Andrews conceded that, if an artist were a politically engaged person, his or her art was likely to be political; but he also noted that many politically minded artists preferred not to create **agitprop** art. Andrews worked in both veins, creating works that were at times personal and at others political.

A product of a large rural Georgia sharecropper family, Andrews's childhood was trying, to say the least. He attended segregated schools when not assisting his family with farming. Andrews had precocious drawing abilities that his parents (who were both creatively gifted—his father was a self-taught artist and his mother was a writer) supported. Graduating from high school in 1948, Andrews moved to Atlanta, where he received his first commission to paint a mural for a local restaurant. He also won a scholarship to enroll at Fort Valley State College, an HBCU. In 1950, when Andrews's scholarship funds were depleted, he joined the U.S. Air Force.

Andrews was discharged in 1954 at the end of the Korean War. Instead of returning to Georgia, he utilized his GI Bill stipend to pay for tuition at Chicago's SAIC, where he received a BFA in 1958. Andrews moved to New

York City, where he settled initially on the Lower East Side near the infamous Bowery—the city's skid row. In response to his harsh surroundings, in 1959 Andrews began creating mixed-media paintings that incorporated paper trash, bits of rope, torn fabric, and other textured materials that seemed to express the detritus of the Bowery itself. This innovative method resulted in invitations that year to exhibit in biennials at both the Pennsylvania Academy and the Detroit Institute of Art (DIA). In 1960, Andrews landed his first one-person exhibit, in Provincetown, where he became acquainted with Thompson and other artists of the popular Massachusetts art colony.

Into the 1960s, Andrews fine-tuned his characteristic style of collaged paintings with highly tactile surfaces that lent palpability and dynamism to his imagery. Thematically, Andrews preferred solitary figures that personified intellectual concepts, political themes, and states of mind, evinced in the works' titles, such as *Sexism*, *Trail of Tears*, *Freedom of the Press*, *War*, and *Religious Revival*. Andrews portrayed the people and places he knew well—friends and families, southern sharecroppers and preachers, pool hustlers, boxers, nightclubs, and domestic genre scenes—as well as subjects close to his heart, such as the Holocaust and images of black rage against an unjust America. Andrews's 1969 *Did the Bear Sit Under a Tree* (Figure 10.4)

▼ **10.4** Benny Andrews, *Did the Bear Sit Under a Tree*, 1969, oil on canvas with painted fabric collage and zipper, 50″ × 61¾″ × 2¼″.

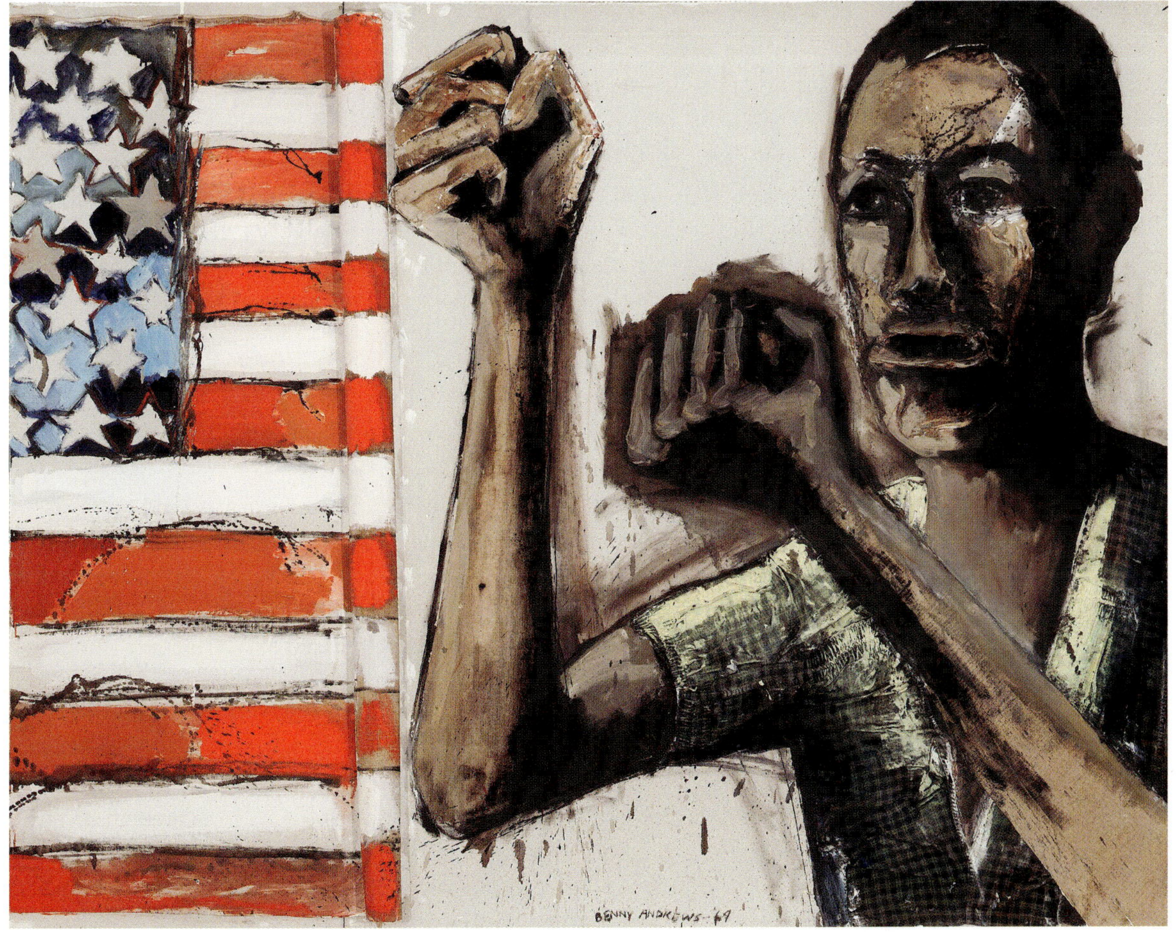

incorporates an oft-utilized Pop Art icon—the American flag—juxtaposed with a black man shaking clenched fists at the banner. This potent mix of Pop and politics was emblematic of the Black Arts Movement. The success of three solo shows during the 1960s enabled Andrews to make the first of several trips to Mexico to study the art of the *los tres grandes* (see Chapter 7).

By the mid-1960s, Andrews's reputation was established. His innovative methods earned him Whitney Fellowships in 1965 and 1966, which funded a lengthy visit to his birthplace in Georgia, where he created a series of autobiographical pictures. On returning to New York in 1968, Andrews joined the faculty of Queens College, where he taught and counseled students in their SEEK (Search for Education, Elevation and Knowledge) program for the next 30 years. Andrews also taught classes at "the Tombs," a correctional facility just west of the Bowery that was notorious for the corruption and brutality of its staff, overcrowding, and a decaying physical plant. The Tombs was the site of an eight-day riot in 1970, after which many of its inmates were transferred to Attica prison, contributing to another major riot there the following year. The Tombs riot disrupted Andrews's art program (which was closed permanently in 1974), but, with the support of the BECC, it was reconfigured to encompass prison facilities nationwide.

In 1971, Andrews was featured in a one-man show at the Studio Museum (a second was mounted in 1988), and he won the first of several grants from the New York State Council on the Arts. The following year, he was awarded the first of five MacDowell Colony residencies and later was appointed to its Board of Directors. In 1974, Andrews won the first of multiple NEA grants before being appointed director of the NEA Arts Program in Washington, D.C., in 1982. Andrews held the position for two years before resigning to focus more time on his art. In 1975, he created a series of works in homage to the U.S. Bicentennial, which traveled to galleries across the country. Andrews continued his commitment to community service and activism when, in 1976, he became involved with the Inner City Roundtable of Youths (ICRY), which was founded by Nizam Fatah (b. 1952), an ex-member of the Chicago gang the Blackstone Rangers. Andrews joined the ICRY board and helped to provide vital counseling, job referrals, vocational training, crisis intervention, and legal services for its clients.

Throughout the 1980s and 1990s, Andrews had many retrospectives and group shows. In 2002, the Andrews Foundation was formed to support young artists and to expand the art collections of African-American museums. As late as 2006, the year of Andrews's death, he was volunteering his services to create an art program for children displaced by Hurricane Katrina. Andrews was also a respected author and art critic who published more than a dozen articles over the course of his career and illustrated a series of successful children's books.

Cliff Joseph

Like Andrews, Cliff Joseph (b. 1927) has maintained a high level of community activism throughout his life. After cofounding the BECC with Andrews, he served as chairman of Action Against Racism in the Arts. The group was formed in 1979 in response to an exhibit held that year at the prestigious, alternative Artists Space in New York's Soho neighborhood. Titled *Nigger Drawings*, the show featured abstract drawings and photographs by a white artist named Donald Newman (b. 1956). The title of the show sparked a torrent of protests and the formation of Action Against Racism in the Arts, which held a show of its own in 1981 to protest racism in the art world. Joseph also participated in the widespread Art Against Apartheid movement of the mid-1980s and organized a touring exhibit in 1984 to protest white minority rule in South Africa. He was likewise an active member of the Cityarts Program, which partnered professional artists with students to create public murals.

A Panama émigré, Joseph grew up in Harlem in the 1930s and majored in illustration at Pratt Institute in the 1940s. He first became involved in the Civil Rights Movement while working as a graphic designer in New York, during which period he traveled to Washington, D.C., for the 1963 march. This experience drove home to Joseph the importance of social protest. Joseph devoted not only his time but also his art to social causes. His imagery of this period advocated for militant social action and school integration, and for specific activist groups such as the SNCC. Joseph's art also addressed police brutality and specific racially motivated atrocities, such as the 1963 Birmingham, Alabama, church bombing by white supremacists that killed four black children.

Joseph's 1966 painting *The Separatists* is typical of his political art (Figure 10.5). The image imprisons two monstrous figures within a square cage, separated from each other by blood-red bars. Teeth bared, eyes aglow with hatred, and fists tearing at their prison bars, these two naked

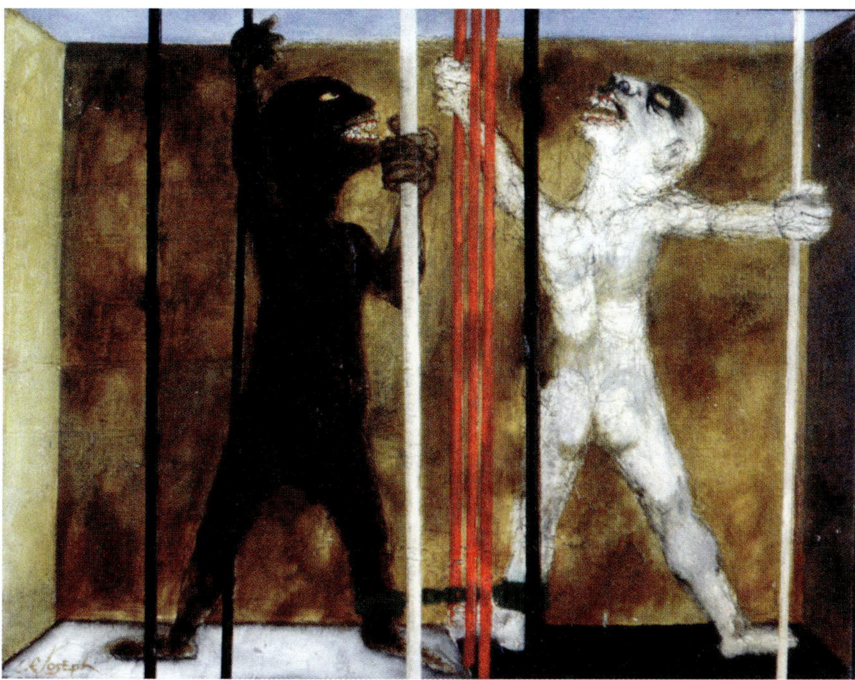

◀ **10.5** Cliff Joseph, *The Separatists: Racial Hatred Keeps All Imprisoned.*

men—one black and one white—are reduced to their most bestial selves. Using expressive brushwork, a limited but bold palette, and ghastly caricature, Joseph makes his point, which is underscored in the painting's subtitle: "Racial Hatred Keeps All Imprisoned."

Over the next several decades Joseph routinely exhibited his politicized art at alternative venues such as churches and community centers, and at New York's Exit Art and JAM (Just Above Midtown) Galleries. He chose established venues as well, with solo shows at dozens of university campuses and public museums both in the United States and abroad, including eight shows at branches of the National Gallery of Vietnam that displayed his antiwar imagery.

As part of his belief in art as a powerful tool for change, Joseph was a frontrunner in the field of art therapy (along with Georgette Seabrooke Powell; see Chapter 7). Art therapy was formalized in the United States in 1969 with the founding of the American Art Therapy Association. Joseph became its first black member in 1969 and served as president of its New York chapter. He worked with Andrews at the Tombs, using art as prison therapy. In 1970, he was appointed director of art therapy at Yeshiva University and he helped to form one of the first ever art therapy master's programs, at Pratt Institute. In 2008, the American Art Therapy Association awarded the 81-year-old Joseph their distinguished Social Justice and Change Award.

An accomplished scholar and author, Joseph wrote an essay entitled "Art Therapy and the Third World," and he cowrote *Murals of the Mind: Image of a Psychiatric Community* with psychiatrist Jay Harris, in which the treatment of schizophrenic hospital patients through cooperative art projects was documented and analyzed. A creative writer as well, Joseph published a science fiction novel entitled *The Revelation of Number 10*, which centers on two visual artists—one in Russia and one in New York—who are compelled by an unseen extraterrestrial force to divert mankind from its path of violence, war, and ultimate self-destruction to one of peace. Joseph currently lives in Chicago and has continued to participate in pacifist causes, including campaigns against NATO and the wars in Afghanistan and Iraq. As a member of Caravan to Cuba, he has opposed the U.S. embargo against that country. Joseph's most recent concerns have focused on environmental issues.

THE WEUSI AESTHETIC

The Harlem-based WEUSI Artist Collective was founded shortly after Spiral, in 1964. Its members believed that art and activism were inseparable. Taking their name from the Swahili word for "black," a key goal of the group was to bring art to the black community. Other major tenets were to include African icons and formal elements in their art and to incorporate African and African-American history, culture, and social concerns into their visual narratives. Several members of this **Afrocentric** group took on African names, rejecting their given names (in the manner of Malcolm X), which were inherited from past slave owners.

Among the early members of WEUSI were Abdullah Aziz (b. 1932), Okeo Pyatt (b. 1942), Taiwo Shabazz Duvall (b. 1933), Otto Neals (b. 1930), Bill Howell (1942–75), Kay Brown and Dindga McCannon (see Chapter 11), Ademola Olugebefola (discussed later in this chapter), and James Phillips (discussed later in this chapter). The group established their own gallery, Weusi-Nyumba Ya Sanaa (Swahili for "black house of art" or "black gallery"), which mounted shows for 10 years, until 1974; their community-based Weusi Academy of Arts and Studies served Harlem art students until 1978. The group mounted a major exhibit at the Studio Museum in 1971. Still viable into the 21st century, its members organized a major historical retrospective at the African American Museum in Nassau County in 2008 and at the Dwyer Cultural Center in Harlem in 2010.

Ademola Olugebefola

Artist and musician Ademola Olugebefola (b. 1941) is the driving force of WEUSI. Born in the Virgin Islands, he grew up in New York and has spent much of his life in Harlem. He works in a wide variety of media, including prints, drawings, sculpture, murals, easel painting, and graphic design. His mixed-media *Emerging Spirit* of 1970 epitomizes WEUSI aesthetics (Figure 10.6). The composition features an abstracted figure with a flame-like cloak, kingly collar, and crown, rising upward toward double moons in a night sky. The figure wears an African-inspired mask. On its torso the artist has collaged a raised circle that alludes to the small receptacles found on Kongo power figures: cavities filled with sacred soil, seeds, and bones and sealed with resin. The images of the two circular moons can be interpreted in different ways. The Yoruba and Vodou spirits of the moon, Yemaya and Kalfu (from the French *carrefour* or "crossroads"), respectively, signify fertility and virility. Kalfu is horned and partial to the color red, as is Olugebefola's spirit figure. Kalfu is also the link between the human and spirit worlds and is vital to Vodou practice. Embodied in the two moons also are Yoruba and Vodou beliefs in the sacredness of twin births, exemplified by the Ibeji and Marassa. Olugebefola's image shares in common with art of the mid-20th-century Haitian Renaissance (which teemed with Vodou imagery) an expressive and abstract formal approach, strong colors, and spiritual iconography.

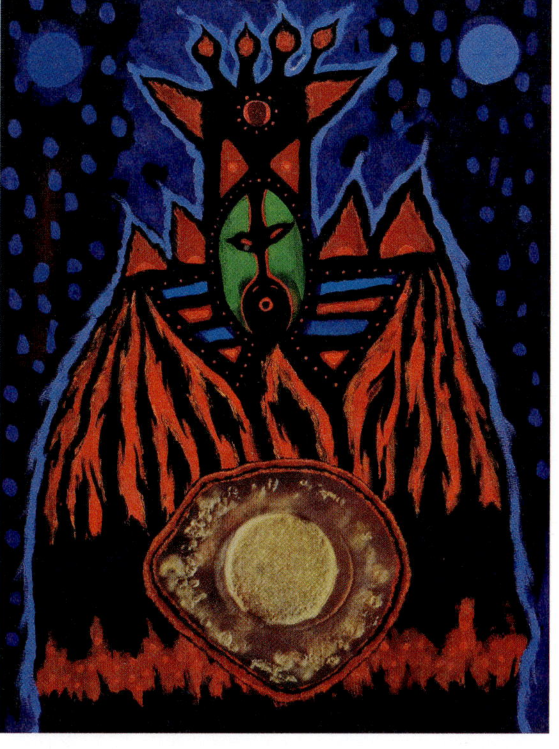

▼ **10.6** Ademola Olugebefola, *Emerging Spirit*, 1970–71, mixed media and collage on paper, 24″ × 18″.

Dedicated to the philosophies of WEUSI, Olugebefola has spent a lifetime expressing black culture through art, not only as an artist but also as a jazz musician, arts educator, art dealer, curator, and arts administrator. He served on the Harlem Cultural Council and was director of education at the WEUSI academy. From 1973 to 1977, Olugebefola was vice president of the National Conference of

Artists (NCA). Founded in 1959, the NCA's mission to "preserve, promote, inspire and support African American Art and Culture through the visual arts" echoes that of WEUSI.

Managing always to advance his artistic agenda without compromising his commitment to community service, Olugebefola exhibited in group shows throughout the 1970s, including FESTAC 1977 in Lagos. One of the artist's myriad interests is "wearable art" such as African-inspired fashion and jewelry design. Olugebefola showcased his creations at his own fashion studio, the House of Umoja on 7th Avenue in Harlem, which opened in 1966. In the early 1970s, he expanded this business to his birthplace of St. Thomas in the Virgin Islands.

From 1969 to 1972, Olugebefola worked in a number of different capacities, from art director to production manager, at several New York theaters. Among these were the New Lafayette Theatre, a Harlem-based company that produced plays, drama workshops, and a theater magazine; the National Black Theatre (NBT), founded in Harlem in 1968 and still a highly active performance space; and the Public Theatre in downtown Manhattan. Beginning in 1975, Olugebefola was president of Caribbean Media Associates, an audiovisual production company, and in 1978 he cofounded with his siblings a fine arts dealership and consulting firm called Tetrahedron. Olugebefola also taught art during this period in the New York City public school system and at community centers citywide.

His entrepreneurial ventures continued through the 1980s and 1990s. With his wife, photographer Pat Davis, in 1980 Olugebefola founded the New York–based advertising and graphic design firm Solar Associates. In 1989, the couple transformed their apartment in the historic Grinnell Building on Riverside Drive into an alternative exhibit space. Other undertakings include a publishing concern that produced, among other things, Kwanzaa-related books and prints, African-American children's books, and a Harlem travel guide.

Ben F. Jones

Multimedia installation artist Ben F. Jones (b. 1941) spent his youth in Paterson, New Jersey, and remains a New Jersey resident. His wide travels, however, have taken him to Europe, Asia, South America, Africa, and the Caribbean—in particular to Cuba, where he has had numerous exhibitions and has participated in a dozen cultural exchange programs since the 1970s.

Jones began sketching portraits of family members while barely a teenager. He received his BFA in 1963 and an MA degree three years later. By 1970, Jones was associated with WEUSI and the subject of a one-person show at its gallery. Jones also participated in the major Black Arts Movement group shows of the decade. His art of the period honored black leaders and creative icons as well as African cultural themes and symbols. Jones's *Black Face and Arm Unit* is among his best-known works of the 1970s and debuted in his solo show at Weusi Gallery (Figure 10.7). Using his own body, the artist cast 15 plaster reliefs of his face and arms and painted them with vivid patterns composed of stripes, circles, and spirals. The inclusion of sequins and metallic paint enliven the installation, which was designed for

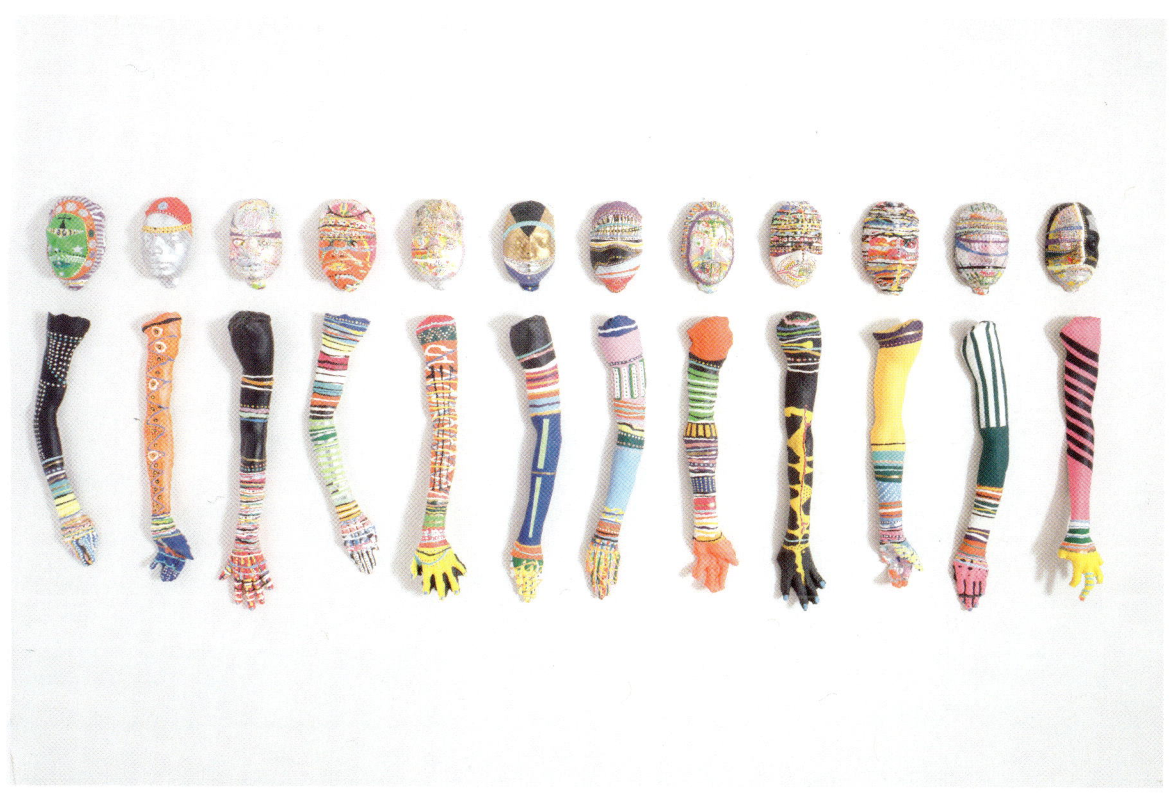

▲ **10.7** Ben F. Jones, *Black Face and Arm Unit*, 1971, acrylic on 30 plaster casts, life size.

Art © Ben F. Jones, Collection of the New Jersey State Museum. Museum purchase FA1984.92a-x. Reproduced with permission.

mounting on a flatly painted wall so that the active shapes and patterns would stand out in bold silhouette. The horizontality of the sculpture conjures up visions of Egyptian wall paintings, and the multihued faces, despite being cast from a single source, suggest the great range of human diversity, even as they remind us of our shared humanity. The first portion of the work's title, "black face," taken from the derogatory minstrel tradition, is here transformed into a positive reinterpretation of a negative stereotype.

Jones won the first of two NEA grants in 1974–75 (a second was awarded in 2007). Over the next three decades, he continued to focus his creative energies on representations of black beauty in myriad variations. His recent *Men Pattern* suite celebrates the black male nude, stripped of outworn myths and obsolete taboos. Jones has also produced artworks dedicated to African theological motifs, such as his room-sized, site-specific installations devoted to Shango (the Vodou and Yoruba warrior *orisha*, or god of fire and lightning) and the power of positive change. In addition, a number of multimedia portraits pay homage to African-American and Afro-Caribbean musicians, including Bob Marley, Dinah Washington, Nina Simone, Sarah Vaughan, and Billie Holiday. Jones's recent works are more existentialist, nonfigurative representations of Zen concepts such as wholeness, peace, hope, and enlightenment, using Abstract Expressionist staining and gestural techniques.

James Phillips

Nonfigurative artist James Phillips (b. 1945) hails from Brooklyn, New York. His geometric canvases incorporate African-inspired forms and

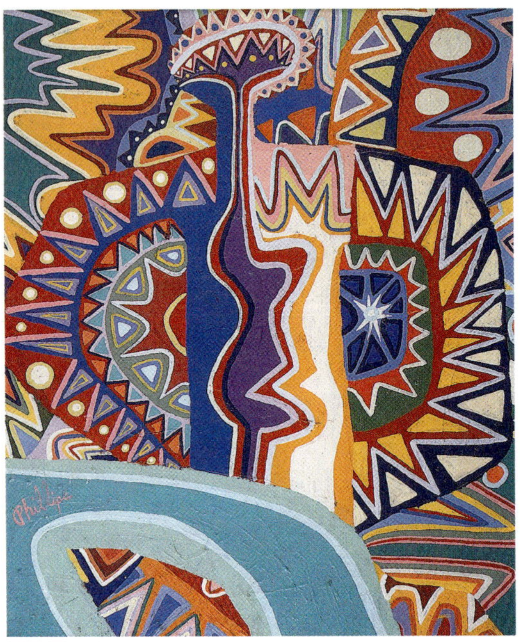

▲ **10.8** James Phillips, *The Dealer*, from the *Junkie in the Twilight Zone* series, 1966, oil on canvas, 20″ × 16″.

symbolism. Phillips began his art studies in the early 1960s at Fleisher Art Memorial School in Philadelphia, which has a century-old tradition of bringing art training to the economically disadvantaged. He attended the Philadelphia College of Art (today the University of the Arts) in the mid-1960s before moving to New York to study at the Printing Trades School, a vocational institution initially funded in the 1930s by the WPA to educate youths ages 16–25. Phillips joined WEUSI at the time of its founding and, inspired by the group's art and philosophies, developed a unique style of painting marked by **chevron** patterns, visual rhythms inspired by jazz music, and a vivid Pop Art palette (Figure 10.8). Through nonobjective line and color, his visual statements celebrated such varied themes as black unity, revolution, African theology, nature, spirituality, and the maelstrom of New York City life. His 1966 *The Dealer*—which Phillips created as part of his *Junkie in the Twilight Zone* series—uses a psychedelic palette and frenetic chevron and linear design elements to embody the rising LSD epidemic in 1960s America.

After securing a Creative Artists Public Service (CAPS) grant in 1971, Phillips became aware of the activities of AfriCOBRA (discussed later in this chapter) and joined the group officially in 1973. Phillips then held a four-year artist's residency at Howard University, after which he participated in Changing Education Through the Arts (CETA), a federally funded program that sought to integrate the arts as a learning tool into all aspects of education. In the 1980s, Phillips spent time in Tokyo under the auspices of an NEA Exchange Fellowship, while also serving as a visiting professor at the University of California, Berkeley. Phillips moved next to Baltimore to teach at the Maryland Institute College of Art (MICA), where he completed his MFA degree in 1998. Since 2001, Phillips has served on the Howard University faculty as supervisor of graduate studies. He has exhibited in more than 70 shows in the United States and abroad. Phillips has also received commissions to create large-scale, site-specific works from the cities of Baltimore, San Francisco, and New York, and from the Philadelphia Airport.

OBAC AND THE WALL OF RESPECT

Another pivotal collective of the Black Arts Movement was the Organization of Black American Culture (OBAC, pronounced "Obasi," which is derived from the Yoruba word for king, *oba*). The group was cofounded in Chicago in 1967 by Jeff Donaldson (discussed later in this chapter), who was then a university professor. Donaldson was joined in OBAC by Africana studies historian Abdul Alkalimat (then Gerald McWorter; b. 1942) and writer and African-American literary historian Hoyt Fuller (1923–81). The visual arts arm of OBAC—which, as a whole, was devoted to many forms of art (music, writing, dance, theater, etc.)—revived the WPA mural tradition with its most historic endeavor, the *Wall of Respect*, painted on an abandoned building on the South Side of Chicago in 1967 (Figure 10.9).

Designed to pay homage to black leaders and to bring an element of visual beauty to the then-depressed South Side, the mural was a collaborative effort consisting of eight panels and some 50 portraits. Among these were depictions of major sports figures like Muhammad Ali and Kareem Abdul-Jabbar; jazz and blues artists Billie Holiday, Miles Davis, and Sarah Vaughan; R & B artists James Brown and Aretha Franklin; civil rights activists Adam Clayton Powell, Jr., Marcus Garvey, Stokely Carmichael, and Malcolm X; actors Sidney Poitier and Cicely Tyson; and literati Amiri Baraka, Gwendolyn Brooks, and James Baldwin. Elijah Muhammad and the black Muslims were also included, but, significantly, Martin Luther King, Jr., was not. By this time, his pacifist and integrationist stances had been rejected by many in favor of black militancy.

Participating OBAC artists included, among some two dozen, Illinois Institute of Technology student Sylvia Abernathy (b. 1939), who was responsible for the overall design of the mural, and Jeff Donaldson, who painted the jazz panel. Wadsworth Jarrell contributed a panel on R & B artists; Barbara Jones-Hogu portrayed theater personalities; Norman Parish (1937–2013)

▼ **10.9** Sylvia and Billy Abernathy, Barbara Jones-Hogu, Myrna Weaver, Jeff Donaldson, Eliot Hunter, Wadsworth Jarrell, Norman Parish, William Walker, Darrel Cowherd, Roy Lewis, Robert Sengstacke, and others, *Wall of Respect*, 1967 (destroyed 1971), approximately 20′ × 40′. Forty-Third and Langley Streets, Chicago, IL.

Photo © 1989 Robert A. Sengstacke, courtesy of Chicago Public Art Group.

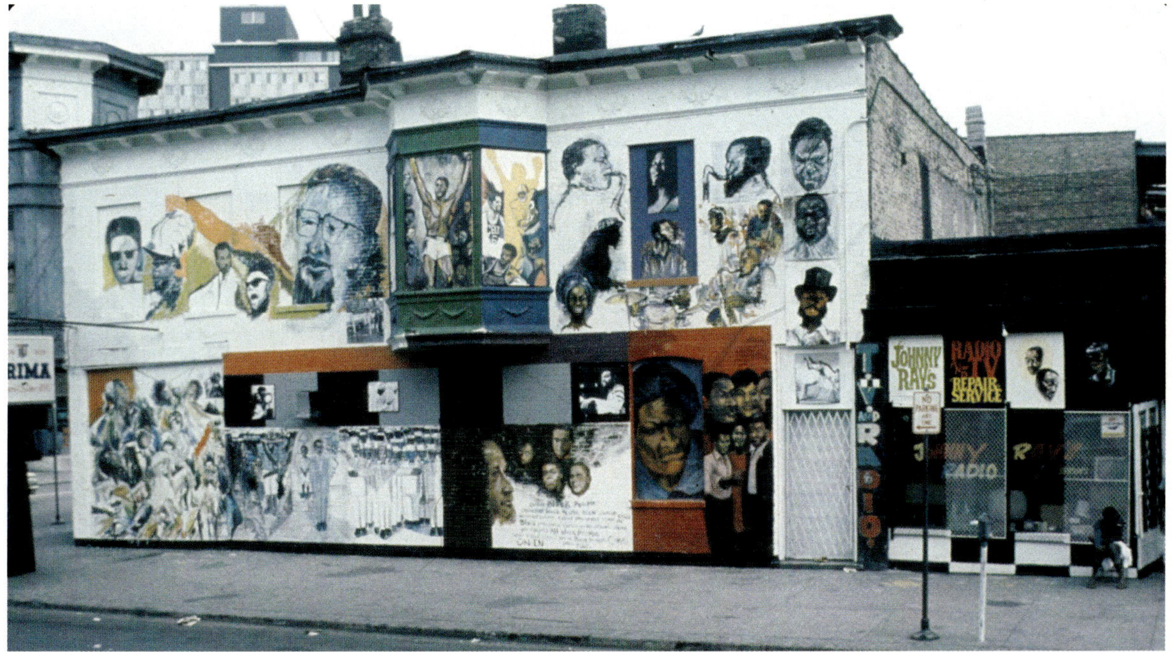

depicted black statesmen in the largest section of the mural; William Walker devoted his section to religious figures; and Carolyn Lawrence (b. 1940) painted an homage to black dancers on an adjacent newsstand. Several photographers also collaborated on the project by mounting their photographs on the wall and by documenting the mural's progress. They included Darrel Cowherd (b. 1940) and Billy Abernathy (b. 1938); Roy Lewis (b. 1937), whose photo of Malcolm X was prominently displayed; and *Chicago Defender* photographer Robert Sengstacke (b. 1943). Because "the Wall," as the mural has become known, was ultimately destroyed when the building was demolished in 1971, the photographic records taken by OBAC photographers have become historic documents and the only remaining chronicles of this significant collaboration, today considered among the most decisive political art **happenings** of the decade.

In contrast to artists hoping to exhibit their works at established venues such as museums and galleries, which required some form of official sanction, the OBAC artists turned to the citizens of the South Side for informal approval and input, making the *Wall of Respect* a genuinely cooperative endeavor. People who lived near the site of the mural at 43rd and Langley Streets watched the artists' progress and provided them with food, drinks, and criticism as they worked. Even the local gang, the Blackstone Rangers, whose turf-identifying graffiti already adorned the walls of the neighborhood, gave their tacit approval by safeguarding the mural from vandals. The enterprise was so successful and widely publicized that it sparked hundreds of similar projects in urban neighborhoods across the country, including the 1969 *Wall of Truth*, located on a facing building; the Detroit *Wall of Dignity* (1968); and the Atlanta *Wall of Respect* (c. 1974).

AFRICOBRA AND THE BLACK AESTHETIC

In 1968, OBAC evolved first into the artists' group COBRA (Coalition of Black Revolutionary Artists) and, later, into AfriCOBRA (African Commune of Bad Relevant Artists). Its members' art emphasized narratives of black history and the African-American struggle for social, economic, and political parity. They utilized symbols derived from African sculpture, hieroglyphic writings, and textile designs. They strove for stylistic accessibility (words and recognizable figures) in their work that would help it connect more readily with their audience: the working-class black community. Other formal elements that composed the "look" of AfriCOBRA art included a saturated and vivid palette, bold patterns, visual improvisation, and jazz-inspired **syncopation**. Wildly popular during the late 1960s and 1970s, the AfriCOBRA visual approach became a hallmark of the Black Arts Movements and had far-reaching influence on artists for more than a decade.

AfriCOBRA held its first major group show, *AfriCOBRA I: Ten in Search of a Nation*, in 1970 at the Studio Museum. It also organized the historic Conference on the Functional Aspects of Black Arts (CONFABA), in Evanston, Illinois. Spearheaded by Donaldson and his African-American art history students at Northwestern University, it drew national attention to the need for art historians to play a proactive role in framing, documenting, and publicizing the history of African-American art. A series of task forces were formed to address five key areas: education, research, resources, dissemination, and aesthetics.

CONFABA organizers invited Catlett, as an "advisor and elder of distinction," to attend the conference. However, she was denied a visa and had to address attendees via telephone. In her remarks, she described herself and her CONFABA compatriots as black revolutionary artists who must remain dedicated to cooperative socialist efforts and to the liberation of black people from oppression. Catlett's address led to a major retrospective of her work at the Studio Museum the following year, in 1971, which earned her the title "foremother of the Black Arts Movement."

AfriCOBRA has had exceptional staying power, holding group exhibits through the 1970s and 1980s. The ensemble's 20-year retrospective was held at the Nexus Art Center in Atlanta in 1990. An historical exhibit, *AfriCOBRA and the Chicago Black Arts Movements*, was mounted at Northwestern University in 2010, and *AfriCOBRA and Beyond* was held at the DuSable Museum in 2013, still featuring original members. AfriCOBRA remains active today, some 45 years after its founding. Its member artists continue to exhibit and inspire younger artists to follow in their aesthetic footsteps.

Jeffrey Donaldson

Arkansas native Jeffrey Donaldson (1932–2004) was a vital member of AfriCOBRA and one of the most influential artists of the Black Arts Movement. He was one of the first-ever visual arts majors at Arkansas AM&N College (today's University of Arkansas at Pine Bluff). He was mentored by the founder of the art department there, African-American artist John Miller Howard (1908–80), who headed the department for more than 40 years. Howard introduced Donaldson to the achievements of African-American artists and instilled in Donaldson a sense of pride in his artistic heritage.

On graduation in 1954, Howard secured for Donaldson his first teaching position at a Jackson, Mississippi, high school, where the young artist founded an art program and taught for one year before he was drafted into the army in 1955, spending two years in France. Once discharged, Donaldson joined his family in Chicago, where they had moved from Arkansas. From 1957 to 1965, he taught art in the Chicago public school system while attending the Illinois Institute of Technology, where he earned a master's degree in art education in 1963. Over the next decade, as Donaldson distinguished himself as a leader in the Black Arts Movement in Chicago, his art became a model for AfriCOBRA's aesthetics.

Donaldson dubbed his style of art "trans-African" because it incorporated African form and content from both sides of the Atlantic. His 1969 *Wives of Shango* embodies this approach. Its title refers to Shango, a god venerated in West Africa, Trinidad, Haiti, Cuba, the Dominican Republic, and Brazil (Figure 10.10). Donaldson portrays Shango's warrior wives as a triad of armed black women. They shoulder rifles and are draped with bandoliers of ammunition. These women signify the code of armed resistance to white

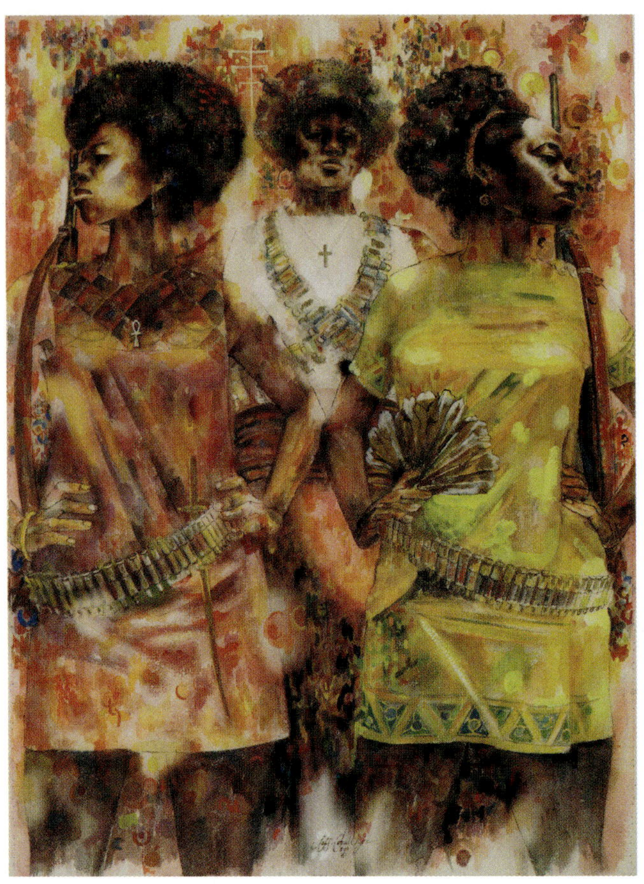

▲ **10.10** Jeff Donaldson, *Wives of Shango*, 1969, watercolor with mixed media on paper, 30″ × 22″.

Brooklyn Museum, gift of R. M. Atwater, Anna Wolfrom Dove, Alice Fiebiger, Joseph Fiebiger, Belle Campbell Harriss, and Emma L. Hyde, by exchange; Designated Purchase Fund, Mary Smith Dorward Fund, Dick S. Ramsay Fund, and Carll H. de Silver Fund, 2012.80.13. © Jameela K. Donaldson.

violence that marked the age. The women-warriors sport the Afro hairstyles that had been adopted by proponents of the Black Power Movement as a prideful acknowledgment of their African heritage. Donaldson decorated the women's simple shifts with chevron trim derived from Kongo textile patterns. One woman wears a Christian cross on a chain around her neck. Another wears an ankh—the Egyptian symbol for life. Together the pendants allude to the fusion of East and West that constitutes African-American culture and Donaldson's Trans-African aesthetic. Formally, the straightforward clarity of Donaldson's style is ideally AfriCOBRA, as is his use of iridescent hues and a shimmering effect.

Donaldson served as an assistant professor at Northeastern Illinois University in Chicago from 1965 to 1968, and in 1974, he became that institution's first black doctoral graduate, and one of the few PhDs in the field of African-American art history. In the 1970s, he served as a delegate to FESTAC in Lagos and joined the faculty of the Howard University Art Department, where his tenure spanned two decades. He taught and mentored literally thousands of students, eventually retiring in 1998, six years before his death from a heart attack.

Wadsworth and Jae Jarrell

Born in Georgia, AfriCOBRA mainstay Wadsworth Jarrell (b. 1929) moved to Chicago after serving in the army during the Korean War. In 1954, Jarrell enrolled in the SAIC to study graphic design. Within a few months, he broadened his focus to include painting. Jarrell completed his degree in 1958 and participated in the institute's prestigious *Chicago Artists* exhibit that year. He also met Donaldson, with whom he would collaborate for many decades. The two artists conceived of a school of black art with a common aesthetic agenda. The concept developed from an idea first voiced by Donaldson in a casual conversation with Jarrell in 1962 into AfriCOBRA six years later.

Jarrell's works at the turn of the 1960s were Cubist in style and depicted abstracted scenes of everyday life in Chicago's black community, such as nightclubs, street scenes, horse racing themes, and jazz performances, a motif that Jarrell contributed a decade later to the *Wall of Respect*. Although Jarrell's painting style would evolve over time, his thematic interests remained constant throughout his life. In 1963, a watercolor by Jarrell entitled *The Art Pub* was included in a SAIC exhibition. (Richard Hunt also participated.) Critical attention from this exhibit set Jarrell's professional art career in motion. Working from his Hyde Park studio, Jarrell began to intensify his palette and energize his brushwork. In 1963, he met Elaine Annette Johnson—Jae Jarrell (b. 1935)—whom he married four years later. The year of their marriage, the artist and his wife joined OBAC and collaborated on the *Wall of Respect*. In the late 1960s, they opened WJ Studio and Gallery, an alternative art space in their multilevel home, which showcased local visual artists and poetry and musical performances. The couple helped to cofound AfriCOBRA, which held meetings in their gallery (the venue also hosted CONFABA).

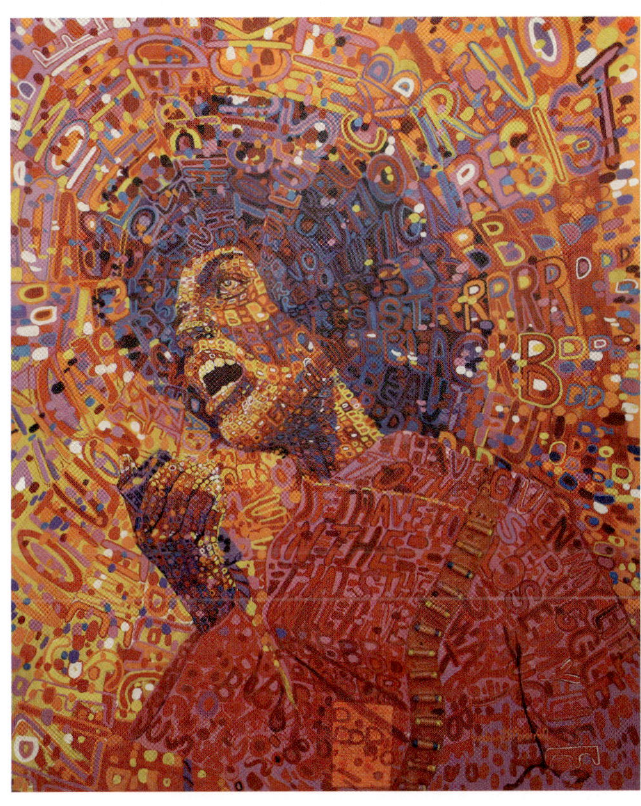

▲ **10.11** Wadsworth Jarrell, *Revolutionary (Angela Davis)*, 1971, acrylic and mixed media on canvas, 64″ × 51″.

Collection of the Brooklyn Museum, gift of R. M. Atwater, Anna Wolfrom Dove, Alice Fiebiger, Joseph Fiebiger, Belle Campbell Harriss, and Emma L. Hyde, by exchange; Designated Purchase Fund, Mary Smith Dorward Fund, Dick S. Ramsay Fund, and Carll H. de Silver Fund. © Wadsworth Jarrell.

Wadsworth Jarrell's painting *Revolutionary* of 1971 was exhibited in the second AfriCOBRA group show at the Studio Museum (Figure 10.11). It is composed of multiples of the letter *B*, shorthand for "black" and "bad" (the latter term indicative of someone with social commitment and artistic integrity). These letters are the buildings blocks for a portrait of Black Panther advocate Angela Davis (b. 1944). In Jarrell's tribute to Davis, the letter *D* also repeats and signifies her name and the word "down," meaning "in agreement" or "in accord" with the Black Liberation Movement. Jarrell worked within a Pop and Op Art aesthetic. He employed Pop Art means by incorporating a widely familiar icon—Davis—as well as text and a dazzling palette of pink, orange, and blue. The end result is a shimmering mosaic image that "speaks" both visually and verbally. Short for "optical," the Op Art trend of the 1960s used optical illusions to confound the viewer's perception. Jarrell's use of hundreds of letters and revolutionary text statements are optically camouflaged within a figurative portrait. Written backwards and forwards, the words "revolutionary," "resist," "sister," "black," and "beautiful" radiate from Davis's head like a neon halo. Her tunic reads, in part, *"I have given my life in the struggle; that's the way it will have to be."*

In the painting, Davis wears a "revolutionary suit" with an ammunition belt and bullets collaged onto the canvas. This element was inspired by Jae Jarrell's *Urban Wall Suit* and her *Revolutionary Suit*, A-line miniskirt and jacket sets, the latter with bandolier trim, complete with bullets, which was also featured in the Studio Museum show. Jae designed wearable art that was influenced by African sculpture and textiles. A graduate of Bowling Green State University in Ohio, Jae also trained at the SAIC, Howard University, and Parsons School of Design. Her designs incorporate elements of graffiti, Pop imagery and texts, geometric patterns, varied textures, and vivid colors. They are fashion incarnations of the AfriCOBRA aesthetic (Figure 10.12).

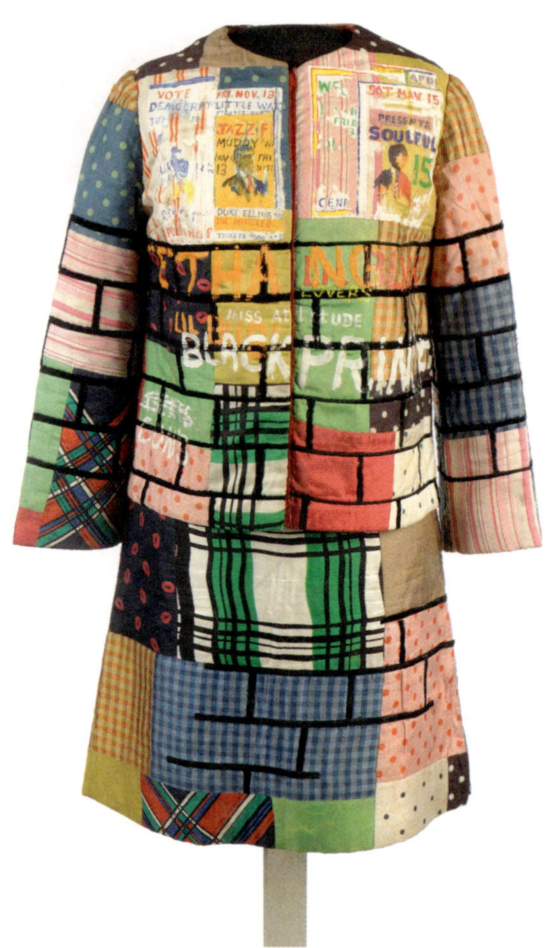

▲ **10.12** Jae Jarrell, *Urban Wall Suit*, c. 1969, sewn and painted cotton and silk, two-piece suit, 37½″ × 27½″ × ½″. Brooklyn Museum, gift of R. M. Atwater, Anna Wolfrom Dove, Alice Fiebiger, Joseph Fiebiger, Belle Campbell Harriss, and Emma L. Hyde, by exchange; Designated Purchase Fund, Mary Smith Dorward Fund, Dick S. Ramsay Fund, and Carll H. de Silver Fund, 2012.80.16. © Jae Jarrell.

After the 1971 AfriCOBRA show, the Jarrells moved to Washington, D.C. Wadsworth joined Donaldson on the Howard University art faculty, where he taught photography for six years and completed his MFA. In 1977, he participated in FESTAC; the festival had a profound influence on his art of the late 1970s, which routinely incorporated imagery derived from the abstract forms of Nigerian Senufo sculpture. After FESTAC, Jarrell accepted a position at the University of Georgia, where he remained for ten years. At the time of his retirement in 1988, Jarrell and Jae moved to New York City and settled in Soho, where Jae opened a vintage clothing shop. In 2009, the couple relocated to Jae's hometown of Cleveland, Ohio, where they currently live.

Barbara Jones-Hogu

The Afrocentric figurative works of AfriCOBRA painter and printmaker Barbara Jones-Hogu (b. 1938) is epitomized by her now-classic 1971 **screen print** *Unite*. It features a pyramid composition composed of bold silhouettes and block lettering (Figure 10.13). Articulated as a unified flat black form is a group of protestors whose raised fists signify their commitment to the Black Power Movement. An ankh dangles from the ear of one activist, whose face, like those of her comrades, is formed by two-toned (tan and brown) reductive forms. To this, the artist added hatching to create modeling and texture. The word "unite" echoes within the context of a chevron kaleidoscope, the colors of which allude to those of the American flag and to the skin color of the African Americans who struggle for equality under its banner.

Jones-Hogu grew up in Chicago and earned her BFA in 1964 at the SAIC. Like Donaldson, she attended Illinois Institute of Technology, where she completed an MS in printmaking in 1970. An original member of OBAC and AfriCOBRA, Jones-Hogu contributed several portraits of actors to the *Wall of Respect*. Her works most often included text messages that underscored the concerns and philosophies of AfriCOBRA and of black America more broadly. Since the founding of AfriCOBRA, Jones-Hogu has consistently exhibited with the group. Recently, she has studied filmmaking and has begun to document African-American artists. Notable is her 2010 documentary film *The Black Age of Comics: Telling Our Stories*.

Nelson Stevens

For Brooklynite Nelson Stevens (b. 1938), jazz themes, portraits of African-American icons such as Stevie Wonder, Angela Davis, and Malcolm X, and the black female nude are favorite painting motifs. Working with small

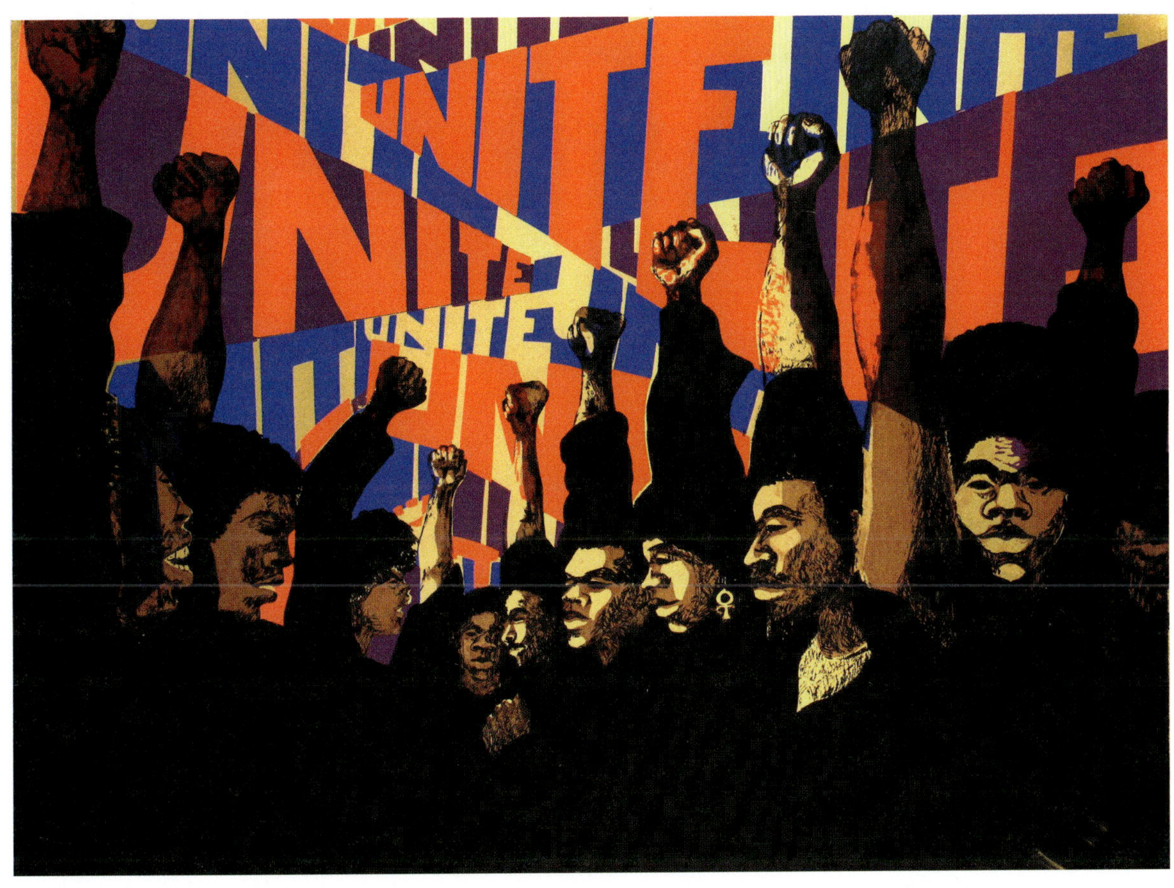

▲ **10.13** Barbara Jones-Hogu, *Unite*, 1971, screen print on paper, 22½″ × 30″.

prismatic and geometric elements, Stevens builds his mosaic forms into larger final images that are organic in shape and marked by monumentality, achieved by the use of a worm's-eye view, and a sense of substantive mass and weight. Stevens's understanding of color harmonies and values unifies the many puzzle-like pieces that give his paintings the quality of stained glass, a feature that has become the artist's hallmark.

Stevens began his career as a graphic designer in the late 1950s and then received a BFA in painting and art education from Ohio University in 1962. He spent the next four years teaching in the Cleveland public school system before enrolling at Kent State University to earn his MFA degree. While a graduate student, Stevens lectured at the Cleveland Museum of Art and was an art instructor at Cleveland's Karamu House and Case Western Reserve University.

Master's degree in hand, Stevens was appointed to the art faculty at Northern Illinois University, where he remained for three years before taking a position on the faculty of the University of Massachusetts, Amherst in 1972. During a 30-year career there, he taught painting, drawing, graphic design, and African-American art history and theory. He also recruited students to create murals on black subjects (completing more than 30 public murals in the Springfield area alone) and promoted murals as a way of educating the community through art. Stevens retired from Amherst in 2003 and settled in Baltimore. In addition to dozens of showings at U.S. galleries and museums, his work has also been exhibited in Africa and the Caribbean. Stevens won a Lifetime Achievement Award from the Anyone Can Fly Foundation in 2013, which is dedicated to honoring African-American artists and bringing their history to youth through education. Throughout Stevens's more-than-fifty-year career, he has remained devoted to the same goal.

THE OBAC AND AFRICOBRA LEGACY: BLACK POWER MURALS

William Walker

Chicago artist William Walker (1927–2011) is perhaps one of the most prolific mural painters to come out of OBAC and AfriCOBRA; he is considered the father of the **Chicago Mural Movement**. Through friend and photographer Billy Abernathy, in 1967 Walker learned about OBAC and suggested to the group that they create a mural at 43rd and Langley Streets, which became the *Wall of Respect*. After his contribution of portraits of religious figures to the Wall, over the next four decades, Walker completed more than 30 murals in working-class Chicago neighborhoods. Themes were invariably sociopolitical and included narratives of black history; messages of black pride, harmony, and peace; critiques of racism, prejudice, and economic oppression; workers' rights motifs; and tributes to black icons such as Martin Luther King, Jr., and Harriet Tubman.

Walker was born in Birmingham, Alabama, but came to Chicago with his family when he was five. Raised initially by his biracial grandmother, Williams learned from her the importance of cross-cultural understanding and engagement. He spent time in the military during World War II and the Korean War. Discharged from service while stationed in Columbus, Ohio, Walker enrolled in the Columbus Gallery School (today Columbus College of Art and Design), where he was mentored by African-American art historian and artist Samella Lewis (b. 1924).

During this period, Walker researched the lives, careers, and art of the Mexican Muralists, whose paintings he greatly admired. He was impressed with the ability of *los tres grandes* to compose murals that responded to the idiosyncrasies of a particular architectural setting. Incorporating elements from the styles of Rivera, Siqueiros, and Orozco into his own work, in 1952 Walker won the Earl C. Derby Award for Figure Portraits at Columbus College's annual exhibition. After graduating in 1954, he traveled south to Tennessee, painting commissioned murals in churches, lodges, and nightclubs in Nashville and Memphis. A road trip to the farmland of Arkansas to map out a mural assignment that called for a plantation scene exposed Walker to the extreme poverty and deprivation of black farmworkers. He was inspired to use his mural painting to draw attention to the needs of the underprivileged.

In 1955, Walker returned to Chicago to realize his goal, although it took him a while to achieve it. For several years, he earned a living as a sign and ornamental painter for local design companies. By the end of the 1950s, he was working as a freelance designer, specializing in architectural painting that incorporated small murals into his commissions, often without charging for them. By the 1960s, he had become an integral part of the African-American artistic community in Chicago. He was affiliated with Burroughs and the SSCAC as well as OBAC and AfriCOBRA. After completing work on the *Wall of Respect*, in 1970 Walker formed the Chicago Mural Group, known today as the Chicago Public Art Group (CPAG), a multiracial collective of muralists. CPAG cofounders included Walker, international public artist John Pitman Weber (b. 1942), and painter Eugene Eda (b. 1939), who collaborated with Walker on the Detroit *Wall of Dignity* in 1968. The Chicago Museum of Contemporary Art hosted the group's first exhibit of portable murals in 1970. The paintings were later donated to the SSCAC, the Angela Davis Legal Defense Fund, the Pedro Campos Peoples' Health Center, and several churches.

Working with members of the community, the collective continues to create public art, including, in addition to murals, sculpture, mosaics, and park and garden design. Another important CPAG mission is the restoration and preservation of public murals, which routinely fall victim to building demolitions, whitewashing, fading, and weather damage over time. In 2009, two years before Walker's death, his mural *Childhood Is Without Prejudice* was restored by CPAG (Figure 10.14). Painted in 1977, the mural was created by the artist as a gift to the Bret Harte Elementary School in Hyde Park, which Walker's daughter had attended, and which advocated cross racial cooperation and friendship. Walker's mural is

▼ **10.14** William Walker, *Childhood Is Without Prejudice*, 1977, enamel on concrete, acrylic restoration, approximately 8′ × 35′. Fifty-Sixth Street Metra station underpass, 56th Street and Stony Island Avenue, Hyde Park, Chicago, IL. Restored in 1993 by Olivia Gude and Bernard Williams.

Photo: Chicago Public Art Group.

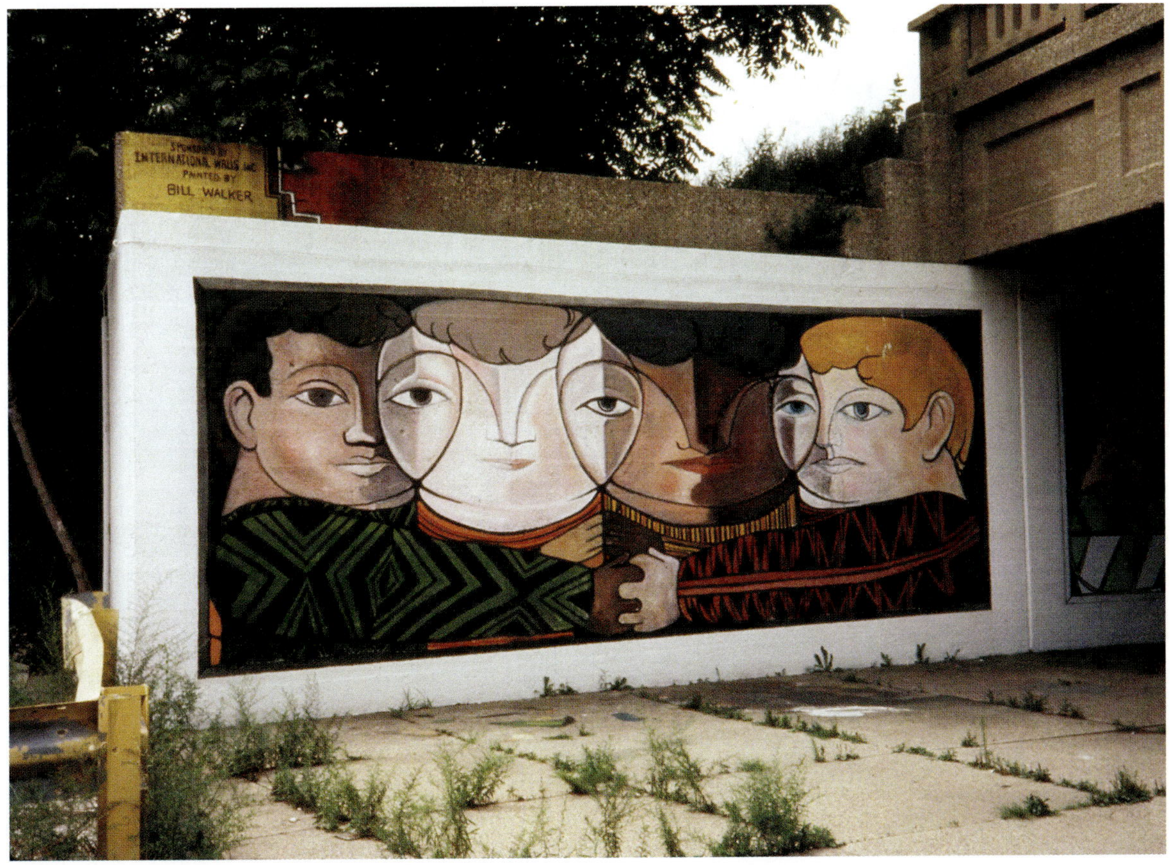

marked by monumentality and reductive forms that reflect the influence of *los tres grandes*. Walker's trademark use of overlapping figures and chevron patterns combines with Mexican-inspired elements to create a commanding visual statement.

In 1980, Walker became the first African-American artist to complete a **Percent for Art** commission for the City of Chicago: *Reaching Children, Touching People* at the Altgeld Garden Center for early childhood care and learning on East 132nd Street (whitewashed in 2005). This coup was soon followed by a major retrospective of nearly four dozen of Walker's paintings and drawings, *Images of Conscience: The Art of Bill Walker*, hosted by Chicago State University in 1984. The works portrayed Walker's observations of African-American urban life in the 1970s and early 1980s. They depicted inner-city violence, drug abuse, and crime in a bleak and disheartening manner. The show's content drew severe criticism from the black community, who felt that the artist had misrepresented them. Walker, however, felt that exposing the rampant crime, poverty, and oppressive conditions of disenfranchised African-American communities was a way to draw attention to the need for socioeconomic reform. Although many venues rejected the controversial exhibition, eventually the Vaughn Cultural Center in St. Louis and the Paul Robeson Cultural Center at Pennsylvania State University both hosted the show.

The streets of Chicago have served as the home for much of Walker's work, although only a few of his iconic murals have survived the years. Walker's final mural was completed at 47th and Champlain Avenue in honor of Harold Washington, Chicago's first black mayor, who died in office in 1987.

Calvin B. Jones and Mitchell Caton

The dedication of AfriCOBRA artists like Walker to murals as a communal art form sparked a mural renaissance that has lasted into the 21st century. Two of the most prolific artists were CPAG members Calvin B. Jones (1934–2010) and his collaborator Mitchell Caton (1931–1998). Jones was born and raised in Chicago and began winning art prizes in primary and secondary school. He won a four-year scholarship to the SAIC, where he studied painting, drawing, and illustration. After receiving his BFA in 1957, Jones's work was included in the 1958 juried *Chicago Artists Exhibition* at the Art Institute. Subsequently, Jones moved to Kansas City to head the Hallmark Greeting Cards advertising division and to establish his own graphic design firm.

A few years later, Jones returned to Chicago to work for the historic Vince Cullers advertising firm—the first major black-owned ad firm in the United States—and for John Plain & Company, which produced a gift and home goods catalog similar to the Sears catalog. By the mid-1960s, Jones had become an accomplished artist and designer, despite the fact that he had developed a visual disorder known as keratoconus. Refusing to allow his hampered vision to stymie his career, Jones worked in the advertising and graphic design fields until 1970, when he became director of Chicago's alternative AFAM Gallery Studio and Cultural Center. With his codirector and fellow muralist Alfred Jackson Tyler (1933–2011), who had also trained at the SAIC, Jones operated one of the city's few exhibition spaces for black artists.

Jones's creative collaborator, Mitchell Caton, was born in Arkansas and also won a college art scholarship to the University of Little Rock. After graduating, Caton traveled first to New York to take classes at the Art Students League and then to Chicago to enroll at the SAIC. He paid for his studies with a day job as a postal worker. In 1969, Caton met Walker and assisted him in repainting sections of the *Wall of Respect* that had been damaged by fire. In 1970 Caton joined CPAG, where he met Jones. By the mid-1970s, Jones and Caton were collaborating on murals in Chicago, Detroit, and Atlanta. The two worked together from 1976 to 1987. Jones conceptualized the compositions and painted the figures and portraits, and Caton painted the abstract design elements.

The first Jones-Caton Chicago mural, *A Time to Unite*, was restored by CPAG in 2003 and is located at 41st and Drexel Avenue (Figure 10.15). Painted to coincide with the U.S. Bicentennial, the mural depicts a massive stone sundial and the title, "A Time to Unite" in bright yellow shadow block letters, a directive to African Americans to reinvest in sociopolitical and cultural unity. Also portrayed are a black family, farmworkers, schoolchildren, tenement buildings, jazz musicians, traditional African drummers, and a black cyborg composed of human flesh and the inner mechanisms of a ticking clock. Uniting these narrative elements are chevron, stripe, and Nigerian ***kente* cloth** patterns. The mural was completed with the collaboration of a third artist, Justine DeVan (b. 1937), who is renowned for her own 1977 mural *Black Women Emerging*, located at 41st Street and Cottage Grove (see Chapter 11).

▼ **10.15** Calvin Bell Jones, Mitchell Caton, and Justine Preshé DeVan, *A Time to Unite*, 1976, restored 2003, oil on concrete, restored with acrylic, 10′ × 40′. Forty-First Street and Drexel Avenue, Chicago, IL.

Photo: Chicago Public Art Group.

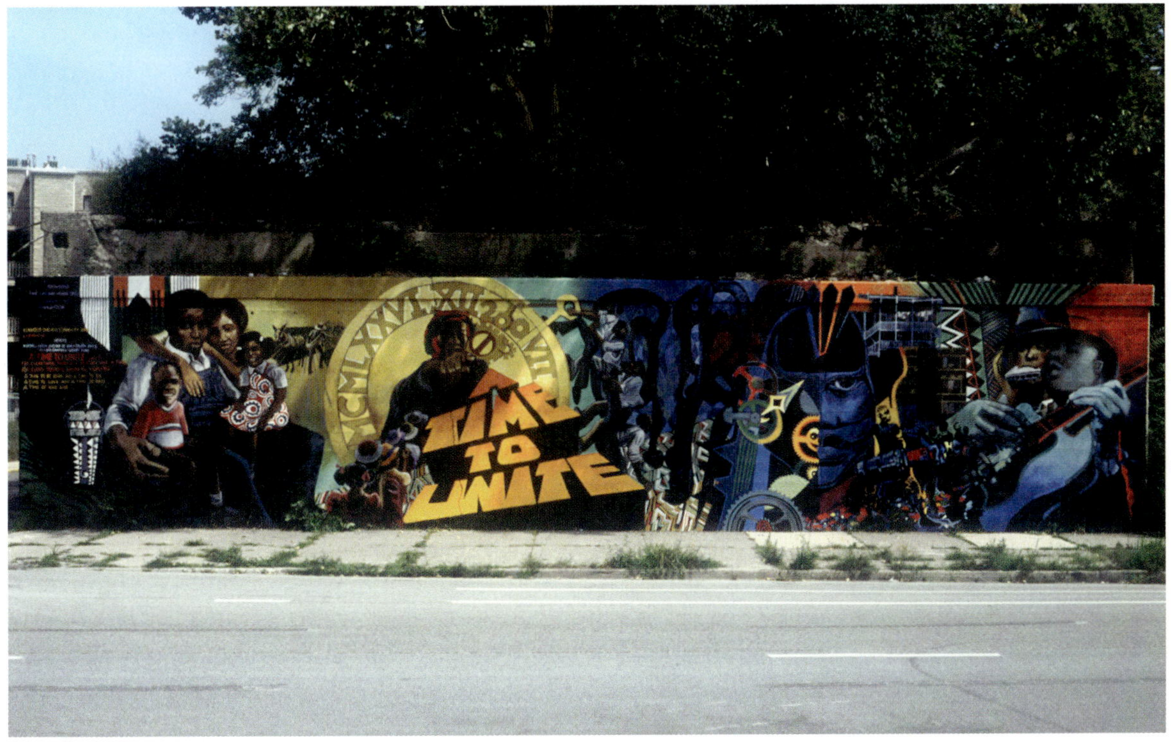

In 1977, Jones exhibited at FESTAC in Lagos. That same year, he had a one man-show at the SSCAC, with which he remained affiliated for 40 years as an artist-in-residence, exhibitor, and teacher. In the 1980s, Jones had a corneal transplant that restored his sight. Afterward, he shifted from figurative art to abstract mixed-media paintings inspired by West African textile patterns, linguistic symbols, and sculpted masks. These paintings are radiantly hued, intricately composed, and sumptuously textured with added elements such as cowry shells, fabric, and papier mâché. The last of the Jones and Caton murals, *Bright Moments, Memories of the Future*, was a multi-portrait mural of legendary black entertainers that celebrated the 1987 opening of Chicago's New Regal Theater. Ailing from a complex of health problems, Jones relocated to the San Francisco area in 2003, where he lived until his death. His last public mural (digitally enlarged panels of six of his paintings) was installed at Chicago's 55th Street Metra station in 2009. Shortly after Jones's passing, in 2011 and 2012 the SSCAC and the Left of Center Gallery in Las Vegas mounted consecutive memorial exhibits of his art.

AGITPROP ART

The term "agitprop" combines two concepts—agitation and propaganda—and refers to art that promotes a very explicit political message. Derived from an early 20th-century Russian term, "agitprop" could be applied, to varying degrees, to the entire Black Arts Movement. However, it is used here to describe art that is exceptionally and deliberately confrontational.

Dana C. Chandler, Jr.

Massachusetts native Dana C. Chandler, Jr. (a.k.a. Akin Duro; b. 1941) is considered one of the most political artists of the Black Arts Movement. His art has been aptly described as "provocative and blatant." Using his art as a protest forum, Chandler spent a lifetime campaigning for racial, gender, and socioeconomic parity as an international speaker and exhibitor.

While still a teenager, Chandler worked with the NAACP and several other civil rights groups. He also won multiple national awards—including the first Boston Technical High School's Annual Art Award in 1959—for his socially engaged art. Chandler attended Massachusetts College of Art (MassArt), graduating with a BS degree in art education in 1967. Chandler later taught at MassArt, as well as at Simmons College from 1971 until his retirement in 2004. Like his art, Chandler's teaching style was rooted in the black experience. He taught from an Afrocentric rather than Eurocentric vantage point.

In the 1960s, Chandler witnessed brazen acts of police brutality (including the beating of a pregnant Boston woman) that compelled him to embrace the militant tenets of the Black Power Movement. Chandler produced pointed works of protest art that became the subject of a 1967 solo show entitled *Black Power Revolution in Art*. His works graphically condemned the war in Vietnam, President Lyndon Johnson, race riots, and racism. At the Boston NAACP's national convention that year, Chandler was named the chapter's Man of the Year. By 1968, he had achieved such notoriety that his art was included in exhibits at Brandeis University and the Studio Museum, and, in

1970 and 1971, at the Boston Museum of Fine Arts and Smith-Mason Gallery in Washington, D.C.

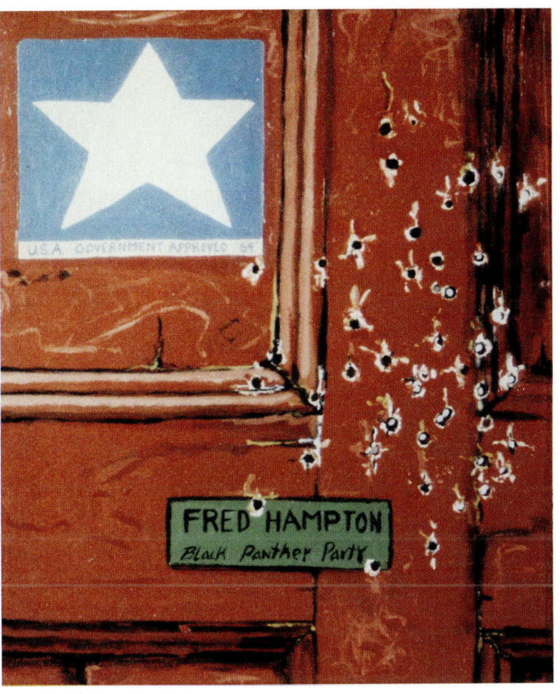

▲ **10.16** Dana C. Chandler, Jr., *Fred Hampton's Door (Hampton Memorial; The Door)*, 1974, acrylic on particleboard, 24″ × 36″.

In 1973, the artist's Boston studio in South End was robbed and vandalized, which prompted Chandler to move to an abandoned factory on the grounds of Northeastern University in the Roxbury neighborhood. Chandler approached university officials about using the space as a studio and establishing himself there as an artist-in-residence. The college agreed and designated 8,000 square feet on the second floor of the building as an artist's residency space. This initiative developed over the next five years into the African American Master Artist-in-Residence Program (AAMARP). Under Chandler's direction, the entire warehouse of some 40,000 square feet was reconfigured into a series of artists' studios, a gallery, a community workshop, and meeting and performance spaces. In 1978, the program was inaugurated with a dozen local artists-in-residence, including Allan Rohan Crite (1910–2007). Chandler served as AAMARP codirector (along with James Reed, associate dean of criminal justice) for more than a decade. He structured the program so that students and the public could have ready access to the artists' studios to observe them at work, participate in art workshops, and discuss their art. Artists were supported, in part, by university stipends and were permitted long-term residencies.

Creatively, the 1970s was an intensely productive time for Chandler. He launched the decade with his iconic *Fred Hampton's Door* (Figure 10.16). For this multimedia piece, the artist shot live ammunition through painted wood to create real bullet holes. The work memorialized the scandalous 1969 shooting by FBI agents and Chicago police officers of Black Panther leader Fred Hampton (1948–69) through his apartment door, reportedly as he slept. Referencing Hampton's spilled blood as well as the American flag, Chandler painted the "door" red and painted a white star in a blue square in the upper-left corner. A nameplate reading "Fred Hampton, Black Panther Party" identifies the door for viewers. Although Hampton evidently survived the initial shots fired through the door, he was reportedly executed immediately thereafter with two shots to the head by police.

Chandler was a dedicated muralist as well. He created political murals throughout the Boston area, often working with fellow artist and poet Gary Ames Rickson (b. 1942). Among these were *Stokely and Rap: Freedom and Self Defense*, which paid homage to SNCC and Black Power Movement activists Stokely Carmichael (a.k.a. Kwame Ture; 1941–98) and H. Rap Brown (a.k.a. Jamil Abdullah Al-Amin; b. 1943). Another was Chandler's 1972 *Knowledge Is Power, Stay in School*, which advocated the importance of education for African Americans in their quest for racial equality. More recently, in the 1990s, Chandler initiated an ongoing monochromatic print series on the history of human violence, including themes of world war, enslavement, genocide, and brutality against women. The series draws attention on a global scale to inhumane atrocities that have occurred in such places as Eastern Europe, the Middle East, and Africa.

In the 21st century, Chandler used the medium of installation art to address issues of economic oppression, international worker exploitation, and out-of-control consumerism in the West. In 2011, Chandler became the host of a weekly public radio program called *Blues Nation*, which airs on KGLP—a radio station at the University of New Mexico, Gallup, where the artist currently resides—and which gives him an opportunity to indulge his love of jazz and the blues; he also continues to paint.

Joe Overstreet

Joe Overstreet (b. 1933) works mainly in the genres of Abstract Expressionism and hard-edge painting. However, his abstractions, particularly in the 1960s and 1970s, often have political import. Overstreet is an intensely intellectual artist with myriad interests in geometry, chemistry, music, aviation, East Indian philosophy, Native American totem and sand paintings, and West African, pre-Colombian, and Egyptian art and architecture, which have influenced his painting over more than 60 years. Of African and Native American descent (his grandfather walked the Trail of Tears), Overstreet grew up in the Deep South. To escape racial hostilities in Mississippi, his family moved to the San Francisco Bay Area in 1941 when the artist was eight. After graduating high school in 1951, Overstreet attended the Oakland School of Arts and Crafts until 1954, where he studied with Nathan Oliveira (1928–2010), an exponent of the **Bay Area Figurative Movement**. Next, Overstreet attended the California School of Fine Arts, where he studied alongside Bay Area figurative abstractionist Richard Diebenkorn (1922–93) and Abstract Expressionist Clyfford Still (1904–80).

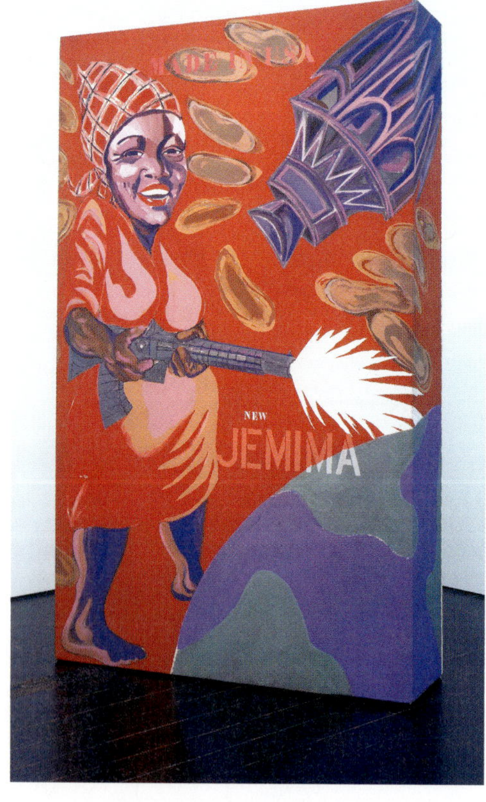

▼ **10.17** Joe Overstreet, *The New Jemima*, 1964, 1970, acrylic on fabric over plywood construction, $102\frac{3}{8}'' \times 60\frac{3}{4}'' \times 17\frac{1}{4}''$.
The Menil Collection, Houston, TX. Photo: Paul Hester.

Overstreet spent seven years in the 1950s as a merchant seaman. When not traveling, he worked out of his studio on Grant Avenue and became an integral part of the beat scene at North Beach, where one of his mentors, artist Sargent Johnson (see Chapter 6), also lived. During these years, Overstreet created paintings inspired by Hard-Edge painter Frank Stella and Abstract Expressionist Willem de Kooning, and he exhibited his paintings at small local galleries and cultural venues. In 1958, Overstreet moved to New York City, settling in the Bowery. He spent his time with newfound artist friends Bearden, Woodruff, de Kooning, Pop artist Larry Rivers (1923–2002), and the Cedar Bar crowd, and visiting the Metropolitan Museum.

In the 1960s, Overstreet began to create Abstract Expressionist and Pop Art–style works of social protest. One of his best-known paintings is the Pop image *The New Jemima* (Figure 10.17). Painted in psychedelic hues, the larger-than-life-size canvas portrays the iconic Aunt Jemima from the pancake box, toting a machine gun that fires on the earth and sends pancakes flying. This tongue-in-cheek image fuses Neo-Dada humor with black liberation politics, as the once-docile maid becomes lethal. Overtly figurative paintings such as *New Aunt Jemima* are, however, rare for the artist, who prefers abstraction.

Overstreet experimented with shaped and unstretched canvases in the 1960s and 1970s, inspired by mandalas, tantric imagery, and Islamic, Mali, Benin, and Aztec patterns and forms. Other impetuses came from mathematical systems such as those used in the construction of the ancient pyramids at Giza, which helped to anchor his dense and weblike abstractions. In New York in 1975, Overstreet met and married Corrine Jennings (b. 1940), daughter of WPA artist and Woodruff protégé Wilmer Jennings (1910–90). That year, the couple cofounded the nonprofit Kenkeleba House/Wilmer Jennings Gallery, a major New York multisite venue for minority visual and performance artists, which the couple continues to direct today. Since its opening, Overstreet has maintained his New York studio above the gallery, which he helped to construct.

The 1980s saw the influence of jazz on Overstreet's work, particularly the *Storyville* series, which paid homage to the New Orleans red-light district, where jazz is believed to have originated. Fluctuating between the painterly and the geometric, Overstreet's later works are marked by color harmonies and allusions to depth within the nonobjective environment.

David Hammons

Since the late 1960s, David Hammons (b. 1943) has created art that centers on racial injustice. In his 1970 *Injustice Case*, Hammons framed the profile of a body (his own), bound and gagged, with an American flag (see chapter-opening image). The work is a graphic reference to the gagging of Black Panther Bobby Seale (b. 1936) during his trial for conspiracy and for inciting a riot. Seale repeatedly rose from his seat and vocally protested the trial and the charges against him, which prompted the judge to order him bound and gagged, and to give him a sentence of four years for contempt. The ghostly silhouette in *Injustice Case* is the result of a **body print** made with powdered pigment and margarine, a technique Hammons often used in the 1970s. His representation expresses the intensity of Seale's anger, through the physical stress of the pose and the constraining quality of the clothing and bindings. By including an American flag border, Hammons highlighted the inequities of the American justice system.

Raised in Springfield and Chicago, Hammons studied in Los Angeles at Chouinard Art Institute (CalArts) from 1966 to 1968 and at Otis Art Institute from 1968 to 1972. A witness to the 1965 Watts riots, he first began creating his now-celebrated agitprop art in Los Angeles. He relocated permanently to New York City in 1974 and continued his studies at Parsons. Following the creation of his flag-framed body print series, Hammons began to incorporate American flag imagery into his art using actual fabric banners. Hammons's now-legendary red, black, and green *Africa American Flag* has become one of his best-known works. When it was hung outside MoMA's avant-garde PS1 space in Queens in 1991 on the occasion of the artist's retrospective there, entitled *Rousing the Rabble*, the flag created controversy among some citizens, who felt that it was an act of desecration to substitute the colors of the Black Liberation Movement and the UNIA for the red, white, and blue of the American flag. Hammons's controversial art won him some of the art world's highest honors, including the 1989–90 Rome Prize to study at the American Academy and a 1991 MacArthur Foundation prize, nicknamed the "Genius Award." Hammons's art has been exhibited and collected by literally hundreds of museums and galleries in the United States and around the world.

Summary

The Black Arts Movement developed in response to the struggle for racial equality that raged in the 1960s and 1970s, embodied in the Civil Rights and Black Liberation Movements. Black artists merged the look of Pop Art, patterns inspired by African textiles, and the iconography of civil unrest to create forceful agitprop imagery. Artists also organized a variety of groups, such as Spiral, WEUSI, OBAC, AfriCOBRA, and the BECC, to achieve a number of goals: protesting social injustice, integrating museum art collections, conceiving a shared visual program or black aesthetic, and bringing art to disenfranchised communities through mural painting and community outreach. While thus engaged, African-American artists also strove to strike a balance between artistic and political concerns.

Key Terms

Afrocentric: refers to that which emphasizes African and African-American culture

agitprop: art that emphasizes a political agenda

alternative space: a public location for the exhibition of art other than a conventional museum or gallery

Bay Area Figurative Movement: an art movement in San Francisco in the 1950s and 1960s that comprised figurative art that was a direct reaction against Abstract Expressionism

black nationalism: an anti-integrationist philosophy popular in the 1960s and 1970s that promoted African-American economic independence and the formation of a separate African-American state

body print: an artwork created by using the human body and pigment to impress an image onto paper or canvas

chevron: a line or form in the shape of a *V*

Chicago Mural Movement: a movement centered in Chicago in the late 1960s and 1970s during which trained artists partnered with low-income community members to create outdoor wall paintings to beautify neighborhoods and engage in social protest or commentary

graffiti: unsanctioned informal urban murals that are often expressive and abstract in form and includes elements of text

happening: a public art performance that incorporates audience participation

kente cloth: a colorful silk and cotton fabric created from interwoven strips of geometrically patterned cloth by the Akan people of Ghana
Percent for Art: legislation requiring that 1% of the budget of a government-funded building be spent on public art
screen-printing: a printmaking technique wherein an image is painted onto mesh fabric using thinned glue; and ink is pushed through the glue-free areas onto paper or other surfaces using a squeegee; differs from silk-screening in that the mesh fabric is a synthetic or other nonsilk fabric
syncopation: placing emphasis on sounds or forms that would otherwise be subordinate elements in work of art or musical composition

Questions for Further Study and Discussion

1. Discuss and debate the validity of Raymond Saunders's statement:

   Some angry artists are using their art as political tools, instead of vehicles of free expression. An artist who is always harping upon resistance, discrimination, opposition, besides being a drag, eventually plays right into the hands of the politicians he claims to despise—and is held there, unwittingly (and witlessly) reviving slavery in another form. For the artist, this is aesthetic atrophy.

2. Debate whether and how black nationalism differs from segregation.
3. What was the value of alternative spaces to black artists?
4. What philosophical differences plagued the Spiral group? Debate these differing attitudes.
5. In addition to creating art, discuss the various ways that African-American artists contributed to the Civil Rights and Black Power Movements.
6. Several Black Arts Movement groups took issue with museum exhibition practices. What advances were these groups able to make to improve the situation?
7. Define the black aesthetic.
8. What was the purpose and significance of the *Wall of Respect*?
9. Research other important artists not discussed or mentioned only briefly in this chapter such as Sylvia Abernathy (b. 1939), Abdullah Aziz (b. 1932), Alexander "Skunder" Boghossian (1937–2003), Bernie Casey (b. 1939), Taiwo Shabazz Duvall (b. 1933), Eugene Eda (b. 1939), Felrath Hines (1913–93), Alvin Hollingsworth (1928–2000), John Miller Howard (1908–80), Bill Howell (1942–75), Wilmer Jennings (1910–90), Winston Kennedy (b. 1944), Carolyn Lawrence (b. 1940), Samella Lewis (b. 1924), Tom Lloyd (1921–1996), Ed (Edward) Love (1936–1999), Otto Neals (b. 1930), Norman Parish (1937–2013), Okeo Pyatt (b. 1942), Gary Ames Rickson (b. 1942), Malkia Roberts (b. 1927), Merton Simpson (1928–2013), Vincent Smith (1929–2004), Alfred Jackson Tyler (1933–2011), and James Yeargans (1908–72), and photographers Billy Abernathy (b. 1938), Darrel Cowherd (b. 1940), and Roy Lewis (b. 1937).

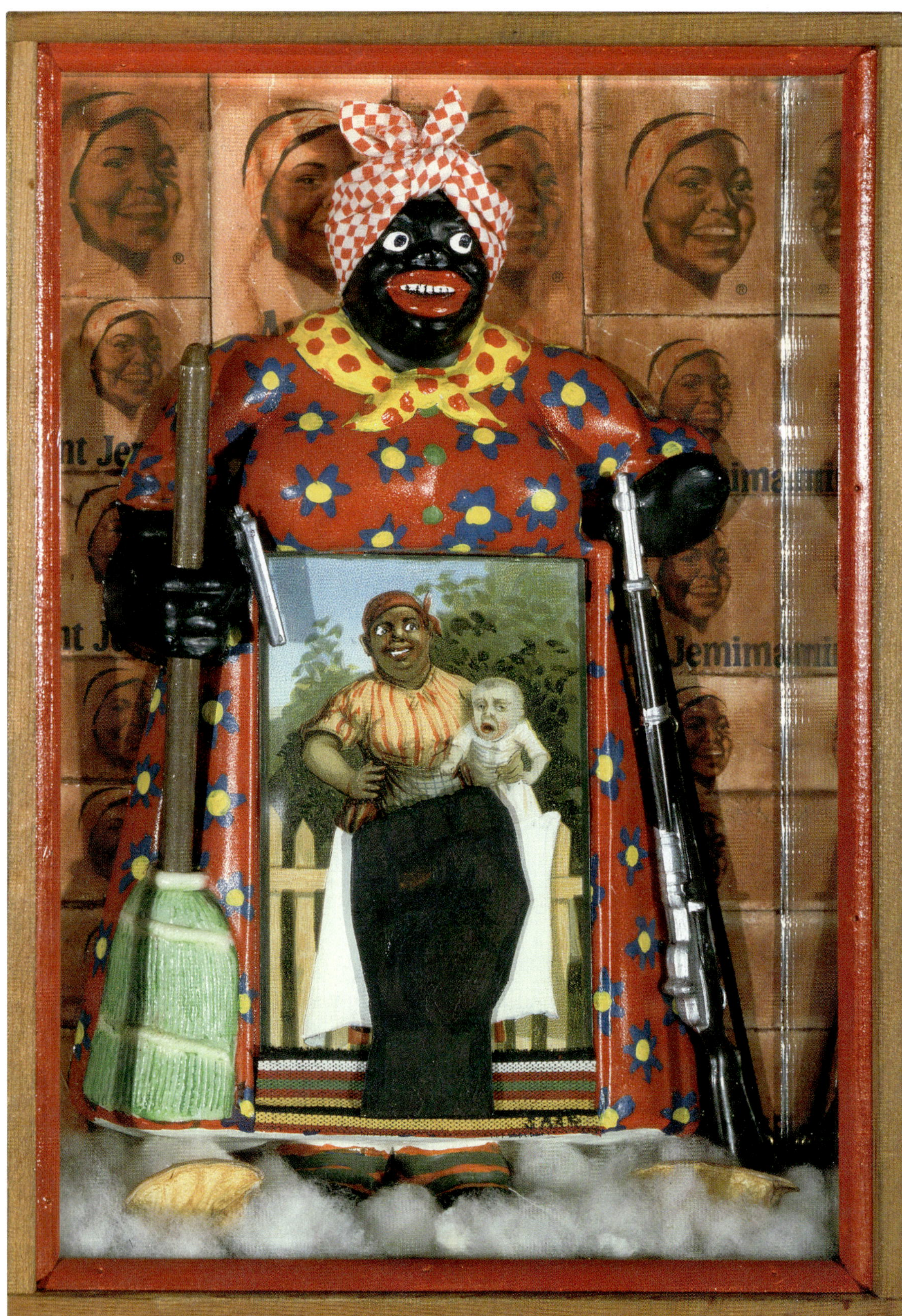

BLACK FEMINIST ART: A CRISIS OF RACE AND SEX

11

Just as the Black Arts Movement emerged from the black power crusade, so the Feminist Art Movement sprang from the broader Women's Movement, which itself was sparked by two significant events. The first was the publication in 1963 of National Organization of Women (NOW) founder Betty Friedan's book *The Feminine Mystique*, which critiqued society's repression of, and discrimination against, women and charted their changing social roles. The second was the passing in 1964 of the Civil Rights Act, which banned sex and race discrimination. By the early 1970s, when the Supreme Court legalized abortion, perceptions of women, their prerogatives, and their status in society had radically changed. In response to this new outlook, women artists began to create work that better reflected their new social identities. Coming together in a vast array of formal and informal coalitions, a new generation of women artists formed the core of the Feminist Art Movement.

Leading feminist art critic Lucy Lippard (b. 1937) defined the feminist art campaign "as a revolutionary strategy and way of life more so than an aesthetic or stylistic phenomenon." The "revolutionary strategies" of the Feminist Art Movement were not unlike those of the Black Arts Movement: they were designed to bring women artists to the attention of museums, historians, gallerists, and collectors. In 1970, the Ad Hoc Women Artists' Committee was founded in New York by Lippard and others to address the limited inclusion of women in the Whitney Museum's exhibitions and permanent collections. Using strategies similar to those of the Black Arts Movement—speaking with the press, letter writing and telephone campaigns, and picketing—within a year, Ad Hoc delegates had persuaded the Whitney to increase the percentage of women in their annual and biennial shows from 5 percent to 22 percent. They also convinced the Whitney to add two women of color—renowned Neo-Dada artist Betye Saar (discussed later in this chapter) and sculptor Chase-Riboud (see Chapter 9)—to their 1971 annual. That same year, the Los Angeles Council of Women Artists launched a similar and equally successful campaign against the Los Angeles County Museum of Art (LACMA) for its underrepresentation of women.

Social attitudes about women were another concern for feminist artists, who routinely had to work harder than men to achieve the same level of approbation and success. However, because society expected them to be mothers and caretakers of the home, those women who put their art careers before their domestic responsibilities were subject to social censure—and sometimes guilt-motivated self-censure. The Feminist Art Movement strove

◀ Betye Saar, *The Liberation of Aunt Jemima*, 1972, mixed-media assemblage, 11¾″ × 8″ × 2¾″.

Collection of University of California, Berkeley Art Museum; purchased with the aid of funds from the National Endowment for the Arts (selected by the Committee for the Acquisition of Afro-American Art). Courtesy of Michael Rosenfeld Gallery LLC, New York, NY. Photo: Joshua Nefsky.

to change this thinking. The most celebrated essay on the subject was art historian Linda Nochlin's (b. 1931) article "Why Have There Been No Great Women Artists," published in *ARTnews* in 1971. Nochlin's thesis adroitly analyzed the fundamental gender chauvinism of Western society and the long history of impediments—such as lack of access to art schools, the demands of childrearing, and social taboos and restrictions—that had prevented women from becoming "great artists" with the same frequency as men. Her argument also successfully countered patriarchal claims that women artists were less talented than their male counterparts and thus less deserving of attention.

Another goal of the Feminist Art Movement was developing a plan to rectify the absence of women artists from the history of art. In 1969, Women Artists in Revolution (WAR) was formed by a coalition of women who had defected from the ranks of the Art Workers Coalition (AWC; see Chapter 10). The AWC, they observed, was monopolized by a white male membership and was only tangentially concerned with women's causes. WAR tasked itself with identifying important artworks by women and researching and writing history, theory, and criticism of women's art.

A CRISIS OF RACE AND SEX

Black women who wished to take part in the Feminist Art Movement were faced with a dilemma. As blacks, they had racial issues to contend with that were being addressed by the Black Arts Movement. As women, they had gender discrimination concerns that were being addressed by the Feminist Art Movement. Deciding which group best suited them was a difficult task, because both movements tended to marginalize the specific concerns of black women. The Feminist Art Movement was composed mainly of white, middle-class women who had little interest in art-world racism. Betye Saar, working on the West Coast, noted a conspicuous lack of support for African-American women artists from their Euro-American colleagues when she remarked, "It was as if we were invisible. . . . The white women did not support [us]." And New York artist Emma Amos declined to join a consortium of Greenwich Village feminists because, as she explained, "From what I heard of feminist discussions . . . the experiences of black women of *any* class were left out."

Unfortunately, to ally with the Black Arts Movement presented similar problems for black women. The Black Arts Movement was endemically **patriarchal**. Historical texts, museum collections, and exhibitions of black art mainly featured men. Its organizations, such as AfriCOBRA and Spiral, were male dominated. In fact, Faith Ringgold (discussed later in this chapter) was flatly refused when she asked Bearden if she could join the group. Spiral's only woman member was Emma Amos, a college student who had been "hosted" into the group by her professor and mentor, Hale Woodruff. Unlike Ringgold, who was an outspoken political artist, Amos "knew her place"; she did not interfere in the group's activities. Those women who chose black power over feminism were compelled to accept and comply with their own marginalization.

Even though black women were being marginalized by both the black and feminist art equations, they had to choose. The challenge of this dilemma was fittingly articulated by Ringgold, who asked, "When there is a group for blacks and a group for women, where do I go?" Literary critic Linda Dittmar qualified the difficulty black women artists faced in negotiating the treacherous territory between race and sex as a problem of conflicting allegiances. Loyalty to one's race and class motivated women to support their male counterparts. According to Dittmar, loyalty to one's gender, however, made allegiances with men problematic. Nevertheless, a courageous contingent of black women artists joined the rank and file of the Feminist Art Movement and grappled with race and gender censure simultaneously, in pursuit of their goals.

WSABAL AND THE WWA

Black women artists decided to create their own professional support groups: for example, the group WSABAL (Women, Students and Artists for Black Art Liberation), whose formation was prompted by a protest action of New York Art Strike Against Racism, War, and Repression.

Launched in 1970 by Minimalist artist Robert Morris (b. 1931) and several of the more militant members of the AWC, Art Strike was initially galvanized to protest the U.S. bombing of Cambodia and the May 1970 mortal police shooting of five unarmed students who were protesting this action at Kent State University in Ohio and at Jackson State University in Mississippi. That month, Morris forced the closure of his one-man exhibit at the Whitney Museum as a way to "underscore the need . . . to shift priorities . . . from art making and viewing to unified action within the art community against . . . repression, war and racism." Hard-edge painter Frank Stella followed suit with the closing of his exhibit at the MoMA. Their actions were designed to increase public awareness of American military atrocities and to pressure museum board members such as the influential Rockefeller and Whitney families to lobby the U.S. government to end its military campaigns. Art Strike members next threatened to withdraw from the prestigious international Venice Biennale art show and to mount a counter-biennale in New York. Their plans for the replacement show, however, excluded minorities and women, despite Art Strike's call for an end to racism and oppression.

Frustrated by their exclusion from even the more radical arts groups such as Art Strike, Ringgold, her daughters, and several other black women artists formed WSABAL to give women of color a voice in the art world. In 1971, WSABAL members persuaded art dealer Nigel Jackson to schedule a showing of their work at his Acts of Art Gallery in Greenwich Village. The exhibit was titled *Where We At, Black Women Artists, 1971*. It showcased more than a dozen black women artists, including Ringgold, Kay Brown, and Dindga McCannon (discussed later in this chapter).

The show's vernacular title *Where We At* was chosen to engage the working-class black community and to frame the artists as integral members of that community. To further emphasize their roles as community members, participating artists prepared home-cooked food for the reception, feeding the attendees as they might their own families. Arguably the first group in U.S. history dedicated solely to professional black women artists, the *Where We At* exhibit was a local and critical success. According to McCannon, "We had a unique opening . . . and it became a media event. The press came; everybody wanted to interview us. All of a sudden [black] women artists were discovered." The success of the show prompted participants to form their own cooperative, named for the show, Where We At, Inc. (WWA).

Headquartered in Brooklyn and led by Kay Brown, the WWA sought to support and empower black women artists to breach the color and gender lines that barred them from ready access to the art world. WWA also worked to bring art to disenfranchised minority communities, a goal they shared with the Black Arts Movement. Like the Feminist Art Movement, WWA members sought professional parity with their male counterparts. But they were as much concerned with racial discrimination in the art world as with gender bias. They did not wish to withdraw their support from black men in their struggles for professional equity with whites.

The WWA partnered with the National Conference of Women in Visual Arts (NCWVA), a Washington, D.C.–based forum, to mount integrated women's art exhibits at various venues in downtown Manhattan in 1972. However, WWA members were disturbed by the flagrant anti-male tenor of the white women artists' works, and by their lack of interest in racial issues. WWA artists preferred the iconography of positive representations of the black family, images of cross gender cooperation and relationships, and themes of civil rights, African and African-American culture and history, and, most importantly, authentic self-portrayals of black women unmarred by prevailing stereotypes. The WWA mounted a group show later that year, *Cookin' and Smokin'*, at the Weusi-Nyumba Ya Sanaa Gallery. Participants included McCannon, Vivian Browne, Ann Tanksley (b. 1934), Ringgold, Carole Byard (b. 1941), Gilbert Coker (see Chapter 12), and half a dozen other members.

Most of the group's efforts during the 1970s were directed toward providing community-based services such as art workshops, youth mentorships, local exhibits, lectures, and art classes. They brought these programs to schools, hospitals, prisons, and community centers. Key among their projects was a 1975 colloquium on black women artists held at Medgar Evers College (CUNY), where Brown served on the humanities faculty and as supervisor of the visual arts programs. The conference was held on the occasion of International Women's Year. Other WWA efforts included a 1975 panel discussion hosted by the Brooklyn Museum and a series of prison workshops in 1978 at New York state's Bedford Hills Correctional Facility for Women and the Arthur Kill Correctional Facility for Men.

The WWA continued its activities into the 1980s. A key project was the publication of *"Where We At": Black Women Artists: A Tapestry of Many Fine Threads* in 1982. By this time, the group had swelled to nearly 40 members. The use of the word "tapestry" in the title was a metaphor for the variety of women and aesthetic approaches within a unified coalition. It also served as an allusion to fabric and textiles as high art media, rather than as "folksy" (and thus undervalued) materials only used by homemakers for quilts and clothes. In 1985, the group collaborated with the male artists of WEUSI to mount *Close Connections*, a cross gender exhibit held in Midtown Manhattan. The following year, a WWA jury chose a selection of male artists, among them Lorenzo Pace (see Chapter 12), to share the stage with them in the show *Joining Forces: 1 + 1 = 3* at Brooklyn's Muse Community Museum. This exhibit was truly collaborative in that men and women artists paired together to create a single work of art. Each couple collaborated over several months in what the WWA described as a "platonic mating ritual." The show's title signified the creation of an art "child" by various artist-couples, the individual outcomes of which constituted a marriage of two artists' visions.

Still going strong, the WWA celebrated its 25th anniversary in 1995. Long aligned with WEUSI, Kay Brown collaborated with WEUSI leader Olugebefola on the text for the catalog of a joint exhibit held at the Jamaica Center for the Arts in Queens, New York. In 1999, the Schomburg Center mounted the exhibit *Black New York Artists of the 20th Century*, which included WWA artists Brown, Ringgold, McCannon, Byard, Onaway K. Millar (1919–2008), and others. Over the course of its existence, the WWA supported the careers of dozens of artists. Key among these were, in addition to those already mentioned, Catti (Catherine James; b. 1940), Robin Holder (b. 1952), Viola Burley Leak (b. 1944), and Coreen Simpson (b. 1942).

BLACK FEMINIST ARTISTS

Kay Brown

WWA director Kay Brown (1932–2012) was a 1968 BFA graduate of New York's City College (CCNY) and a 1986 MFA graduate of Howard University. She was also a multitalented writer, printmaker, and graphic and fashion designer. Brown joined WEUSI beginning in 1968, becoming one of only two women to belong to WEUSI's 16-artist coterie (the other was McCannon). At WEUSI, Brown was exposed to the idea of a black aesthetic for the first time. Within the nurturing environment of the group, she refined her skills as a painter, printmaker, and multimedia artist, adopting WEUSI's Afrocentric approach to art. Brown's involvement with WEUSI led to her inclusion in the historic 1968 Brooklyn Museum survey show *Contemporary Afro-American Arts*.

Although Brown felt especially enriched by her WEUSI affiliation, she also desired to connect with a collective specifically dedicated to black women artists, their needs, and their concerns. Much of what she learned and absorbed at WEUSI she brought to the WWA, in particular the community-oriented nature of WEUSI's efforts and its interest in black subject matter, aesthetics, and issues. She also imbued her art with her concerns and experiences as a woman artist. The etching *Sister Alone in a Rented Room*, for example, differs from the artist's prefeminist images (such as the 1968 *Devil and His Game* and the 1969 *Black Soldier*, both of which center on the male protagonists of black liberation) in its focus on a single woman. Presumably the artist, depicted is an isolated figure in drab clothing and similarly dreary surroundings (Figure 11.1). She is seated on a cot and hunched over as if

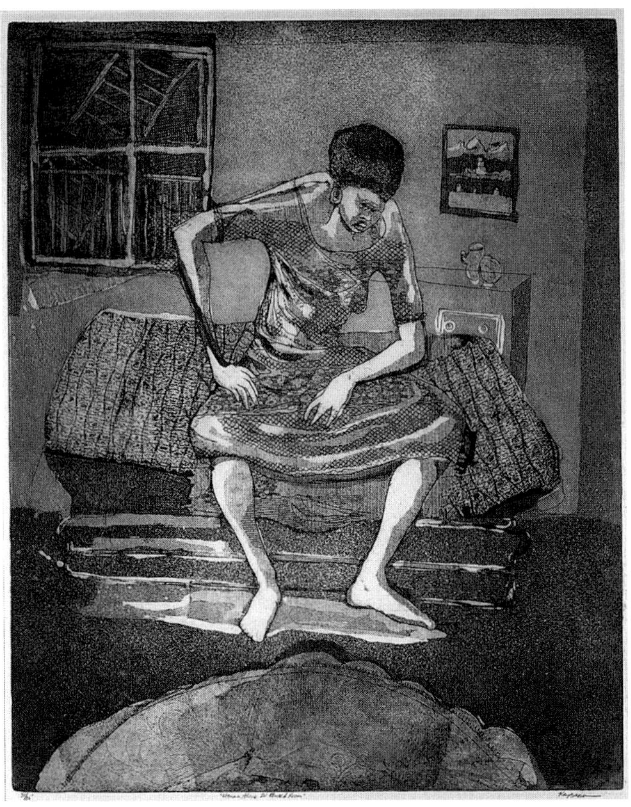

▲ **11.1** Kay Brown, *Sister Alone in a Rented Room*, 1974, etching 30/35, 20″ × 16½″.
Courtesy of the artist.

unable to bear the weight of her personal and professional struggles and her poverty. One is instinctively reminded of Vincent Van Gogh's 1889 *Bedroom at Arles* which likewise exudes a sense of destitution and loneliness.

After the founding of the WWA, Brown continued to express her concern for the civil rights campaign and her solidarity with black male artists by participating in the show *Black Motion*, mounted at New York's Tribal Arts Gallery as part of the SCLC Black Expo in 1972. In this exhibit, Brown shared the stage with WWA members Ringgold, Millar, Camille Billops (b. 1933), and Vivian Browne, as well as with Jacob Lawrence, Benny Andrews, Raymond Saunders, Charles White, Cliff Joseph, Norman Lewis, and members of the Kamoinge Workshop (see Chapter 8).

The following year, when an all-black curatorial jury chose 42 of the most outstanding African-American artists for *Blacks: US: 1973*—a major exhibit at the New York Cultural Center—a significant number of women, including Brown, were selected. Others included WWA members Billops, Browne, and Byard and nonmembers Saar, Marie Johnson Calloway (b. 1920), Howardena Pindell (b. 1943), and Valerie Maynard (b. 1937). Brown maintained an impressive exhibition schedule throughout the 1970s, showing with the WWA and WEUSI. Simultaneously she taught at Medgar Evers College and served as president of the WWA, a post from which she resigned in 1980.

Brown left her teaching position at Medgar Evers in 1989, relocating in the early 1990s to northeastern Washington, D.C. Brown taught art and creative writing throughout the decade, working for several public institutions. In the later 1990s, she was a member of the WPA-inspired Writers Corps, a coalition of service-oriented artists. Brown also authored a young adult novel, *Willy's Summer Dream* (1989), which was inspired by the experiences of Brown's youngest son as an educationally challenged child. Despite her relocation, Brown maintained ties with New York and WEUSI, appearing in the group's shows through the 21st century. Brown was also included in the 2000 retrospective at Cornell University entitled *Blackness in Color: Visual Expressions of the Black Arts*.

Brown spent the last ten years of her life at an historic senior residence in the American River City Park neighborhood of northwestern Washington, D.C. She was something of an artist-in-residence there: she organized museum tours for her neighbors and lectured on black history. Even at the end of her life, Brown was dedicated to improving her community. "People always need more activities to inspire them," she told a reporter a few years before her passing. The year she died, Brown published an article detailing the founding years of the WWA in *Nka: Journal of Contemporary African Art*. It is the most detailed history to date on the group's activities.

Faith Ringgold

Like Brown, WSABAL founder Faith Ringgold (b. 1930) actively engaged in both the Black Arts and Feminist Art Movements. She was born and raised in Harlem, where she attended CCNY, receiving BA and MA degrees in art and education in 1955 and 1959. Ringgold was mentored by American Social Realist artist Robert Gwathmey (1903–88), whose nurturing teaching techniques gave Ringgold the confidence to act on her own artistic impulses. After receiving her BA, Ringgold spent the next two decades teaching art in the New York City public school system, raising her two daughters, and working to make a name for herself in the New York art scene.

Committed to engaging with the Civil Rights Movement, Ringgold contacted Spiral cofounder Bearden and asked to join the group, with which she felt a genuine kinship. However, after reviewing slides of her work, Bearden wrote a letter to Ringgold in which he unfavorably assessed her idiosyncratic painting style. He complained that Ringgold's deployment of a shallow and condensed picture space prevented her figures from "breathing." Although deflated by the rejection, Ringgold persisted in her own distinctive, semiabstract style, which merged figural distortion, compressed space, flat planes of color, and geometric design elements with sociopolitical symbolism. In subsequent years, her art would be celebrated for the very characteristics that had prevented her acceptance into Spiral.

In 1966, Ringgold joined the Spectrum Fine Art Gallery, a cooperative space. In contrast to Spiral, Spectrum included an all-white membership of, for the most part, abstract painters and sculptors. Ringgold's presence was a welcomed way to integrate the gallery and to diversify the group's art offerings. Likewise, Ringgold benefited from Spectrum's policy of affording its artists time and space for solo exhibits. Her first show, in December 1967, showcased her *American People* series, which she had begun in 1963. Composed of depictions of African Americans as uneasy players in a hostile white environment, the nearly two dozen tableaux were graphic distillations of Ringgold's encounters with racial integration, which, although progressing in the 1960s, was still fraught with conflict.

Several key works in the show included images of the American flag, an interest stimulated by the flag paintings of Pop artist Jasper Johns (b. 1930). However, Ringgold felt that his images were "incomplete" because they remained politically neutral and made no reference to the racial, gender, and antiwar protests that had erupted throughout the country. Ringgold joined the many Americans who burned or in some way defaced the flag as an oft-employed, if then illegal, form of political protest. In 1970, Ringgold joined an integrated group of nearly 200 artists in an exhibit titled *The People's Flag Show*, which was installed at the Judson Memorial Church Gallery in Greenwich Village. The participating artists adapted the icon of the flag to express their displeasure with the U.S. offensive in Vietnam and with the oppression of women and minorities at home. Images in the show included Ringgold's *The Flag Is Bleeding*, which portrayed an American flag dripping blood. Kate Millet's (b. 1934) U.S. flag emerging from a toilet and AWC cofounder Alex Gross's (b. 1923) flag-covered penis provided metaphors for the deteriorating state of American politics and the menace of U.S. military chauvinism.

Conceived to challenge flag desecration laws, the show was organized and curated by Ringgold, Belgian arts activist Jean Toche (b. 1932), and Judson Gallery curator Jon Hendricks (b. 1939). All three were members of the AWC, and Toche and Hendricks were also founders of the militant Guerrilla Art Action Group (GAAG). Later nicknamed "the Judson Three," on the closing day of *The People's Flag Show*, they were arrested and jailed on charges of flag desecration. Their plight quickly became an international cause célèbre, and donations to pay for their bail and legal defense poured in. Art world titans, such as Lippard, MoMA director John Hightower, and the Metropolitan Museum's Allon Schoener, testified for the defense, but to no avail. The Judson Three were convicted on May 14, 1971, and each was sentenced to a fine or one month in prison. Ringgold chose the fine.

Ringgold continued her activism in the early 1970s with the creation of a series of Pop and Op Art political posters designed to help raise money for the Black Panther Party's legal defense fund. Selections from this cycle boldly displayed popular Black Panther maxims such as "Free All Political Prisoners," "All Power to the People," and "Free Angela." Her designs incorporated the hallmark colors of the Black Power Movement: red, black, and green. She also worked assiduously with the UBAC to compel MoMA to include black artists in its galleries and was successful in securing two one-man shows for Bearden and Hunt. Ringgold chafed, however, against the idea that the museum would only showcase black men. It was no comfort to her that Bearden, who had earlier rejected her from Spiral, benefited from her politicking. By the early 1970s, Ringgold believed that any arts activism that was not specifically feminist could not effectively serve her needs, and she allied herself with the Feminist Art Movement.

▼ **11.2** Faith Ringgold, *Woman Freedom Now*, from the *Political Poster* series, 1971, cut paper (original) and offset litho, 30″ × 20″.

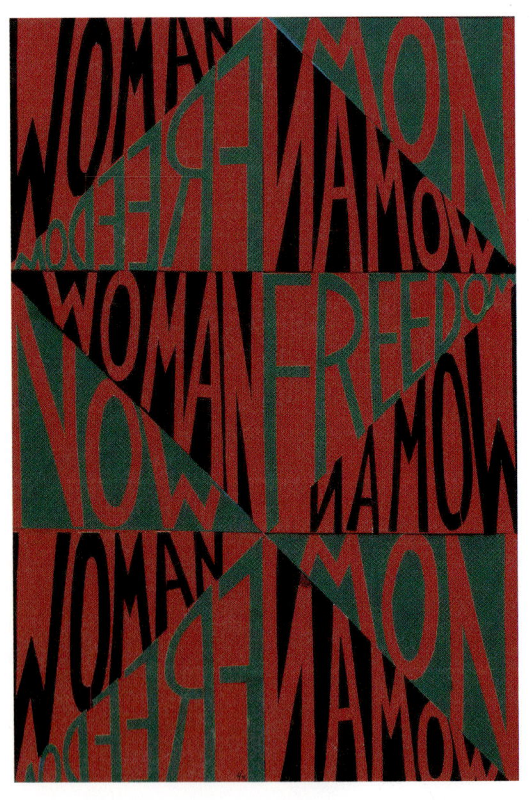

Ringgold's art of the 1970s has been described as **Afrofemcentric**, owing to its consolidation of her interests in both black liberation and women's causes. According to art historian Frieda High, who coined the term, Afrofemcentric art fuses conventional and **alternative media** (especially fabric) and racial and gender motifs. In Ringgold's feminist works, such as her "political poster" *Woman Freedom Now*, she deftly synthesized feminism and black power into a single kaleidoscopic Op Art vision of red, black, and green block letters within a Bakuba chevron textile pattern (Figure 11.2). Amiri Baraka said of *Woman Freedom Now* that it was a "modern classic" because it was one of the first, and one of the very few, political posters designed to address the issue of feminism within the context of black power.

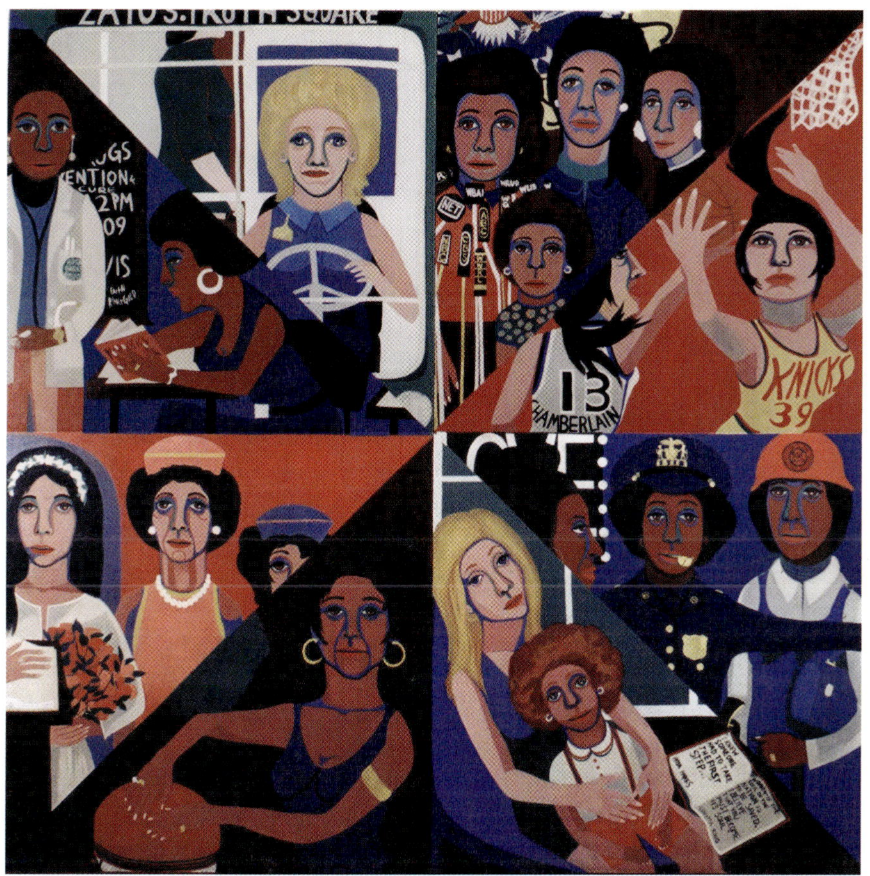

◀ **11.3** Faith Ringgold, *For the Woman's House*, 1971, oil on canvas, 96″ × 96″.

Faith Ringgold © 1971, collection of the Rose M. Singer Center, Rikers Island, New York, NY.

In 1971 Ringgold further expressed her dedication to women's causes, especially those of disenfranchised women, when she painted the mural *For the Woman's House* for the Riker's Island Women's House of Detention (Figure 11.3). The painting depicts a series of women in nontraditional female roles, including a bus driver, priest, basketball star, U.S. president, policewoman, construction worker, and doctor. Each vignette is set within a triangular chevron space inspired by Kongo Bakuba textile patterns and by the prevailing black aesthetic. Each scene was prompted by the women inmates at Riker's, whom Ringgold interviewed to learn which images they would find most inspirational.

The following year, Ringgold created her Tibetan tanka-inspired *Feminist* series. Having seen fabric tankas at the Amsterdam Rijksmuseum while on a tour of Europe that year, Ringgold abandoned the canvas stretcher and began framing her paintings in brocaded textiles, a practice that would mark all her future work. The cloth-framed paintings in the *Feminist* series combined calligraphic landscapes over which the artist inscribed poignant quotes from famous black women, such as Congresswoman Shirley Chisholm (1924–2005), who said: "Of my two handicaps, being female put more obstacles in my path than being black."

For the petite Ringgold, abandoning the stretcher made it possible for her to easily, cheaply, and efficiently pack, store, and ship her paintings. Having a limited income and a modestly sized apartment, creating large-scale paintings on wooden stretchers was a financial and logistical burden for Ringgold. Furthermore, she could not carry large canvases (which were too bulky for her elevator) up 14 flights of stairs to her Harlem apartment without help. The tanka format solved all of these problems and led directly to the "story quilts" for which Ringgold eventually became famous. The story quilts, first conceived in 1980, are paintings and quilts at the same time. After painting a scene—invariably on a feminist or Afrocentric theme—Ringgold adds batting and backing and stitches right through the painting to create the final work of art. Ringgold's approach is referred to as **femmage**, a term coined by renowned feminist artist Miriam (Mimi) Schapiro (b. 1923) to describe art that combines painting and fabric while addressing women's themes. Ringgold's art helped to reconstitute the perception of quilts from "women's work" to high art. Between 1972 (when Ringgold made her first tanka) and 1978, femmage practitioners coalesced to form a significant art movement known as the **Pattern and Decoration Movement**, which gave long-overdue precedence to textile art forms.

Ringgold resigned from her job teaching in the New York City public school system in 1973 to create art full time. She rapidly became the darling of the Feminist Art Movement and was the recipient of many invitations to exhibit and lecture about her art. In 1984 the Studio Museum hosted a 20-year retrospective of Ringgold's art, and the University of California, San Diego appointed her to a professorship, a position she held until her 2002 retirement. In the 1990s, Ringgold's quilts inspired her to create an ongoing series of award-winning children's books. The best known is *Tar Beach* (Crown, 1991), which Ringgold based on her 1988 quilt. In 1994, she published her autobiography, *We Flew over the Bridge*. Ringgold's artworks are today in the collections of virtually every major museum in the country and many in Europe, Asia, and Africa. Her narrative mural of the Harlem of her childhood graces the New York City subway station at 125th Street, not far from where the artist still maintains her studio; and the artist's Anyone Can Fly Foundation, headquartered there, is devoted to bringing the history of African-American art into educational curricula.

▼ **11.4** Dindga McCannon, *Revolutionary Sister*, 1971, mixed-media construction on wood, 62″ × 27″.

Brooklyn Museum, gift of R. M. Atwater, Anna Wolfrom Dove, Alice Fiebiger, Joseph Fiebiger, Belle Campbell Harriss, and Emma L. Hyde, by exchange; Designated Purchase Fund, Mary Smith Dorward Fund, Dick S. Ramsay Fund, and Carll H. de Silver Fund, 2012.80.32. © Dindga McCannon.

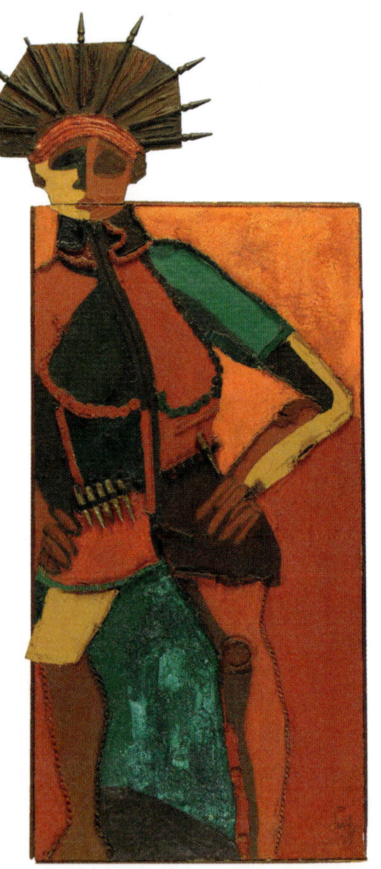

Dindga F. McCannon

Multimedia artist and WSABAL member Dindga F. McCannon (b. 1947) created one of the most iconic black feminist works of the 1970s: *Revolutionary Sister* (Figure 11.4). Painted on shaped and hinged wood (the top folds down for storage and shipping), the construction includes sequins and bullets and is predominated by the black power color scheme of red, black, and green. Breaching the rectangular confines of the picture space is the head of a female soldier, whose Afro hairstyle is decorated with spikes that imply a crown, a helmet, and a halo. The high collar of her T-shirt suggests a military uniform. The flat and abstract planes of her face create a mien that is alluring and unyielding at once. McCannon created *Revolutionary Sister* in 1971, the same year that Wadsworth

Jarrell painted *Revolutionary* (Figure 10.11). A comparison of the two works highlights the nuances that distinguish art about women by men from art about women by women.

Jarrell and McCannon's works both feature the word "revolutionary" in their titles as a reference to the Black Power Movement. Both portray empowered black women: Jarrell's Angela Davis and McCannon's unnamed warrior. Both artists use bullets in their works, an allusion to the Black Panther Party's credo of armed self-defense against police brutality. And both paintings are boldly hued and figurative. Differences occur in their angles of vision and constructions of gender. The worm's-eye view used by Jarrell elevates Davis to a larger-than-life position vis-à-vis the viewer. This tactic both monumentalizes Davis and distances her from us. McCannon's vantage point places the viewer face to face with the figure, who gazes calmly out at her audience. Although clearly a powerful woman, she connects with the viewer on equal footing. In Jarrell's picture, the woman is the adored "other"; in McCannon's, the woman is the "self."

Like Ringgold, McCannon was born and raised in Harlem. She graduated from Fashion Industries High School in 1962 and went on to study at the Art Students League, CCNY, the Weusi-Nyumba Ya Sanaa Academy (also joining and exhibiting with the group), and Bob Blackburn's printmaking workshop and privately with Richard Mayhew, Charles Alston, and multimedia artist Alvin Hollingsworth (1928–2000). Throughout the 1960s, McCannon exhibited in the annual Harlem and Greenwich Village outdoor art shows. Her media included painting; printmaking; jewelry; wearable art (including men's and women's clothing, hats, and accessories); textile art, including quilts (dubbed by McCannon as "fabric collages"); and public murals that she created while working for New York's Cityarts Workshop.

McCannon wrote and illustrated two children's books, *Peaches* (1974) and *Wilhemina Jones, Future Star* (1977). Semi-autobiographical, they detail the life of a Harlem teenager who aspired to become an artist. McCannon also collaborated with Caribbean playwright Edgar White (b. 1947), creating illustrations for three books. McCannon exhibited at Acts of Art on six occasions from 1971 to 1975, including the Whitney Rebuttal and WSABAL shows. Her work has since been shown at multiple Harlem venues, major national museums, and university and commercial galleries.

Betye Saar

In 1969, California artist Betye Saar (b. 1926) created one of her first feminist artworks, a mixed-media work entitled *Black Girl's Window.* It portrays the silhouette of a black girl trapped behind the glass of an aged window frame as a metaphor for the social limitations faced by black women. Three years later, she created one of the most powerfully engaging images of the Feminist Art Movement, her 1972 *The Liberation of Aunt Jemima* (see chapter-opening image). In this startling found object construction of grotesque caricature, pop imagery, and symbols of violence, Saar critiques the ubiquitous stereotype of the black mammy. Aunt Jemima's image, co-opted by Saar from the well-known pancake box, is repeated in a patterned backdrop. In front of this Warholesque Pop Art screen stands a modified version of the same icon: a vintage black figure that was originally designed as a memo holder. The figure's bulging eyes, thick intensely red lips, and grimace are evidence of the demeaning nature of these vintage items, which, ironically, have lately become prized collectibles for African-American antiquarians.

The rotund Jemima wears her traditional bandana and apron, on which is embedded another variation on the theme: a third mammy, who holds an infant in her left arm. This last figure is partially obscured by an enlarged fist—the black power sign—and the infant she holds is resting on the apex of that fist. The baby cries, and its brows are deeply furrowed with anxiety. This is hardly a conventional rendition of the subject, which would normally show the mammy as a helpful caregiver to white children. Instead, Saar offers viewers a disturbing alternative: a child of mixed race, the product of the mammy's forced submission to her white master and a signifier of the enslaved woman's servile status as breeder and chattel. According to Saar, the work symbolizes the degradations of slavery, Jim Crow segregation, and ongoing racism. A further jarring element is the small pistol that the main figure holds in the same hand as the broom. A second weapon—a rifle—is positioned at the left side of the figure, counterbalancing the broom. Art historians Moira Roth and Yolanda Lopez have described this gun-toting Aunt Jemima as "psychologically as well as politically explosive." In their eyes, Saar has transformed the conventional icon from a docile maid into a self-liberating woman. The combination of grotesquery, pop icons, and symbols of violence in *The Liberation of Aunt Jemima* encapsulates the fury of both the Black Arts and Feminist Art Movements.

Emma Amos

Atlanta-born artist Emma Amos (b. 1938) made this provocative statement: "For me, a black woman artist, to walk into the studio is a political act." This pithy observation aptly describes what it means to be perennially at the mercy of race and gender bias in the art community, a circumstance Amos knows well. She was born in segregated Georgia to upper-middle-class parents who owned and operated a drugstore in Atlanta. Her parents encouraged her interest in art from an early age. When the artist was 11, they arranged for her to study privately with Ruth Hall Hodges (1907–87), a member of the art faculty at Morris Brown College. Her work was selected by Hale Woodruff for three of the Atlanta University annuals, beginning when she was 15. After graduating from high school, Amos spent a summer in Hampton University's precollege program before attending Antioch College in Ohio from 1953 to 1958. There she studied fine arts and textile weaving under art department chair Robert Metcalf (1902–78). She also spent one year abroad studying printmaking techniques at the Central School of Art in London. After graduating from Antioch, Amos returned to London's Central School to complete a diploma in etching in 1959.

Following her European trip, Amos moved to New York, where she joined several prestigious printmaking workshops operated by Letterio (Leo)

Calapai (1902–93), Riva Helfond, Robert Blackburn, and her London teacher Anthony Harrison, who had relocated to New York. In New York, Amos attained immediate, if moderate, success. Through contacts made at Calapai's workshop, she developed a relationship with Sylvan Cole, director of the Associated American Artists Gallery, where she was invited to exhibit her prints. It would be some years, however, before Amos could make a living selling her works. In the interim, she married and raised her children while working as a teaching assistant at the Dalton Elementary School (where she met her husband, Robert Levine). Amos also earned her master's degree in 1965 from NYU, where she reacquainted herself with Woodruff, who, by this time, was on the NYU faculty and was a member of Spiral.

Woodruff arranged for Amos to join Spiral, where she thrived creatively and intellectually. From conversations with Romare Bearden, she learned about African-American artists such as Jacob Lawrence, whose work had previously been unknown to her. Likewise, she was exposed to the idea of a black aesthetic and to agitprop art. Although resistant to the deliberate creation of "black art" per se (Amos felt at the time that there was something essentially disingenuous in placing emphasis on race rather than individual creativity), she believed that ethnicity could factor into creative decision making without necessarily dominating the process. For example, she felt that jazz music was the ideal artistic embodiment of a black aesthetic. She also believed that Spiral might have survived longer as a group, and perhaps had greater impact, if its members had been able to create a visual arts program that was in some way comparable to jazz: unique to the black community and yet expansive enough to encompass myriad individual tastes and styles.

Although flattered to have been invited to join Spiral, even as a young artist Amos was aware of the conspicuous absence from the group of any other women. She quickly came to realize that the New York art scene was, in her words, "a man's scene, black or white." Her participation in Spiral was usually limited to that of an observer rather than a participant in the group's discussions, particularly when, as she put it, "the old boys settled into age-old fights with each other." She felt isolated in Spiral, where even a distinguished artist like Elizabeth Catlett was referred to by male members as "the wife of Charles White," whom Catlett had long since divorced.

From 1961 to 1971, Amos worked for noted textile designer Dorothy Liebes (1897–1972), who was one of the most renowned fabric artists in the country. Many of Amos's designs were translated into unique carpets, produced for the Hilton Hotel chain and other upmarket clientele. Amos also designed patterns for upholstery, window treatments, and clothing fabrication. This virtuosity is evident in her meticulous selection of the textiles with which she, like Ringgold, frames her paintings, which are at once sumptuous, harmonizing, and vigorously graphic. Amos prospered as a weaver during this time, when a momentary boom in the popularity of textile crafts occurred, thanks to the Pattern and Decoration Movement. Yet she knew better than to advertise herself as a weaver in fine arts circles, where conventional hierarchies of high and low art persisted.

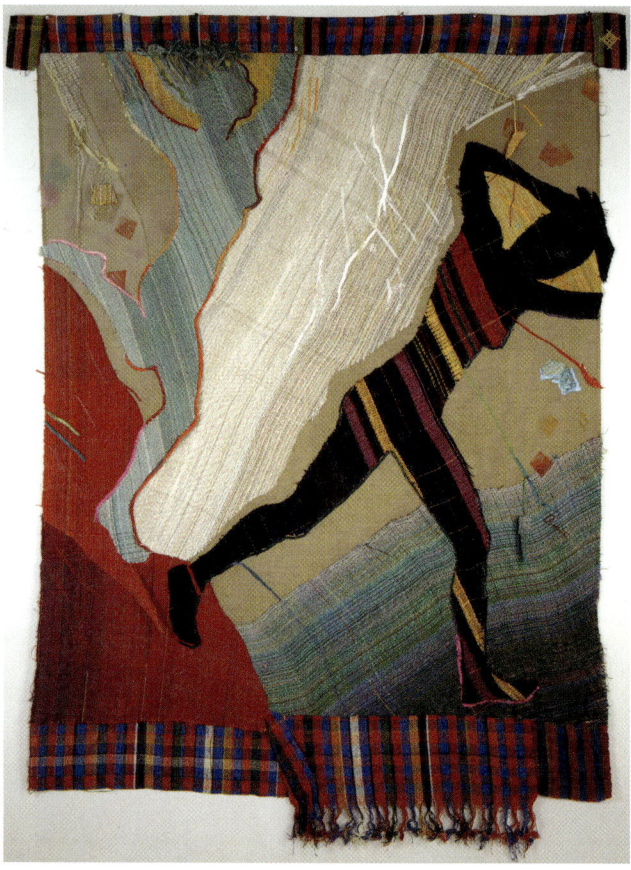

▲ **11.5** Emma Amos, *Out in Front*, 1982, handwoven linen, 76″ × 84″.

Art © Emma Amos / licensed by VAGA, New York, NY. Photo: Becket Logan.

In 1977, Amos became cohost, with quilt maker and best-selling novelist Beth Gutcheon (b. 1945), of a WGBH Boston public television series on crafts, entitled *Show of Hands* (for which Amos wrote the pilot). The series aired in 13 episodes over 18 months and featured local woodworkers, ceramicists, weavers, and stained glass, quilt, and jewelry makers. Amos's experience with the series helped her to resolve her "closet" weaver predicament. Because the show presented craftsmen and craftswomen to TV viewers as fine artists in their own rights, Amos was able to create a fusion of craft and high art by taking the femmage approach.

Amos's fabric painting *Out in Front* incorporates sections of solid, striped, and checked warp-edge cloth (which the artist wove herself) into what is essentially a two-dimensional painting (Figure 11.5). It depicts two lithe female nudes sprinting across the picture plane with joyous abandon. The lines of the warp and weft of the cloth alternate between emphatic vertical and oblique thrusts and nervous meandering threads evocative of flowing water. Amos handles fabric as nimbly as she manipulates paint (colorful strokes of which underscore the dynamic action of the figures). The turquoise material that comprises the form of the left-hand figure culminates at the top of the figure's head in frayed edging that approximates braided hair tossed high as the figure moves through the air. The second body hurtles forward (hence the title, *Out in Front*) with considerable momentum, created by the artist's choice of brightly striped fabric, angled to intensify movement.

Beginning in the mid-1980s, rather than weaving her own cloth, Amos traveled to Europe and Africa to select fabrics for integration into her paintings and multimedia prints (the latter of which include **silk collagraphs** and hand-cut stencil prints on plush fabrics). Amos favors West African *kente* cloth and southeast African *kanga* cloth. She also utilizes symbolically printed ***bogolanfini*** **textiles** of the Bamana people and wax-dyed batiks made in Holland. Amos expertly manipulates these exotic fabrics to flank and complement her unstretched canvases and to enliven the surfaces of her prints.

In 1980, Amos took a faculty position at Rutgers University, where she eventually became the Art Department chair. In addition, Amos served on the editorial board of the feminist journal *Heresies*, and she wrote for the New York artists' magazine *M/E/A/N/I/N/G*. Her articles targeted the difficulties faced by black women artists and offered strategies for dealing with art world racism. Amos also made a determined effort to work with other women artists whenever possible. In addition to the time she spent with Dorothy Liebes, she studied papermaking with Indian-born artist Zarina (Zarina Hashmi; b. 1937) at the New York Feminist Art Institute (NYFAI). She also joined Fantastic Women in the Arts, an ensemble that attempted to close the gap between black and white feminists.

Although Amos was well aware of the racial divide that existed in the Feminist Art Movement, she found that some artists' collectives were sympathetic to the needs of both black and female artists. These groups included the integrated Guerilla Girls, which promoted anonymous membership and "guerilla" public relations tactics to spotlight art world chauvinism. Another supportive group was Entitled: Black Women Artists, a coalition that provided moral support, professional networking, promotional opportunities, and public exposure for its members. To honor her many women supporters, in 1990 Amos began an extensive series of portraits entitled *The Gift*, which she bequeathed in its entirety to her daughter, India (named after the artist's mother) for her twentieth birthday. *The Gift* consists of more than 40 watercolor portraits on paper of Amos's friends and colleagues, including African-American artists Billops, Ringgold, Catlett, Browne, and Byard; Euro-American artists Schapiro and Joyce Kozloff (b. 1942), critic Lippard, and historian Roth; and Native-American artist Kay WalkingStick (b. 1935). Amos summed up the objective of *The Gift* by stating, "There's something powerful and strong about women artists, about womanhood."

In addition to Amos's iconographic motifs featuring active and empowered women and narratives, she has created cycles that focus on racism, black hair, black athletes, entertainers, and historic figures over the last four decades. Still others address patriarchy within the Western art historical canon, African-American history, and her own family history. Formally, Amos is a colorist in the classic sense, preferring a robust palette. In a metaphoric sense, Amos is a different kind of colorist in that she paints on her figures the entire range of black skin tones from dusky to dark. She believes that skin color is as integral to African-American existence as pigment is to painting, and she enjoys creating works that play on both concepts simultaneously.

In 2008, Amos retired from her position at Rutgers. She continues to work from her home studio in New York's East Village.

Nellie Mae Rowe

Nellie Mae Rowe (1900–82) is usually described as a folk or **yard artist** by art historians. However, if judged by her achievements, rather than her preferred display space (her yard) and lack of formal training, Rowe fits well within the feminist art domain. Critic Lucy Lippard remarked in a comprehensive survey of self-taught artists, *Souls Grown Deep*, that feminist artists were so busy rediscovering past quilt making and other fabric art traditions that they overlooked many self-taught living women artists who were creating nontraditional art right under their noses, without notice or sanction.

Not until a decade after the founding of the Feminist Art Movement, with the mounting of the 1982 Corcoran show *Black Folk Art in America*, were many of these artists given their due. In addition to Rowe, the Corcoran exhibit exposed some 20 vernacular artists to the art-going public. Following this exhibition, interest in Outsider Art skyrocketed; and by the end of the 20th century, self-taught artists such as Rowe had become art world "insiders" rather than "outsiders."

Like so many women artists, Rowe began as a doll and quilt maker (Ringgold is also famed for both skills). She learned these crafts as a child, and by the time she reached her teens, Rowe had become an accomplished artist. She credited her love of art to the encouragement of her parents. Her father (ex-slave Sam Williams) was an enterprising cotton, vegetable, and fruit farmer, as well as a blacksmith and basket weaver; her mother, Luella Swanson Williams, was a quilt and dressmaker. Rowe began to explore her artistic gifts a few years after the 1948 death of her second husband, an elder widower named Henry "Buddy" Rowe. Until that time, she had been fully engaged, first as a child fieldworker with her nine siblings in Fayetteville, Georgia; later as a wife and homemaker; and finally as a domestic employee.

Art making offered Rowe a welcomed release from the daily grind of housekeeping (work that she continued to do well into the 1970s). Between 1948 and 1960, Rowe had created so many works of art that her home in Vinings, Georgia, became an outdoor gallery where her handmade and found object art was on public display. Items in her "gallery" included her quilts, life-size dolls, sculptures, stuffed animals, drawings, Christmas ornaments, plastic toys, and other cherished objects that adorned the artist's fence, clothesline, and trees. Rowe even trimmed her hedges topiary-style in the shapes of animals such as sheep, birds, and pachyderms. Rowe kept a guest book and gave tours of her yard and home, as well as musical performances, for hundreds of curious art aficionados.

Rowe's sculpture incorporates unorthodox materials such as human hair, rhinestones, pearls, marbles, ribbons, and chewing gum, which substitutes for sculpture clay. Her two-dimensional works (usually drawings on paper) depict fantastical environments and amorphous figures that evoke the Surrealist fantasies of Marc Chagall (1887–1985). Rendered in intense Crayola hues, Rowe's drawings portray farm animals, house pets, domestic scenes, and genre subjects such as picking cotton, washing clothes, and making soap—the realities of her life. She also depicted more serious subjects such as the 1981 Atlanta child murders, as well as creating numerous self-portraits that are especially revealing.

Sadly, Rowe was diagnosed with terminal cancer in 1981, within a year of the Corcoran show, and died soon after. Rowe reacted to the news of her illness by raising the stakes of her creativity. In her last year, according to collector and *Souls Grown Deep* editor William Arnett, "her vision, ambition, skill, and the complexity of her work expanded considerably." Rowe's last paintings were rich with symbols of her own mortality, such as cliff edges, demonic figures, and empty chairs. A recurring motif was a self-referential canine coupled with phrases like "I Am Worrie[d]," "I Might Not Come Back," and "I'm [on] the Wrong Road"—words that express the artist's state of mind as she struggled with terminal cancer.

Shortly before her death, Rowe was invited by First Lady Nancy Reagan to produce a Christmas card for the White House. The artist declined the commission, allegedly due to her poor health; but she admitted to a friend that she was not enthusiastic about designing a holiday greeting that would be shared with few, if any, African Americans and certainly none who were poor or disadvantaged, as she had been for most of her life. While many Rowe admirers have taken pleasure in imagining her as a social naïf, plainly she was not. She intended for her art to be shared with the black community. She believed that her paramount gift was the ability to "make something out of nothing"—an apt metaphor for her own evolution from dire and humble beginnings to distinguished stature as a revered artist.

BLACK FEMINIST MURALS

Vanita Green and Justine Preshé DeVan

As a Chicago teenager, Vanita Green (b. 1952) happened to see Black Arts Movement muralist William Walker painting his *Peace and Salvation: The Wall of Understanding* in 1970. Observing that his mural portrayed men almost exclusively as arbiters of "peace and salvation," Green borrowed Walker's paints and brushes and, on a nearby brick structure, painted portraits of iconic black women including Angela Davis, Mary McLeod Bethune, Nina Simone, and Harriet Tubman. She called it *Black Women*. Within a few days, vandals had defaced the mural with white paint thrown at the wall in broad splatters. Green commented: "Before, it was just a pretty picture; but now it says more"—more, indeed, about the resistance to black female assertiveness that came from so many quarters.

Green was one of a number of African-American women artists who saw mural painting as a powerful way to address issues specific to black women. One notable example is the 1977 mural by Justine Preshé DeVan (b. 1936), *Black Women Emerging*, which is located at 41st Street and S. Cottage Grove Avenue in Chicago (Figure 11.6; restored in 2000). Funded by the National Endowment for the Humanities (NEH), the project was a genuine community effort. DeVan invited women of all ages from the surrounding Bronzeville neighborhood to assist her in priming the wall and painting the design. Rendered in the Social Realist style of the 1930s, the mural portrays black women taking active part in their own betterment and liberation.

The mural's central figure wears graduation robes and grasps a diploma to symbolize educational achievement. Another figure raises a judge's gavel to signify advances in the justice system for women. Depictions of the symbol of medicine (the caduceus, a staff with two entwined serpents around it) and the Capitol Building allude to women's roles in medicine and government. Broken chains, brooms, children, and books symbolize liberation from

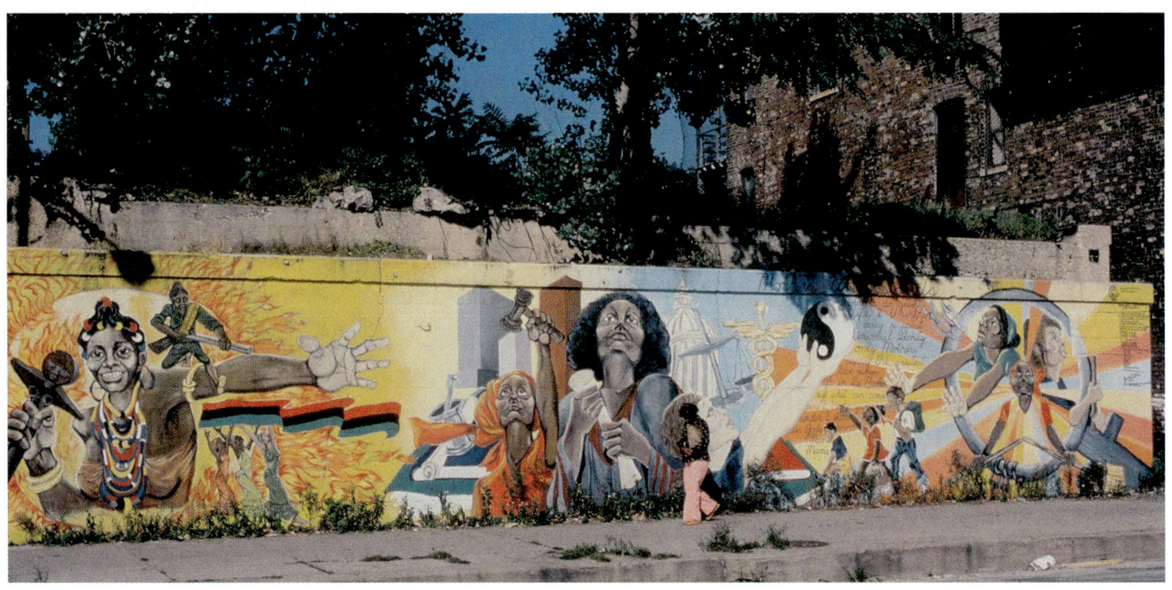

▲ **11.6** Justine Preshé DeVan in collaboration with Mitchell Caton, *Black Women Emerging*, 1977, mural, 4120 South Cottage Grove Avenue, Chicago, IL.

Photo: Chicago Public Art Group.

domestic servitude through education. Finally, the left quadrant of the mural depicts a powerful African woman holding an *akua'ba* fertility sculpture and emerging from a ring of fire. It is accompanied by an African woman guerilla fighter sporting a fully loaded bandolier and musket, and a group of dancers carrying a red, black, and green banner.

DeVan began making murals in 1968 and is considered one of the founders of the Chicago Mural Movement. She was born and raised in Philadelphia, where she received her teaching certification and art training. After college, DeVan worked for many years as a teacher in the Philadelphia public school system before taking time off in the 1970s to study at the SAIC. From 1973 to 1977, DeVan was associated with the Chicago Mural Group and completed a number of projects. Most notably, she worked with Calvin Jones and Mitchell Caton on their first mural collaboration, *A Time to Unite*, in 1976 (Figure 10.15). In recent years, after retiring from teaching, DeVan served as board secretary of the National Conference of Artists. She remains committed to art education as a path to empowerment for women.

Sharon Haggins Dunn

Artist and photographer Sharon Haggins Dunn (b. 1946) carried out a mural initiative at Yarmouth and Columbus Avenues in South Boston in 1970. The mural, *Maternity*, was completed the year she received her BFA degree from Boston University (Figure 11.7). The work was sponsored by Summerthing, an urban mural art initiative funded by the city. *Maternity* was radiantly hued, figurative, and enlivened with rhythmic shapes and patterns. It is dedicated to black mothers and is considered among the first works—if not *the* first work—of its kind. A frieze of larger-than-life-size women, pregnant or partnered with their children,

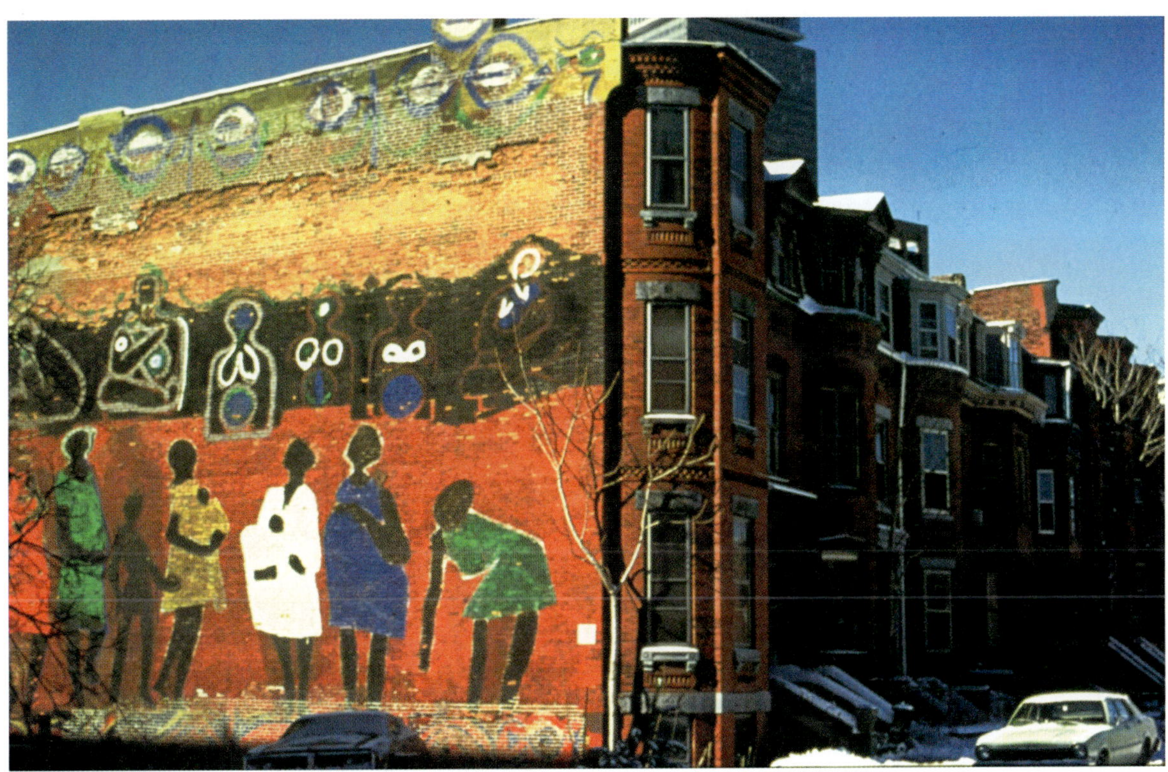

▲ 11.7 Sharon Haggins Dunn, *Maternity*, 1970, mural, Yarmouth and Columbus Avenues, South Boston, MA.

Reproduced by permission of the artist.

anchors the composition. Above this panel is a second procession of transparent bodies whose breasts and uteri are revealed as if by X-ray, underscoring women's roles in procreation. Dunn's identification with her subject was likely heightened by the fact that she herself was pregnant at the time.

Dunn attended New York's High School of Music and Art before relocating to Boston to complete her BFA. In 1983 she earned a master's of science degree in visual studies from the Architecture Department of MIT. Her work is influenced by global cultures and embodies her concerns for the welfare of African Americans, as well as their obscured and distorted history. She is an accomplished photographer, painter, and digital artist whose art today documents changes in ecosystems, topography, and climate. Dunn has worked as an arts educator since the 1980s, as chair in the Studio Foundation Department at MIT.

Summary

Black feminist artists declined to succumb to social pressures requiring them to subordinate their personal interests to those set out by social convention. They refused to accept patriarchy as a given. And they skillfully negotiated the precarious tightrope between gender and ethnicity with grace and aplomb. Furthermore, they understood instinctively that, from their vantage point apart from the mainstream, they could see their path more clearly. Each chose to create art at a time when women artists of color were being actively marginalized; they chose feminist form and content even as art world chauvinism worked actively against them; and they achieved their creative and professional goals without so much as a backward glance.

Key Terms

Afrofemcentric: refers to that which emphasizes African and African-American culture within a feminist context

alternative media: in visual art, unconventional or nontraditional materials used to create art

bogolanfini textile: a handwoven cotton fabric believed to protect the wearer that is made and worn by the Bamana people of Mali; it is created using a resist-dye technique wherein a mud solution is painted onto the fabric to create abstracted animal designs

femmage: assemblage or collage art created by women, often with a feminist theme

patriarchy: a sociopolitical system in which men are empowered and women disempowered

Pattern and Decoration Movement: a 1970s American art movement that reacted against Minimalism with art composed of colorful all-over floral and geometric patterns

silk collagraph: also known as silk aquatint, a form of print created by painting an image onto a black, silk-covered plastic printing surface with white acrylic paint; the image is then inked and printed on an etching press

yard artist: one who displays his or her own works of art in his or her yard or garden as an alternative exhibition space

Questions for Further Study and Discussion

1. What were the major goals of the Feminist Art Movement?
2. What concerns of black women artists were not specifically addressed by either the Black Arts or Feminist Art Movement?
3. What obstacles historically prevented women from becoming professional artists?
4. Discuss two black feminist art groups, their goals, and their activities.
5. Choose two paintings of women from your local museum—one by a male artist and one by a female artist. Discuss their differences.
6. Research and discuss the activities of the Guerilla Girls (different from the Guerilla Art Action Group).
7. What was the significance of femmage to the Feminist Art Movement?

8. Debate the validity or lack thereof of yard art as an art form.
9. Research other significant artists not discussed at length in this chapter, including Camille Billops (b. 1933), Carole Byard (b. 1941), Marie Johnson Calloway (b. 1920), Catti (Catherine James; b. 1940), Robin Holder (b. 1952), Viola Burley Leak (b. 1944), Valerie Maynard (b. 1937), Onaway K. Millar (1919–2008), Coreen Simpson (b. 1942). Ann Tanksley (b. 1920), and Ruth Waddy (1909–2003).

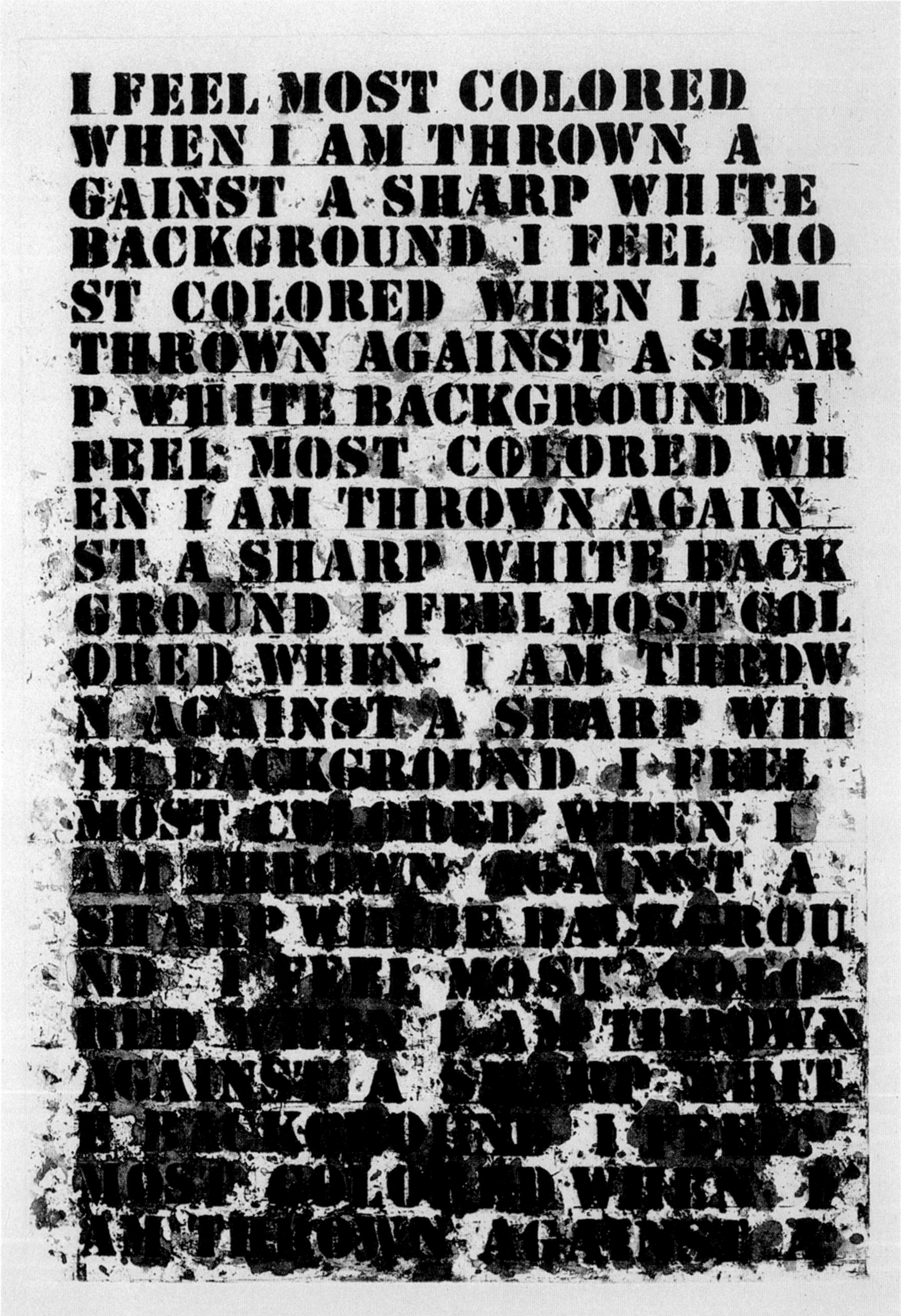

I FEEL MOST COLORED
WHEN I AM THROWN A
GAINST A SHARP WHITE
BACKGROUND I FEEL MO
ST COLORED WHEN I AM
THROWN AGAINST A SHAR
P WHITE BACKGROUND I
FEEL MOST COLORED WH
EN I AM THROWN AGAIN
ST A SHARP WHITE BACK
GROUND I FEEL MOST COL
ORED WHEN I AM THROW
N AGAINST A SHARP WHI
TE BACKGROUND I FEEL
MOST COLORED WHEN I
AM THROWN AGAINST A
SHARP WHITE BACKGROU
ND I FEEL MOST COLO
RED WHEN I AM THROWN
AGAINST A SHARP WHIT
E BACKGROUND I FEEL
MOST COLORED WHEN I
AM THROWN AGAINST A

POSTMODERNISM

12

"Postmodernism" as a term came into wide use in the 1970s, in the wake of Abstract Expressionism and Minimalism. Initially applied to architecture, by the 1980s it was also being used to describe visual art. A broadly defined movement, Postmodernism embodies a rejection of several characteristics of Modernism. Among these are the idea that art must be a unique, sustainable object such as a painting or sculpture; that art is a marketable commodity; that the perceptual aspects of art—what it looks like—are key to its significance; and that art must be hand made by the artist. Rejecting these concepts, Postmodernists supplanted the conventional art object with what has been termed "Post-Object" Art: new forms of artistic expression such as performance, videos, installations, found art, assemblage, and texts. Postmodernists also used alternative media such as industrial plastics, poured concrete, architectural insulation, and other low-grade metals.

POST-MINIMALISM

An early variation on the Postmodern theme, Post-Minimalism was a reaction against the strict focus of Minimalist sculpture on elemental geometric forms. Post-Minimalists believed that pure formalism—the assertion of the art object as unique and iconographically hermetic—was cold and disengaging. Although attracted to the pristine shapes of Minimalism, Post-Minimalists wished to infuse them with personal and political portent. They were also interested in the use of unconventional and industrial materials, such as polymer plastic or stainless steel, and with new interpretations of traditional materials.

Fred Eversley

Fred Eversley (b. 1941) is a Brooklyn native, the son of a teacher and an aerospace engineer. Eversley, too, was scientifically inclined, earning a BS degree in electrical engineering from the Carnegie Institute of Technology (today, Carnegie Mellon University). After graduating in 1963, he took a break from engineering to spend the summer at the Instituto Allende in Mexico studying mural techniques. He then moved to California to pursue a career in the fields of electronics and aerospace technology, working for NASA from 1963 to 1967.

Living in Venice Beach at the time, Eversley became acquainted with the kinetic sculptor Charles Mattox (1910–96) (who had worked with Diego Rivera) and with the **Light and Space Art Movement**, which dovetailed with Eversley's dual interests in science and art. Exponents of Light and

◀ Glenn Ligon, *Untitled (Four Etchings)*, 1992, one of four soft-ground etchings, 23-9/16″ × 15¾″ (plate, each), 25⅛″ × 17⅜″ (sheet, each).

Space Art used new media to manipulate light and alter spatial perception. Eversley's early sculptures were translucent polished resin pieces. They were inspired by the Minimalist-related **Los Angeles Look** style, which popularized the use of resin as a glossy sculptural medium in the 1960s. Within a few short years of his early experiments, Eversley was creating sculptures from cast acrylic polymer, stainless steel, and bronze. Although the shapes of his cast pieces feature the elemental severity of Minimalist form, Eversley added light and color manipulation to the genre.

Eversley's Post-Object Art engages viewers interactively. Instead of viewing his sculptures as standalone art objects, viewers are invited to look through them as they transform the surrounding environment. Eversley's U-shaped parabolic, elliptic, and triangular polymer sculptures are designed much like optical lenses. They actualize the artist's interest in reflecting and refocusing light energy (see, for example, his *Big Red Lens*, Figure 12.1). As they are observed, the apparent rigidity of Eversley's sculptures quickly gives way to a mercurial fluidity. Their mirrorlike surfaces add to this malleability and draw viewers inexorably into their own reflections. However, their reflections disappear as the translucent sculpture leads their gaze to the vista beyond the object, which has been transformed by the shaped and dyed polymer into myriad spatial, temporal, and dimensional possibilities. Eversley creates sculptures that disintegrate the Modernist barrier between

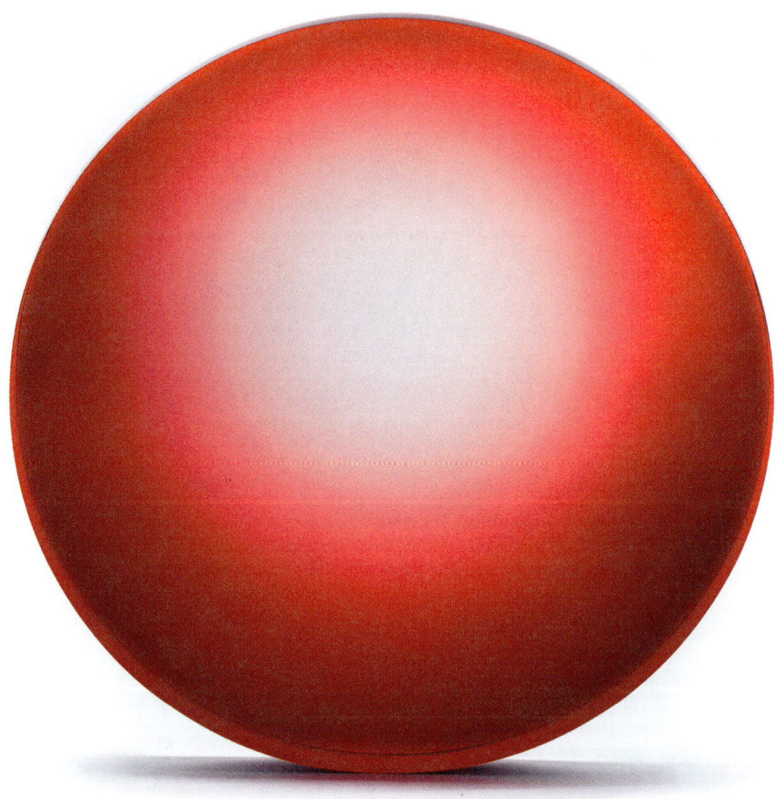

▶ **12.1** Frederick Eversley, *Big Red Lens*, 1985, cast polyester, 40″ × 40″ × 6″.

© Frederick Eversley. Crystal Bridges Museum of American Art, Bentonville, AR. Photo: Edward C. Robinson III.

object and viewer. His aim is to make art that is kinetic—not that his solid sculptures move, but the observer is seduced to move around them as light, ever changing, moves through or reflects from their surfaces.

Since his first one-man show at the Whitney Museum in 1970, Eversley's art has been shown at hundreds of museum and galleries around the globe, and he has received dozens of awards. Key among these are an NEA grant and a three-year artist's residency from 1977 to 1980 at the Smithsonian Institution's Air and Space Museum—the first-ever such award. Today he works from studios on both coasts, in Venice Beach and New York's Soho district.

Lorenzo Pace

Along with abstract sculptor Chase-Riboud (Chapter 9) and half a dozen other artists, sculptor and performance artist Lorenzo Pace (b. 1943) contributed to New York City's African Burial Site memorial project in 1991. He was chosen to design a towering outdoor monument. Installed in Foley Square Plaza facing the Federal Court Building, the 300-ton, 50-foot-high black granite monument was a decade in the making. Entitled *Triumph of the Human Spirit*, the sculpture is one of the largest site-specific sculptures in the world to pay tribute to those who lost their lives to the African slave trade (Figure 12.2).

The sculpture's austere design was inspired by the Chi Wara—ancestor deities of crops and fertility—antelope sculptures of the Bamana people

▼ **12.2** Lorenzo Pace, *Triumph of the Human Spirit*, commissioned 1991, installed 2000, black granite, 50′ high, Foley Square, New York, NY.

Commissioned by the New York City Departments of Parks and Cultural Affairs; funded by the Percent for Art Program. Artwork © Lorenzo Pace. Photo: Jerome Ryan, Mountains of Travel Photos.

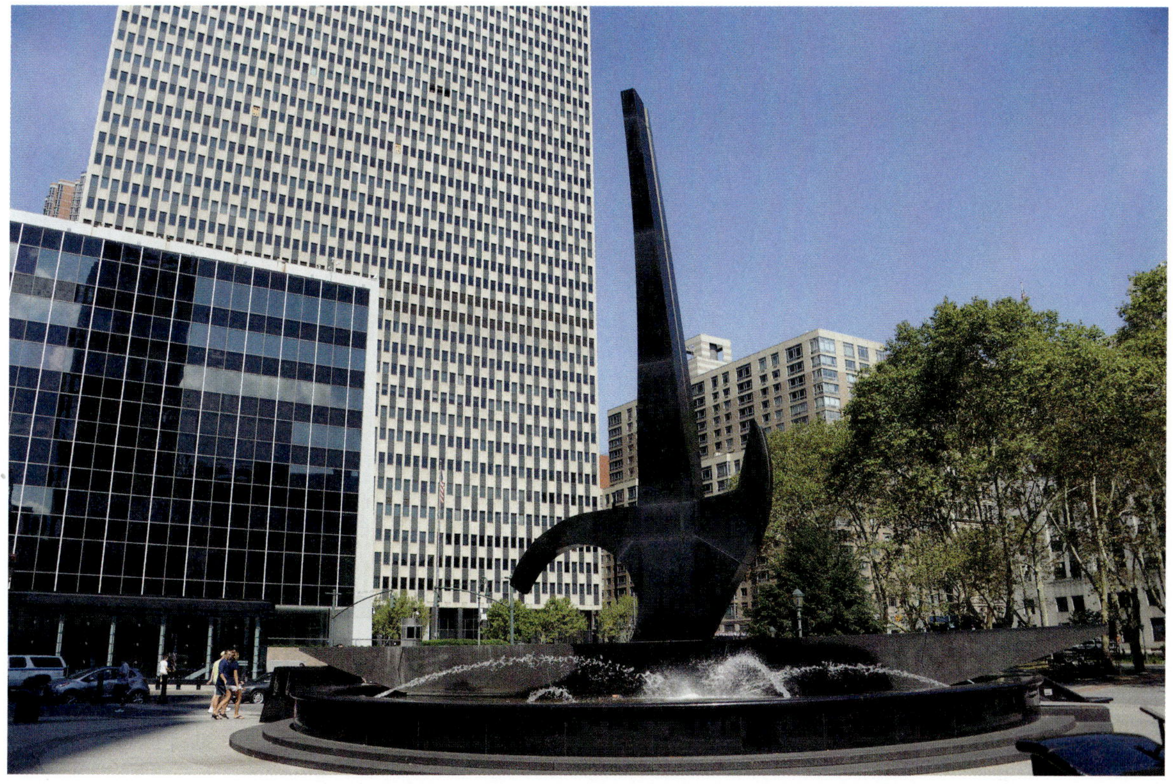

of Mali. The support base on which the abstracted antelope stands takes the elemental form of a long ship, symbolic of the Middle Passage, which brought the African slaves to the United States, and of life journeys. Interred in this base is an iron padlock reproduced from the original antique one that once shackled Pace's great-great-grandfather's slave chains. In 2001, Pace published a bestselling children's book, *Jalani's Journey*, detailing his ancestor Steven Pace's enslavement and passage to the New World. *Jalani's Journey* developed into an interactive Postmodern artist's performance called *Jalani and the Lock*, which involves narrative, theater, and musical components including drums, flute, rattles, and whistle, all played by Pace. The book and the performance were designed to engage the minds and spirits of viewer-participants, young and old, in African-American history, slavery, oppression, and triumph.

The son of a Birmingham, Alabama, minister and one of 13 siblings, Pace was employed as a factory worker when, at age 19, he decided on a whim to travel to Paris. He immersed himself in the expatriate community and in the art, culture, and jazz nightlife of the city. After a year, he returned home and settled in Chicago. While strolling in Hyde Park along the shores of Lake Michigan, he came upon an artist sculpting a religious scene in wood. Impressed by the man's talent, Pace tried his own hand at woodcarving. Five self-taught years later he had his first solo show at the South Side Community Art Center. A dean from the University of Illinois–Chicago who saw Pace's show offered him a full scholarship to attend the university, agreeing to enroll him as a third-year student due to his advanced skills. Pace subsequently studied at the Art Institute of Chicago, where he also received a full scholarship, earning BFA and MFA degrees there over the next three years. Pace then completed his doctorate in 1978 at Illinois State University.

Pace joined the faculty of the University of Illinois in Chicago briefly before relocating to New York, where he established a Brooklyn studio and became an integral part of the Postmodern New York scene. He was best known for his Afrocentric performances and installations that incorporated live and recorded music and oration, recycled objects, wood sculpture, and found materials. A 1986 installation dedicated to musician Stevie Wonder included a vintage poster of Wonder at age 14 from a performance at Harlem's Apollo Theater that Pace had discovered in a trash bin. Pace's aesthetic motifs are inspired by Afrocentric culture and history, cycles of life and death, issues of justice, stories of family, ecological preservation, and pacifism. In the 1990s, he served as director of the Montclair (New Jersey) State University Art Galleries, and since 2007, he has served as a full professor of art at University of Texas–Pan American in Edinburg.

Martin Puryear

Sculptor Martin Puryear (b. 1941) works with a range of media among which are bronze, stainless steel, rawhide, and stone. He is also renowned for his ability to transform the traditional medium of wood into art objects that take advantage of the many ways that wood can be used. His forms take on the appearance of woven fiber baskets, haystacks, metal mesh, bronze, cornucopias, musical instruments, balls of yarn, mollusk shells, reeds, rope, and spider webs, although, as an abstract artist, Puryear does not intend these effects so much as they are inferred by the viewer. Puryear's 1995 *Alien Huddle*, for example, although constructed from red cedar and pine, takes on the pristine shape of a snail or mollusk shell, with a surface so smooth as to suggest the mechanistic perfection of an organic life form.

The shapes, planes, textures, and colors that Puryear chooses for each work are visually and structurally stunning. His aesthetic influences include African sculpture and basket-weaving, carpentry, and the woodwork of coopers, boatwrights, and musical instrument designers. In fact, Puryear has been a proficient designer of wood instruments and tools such as guitars and archer's bows since childhood. Puryear's abstractions are often imbued with references (sometimes revealed in their titles) to African-American icons, autobiographical subjects, death, desire, faith, memory, human relationships, and other existentialist topics. Other works are about process and form, in the classic Modernist sense, without narrative meanings. In either case, his sculptures speak for themselves, in their own formal languages, offering visions that are both austere and allusive.

Born and raised in Washington, D.C., Puryear received a BA in biology and art from Catholic University in 1963. After college, he joined the Peace Corps and taught high school in Sierra Leone for two years, from 1964 to 1966. While in West Africa, he sought out indigenous craftsmen, with whom he studied traditional woodworking and carpentry. Puryear next traveled to Stockholm, attending the Royal Swedish Academy to study printmaking and sculpture from 1966 to 1968. He further explored wood as a sculptural medium visiting the workshop of master woodworker and furniture designer James Krenov (1920–2009) several times. The spare, clean lines of Scandinavian furniture design had a definitive influence on Puryear, whose later works blurred the boundaries between sculpture and furniture.

Puryear's organic abstract sculptures created while in Sweden landed him his first one-man show in Stockholm in 1968 of etchings and sculptures. The following year, he returned to the United States, where he was awarded a scholarship to attend the Yale University School of Art and Architecture. Over the next two years at Yale, Puryear worked for a semester as an undergraduate teaching assistant and completed an MFA in sculpture (he would later receive an honorary PhD there in 1994). Puryear also was exposed to the works of several of the resident artist-faculty, including Minimalists Robert Morris and Richard Serra (b. 1939), whose monolithic approaches to sculpture influenced Puryear's aesthetic development.

Over the next decades, Puryear taught at Fisk University (1971–73), the University of Maryland in College Park (1973–77), and the University of Illinois (1978–87). He also established a studio in Williamsburg, Brooklyn, until it was destroyed in a fire in 1977. Puryear won several creative arts grants and awards, including a 1978 NEA Fellowship and a Guggenheim Fellowship, which he used to travel to Japan in 1983 to study the spare forms of Japanese architecture, landscaping, and Zen garden design. A subsequent Rome Prize took Puryear to Italy for a residency at the American Academy in 1986 (he won a second such award in 1997).

By the end of the 1980s, Puryear had developed an impressive international reputation with dozens of exhibits, commissions, and art awards to his credit. Key among these were a MacArthur Foundation Genius Award in 1989; major showings at three Whitney Biennials (1979, 1981, and 1989); and solo shows in major museums in the United States and abroad. He also received commissions, including site-specific installations at public and private spaces in major U.S. cities and in Germany, Japan, and China. From 2007 to 2009, a 30-year retrospective of Puryear's work traveled throughout the United States. Puryear retired from teaching in 1990 and returned to New York where he lives and works.

CONCEPTUAL ART

Another major Postmodern trend was Conceptualism, which rejected artistic skill, technique, style, and even media in favor of theoretical substance and cognitive expression. The artist's thought processes took precedence over other concerns. Consequently, language in the form of written texts became integral to the art-making process (and sometimes was the sole element). An article published in 1967 by Minimalist and Conceptualist artist Sol LeWitt (1928–2007) encouraged visual artists to embrace words as a potential medium. In subsequent years, LeWitt's views were echoed and expanded by artist Joseph Kosuth (b. 1945), who launched the Conceptual Art Movement to foster art as intellectual discourse rather than as objects of visual interest.

Howardena Pindell

Multimedia artist Howardena Pindell (b. 1943) has a freewheeling aesthetic approach that draws on a multiplicity of sources. Among these are Abstract Expressionism, Conceptualism, Minimalism, Color Field painting, graffiti art, **adire-eleko dyeing** techniques, and photography. Equally diverse are her narrative scenarios, which derive from personal, universal, racial, and feminist sources. After earning a BFA from Boston University in 1965 and an MFA from Yale in 1967, Pindell worked as an associate curator at MoMA, where she experienced hostility from some members of the staff. Believing this treatment to be motivated by both her race and her gender, Pindell addressed the experience in her art, activism, and writing, treating the three vehicles as interrelated media.

Pindell's publication of "Art (World) and Racism: Testimony, Documentation, and Statistics" exposed through interviews and carefully gathered and verified data the institutionalized racism within prestigious New York museums and galleries. In 1973, Pindell's concerns prompted her to become a founding member of the Soho-based women's art gallery A.I.R. (Artist-in-Residence) and later a founder of the Committee Against Racism in the Arts. To highlight the racial biases of the art community, Pindell produced and starred in a film short entitled *Free, White, and 21* (1980). Employing a bitingly satirical inverse of blackface, Pindell camouflaged her own brown skin with white makeup and donned a blond wig. Enunciating in imperious tones, her whiteface persona engaged in a dialogue with an off-screen narrator (the voice of the artist, as herself). The film's "free, white, and 21"-year-old protagonist made light of her black counterpart's complaints about institutional racism. The film is an autobiographical reflection of Pindell's personal encounters with race, gender, and class inequities.

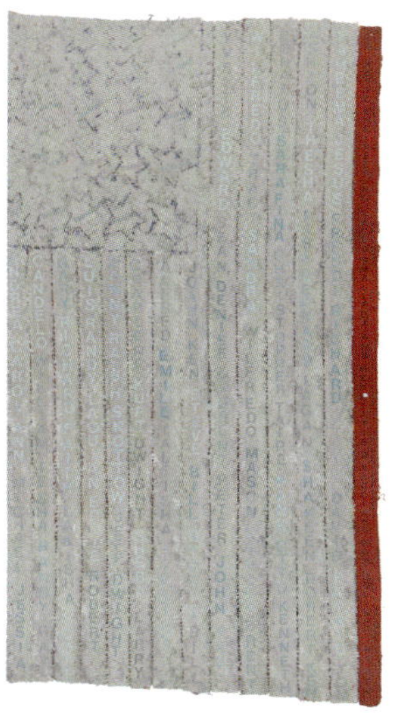

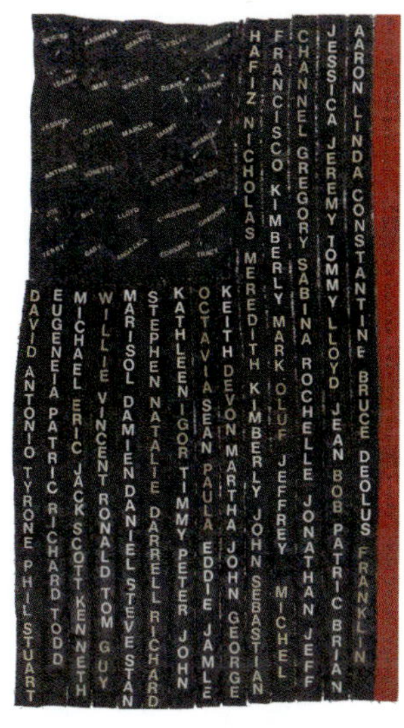

▲ **12.3** Howardena Pindell, *Separate but Equal Genocide: AIDS*, 1991–1992, acrylic on canvas, 75½″ × 91″.

Courtesy of the artist and Garth Greenan Gallery, New York, NY.

Pindell's 1992 *Separate but Equal Genocide: AIDS* is a two-part unstretched conceptual painting of a blanched and a black American flag (Figure 12.3). Bordered with a bold red stripe suggestive of human blood, each flag is covered with dozens of names of AIDS victims. The white and black versions of the work underscore that the AIDS virus is colorblind and attacks people across the racial divides. Its title echoes the premise of the Jim Crow laws, a bleak reminder that illness does not discriminate, even if humans do.

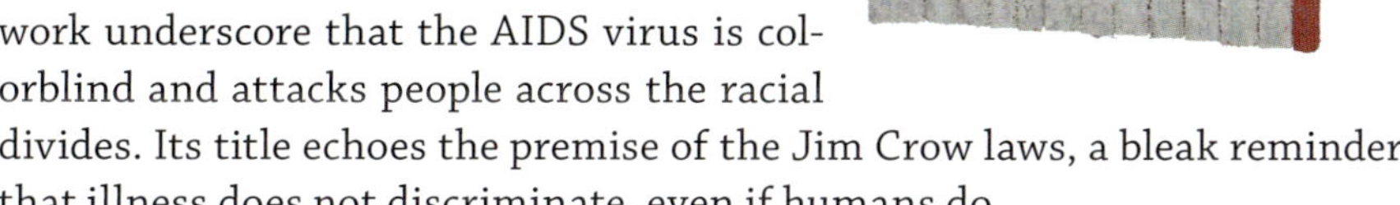

Despite Pindell's preoccupations with pressing sociopolitical, health, and cultural issues, she does not compromise aesthetics for the sake of polemics. Instead she gives equal precedence to both with incisive wit and intellectual acumen. After choosing a conceptual catalyst, Pindell embarks on a creative journey that is primarily about form. In 1990, Pindell won the College Art Association Award for Distinguished Body of Work. During the latter 1990s, she held a five-year position as a visiting professor at the Yale University School of Art and currently teaches at the State University of New York at Stony Brook. She continues to create and exhibit her work, most notably in a 2007 solo exhibition at the Louisiana Museum of Science and Art in Baton Rouge.

Pat Ward Williams

Conceptual artist Pat Ward Williams (b. 1948) uses photography, texts, video, and found objects to create provocative assemblages and installations. Her art also focuses on race and gender identity politics, from both autobiographical and universal vantage points. Her best-known work, *Accused/Blowtorch/Padlock*, from 1982, combines a page from a 1937 issue of *Life* magazine, silver print photographs, a found window frame, and painted text. The uncredited *Life* photo (accompanied by three enlargements) portrays a black lynch victim hogtied and padlocked to a post (Figure 12.4). He is covered in burns, and the rope around his waist literally cuts into his body. Mounted in a distressed wooden frame, the photos are centered on black tarpaper covered with handwritten texts that look like chalk scrawls on a blackboard. The words read:

> *There's something going on here. I didn't see it right away. After all, you see one lynched man you've seen them all. He looks so helpless. He doesn't look lynched yet. What is that under his chin? How long has he been LOCKED to that tree? Can you be BLACK and look at this? Life magazine published*

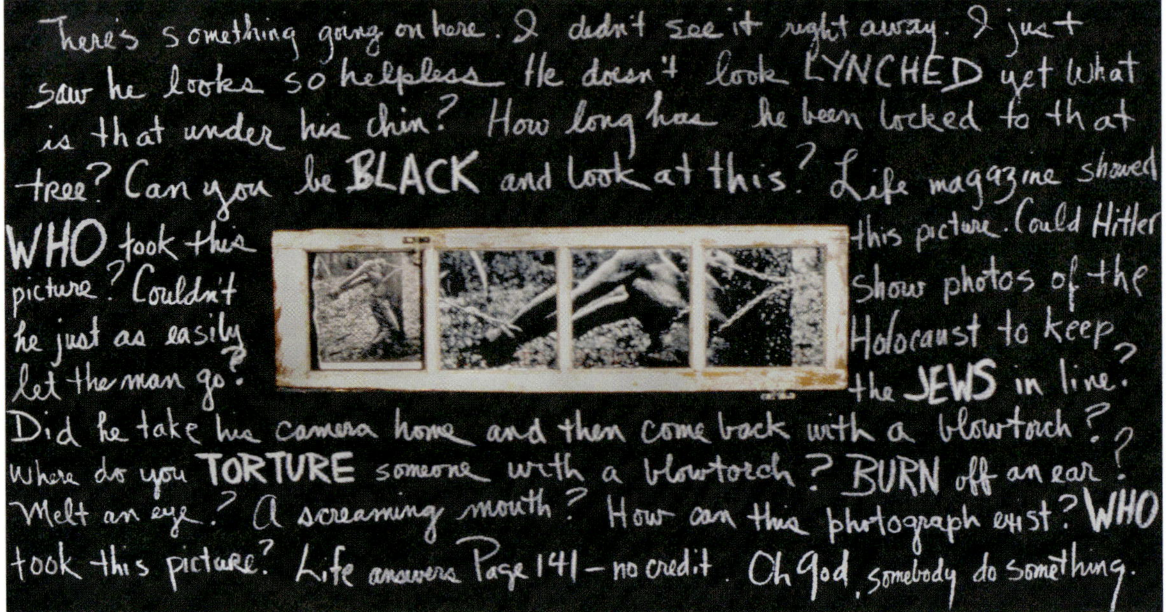

▲ **12.4** Pat Ward Williams, *Accused/Blowtorch/Padlock*, 1982, silver print, tarpaper, wood frame, magazine page, approximately 4′ × 6′.

this picture. Could Hitler show pictures of the Holocaust to keep the JEWS in line? WHO took this picture? Couldn't he just as easily let the man go? Did he take his camera home and then come back with a blowtorch? Where do you TORTURE someone with a blowtorch? BURN off an ear? Melt an eye? A screaming mouth. How can this photograph exist? WHO took this picture? Oh, God. Life answers—page 141—no credit. Somebody do something.

The nature of the scrawl—its size and width inconsistencies, letterform variations, and the strategic use of capital letters—denotes the artist's reaction to seeing this image in a popular magazine. This manipulation of typography to express sounds, ideas, and emotions transforms the viewer into a listener who is almost able to hear chalk tapping and scraping rapidly across a blackboard, keeping pace with the writer's tumultuous reactions and thoughts. The white words scratched onto the black background further signify the attack by whites on the body of the black lynch victim, and the use of tarpaper alludes to the tar and feathering of blacks, which often accompanied their lynching. In its entirety, the work is an indictment of racial violence and America's reprobate legacy of lynching its black citizens—and of those who did nothing in the face of such atrocities.

Born in Philadelphia, Williams attended that city's Moore College of Art and Design and received a BFA in 1982. She completed a master's degree in 1987 at the Maryland Institute College of Art (MICA). While completing her master's, Williams taught at the Baltimore School for the Arts. She then taught at Bowie State University (1986) and the College of Notre Dame in Baltimore (1987–89). At this time, Williams was chosen to participate in the Photo-Active Feminist Visiting Artists Series—an NEA-funded two-semester course. Williams co-taught the course with seven of the country's most politically engaged feminist photographers, including renowned conceptualist Barbara Kruger (b. 1945).

In 1989, Williams moved to the West Coast to accept a two-year position at CalArts. After winning another NEA award in 1990, she joined the faculty at UC Irvine and remained there for the next decade. Since 1995, Williams has completed several major multimedia public commissions in California. She is the winner of several national and international residencies and has exhibited globally at leading museums. Since 2000, Williams has made her home in Florida, where she works at Florida State University, teaching film and photography.

Glenn Ligon

Bronx native and mixed-media conceptual artist Glenn Ligon (b. 1960) studied at the Rhode Island School of Design (RISD) and Wesleyan University, receiving a bachelor's degree in 1982. In 1985, he won a coveted spot in the Whitney Museum Independent Study Program. Within ten years, his text-based black-and-white paintings that addressed personal and political themes of slavery, civil rights, race, and homosexuality garnered Ligon two NEA awards. Ligon's works appropriate texts from a diverse group of writers such as Walt Whitman, Zora Neal Hurston, Gertrude Stein, James Baldwin, Ralph Ellison, and Richard Pryor. Carefully chosen and sometimes cryptic excerpts are transferred by Ligon onto white canvas, using black oil crayon or coal dust and letter stencils.

Ligon's iconic *Untitled (I Feel Most Colored When I Am Thrown Against a Sharp White Background)* of 1990 began with a found wooden door primed by the artist with gesso (see chapter-opening image). Using stencils, he lettered the work's title repeatedly in black oil stick and black graphite. The juxtaposition of black letters against bright white gesso actualized the meaning of the words, which were excerpted from a 1928 essay by Zora Neale Hurston entitled "How It Feels to Be Colored Me." In Ligon's work, Hurston's words and experience become his own and, when read by a third party, that of the viewer. In this way, Ligon transforms words into art and communicates the experience of being black in America with profundity. According to the artist, he intended to stencil the letters sharply and clearly, but the oil medium was uncooperative. Ligon realized that the oozing of the oil and the blurring and overlapping of the words gave the work deeper meaning, in that racial identity is indeed fluid, unsettling, confusing, and problematic.

For his lifelong dedication to art-as-idea, Ligon has been awarded multiple fellowships and art prizes. His works are in the public collections of virtually every major art museum in the United States and have been exhibited in museums in dozens of countries.

INTERMEDIA ART

Many Conceptual artists communicate through performance and installation. Performance art involves a theatrical presentation performed for an audience often, but not necessarily, at a cultural venue or event, such as a gallery. Conversely, many historic performances have been staged in parks, on city streets, and in other nontraditional venues. Although the term "performance" was not widely applied to artists' actions until the late 1970s, the art form was popularized in the mid-1960s by the international artists group **Fluxus**. Drawing on a mode of Conceptualism, Fluxus artists combined many forms of media, such as Minimalist art, music, and poetry, to create spontaneous and improvised **intermedia** activities. The media routinely associated with performance art include—in addition to theater, music, and poetry—sculptural assemblage, dance, and video. Furthermore, as an ephemeral art form, performance is an ideal exponent of Post-Object Art because, whether minutes, hours, or days long, a performance has a limited lifespan. As such, it can neither be purchased by collectors nor preserved in a museum (although many performances have been documented in video and photographs). The term "happening" is often used synonymously with "performance art" and involves audience participation rather than mere observation.

Like performance, installation art is also temporary and not intended for sale—at least it wasn't in its early incarnations. (By the 1990s, artists had begun to create "packaged" installations that could be sold in whole or in part.) Installations comprise large, often room-size spaces filled with found and handcrafted objects. Installations are created for a particular gallery or alternative space and, even if installed elsewhere, can never be composed exactly the same way twice, because spaces differ. Installations provide viewers with the experience of being surrounded by art rather than observing it. One "enters" an installation and becomes part of it.

Houston Conwill

Installation and performance artist Houston Conwill (b. 1947) was a pioneer in intermedia art. His fusions of installation, live and recorded music, dance, theatre, and conceptual elements such as narrative and song are multisensory experiences intended to live in memory rather than in physical form.

Conwill was born in Louisville, Kentucky, and planned to enter the priesthood before becoming an artist. In the 1950s, he entered a Benedictine monastery in Indiana but found the austere lifestyle unsuitable to his temperament. In 1966, Conwill left the monastery and joined the U.S. Air Force, serving for three years during the Vietnam War. After his discharge, he settled in Washington, D.C., and became an art student at Howard University, where he was trained in design, painting, and printmaking under Lois Jones and Black Arts Movement artists Skunder Alexander Boghossian (1937–2003) and Jeff Donaldson, among others. Conwill also worked as an artist's assistant for Color Field painter Sam Gilliam (see Chapter 9). Specializing in printmaking, Conwill earned his BFA in 1973.

From D.C., Conwill relocated to the West Coast to study at UCLA. In Los Angeles, Conwill joined with his wife, artist/curator Kinshasha Holman Conwill (b. 1951); multimedia and assemblage artist Alonzo Davis (b. 1973); and half a dozen other black artists to form the Brockman Gallery Street Graphic Committee, an LA mural collective. The group completed a number of community murals in the city. They also exhibited collectively at Brockman Gallery, which was founded in 1967 as a gallery and studio space for minority artists by Davis and his brother, assemblage artist Dale Brockman Davis

(b. 1945). Conwill met and collaborated on performances with Betye Saar, Hammons, Maren Hassinger (b. 1947), and Senga Nengudi (Sue Irons; b. 1943), among others.

Conwill's performances, which began in the 1970s, expressed his experiences as a southern-born black man and practicing Catholic. Functioning as both art and sociological documents—and incorporating a variety of objects such as altars, maps, clay, dirt, sculpture, and found items—Conwill's art actualizes African-American history, culture, folklore, and spirituality. Among his earliest works is the *JuJu* series, staged in 1975 and 1976. The performance incorporated an installation of imprinted latex sheets, West African "juju" (good luck) pouches, a carved wooden stool derived from Shona (Zimbabwe) stools and Ashanti (Ghana) headrests, beaded vessels, blues and jazz music, written cyphers, and other found and made objects. These elements were combined with the actions of the artist—assembling the installation, dancing, chanting, and painting his body and other objects. The performance engaged the audience in a "conjuring up" of African cultural memory and sacred traditions.

Later Conwill installations and performances explored themes of death, memory, and transcendence. His *Open Secret* is a pyramid-shaped diptych inlaid in the tile wall of the East 125th Street station of the New York City subway. One of the first works commissioned by the city's Arts for Transit program, *Open Secret* is a 1980s time capsule revealed by an open-grid covering, through which straphangers observe cryptic forms and objects, as if peering into the collective memory of the 1980s. Acknowledging the uniqueness and cultural profundity of Conwill's art, the MoMA awarded him an artist's residency at its alternative PS1 space in 1980, which prompted Conwill's relocation to New York. His stay at PS1 culminated the following year in an installation: *Easter Shout!*, a glittering and brilliantly painted apse, complete with benches, altar, chalice, and candles.

In the 1980s, Conwill developed the **cosmogram** installation, for which he is best known. A circular, floor-based design related to Kongo religious art, the cosmogram infuses the artist's installations with a sense of ritual movement akin to Buddhist circumambulation. In 1983, Conwill began a series of cosmographic performance installations titled *Cakewalk*. The title refers to a traditional African-American dance that was performed at the 1876 Philadelphia Centennial, where prizewinning dancers were given a large, wedding-sized cake in lieu of a trophy—hence "cakewalk." Composed of stiff, high-stepping movements, the cakewalk is rooted in the antebellum slave practice of mimicking white dances such as the waltz and the polka. By the 20th century, blackface minstrels had turned the cakewalk back on itself by using it to mock African Americans.

Conwill's 1983 *Cakewalk* involved dance movements performed around the perimeter of a circular, floor-based cosmogram. The work channeled Yoruba and other African philosophies through live and vintage videotaped dance performances. Installed over several years in changing versions, in 1989 the series was reified as *The New Cakewalk*, with the inclusion of sculpture and texts. That year, the performance toured to the High Museum in Atlanta, the Aspen Art Museum, and MoMA. The MoMA Projects Gallery version was entitled *The Cakewalk Humanifesto: A Cultural Libation* and comprised an oversized 8-foot by 8-foot window. On the glass pane of the window Conwill etched a cosmographic dance floor that, like a Gothic stained glass window, cast light onto the gallery floor in patches that served as a diagram for dance steps. Maps of several cities—New Orleans, Atlanta, Memphis, and Louisville—were also etched on the glass and referred to periods of the artist's life and to events in African-American history. Facing the window, a long table with allusions to the Last Supper held bowls of soil and water from the named cities. The installation was aptly described at the time by MoMA curators as "a ritual dance of remembrance." More specifically, it signified a ritual journey or "cakewalk" through the African-American South and through the artist's past.

Throughout the 1980s, Conwill received many honors. He also continued to create many site-specific pieces. Key among these is the award-winning *Rivers* of 1991, a terrazzo floor design for the Schomburg Center theater lobby that Conwill created in collaboration with artist and poet Estella Conwill Majozo (his sister; b. 1949) and architect Joseph De Pace (b. 1954), whom Conwill met when they were both Prix de Rome winners in Italy. The group attributes their work jointly as created by Conwill, Conwill, and De Pace. *Rivers* marks the grave of Langston Hughes, whose ashes are buried beneath the Schomburg floor. The cosmogram, indicative of the cycles of life and death, is inset with excerpts from Hughes's poems, most significantly, "My soul has grown deep like the rivers" from Hughes's 1920 *The Negro Speaks of Rivers*, for which the installation was named.

Conwill, Conwill, and De Pace are perhaps best known for their 1994 installation *The New Ring Shout: A Tribute to African Burial Ground in New York City* (Figure 12.5). Located in the lobby of the building adjacent to the burial site, Conwill's 40-foot-diameter terrazzo and polished brass floor design is named for a southern Christian form of prayer that is derived from the religious practices of enslaved Africans. A "ring shout" describes a circle of worshippers dancing with ecstatic energy at the close of a church service. Also in the form of a Kongo cosmogram, *The New Ring Shout* lists the names of 24 African ethnic groups who were targeted by the slave trade, in a circular formation around a map of New York. As permanent collaborators, Conwill, Conwill, and De Pace embody the Postmodern rejection of single-media art and solitary creative genius. Instead the trio embodies the concept of communal activity and social purpose integral to the activities of so many African-American artists since the socialist era of the 1930s.

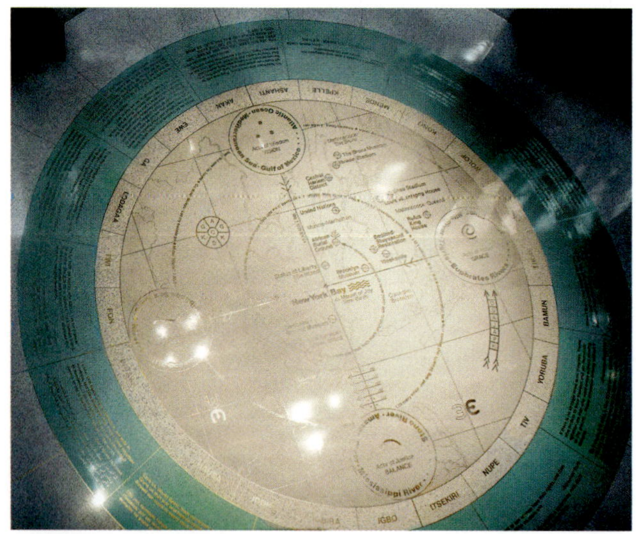

▼ **12.5** Houston Conwill (sculptor), Joseph De Pace (architect), and Estella Conwill Majozo (poet), *The New Ring Shout*, installed 1994, terrazzo and polished brass, 40′ diameter.

Ted Weiss Federal Building, 290 Broadway, New York, NY. Photographs in the Carol M. Highsmith Archive, Library of Congress, Prints and Photographs Division, LC-DIG-highsm-02822.

Terry Adkins

Intermedia artist Terry Adkins (1953–2014) transforms the physicality of sculpture into a musical abstraction and the immateriality of sound into concrete reality. His art fuses elements of time and space by combining live and recorded music, video, spoken-word poetry, costumes, sculpture, architectural elements, found object assemblage, and handmade instruments such as his 18-foot-long horns, dubbed "arkaphones" (Figure 12.6). Both playable instruments and sculptures, Adkins's arkaphones typify his cross-disciplinary approach to art. They were played during Adkins's "Last Trumpet" recitals with his band, the Lone Wolf Recital Corps. According to the artist, the number of arkaphones (four) and their colossal size allude to the trumpets of the four angels who herald the Last Judgment in the biblical Book of Revelation, thus adding an element of both the spiritual and the apocalyptic to this moving sculptural performance.

Adkins's subjects include African and African-American history, culture, and icons, and great musicians and composers. Adkins has created individual artworks in honor of Beethoven, Bessie Smith, John Coltrane, and Jimi Hendrix and commemorative pieces for writers Zora Neale Hurston, Ralph Ellison, and Jean Toomer; inventor George Washington Carver; activists Sojourner Truth, Martin Luther King, Jr., and John Brown; and explorer Matthew Henson. Concerned with biographical authenticity, for his Henson piece, Adkins actually traveled to the North Pole; similarly, in his *Meteor Stream: Recital in Four Dominions* for John Brown, Adkins included Brown's own writings.

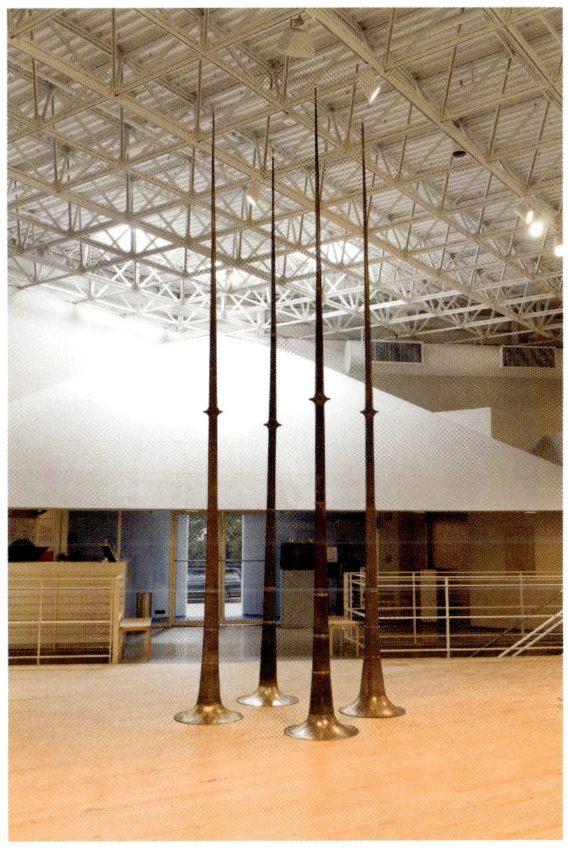

▲ **12.6** Terry Adkins, *Last Trumpet*, installation, detail, 1995, four brass arkaphones, 216″ × 24″.

Installation view, Radical Presence: Black Performance in Contemporary Art, Contemporary Arts Museum, Houston, TX, 2013. Courtesy of the Estate of Terry Adkins and Salon 94, New York, NY. Photo: Jerry Jones.

Adkins was born and raised in the Washington, D.C., area. In the 1960s, he was the only African-American student in the Catholic boys' school that he attended on an academic scholarship. He next attended Fisk University, where he was mentored by Aaron Douglas and Martin Puryear. After receiving a BS in 1975 and an MS in printmaking in 1977, he was awarded an MFA in sculpture in 1979. Adkins mounted his first major solo exhibits in Virginia in 1980–81 and in 1982 moved to New York to accept an artist's residency at the Studio Museum. This honor was followed in 1986 by an NEA grant that supported a one-year residency in Switzerland. While in Zurich, he founded his sound artist band, the Lone Wolf Recital Corps, which he enlisted to play a variety of instruments (including his arkaphones) during his "recitals," as Adkins calls his intermedia works.

In the 1990s, Adkins began a teaching career at SUNY New Paltz while maintaining a home and studio in Brooklyn. From 2000 until his untimely death from heart failure at age 60, Adkins served on the faculty of the University of Pennsylvania School of Design. Over three decades Adkins had dozens of solo exhibitions at major museums, universities, and private galleries in 17 states and half a dozen countries.

Lorraine O'Grady

Through multimedia installations and pioneering performances, artist Lorraine O'Grady (b. 1934) critiques the hypocrisies of the black middle class from which she hails and seeks to reconfigure images of black women from sexual objects to subjects of conceptual discourse. Her work also focuses on issues of miscegenation, racial self-identity, American cultural history within the context of race, and the nature and meaning of art.

O'Grady's parents were West Indian immigrants and members of Boston's black elite. They provided her with the best education, although not in the visual arts. O'Grady received a BA in economics from Wellesley College in 1961 and an MFA in fiction from the University of Iowa in 1967. She moved to New York in 1970 to work as a columnist for *Rolling Stone* magazine and the *Village Voice*. Inspired by the ongoing Conceptual Art Movement, by 1980 O'Grady had launched an art career that blended her many talents and interests, from fiction writing to documentary photography. Utilizing texts, photographs, drawings, and sound, she created installations and performances that intrepidly critiqued conventional social attitudes.

At a reception held at JAM Gallery in 1980 and again at the New Museum in 1981, O'Grady executed her first major "guerilla" performance, in the guise of her legendary alter ego, Mlle Bourgeoise Noire. Dressed in a tiara, beauty contestant's sash, and an evening gown and cape fashioned from nearly 200 pairs of white gloves, she strode in a stately manner amid unsuspecting gallery guests. In her hands she carried a whip that she used to flagellate herself. She shouted to the crowd, "That's enough! No more bootlicking. . . . No more ass-kissing. . . . No more buttering-up. . . . No more posturing of super ass-imilates. . . . Black art must take more risks!" The performance ridiculed black artists for having abandoned the agitprop art of the Black Arts Movement for fear of offending conservative members of the art community. O'Grady described her performance technique as a "hit-and-run" operation designed to disrupt cultural events and to provide an "electric jolt" to viewers.

O'Grady has presented her performances at the Whitney Biennial, MoMA, Kenkeleba Gallery, MICA, and other museum sites, as well as at pubs, on the streets of Harlem, and in New York's Central Park. Her 1982 Central Park performance *Rivers, First Draft* was curated specifically for (and about) O'Grady by renowned art historian and artist Gylbert Coker (b. 1944). As co-curator with the equally prolific art historian Horace Brockington (b. 1950) of New York City's Art Across the Park program, Coker arranged for O'Grady's piece to be performed in Central Park's Loch, a wooded waterfall area near 103rd Street at park center. *Rivers* included several actors and props, such as a door, chair, and table (Figure 12.7). The performance detailed the evolution of the artist from child to teenager to adult, and from the Caribbean to New England. In the narrative, after being rejected by a group of black male artists, the protagonist symbolically merges with her other "selves" and claims her own identity as a woman and an artist.

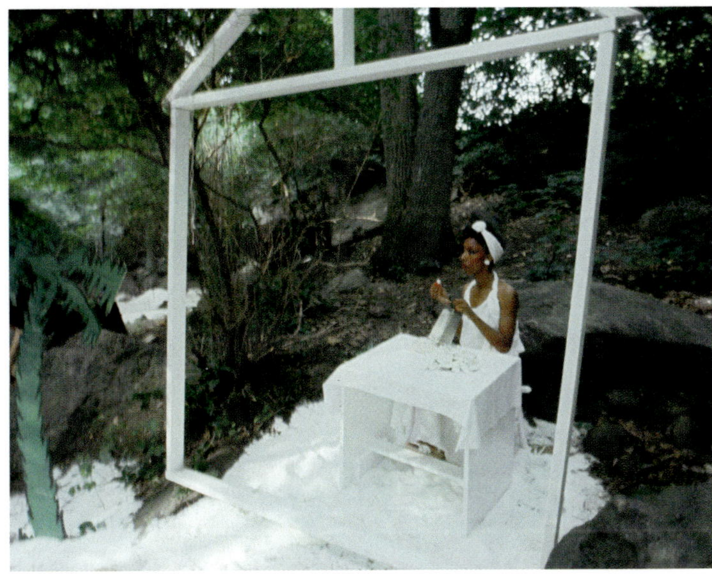

▲ 12.7 Lorraine O'Grady, *Rivers, First Draft (The Woman in the White Kitchen Tastes Coconut)*, 1982/2015, digital C-print in 48 parts, 16″ high × 20″ wide.

Courtesy of Alexander Gray Associates, New York, NY. © 2015 Lorraine O'Grady / Artist Rights Society (ARS), New York, NY.

Adrian Piper

Philosopher Adrian Piper (b. 1948) was among the first major artists to embrace Conceptualism, an interest sparked by her employment in the 1960s as an assistant to Sol LeWitt. Through performances, installations, and the use of archival documents and written and oral texts, Piper addressed a number of controversial topics, most significantly white fears of miscegenation and myths associated with the black male.

Born in Harlem, as a teenager Piper took classes at the Art Students League. Soon after her high school graduation, she began exhibiting her Minimalist-inspired art on two continents. In a single year between 1969 and 1970, at age 21, Piper earned an associate's degree in painting and sculpture from the School of Visual Arts (SVA) and exhibited her work in major galleries in Germany, New York, and Seattle, and at Oberlin College. Piper also enrolled that same year at CCNY as a philosophy major, completing her BA in 1974.

By the mid-1970s, Piper's earlier Minimalism had given way to Conceptualism in the form of sociopolitical happenings. One of the artist's earliest such performances was *Mythic Being* (1972–76), for which she cross-dressed as an African-American man in dark sunglasses, Afro wig, bell bottoms, and a fake mustache. In this camouflage, Piper toured New York theaters, gallery openings, concerts, films, and plays. She wandered city streets, rode buses and trains, and accosted white students on the Harvard University campus. Piper went so far as to enact mock public muggings while her unwitting audience either ignored the skirmish or observed it with alarm and panic.

As the much maligned and stereotypical "black brute," Piper was able to incite many reactions from her audience, including fear, distrust, aversion, and belligerence, while seeming to remain emotionally detached from their responses. The performance was documented in drawings, collages, and photographs, and in *Village Voice* ads that featured retouched photos of Piper in her disguise. As a happening, *Mythic Being* was seamlessly aligned with the ethos of Conceptualism, in that it was performed in locations that existed beyond the boundaries of the conventional gallery system. Piper's rejection of the establishment underscored her desire to connect directly with her audience: the everyday xenophobes who perpetuated race and gender discrimination. Piper's wish was to make art that would help to develop a world free of racism and stereotypes.

Other now-historic Piper guerilla performances include *My Calling Card #1 (For Dinners and Cocktail Parties)*. This happening was played out on multiple occasions. The biracial Piper, whose fair skin causes her to be mistaken for white, was often unwillingly made party to racist conversations. In such instances, she silently distributed calling cards to the offenders, printed with the following statement:

> *Dear Friend, I am black. I am sure you did not realize this when you made/laughed at/agreed with that racist remark. In the past, I have attempted to alert white people to my racial identity in advance. Unfortunately, this invariably causes them to react to me as pushy, manipulative, or socially inappropriate. Therefore, my policy is to assume that white people do not make these remarks, and to distribute this card when they do. I regret any discomfort my presence is causing you, just as I am sure you regret the discomfort your racism is causing me.*

The performance permitted Piper to disengage herself from social confrontation while at the same time making her feelings known.

My Calling (Card) #2: Reactive Guerilla Performance for Bars and Discos likewise undermined the recipient's expectations by suggesting that all women who visit nightclubs are not, in fact, interested in sexual encounters. The card read in part: "I am not here to pick up anyone or to be picked up. I am here alone because I want to be alone." The performance was prompted by Piper's experiences with sexism, not the least of which occurred while she worked as a go-go dancer in a Manhattan nightclub in the mid-1960s. Both *Calling Card* performances are predicated on the Minimalist renunciation of overt "signs of artistic personality and effort." The performances are also based on the Kantian theory that the mind compulsively imposes order on the world around it, by way of artificial categories and preconceptions that disallow the existence of countless individual identities. Piper's performances insist that presumptions about race and gender are imprecise at best and destructive at worst.

By 1981, Piper had earned master's and PhD degrees in Kantian philosophy from Harvard University and spent a year of study abroad at the University of Heidelberg in Germany. She also won a Guggenheim Fellowship and two NEA Fellowships during this period, which helped to fund the next stage of her creative experimentation: video installation. Between 1988 and 1990, Piper took on the subject of miscegenation with the installations *Cornered* and *Out of the Corner*. In these works she arranged video monitors and overturned furniture in a gallery room with two birth certificates hanging on the wall; one certificate identified her as black, and the other identified her as white. Each video monitor displayed either Piper or an anonymous player reciting simultaneous litanies about the probable presence of African blood in most self-proclaimed white Americans.

The orations argued logically and dispassionately that, given the many centuries of racial mixing in America, the existence of substantive numbers of Americans of either "pure" European or "pure" African blood was highly improbable. The capsized furniture signified the "overturning" of fallacies of racial difference and suggested a vehement struggle of either physical (as in the racial and sexual violence associated with miscegenation) or metaphysical (as in the mental struggle of Piper's audience to accept the facts that she was presenting) proportions. The goal of *Cornered* and its outgrowth, *Out of the Corner,* was to prevail on white viewers to, in Piper's words, "transcend that deeply entrenched, carefully concealed sense of privilege, specialness, and personal superiority" that is associated with whiteness. By pointing out that the blood of all Americans is intermingled, *Cornered* exposed racism as a visual pathology—"an anxiety response to the perceived difference of a visually unfamiliar 'other.'"

Piper has received numerous fellowships, grants, and awards. In 2012 the College Art Association acknowledged Piper with their Artist Award for Distinguished Body of Work, and in 2014 the Women's Caucus for Art gave Piper their Lifetime Achievement Award. Piper's impressive exhibition history includes six retrospectives, most recently at the Museum of Contemporary Art of Barcelona in 2004, among many other solo exhibits in the United States and abroad. A scholar as well as an artist, Piper publishes in the areas of art, culture, aesthetics, Kantian philosophy, ethics history, and **metaethics**. Her collected writings, *Out of Order, Out of Sight*, were published in two volumes in 1996. A second edition of collected writings, *Margins Behind the Lines: Collected Writings*, is scheduled for publication as an e-book, and her work on Kantian metaethics, *Rationality and the Structure of the Self,* is already available as an open e-book.

Since the 1980s Piper has taught philosophy at half a dozen universities, including Georgetown, Harvard, and Stanford. At the end of the 1980s, she joined the faculty at Wellesley College, where she remained for 20 years. Seemingly cursed by the very xenophobia that she worked so long to dispel, Piper's persistent international travel schedule was deemed "suspicious" by the U.S. Transportation Security Administration (TSA) in the wake of 9/11, and she subsequently lost her tenured position at Wellesley in 2008. Despite these setbacks, in 2011 Piper was named professor emeritus by the American Philosophical Association. In 2012 she officially "retired from being black" after 64 years of exhaustive engagement with the color line. One can interpret her gesture as a final work of conceptual art, as it compels a re-evaluation of cultural and identity constructs. Piper today lives and works in Berlin, where she is director of the APRA (Adrian Piper Research Archive) Foundation Berlin, a physical and electronic resource that documents, interprets, and preserves Piper's lifework and funds intellectual research.

Renée Green

Born in Cleveland, Renée Green (b. 1959) received her BA in 1981, followed by coursework at the Parsons School of Design in 1982 and 1984; in 1989, she was accepted into the Whitney Museum's Independent Study Program. Green focuses her artwork on examinations of how information is gathered, collated, displayed, and disseminated in the digital age. She begins her assessments with a particular document, object, artwork, image, structure, place, or written text (or multiples of these) and proceeds to deconstruct their superficial or accepted meanings in order to reveal new, even contradictory

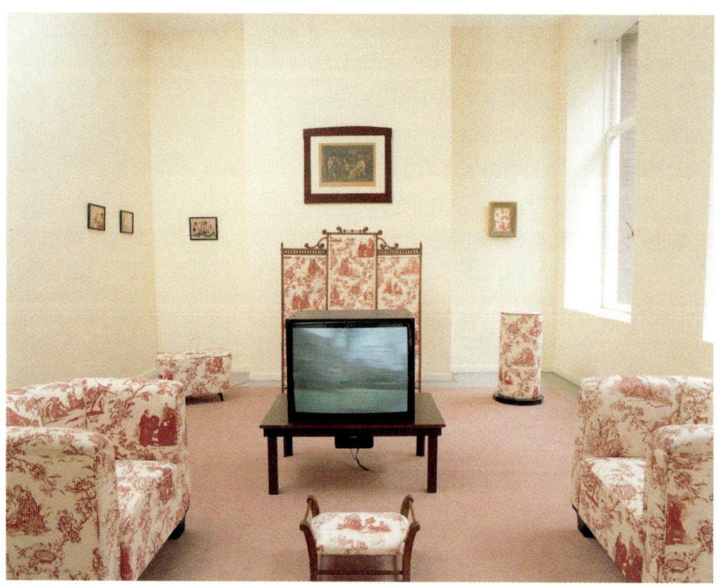

▲ **12.8** Renée Green, *Mise-en-Scène: Commemorative Toile*, 1991.

Installation view, Stichting De Appel, Amsterdam, 1996. Courtesy of the artist and Free Agent Media.

meanings. Depending on the nature of the project, Green presents her "findings" in a range of configurations that might include photography, video, film, sculpture, prints, texts, interactive installations, and, more recently, websites and other digital media.

Green's 1992 installation *Import-Export Funk Office* maps the trajectory of hip-hop from the United States to Germany. Composed of wall signage, video displays, and metal archival shelving filled with books and articles, the "office" is a repository of records that chart the means and routes through which elements of hip-hop were "exported" from the United States to Europe and back again. In another architectural installation, the artist's *Mise-en-Scène* of 1991, viewers are presented with what appears to be a typical 18th-century French parlor decorated with furniture that has been upholstered in classic magenta and cream toile (Figure 12.8). On closer examination, it becomes evident that the toile fabric (which also serves as wallpaper and drapes) has been silk-screened with images of slave abuses. The tastefully appointed salon is suddenly transformed into a reminder of a source of French wealth during the age of slavery. Its audio and video components include harpsichord period music and interviews with contemporary French officials about the transformation of the city of Nantes into the country's largest port thanks to the lucrative slave trade.

A consummate Conceptualist, Green composes explicative videos and catalogs to accompany her works, so that viewers can best navigate their complexities. These discrete components then become works of art in themselves as standalone films, artists' books, exhibition catalogs, archival collections, and audio transcripts. Since the 1990s, Green has had, in addition to her art career, a prolific teaching and curatorial career. She taught at the Whitney Independent Study Program beginning in 1991 and served as its director in 1996–97. From 1998 to 2003, Green taught at the Akademie der bildenden Künste (Academy of Fine Arts) in Vienna, Austria. Returning to the States in 2003, she spent two years at the University of California, Santa Barbara, before becoming dean of graduate studies at the San Francisco Art Institute from 2005 to 2011. Presently, Green is professor and director of the Art, Culture and Technology (ACT) Program at MIT.

Fred Wilson

Bronx, New York–born Fred Wilson's (b. 1954) work critiques conventional museum and gallery installations of art and artifacts. He believes these are falsely constructed paradigms designed to obscure the true nature and history of objects, particularly objects related to slavery and racial oppression. Wilson manipulates the customary museum paraphernalia, such as wall texts, pedestals, vitrines, and lighting, in order to heighten viewer awareness of object manipulation, curatorial agendas, and art historical context.

In the mid-1980s, Wilson began creating simulated museum environments, which led, in 1992 to an "intervention" (rather than an installation) titled *Mining the Museum*. It reconfigured an already-existing museum space at the Maryland Historical Society. Using the museum's own collection and galleries, Wilson critiqued how the history of American slavery and Native-American genocide was presented or, more fittingly, not presented to museum-goers. Key for Wilson was that the Maryland Historical Society presented this history from a white, male vantage point almost exclusively, while overlooking the viewpoints of women, Native Americans, and blacks in Maryland history.

In Wilson's 1991 installation *Guarded View* (which was part of the Maryland Historical Society exhibit), he presented headless brown-skinned museum guards in uniform to highlight the often ignored role played by blacks and other minorities in safeguarding our nation's treasures (Figure 12.9). In a related performance, Wilson gave a tour of *Mining the Museum* to museum staffers, and, during a brief intermission, he left the tour group to secretly don a guard's uniform. Returning to the gallery, Wilson (a brown-skinned man with an Afro hairstyle) stood quietly, arms folded, without identifying himself. No one in the group either noticed or acknowledged him until he spoke up and made his presence known. Part of Wilson's intention was to highlight the fact that many museums that claim to have a diverse workforce in fact hire most of their minorities for low-level rather than administrative or curatorial positions.

▼ **12.9** Fred Wilson, *Guarded View*, 1991, wood, paint, steel, and fabric, four parts, dimensions variable.

Whitney Museum of American Art, New York, gift of the Peter Norton Family Foundation 97.84a-d. © Fred Wilson, courtesy Pace Gallery. Photo: Sheldon C. Collins.

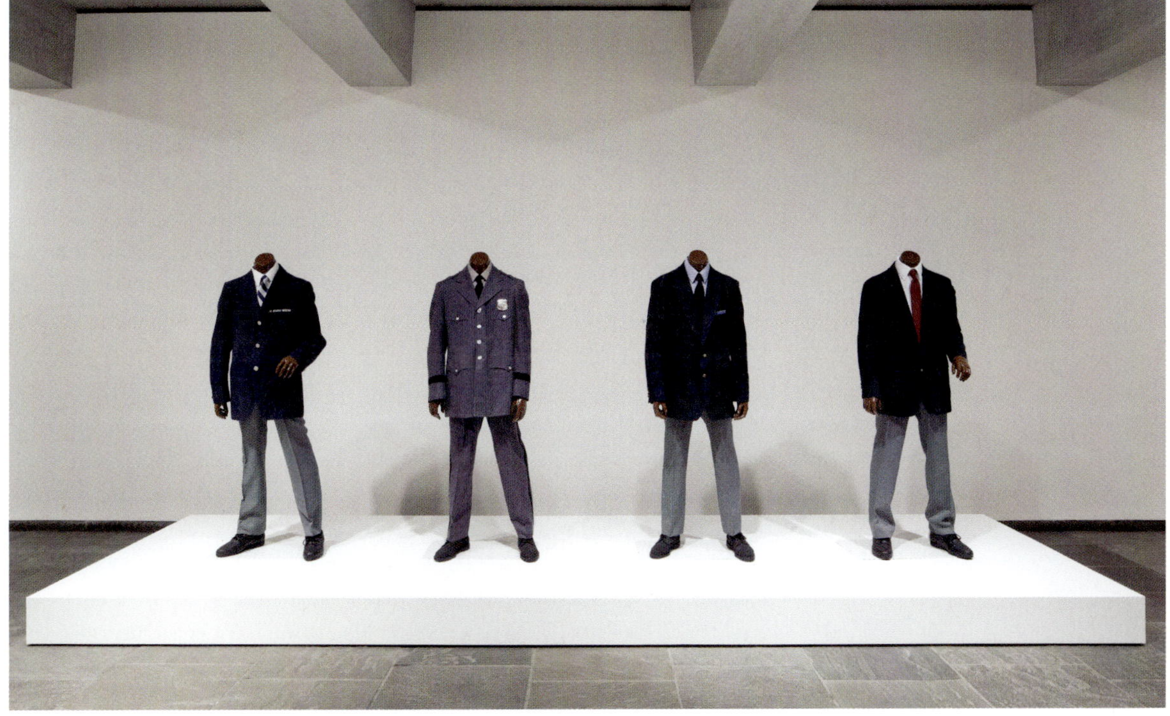

Wilson's work was predicated on his inside knowledge of museums. He began his career as a part-time educator and preparator (art handler) at the Museum of Natural History, the Metropolitan Museum of Art, and the American Craft Museum in New York City. Also, he had previously worked as a security guard at the SUNY Purchase Neuberger Museum when he was a university student. Wilson was raised in New York and attended the High School of Music and Art before going on to complete a BFA in art performance and dance at SUNY Purchase in 1976. By 1979, he was back in New York and conceiving, creating, and exhibiting his conceptual pieces. In 1987, he became director of the Longwood Arts Project, an alternative space in the South Bronx.

In 1992, he was chosen to represent the United States at the Cairo Biennale. The following year, Wilson's Egyptian-themed installation *Re: Claiming Egypt* was featured in the Whitney Biennial, and in 1993, *Guarded View* was the centerpiece of the Whitney's now-famous *Black Male* exhibit. (*Guarded View* is presently part of the Whitney's permanent collection.) Wilson received a MacArthur Foundation Genius Award in 1999 and was invited to be a U.S. delegate to the 50th Venice Biennale in 2003.

Martha Jackson-Jarvis

Although installation is a preferred method of artist Martha Jackson-Jarvis (b. 1952), she is also an Earth artist. Variously termed Land Art, Earthwork, and Environmental Art, depending on the materials used and the type of intervention, Earth Art is an outdoor incarnation of installation art. The artist reshapes or transforms a natural setting to draw attention to issues such as changing ecosystems, environmental decay, pollution, and concepts of life, death, and the human connection to the environment. Natural and manmade materials are used to alter a particular environment, and such alterations take myriad forms. Earth artists also bring nature into the gallery spaces to create indoor landscapes.

Jackson-Jarvis's *Ochun: Earth Mounds* was conceived in 1999 and installed permanently the following year at the 295-acre site of the South Carolina Botanical Garden (Figure 12.10). Using cast-iron cauldrons as molds, the artist used a mixture of red adobe clay, river sand, and cement to create semi-spherical forms of varying sizes. Placed amid moss and ferns near a fallen red oak tree and a curving stream, Jackson-Jarvis's mounds are an homage to the Yoruba mother goddess of love and beauty, who reigns over natural bodies of water. Ochun's consort, the ***orisha*** Ogun, who presides over iron (weaponry, sculpture, and blacksmithing), hunting, and war, symbolically resides in the garden as well, in the form of the iron cauldron molds themselves, which were imbedded into the landscape. The installation is a metaphor for what the artist terms the "landscape of our lives" and is symbolic of birth, death, and rebirth. In the intervening years since *Ochun* was installed, the mounds have slowly become enveloped by earth—a reminder of the inexorability of the life cycles.

Jackson-Jarvis has spent a lifetime creating art that expresses her concerns regarding the misuse of natural and human resources. These leitmotifs extend

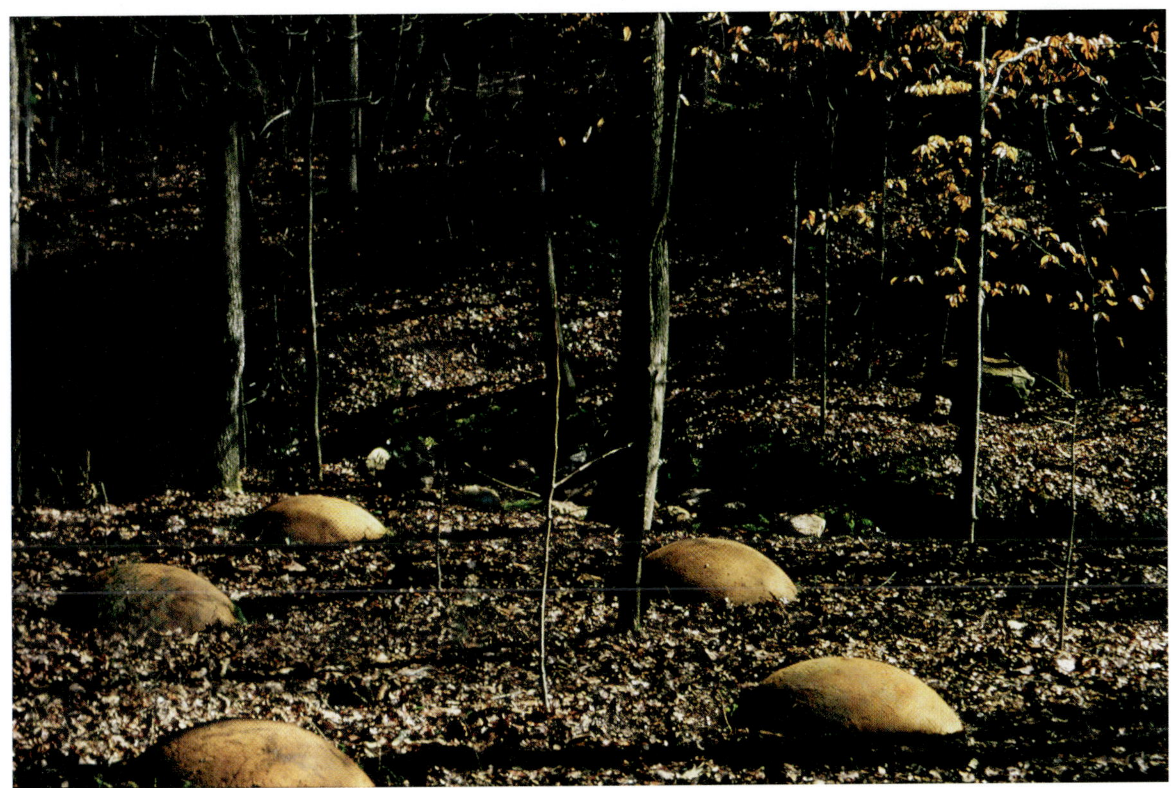

▲ **12.10** Martha Jackson-Jarvis, *Ochun: Earth Mounds*, 1999–2000, iron molds, red clay, river sand, and cement. South Carolina Botanical Garden, Clemson University Campus.

Photo courtesy of Martha Jackson-Jarvis, artist.

to war, starvation, economic oppression, bigotry, misogyny, psychological isolation, and spiritual dispossession. Jackson-Jarvis's multimedia art takes the form of monumental mosaic spheres, public wall installations, shell-encrusted mausoleums, and stone burial site formations. They function as poignant reminders of the interconnectedness of all the earth's inhabitants, the cyclical nature of existence, and the importance of treating one another and our shared environment with nurturing respect.

ASSEMBLAGE ART

Assemblage art comprises the piecing together or "assembling" of already existing objects (found objects) to create a work of three-dimensional art. Take, for example, the wooden window frame used by Conceptual artist Pat Ward Williams to frame photos in her *Accused/Blowtorch/Padlock* (Figure 12.4). The found objects used in assemblages are often ordinary, low-cost, manufactured, or even discarded items: bits of wood, scrap metal, old toys, tools, rags, and so on. Assemblage artists have unlimited aesthetic options. They can leave the found items in their original states, paint them, or combine them to create an entirely new object. Assemblage, which has roots in early 20th-century Modernism, experienced a revival among Postmodernists because it rejected traditional painting and sculpture in favor of recycled objects that, through the creative mind of the artist, could be transformed.

Noah Purifoy

An early and prolific Postmodern assemblage artist, Noah Purifoy (1917–2004) came to Los Angeles in 1952 from Alabama by way of Cleveland (where his family moved when he was 12) and remained there for the rest of his life. He greatly influenced the next generation of West Coast assemblage artists, such as Hammons, Nengudi, and John Outterbridge (discussed later in this chapter). Purifoy received a degree in history from Alabama State Teachers College in Montgomery (1939) and a master's degree in social work from Atlanta University (1948). He held a variety of jobs, teaching high school carpentry in Montgomery, Alabama, from 1939 to 1942; serving in the navy from 1942 to 1945; and working as a social worker in Cleveland from 1950 to 1952.

On his arrival in California, Purifoy continued as a social worker until 1954. He then enrolled at Chouinard (CalArts), where he completed a second master's degree in 1956. For the next decade, Purifoy worked in LA as a window display artist, furniture designer, and freelance interior designer. In 1964, he cofounded the Watts Towers Community Arts Center and served as its director until 1966. The center was located at the famed Watts Towers, 100-foot-high historic landmark constructions made entirely of found objects by Italian tile setter Simon Rodia (1879–1965) in the 1950s. Constructed of castoff tiles, glass, and crockery cemented to a steel rod skeleton, Rodia's creation inspired a generation of California artists to make "something out of nothing." From its historic location, the Watts Art Center organized free art classes, concerts, and plays for Watts residents in Rodia's abandoned four-room home. Hammons, John T. Riddle (1933–2002), Saar, and Outterbridge were among many young artists affiliated with Purifoy and the center who went on to become renowned assemblage artists in their own rights.

A year after the center's founding, the infamous Watts Riots occurred, and Purifoy witnessed firsthand the looting and burning of his beloved neighborhood. Afterward, he and his colleagues wandered through the rubble and, over several weeks, gathered literally tons of debris such as bits of metal, shattered and melted glass, and scorched wood. The collection of destroyed objects became a record of a lost community. Sensing the gravity of the neighborhood's "remains," Purifoy began to repurpose this massive collection of wreckage into works of assemblage art. Of particular interest to Purifoy were industrial materials and consumer items that spoke to the era. His interest dovetailed with Pop Art's focus on these items. However, Purifoy chose rusted, broken, and used objects rather than the pristinely painted Campbell's soup cans of Andy Warhol or the artfully constructed giant hamburger sculptures of Claes Oldenburg (b. 1929). Purifoy was less interested in poking fun at consumer culture than he was in expressing his sociopolitical concerns. For Purifoy, the value of art rested in its function as a vehicle for intellectual engagement and social change.

In 1966, Purifoy and Watts Art Center cofounder Judson Powell (b. 1932) organized a now historic exhibit, *Junk Art: 66 Signs of Neon*. The show included an interracial group of eight artists and debuted at the Simon Rodia Commemorative Watts Renaissance in the Arts Festival, which was initiated that year and which continued annually until 1973. *Junk Art: 66 Signs of Neon* consisted of assemblage pieces created from materials the two had collected after the riots. Among these items were melted neon signs (hence the show's title), wood, smashed windows, scorched rail tracks, and lumps of partially liquefied (from fire) metal.

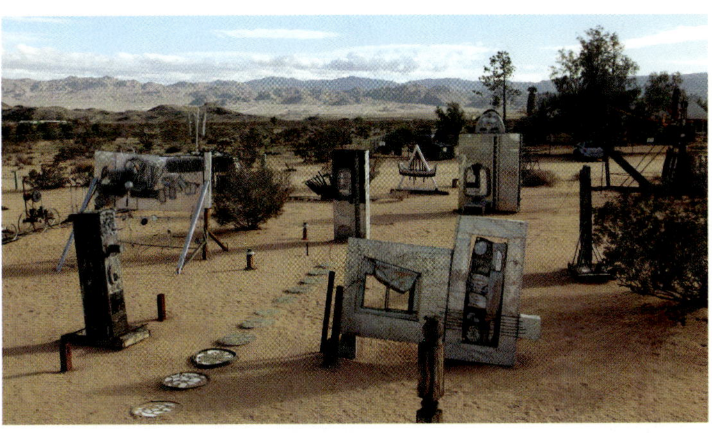

▲ **12.11** Noah Purifoy, *The Sculpture Garden* (Joshua Tree, CA). Outdoor Desert Art Museum of Sculpture, panorama of Purifoy sculptures.

Courtesy of the Noah Purifoy Foundation, www.noahpurifoy.com. Photograph by Drew Tewksbury.

From 1966 to 1973, Purifoy organized the annual Watts Art Festival, supervised the art center, and also taught classes and workshops at several local colleges. From 1973 to 1976, he was director of community services at LA's Central City Community Mental Health Facility, before he joined the California Arts Council. As chair of the council's Subcommittee on Art-in-Education, beginning in 1977 Purifoy organized the Artists in Social Institutions program, which brought art classes and workshops to state prisons. Purifoy dedicated himself to the council for more than a decade, which left him little time to focus on his own art career.

In 1989, Purifoy moved to the Mojave Desert and directed his energies entirely to art making. Residing on a 7.5-acre property in the town of Joshua Tree, owned by Watts Art Center artist and friend Debbie Brewer, Purifoy slowly transformed the location into a massive outdoor museum filled with assemblage sculptures (Figure 12.11). The location became a surreal environment that, like the Watts Towers, was intended to exist permanently in the open air. Now a museum, park, and foundation (the Noah Purifoy Foundation [NPF]), the Joshua Tree site features assemblage art composed of everything from used bowling balls to rusted refrigerators. The NPF and its site are an enduring tribute to Purifoy and his philosophy of art for social change.

John Outterbridge

Another Watts Art Center assemblage artist, John Outterbridge (b. 1933), began his career in 1952 as an engineering student at North Carolina A&T University, near his birthplace of Greenville. There he met several art students who thought he had creative potential and encouraged him to pursue art. Unable to meet tuition demands, Outterbridge decided to join the army to take advantage of the GI Bill, which he hoped would allow him to attend art school after his discharge. Stationed in Germany, Outterbridge trained as a weapons specialist by day, but in the evenings he took classes in German language and traversed the nearby countryside painting (and sometimes selling) watercolor landscapes. When an officer found his paintings during a barracks inspection, he promptly purchased several and located a studio space for Outterbridge on the army base. He also assigned Outterbridge to sign- and mural-painting duties.

After his 1956 discharge, Outterbridge moved to Chicago and attended classes in graphic design and illustration. To support himself, he worked as

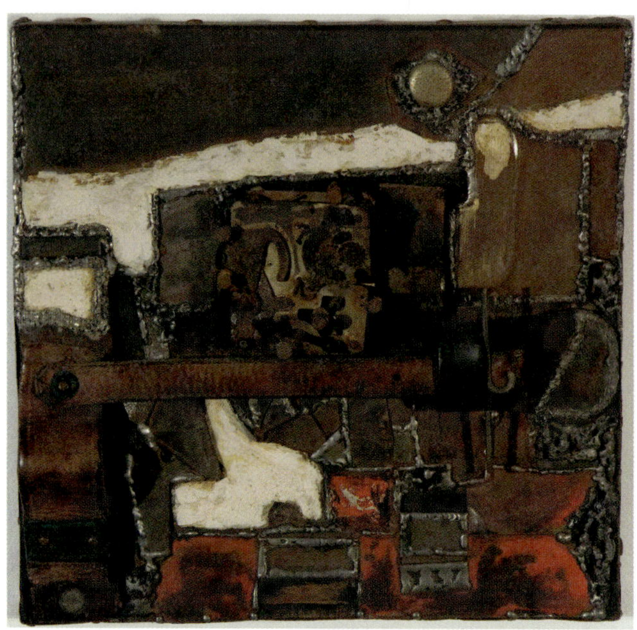

▲ **12.12** John Outterbridge, *Strange Fruit, Containment* series, 1969, mixed media with metal, 10.5″ × 12″ × 1¾″ or 11″ × 11″ × 4.3″.

Private collection, courtesy of the artist and Tilton Gallery, New York, NY.

a messenger for a graphic design firm and then as a city bus driver for eight years. He also joined the SSCAC and exhibited his work there. In 1963, after what the artist described as several financially, personally, and professionally difficult years, Outterbridge married and moved to Los Angeles, which he hoped would be a better place to raise children. Once there, he met Purifoy, who encouraged him to work with found objects. While experimenting with materials, Outterbridge taught at community art centers in Compton and Watts. Inspired by Purifoy, he began collecting castoff objects that he found in the streets, using them to make assemblages that expressed inner-city LA life.

Outterbridge's art-making of the period was influenced by the abstract sculptures of Mark di Suvero (b. 1933) made from demolition site refuse, the monumental sheet-metal sculptures of Richard Serra (b. 1939), and the Postmodern "combines" (painting and assemblage) of Robert Rauschenberg—artists whom Outterbridge met while installing their exhibits at the Pasadena Museum, where he worked between 1967 and 1973. His 1969 *Containment* series is an abstract, wall-mounted assemblage suite composed of discarded bits of leather and soldered metal, "contained" within rectangular casings. His *Strange Fruit/Time for a New Direction* from the series (Figure 12.12) presents an abstract specter of a map of Watts, just east of South Alameda. The title and the work allude to the police practice during the Watts rebellions of "containing" (rather than ending) the violence and looting within the black Watts neighborhood to prevent it from spilling over into the abutting South Gate area, which was then home to several white gangs. Outterbridge's presentation of crisscrossing soldered seams, the inner workings of a clock, a leather belt, a metal hook, and areas of red suggest crushing summer heat, urban mayhem, violence, fire, destruction, and the "time for a new direction" suggested in the title.

In 1973, Outterbridge became director of the Compton Communicative Arts Academy, which, until its closing in 1976, provided arts and humanities programming for local residents. After several years at the academy, Outterbridge replaced Purifoy as director of the Watts Towers Community Arts Center, where he remained from 1975 to 1992. After retiring from that position, Outterbridge devoted his full-time attention to art making. He has since been featured in half a dozen solo exhibits at museums in New York and California, and he has been the recipient of major public commissions, honorary degrees, and awards.

Aminah Brenda Lynn Robinson

Artist and children's book illustrator Aminah Brenda Lynn Robinson (1940–2015) grew up in the Poindexter Village Housing Project in Columbus, Ohio.

A compulsive sketch artist as a child, Robinson had already trained herself in figure drawing by the time she enrolled in Columbus School of Art (later Columbus College of Art and Design) in 1956. After four years there, Robinson studied art history and philosophy at Ohio State University from 1960 to 1963. In 1964, she married Korean War veteran and career military man Charles Robinson and, throughout the 1960s, worked as an illustrator, first in Columbus and later in various cities in Nebraska, Idaho, Mississippi, and Puerto Rico where her husband was stationed.

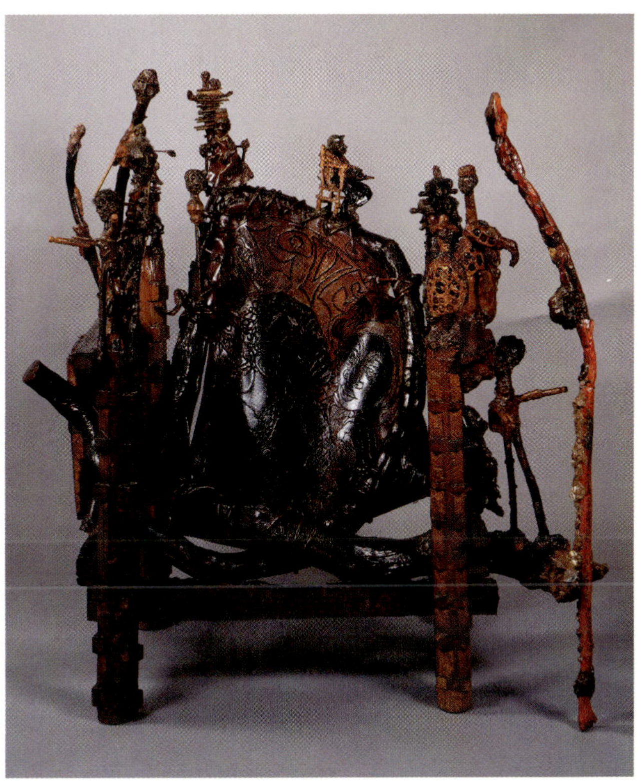

▲ **12.13** Aminah Brenda Lynn Robinson, *Gift of Love*, 1974–2002, wood, leather, hogmawg (mud, pig grease, dyes, glue, and lime), leather, and found objects, 61″ × 35″ × 56″.

Columbus Museum of Art, OH. Gift of the artist, 2008.005.

After a 1971 divorce, Robinson returned to Columbus with her four-year-old son Sydney and, for nearly two decades from 1972 to 1990, taught art in her childhood neighborhood at the Beatty Recreation Center, a community center run by the Columbus Recreation and Parks Department. A low-paying position, the job barely provided a livable income. Unable to afford new furniture for her home, in the mid-1970s Robinson began work on a now-legendary oversized chair, which she later entitled *Gift of Love* (1974–2002; Figure 12.13). Made of hand-tooled and tanned animal hide, tree roots, and other found items, the chair marked Robinson's first formal foray into assemblage art. Significantly, she worked on the chair intermittently for 40 years.

Encouraged by friend and Columbus wood sculptor Elijah Pierce (1892–1984), whom Robinson had met in 1968, she created other sculpture and multimedia assemblages using whatever materials she could find. These materials included found bits of plastic, metal, and glass; all manner of fabrics, textiles, and leather; a homemade sculptural medium—dubbed "hogmawg"—made from clay, pulverized brick, and twigs with pig fat as the mixing agent; and more traditional materials such as pen and ink, paint, and drawing charcoal. Robinson also worked in larger formats, sometimes creating multimedia elongated textile works of more than 200 feet in length. She nicknamed these scroll-like pieces "RagGonNons" because they were made using old rags and other fabrics adorned with buttons and beads.

Robinson was a narrative artist whose work depicts epic tales of her beloved Columbus and its African-American populace, as well as stories of her family's history. Robinson also portrayed African-American abolitionists, civil rights leaders, musicians, and writers. Over time, her home and yard overflowed with her art, and its visibility brought her to the attention of the local art community.

In 1979, the Cleveland American Forum for Study arranged for Robinson to travel abroad for the first time. She visited Africa, in particular the historic sites of the slave trade. She also toured Egypt, where she was christened

Aminah by an Egyptian cleric whom she met while there. (The name derives from Aamina, the name of the Prophet Muhammad's mother.) After her return to the States, Robinson's reputation grew, mostly by word of mouth, thanks to her many local fans. The artist began receiving invitations to exhibit her work at museums and galleries. Between 1980 and 1990, she exhibited in group shows at various university and civic galleries, and she was honored with the Ohio Governor's Award for the Visual Arts and several fellowships from the Ohio Arts Council.

In addition to mounting a solo show at the Columbus Museum, in 1990 Robinson was commissioned by the Columbus Metropolitan Library to paint a 40-foot multi-paneled mural for the library's open staircase. It depicts the history of two bygone black Columbus communities of the 19th and early 20th century—Sellsville and Blackberry Patch—which the artist researched exhaustively as part of her creative process. The income from this commission made it possible for Robinson to give up her job at the Beatty Community Center and become a full-time artist. Just when her star was rising, however, in 1994 the artist's son Sydney, who had long suffered from depression, committed suicide at age 27. Having saved his baby teeth, she chose to include them in several of her artworks, allowing this organic part of his body to live on in her art.

During the 1990s, Robinson illustrated a series of children's books, including *Elijah's Angel* (1992), *Sophie* (1994), *A School for Pompey Walker* (1995), and *To Be a Drum* (1998). In 2002, a major retrospective entitled *Symphonic Poem: The Art of Aminah Robinson* was organized by the Columbus Museum of Art and traveled around the country. Robinson's career was crowned with the coveted MacArthur Foundation Genius Award in 2004 and with the Anyone Can Fly Foundation Lifetime Achievement Award in 2010.

Alison Saar

The sculpture, assemblage, and installation art of California native Alison Saar (b. 1956; daughter of artist Betye Saar) is framed by her eclectic interests in ethnicity and gender; by European, Asian and African art; by her knowledge of art history; and by neo-African religions such as Vodou. Saar's interest in reprocessing secondhand odds and ends was triggered by a childhood visit to the Watts Towers, where her mother worked. Her materials include found objects such as tree trunks and branches, old ceiling tin, coat hangers, barbed wire, wooden dolls, rusted nails, broken glass, and plastic bottles. Saar works with low-tech tools such as wood chisels and chainsaws to hammer, reshape, assemble, and paint her found materials, giving them new meaning and form. Saar relishes the use of recycled materials because she believes that these objects (which she collects copiously from city streets and flea markets) have their own "memory" and hence bring something unique to the work.

Saar's work, most often human figures, is imbued with emotional, spiritual, sexual, and political import. Her 1999 *Compton Nocturne* portrays a woman caught between dream and waking states. The figure's body reclines, but its head is upright (Figure 12.14). Hair coifed from tree branches grows

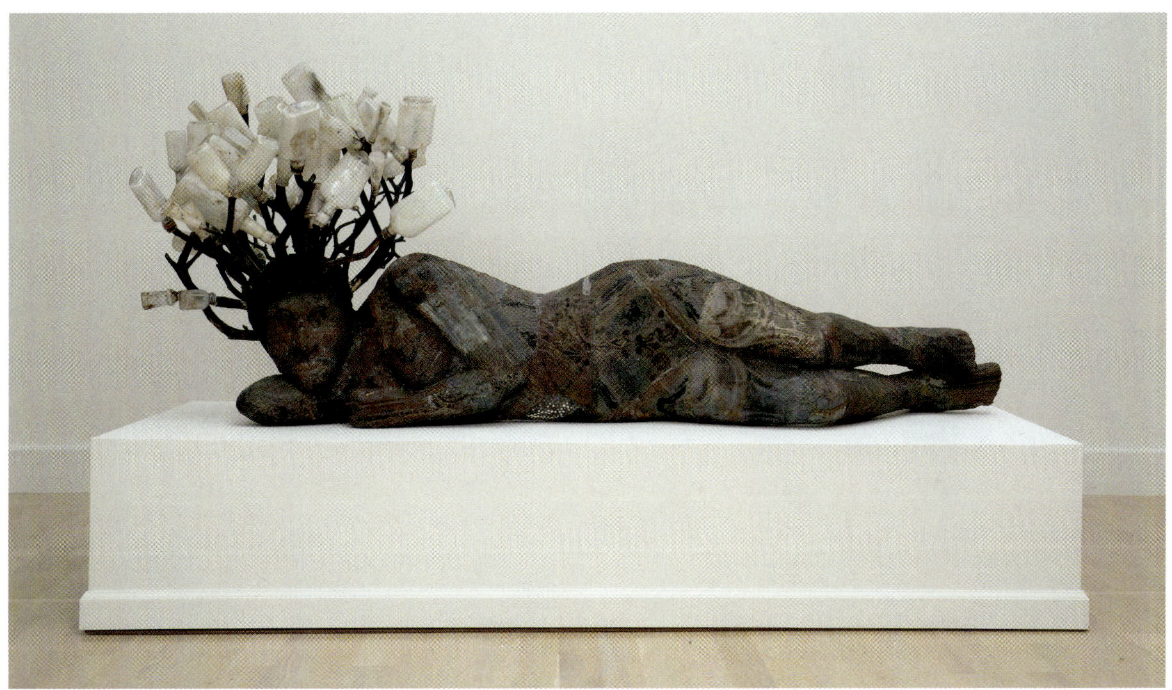

▲ **12.14** Alison Saar, *Compton Nocturne*, 1999, wood, tin, bottles, paint, and tar, 33″ × 80″ × 28″.
Weatherspoon Art Museum, the University of North Carolina at Greensboro, museum purchase with funds from the Benefactors Fund, 1999.

out of her head like Medusan snakes. At the end of these tendrils sprout bottles, an allusion to traditional African-American bottle trees, which have adorned yards in the southern United States since the 18th century. Meant to capture spirits, the bottle tree is reified in Saar's *Compton Nocturne* as a dream catcher. Hammered ceiling tin forms the figure's skin. Saar allowed the stamped decoration of the original tin to remain visible, so that old and new forms exist concurrently. To create a heightened sense of the figure's raw energy, in places Saar deliberately left the gouges of her chisel visible. Finally, Saar's title indicates that this woman is from the LA neighborhood of Compton, infamously associated in the popular mind with hip-hop and gang violence. Through this work, Saar compels us to rethink the myopic stereotypes that qualify such a diverse community as a unidimensional universe of Crips and Bloods.

Saar is a devotee of African-American folk art, which was the subject of her undergraduate thesis at Scripps College, completed under the supervision of her advisor, artist/historian Samella Lewis. In the thrall of folk inspiration, Saar produces works that evoke the vernacular, to which she adds cultural narratives of a decidedly urbane nature, revealing her training as an art historian. The trademark rusticity of Saar's sculptures owes something to family influences, following the example set by her mother and her father, Richard, who was an art conservator. Mr. Saar exposed his daughter to museums and art books as a child, and, by hiring her as his assistant (working mainly on the restoration of African and Afro-Caribbean artifacts), he taught her the value of preserving old and decaying objects. Her unique methods and unsettling visual statements merge to form evocative and commanding structures of extraordinary vitality.

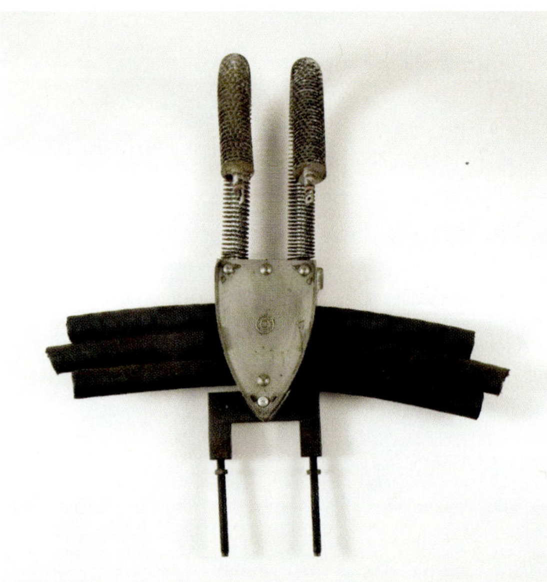

▲ **12.15** Willie Cole, *Neo-Senufo*, 1988, assemblage of found objects and concrete, 21½″ × 20″ × 9¼″.

Photo courtesy of Alexander and Bonin, New York, NY.

Willie Cole

Willie Cole (b. 1955) is a New Jersey native who was already studying art at the Newark Museum in his preteens. He enrolled in Newark's Arts High School and won his first art award at a local teen art festival. After graduating from high school, Cole attended the School for Visual Arts in New York, graduating in 1976. Over the next several years, Cole continued his arts education at the Art Students League while earning a living as a freelance illustrator and graphic designer. By the mid-1980s, Cole was creating and exhibiting video and installation art. In 1988, he secured an artist's residency at the Studio Museum.

Cole is best known for his use of mask-like impressions burned onto paper and canvas using an ordinary clothing iron—a motif he began using at the Studio Museum. A review of Cole's work of this period reveals its allure, which is both visual and conceptual. For example, in an early assemblage from 1988, Cole combined found rubber tubing, heating coils, and a metal household iron to create an African sculptural form entitled *Neo-Senufo* (Figure 12.15). Extrapolated from sacred helmet masks created by the Senufo people of Mali, Burkina Faso, and the Ivory Coast, Cole's variation on the theme alludes to his African heritage and to women domestic workers through its transformation of household objects, fusing race and gender into a witty Neo-Dada construction.

A master of the **ready-made** art form, Cole creates two- and three-dimensional figurative art using household objects such as blow-dryers, irons,

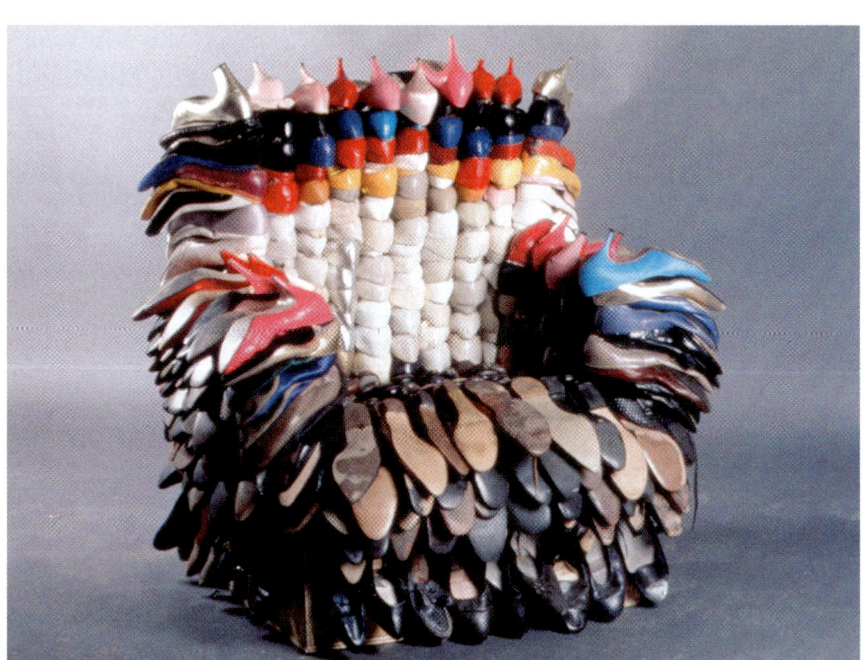

▶ **12.16** Willie Cole, *Made in the Philippines*, 1993, shoes, PVC pipe, and wood, 46″ × 38″ × 38″.

Photo courtesy of Alexander and Bonin, New York, NY.

and ironing boards, transforming them into masks, ellipses, robots, and warrior shields. Cole's alchemical skills are nowhere more evident than in his tongue-in-cheek throne made from women's high-heeled shoes (Figure 12.16). Titled *Made in the Philippines*, it is an allusion to the widely publicized shoe fetish of Filipino First Lady Imelda Marcos, to consumer waste, and to America's dependence on underpaid Asian labor. Cole has made equally intriguing shoe "masks" using stiletto heels to create bared teeth and red pumps to fashion minstrel-like red lips for a blackface countenance.

Cole's provocative and witty art garnered him his first major solo exhibit at the Mint Museum in Charlotte, North Carolina, in 1989. Since then he had been commissioned by Paramount Pictures to create paintings for the sets of the Eddie Murphy film *Boomerang*, and he has received multiple artist's residencies and major grants from the Tiffany and Joan Mitchell Foundations, among others. Cole won the Driskell Prize, awarded by Atlanta's High Museum; and dozens of key museums permanently house his art.

POSTMODERN PHOTOGRAPHY

The late 20th century saw a drastic rise in image-based technologies, from conventional television and film to video, LED advertisements, computer-generated imagery, and digital photography. These advancements led to the widespread acceptance of photography as a valid art form central to Postmodernism. Because photography had historically been viewed as distinct from high art forms such as painting and sculpture, Postmodern artists enthusiastically embraced the medium, in part as a way to deconstruct such conventional thinking. The outcome was the development of wide, varied, and entirely new artistic approaches to photography as both a conceptual and anti-Modern art form.

Carrie Mae Weems

Portland, Oregon–born photographer and multimedia and installation artist Carrie Mae Weems (b. 1953) is an innovator in conceptual photography. Weems earned a BFA from CalArts in 1981 and an MFA from UC San Diego in 1984 and studied African-American folklore at UC Berkeley from 1984 to 1987. Her Berkeley research in storytelling (particularly the narratives of Zora Neale Hurston) inspired her to incorporate literary components into her visual arts projects. Texts function to clarify and enhance her otherwise enigmatic iconography. Weems's oeuvre can best be described as a balance between pictorial and verbal narratives that pivot on questions of ethnic, cultural, and sexual identity. Her famed 1995 suite *From Here I Saw What Happened and I Cried* embodies this balance. The suite is composed of more than 30 reconstituted photos appropriated from archeological daguerreotypes of American slaves taken in 1850 (Figure 12.17). The original photos were intended for use by Swiss racial theorist Louis Agassiz (1807–73) to prove the inferiority of Africans and to codify racial types.

Rephotographing the original images through a red filter, Weems placed the new photos in vintage-styled frames and overlaid them with etched glass. Each glass overlay bears a unique phrase: "You Became a Scientific

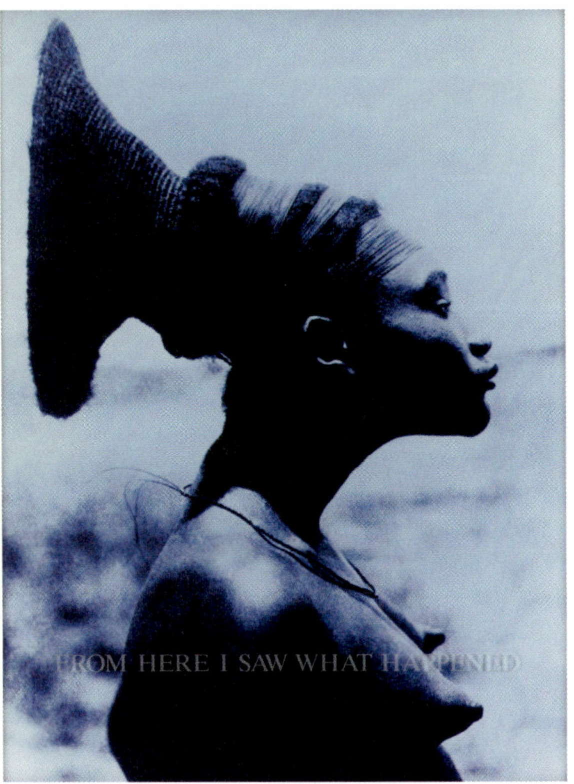

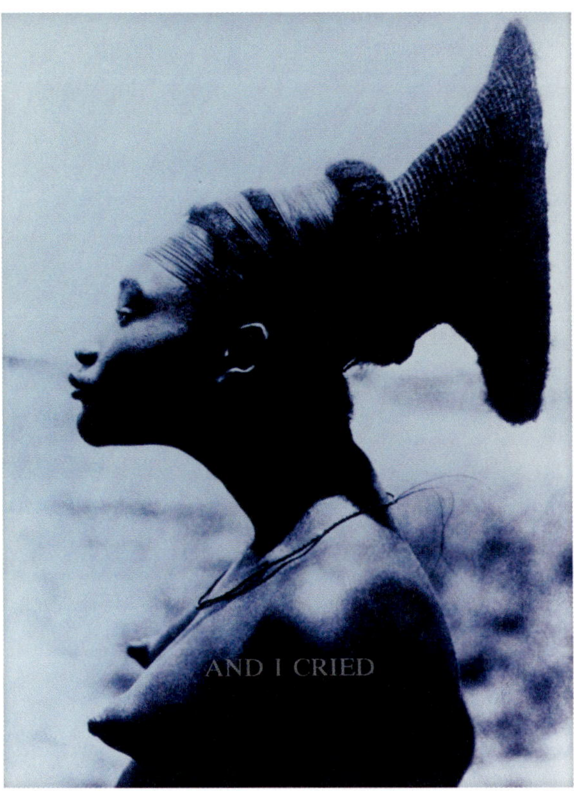

▲ **12.17** Carrie Mae Weems, *From Here I Saw What Happened and I Cried* (two images from the series), 1995/1996, C-prints, sandblasted text on glass, 43″ × 33″.

© Carrie Mae Weems. Courtesy of the artist and Jack Shainman Gallery, NY.

Profile," "A Negroid Type," "An Anthropological Debate," "A Photographic Subject," and similar pithy descriptors that remind viewers of the efforts of the 19th-century scientific community to reduce African genealogy to the level of animals. As the series unfolds, the texts become more elaborate and incensed. The words "Black and Tan Your Whipped Wind of Change Howled Low Blowing Itself Ha—Smack Into the Middle of Ellington's Orchestra," for instance, accompanies a photograph of the brutally scarred back of a male whipping victim. The series of images is flanked by two grisaille prints of a classic photo of the exquisite Mangbetu queen Nobosodru, taken in 1925 by George Specht and Leon Poirier while they traveled in the Congo (Figure 12.18). The two profiles of Queen Nobosodru are accompanied by the title words, "From Here I Saw What Happened and I Cried." Sentinel-like, she watches from her perch in the African past as her descendants are debased and oppressed. Weems's deconstructionist intent is to recontextualize the original photos so as to ascribe to them new meanings and, in her words, a "level of humanity and . . . dignity that was originally missing."

Weems's photographic art is centered on debunking the notion that "the camera never lies." As French literary theorist Roland Barthes argued in his 1964 structuralist essay "Rhetoric of Images," a photograph by virtue of its promise of veracity is, in fact, more deceptive than other two-dimensional media such as painting and drawing, which viewers recognize as modified interpretations of reality. Those who suppose that photography captures objective truth overlook the fact that the camera is manipulated by a

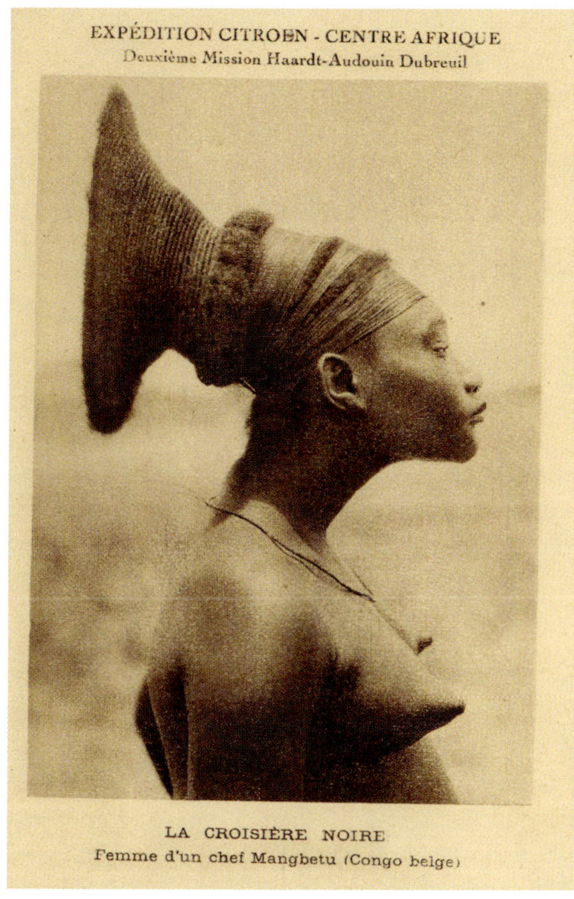

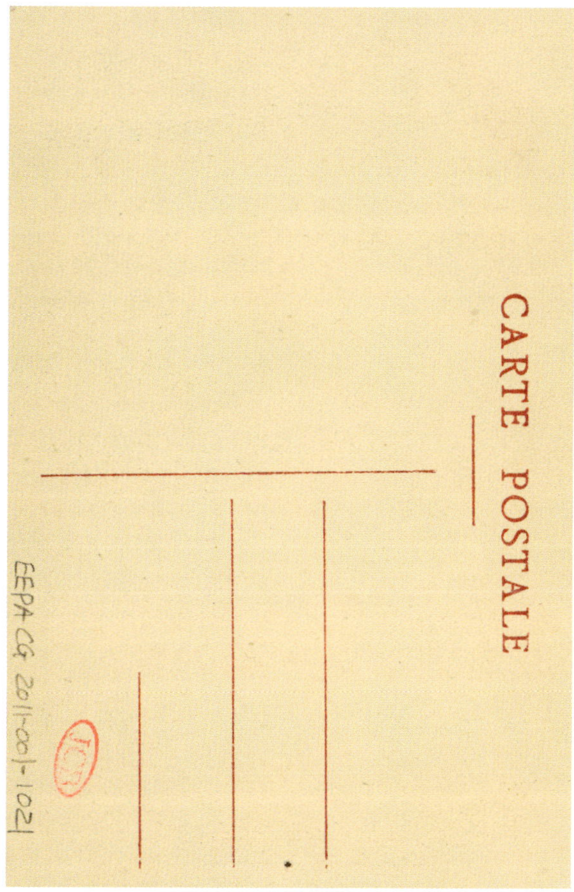

▲ **12.18** Leon Poirier and George Specht, *La Croisière Noire: Femme d'un chef Mangbetu (Congo Belge), Expédition Citroen—Centre Afrique, Deuxième Mission Haardt-Audouin Dubreuil,* March 1925, photogravure postcard, 5.5″ × 7″.

Photo: Léon Poirier and Georges Specht, 1925. Photogravure, postcard EEPA Postcard Collection, CG-20-76. Eliot Elisofon Photographic Archives National Museum of African Art Smithsonian Institution.

subjective and very human photographer whose agendas and predispositions affect creative decisions such as subject matter, lighting, cropping, and vantage point. In light of Barthes's observations, it would be more accurate to assume that the camera always lies, or at least tells an especially partisan tale. Weems's work reinterprets archeological photos from the point of view of a contemporary artist of African-American descent whose **gaze** is by far more elastic and sophisticated than the white gaze for and by whom the original photos were taken.

Weems's conceptual photography extends to large-scale installations wherein she digitally enlarges photos and prints them onto fabric, transforming entire galleries. Her themes include intimate portraits of family and friends, Sea Island landscapes, and African architectural monuments. She has also explored the origin and nature of historically black colleges and universities (in her controversial *Hampton Project* of 2000), and the intricate genealogical web that links white and black Americans (the *Jefferson Suite* of 1999). For her insightfully critical art, Weems has received honorary degrees from Colgate University and CalArts and won the MacArthur Genius Award, the Skowhegan Medal for Photography, a Rome Prize, a Pollack-Krasner Foundation grant, and many more accolades. She continues today to create from her New York studio.

Dawoud Bey

Originally from the New York City borough of Queens, photographer, musician, and writer Dawoud Bey (b. 1953) currently lives and works in Chicago. Trained since childhood as a drummer and pianist, Bey was working as a professional musician when a 1969 visit to the *Harlem on My Mind* exhibit at the Metropolitan Museum inspired him to become a photographer. A year earlier, his godmother had given him a single-lens reflex camera that he taught himself to use. During this period, Bey also changed his first name from David to Dawoud, the Arabic pronunciation of David, and his last name from Smickle to Bey—a name he borrowed from a favorite drum teacher. By the mid-1970s, he was working as a photographer full-time.

Bey gained international attention for his sizeable, sobering, and striking color portraits of minority and bohemian youth culture personae taken beginning in the 1980s. His first major series, however, was conceived in 1975 and was composed of modestly sized black-and-white images of Harlem locals—a project directly inspired by the Van Der Zee photos in the *Harlem on My Mind* show. Bey's now-celebrated Harlem series was exhibited in 2012 at the Art Institute of Chicago, where it now resides.

Bey studied for two years at SVA before leaving in 1978 to work as an artist-photographer for the CETA (Comprehensive Employment and Training Act) Program, which provided temporary employment for low-income applicants. While at CETA from 1978 to 1981, Bey met his future wife, abstract painter Candida Alvarez (b. 1955). At this time, the exceptional quality of Bey's photography led to his first teaching experience: the Studio Museum hired him to teach a photography class in 1976. Teaching became Bey's chief means of financial support during the 1980s, in addition to grants. He also occasionally sold and often exhibited his photographs, locally and nationally. He continued his education at SUNY's Empire State College in Saratoga Springs, where he earned a BFA in photography in 1990; three years later, Bey earned an MFA from the Yale University School of Art.

In the 1990s, Bey developed his signature photographic style: large-format color portraits, exemplified in the decade-long series *Polaroid 20 × 24*. Composed of introspective single- and multiple-print portraits sometimes cropped and reassembled like puzzle pieces, the series includes shots of edgy urban teenagers, and of Bey's family members and artist-friends: Hassinger, Whitfield Lovell (b. 1959), Lorna Simpson (b. 1960), and Sol LeWitt (in a diptych with LeWitt's wife, Carol), among others. Often shot at close range, images in the *Polaroid 20 × 24* series focus on facial expressions, hands, gestures, and the sitter's gaze. In Bey's 1996 *Syretta* from the series, a somber teen is captured in six prints with borders and sections that are slightly misaligned so that the overall feeling is one of disjuncture and unease (Figure 12.19). Through this technique, Bey communicates the sitter's state (or states) of mind. His images offer multifaceted psychological readings that transcend race, age, and gender.

In 1992, Bey's photography garnered him the first of three artist's residencies at the Addison Gallery of American Art in Andover, Massachusetts. His project there involved photographing private and public school students to explore issues of class difference. Inspired by the experience, Bey continued to photograph young people into the 21st century. His studies of youth culminated in a 2007 book and accompanying exhibit underwritten by the Aperture Foundation entitled, appropriately, *Class Pictures*: an allusion to both the student status of the subjects and their differing socioeconomic classes. The images each feature captions, written by the various sitters. An Indian teen named Usha wrote, "I can speak four languages. I am an actress." Omar ruminated, "I know that I shouldn't but sometimes I wonder how other people look at me." And Kevin observed, "When I was about six or seven, my father died. This was either the worst or the best thing that ever happened to me. In fact, now that I think about it, it was both." The images and the remarks reveal that race and class—and even age—have very little to do with our shared humanity. A national solo tour of his *Class Pictures* traveled from 2007 to 2011.

Since 1998, Bey has served as professor of photography at Chicago's Columbia College. Bey's recent photographic suites include *The Birmingham Project*, in honor of the 50th anniversary of the Atlanta church bombings, which debuted at the Birmingham Museum of Art in 2013.

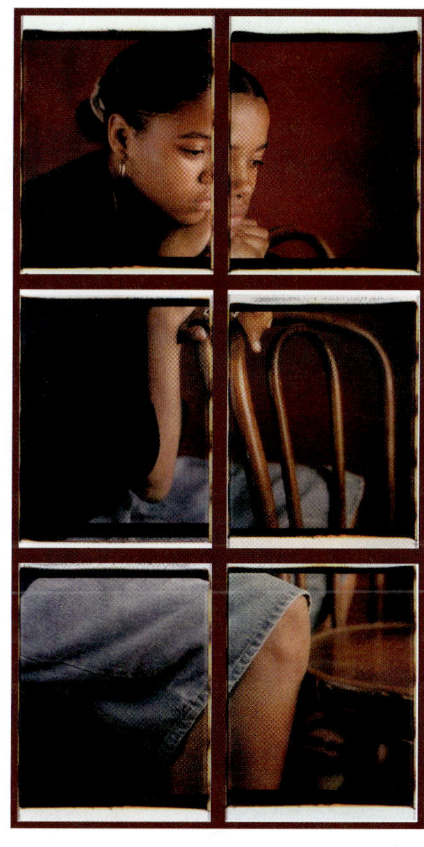

▲ **12.19** Dawoud Bey, *Syretta*, 1996, dye diffusion transfer prints.

Museum purchase with funds from Ms. Joanna Sturm by exchange. © Dawoud Bey. The Haggerty Museum of Art. Marquette University, Milwaukee, WI.

Lyle Ashton Harris

Lyle Ashton Harris (b. 1965) was born and raised in the Bronx. Additionally, his family spent two years in Dar Es Salaam, Tanzania, from 1974 to 1976. After receiving a BA from Wesleyan University in 1988 and an MFA from CalArts in 1990, Harris attended NYU's National Graduate Photography Seminar in 1991. That same year he was awarded an NEA Fellowship, followed in 1992 by a coveted spot in the Whitney Museum Independent Study Program. During the remainder of the 1990s, Harris was featured in half a dozen solo exhibitions. Since 1996, he has served as director of NYU's Global ArtSites Program. While an artist-resident at the American Academy in Rome in 2001, Harris developed his *Blow Up* series—a collection of site-specific collages and photomontages consisting of images that interrogate gender and sexual identity. After returning to the United States, he rejoined NYU's faculty. He spends time each year at NYU's extension school in Accra, Ghana, where, among other assignments, he has been on the Board of Directors of Art in Social Structures (AISS) since 2009.

Harris's artistic media include photography, film, collage, installation, and performance; his iconography centers on race, ethnicity, gender, and social identity; and his preferred form is portraiture. Through these "lenses," he examines pop icon identity (notably that of Billie Holiday and Michael Jackson), masquerade and costumes as metaphors for latent identities, and manifestations of acute masculinity in the military, law enforcement, and sports arenas. Consistent throughout his oeuvre is beauty: beautiful people in beautiful settings and elegant poses who communicate identity by cross-dressing, exposing themselves, painting their faces, shaving their heads, coifing their hair, and wearing costumes and masks.

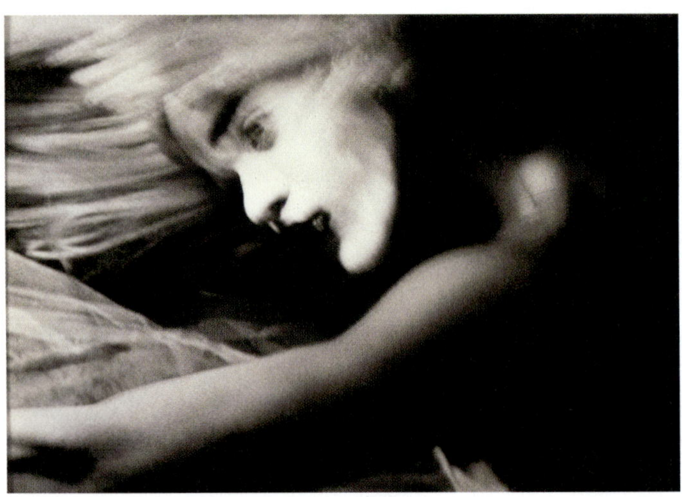

▲ **12.20** Lyle Ashton Harris, *Untitled #1*, 1987–88, black-and-white silver gelatin print, 30″ × 20″.

Courtesy of the artist.

Harris's late 1980s black-and-white photographic series *Reflection of Past Life Through Glass* includes several self-portraits wherein the artist is veiled in white organza. A metaphor for veiled identity, the photographs represent the black male as vulnerable, elusive, and attractive. The gossamer veiling, like a bridal veil, belies the artist's powerful physical presence, just as the black male body—and all its attendant stereotypes—belies the fact of black male homosexuality. In his *Americas* and *Constructs* series of the same period, a nude Harris wears blond wigs, tutus, and whiteface as a riposte to blackface minstrelsy (Figure 12.20). He strikes provocative dance poses in front of the camera in a critique of black male stereotypes, Western ideals of beauty, and the pervasiveness of false social and gender constructs. More recent Harris suites comprise color photography, photomontage, and video and explore similar issues of ethnicity, homosexuality, gender, and masculinity.

Lorna Simpson

The art of Lorna Simpson (b. 1960) integrates a destabilizing mix of sentence fragments, word lists, and photography. Her 1991 *Five Day Forecast* juxtaposes five black-and-white photos of a nonspecific black woman whose head has been cropped off (Figure 12.21). She wears a white shift and stands frontally with arms folded. Each image is accompanied by a day title and a caption: "Monday: Misdescription, Misinformation," "Tuesday: Misidentity,

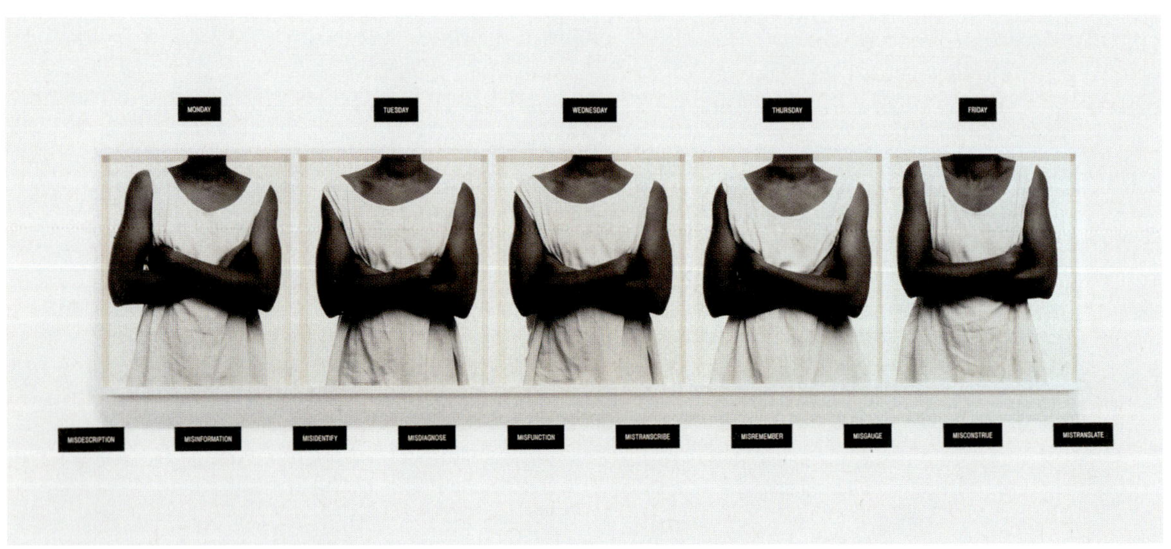

▼ **12.21** Lorna Simpson, *Five Day Forecast*, 1991, five 20″ × 24″ Polaroids mounted in one frame, with 15 plastic plaques.

The Tate Britain Gallery, purchased with funds provided by the 2010 Outset/Frieze Art Fair Fund to benefit the Tate Collection 2010. © Lorna Simpson, courtesy Salon 94, New York, NY.

Misdiagnose," "Wednesday: Misfunction, Mistranscribe," "Thursday: Misremember, Misgauge," and "Friday: Misconstrue, Mistranslate." Simpson's words and images suggest the myriad ways in which our assumptions about black woman—indeed, about anyone—can be erroneous.

A Brooklynite, Simpson initially trained as a documentary photographer at the SVA (BFA, 1983) and at the University of California, San Diego (MFA, 1985). Formally, Simpson's imagery is inspired by the compositional poise and equanimity of Roy DeCarava's work. Conceptually, Simpson creates pictures that expose photography as a subjective rather than objective medium. Simpson's images are often political in content and frequently focus on the problems faced by women, such as sexual harassment and domestic violence. Although, like many conceptual photographers, Simpson accompanies her photographs with texts, her use of language is designed to provoke rather than dictate critical thinking.

Simpson's photographs are renowned for their narrative restraint. Her spare settings and anonymous subjects impede any reading of personality and make her sitters difficult to pigeonhole. Simpson's characters may be interpreted in any number of ways: as angry, stubborn, recalcitrant, or shy. In this way, Simpson allows her audience a great deal of interpretive freedom and ensures their active participation in the work. Furthermore, Simpson universalizes her subjects by denying viewers a face with which to identify, and by utilizing the least culturally charged props available to her, such as her oft-employed plain white dress. The interpretive possibilities are myriad, making the work obstructive and enticing at the same time. The viewer cannot hope to wholly know the subject and is permitted only the narrowest glimpse of his or her existence.

In recent years, Simpson has created a series of films centering on complicated women characters whose roles blur distinctions between binary concepts such as black and white, male and female, good and bad, celibate and sexualized, and aggressive and passive. Her film work is informed by 1940s film noire, the independent films of John Cassavetes (1928–89), the experimental works of Jean-Luc Goddard (b. 1930), and method acting. Highly regarded for its provocative formal orientation and conceptual complexity, Simpson's art is shown and collected in the United States and Europe. As a testament to Simpson's revered status and that of her art, she was awarded the International Center of Photography's Infinity Award in 2010.

Summary

As a reaction against the object-based nature of late-era Modernist movements such as Abstract Expressionism and Minimalism, Postmodern art embraced eclectic forms and methods. Post-Minimalist sculptors created sculpture that engaged the space around it as well as the viewer's senses. Conceptual artists emphasized words and ideas as integral to art making. Performance and installation artists took advantage of varied media—sculpture, dance, music, and video—to create ephemeral and dynamic art experiences rather than permanent, static art objects.

Assemblage artists revived the early 20th-century interest in found and ready-made materials to create art from preexisting non-art items, which they recycled into iconographically complex works of art. The Postmodern era also mainstreamed photography as a significant form of conceptual art.

Key Terms

adire-eleko dyeing: a starch resist dying technique used by the Yoruba people of Nigeria to create indigo patterned textiles

cosmogram: a circular symbol representing the cyclical nature of life

Fluxus: an international and interdisciplinary group of performance artists founded in the 1960s

gaze: in art, refers to how and what is seen or observed by either the viewer or the sitter; suggests a particular point of view

intermedia art: art created across creative disciplines and with multiple media

Light and Space Art Movement: a sculpture movement centered in 1970s Los Angeles that used light, spatial effects, and new media such as fiberglass and resin to undermine the static nature of art objects and to engage the sensory perceptions of the viewer

Los Angeles Look style: a 1960s California-based predecessor to the Light and Space Movement, which popularized the use of fiberglass and resin to create glossy two- and three-dimensional abstract art

metaethics: the study of the origin and meaning of morality, including the psychological bases for morality and whether or not morals are a human construction or a transcendent truth

orisha: a Yoruba deity

ready-made: a work of art composed of common manufactured objects recontextualized by the artist

Questions for Further Study and Discussion

1. What aspects of Modernism did Postmodernism reject?
2. Define Post-Object Art.
3. How did Post-Minimalism differ from Minimalism?
4. Debate whether a work of art should be a permanent object.
5. Create your own business cards like the cards of Adrian Piper, using a statement of your choice designed to mitigate verbal confrontation. Rather than distributing them, discuss in class.
6. Identify, collect, and assemble several found objects into a new and unique work of ready-made art. Write an essay on the iconography of your assemblage.
7. How did the urban riots of the 1960s fuel the Postmodern assemblage art movement, particularly in Los Angeles?
8. Read Roland Barthes's "Rhetoric of Images" and discuss/debate his argument that photographs are not reflections of "truth."

9. Reseach other artists not discussed in detail in this chapter, such as Skunder Alexander Boghossian (1937–2003), Beverly Buchanan (b. 1940), Gylbert Coker (b. 1944), Maren Hassinger (b. 1947), Kinshasha Holman Conwill (b. 1951), Alonzo Davis (b. 1973), Dale Brockman Davis (b. 1945), Bessie Harvey (1929–94), Lonnie Holley (b. 1950), Ulysses Jenkins (b. 1946), Daniel LaRue Johnson (b. 1938), Whitfield Lovell (b. 1959), Senga Nengudi (Sue Irons; b. 1943), Franklin Parker (1945–2001), Judson Powell (b. 1932), John T. Riddle (1933–2002), Gary Simmons (b. 1964), Coreen Simpson (b. 1942) and Renee Stout (b. 1958). How does their work compare with the artists studied in this chapter?

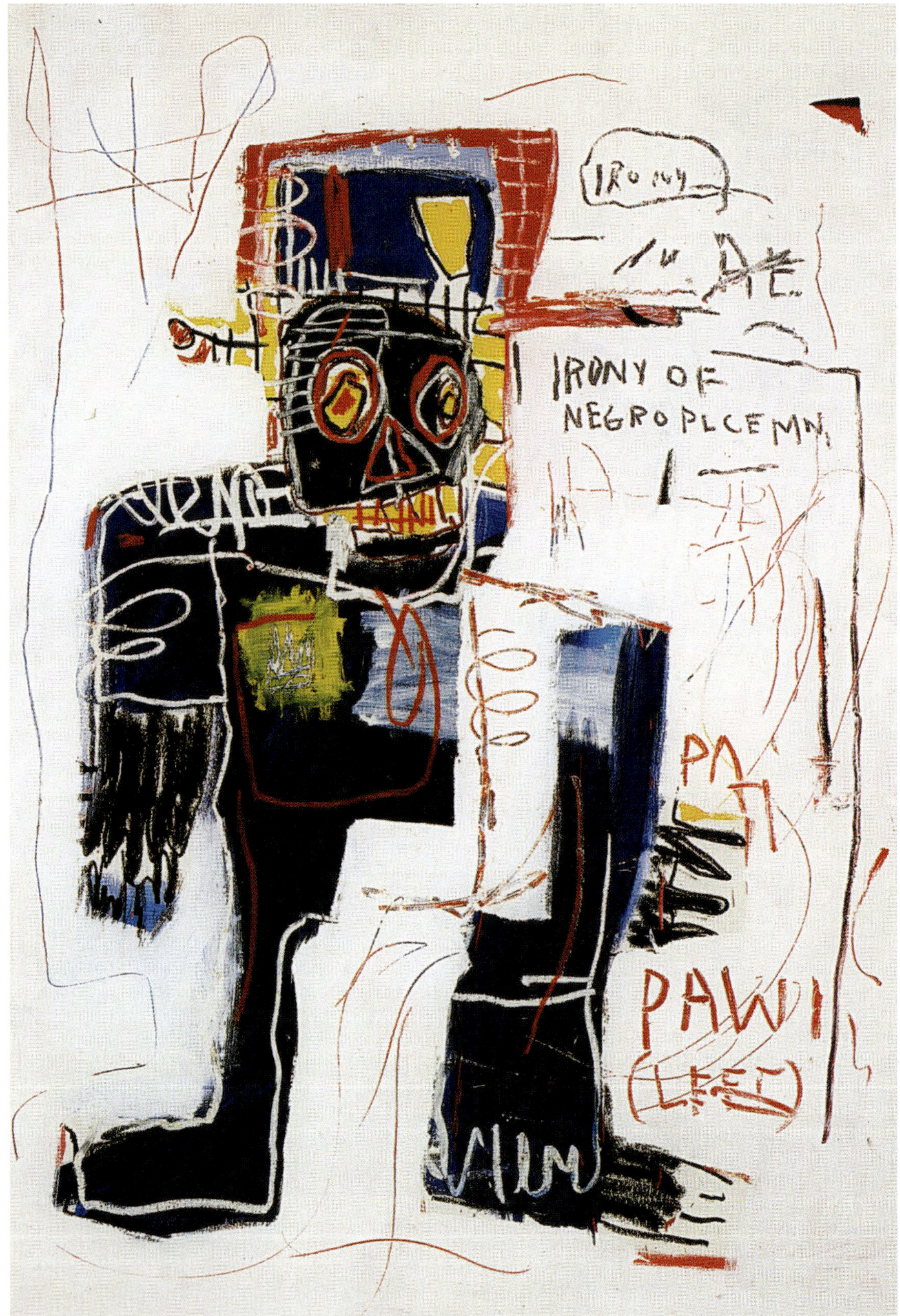
IRONY
IRONY OF
NEGRO PLCEMN
PA

NEO-EXPRESSIONISM, THE NEW ABSTRACTION, AND ARCHITECTURE

13

The art of the late 20th and early 21st centuries shows a persistence of both figurative and abstract styles, suggesting a look backward and a resistance to change. At the same time, it incorporates distinct differences indicative of changing New Millennium sensibilities. Neo-Expressionist painting merges the dynamic surface textures of Abstract Expressionism with recognizable figures and a tongue-in-cheek wit. New Abstraction, on the other hand, brings to Abstract Expressionist art a more lyrical palette, fluid paint application, and the incorporation of non-traditional media. In contemporary architecture, Neomodernism updates the cubic forms of the International Style; Neo-Historicist architecture offers streamlined versions of Neoclassic and Gothic Revival structures; and Postmodern buildings deconstruct the box so typical of 20th-century skyscrapers, to create entirely new architectural shapes.

NEO-EXPRESSIONISM

As early as 1980 and continually into the 21st century, Postmodernism's success prompted a reaction from artists who longed to return to traditional painting and sculpture materials and to straightforward representations of the figure. Neo-Expressionism exemplifies this trend. It embodied a rejection of assemblage, installation, performance, found objects, and Earth Art—all the innovations that Postmodernism had brought into play. Some exponents refute the sober and cerebral bent of Conceptualism in favor of a more humorous, even sarcastic approach. Others, while forgoing humor, share a common interest in straightforward storytelling. Whereas both Modernism and Postmodernism were often **ahistorical** and predicated on the idea of newness and originality, many Neo-Expressionists are fascinated by art of the past, which they routinely **appropriate** or reference in their own art. Despite these commonalities, Neo-Expressionism embraces a diversity of pictorial styles, from figurative expressionism with tactile, energetic, and colorful surfaces to straightforward illusionistic painting (sometimes referred to as New Image Painting).

Iconographically, Neo-Expressionism is equally eclectic, covering a range of subjects from contemporary politics to personal experience, and from world history to art history. Neo-Expressionism often borrows icons and representational styles from the same sources as 1960s Pop Art: comic books, advertisements, graffiti, media, and mass culture. Unlike the earlier incarnation, however, Neo-Expressionism employs Pop Art sources to critique, mock, and lampoon society. The same can be said of its later iteration,

◀ Jean-Michel Basquiat, *The Irony of a Negro Policeman,* 1981, acrylic and oil stick on wood, 72″ × 48″.

Neo-Pop. Similar in subject matter, the two styles differ in appearance. The textured, active, and painterly surfaces of Neo-Expressionism contrast with the more mechanical imagery of Neo-Pop, which developed at the end of the 20th century. Though dissimilar in form, Neo-Expressionism and Neo-Pop both present critiques that are often harshly biting—even shocking. A common approach of African-American Neo-Expressionists is to use taboo stereotypes to **deconstruct** these clichés, a practice that has subjected some of them to tough criticism.

Robert Colescott

Robert Colescott (1925–2009) was a forerunner of the Neo-Expressionist Movement who bridged the gap between old and new variations on the Pop-Art theme. His images have been described as masterfully absurd, grotesque, and politically incorrect—all relatively accurate descriptions. From the mid-1970s until his death, he painted vividly hued and bawdy group scenes that ridiculed and satirized racism and sexism in America with fearless abandon.

Although he had been exhibiting abstractions for decades, Colescott's work did not come to national attention until he turned to figurative art. Populated with African-American characters who display a wide range of skin tones, personalities, and iconography, Colescott's pictures depict derisory and profane stereotypes that compel viewers to laugh, experience guilt, or express indignation, depending on the mindset, age, and ethnicity of the viewer.

Plundering U.S. political history and international art history, Colescott's paintings achieve their shocking effect through the appropriation and perversion of well-known artworks from the Renaissance to the 20th century. Replacing European subjects with African-American ones, Colescott pillages the heretofore revered art historical past to spotlight persistent fallacies in the contemporary age. His earliest works in this vein include the famed 1975 *George Washington Carver Crossing the Delaware*, which borrows from the revered painting by Emmanuel Leutze (1816–68), *George Washington* (not Carver) *Crossing the Delaware*. Subtitled *Page from an American History Textbook*, Colescott's painting affronts with the kind of mockery not seen since Dada artist Marcel Duchamp (1887–1968) mounted a urinal on a pedestal and signed it as a work of art in 1917.

In Colescott's painting, George Washington is replaced by African-American scientist George Washington Carver, and his men are exchanged for a black contingent in tattered clothing. Among them are a mammy, a banjo player, a cook, a drunk, and a shoeshine boy. Colescott's figures are painted in cartoon-like fashion as minstrels, with broad, white-toothed grins; bulging red lips; and white eyes aglow against their dark skin. The one well-dressed black rower included in the Leutze painting is missing entirely from Colescott's composition. Although his blatant representation of black stereotypes has upset a segment of the African-American art community, Colescott's satires are meant to highlight—and hence defuse—the absurdity of racial fallacies.

Other Colescott paintings in this genre include his 1975 *Eat Dem Taters*, a perversion of Van Gogh's 1885 *Potato Eaters* that replaces Van Gogh's impoverished Dutch peasants with a black family marked by large pink lips and toothy grins, and his 1985 *Demoiselles d'Alabama*, in which the female nudes from Picasso's 1907 *Demoiselles d'Avignon* are garishly clothed and the African masks used by Picasso are transformed into black female faces. Colescott's images, which bear comparison to the burlesque art of Ashcan artist Reginald Marsh, make use of a variety of figural distortions such as enlarged heads, warped bodies, and exaggerated features. He employs a complex compositional approach that overlaps multiple figures and compresses them into a crowded and visually confounding space.

Born in Oakland, California, to musician parents who were friends of artist Sargent Johnson (see Chapter 6), Colescott was trained from childhood as both a drummer and a visual artist. As a young man, he spent the years from 1942 to 1945 in Europe during World War II as part of the all-black 92nd Division. From the end of the war until 1952, he attended the University of California, where he earned his undergraduate and graduate degrees and adopted the Hard-Edge painting style. During a year in Paris between degrees, Colescott studied with French Modernist Fernand Léger and spent many hours examining masterworks in the Paris museums. In 1957, he began a teaching career at Portland State University that lasted for 11 years. He spent his 1964 sabbatical in residence at the American Research Center (ARCE) in Cairo, Egypt. The experience led to a one-year visiting professorship at the American University in Cairo in 1966 that was followed by a three-year stay in Paris from 1967 to 1970.

Back in California, Colescott was inspired by the figurative Pop Art trends that had developed there. Using Pop as a springboard, he redefined and developed his trademark style. In the 1980s, Colescott relocated to Tucson to accept a teaching position at the University of Arizona, where he remained until his retirement in 1998, a year after he became the first black artist selected for the Venice Biennale. Colescott received three NEA grants in 1976, 1980, and 1983, and a Guggenheim award in 1985; and he was appointed to the National Academy of Design in 1997. In his later years, Colescott's work became more painterly and abstract, though no less satirical or political.

Joyce J. Scott

Joyce J. Scott's (b. 1948) art is a figurative hybrid of fine art and craft. Working in a variety of media, including printmaking, fabric, and blown glass, Scott is best known for her sculpture and jewelry, intricately crafted from colored glass beads. Scott's investigations of craft as high art are coupled with hard-hitting subject matter, including lynching, apartheid, domestic violence, and cultural imperialism, presented within a Pop Art idiom. Her 1986 *Man Eating Watermelon* engages one of the artist's favorite themes: racial stereotypes (Figure 13.1). An entire series of Scott's constructions focuses on the image of the watermelon as a marker of racist pop culture, which so often lampooned African Americans as

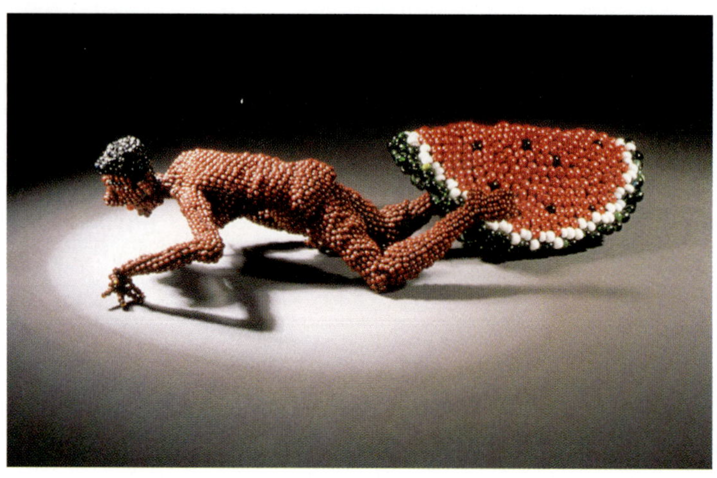

▲ **13.1** Joyce J. Scott, *Man Eating Watermelon*, 1986, glass beads, 8″ × 3″.
Private collection. © Joyce J. Scott. Photo: Kanji Takeno.

watermelon-eating **Sambos**. The series features facetious titles such as *Aunt Jemelon* (a conflation of Aunt Jemima and watermelon), *Venus de Melon* (a parody of the classic Greek Venus de Milo), and *Man Eating Watermelon*, which suggests that the fruit is devouring the man (as in "man-eating") rather than vice versa. Indeed, Scott's beaded melon slice in *Man Eating Watermelon* impedes the nude male's desperate attempts to escape from its symbolic import as a terrorizing stereotype.

Scott was born in Baltimore to a creative family with a history of blacksmithing, basket-weaving, and canoe building. Her mother, with whom the artist collaborated on several projects, was the renowned quilter and fiber artist Elizabeth Talford Scott (1916–2011), known for her innovations in appliqué and embroidery. Scott the younger earned a BFA from MICA in 1970 and an MFA from the Instituto Allende in Mexico in 1971. With more than 100 exhibits to her credit, Scott's art has been the subject of solo shows at many American museums. In 2010, Scott won the Women's Caucus for the Arts Lifetime Achievement Award—one of many grants, fellowships, and residencies that have acknowledged her innovation, creativity, and commitment to her craft.

Michael Ray Charles

Michael Ray Charles (b. 1967) is a Louisiana native who attended McNeese State University to study graphic design and illustration. After receiving his BFA in 1989, he completed graduate work at the University of Houston, receiving an MFA in 1993. After graduate school, Charles joined the faculty at the University of Texas at Austin, where he continues to teach today. His controversial paintings depict a plethora of Sambo, mammy, and **pickaninny** images derived from the pop culture graphics of the 19th and early 20th centuries, when such imagery was intended to humiliate African Americans as absurd, feral, and grotesque. For his foregrounding of demeaning icons in his art, Charles has drawn much criticism. The often-vehement emotional responses to his works, however, have convinced him that these images *must* be explored if they are ever to be expelled completely from the popular mind.

According to Charles, the blackface minstrel was one of the first widespread American pop culture phenomena. As such, it is laden with meaning about the roots of the American racial divide. The artist believes that such icons continue to distress Americans, both black and white, because the social ills of the past that the images represent live on in the present. Charles observed that Americans routinely try to hide that which they find ugly, such as racism, in the hope that it will somehow go away on its own. However, if antiblack racism were really gone from the American cultural mind, as some claim, Charles's images—which expose an ugly side of our culture—would have no ability to discomfit.

Charles's paintings and prints deliberately evoke America's past history of bigotry in order to evoke its reverberations in the present. His poster-style art first appropriates pop images from the past and then alters them in disturbing ways. He begins by recreating the worn look of antique posters, to which he adds **double entendre** texts. His 1997 *Forever Free* features a demonic black face and the words "Hello, I'm Your New Neighbor," to highlight white fears of integration. Another portrays a Sambo character taking a large bite out of a basketball (as if it were a watermelon; Figure 13.2). The image is accompanied by the caption "Lifesaball, Eat It Up." The work alludes to the presence of so many African Americans in the NBA, and to their function not so much as athletes but as entertainers and throwbacks to the blackface minstrels pictured in Charles's paintings.

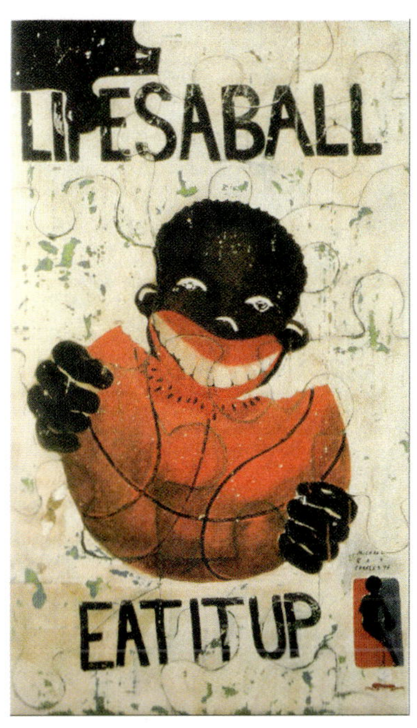

▲ **13.2** Michael Ray Charles, *(Forever Free) Lifesaball*, 1995, acrylic, latex, and copper penny on paper, 60″ × 36″.

Despite a staunch contingent of detractors, Charles's provocative art has garnered a select group of loyal followers. Among them is actor/director Spike Lee, on whose 2000 film *Bamboozled* Charles worked as visual consultant and for which Charles created two paintings, including the film's lead ad image of a pickaninny eating watermelon. Charles has won an NEA Fellowship and jury position and has had one-person shows in Spain, Belgium, Germany, Paris, and Norway, as well as in several U.S. cities.

Kara Walker

One of the youngest and most controversial of the Neo-Expressionist artists is Kara Walker (b. 1969), whose work has been influenced by Robert Colescott. At the age of 28, after earning an MFA from RISD, in 1997 Walker won the MacArthur Genius Award, the youngest artist ever to do so at that time. The award was for art that, among other things, had provided some of the most provocative visual fare that year at the already controversial Whitney Biennial. Once referred to as "the exhibit that people love to hate," the biennial undertakes to showcase art by the most trailblazing exponents of the avant-garde. Artists, such as Walker, who are invited to participate often find themselves catapulted, literally overnight, into positions of national and even international prominence. Walker's black paper cutouts are precisely the kind of art that made the biennial so legendary, and their display at the 1997 biennial brought a barrage of both acclaim and vilification to the artist.

Walker's large-format, lyrical, and vintage-style black silhouettes are routinely mounted on white gallery walls and sometimes accompanied by mood-invoking lighting and video. Her imagery, which takes the form of Victorian-style **silhouette art**, at first beguiles, only to rivet or repel once it is closely inspected. Walker's silhouettes depict fetishism, slavery, death, interracial violence, and biological and sexual depravity acted out by characters from a lost antebellum era. Walker's images relentlessly challenge cultural memory, high art sensibilities, and the viewer's sense of decorum.

In order to fashion her terse tragicomedies, like Charles, Walker draws from racial clichés such as mammies, Sambos, and pickaninnies. Her scenarios also include white plantation masters, mistresses, and children. Virtually all of the protagonists are demeaned, and the entire history of slavery becomes, within this context, a ghastly farce.

In her graphic dramas, Walker self-identifies with the character of the "slave mistress," as the oft-abused young slave woman in her narratives has been termed. With unflinching candor, Walker admits that her own experiences of racial intolerance—particularly while dating white men—have psychologically scarred her, and that one of her fantasies had long been "to create a new identity for herself as the wife of a white man," so as to foil her own negative self-image. Indeed, her real-life marriage to a German man prompted extravagant speculation on the psychobiographical nature of Walker's imagery. She has been described, in psychoanalytic terms, as a victim of abjection (defined by psychoanalyst Julia Kristeva as an unbearable state of self- and other-awareness) who experiences self-loathing and internalized racism and sexism, a condition that the unabashed Walker refers to as her "inner plantation."

Walker's inner plantation can be seen in her very first silhouette piece, the 1994 *Gone: An Historical Romance of a Civil War as It Occurred b'tween the Dusky Thighs of One Young Negress and Her Heart* (Figure 13.3). It is inspired by the 1936 Pulitzer Prize–winning Margaret Mitchell novel and 1939 Oscar Award–winning film *Gone with the Wind*. The work captures the artist's own ambivalence about the novel, which sparked in her a wish to be like its heroine and, simultaneously, resentment because she, a black woman, could never possess the pale skin, long, silky hair, and frail beauty of Scarlett O'Hara. According to Walker, it is this love-hate tension that exemplifies black-white relations in America and that is embodied in her art.

Walker's panoramic *Gone*, now in the MoMA collection, depicts—among a dozen scenes—a Victorian couple on the verge of a kiss under a moss-hung oak tree. As the male paramour leans forward, his rapier shifts back and upward from under his frock coat and threatens to anally rape a black pickaninny who bends forward and strangles a duck by the side of a lake. Another vignette depicts a black girl child with her leg raised, depositing newborns onto the ground like feces. Yet another black girl is engaged in fellatio with a white boy, and a charwoman with a broom is mounted on the shoulders of a white slave master, whose head is subsumed beneath her

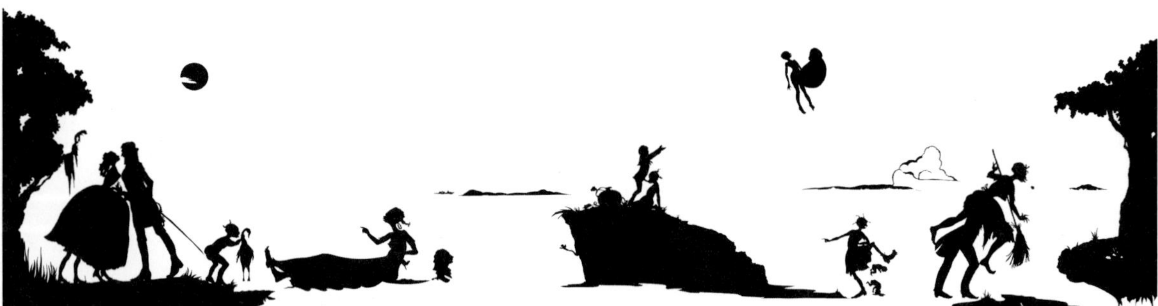

▼ **13.3** Kara Walker, *Gone: An Historical Romance of a Civil War as It Occurred b'tween the Dusky Thighs of One Young Negress and Her Heart*, 1994, cut paper on wall, installation dimensions variable, approximately 156″ × 600″.

Collection of the Museum of Modern Art, New York, NY. Gift of the Speyer Family Foundation in honor of Marie-Josée Kravis. © 2014 Kara Walker.

skirt. Beneath the initial and superficial resemblance of her images to harmless and playful cartoons lie specters that stagger the imagination.

Walker's supporters applaud her peculiar tribute to Jim Crow stereotypes and her use of irony, caricature, and alarming narrative as a means to deconstruct African-American stereotypes. Other advocates see her work as an urbane and cutting-edge critique of racism. In the estimation of Walker acolytes, rather than "denying the unspeakable crime of slavery for fear of reawakening the nightmare," to paraphrase scholar Françoise Verges, Walker's work opens the graves, frees the ghosts, and mourns the dead. Some, less certain as to the value of Walker's vision, grant that, at the very least, she should be allowed the artistic freedom to express herself as she wishes, even if it hurts.

Less empathetic critics argue that despite the ability of Walker's images to radically engage the viewer, they ultimately function to reinforce, rather than subvert, negative stereotypes. Opponents have characterized Walker's work as "coon art" that panders to the tastes of the white art establishment. The staunchest opponents of Walker's brand of "visual terrorism" contend that her reprocessing of stereotypes is degrading and should not be allowed a public forum. They have accused her of building her career on the suffering of her own people. Especially suspect, in the eyes of Walker critics, is the unprecedented rapidity with which the mostly white community of museum curators, gallery owners, collectors, academics, and patrons have embraced Walker's imagery. One of her most resolute detractors has been the artist Betye Saar, who herself, ironically, collects and integrates images of black stereotypes into her own work (see Chapter 11 chapter-opening figure). Saar, however, feels that her own use of racially offensive icons differs greatly from Walker's because Walker proffers her degrading images without explanation, leaving ample room for misinterpretation on the part of her audience; Saar strives, conversely, for a more explicit critique of racial casts through art that deconstructs and empowers unequivocally.

Walker is fully aware that she is a bane to many, but she sees her art as a means to an end. She noted: "To achieve success as an African American, one must spill one's guts constantly—like the old sharecropper in Ellison's *Invisible Man* who raped his daughter and kept telling his horrible story over and over. He's an embarrassment to the educated blacks and a fascination to the whites." Clearly, Walker is mindful of the fact that her success is contingent on the appeal of her works to an art intelligentsia and art-buying public that is, by and large, Euro-American. That her strategy is perceived as a sellout is of lesser importance to Walker than that her voice be heard. For good or bad, she is clearly unwilling to exult in professional obscurity for the sake of political correctness. Walker's art delves into the specifics of slavery, which most modern-day Americans, black or white, would prefer not to contemplate. But as scholar Elizabeth Sharpe pointed out, "some corpses refuse to stay in the ground."

Kerry James Marshall

Winner of the 1997 MacArthur Genius Award, Kerry James Marshall (b. 1955) is known for his darkly pigmented figures that tell narratives about African-American history and society. Marshall adopts a range of formal methods in his work, from multilayered painting and collage pieces, to comic-strip illustrations, and to a synthesis of flat, unmodulated figures and gestural, graffiti-inspired backgrounds.

Marshall was born in Birmingham, Alabama, but was raised from age eight in a Watts housing project. An interested high school teacher arranged for Marshall to receive a small stipend to attend a drawing class at the Otis Art Institute. As a result, in the early 1970s Marshall enrolled at Otis and studied under the mentorship of Charles White. Marshall graduated with a BFA in 1978. By the 1980s, he was exhibiting at various university and commercial gallery venues.

During this period, Marshall became visual arts coordinator at the Brockman Gallery, through which he met many of LA's most prolific black artists, including David Hammons, Carrie Mae Weems, and Lorna Simpson. In 1985, Marshall was awarded an artist's residency at the Studio Museum, which brought him to New York City. During this period, Marshall met his future wife, actress Cheryl Lynn Bruce. At the end of his museum residency, they moved to Chicago and made the city their permanent home. Marshall taught at the University of Illinois School of Art and Design and worked as a production designer for the award-winning film *Daughters of the Dust* (1991), in which his wife played the role of Viola Peazant. By the 1990s, Marshall had developed a distinctive style of art.

In his *Garden Project* (Figure 13.4) paintings, Marshall portrays well-dressed black teenagers tending to various outdoor gardens filled with flora, fountains, birds in flight, palm trees, a romantic setting sun, and heraldic

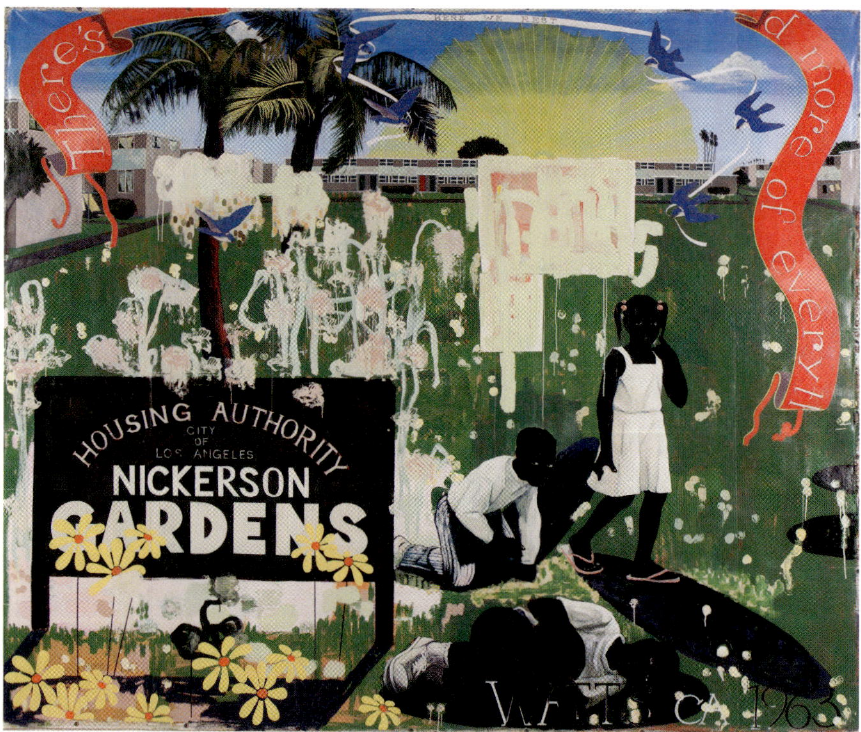

▶ **13.4** Kerry James Marshall, *Watts 1963*, 1995, acrylic/collage on canvas, 114″ × 135″.

banners printed with pleasant phrases such as "Better Homes Better Gardens" and "There's More of Everything." The series offers an ironic counterfoil to the actual poverty-ridden conditions of LA's and Chicago's public housing projects, which bear bucolic names such as "Atgeld Gardens," "Nickerson Gardens," "Wentworth," and "Stateway Gardens." Each picture is marked by Neo-Expressionist gestural strokes and spatters of the brush, which destabilize the otherwise carefully and flatly conceived compositions. Several works in the series are overpainted with their housing authority alphanumerical names—IL 27, IL 28, IL 222—to further remind the viewer of the lack of humanity and community associated with inner-city government housing projects.

Other Marshall suites, such as *Lost Boys* (c. 1993), address the cycle of poverty that traps black youths in the projects and in lives of crime and incarceration. In these paintings, Marshall created head-and-shoulder portraits of black-skinned boys trapped against graffiti-covered walls. Still other series, such as 1992's *Voyager*, critique the transatlantic slave trade. A more recent 2011 work, *Portrait of Nat Turner with the Head of His Master*, appropriates from popular Baroque paintings of Judith with the head of Holofernes, which likewise portray the decapitation of an oppressor by a member of the oppressed. Other Marshall works comprise text-based block letters painted on canvas. Reading like ads or street signs, they feature phrases such as "Why Pay More," "Buy Black," "On Sale Black Friday," and "Black Owned" as critiques of consumerism, racial economics, and the art market. Marshall's *99 Cent Piece* installation from this series is made up of oversized brass coins placed randomly on gallery floors.

Jean-Michel Basquiat

Brooklyn native Jean-Michel Basquiat (1960–88) was a practicing artist for barely a decade before his death from a heroin overdose at age 27. Basquiat began his public career as a graffiti artist working with collaborator Al Diaz (b. 1960) in 1977. For three years, the team's tag, "SAMO" (as in "same old"), accompanied their epigrammatic art, which could be found on subway cars and building walls throughout lower Manhattan. Basquiat's earliest artistic influences were childhood ones: comic book graphics and the burlesque imagery found in pop culture publications such as *Mad* magazine. After living in Brooklyn and Puerto Rico with his family, dropping out of high school, and running away from home twice, in 1976 Basquiat enrolled in an alternative Manhattan high school, City-as-School, which emphasized experiential learning through internships, seminars, and portfolios.

By age 18, Basquiat had left City-as-School and was bunking with friends in New York's Alphabet City and East Village. He earned a living as a freelance artist and promoted his art by selling postcards and T-shirts on which he painted his Expressionist and graffiti-style images and texts. During this period, Basquiat met Pop and graffiti artists Kenny Scharf (b. 1958) and Keith Haring (1958–90) at the SVA (although Basquiat was not officially enrolled there), who shared his stylistic approach. In 1978, Basquiat had a fortuitous meeting with famed Pop artist Andy Warhol and New York City commissioner of cultural affairs Henry Geldzahler while the two were dining at a downtown restaurant. Basquiat convinced the celebrated painter to purchase some of his postcards, and, when he met Warhol again four years later, the elder artist became his friend and artistic collaborator. Meanwhile, Geldzahler became one of Basquiat's first major collectors.

In 1980, Basquiat joined with David Hammons, Kenny Scharf, Pop-inspired sculptor Tom Otterness (b. 1952), text-based Conceptualists Barbara Kruger and Jenny Holzer (b. 1950), and Neo-Expressionist Kiki Smith (b. 1954) to mount an exhibition in an abandoned building near Times Square. The show was organized by two artists' collectives: the Lower East Side's Collaborative Projects Inc. and a South Bronx graffiti coalition known as Fashion Moda. Basquiat's contribution was a SAMO work painted directly onto the wall of the space. The work was hailed in an *Art in America* magazine review as a "knockout" combination of Abstract Expressionism and subway art. From this point on, Basquiat rose quickly to the rank of art world superstar, and his art was avidly sought after by collectors and dealers.

In 1981 alone, Basquiat had high-profile showings at PS1 with African-American Neo-Expressionist Arturo Lindsay (b. 1946) and two solo shows at the gallery of prominent New York dealer Annina Nosei and at Gallerie d'Arte Emilio Mazzoli in Modena, Italy; and he was profiled in an article entitled "Radiant Child" in *Artforum* magazine (a Basquiat documentary of the same name was released in 2010). By the following year, Basquiat had become an international phenomenon, with shows in commercial galleries and major museums on two continents. By 1985, his collaborative works with Warhol and Neo-Expressionist Italian artist Francesco Clemente (b. 1952) had been exhibited in Zurich and Marseille. After Warhol's death in 1987, however, Basquiat became less productive and increasingly despondent. He outlived his friend by only one year.

Basquiat's painting style ranged from expressive and gestural words and images on canvas, paper, objects, and walls in the early 1980s to palimpsest word-based collaged paintings by mid-decade. The earlier pictures featured, in addition to pithy phrases about the artist's life and observations about society, skeletal forms akin to X-rayed bodies that referenced death, masked faces, and renderings of urban symbols such as cars, uniformed policemen, and skyscrapers. His paintings after 1983 addressed the artist's cultural heritage as the son of a Haitian father and a Puerto Rican mother. Noted for his use of emblems such as crowns and halos (symbols of paternity and apotheosis), grimacing faces with garishly bared teeth, rats, ducks, monstrous figures, nondescript scrawls and doodles, and cryptic phrases, Basquiat's art has been described as raw, urban, edgy, and sharp-witted. His 1981 *Irony of a Negro Policeman* embodies all of these attributes (see chapter-opening image). Painted in vivid blue, red, and yellow on a white ground, the work portrays a man in dark blue uniform with a cap and black skeletal face. The title of the painting and the word "pawn" are scrawled next to the figure, suggesting that black policemen were little more than ironic instruments of a racist judicial system. In Basquiat's view, because so many of those either incarcerated or victimized by police brutality were black men, the specter of a black policeman was nothing short of a cruel joke.

A 1985 *New York Times* Sunday magazine cover article, "New Art, New Money: The Marketing of an American Artist," questioned Basquiat's meteoric rise to fame (as well as that of Keith Haring and Kenny Scharf) as resulting from marketing strategies rather than from legitimate creative genius. However, despite many doubters, Basquiat's work has stood the test of time, as evidenced by the many exhibits of his work at museums and galleries around the globe, even today, some 25 years after his death. Clearly an iconic figure whose persona and art continue to impress, Basquiat made history in 2012 when his *Irony of a Negro Policeman* sold at auction in London for more than £8 million.

Danny Simmons, Jr.

Author, poet, philanthropist, and artist Danny Simmons, Jr. (b. 1954) describes himself as a "neo-African Abstract Expressionist" rather than a Neo-Expressionist. The gestural style of Simmons's paintings of the 1990s fuses Neo-Expressionist figuration with a nonobjective approach reminiscent of the "psychic automatism" employed by Surrealists. However, there is little that is random or automatic about Simmons's pictures. Much of his early imagery derives from the shapes and patterns of traditional African masks, power figures, vestments, and other sacred objects that Simmons collects.

Simmons's 1993 autobiographical composition *The Painter* portrays a living Kongo *nkisi nkondi* figure, complete with nails hammered into its limbs to generate power (Figure 13.5). The nude, one-eyed figure holds aloft a paintbrush as he renders a dripping, swirling sun that doubles as a second

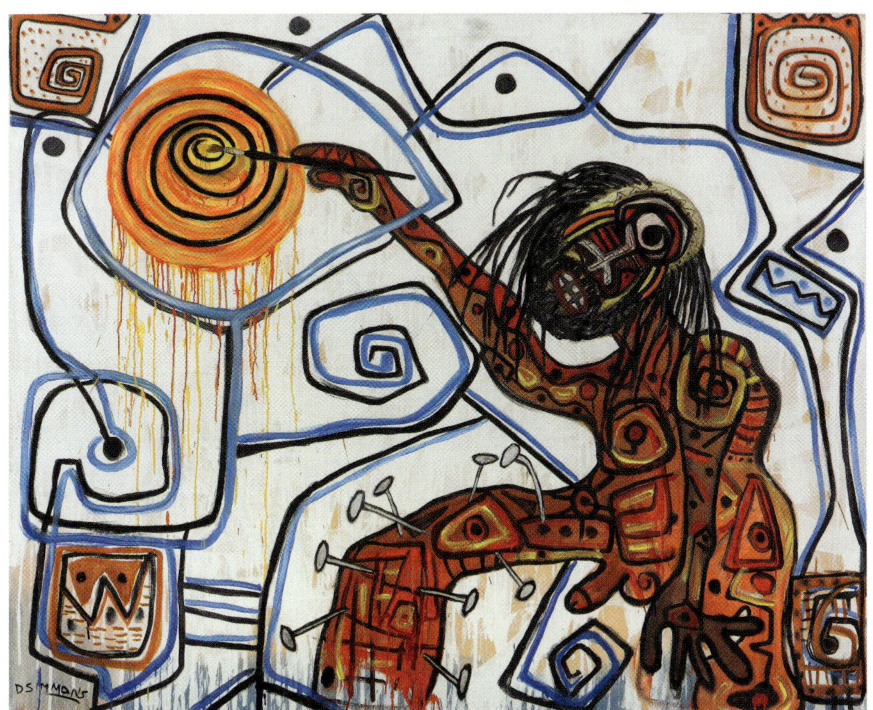

◀ **13.5** Danny Simmons, *The Painter*, 1993, oil on canvas, 72″ × 72″.

eye: the gaze and vision of the artist. Its phallic motifs—from the exposed genitalia and elongated painting arm to the penetrating nails—recall the masculine energy of both African shamans and art historical master painters of the past. The painter figure itself is covered in a Marquesan-like tattoo pattern (repeated in the white negative space of the design and as corner medallions) similar to Burkina Faso masks of the Bwa people.

Simmons's later works of the 2000s eliminate the figure while retaining the meandering quality of the artist's brush. Judiciously configured, his nonrepresentational paintings feature linear upsweeps, uninterrupted cyclical ribbons of color, undulating directional elements, concentrated areas of gesture and energy, and tempered all-over patterns. Equally deliberate are the artist's color choices, which are well balanced and modulated to achieve a variety of desired effects.

Simmons was born into a highly creative family in the New York borough of Queens. His father was a poet; his mother was a painter; and his brothers are musicians. He earned a bachelor's degree in social work from NYU and a master's degree in public administration from Long Island University in Brooklyn, where he lived for much of his adult life. After spending the early part of his professional career as a social worker, Simmons turned to the arts. Fulfillment for Simmons came not only from painting but from writing, philanthropy, and arts education. Simmons has authored half a dozen books on life, love, and the art scene, and an illustrated book of poetry entitled *I Dreamed My People Were Calling but I Couldn't Find My Way Home* (2007). He coproduced the hit 2002–2007 HBO series and Broadway play *Def Poetry Jam*, which gave voice to the spoken word poetry of 21st-century youth culture.

Harkening back to the Last Poets, a group of militant 1960s recording artists who are among hip-hop's earliest influences, *Def Poetry Jam* was an outgrowth of Russell Simmons's *Def Comedy Jam*, which was hosted by actor and hip-hop recording artist Mos Def and which also aired on HBO from 1992 to 1997. Other creative Simmons ventures include the cofounding with his brothers Russell and Joseph ("Run" of the hip-hop group Run-D.M.C.) of Rush Arts Gallery in New York's Chelsea art district and of the Rush Philanthropic Arts Foundation, which is dedicated to empowering disadvantaged youth through art and bringing public attention to artists of color. Simmons also directed a second gallery in Brooklyn—Corridor—which hosted art classes and community workshops. In 2012, Simmons was awarded an honorary doctorate from his alma mater, Long Island University.

THE NEW ABSTRACTION

Despite the wave of Neo-Expressionism, abstract art was hardly swept aside by figuration. In many instances there was a fusion of the two, similar to the figurative abstraction of the 1950s and 1960s. Late-century abstractionists, however, added elements of passion and unruliness to the purity of form and lack of emotion associated with traditional Modernism, which likens New Abstractionists to their Neo-Expressionist contemporaries in character if not in appearance. Evolving out of the Postmodern pluralism of the 1970s, which relaxed the rigid rules of art media and styles, late-century abstraction allowed for differing modes to coexist within the genre and even within a single work of art.

Jack Whitten

Considered one of the first exponents of the New Abstraction, artist Jack Whitten (b. 1939) came to New York from Alabama in 1960 to study at Cooper Union, just about the time that Abstract Expressionism was giving way to Pop Art. Initially enrolling at Tuskegee Institute in 1959 to study medicine, by 1960 Whitten was majoring in art at Southern University in Baton Rouge, Louisiana. He transferred to Cooper Union, where he completed his BFA in 1964. Choosing to settle permanently in New York, Whitten came under the sway of the New York School as well as the Black Arts Movement. His works of the 1960s, though formally indicative of Gestural Abstraction, were influenced in content by the racial unrest of civil rights and black power. A 1968 oil painting, *Martin Luther King's Garden*, includes several phantom portraits of the civil rights leader, camouflaged within an otherwise nonobjective composition of high-key color and dense brushwork. Within a short few years, however, Whitten had forsaken both oil paint and paintbrush for polymer paints and trowel-like applicators such as squeegees, combs, and rakes. These tools gave his paintings the quality of striated metal grates or monochromatic plowed fields viewed aerially and interrupted occasionally by rippling lines and color stains.

In the 1980s, Whitten pushed his painting experiments to new heights by mixing acrylic paint with viscous compounds that he then cast into various three-dimensional shapes to create works that were as much sculptures as they were paintings. By the 1990s, he was casting his paint compounds into solid tiles, from which he then constructed mosaic-like surfaces by mounting the tiles directly onto canvas. Formally subtle and iconographically enigmatic, Whitten takes abstraction to new heights. Despite their nonobjectivity, many of Whitten's works are commemorations of people or events (Figure 13.6), such as a tribute to the 9/11 disasters composed of paint and ashes, and memorials to poet Jayne Cortez, the wife of the sculptor Melvin Edwards, who died in 2013. Whitten had his first major solo exhibition at the Whitney Museum in 1974 and has since had showings at commercial galleries and museums in Europe and the United States. He also participated in two Whitney Biennials in 1969 and 1972, and in numerous other group shows, including the blockbuster 2013 traveling exhibit *Blues for Smoke*. Most recently, in 2014 Whitten was awarded an honorary doctorate from the San Francisco Art Institute.

Thornton Dial, Sr.

Thornton Dial, Sr. (b. 1928), straddles the divide between Postmodern assemblage and New Abstraction. Although he creates his monumental abstract works using found objects, the end results share more in common visually with Abstract Expressionist painting than with found object art. Dial spent his early childhood as a farmworker in rural Alabama, where he

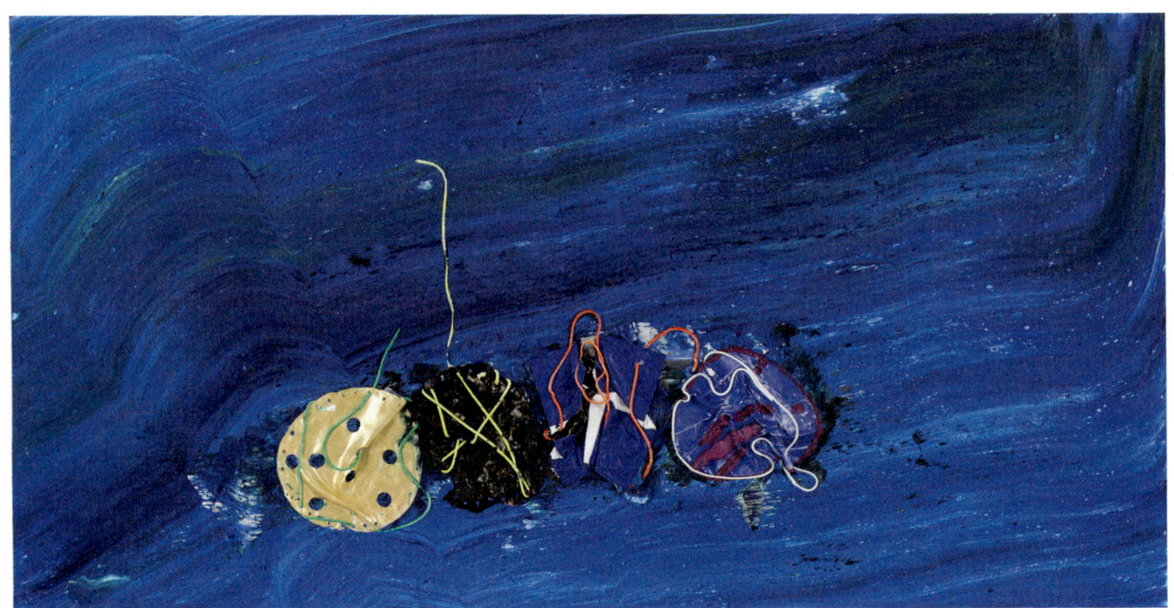

▲ **13.6** Jack Whitten, *Byzantine Quartet (for Stephen Antonakos)*, 2013, acrylic on canvas, 45″ × 87″. Alexander Gray Associates. © 2015 Jack Whitten / Artist Rights Society (ARS), New York, NY.

had minimal access to formal education. He eventually moved to Bessemer, near Birmingham, and spent 50 years as a construction and factory worker. He expressed his creative side by making abstract sculpture from found objects he picked up on jobs sites, a talent he learned as a child from a cousin who constructed toys from farmyard detritus. The abundance of yard art in Birmingham also influenced his creations. When the Pullman boxcar factory where he had worked for 30 years closed its doors in 1981, Dial, in his fifties, retired to a life of raising turkeys, making wrought-iron patio furniture, and creating art.

In 1987, Dial met collector William Arnett through a friend, artist Lonnie Holley (b. 1950). Arnett helped to organize a 1988 showing of Dial's art at the High Museum in Atlanta, followed quickly by several others in key cities such as New York. Within ten years of meeting Arnett, Dial had gained a national reputation, and in 1997 he received critical praise from major media outlets for his work in the Schomburg exhibit *Bearing Witness: African-American Vernacular Art of the South*. Dial creates sizeable found object assemblages and mixed-media paintings and drawings. His choice of found materials is vast and includes everything from bones, tree branches, paper trash, and rope to pop bottles, rubber hoses, plastic dolls, and old bits of metal, fabric, and plastic. His tools are welding torches and paintbrushes. Color also is key to his art, which he invigorates with sometimes vivid and other times subdued color harmonies. Iconographically, Dial's art centers on sociopolitical concerns such as civil rights, poverty, war, and gender and familial relationships.

Dial's frenzied conceptualization of an apocalyptic world, *Blood and Meat* (Figure 13.7), uses black, white, red, and yellow colors to create a near abstract design that is a visual incarnation of Armageddon. In the upper-right and left quadrants of the composition, as well as in the lower-left corner, faces emerge like horrified masks peering through a maelstrom. One sees or

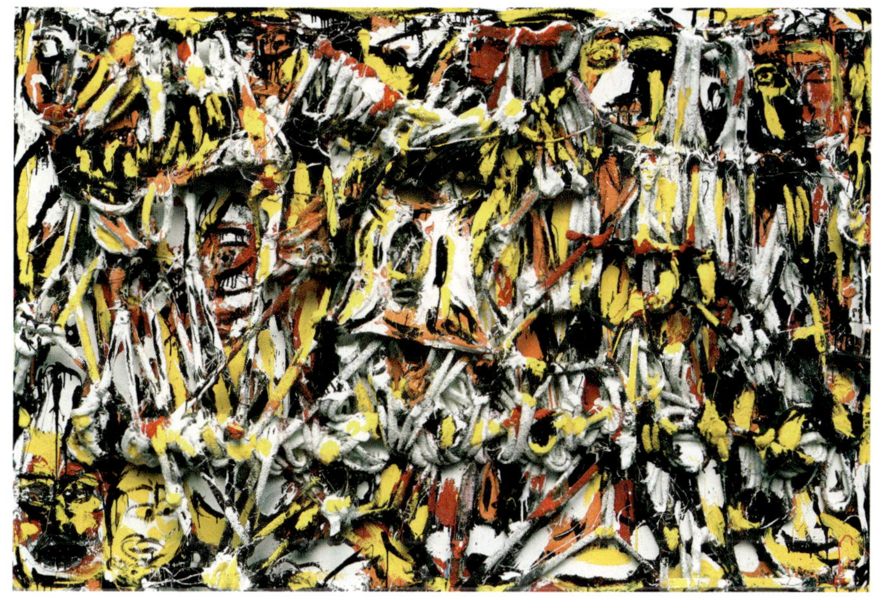

◀ 13.7 Thornton Dial, *Blood and Meat: Survival for the World*, 1992, rope carpet, copper wire, metal screen, canvas scraps, enamel, and Splash Zone compound on canvas on wood, 65″ × 95″ × 11″.

Photo: Stephen Pitkin / Pitkin Studio. Courtesy of Souls Grown Deep Foundation.

imagines bared white teeth tearing at red and pink meat and flesh in a violent bid for survival (the work's subtitle is "Survival for the World"). Thick with impasto, the three-dimensional painting is composed of rope, metal, wire, torn canvas, epoxy compound, and paint. It is unlike any other assemblage art in its total fusion of all its elements.

In 2011, Dial's art was the subject of a *Time* magazine feature story written in response to works such as this; in the article Richard Lacayo described Dial as anything but an Outsider artist, finding the term demeaning and misleading. He wrote that Dial's works were among the most assured and powerful of any he'd seen. Likewise, Michael Kimmelman of the *New York Times* likened Dial's style to the paintings of Abstract Expressionists Jackson Pollock and Willem de Kooning. Others remarked on Dial's affinity with renowned Neo-Expressionists Julian Schnabel (b. 1951) and Anselm Kiefer (b. 1945), neither of whom were familiar to Dial as recently as 2011 when an interviewer questioned him on the subject.

The art world has responded with great enthusiasm to Dial's diverse body of work, evident in the artist's many solo exhibitions, which include a 1993 survey at two major New York museums—the New Museum of Contemporary Art and the American Folk Art Museum—a 2005–06 show entitled *Thornton Dial in the 21st Century* at the Houston Museum of Fine Arts, and other solo shows. Another major acknowledgment came when Dial's work was included in the 2000 Whitney Biennial. For Dial, now in his eighties, art making has become a family affair: his sons Richard and Thornton Junior; his half-brother, Arthur; and his cousin Ronald Lockett are also visual artists.

Mildred Thompson

The art of Atlanta-based painter, sculptor, and printmaker Mildred Thompson (1935–2003) was greatly influenced by music. In particular, she was

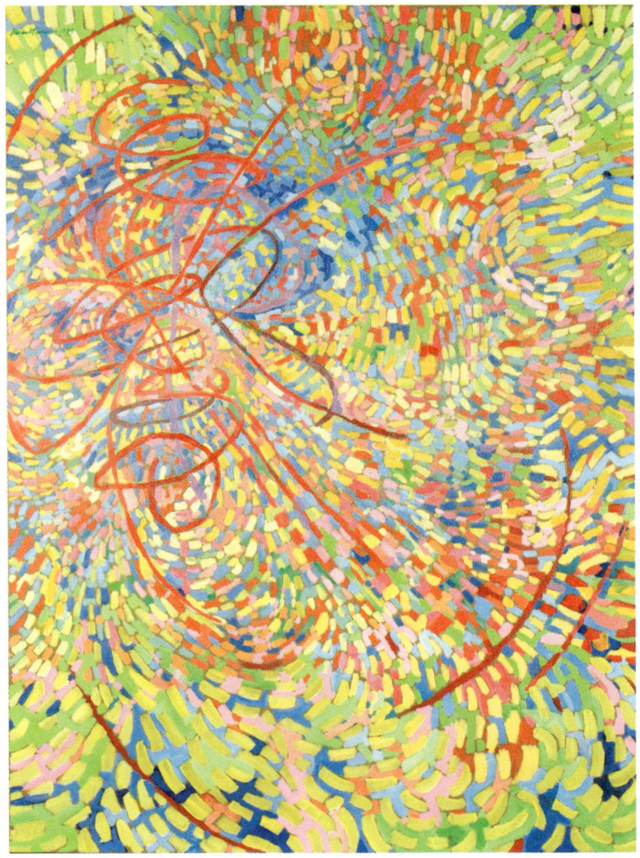

▲ **13.8** Mildred Thompson, *String Theory VI*, 1999, acrylic on canvas, 61″ × 46″ (sight).

Georgia Museum of Art, University of Georgia; The Larry D. and Brenda A. Thompson Collection of African American Art.

inspired by the jazz compositions of Eric Dolphy, Charles Mingus, and Thelonious Monk, and the classical music of Johann Sebastian Bach (1685–1750). Her music-inspired abstractions reflect the artist's visualization of sounds.

Profoundly influenced by Kandinsky, Thompson created her large-scale 1990s painting series *Music of the Spheres* and *String Theory* using rich and radiant hues and gestural drawing to present a symphony of the solar system and unseen dimensions (Figure 13.8). Combining her love of music with her passionate interest in astronomy and metaphysics, Thompson produced images that embodied the wonder of the cosmos and the ability of music to elevate the soul. Like Kandinsky, Thompson saw nonrepresentational art as the most direct way for the viewer to access a state of spirituality. Indeed, Thompson studied at length the writings of German existentialist author and artist Hermann Hesse (1877–1962) about self-exploration and transcendence and those of Swiss psychiatrist Carl Jung (1875–1961) on the **collective unconscious**.

Thompson hails originally from Jacksonville, Florida. She earned her BFA at Howard University in 1953, where she was mentored by James Porter. During a summer break, she won a residency to attend the Skowhegan School in Maine. After completing her undergraduate degree, Thompson won a Max Beckmann Scholarship for postgraduate work at the School of the Brooklyn Museum of Art, where she studied painting with Reuben Tam. An early abstractionist who came of professional age in the first years of the 1960s, Thompson found few gallery or patron outlets for her work. As a result, she did not begin exhibiting in her native country in earnest until the 1980s.

Deciding, rightly, that she would have a better chance at recognition abroad, Thompson earned passage to Europe by teaching for a summer at Florida A&M University before embarking for Germany. She enrolled in the Hochschule für Bildende Künste (the School of Fine Arts) in Hamburg and remained in the city for several years, studying painting and printmaking with abstract sculptor Walter Arno (b. 1930), Abstract Expressionist painter Emil Schumacher (1912–99), figurative expressionist Willem Grimm (1904–86), and Surrealist Paul Wunderlich (1927–2010). Her achievements at the academy in Hamburg garnered Thompson a scholarship that allowed her to remain in Hamburg until 1961, when she returned to the United States. From the 1960s through the mid-1980s, Thompson divided her time between residencies in the United States and living and working in Europe. In 1986, she finally settled permanently in Atlanta and embarked on a painting, writing, and academic career. She taught at various Atlanta colleges and universities and, in 1987, became an editor for the nonprofit contemporary art journal *Art Papers*.

The recipient of multiple residencies at the Spruce Pine workshop of glass sculptor Harvey Littleton (1922–2013), during the last years of her life Thompson worked in vitreography—a print process that replaces the metal, wood, fabric, or stone surfaces typical of printmaking with glass—and produced several series of prints based on the solar system and electromagnetism.

Gaye Ellington

Colorist Gaye Ellington (b. 1947) works principally with acrylic paint on canvas, although she has also created relief sculpture in hammered metal. While studying at Howard University, she came under the influence of the Washington Color School and its exploitation of color as an expressive medium. Returning to her native New York after college, Ellington developed her signature style while studying at CUNY and at the Art Students League under the tutelage of well-known watercolorist Timothy J. Clark (b. 1951). In Ellington's paintings, a kaleidoscopic high-key palette is employed to create imagery that, although partly abstract, resonates with representational phantoms. Like visual riddles, Ellington's renderings at first appear to be purely formal: a series of flamelike brushstrokes that animate the canvas surface. On closer examination, specters of human faces and figures emerge to draw observers into the artist's labyrinthine compositions. Ellington's subjects include vaguely discernible still-lifes, street scenes, figures, and portraits that have the effect of light passing through stained glass.

In addition to nature and the human form, Ellington has long been inspired by the music of jazz, particularly the cadences of her grandfather, "Duke" Ellington. Many of her compositions are, indeed, visual translations of the orchestral arrangements of Duke and Mercer Ellington, as well as of Ellington's arranger, Billy Strayhorn. The artist's *The Blues Ain't* grew out of her grandfather's 1963 recorded stage performance of the same name (Figure 13.9). The concert included Duke Ellington telling a call-and-response tale (entitled "My People") of the contributions of African Americans to American history and evolution, followed by a stirring blues number. While playing this particular recording, Gaye composed her painting. The emotional and orchestral highs and lows of the musical composition become lights and darks in the painting. More than this, a figural embodiment of both artists—grandfather/musician and granddaughter/painter—appear in an ethereal three-quarter view face and torso that soars diagonally across the canvas toward each other. In a 2003 suite that the artist titled *My People* after the same recording, her latent penchant for figuration found expression in a visually stunning collection of portraits of Ellington family and friends.

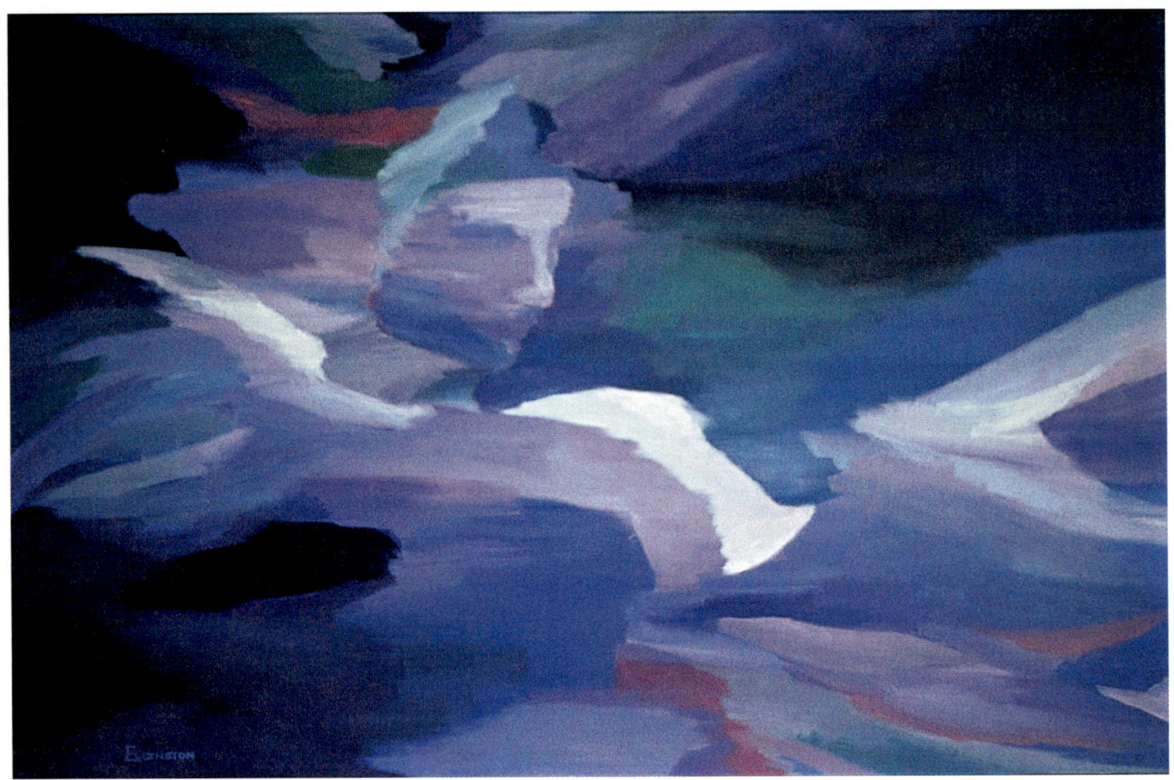

▲ **13.9** Gaye Ellington, *The Blues Ain't*, 1989, acrylic on canvas, 24″ × 36″.

Courtesy of the artist.

ARCHITECTURE

At the close of the 20th century, the United States boasted more than a quarter of a million professional architects, of whom nearly 10,000 were African-American. They have designed in every major genre, including the **Neomodern**, **Neo-Historicist**, and **Postmodern** styles. In addition to embracing the need for environmentally conscious **sustainable design**, African Americans have also promoted architecture that expresses, through form and concept, the multifaceted nature of American culture and that enriches the lives of those who experience their designed spaces.

J. Max Bond, Jr.

One architect who belongs to this new generation is J. Max Bond, Jr. (1935–2009), who initiated the design of the National September 11 Memorial Museum in New York City. Bond hailed from a prominent African-American family of artists, educators, and civil rights activists. His father was president of the University of Liberia in Monrovia; his mother, Ruth C. Bond, was a teacher and quilt maker. His uncle Horace Mann Bond was the first black president of Lincoln University in Pennsylvania, and his cousin Julian Bond was a six-term Georgia senator and chairman of the NAACP from 1998 to 2014.

J. Max Bond, Jr., received both BA and MA degrees from Harvard University in 1955 and 1958. Before founding his own firm in 1970, he worked in France with modern architect André Wogenscky (1916–2004) and with the

New York firms Jordan Gruzen & Partners and Pedersen & Tilney. He next was employed by the Ghanaian government, for which he designed an eco-friendly and avant-garde self-cooling multistructure, the Bolgatanga Regional Library, in 1967. On his return to the United States, Bond directed the Architects Renewal Committee of Harlem for three years before cofounding his own architectural firm, Bond Ryder Associates, with Donald P. Ryder (b. 1926). The firm specialized in housing, university, and cultural projects. Over the next two decades, Bond Ryder (later Bond Ryder James, with the addition of a third partner—John A. James—in 1983) developed into a one of the most sought-after architectural firms in the country.

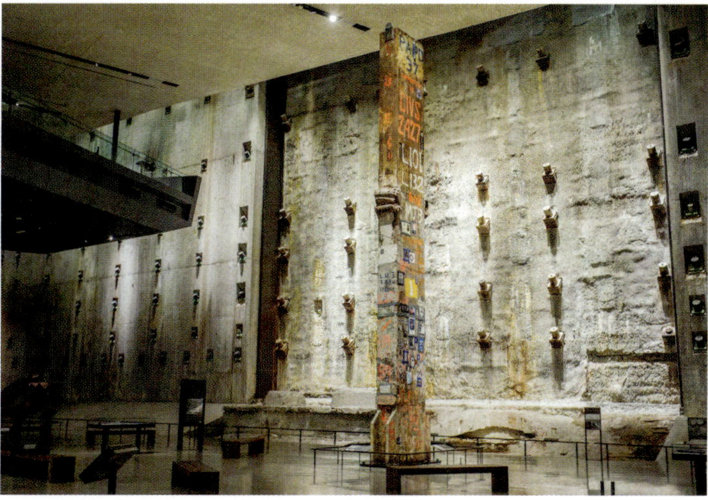

▲ **13.10** Davis Brody Bond, LLP, *National September 11 Memorial & Museum, New York City*, 2014.

Photo: Jin Lee, courtesy of 9/11 Memorial.

In 1990 Ryder announced his retirement, prompting Bond to merge his firm with that of Davis, Brody & Associates. While a principal in the new firm—Davis Brody Bond—Bond himself was responsible for the early stages of the 9/11 museum project (Figure 13.10), which was ultimately dedicated by President Barack Obama in 2014, five years after Bond's death from cancer. Situated beneath the 9/11 memorial in lower Manhattan (for which the firm is also responsible), the museum is accessed through a Neomodern entry pavilion designed by the Norwegian firm Snøhetta. The museum's interior employs an open plan with vast spaces (intended to signify the enormity of the 9/11 events), the Postmodern look of industrial materials, muted gray tones, clean lines, and lack of decoration. Incorporated into its structure are the original retaining wall of the World Trade Center towers and the Vesey Street stairs (dubbed the "Survivors' Stairs"), down which so many fled to escape the collapsing buildings.

In addition to the 9/11 museum, Bond and his firm implemented dozens of new, redesigned, and expansion projects nationwide. Key among these are the Martin Luther King Jr. Center in Atlanta (including Dr. King's burial site), the Frederick Douglass Circle in Harlem, and New York's Harvard Club, Schomburg Center, Studio Museum, and Columbia University Audubon Biomedical Science and Technology Park. This project includes five buildings and the reconstructed Audubon Ballroom—the site of Malcom's X's assassination.

As active as he was as a working architect, Bond was equally productive as an educator. He was a professor at Columbia University for more than 15 years and then served as dean of architecture and environmental studies at City College for 7 years. Bond also served on the New York City Planning Commission, the Board of the American Architectural Foundation, the New York State Council on the Arts, the NEA Arts Jury, the Presidential Design Awards Jury, and the Studio Museum Board.

Norma Merrick Sklarek

Norma Merrick Sklarek (1926–2012) was the first African-American woman to be licensed as an architect, in New York in 1954 and in California in 1962. She is possibly preceded in this honor by Beverly Lorraine Greene (1915–57), who was registered as an architect with the state of Illinois in 1942 (and who helped to design of the UN headquarters in Paris in 1958). Sklarek was born and raised in Harlem, the daughter of West Indian immigrants. Her father was born in St. Vincent; after attending Howard University, he became a physician. Her mother was a seamstress from Barbados. Sklarek attended Columbia University's School of Architecture, where she received her bachelor's degree in 1950. Shortly after receiving her license, in 1955 Sklarek was hired by Skidmore Owings & Merrill (builders of the Sears Tower in Chicago), where she remained for nearly five years before moving to California.

In 1960, Sklarek joined the Los Angeles firm of Austrian-born architect Victor Gruen, a pioneer in designing large-scale shopping complexes. By 1966, Sklarek had become the company's first African-American director of architecture (she also married Gruen architect Rolf Sklarek in 1967). She spent 20 years at Gruen, where she was responsible for realizing the designs of renowned architects such as Cesar Pelli (b. 1926), who was director of design at Gruen from 1968 to 1977, and Postmodern architect Frank Gehry (b. 1929), who apprenticed with, and later designed for, Gruen before founding his own firm. As production architect for Gruen, Sklarek supervised several significant projects, including the historic California Mart in Los Angeles (1963; the city's first wholesale clothing complex), the Fox Plaza in San Francisco (1966), the Fashion Mall in Queens, New York (1973), and the American Embassy in Tokyo (1978), the latter of which she codesigned with Pelli. The embassy's transitional position between the austerity of Modernism and the eclecticism of Postmodernism is evident in the use of International Style reinforced concrete ribbon windows alongside its horizontal rather than vertical emphasis, razor's-edge sharp contours, and polished surfaces (Figure 13.11).

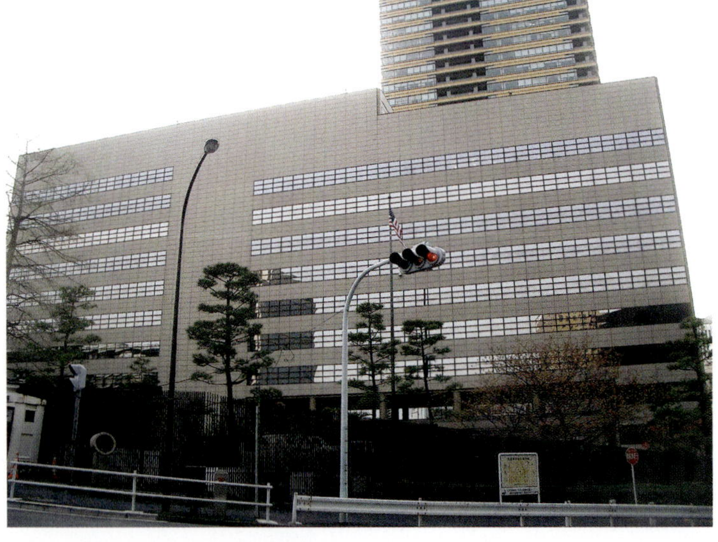

▼ **13.11** Cesar Pelli with Norma Sklarek and Gruen Associates, *U.S. Embassy Office Building, Tokyo*, 1976.

Photo: Ons-commonswiki, licensed under CC BY-SA 3.0 via Wikimedia Commons.

In 1980, Sklarek became the first black woman to be appointed a Fellow by the Los Angeles chapter of the American Institute of Architects (AIA). That same year, she left Gruen to become senior architect at Welton Becket Associates, a major LA firm responsible for the Capitol Records Tower, the **geodesic** Cinerama Dome, the Beverly Hilton Hotel, and several UCLA campus buildings. Sklarek's most significant project there was as lead architect for Passenger Terminal One at Los Angeles International Airport (LAX). The $50 million project was completed in time for the

1984 Olympic Games. It accommodated the event's massive crowds with a pier design that extended from a central concourse and linked 15 gates.

In 1985, Sklarek founded Siegel, Sklarek, Diamond with German-born Margot Siegel (b. 1932) and Chicago-born architect Katherine Diamond (b. 1954). Achieving yet another milestone as the first African-American woman to cofound and direct her own architectural firm—the largest woman-owned architectural firm in the country—Sklarek and her partners designed for several California townships, three University of California campuses, and the Los Angeles Unified School District. In 1989, Sklarek became a principal at Jon Jerde Inc. (today the Jerde Partnership) in Venice, California, where she worked until 1992, most notably on the Mall of America in Minneapolis, before retiring.

Mario Gooden and Ray Huff

Mario Gooden (b. 1965) sees architecture not in a vacuum but as part of a larger conversation about art, culture, society, and knowledge. As a partner with fellow African-American architect Ray Huff (b. 1948) in Huff + Gooden, he is dedicated to architecture that engages the human mind and soul, as well as physical space.

Gooden was born in Orangeburg, South Carolina, about 75 miles northwest of Charleston. He created his first architectural drawing of a futuristic dome-shaped house when he was 11 years old; seven years later, in 1983, he enrolled at Clemson University to study design. After receiving his BS in 1987, Gooden attended Columbia University's Graduate School of Architecture, Preservation and Planning (GSAPP), where he earned a master's degree and the Charles McKim Prize for Excellence in 1990.

Just prior to graduation, Gooden landed a one-year position at the London offices of the international design firm Zaha Hadid Architects. Founded by an Iraqi-born, Pritzker Prize–winning woman architect (b. 1950), Hadid's **Deconstructivist** structures are renowned for their stunning organic contours and allusions to futuristic transport vessels and otherworldly architectural landscapes. Three years later, in 1992, Gooden returned to New York to work with the firm of Steven Holl, one of his former Columbia University professors. Gooden simultaneously carved out an impressive teaching career. Throughout the 1990s, he taught at CCNY and the University of Florida in Gainesville. He is currently a professor at Columbia University's GSAPP, where he teaches architectural design and theory. As a theorist on architecture that, in Gooden's words, "helps us confront contentious topics," he has written *Layered Urbanisms* (2008) and *Global Topologies: Converging Territories* (2013).

In 1997, Gooden partnered with Huff to form Huff + Gooden. Also from Orangeburg and a graduate of Clemson, Huff had been director of the Clemson University Architecture Center in Charleston (CACC) for 20 years. Gooden + Huff maintains offices in Charleston, South Carolina (supervised by Huff), and New York City (supervised by Gooden). Working symbiotically, the team won the AIA Honor Award during the first year of their collaboration, for a Neomodern Sullivan Island beach house. It features a latticed wooden screen surrounding a cube-shaped inner glass and concrete living structure. Raised off the ground to accommodate hurricanes and featuring a fully open space between the lattice façade and the interior, the sustainable design blurs the boundaries between indoors and out. It pays homage to both Modernism and traditional Charleston-area homes.

In 2011, Huff + Goodman was awarded a $67 million commission to redesign of the California African American Museum (CAAM) in Los Angeles, which will include renovation of the current 37,000-square-foot building and a 77,000-square-foot addition to accommodate art galleries, a sculpture garden, a theater, a research facility, and administrative offices. Besides having their designs featured in many major exhibitions, Huff and Gooden co-curated an installation at the Gibbes Museum of Art in Clemson in 2006 entitled *Un/Spoken Spaces: Inside and Outside the Boundaries of Class Race and Space*. The show appropriated 19th-century portraits and slave-era plantation scenes from the museum's permanent collection to critique how museum spaces and collections support prevailing class and racial paradigms.

One of Huff + Gooden's most prestigious commissions was for its entry in a 2003 international competition for the Virginia Key Beach Park Museum. Planned for the 1,000-acre island in Miami's Biscayne Bay, the museum would commemorate the historic "Negroes-only" beach that served the black community from 1945 until the mid-1960s. Completed in 2008, the design incorporates multileveled **cantilevers**, extensive **glazing**, a reedlike building support system, and integrates elements of the landscape. The designers named these elements "Dune Garden," "Commemorative Palm Walk," and "Memory Field," to honor the site's topology and history. They developed the site with the input of African-American landscape architect Walter Hood (b. 1958), another southerner, who was born in North Carolina and later became professor and chair of landscape architecture at the University of California, Berkeley.

Phil Freelon

Also a competing finalist for the Virginia Key Beach Museum project was the Freelon Group, founded in 1990 by Philadelphia-born Phil Freelon (b. 1952). Freelon specializes in cultural, civic, and academic buildings. He is dedicated to designing spaces in which diverse populations can interact and that are creatively, aesthetically, and intellectually edifying. The firm's designs include the National Center for Civil and Human Rights in Atlanta, Emancipation Park in Houston, the Museum of the African Diaspora in San Francisco, and numerous projects in Washington, D.C. Most notable among these is the Smithsonian's $500 million, 313,000-square-foot National Museum of African American History and Culture (NMAAHC), presently under construction near the Washington Monument (Figure 13.12).

Awarded in 2009 to the team of Phil Freelon, Afro-British architect David Adjaye (b. 1966), Davis Brody Bond (see previously), and the 160-year-old Smith Group of architects (officially, the Freelon Adjaye Bond/Smith Group),

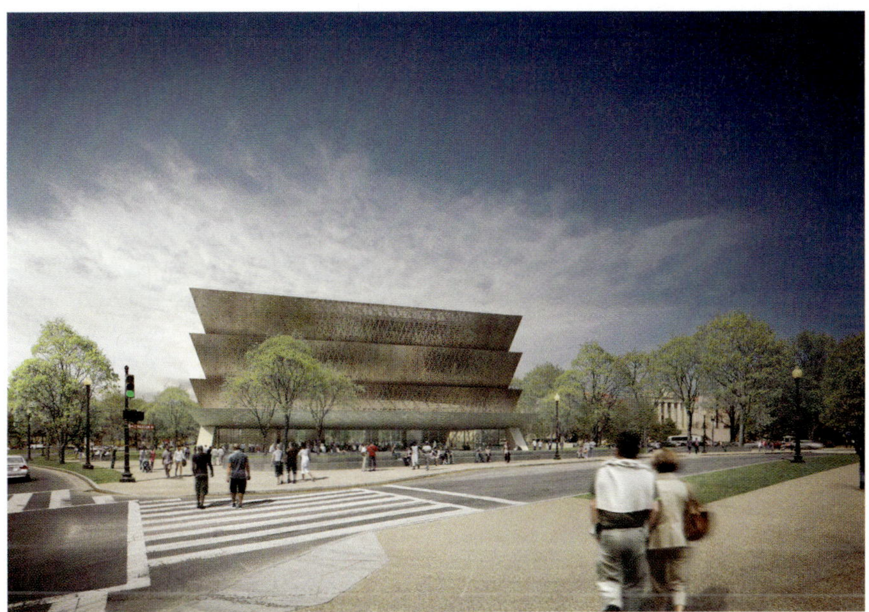

◀ **13.12** Freelon Adjaye Bond/Smith Group, *Plan for National Museum of African American History and Culture*, 2016.

Image: Phil Freelon; rendering by Imaging Atelier.

the commission was the outcome of an intensely competitive international search. With Freelon as lead architect and Adjaye as designer, the team adopted an inverted **ziggurat** shape borrowed from **Yoruban** column design as the building's leitmotif. Sheathed in bronze to signify African-American skin color, the museum's exterior takes the shape of a three-tiered Yoruban crown. In its skyward-reaching design, it is intended to embody the spiritual uplift of the African form that inspired it. The theme of uplift also alludes to the irrepressible nature of African Americans in their historic struggle for equality. Echoes of the trapezoid form can be found throughout the museum: in the walkways, reflecting pool, cantilevered entry awning, and landscape. Skylights punctuate a wooden plank ceiling in the lobby, which will be lit from above to create an ethereal environment intended to inspire visitors. The building is planned for a 2016 opening.

The Freelon Group won 26 AIA awards. Freelon is now managing and design director of the recently merged Freelon Group and Perkins + Will of South Carolina, a global firm founded in 1935 that shares with Freelon a philosophy of designing to improve the lives and communities of those they serve. In addition to his achievements as an architect, Freelon is currently a professor at MIT.

The McKissack Legacy

Howard University civil engineering graduate Deryl McKissack (b. 1961), who founded her architectural firm in 1990, can trace her roots as an architect back to the mid-19th century, when her ancestor, an enslaved **Ashanti** man named Moses, first learned the trade. He was a carpenter and builder for the Charlotte, North Carolina, slave owner William McKissack, from whom Moses took his last name. Moses passed his knowledge of building onto his son Gabriel, who trained his own son, Moses

McKissack III (1879–1952). After working for 15 years as a designer, draftsman, and builder for several white firms, in 1905 Moses III founded the country's first minority-owned architecture and engineering concern in Nashville, Tennessee. He was eventually joined by his brother Calvin Lunford McKissack (1890–1968). Calvin taught architectural drawing at Tennessee Agricultural and Industrial Normal School (today's Tennessee State University [TSU]) and headed the Department of Industrial Arts at Nashville's Pearl High School before partnering with Moses in 1922 to form McKissack & McKissack. At the time the brothers were the first black architects to be licensed in the state (they later were licensed in four additional states).

The firm thrived through the first half of the 20th century, specializing in domestic, church, commercial, and university buildings (such as the Fisk Carnegie Library) in the Neoclassical style. They received their first multimillion-dollar commission in 1942 from the military to design and construct an airfield and flight school facility for the African-American 99th Pursuit Squadron near Tuskegee, Alabama, where the famed Tuskegee Airmen were trained. This was, at the time, the largest ever such project awarded to a black firm. (Other buildings on the airbase were designed by African-American architects Hilyard Robert Robinson [1899–1986] and David Augustus Williston [1868–1962].) In deference to his achievements, President Franklin Roosevelt appointed Moses to the White House Conference on Housing Problems and awarded the firm the Spaulding Medal for Outstanding Negro Business.

After Moses's death in 1952, his brother Calvin headed the firm until his own passing in 1968, at which time Moses's son, William DeBerry McKissack (1925–88), became the firm's president. After suffering a stroke, he was succeeded in 1975 by his wife, Leatrice Buchanan McKissack (b. 1930), who oversaw projects at Fisk, TSU, Howard University, and other campus sites. In 1990, her daughter Deryl founded the second McKissack & McKissack firm in Washington, D.C. Six years later, Deryl received a major contract to rebuild and renovate the 500,000-square-foot U.S. Treasury Building that had been damaged by fire. By the turn of the 21st century, Deryl's company had opened offices in Chicago and received commissions from the Chicago public schools, the Chicago Housing Authority, and O'Hare Airport.

In 2007, McKissack & McKissack was awarded one of its most innovative projects: the Martin Luther King, Jr. Memorial, located on four acres adjacent to the Tidal Basin in Washington, D.C. (Figure 13.13). Chosen as executive architect from 900 competitors, McKissack & McKissack partnered with Devraux and Purnell/ROMA Design Group and Chinese sculptor Lei Yixin (b. 1954), among others, to implement an integrated plan that is as much sculpture and landscape as it is architecture. Unveiled in 2011 at a ceremony attended by President Obama, the main features of the $120 million memorial are three monolithic granite stones: two entitled the *Stones of Despair*, through which visitors pass in order to reach the 30-foot-high *Stone of Hope*, on which King's likeness is carved. Together, the *Stones of Despair*

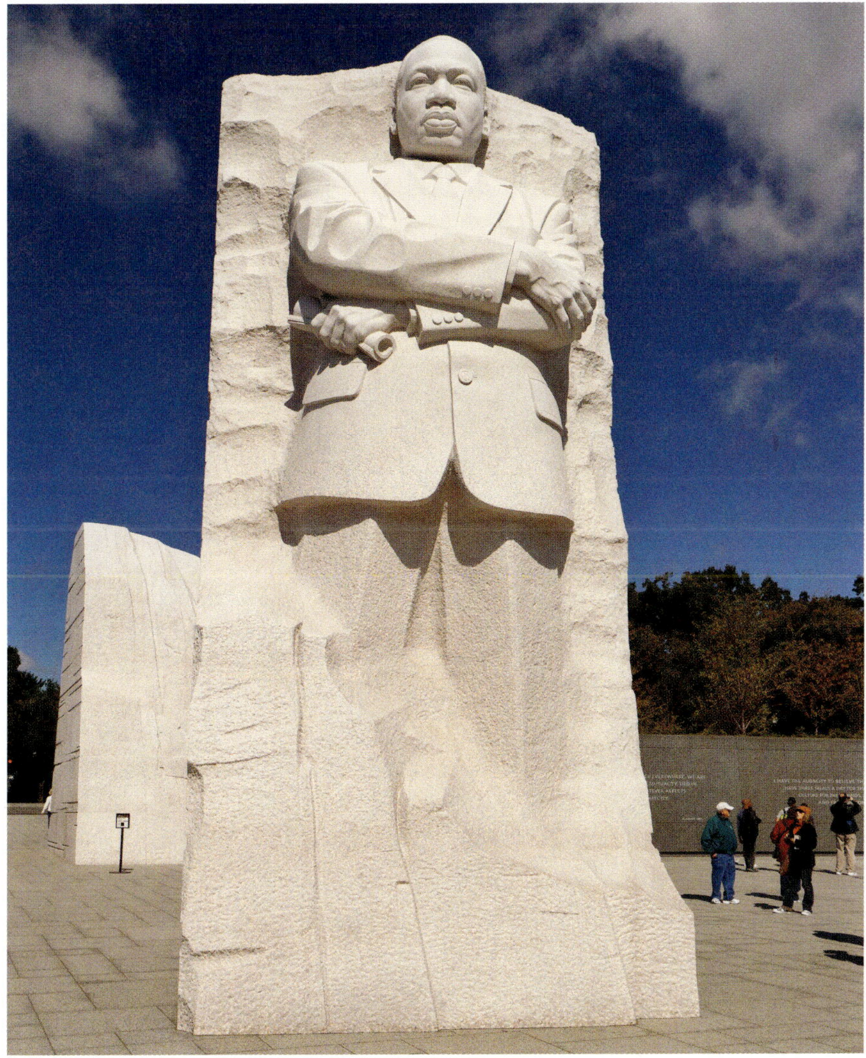

◀ **13.13** McKissack & McKissack, Lei Yixin and Devraux and Purnell/ROMA Design Group, and others, *Martin Luther King, Jr. Memorial, Washington, D.C.*, 2011, granite.

take the form of a mountain that has been cleaved in two, alluding to Dr. King's 1968 "I've Been to the Mountaintop" speech. Extending out from either side of the *Stones of Despair* is a 450- by 10-foot curving granite wall incised with inscriptions excerpted from Dr. King's speeches. The polished gray wall offers an ideal foil for the roughhewn texture of the monoliths. It also shields the space (which includes several bean-shaped gardens) from car and foot traffic. The memorial is further enclosed by a crop of cherry trees and the waters of the Tidal Basin. It has met its aim of offering to visitors a serene sanctuary in which to honor Dr. King and contemplate his vision for a racism-free America.

In 2008, the McKissack & McKissack firm expanded to Los Angeles to design for the LA Metropolitan Transit Authority, Los Angeles World Airports (which oversees LAX), and the LA Unified School District. Today the McKissack firm boasts additional offices in Miami and Baltimore. A separate McKissack construction firm headquartered in New York City is under the direction of Deryl's twin sister Cheryl McKissack, also a Howard graduate.

Other Notable Architects

Others of the thousands of gifted African-American architects who have made major contributions to the field in recent decades include the award-winning Yale University MA (1984) graduate Michael Marshall (b. 1957). His firm, Marshall/Moya, designed the Chuck Brown Memorial Park, which opened in Washington, D.C., in 2014 and honors the famed black guitarist after whom the park is named. Donald Stull (b. 1937) and David Lee (b. 1945) of the Boston firm Stull + Lee both trained at the Harvard Graduate School of Design and have taught there. Working mainly in the Boston area, their firm is responsible for dozens of schools, churches, and civic and university buildings. They also supervised the construction of the Hurricane Katrina Memorial in New Orleans. Finally, Harvey Gantt (b. 1943) of Gantt Huberman Architects in Charlotte, North Carolina, is a Clemson and MIT graduate whose award-winning University of North Carolina Charlotte Center City Building deconstructs the conventional modern cube with a glass-sheathed, three-tiered design that seems to spin on a central axis (Figure 13.14).

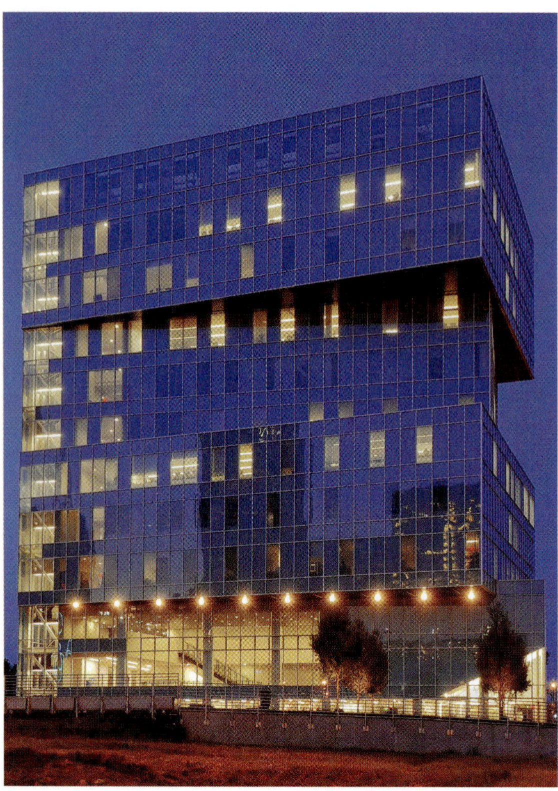

▲ **13.14** Gantt Huberman Architects, *University of North Carolina Charlotte Center City Building*, 2011.
Photo: T. W. Bruton.

Summary

Neo-Expressionist, Neo-Pop, and New Abstract art reflected the tension between 20th-century Modernism and the lure of the "new" that the 21st century promised but had not yet codified. Despite the onset of the New Millennium, many artists rejected the media innovations of Postmodernism and longed for more tried-and-true methods of art-making and expression, such as painting on canvas. Others—such as Scott, Whitten, and Dial—merged Postmodernism's interest in new and alternative media with Modernist abstraction, figuration, and humor with an eclecticism that ultimately marked the era. This same eclecticism can be seen in developments in architecture that displayed characteristics of both Modernism and Postmodernism. Most importantly, what many of the artists and architects of this period shared in common was a continued desire to express their cultural heritage in their work—a continuing thread in the history of African-American art.

Key Terms

ahistorical: refers to that which rejects or exists independently of the historical past

appropriate: to include in a work of art an image or design taken from another work of art

Ashanti: people of Ghana and the Ivory Coast in West Africa who speak the Akan language

cantilever: an architectural element such as a balcony, awning, roof, or beam that is supported at only one end and projects outward with no visible support at the other end

collective unconscious: that part of the memory, such as instinctive behavior, that predates birth and is inherited from biological ancestors

deconstruct: to take apart or dissect something for purposes of in-depth analysis, reevaluation, or reinterpretation

Deconstructivist: a style of Postmodern architecture marked by a rejection of the cubic shape of Modernist buildings and a discontinuity of forms and contours

double entendre: a word or phrase that has two meanings, one straightforward and one indirect and often sexually suggestive

geodesic: in architecture, describes a type of dome constructed of openwork triangles and polygons

glazing: installation of glass windows and walls

Neo-Historicist: refers to 20th- and 21st-century architecture that utilizes premodern styles such as Neoclassicism and Gothic Revival

Neomodern: refers to contemporary architecture that persists in the use of monolithic cubic forms associated with 20th-century Modernism, particularly International Style high-rise construction

Neo-Pop: a 1980s and 1990s art movement inspired by 1960s Pop Art but with emphasis on more contemporary subjects and high-tech materials

pickaninny: a derisive caricature of a black child, often with bulging eyes and large lips

Postmodern architecture: architecture since the 1960s that rejects the monolithic austerity of modern buildings for such features as organic forms, colorful façades, and references to premodern styles

Sambo: a derogatory slave-era term for an unintelligent black male

silhouette art: initiated in England in the 1700s, a type of portrait made by cutting the silhouette likeness of a person from black paper

sustainable design: the use of eco-friendly materials and systems to reduce negative environmental impact

Yoruban: pertaining to the Yoruba-speaking people of Nigeria and Benin in West Africa

ziggurat: originating in ancient Mesopotamia, a stepped temple constructed of trapezoid-shaped levels that decrease in size from bottom to top

Questions for Further Study and Discussion

1. Read these articles:

   [Bowles, Juliette, ed.], "Extreme Times Call for Extreme Heroes." *International Review of African American Art* 14, no. 3 (1997): 2–15.

   Walker, Kara. "The Debate Continues: Kara Walker's Response." *International Review of African American Art* 15, no. 2 (1998): 44–47.

   Based on the two differing opinions expressed in the articles, divide into debate teams and take opposing sides to argue the pros and cons of Kara Walker's art.

2. Choose an appropriated painting by Robert Colescott not illustrated in this chapter. Identify the historical painting from which Colescott appropriated his image. Identify and discuss Colescott's alterations to the original image and their iconography.
3. Artist Michael Ray Charles believes that his art disturbs viewers because racism is still so prevalent in our culture, despite official and media efforts to camouflage its existence. Debate whether or not racism is dead.
4. Kara Walker's critics have attempted to have her work banned from museums and believe that she has no right to profit from such demeaning images. Debate whether or not there should be limitations on artistic freedom. What might be the positive and/or negative outcomes of such censorship?
5. Research and discuss Jean-Michel Basquiat's meteoric rise to fame and why his art continues to fascinate art collectors.
6. Mildred Thompson was told by Black Arts Movement artists in the 1970s that her abstract art was not "black enough." Discuss the expectation that black artists should create art related to their ethnicity, history, or politics.
7. Discuss the significance and the effect on visitors of incorporating structural elements from the original World Trade Center into the 9/11 museum by Bond.
8. The National Museum of African American History and Culture by Freelon incorporates design elements derived from African culture. Discuss the ability of architecture to express a specific cultural heritage.
9. Research and discuss the work of several other significant African-American artists and architects working at the end of the 20th century, including Camille Billops (b. 1933), Beverly Lorraine Greene

(1915–57), Walter Hood (b. 1958), Margo Humphrey (b. 1942), Varnette Honeywood (1950–2010), Arturo Lindsay (b. 1946), Keith Anthony Morrison (b. 1942), Evangeline (E. J.) Montgomery (b. 1933), Mary Lovelace O'Neal (b. 1942), and Elizabeth Talford Scott (1916–2011); as well as those architects mentioned in the "Other Notable Architects" section at the end of this chapter. How does their work compare with that of the other artists discussed in this chapter?

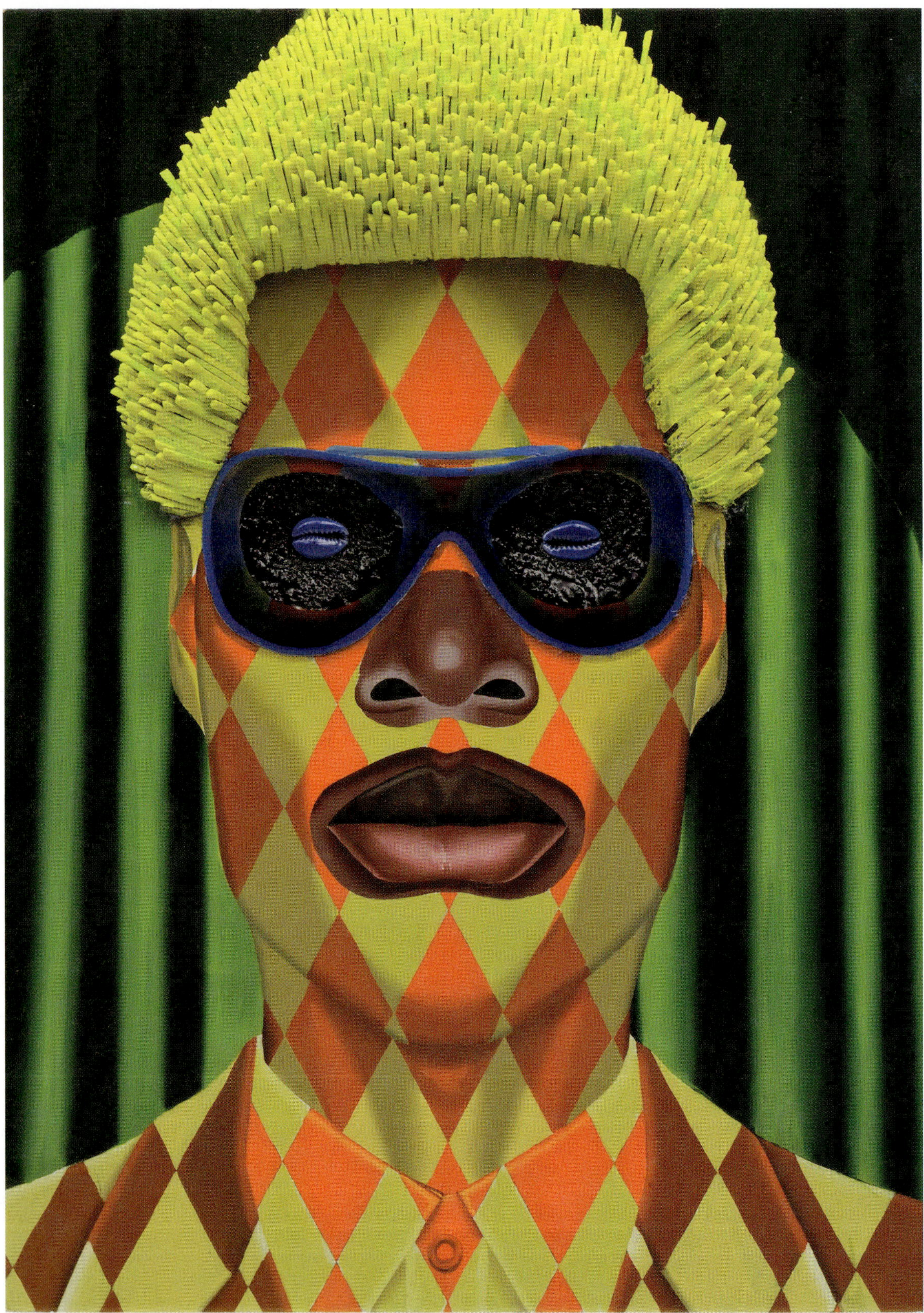

POST-BLACK ART AND THE NEW MILLENNIUM

14

In 2000, Studio Museum director Thelma Golden popularized the term "**Post-Black**" as a way of describing an age in which social biases no longer affected the creation and reception of African-American art. There has been disagreement over the validity of both this term and its underlying premise: that ethnic markers no longer influence black artists' personal and aesthetic identities. "Post-Black" describes an ideal circumstance in which prejudice has been not only contested but eliminated—a condition in which black artists no longer feel compelled to use art as a form of social protest or ethnic self-expression, because this racial identity has lost meaning.

Proponents of a Post-Black era cite as evidence the fact that a white majority voting public elected Barack Obama as America's first black president in 2008—and reelected him in 2012. For them, the sociopolitical changes that made Obama's presidency possible are proof positive that the age of identity politics in which African-American artists (and African Americans more broadly) have been so long immersed has seen its last days. Indeed, some social theorists saw identity politics as a dated notion as early as the 1990s. This assessment was supported by the 2000 national census, which revealed that an increasing segment of the U.S. population had begun to reject racial labeling. "Other" had become the self-identification of choice for a growing number of Americans whose racial profiles were composites of two or more ethnicities, and many claimed entitlement to several cultural birthrights.

Theorists such as artist and critic Keith Morrison have recently questioned the use of words such as "black" and "white" as valid racial labels, although he stopped short of heralding their total demise. According to Morrison, racial labels have become little more than descriptors, adjectives that describe differences in hue, rather than nouns that define identity. Nonetheless, he concluded, this has not eliminated racism:

> *As color distinctions proliferate, white may become not a race apart, but another color among many. But will this eliminate racism in America? The likely answer is no, since without a mass redistribution of wealth . . . people of color will remain the poorest. By virtue of being poor—and disenfranchised—artists of color will likely continue to work outside of the art establishment for the foreseeable future.*

New York Times art critic Holland Cotter echoed this sentiment, arguing that an era of postethnicity may yet prove to be "another exercise in control from above, a marketing label of greatest benefit to the privileged . . . a

◀ Jeff Sonhouse, *The Spirit of a Hypeocrite*, 2008, mixed media.

Courtesy of the artist and Tilton Gallery, New York, NY.

rejection of identity-based art at the behest of a white-dominated art market." What, after all, posits Cotter, can "Post-Black" really mean to an art establishment that continues to be overwhelmingly white?

The contradictory opinions about Post-Black art tend to break along generational lines, with older artists and scholars who lived through the civil rights struggles of the 20th century resisting what they perceive as the false hopes proffered by an alleged Post-Black age. Yet much has surely changed in recent years. Social networking has made millions of formerly disconnected Americans (indeed, populations around the globe) friends across cultural and ethnic boundaries. Twenty-first-century television, digital, and print media are replete with mixed-race couples and biracial children, such as the pairing of the white, blond-haired Kelly Ripa with the robust, black ex–football player Michael Strahan as cohosts of the Emmy Award–winning television show *Live! With Kelly and Michael*, which, in 2014, was rated one of the most-watched syndicated talk shows in the country. In this new age, President Obama's own biracial identity has prompted noticeable shifts in American attitudes about miscegenation. Easily accessible DNA analyses have revealed (as already asserted by Adrian Piper in her 1990 video installation *Out of the Corner*) that most black Americans share blood with their white compatriots. The zeitgeist of younger black artists—many of whom had yet to be born or, at best, were toddlers during the Black Arts Movement—is vastly different from that of their predecessors.

That having been said, the best assessment of whether or not an era of Post-Black art is at hand is in the actual art—which, fortunately, speaks for itself. As an invaluable primary source record, New Millennium art tells us that racial identity is alive and well, and that a bias-free, multicultural, Post-Black age has not yet been realized. Twenty-first-century artistic genres—from Afrofuturism to intervention art—reveal the persistence of identity politics among most young black artists. In the globally interconnected age in which they practice, however, these artists consider race more fluidly and flexibly than did prior generations. They allow multiple racial, gender, and ethnic influences to converge in their art. Beyond this, there are myriad other contemporary stimuli that inform their work, from hip-hop culture to cybergaming and from science fiction to YouTube.

PORTRAITURE AND IDENTITY POLITICS

Deborah Willis

An example of the changing viewpoint of race and sexuality is the series of photographic portraits of champion bodybuilder Nancy Lewis by Philadelphia-born artist Deborah Willis (b. 1948). Willis's representations of Lewis depict the black female body as the gender-bending embodiment of physical prowess—traditionally the purview of men—rather than as an object of sexuality (Figure 14.1). Willis trains her camera on the sinews, veins, taut skin, and tensile strength of her subject; her presentation is bereft of metaphor and dated clichés regarding the spiritual or inner strength of black women. We see instead a literal, corporeal strength that undermines gender typecasting.

A winner of the MacArthur Foundation Award, Willis is a curator, author, historian, and photographer. She has had a long and distinguished career that has culminated in a suite of photographic studies based on the events of 9/11, shotgun houses, hip-hop culture, bodybuilders, family, and motherhood. Willis received a BA from Temple University in 1972 and a BFA from the Philadelphia College of Art in 1975, before moving to New York, where she earned two master's degrees—in fine arts from Pratt Institute in 1979 and in art history from City College in 1986. Concurrently, Willis served as curator of prints and photographs at the Schomburg Center for 12 years, from 1980 to 1992. Relocating to Washington, D.C., in 1992, Willis worked as curator for the Smithsonian's Anacostia Museum while she completed a PhD in culture studies at George Mason University. After receiving her doctorate, in 2001, Willis joined the faculty of NYU, where she now serves as professor and chair of the Tisch School Department of Photography and Imaging. Although best known as an historian and chronicler of African-American photography and the black image in photographic history, Willis is equally prolific as a fine arts photographer. Her works depict, deconstruct, and explore gender, race, and identity paradigms, perceptions of black beauty, and icons of African-American cultural history.

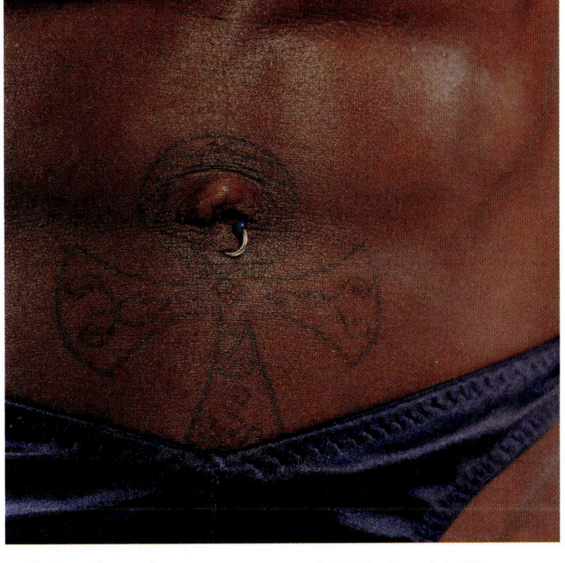

▲ **14.1** Deborah Willis, *Untitled 2—(washboard stomach)*, from *Nancy Lewis Bodybuilder* series, 2000, C-print.

Courtesy of Material Life/ NOLA and the artist.

As a scholarly author, Willis has published some dozen in-depth historical and critical studies of photography. Significant among these are *Out of Fashion Photography: Embracing Beauty* (2013); *Envisioning Emancipation: Black Americans and the End of Slavery* (2012), coauthored with Barbara Krauthamer; *Harlem: A Century in Images* (2010); *The Black Female Body: A Photographic History* (2002), with Carla Williams; and two coauthored books chronicling Michelle and Barak Obama in pictures.

Jeff Sonhouse

Jeff Sonhouse (b. 1968) is best known for his sardonic and commanding portrayals of black men (although he works with equal efficacy in Surrealist and abstract genres), many of which bear his own imposing countenance. A lifelong New Yorker, Sonhouse imbues his portrait busts and figures with an urban edginess worthy of the city. His elegantly attired characters—including portraits of black luminaries and pop icons such as Michael Jackson, P. Diddy (Sean Combs), General Colin Powell, and Cardinal Francis Arinze—stare frontally and unflinchingly at the viewer from behind decorative "skins," masks that camouflage skin color but expose just enough details of the mouth, nose, and eyes (unless obscured by sunglasses) to ensure recognition of the sitter's black identity. The dermis of his subjects is decorated in a seemingly limitless array of brightly colored patterns. Some are adorned with diamond shapes, **Pierrot**-style; others bear checked, polka dot, plaid, chevron, striped, paisley, or polygonal patterns (see chapter-opening image). Still others are starkly white and unembellished. Clothing—suits, ties, bowties, fedoras, papal tiaras, boutonnieres, and so on—is also patterned and vividly hued. This cacophony of color and design serves not to mitigate the power of the black male gaze—a j'accuse glare that marks most of Sonhouse's portrayals—but to underscore its intensity.

Sonhouse adds to many of his paintings three-dimensional elements such as blackened or painted matchsticks or steel wool to replicate the curly texture of black hair, either conservatively cropped or youthfully abundant. Other additive items include feathers, cowrie shells, paper clips, and jewelry that the artist incorporates into his works with ingenuity to suggest speech, bend gender, or approximate bouclé fabric. Routinely appropriating poses and motifs from the works of past artists such as Picasso, Diego Velazquez (1599–1660), and Francis Bacon (1909–92), Sonhouse transforms these renderings entirely. In one Sonhouse portrait, the artist transmutes Constantin Brancusi's (1876–1957) famed sculpture *Bird in Space* into the feather in a black man's cap. Clever titles such as "Pawnography," "The Sacrificial Goat," and "The Spirit of a Hypeocrite" allude to black men as political pawns, scapegoats, and purveyors of hype and suggest the depth of the artist's iconography in his gaze-fixing examinations of black male identity.

A 1998 BFA graduate of the SVA and 2001 MFA graduate of CUNY's Hunter College, Sonhouse has garnered several one-man shows and has been featured in group exhibits in Europe and the United States. He has also earned fellowships from the Joan Mitchell Foundation and the New York Foundation for the Arts.

Mickalene Thomas

Brooklyn-based artist Mickalene Thomas (b. 1971) works in a wide range of media, including painting, collage, photography, film, video, and installation. Her signature art, however, consists of large-scale figurative images of empowered black women created with enamel and acrylic paint and adorned with crystals. Her imagery concentrates specifically on black female beauty and glamour. She appropriates visual themes from the art historical past, including 19th-century portraiture; Hudson River School landscapes; traditional still-life painting; the Modernist visions of Matisse, Picasso, and Bearden; Pop Art; and contemporary culture. Her work is particularly inspired by the authoritative female images of Renée Cox (discussed later in this chapter).

One of Thomas's most renowned works takes multiple forms as a photograph, painting, installation, and collage commissioned by MoMA in 2010. Adapted from French artist Edouard Manet's famed 1963 *Le Déjeuner sur l'Herbe* (also a motif used by Cox), Thomas's *Le Déjeuner Sur l'Herbe: Les Trois Femmes Noires* (*Luncheon on the Grass: Three Black Women*) is based on a mise en scène that the artist staged with models and props in the MoMA outdoor garden in New York City and then photographed. The initial photo was then torn, reassembled, collaged, Photoshopped, and otherwise altered to create a photomontage that pays homage to the media experiments of Picasso and Bearden (Figure 14.2). Sections of woodgrain and patterned fabric are integrated like puzzle pieces with flat areas of bright color and serve as the setting for three seated black women wearing minidresses, 1970s hoop

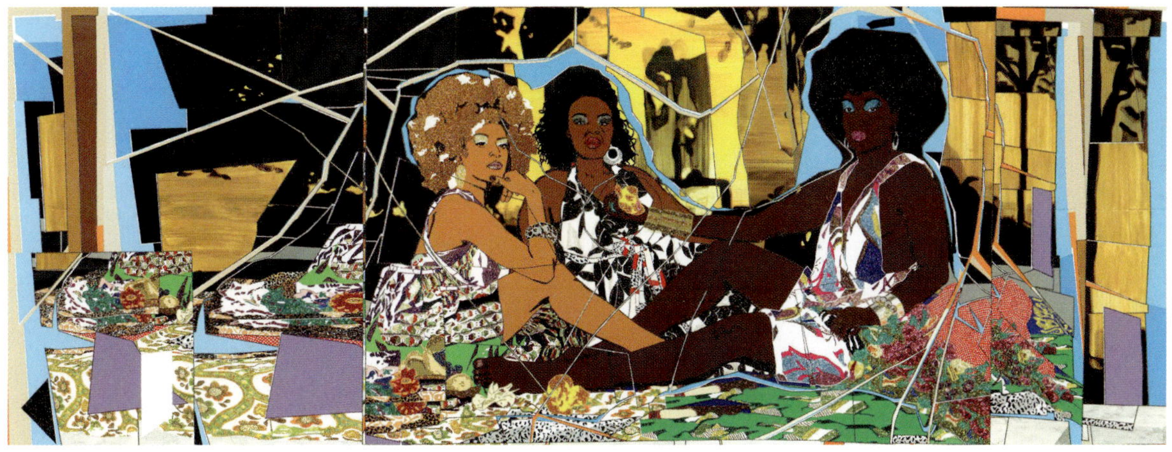

▲ **14.2** Mickalene Thomas, *Le Déjeuner sur l'Herbe: Les Trois Femmes Noires*, 2010, rhinestones, acrylic, and enamel on wood panel, 120″ × 288″.

earrings, bright eyeshadow and lipstick, and Afro hairstyles. They gaze calmly and with self-possession at the viewer, fusing elements of masculine and feminine with casual ease. During the winter of 2010, the photograph and collage adorned the large plate-glass window display of MoMA's 53rd Street façade; a painted version was displayed in the museum restaurant; and the collage was used as part of an installation at MoMA PS1 in Queens. Subsequently in 2012, the collage was featured in a solo Thomas exhibit at the Brooklyn Museum.

Thomas's more recent 2014 *Tête de Femme* images explore Cubism rather than figuration. These works were inspired by Picasso's 1930s *Têtes de Femme* paintings of his mistress, Marie-Thérèse Walter. Thomas worked in collaboration with renowned makeup artist Vincent Oquendo, who styled various models for the work using elaborate makeup techniques. The series transforms photographs of the models into abstracted heads that, despite their distortion, retain an overtly feminine and glamorous appearance, marked by languid eyes, long lashes, ruby red lips, and Pop Art colors. Also a filmmaker, Thomas's documentary *Happy Birthday to a Beautiful Woman* debuted on HBO in 2014. It is a tribute to the artist's mother and muse, runway model Sandra Bush (d. 2012). The film features portraits of Bush by Thomas intermingled with film of Bush discussing her life, its trials, and its triumphs, in poignant detail.

Thomas is a New Jersey native. She received her BFA from Pratt Institute in 2000 and her MFA from Yale in 2002, after which she moved to New York. Since 2006, Thomas has had more than a dozen solo shows and has shown internationally at major museums and galleries.

Kehinde Wiley

Celebrated portraitist Kehinde Wiley (b. 1977) has drawn from the great **alpha male** portraits of 16th-, 17th-, and 18th-century Europe—gentry, royalty, kings, and military officers—to bestow analogous auras of power and dominance on the African-American men he portrays. (He also creates portraits of black women and children.) His sitters are sometimes hip-hop icons such as LL Cool J, Ice T, and Grandmaster Flash and the Furious Five

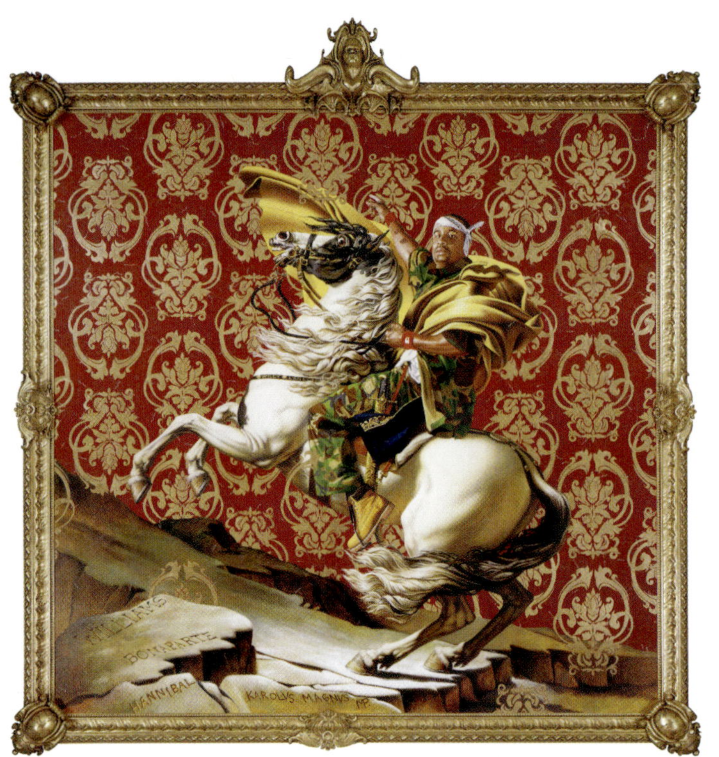

▲ **14.3** Kehinde Wiley, *Napoleon Leading the Army over the Alps*, 2005, oil on canvas, 108″ × 108″.

Courtesy of Roberts & Tilton, Culver City, CA; Sean Kelly, New York, NY; Galerie Daniel Templon, Paris; and Stephen Friedman Gallery, London. © Kehinde Wiley. Used by permission.

and at other times lesser-known models who, nevertheless, exude the same sense of privilege and supremacy. In response to his commanding portrait style, in 2005 VH1 commissioned Wiley to paint several of its Hip Hop Honors awardees who represented the best of the genre's up-and-coming musical talent. Working in a large-scale photorealist style, Wiley used ornate gilded frames and Art Nouveau–inspired patterning—floral, vine leaf, and whiplash motifs—as backdrops for his subjects. This sumptuous combination recalls the clothing and upholstery fabric of several key Western art eras—the Italian Renaissance, the Dutch Baroque style, the French Rococo style, Neoclassicism, and Romanticism—from which Wiley draws inspiration.

Wiley's subjects are sometimes depicted in equestrian poses appropriated from such sources as Jacques-Louis David's 1801 *Napoleon Crossing the Saint Bernard Pass* and Theodore Gericault's 1812 *Charging Chasseur*. In Wiley's *Napoleon Leading the Army over the Alps* from his *Equestrian* series (Figure 14.3), the artist portrays a young black man from south-central Los Angeles, who symbolizes a population historically excluded from Western art. The series addresses that omission by depicting black men as images of power and status. In Wiley's words, "Painting is about the world that we live in. Black men live in the world. My choice is to include them. This is my way of saying yes to us." Whether his subjects are on horseback or enthroned like Napoleon in the 1806 portrait by Jean-Auguste-Domonique Ingres (1780–1867), Wiley's poses are hardly chosen at random. Instead, they consciously reflect something of each sitter's personality: regal, sportsmanlike, effeminate, confrontational, playful, fashion-conscious, introspective, or vain. Furthermore, his paintings do more than appropriate; they deconstruct the concept of the master, as in "master painter," "slave master," and even "Grandmaster Flash." In Wiley's art, the identity, the role, and the meaning of the word "master" is questioned and critiqued. Viewers are reminded that sociopolitical and cultural hierarchies are always in flux. In Wiley's oeuvre, the coveted place of past masters of European painting—the rock stars of their eras—has been usurped by Wiley himself. Likewise, the specter of the white slave master has been supplanted by new images of black men in control of their own destinies and comfortable in their own skin.

Wiley was born in Los Angeles and trained on the West Coast, before relocating to New York to accept an artist's residency at the Studio Museum.

He received his BFA from the San Francisco Art Institute in 1999 and an MFA from Yale in 2001. His work has been shown in solo and group exhibitions throughout the United States and internationally. Wiley currently lives and works in New York City and Beijing, China.

AFROFUTURISM

Initially a music and literary movement, **Afrofuturism** refers to art that interrogates, deconstructs, and reimagines the past, present, and future of Africans in the diaspora through the lenses of **technoculture**, science fiction, futuristic fantasy, and Eastern and African belief systems. The term was first used in print in the mid-1990s by American literary critic Mark Dery (b. 1959) in his book *Flame Wars: The Discourse of Cyberculture*, to describe artists and writers who envision a very different future for blacks than that which has thus far been imagined. Their art defies the negatively constructed African past born of the slave trade, and the seeming inevitability of its legacy in the future. Afrofuturist artists achieve this goal through the use of topsy-turvy takes on old themes, positive spins on once-negative icons, reimagined superheroes, and utopian future societies wherein time and space collapse and conflate and race becomes a malleable concept.

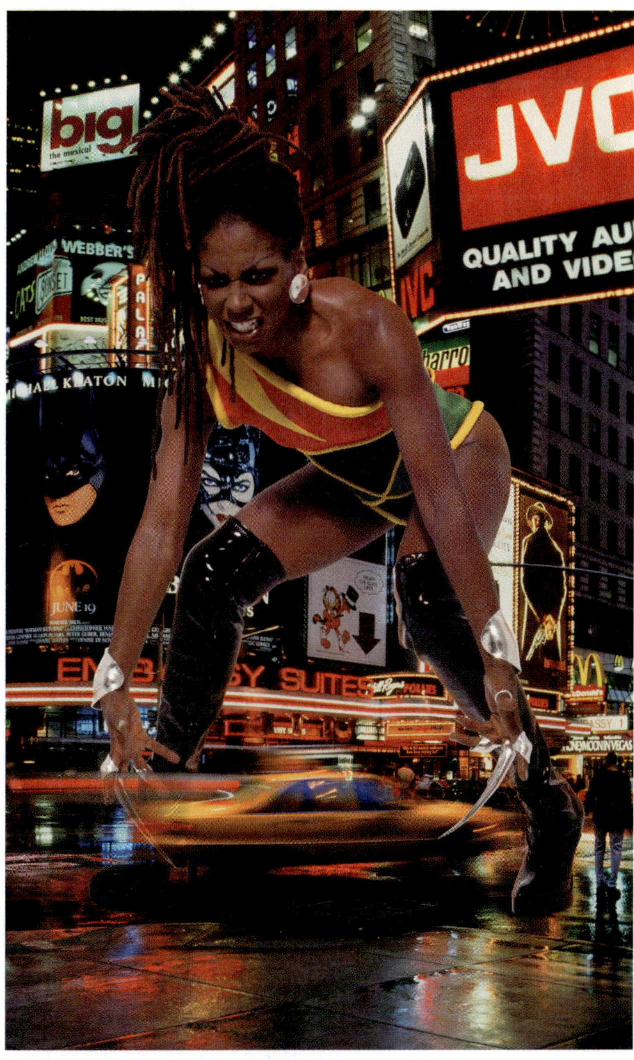

▼ **14.4** Renée Cox, *Taxi*, the *Rajé* series, edition of 3, 1998–2001, cibachrome print, 60″ × 48″.

Renée Cox

One of the most famous images of artist-photographer Renée Cox (b. 1958) is her Afrofuturist self-styled superhero Rajé. Rajé takes form as the artist in thigh-high black patent leather boots and an off-the-shoulder swimsuit of red, black, yellow, and green (a combination of the colors of the Jamaican and black nationalist flags). Rajé appears in a variety of Cox's photomontages, including *Taxi*, a 1998 cibachrome in which the superhero forcibly stops a speeding taxicab. The image critiques the erstwhile notorious penchant of many New York City cab drivers for passing up black passengers in favor of whites (Figure 14.4). Other incarnations of Rajé show her rescuing Uncle Ben and Aunt Jemima from their respective food boxes, perched atop the Statue of Liberty with legs crossed, and flying over the Great Sphinx at Giza. In each instance, Rajé rights injustice, rewrites history, and subverts stereotypes.

Cox's use of her own body in her work was the subject of heated public debate when, following the showing of her *Yo Mama's Last Supper* at the Brooklyn Museum in 2001, New York mayor Rudolph Giuliani condemned the photograph of a nude Cox posing as Christ with black apostles as "disgusting" and "outrageous." In order to "consecrate" black bodies and draw attention to their absence in Western visual culture, in this and other works from Cox's *Grand Salon* and *Flippin' the Script* series, the artist plundered canonical paintings such as Leonardo da Vinci's *Last Supper* (1495–98), Andrea Mantegna's *St. Sebastian* (c. 1460), Michelangelo's *Pieta* (1499), Antonio Canova's *Paolina Borghese as Venus Victrix* (1808), and Edouard Manet's *Le Déjeuner sur l'Herbe*, replacing historical white icons with contemporary black ones.

Cox emigrated to the United States with her family from Jamaica in the West Indies. She began her career as a fashion photographer for *Details*, *Cosmopolitan*, *Essence*, and *French Glamour* magazines. As she became aware of the debates about the black female body and the scarceness of its presence in the fashion industry, Cox began to use her own body in conjunction with the "scrutinizing eye" of her camera to consider matters of black female beauty and sexuality. Over the last several decades Cox has produced a variety of art suites that are both conceptual and formal in emphasis. The text-based series *Surprise Surprise* (1995) draws attention to the internalization of racist stereotypes by blacks themselves. *Queen Nanny: Maroon Series* (2004) offers scenes of an empowered Caribbean woman and escaped slave. *The Discreet Charm of the Bourgeoisie* (2008) presents satirical scenes of Cox as an upper-middle-class suburban housewife. And *Sacred Geometry* (2014) digitally manipulates nudes and portraits of black models into kaleidoscopic fractal-like forms.

Ellen Gallagher

The art of Ellen Gallagher (b. 1965) encompasses a variety of media and techniques, including collages, assemblages, drawings, paintings, prints, paper reliefs, video, and sculptures, often installed as composite ensembles. She works in an amalgam of Minimalist, conceptual, and figurative genres that are at once hermetic and revelatory. Gallagher is best known for her appropriation of mid-20th-century print ads for black hair-straightening and skin-lightening products. À la Duchamp's mustached Mona Lisa (*L.H.O.O.Q.* of 1919), Gallagher alters these ads with painted red lips, cutout eyes, and bright yellow wigs to problematize the legacy of African Americans who—via hair weaves, blond hair dye, skin lighteners, and rhinoplasty—actively pursue Europeans ideal of beauty. Other persistent motifs in Gallagher's eclectic vision are blackface minstrelsy, science fiction, and surrealist fantasy, placing her squarely within the Afrofuturist firmament.

Gallagher's 2001–ongoing *Watery Ecstatic/Coral Cities* series incorporates vintage images from iconic black publications such as *Ebony* and *Sepia* to actualize a Postmodern fable conceived by the electro/nouveau disco musical duo Drexciya, composed of James Stinson and Gerald Donald. Their fantasy lyrics describe an African Atlantis, the home of a subaquatic race born from pregnant slaves who were drowned by slavers during the Middle Passage. Delivered from the amniotic fluid of their mother's wombs directly into the ocean, these deep-sea dwellers were able to breathe water and thus survive where their mothers perished. Gallagher's interest in visualizing this fantastical allegory was further inspired by a season she spent as an oceanography student on a research vessel in 1986. During her year at sea, she made detailed drawings of microscopic marine organisms that, in actuality, take bizarre forms not unlike those of science fiction creatures. Gallagher's artistic visions of Drexciya's underwater world synthesize imagined and authentic versions of fish, plankton, crustaceans, and pteropods (marine invertebrates) with humanoid figures that grow algae for hair.

A native of Providence, Rhode Island, in the 1980s Gallagher studied writing, oceanography, and visual art at several prestigious institutions. Her art has been the subject of solo and group exhibits both at home and abroad. Gallagher maintains studios in New York City and Rotterdam.

Laylah Ali

Laylah Ali (b. 1968) came to prominence with her invention of a population of cartoon-like characters dubbed "Greenheads." The Greenheads are brown-skinned anthropoids with painfully thin and rigidly uniformed bodies topped by circular green, disproportionately large heads. They bear a not-so-vague resemblance to the animated players in the popular cartoon series *South Park*. Ali's vignettes portray sadistic behaviors that signal the widespread acceptance of violence in children's television. In one painting, a female Greenhead stands in her underwear while using her panties (still on her hips) to lash to her side the neck of a gasping child and a bundle of dynamite. In another, three men hang from their necks while holding the severed limbs of a living figure who witnesses their hanging. Yet another composition portrays Ku Klux Klan Greenheads in tall, cone-shaped white hats, examining a decapitated head as if it were a strange toy. What astounds in Ali's "parables of race," which are comparable to Kara Walker's antebellum horrors (Chapter 13), is the anomalous rendering of savage narrative and Spartan color schemes, empty background fields, and graphic precision. These works provide a fitting comment on the insensitivity to violence that is part and parcel of New Millennium culture and a direct result of the profusion of brutality made available through all forms of media, from "Taliban" computer games, to hip-hop lyrics, and to untold numbers of grisly sci-fi and action films.

In 2004, Ali developed a new mythical race in a series she calls *Typology*, a pun that describes the artist's rendering of human (or humanoid) "types" as if it is a scientific study (Figure 14.5). Like her Greenheads, Ali's *Typology* characters are rendered in a cartoon-like fashion that obscures the dark and complex portent of the artist's iconography. Her anthropoids act our interpersonal power plays through Ali's deployment of hierarchic proportions, physical disabilities, poses, gestures, and situational narratives. Rather than depicting overt acts of violence, as with the Greenheads, in

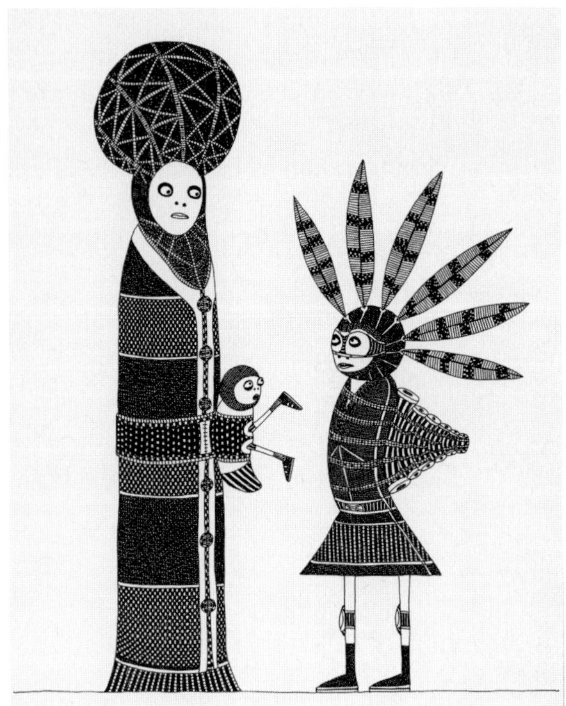

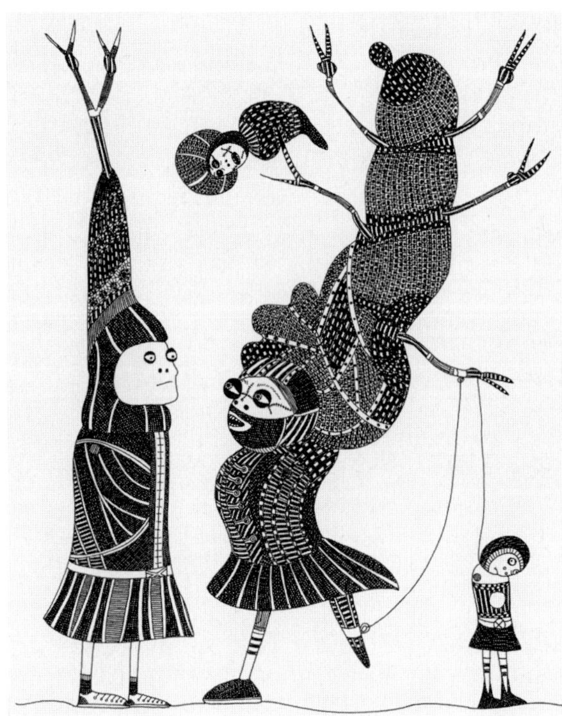

▲ **14.5** Laylah Ali, *Untitled*, from *Typology* series, 2005, ink on paper, 14″ × 11″ each of two drawings.

the *Typology* vignettes Ali alludes to violence with more subtlety. Some figures are, indeed, limbless, bound, dangling from a hangman's noose, or speared by a tree branch, but these misfortunates are often rendered tangentially to a core scene in which the dominant characters converse and interact.

Also unlike the Greenheads—whose racial identities can be culled from their skin color and behavior—Ali's new players present multiple ethnicities or none at all, depending on the drawing and one's point of view. Because the images are configured mainly in black and white, skin color becomes irrelevant to this "race" of otherworldly beings. Although their towering and implausible hats and hairdos, intricately patterned cloaks, costumes, masks, and other accoutrements give hints as to each character's importance or lack thereof, a thoroughgoing understanding of their social order eludes us. Viewers are simply reminded that any hierarchical social system that involves better and worse, powerful and weak, dominant and subordinate, or master and slave is an evolving construct rather than a fixed reality. One's position on any given level of the sociopolitical totem pole is impermanent.

Ali was born and raised in Buffalo, New York. In 1991 she earned a bachelor's degree from Williams College. She was awarded a residency at the Whitney Museum Independent Study Program in 1991 and another at Skowhegan in 1993, after which she completed an MFA at Washington University in St. Louis in 1994. In Williamstown, Massachusetts, where she currently lives and works, over the next 20 years Ali earned an impressive array of honors and exhibitions.

Sanford Biggers

Los Angeles–born artist Sanford Biggers (b. 1970) merges improvisational performance, music, film, video, installation, sculpture, and sculptural performance into his intermedia art. His sculpture and installation materials include such varied components as quilts, lighting, furniture, musical instruments, plastic flora, aluminum, Plexiglas, and even his own body. Biggers's subject matter incorporates hip-hop, jazz, and pop music, and African and Asian religions. He addresses such issues as racial stereotypes, slavery, and the Middle Passage, often including more than one motif within a single piece.

Biggers's sculptural installation *Cheshire* vastly enlarges the full red lips associated with minstrelsy into an oversized apparition of the grin of the Cheshire cat from Louis Carroll's *Alice in Wonderland* (Figure 14.6). Partly by naming the work "Cheshire" and partly by extracting the lips from the context of a black face, Biggers wholly alters the erstwhile derogatory signification of the toothy minstrel grin. Using painted aluminum, Plexiglas, and LED lights, Biggers created a five-foot-wide smile that flashes white lights—its "teeth"—at the audience with the magical delight of Carroll's mischievous cat. Whether hung from a gallery ceiling, displayed on a billboard, or perched in a tree in an outdoor setting (where Carroll's cat appeared to Alice), Biggers's smile critiques the stereotype while simultaneously dissociating it from its past.

Other Afrofuturist works by Biggers reimagine Harriet Tubman as an astronaut, slave ships as Buddhist lotus flowers, and the origin of the universe

▼ **14.6** Sanford Biggers, *Cheshire (Hanging/Orange)*, 2010, digital C-print, 24″ × 34″.

Courtesy of the artist.

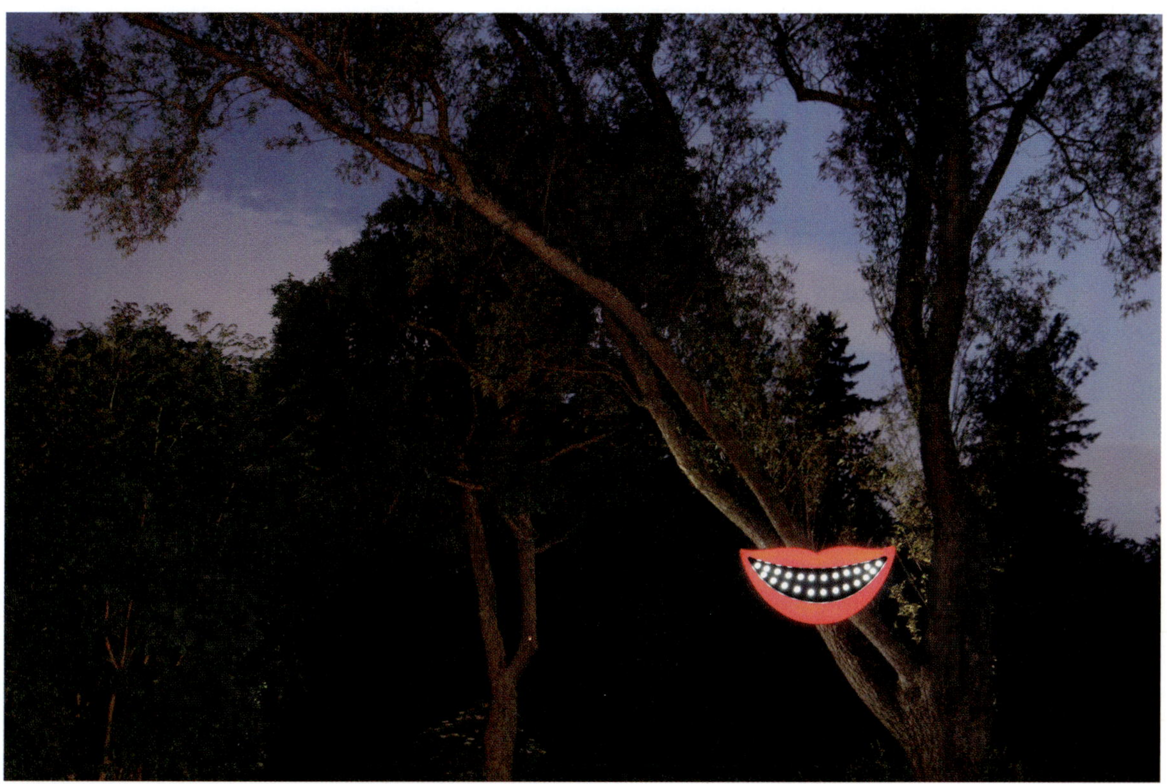

celebrated by an invisible performer of the calenda (Afro-Caribbean martial arts movements). To create the latter work, Biggers used a lighted disco ball with a mirrored surface that cast fragments of light onto the gallery walls to suggest a primordial Big Bang explosion.

Biggers received his BA from Morehouse College in Atlanta in 1992 and his MFA from the SAIC in 1997. Before moving to New York in 1999 to accept a teaching position at Columbia University, Biggers taught at Virginia Commonwealth University and was a visiting scholar at Harvard University. Solo and group performances and shows of his work have been hosted around the world.

Xaviera Simmons

Xaviera Simmons (b. 1974) works in photography, text-based conceptual art, assemblage, performance, installation, video, sound (including working as a DJ), and sculpture. Her photographs are often artistic records of her performances and assemblages. Because Simmons's assemblages often incorporate human bodies (frequently her own), her photographs serve as records of these necessarily ephemeral art objects. They also function as standalone works of art in their own right. A Simmons human assemblage camouflages the body beneath a mass of disparate found objects, such as Polaroid snapshots of black models and musicians, antique **blackamoor** figurines, fabric, pottery, African and Mardi Gras masks, feathers, clothespins, hair extensions, palm leaves, and animal skulls. The assemblage is then photographed and the photo manipulated so that it is impossible to tell what is real and what is invented.

Best known for her photographs of carefully staged performances and stationery vignettes, Simmons's imagery explores black female identity and racial stereotypes. The artist's various models are presented nude and painted entirely black or clothed in black attire with bright red minstrel's lips and are posed eating watermelon in a vintage 1950s kitchen or seated in a rattan throne among tall reeds wearing massive Afro wigs. In Simmons's photograph *One Day and Back Then*, the past and future are merged in a field of reeds that alludes to the African motherland before imperialism, colonialism, and the slave trade (Figure 14.7). In Simmons's fantasy world, a recontextualized minstrel in a black velour robe and blackface stares solemnly at the viewer from the safety of her reed "jungle," as metaphorically distant from the stereotype to which it alludes as the African past is from its future. Simmons sets up problematizing contrasts: a black figure against pale gold reeds, tightly coiled black hair against the long, silken blond "hair" in the form of those reeds, and red minstrel lips that frown rather than grin.

Simmons's art obfuscates the boundaries between herself as the subject and as the maker of her art. She describes her images as portraits and self-portraits that aim to translate paradigms of blacks, Africans, Afro-Americans—the sundry words that define people of African descent—into a visual language that is both intriguing and unpredictable. She hopes her art prompts new ways of seeing and understanding blackness as a shifting hypothesis rather than a fixed idea. A New Yorker, Simmons earned a BFA from Bard College in 2005 and was chosen that year for the Whitney

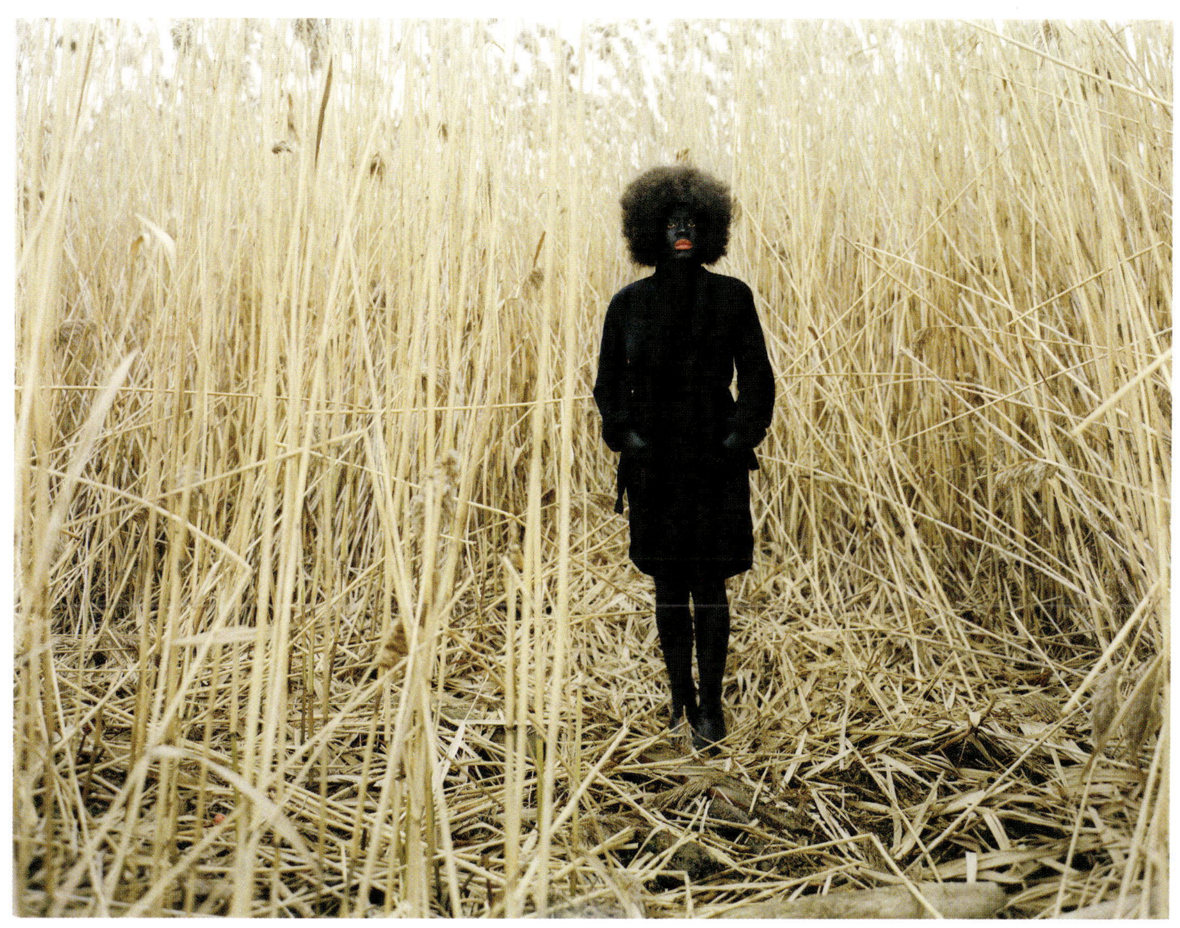

▲ 14.7 Xaviera Simmons, *One Day and Back Then (Standing)*, 2007, Chromira C-print, edition 2/5, 30″ × 40″.

Independent Study Program. Since then she has earned several major awards and exhibitions.

Trenton Doyle Hancock

Oklahoma City–born Trenton Doyle Hancock (b. 1974) grew up in Paris, Texas, and received a BFA from Texas A&M University in 1997. In 2000, at age 26, Hancock became one of the youngest artists ever to participate in the distinguished Whitney Biennial (he was invited back two years later in 2002). His media are prints, drawings, installations, and paintings, collaged with felt fabric. Influenced by pulp fiction and the serial sagas of comic book superheroes, Hancock's iconographic leitmotif is a fantastical society of flora and fauna hybrids named (and shaped like) "Mounds." Horizontally striped in black and white, these wobbling, egg-shaped beings with their garish heads live epic and tragic lives that are played out in Hancock's art.

Through the bizarre experiences of his mythic Mounds and their archenemies, the Vegans, Hancock addresses the range of human experiences, dilemmas, and challenges, most significantly the clash between good (embodied by the Mounds) and evil (personified by the Vegans). The Mounds ruminate on such topics as aesthetics, morphology, body image, civil unrest, memory, disease, and the psyche. A griot by nature, Hancock frequently uses texts in his paintings and installations to clarify his narratives. In the 10-foot-high unstretched canvas *The Legend Is in Trouble* (2001), Hancock combines felt, glue, collaged lettering, hair, painting, and drawing to create his allegory of evil triumphing over good. A protagonist—the Legend—is attacked by Vegan rebels and mortally wounded, such that his bodily contents—his life's blood, called "moundmeat"—ooze out of multiple wounds, portending the Legend's death. Even the saga's superhero, Torpedo Boy—an avatar of Hancock in yellow tights that appears in numerous episodes—is helpless to save him.

Perhaps due to its narrative and discursive nature, Hancock's art has lent itself to reifications in other art forms—specifically ballet. The two-act *Cult of Color: Call to Color* was conceived by Hancock following a commission from Ballet Austin in Texas. Choreographed by the company's artistic director, Stephen Mills, and scored by German composer and jazz musician Graham Reynolds, it premiered in Austin in 2008.

Other Hancock commissions include a mural for the Dallas Cowboys Stadium and a site-specific Olympic Sculpture Park installation sponsored by the Seattle Art Museum. He has received many awards, fellowships, and grants, and his work has been featured in exhibitions around the world.

NEW MILLENNIUM PERFORMANCE ART

Performance art (see Chapter 12) continued into the New Millennium as a dynamic form of creative expression. A new generation of African-American artists took up the gauntlet with updated themes, high-tech methods, and futuristic costuming.

Nick Cave

One of the leading lights among the new performance art practitioners is artist Nick Cave (b. 1959). Straddling the divide between Afrofuturism and performance, Cave's "soundsuits" defy media categorization. Hand-sewn and crafted from colorful flea market finds such as faux fur, brilliantly dyed human hair, sisal, feathers, fabric, beads, sequins, rugs, and even board games (used to create faces), these works of art are both sculptures and costumes at once (Figure 14.8). Visually captivating, Cave's soundsuits are designed to fully camouflage the wearer's (Cave's) identity. Thus disguised, the artist then acts out choreographed movements that bring the suit to life. Able to transform himself into a vehicle of protest or anger, exuberance, or introspection, Cave communicates more forcefully and earnestly from within the soundsuit than he might without it. Behind the soundsuit veil, he becomes a shaman of sorts. His goal is to coax viewers into a transcendent, dreamlike state in which they might derive a sense of pleasure, awe, tranquility, or harmony from the sensory experience he provides.

Cave's suits are comparable in their surreal nature to such fictional costumed characters as the futuristic Darth Vader from the *Star Wars* films, hairy Cousin Itt from the Adams Family, and the Claymation icon Gumby. No two costumes are alike, and, depending on the materials used, each makes a different sound when enlivened by the artist's movements: metal toy tops clank against one another, long hair or fibers swish through the

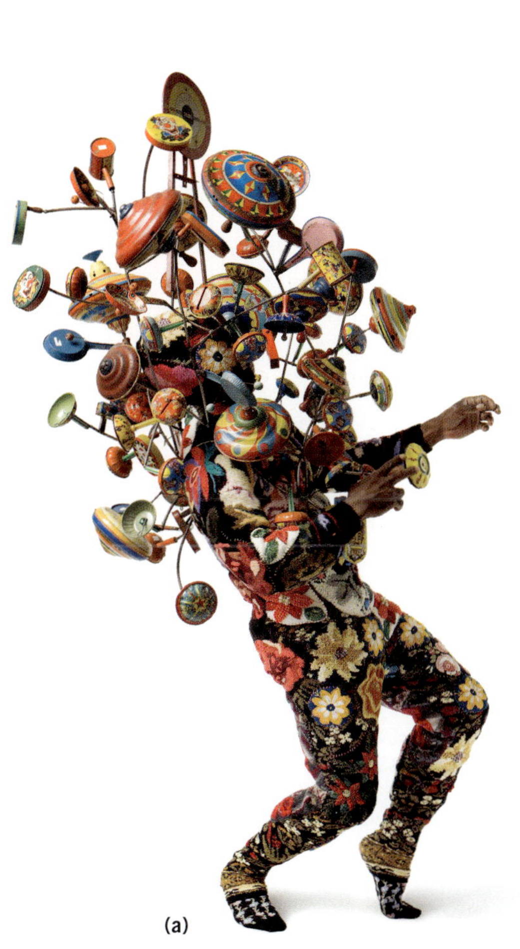
(a)

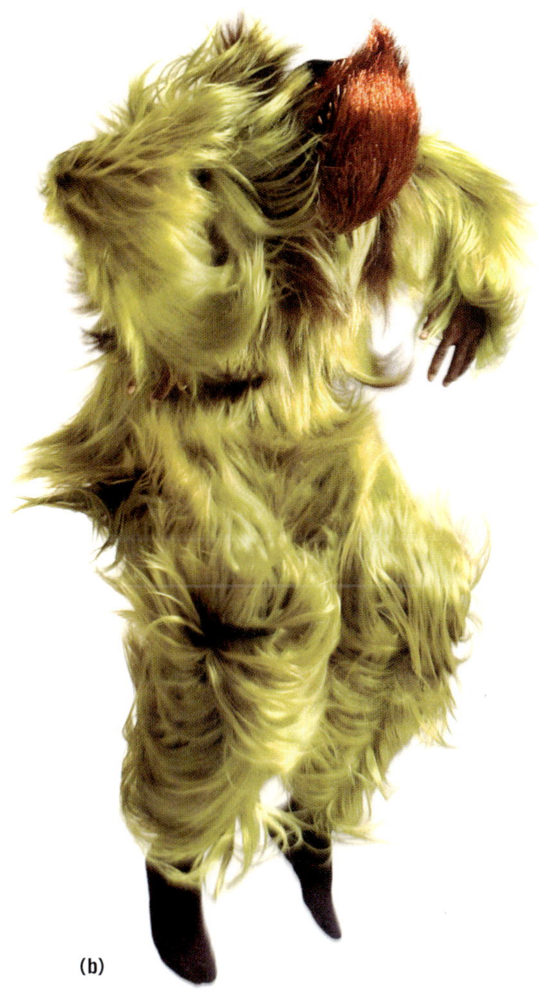
(b)

▲ 14.8 Nick Cave, *Soundsuit*, 2006–13, (a) faux fur and mixed media, (b) toy tops and mixed media.

air, and beads click against sequins. Since 2010, Cave has developed his performance-wear into standalone sculptures, video and sculptural installations, and mandala-shaped relief paintings. Adding to his already eclectic repertoire of materials, Cave's paintings and sculptures are constructed from artificial flora, ceramic and plastic animal figures, appliquéd fabric, natural and synthetic fibers, wire, and even furniture. His three-dimensional works comprise majestic animals with neon manes that have the look of prehistoric mammals, floating figures in spacesuits that hang from gallery ceilings, and anthropoids with human bodies and surrealistic chandelier heads.

The Missouri-born Cave was one of six siblings in a family of modest means—a situation that required him to design his own clothes from his brothers' hand-me-downs. (His eldest brother, Jack, also became a fashion designer.) Cave earned a BFA from the Kansas City Art Institute in 1982 and then an MFA from the Cranbrook Academy of Art. During the 1980s, he studied modern dance with the Alvin Ailey Company, which is reflected in his expertly choreographed performances. He created his first soundsuit following the infamous 1991 police beating of Rodney King, which compelled Cave to rethink his status as a black man in America—as someone "discarded, devalued, and viewed as less than [a man]." Cave decided to express his feelings through his art. With the soundsuit and in the time-honored tradition of masquerade, he found a way to become whomever he wished, and to communicate freely without being judged because of his race or gender.

Ironically, Cave's first soundsuit was not intended to create sound at all, but, due to the materials used to make it—twigs collected from a local park—the suit rustled when he moved inside it, much to the artist's surprise and delight. Made of hundreds of tree sprigs cut to three-inch lengths and wired to an ordinary fabric bodysuit, the noise created by this first soundsuit inspired Cave to choreograph his movements so as to generate specific sound rhythms. Over time, Cave's award-winning suits (which today number in the hundreds) evolved to include more diverse and colorful materials, and his performances progressed to include additional dancers, video components, musicians, and even contemporary DJ performers. Cave currently lives and works in Chicago and since 1989 has served on the faculty at the SAIC, where he has chaired the Fashion Department.

Camille Norment

Camille Norment (b. 1970) is an intermedia performance, video, and installation artist whose works are rooted in the traditions of Op Art, Conceptualism, and Minimalism. Through resonant acoustic compositions, Op Art image elements, and carefully designed site-specific spaces, Norment strives to heighten viewer-listener awareness of their own physical and psychological states. Consumers of Norment's art are invited to become active participants in the creative process as they move through her installations and engage both visually and aurally in their intermedia components. Simultaneously sensory and perceptual, Norment's sound, light, and visual art forms subvert art-consumer expectations. Her sound works comprise such elements as inaudible vibrations that are felt by the body rather than heard. Norment's musical performances, on the other hand, are at once cacophonic and melodic. They are created using a combination of electronic sound, a Norwegian Hardanger fiddle, and a crystallophonic "armonica" wherein sound is formed by the friction of stacked glass bowls rubbing against one another.

In Norment's visual and spatial art, optical illusions abound. An observer might be confronted by eerie cast shadows, ambient lighting, a coin that spins continually and mysteriously on a pedestal top, or a light bulb that oscillates hypnotically without any visible impetus, in tandem with a laser light beam. Viewers might gaze into a painting that is, in fact, a mirror and find themselves inserted into a Surrealist landscape. Conversely, viewers might gaze into a mirror that offers no reflection at all—like the empty mirror in Surrealist painter René Magritte's 1938 *Time Transfixed*. However, Norment's mirror is not an illusory painted image but an actual mirror—a solid, three-dimensional object—in which the viewer has become invisible. Norment configures her art within galleries or unorthodox architectural environments (such as stairwells), which she transforms into padded asylum cells, rooms of near total darkness, or industrial spaces.

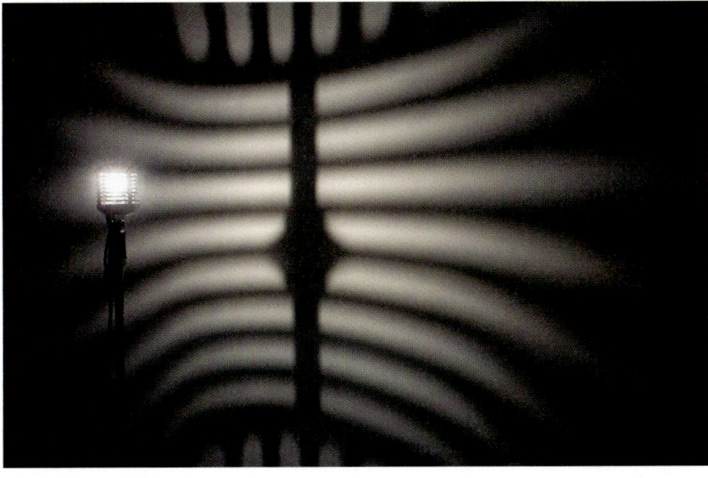

▲ **14.9** Camille Norment, *Triplight*, 2008, 1955 Shure microphone cage, stand, light, electronic components, dimensions variable.

Norment's artworks also proffer abstruse references to African-American culture and history—references that each observer may choose to read, expand on, or ignore. The kinetic sculpture *Juke* features a "dancing" penny that spins atop a black "stage" (in the form of a black pedestal)—alluding to a black dancing minstrel. Its title refers to juke joints (dance halls with jukebox music), African-American dance traditions, and to synonyms for "juke," such as "escape" and "evade." The latter references suggest escape from slavery, which refers back to the spinning penny—the focus of *Juke*—a coin that bears the portrait of Abraham Lincoln, whose efforts led to abolition. Similarly abstruse is the iconography of Norment's 2008 *Triplight* installation, which centers on a vintage jazz microphone (Figure 14.9). The metal casement of the microphone is illuminated from the inside, so that it casts a skeletal shadow on the gallery walls. The coupling of the actual standing microphone with its own shadow creates the appearance of a shadowy singer crooning into the mic. Norment manipulates the installation's optical elements so that the light pulsates rhythmically as if to the beat of a musical composition. Despite the fact that the light pulses are soundless, viewers often imagine that they hear a tune faintly playing.

In their similarity to a skeletal rib cage, the shadows of *Triplight* suggest both death and a cage, which may be interpreted in a variety of ways. The jazz great Billie Holiday appears in numerous iconic photographs singing into the same style of microphone. The shadows might reference Holiday's tragic death at the age of 44 from alcohol-induced liver and heart failure, the "death" of her virginity as a result of her experience as a rape victim and prostitute before reaching age 14, and/or the tragedy of her life as a major recording and performance artist whose success was overshadowed by racial discrimination, drug addiction, and imprisonment (being caged). Indeed, Holiday's once-beautiful face and body were described at the end of her life as a grotesque and skeletal caricature destroyed by excess. Norment's choice of the title *Triplight* carries within it additional allusions to dance (as in the phrase "trip the light fantastic"), to a drug-induced trip, and to a semiprecious brown stone known as triplite—each emblematic of Holiday.

Norment was born in Silver Spring, Maryland, a suburb of Washington, D.C. In addition to creating artwork, Norment performs with the Camille Norment Trio, which includes the artist, guitarist Håvard Skaset, and folk fiddler Vegar Vårdal. She has created both permanent and ephemeral visual and sound installations for numerous galleries and museums around the world.

INTERVENTION ART

Intervention art combines elements of the Conceptualist, installation, and performance art of the latter 20th century but ups the ante considerably. It involves a radical, performance-based engagement with an urban or cultural space (think flash mob) and with a particular and often unsuspecting audience or with any variety of already existing objects, such as works of art and architecture. In an intervention, an artist (or artists) might perform impromptu in a public park or museum lobby by transforming their own bodies into living works of public art (think mimes). Alternatively, a city sidewalk might become the canvas for an elaborate interventionist chalk drawing. A commercial billboard might be transformed into a work of conceptual text art or used to display a painting. The aims of intervention art vary, but, as an art form, intervention is invariably interactive. Rather than being carried out privately, interventions involve some segment of the public and aim to alter a given circumstance, make a political or social statement, draw attention to a social ill, or critique or mock some aspect of contemporary culture. Furthermore, interventions last for varying lengths of time, from minutes to years.

Intervention art is viewed by many as subversive and an affront to the very idea of art (particularly when acts of vandalism or trespass are involved). Nonetheless, many interventions are carried out with the full support of the art community. This depends entirely on whether or not the ultimate goal of the intervention is deemed to enhance or improve a given situation, space, or mindset—although even this caveat is a fluid one. Since its germination at the end of the 20th century, intervention art has become increasingly more positive and less destructive. As a result, it has also become more popular among the art establishment, even serving as fodder for significant art exhibitions such as *The Interventionists: Art in the Social Sphere*, held at the Massachusetts Museum of Contemporary Art (MOCA) in North Adams in 2005.

William Pope.L

William Pope.L (b. 1955) is celebrated for his urban interventions and conceptual projects. His body and wit are key tools used to articulate his concerns about language, gender bias, gay issues, race, and the shortcomings of capitalism. His 1997 *ATM Piece* was created to challenge a New York City mandate requiring panhandlers to stay ten feet away from any cash machine. At the time, homeless men asked for tips by holding ATM doors open for banking customers. In a deconstructive twist, Pope.L chained himself to a 24-hour banking facility near Grand Central Station. While dressed in a skirt made of 80 one-dollar bills, instead of asking for money, he tore a dollar in half and offered one half to each customer as he held the door open for him or her.

Born in Newark, New Jersey, Pope.L studied at Pratt Institute in New York City, later completing a BFA at Montclair State College (1978), followed by an MFA at the Rutgers University Mason Gross School of the Arts (1981). To augment his skills as an artist, he studied as an artist-in-residence in the Re.Cher.Chez performing arts program at New York's Mabou Mines Theatre Company from 1983 to 1985. In 1990, Pope.L began teaching theater and film in the Department of Theater and Rhetoric at Bates College in Lewiston, Maine.

From the 1980s to the 2000s, Pope.L enacted some 40 urban performances, by walking or crawling through New York's streets while utilizing various props and costumes. In Pope.L's 1997 intervention *Member (Schlong Journey)*, he paraded the streets of Harlem while carrying a white cardboard penis supported by a structure on wheels. In several iterations of *Eating the Wall Street Journal*, he chewed and then spat out bits of paper from the *Wall Street Journal* while seated on a toilet, mounted on a 10-foot pedestal. Lampooning Duchamp's 1917 Dada *Fountain* (an inverted urinal mounted on a pedestal), emphasizing the disparity between the haves (symbolized by the white penis and the Wall Street Journal) and the have-nots, as well as their common connection to capitalism, Pope.L's intervention typified the polemical spirit of first-generation intervention art.

In the 1990s, Pope.L undertook two memorable interventions. In *The Great White Way* (the nickname for New York's theater district and a racial pun), Pope.L crawled on hands and knees along the full length of Broadway dressed in a Superman costume with a skateboard strapped to his back (Figure 14.10). The 22-mile crawl was carried out in installments over five years. In *Tompkins Square Crawl*, Pope.L writhed through the gutter in business attire to protest the forcible ejection by the NYPD of homeless people from the Lower East Side park. From 2000 to 2005, Pope.L performed both solo and group crawls in Portland (Maine), Boston, Philadelphia, Houston, Cleveland, Montreal, Prague, Budapest, Berlin, and Tokyo.

More recently, his celebrated and witty tour *The Black Factory*, first exhibited in 2004, was installed in a white former ice cream truck containing a gift shop with an inflatable archive of donated black objects. Pope.L invited the public to donate to the Black Factory items that they associated with black culture (everything from Afro picks to R & B LPs and ice cubes), which he and his collaborators reappropriated and reconfigured into new and different "products," such as "Black Factory evaporated milk," "Black Factory rubber ducks," and "Black Factory bottled water" (complete with appropriate labeling and cataloged on the Black Factory's website, www.theblackfactory.com). These items were then sold in the gift shop

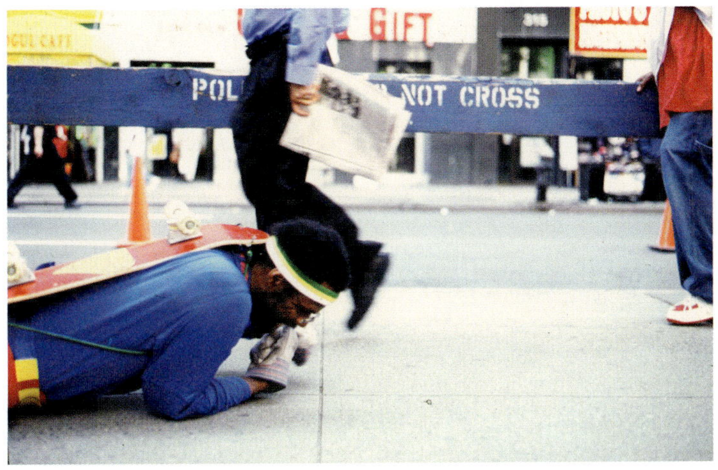

▼ **14.10** William Pope.L, *The Great White Way, 22 miles, 9 years, 1 street (Whitney version)*, 2001.

Photo by Lydia Grey, courtesy of the artist and Mitchell-Innes & Nash, NY. © Pope.L.

to help fund the continuation of the intervention; a percentage of their earnings were also donated to charity.

The Black Factory toured the country to irreverently insert contradictory concepts of "Blackness" and black culture into places where it is usually absent, such as government offices, museums, and art fair sites. The stated aim of the intervention was to introduce visitors to the notion that perceptions of "Blackness" should be limited not by race but only "by our courage to imagine it differently." The intervention also addressed the issue of navigating difference beyond that of race. The crew of performance artists who manned The Factory engaged in improvisations and burlesque antics that underscored this agenda. The project sparked discussion among visitors and the press concerning changing conceptions of gender, politics, race, and social constructions as "playgrounds" and "battlefields" of malleability rather than as fixed realities. In 2009 Pope.L transformed the ice cream truck into a stationary art installation by half-burying it in granular black silica and outfitting it with a booming sound system. This iteration of the Black Factory debuted at Art Basel in Miami Beach, where it was installed in the Botanical Garden.

Theaster Gates

Chicago artist Theaster Gates (b. 1973) uses his considerable skills as a sculptor, architect, real estate developer, musician, and performance and installation artist to devise urban interventions on a grand scale in South Side Chicago. Blurring the boundaries between art and community redevelopment, Gates has revived an entire neighborhood—what he describes as a re-envisioning of "black space"—through a combination of art installations, home remodeling, urban planning, cultural fundraising, pottery production, lumber milling, and arts education. His road to this visionary state of ongoing intervention began in earnest in 1996, when Gates received his degree in urban planning from Iowa State University. In addition to classes in his declared major, Gates took a number of art courses with respected ceramicist and mixed-media sculptor Ingrid Lilligren (b. 1949), which sparked his interest in the arts.

Propelled by his undergraduate fine arts training, within two years of graduating, Gates had earned an MA in fine arts and religious studies from the University of Cape Town in South Africa. With expertise in both urban planning and fine arts, he was hired in 2000 by the Chicago Transit Authority (CTA) as an arts programmer, which gave him insight into the workings of civic administration—knowledge that would later serve his interventionist pursuits. According to Gates, "Understanding how bureaucratic systems work . . . is a very big part of my practice. I'm not a good perspective drawer, but I can write a really good memo." While working for the CTA, Gates decided to re-enroll at Iowa State, where, in 2006, he earned a second interdisciplinary master's degree in community planning, ceramics, and religion. He was subsequently hired by the University of Chicago as director of arts and public life, a post that he continues to hold today. This position ideally suits his two key interests: art and the community.

One of Gates's first artistic projects was a performance at a small community arts center. The performance consisted of Gates, in the guise of a mythic Japanese potter (Gates has a keen interest in Asian culture), hosting a formal soul food dinner in the decorous manner of a Japanese tea ceremony. Art center members were treated to a community meal, were exposed to Japanese culture, and could avail themselves of ceramic art (the fictional Japanese potter's wares were made by Gates), all in a single event. Several years later at the 2010 Whitney Biennial, Gates reconstituted this earlier performance. Using a few architectural and assemblage pieces, he converted the museum's garden into a Zen garden in which the artistic community might feel free to perform, engage with one another, meditate, or enjoy live concerts performed by Gates's band, the Black Monks of Mississippi.

Recalling again the fusion of Asian and African-American culture, in 2012 and 2013 Gates repurposed drawers from an old desk, wood planks, and worn wooden cart wheels to create his tongue-in-cheek *Rickshaw for Black Brick* (Figure 14.11). Part of a larger series of working rickshaws that carry everything from building materials to sleeping bags, Gates's sturdy, mobile, and culturally conflated carts symbolize both architectural and human community building.

Gates's belief that nothing is useless and that all things have value extends to his South Side Chicago neighborhood, which has long suffered from fiscal, cultural, and financial neglect, and which, until recently, was known for the decaying conditions of its public housing. Making the decision to reside in one of the area's poorest districts, Gates purchased a defunct candy store on South Dorchester Avenue and transformed it into his studio and home using found materials and local labor. In 2009, when an adjacent home became available for $16,000, he purchased it; and his first major urban intervention was launched. Known today as the Dorchester Projects, Gates's intervention employed local laborers (to bring income to the

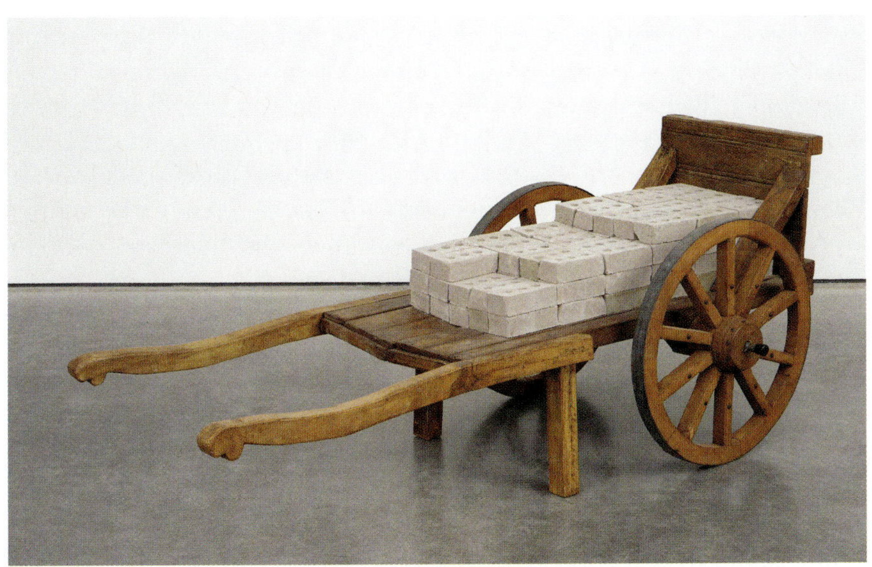

◀ **14.11** Theaster Gates, *Rickshaw for Black Brick*, 2013, wood, metal, and clay, 36″ × 96″ × 48″.

community), who worked with found wood salvaged from a forgotten neighborhood bowling alley. (Gates later repurposed materials from the Dorchester Projects demolition to refurbish a house in Kassel, Germany, which was featured at the international Documenta 13 exhibition in 2012.) With minimal resources, Gates and his team transformed the building into an art and architecture library with 14,000 books appropriated from an out-of-business bookstore and 60,000 vintage glass lantern slides that the University of Chicago no longer used. The artist's library was subsequently augmented with 8,000 LPs recovered from an out-of-business South Side record shop. The Dorchester Projects quickly became a place of intellectual and community exchange that offered, in addition to printed matter, private music-listening rooms, DJ performances, and art and design classes for children and adults. The project has since expanded to include artists' residencies and a film-screening site.

Building on the success of the Dorchester Projects, in 2012 Gates took on another major urban intervention when he purchased an old bank building on South Stony Island Avenue and East 68th Street in Calumet Heights that was earmarked for demolition. With the intention of transforming the bank into an art center, Gates convinced Chicago mayor Rahm Emanuel to sell the 1923-built Illinois State Bank structure to him for $1 by promising to raise nearly $4 million to renovate the building. Gates raised the money by removing 100 marble slabs from the run-down edifice, engraving each with the phrase "In ART We Trust" (a twist on the phrase "in GOD we trust," which appears on bank notes), and selling them to patrons as works of Gates's own art, for $5,000–$50,000 each. Playing on the banking theme, Gates referred to the reconfigured marble slabs as "bonds," because, like paper bonds, their value would increase over time, from that of mere stone to that of high art. The investment concept further appealed to Gates because his marble "bonds" would fund the restoration of a onetime bank.

Similarly efficient and sustainable is Gates's $1.3 million commission from the CTA to redesign a train station on Chicago's South Side. For this intervention, Gates plans to hire local masons to cast the bricks required for the rebuild. They will carry out this work in the artist's own brickworks, installed in the Dorchester Projects. The heat generated from the brick-firing process will be used to dry trees culled from the Chicago Park District; the milled trees will be used as lumber to refurbish the projects, and the sawdust from the milling process will create fuel for a kiln where Gates and fellow artists can create pottery for exhibition and sale.

Gates now directs the Rebuild Foundation, which is currently revamping once-dilapidated buildings in Chicago, St. Louis, and Omaha into further art, culture, and community spaces. Most recently, the foundation has partnered with a commercial developer to create (from an abandoned Chicago housing project) a 32-unit, mixed-income residence and art colony for emerging artists, who will staff the site's art center. Gates is now casting his eye on similar sites on the East Coast. Redefining the meaning of art and reinvigorating art's power to create change, Gates's enterprises produce art, support artists, make art available to the public, provide arts education and edification, improve the financial and cultural state of communities, and bring rich and poor together—at comparatively little cost. As such, his interventions offer a paradigm for others who seek to resolve problems of poverty, lack of community, ethnic isolation, education, and ecology through creative thinking and action.

NEW MEDIA ABSTRACTION

In addition to other trends, a continuing thread of abstract art has carried forward into the 21st century, with a twist. Contemporary abstractionists are exploring a range of nontraditional materials from crochet to rubber tires to vinyl-based paint (Flashe). Their content as well as form diverges from earlier styles of abstraction. Today's practitioners are inspired by computer, information, and sound technology; interplanetary exploration; satellite photography of the Earth's surface; DNA science; and any number of New Millennium phenomena.

Chakaia Booker

Newark, New Jersey–born Chakaia Booker (b. 1953) transforms alternative media—most notably recycled rubber tires—into densely textured, abstract forms that are both aesthetically and conceptually sumptuous. Booker is a successor to the legacy of Neo-Dada abstractionists such as Louise Nevelson (1899–1988), whose mid-20th-century wood assemblages inform the younger artist's aesthetic. Booker, however, has brought the genre into the 21st century by fusing a Minimalist interest in industrial materials, a Dada concern for the obfuscation of high and low art, her concern for environmental sustainability, and thematic foci as wide-ranging as race, beauty, privilege, and spirituality. Her themes manifest themselves not in narrative form but, rather, in the overwhelming blackness of her rubber pieces, in their inherent physicality, and in their evocative titles: *Echoes in Black*, *Spirit Hunter (Industrialized Nkisi Nkondi)*, and *Repugnant Rapunzel (Let Down Your Hair)*.

Booker manipulates her materials—truck, car, and bicycle tires and inner tubes—into variegated forms by cutting, folding, twisting, and turning them inside out to create an assortment of curving, whiplike projections and orbicular shapes that are anchored to wood or metal armatures. The end results are nothing short of startling: from animate, monumental outdoor works and wall-sized reliefs—including the critically acclaimed *It's So Hard to Be Green*, which was exhibited at the Whitney Biennial in 2000—to free-floating sculptures such as *The Fatality of Hope* (2007; Figure 14.12), which writhes like some primordial Medusan creature. Fragile forms surge away from the rectilinear core of the sculpture like arabesque script—signifiers of hope as a human folly. These arcing elements are inexorably pulled back, like so many spring coils, into the sculpture's unyielding nexus—a proverbial black hole by which hope is crushed. Booker earned a BA at Rutgers in 1976 and an MFA from CCNY in 1993. After graduate school, she remained in New York, where she currently lives and works. Booker began her career making wearable art (clothing and jewelry) and

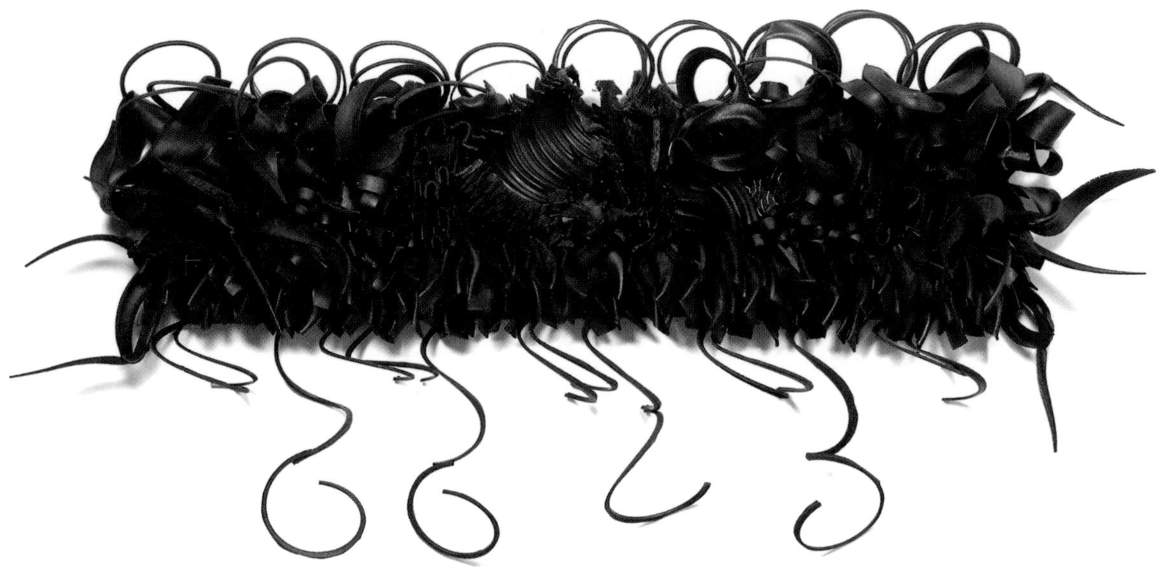

▲ **14.12** Chakaia Booker, *The Fatality of Hope*, 2007, rubber, tires, wood, and steel, 85″ × 201″ × 32″.
Courtesy of Chakaia Booker.

assemblages from castoff furniture, plumbing, and debris found at construction sites. She continues to work as a weaver, ceramicist, and assemblage artist exhibiting in the United States, Europe, and Asia.

Xenobia Bailey

Xenobia Bailey (b. 1955) employs intricate, labor-intensive crochet, beadwork, and embroidery techniques to create vivid chromatic abstractions that take the form of mandalas, soft architectural structures, and wearable art. Capitalizing on her own superior color sense and sculptural abilities, Bailey produces hats, outerwear, rugs, tents, and crocheted "paintings" inspired by the shapes and patterns of African ceremonial adornment, Afro-Caribbean *mas* costumes, and Asian and Native-American aesthetics, and by the improvisation and rhythms of 1970s funk music. The resulting works are scintillating hybrids of fashion design, millinery art, beading, painting, and sculpture.

Born in Seattle, Bailey attended University of Washington to study ethnomusicology before turning to the visual arts. In 1974, she moved to the East Coast under the auspices of a national organization of women of color (the Links) and the Benefit Guild of Seattle. She continued her education at Pratt Institute, gaining a foundation in painting and sculpture before choosing industrial and product design as a major. Bailey graduated from Pratt in 1978, after which she launched a professional career as a costume designer for community theater productions. She also taught at community art centers and spent a year as a social worker. By the 1980s, however, Bailey had developed a unique line of wearable art that she marketed initially at city flea markets and street fairs. After sending photos of her hats to *Elle*, the women's magazine began to regularly feature Bailey's designs.

The *Elle* magazine features led to similar interest from other magazines, giving Bailey's art unprecedented public exposure, which earned her commissions from such high-profile clients as Benetton clothing, Spike Lee, and Bill Cosby, who featured her clothes in their movies and televisions shows. Later in her career, Bailey introduced large-scale, shaped fabric sculptures into her repertoire, evocative of the works of Hard-Edge abstractionist Frank Stella. These later works by Bailey were configured of dazzling concentric forms and constituted sculpture, painting, and craft combined (Figure 14.13).

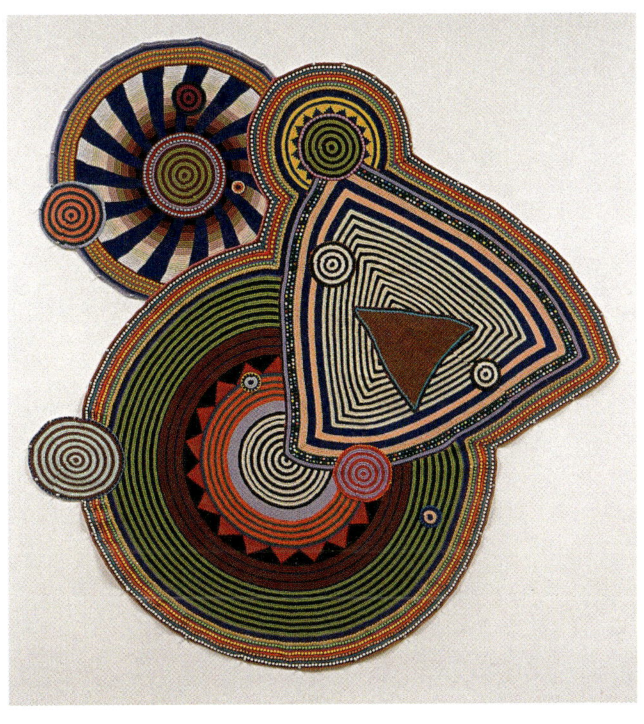

▲ **14.13** *Xenobia Bailey, Trilogy*, 2000, 4-ply acrylic, cotton yarn, plastic pony beads, hand-crocheted, single-stitched, attached with embroidery stitches and cotton canvas backing, 8′ × 7′.

Mark Bradford

MacArthur Foundation Fellow Mark Bradford (b. 1961) is best known for his large-scale *papier collé* (paper collage) art created from reclaimed materials. Although, due to its abstract form, his work is not overtly agitprop or racially charged, like certain of his Abstract Expressionist forbears (see Chapter 9), Bradford imbues distinctly readable elements of race into his nonobjective idiom. Weblike in configuration, Bradford's art has many visual wellsprings, among which are city street grids, topographical maps, and documentary photographs. His collages comprise multiple strata of materials and meaning and are physically demanding and time-consuming to create. His process involves painting and layering found paper—newspaper, printed posters, used copy paper, and even hair salon end papers (his mother owned a hair salon)—which he adheres to canvas with acrylic gel and then strips away to reveal sections of the underlayers. Some works resemble bird's-eye views of dense cities; others appear distinctly Minimalist in their repetition of geometric shapes and near-monochromatic palettes; while still others have active and expressive surfaces reminiscent of the paintings of Jackson Pollock.

Bradford's iconography derives from inner-city culture, politics, poverty, racism, discrimination, demographics, and socioeconomics, both historically and in the present. In his *Scorched Earth* of 2006, Bradford layered black carbon paper, torn and cut billboards, printed copy paper, paint, and gel to fashion an abstracted city of black, white, and primary colors (Figure 14.14). Part aerial view and part elevation, skyscrapers appear to topple apocalyptically even as they form a grid of blackened streets under a blood-red sky. Circumscribing the "scorched" area of the collage are dozens of bits of paper and daubs of paint that transmute into multitudes of people stacked row upon row. These forms represent the African Americans killed or left homeless after the 1921 Tulsa, Oklahoma, race riot, considered the worst in the country's history. Sparked by the complaint of a white woman that a black

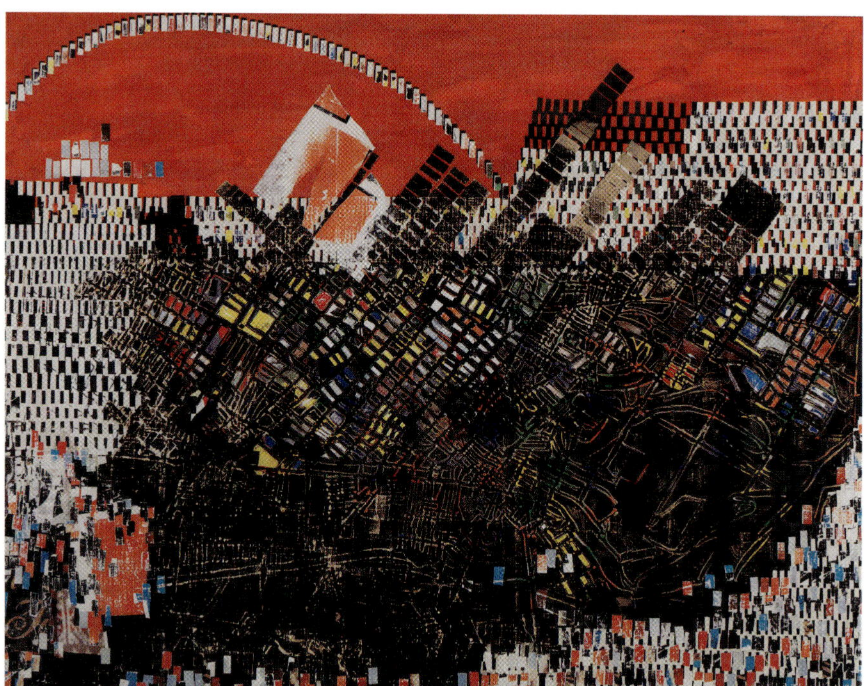

▶ **14.14** Mark Bradford, *Scorched Earth*, 2006, collage on paper, mounted on canvas, 94.5″ × 118″.

Courtesy of the artist and Hauser & Wirth. Photo: Bruce White.

man had accosted her in an elevator, within a few hours the second-largest black community in the United States had been burned to the ground by angry whites and as many as 300 Tulsa residents lay dead.

Hailing from South LA and Santa Monica, Bradford enrolled at CalArts in 1991 and completed BFA and MFA degrees there in 1995 and 1997, respectively. A video and sculpture installation artist as well as a collagist, Bradford has shown in major exhibitions in the United States and internationally. In 2009, he collaborated with the Getty Museum and a team of teachers and artists (including Kara Walker; see Chapter 13) to design an arts curriculum for primary and secondary schools. In 2011, the Museum of Contemporary Art in Chicago supported him in a similar enterprise—the Mark Bradford Project—through a one-year artist's residency. Designed to engage the Chicago community—particularly students—with the arts, the interactive project involved artist workshops, outreach, lectures, and a solo exhibit.

Jennie C. Jones

Jennie C. Jones (b. 1968) is an audio abstractionist who creates Minimalist geometric paintings, prints, drawings, collages, and sculptures, which she couples with digitally manipulated jazz, electronica, classical, and Minimalist music. By slowing the tempo of recorded excerpts, and by altering their frequency and tone, Jones creates new sounds that invoke spiritual states of mind. Her accompanying Minimalist imagery has been compared to the painted squares of Piet Mondrian, Kazimir Malevich, and Ad Reinhardt and to the spare white paintings of Robert Rauschenberg. However, Jones's use of fabric acoustic panels in lieu of paint and her highly evolved sense of color and balance distinguish her visual art from that of her predecessors. Her

2013 *Bold, Double, Barline (Variation #2)* pairs a gray fabric rectangle with a narrower black panel and separates them with a thin, lemon-yellow line (Figure 14.15). Although large and paler than the black section of the "painting," the gray panel does not tip the weight of the composition to the left, thanks to the intensity of the yellow line, which pulls the eye back toward the dark area.

▲ **14.15** Jennie C. Jones, *Bold, Double, Barline (Variation #2)*, 2013, acoustic absorber panel and acrylic paint on canvas, 48″ × 36″.

Art © Jennie C. Jones. Photo: Cathy Carver.

In her three-dimensional art, Jones incorporates, in addition to sound, musical found objects such as lengths of audiotape, earplugs, wire, speaker cables, and plastic audiocassette sleeves. Jones defines her three-dimensional works as "the physical residue of music." Her sculptures depart from her painting style in that their surfaces are gestural and highly active rather than Minimalist. Audiotape, cables, and wire are arranged in the manner of Surrealist automatic writing, with dense areas of looped and coiled material creating the appearance of frenetic script balanced by serene negative space. Whether in painting, sculpture, or sound compositions, for Jones balance is key.

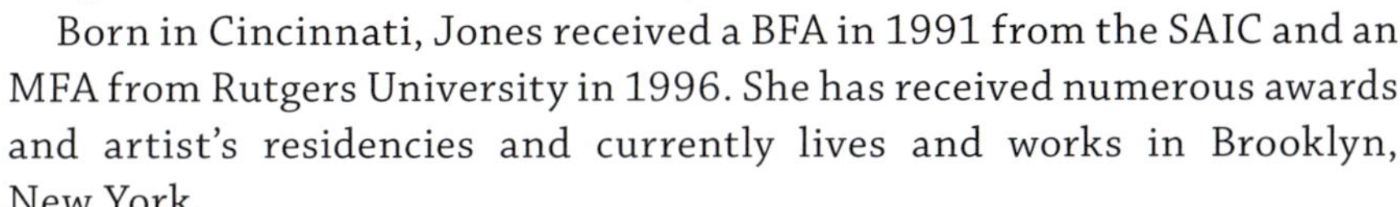

Born in Cincinnati, Jones received a BFA in 1991 from the SAIC and an MFA from Rutgers University in 1996. She has received numerous awards and artist's residencies and currently lives and works in Brooklyn, New York.

Shinique Smith

Shinique Smith (b. 1971) creates site-specific and stand-alone sculptures and collages that utilize found fabric as a key media component. Her multimedia abstractions are both lyrical and colorful. They merge disparate textile items such as ribbon, rope, twine, bamboo fiber, pillows, and clothing, as well as paper and acrylic paint. Smith uses sweeping arabesque and calligraphic strokes of the brush to create highly active painted environments within which cut, folded, twisted, tied, and draped cotton, lace, gingham, burlap, feathers, and tulle are seamlessly integrated. Each bit of fabric, carpet, or found object element in her art (such as a stuffed animal or denim overalls) bears its own lively printed pattern, faded dye, or worn and torn areas and, thus, resonates with a personal history, even as these discrete elements are reworked to create an object that is more than the sum of its parts. Smith's sculptures are often three-dimensional incarnations of her collages; and her installations are dazzling fusions of both (Figure 14.16).

Smith was born and raised in Baltimore. She attended MICA and received a BFA in 1992 and a master's degree in art education from the School of the Museum of Fine Arts in Boston in 2000. Returning to MICA, Smith received a second master's, in fine arts, in 2003. Since then she has had an impressive career, with solo exhibits and group shows in the United States and Europe. Smith lives and works in northern New York State.

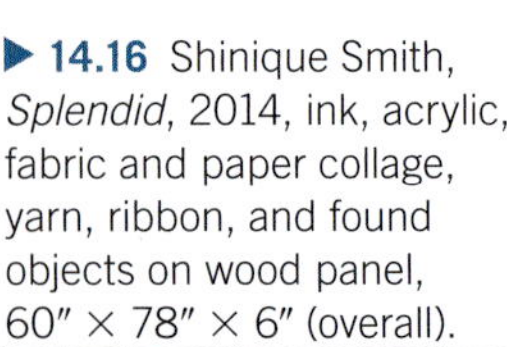

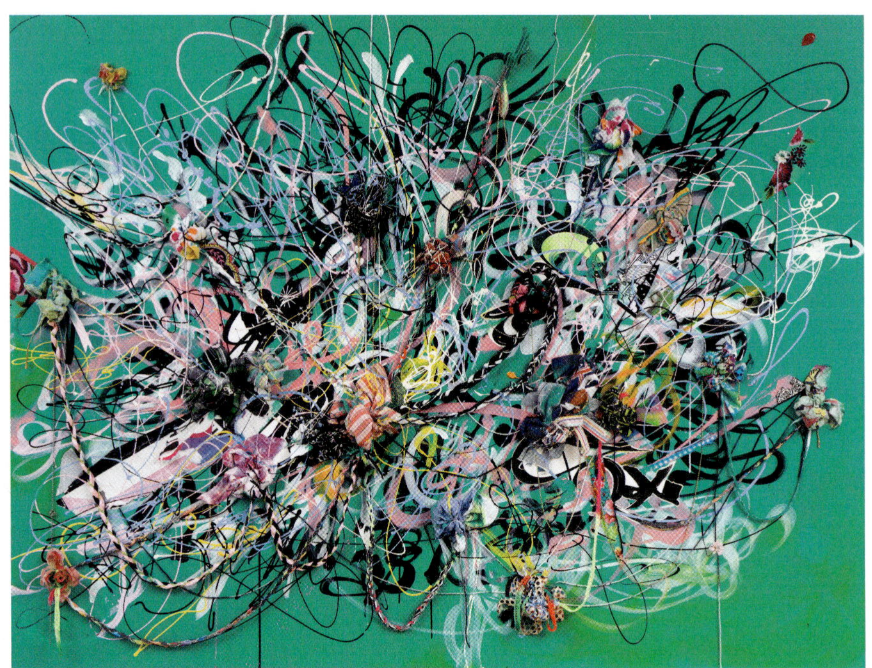

▶ **14.16** Shinique Smith, *Splendid*, 2014, ink, acrylic, fabric and paper collage, yarn, ribbon, and found objects on wood panel, 60″ × 78″ × 6″ (overall).

Museum of Fine Arts, Boston, MA. Museum purchase with funds donated by Barbara Karp Shuster through the Heritage Fund for a Diverse Collection in memory of her mother, Mrs. Harold Karp, 2015. © Shinique Smith. Photo courtesy of the Museum of Fine Art, Boston.

Summary

The New Millennium has brought with it major changes in the art of African Americans. More globally connected than ever before, African-American artists see themselves as part of an international community. Their art merges American, African, Asian, and European themes and confounds boundaries between art and community service, traditional and alternative media, and private and public spaces. The growing population of African Americans who self-identify as bi- and multiracial suggests that black art and blackness, as they have been understood in the past, are being reevaluated. Black stereotypes that were once taboo not only have been incorporated into African-American art but have given way to Afrofuturist portrayals of fantasy identities that are only tangentially concerned with racial typecasting. Twenty-first-century African-American artists place no limits on either their formal or their iconographic sources, which are as varied and complex as the artists themselves.

Key Terms

Afrofuturism: an art movement that incorporates science fiction and fantasy with themes concerning Africans in the global diaspora

alpha male: the dominant male leader of a group

blackamoor: refers to 18th- and 19th-century ceramic figures of African Muslims (called Moors) portrayed with black complexions and wearing turbans

Pierrot: similar to a harlequin, a French traditional performer who wears a white costume and pointed hat, white face paint and painted red lips like a clown. Usually a male character, he performs with a sorrowful rather than happy expression

Post-Black: a period beginning in the 1990s when many African-American artists rejected being identified by their race

technoculture: culture influenced by Internet technology

Questions for Further Study and Discussion

1. Many critics reject the idea that a Post-Black era has arrived in the United States. Forming debate teams—for and against—debate whether or not Post-Black culture exists.
2. Research and write an essay on the origins and evolution of Afrofuturist art in other genres besides the visual arts, specifically music or literature.
3. Appropriation is used by several artists in this chapter. Discuss how appropriation, unlike direct plagiarism, is a valuable tool for artistic expression.
4. Several artists in this chapter, such as Renée Cox, Sanford Biggers, Ellen Gallagher, and Xaviera Simmons, use racial stereotypes to deconstruct these self-same stereotypes. Discuss how they achieve this and whether or not each artist is successful.
5. Debate whether the major urban interventions of Theaster Gates should be defined as art.
6. Several artists are also significant exponents of contemporary African-American art. Research and discuss or write a paper on Mequitta Ahuja (b. 1976), Iona Rozeal Brown (b. 1966), Leslie Hewitt (b. 1977), Leonard Drew (b. 1961), Simone Leigh (b. 1968), or Amy Sherald (b. 1973), Roberto Visani (b. 1970).

GLOSSARY

Terms below are defined specifically with reference to the subject matter and contents of this book. Note that any number of the terms below may have alternate definitions.

A

academy: a formal art school, traditionally government sponsored, where acknowledged master artists set curricula and serve as faculty

Action painting or Gestural Abstraction: a form of paint application that results in an abstract visual record of the artist's gestures or actions during the painting process

adinkra: a set of ideographic or conceptual symbols used by the Akan people of Ghana

adire-eleko: a resist-dying process in which designs are hand painted onto cloth with starch paste

aestheticism: a philosophy that advocates that the arts should not be judged by political, social, or moral standards, but by artistic ones only

Afrocentric: refers to that which emphasizes African and African-American culture

Afrofemcentric: refers to that which emphasizes African and African-American culture within a feminist context

Afrofuturism: an art movement that incorporates science fiction and fantasy with themes concerning Africans in the global diaspora

agitprop: art that emphasizes a political agenda

ahistorical: refers to that which rejects or exists independently of the historical past

akonting: a three-stringed instrument constructed from a hollowed gourd and stretched animal skin, with a wood neck

album amicorum: from the Latin, refers to a friendship album or autograph book

allegory; allegorical: a narrative or image that symbolizes an idea or concept—such as freedom, victory, or justice—or that has a moral or political meaning

alpha male: the dominant male leader of a group

alternative media: in visual art, unconventional or nontraditional materials used to create art

alternative space: a public location for the exhibition of art other than a conventional museum or gallery

Amarna: refers to art produced during the 14th century B.C.E. under the direction of the Eighteenth Dynasty Egyptian pharaoh Akhenaten and his wife Nefertiti

ambrotypes: negative photographs on glass that, when placed on a black background, appear to be a positive image

American Empire style: Federal-style furniture patterned after the Neoclassical designs created during the reign of the French emperor Napoleon at the turn of the 19th century

American Regionalist style: a painting style of the 1930s that focused on themes of American rural life

American Renaissance: in visual art and architecture, the period from 1876 to 1917 when American artists associated themselves with the achievements of the 15th-century Italian Renaissance masters

Analytic Cubism: the first stage of Cubist painting, from 1909 to 1912, characterized by a monochromatic palette and highly abstracted compositions

anamorph: an extremely distorted image whose form is revealed only by viewing it from a specific angle

appliqué: in needlework, the process of cutting pieces of material and sewing them onto another larger piece

appropriate: to include in a work of art an image or design taken from another work of art

apron: in furniture design, a panel placed at a right angle to the surface or seat of a table or chair that connects to the legs

aquatint: a form of printmaking using acid and rosin (solid resin) on a metal plate to create a subtly toned image for transfer to paper using ink and a printing press

Arawak: an indigenous people of the Caribbean who occupied the present-day locations of Haiti, the Dominican Republic, Cuba, Jamaica, Puerto Rico, and the Cayman Islands before the arrival of Columbus; also refers to their language

arbitrary color: color that is chosen for visual, symbolic, or emotional effect rather than for visual accuracy

Art Brut: art created outside of the institutions and traditions of the academic art world

Art Deco: an architecture and design style of the 1920s and 1930s characterized by geometric motifs

Art Nouveau: a late 19th-century French architecture and design movement characterized by floral and vine motifs and curving linear forms

art-for-art's-sake: a philosophy that asserts that art should be created for the sake of its appearance alone and should not be required to serve any other purpose

Ashanti: people of Ghana and the Ivory Coast in West Africa who speak the Akan language

Ashcan School: an art movement characterized by scenes of urban poverty and the working class

ashlar stone: a building façade stone that has been squared and smoothed to fit snugly with adjoining stones

assemblage: a work of art created by assembling preexisting objects

asymmetrical balance: the property of an artwork that is irregular or unbalanced in composition or form

automatism: the creation of art through subconscious rather than deliberate action

avant-garde: French for "look ahead," refers in art to those who are innovative or cutting-edge

B

Bakuba: refers to people of the Kasai River region in the Democratic Republic of the Congo

Barbizon School: 19th-century French landscape painters, including Théodore Rousseau, Charles Daubigny, and Jean-François Millet, who painted outdoors, directly from nature, in the town of Barbizon on the edge of the Fontainebleau forest, 30 miles southeast of Paris

Baroque period: in visual art, a 17th-century European style marked by dramatic content and lighting contrasts, exaggerated movement, monumental themes, and ornamentation

bas-relief: meaning "low relief," refers to sculpture that projects only slightly from a background surface

Bauhaus: a German school of modern architecture and design active from 1919 to 1933 and headed by Walter Gropius

Bay Area Figurative Movement: an art movement in San Francisco in the 1950s and 1960s that comprised figurative art that was a direct reaction against Abstract Expressionism

Beaux Arts: a style of 19th-century architecture that took its name from the Paris École des Beaux Arts (School of Fine Arts) and is marked by dramatic visual statements, oversized proportions, and ornate sculptural decoration that enhance an otherwise classical framework

Biedermeier: an early to mid-19th-century Central European furniture style characterized by functionality, restrained curves and scrolls, and streamlined classical motifs

Black Chicago Renaissance: an interdisciplinary arts movement of the 1930s and 1940s akin to the Harlem Renaissance

black nationalism: an anti-integrationist philosophy popular in the 1960s and 1970s that promoted African-American economic independence and the formation of a separate African-American state

blackamoor: refers to 18th- and 19th-century ceramic figures of African Muslims (called Moors) portrayed with black complexions and wearing turbans
blackface minstrels: a genre of popular 19th-century entertainers who wore black stage makeup and performed in the guise of a black person; performances were characterized by stereotypical exaggerations and comedic caricature
body print: an artwork created by using the human body and pigment to impress an image onto paper or canvas
***bogolanfini* textile:** a handwoven cotton fabric believed to protect the wearer that is made and worn by the Bamana people of Mali; it is created using a resist-dye technique wherein a mud solution is painted onto the fabric to create abstracted animal designs
British Regency style: an early 19th-century furniture style incorporating ancient Egyptian and Greco-Roman decorative elements such as columns, animal legs, lyres, and scrolls
broderie perse: meaning "Persian embroidery," a style of quilt making in which cotton floral-print fabric is cut around the perimeter of each flower and sewn onto a larger cloth
burnish: to hand or tool polish an object to create a lustrous surface
buttresses: an architectural reinforcement built against or projecting from a wall as support for the weight of the roof

C

cabinetmaker: a designer and maker of cabinets, shelving, and furniture
cabriole leg: an S-curved furniture leg that derives from ancient China and classical Greece
cantilever: an architectural element such as a balcony, awning, roof, or beam that is supported at only one end and projects outward with no visible support at the other end
carborundum mezzotint: a form of printmaking using a gritty silicone carbon compound ground into a metal plate to create an image of subtle tones for transfer to paper using ink and a printing press
cartoon: a preliminary sketch for a mural or other painted composition
cartouche: in architecture, a decorative oval form, often embellished with scrolls that frames a symbol, letters, or a secondary design
Cézannesque: in the style of French Post-Impressionist founder Paul Cézanne (1839–1906)
chevron: a line or form in the shape of a *V*
chiaroscuro: the use of strong contrasts of light and dark to create the illusion of three-dimensional form on a two-dimensional surface
Chicago Mural Movement: a movement centered in Chicago in the late 1960s and 1970s during which trained artists partnered with low-income community members to create outdoor wall paintings to beautify neighborhoods and engage in social protest or commentary
chinking or *bousillage*: substances used to fill cracks, holes, or spaces between logs in log cabins; substances range from plaster or clay to plant fibers or wood chips
chintz: polished cotton fabric traditionally made in India and printed with floral designs
chromolithograph: a color image printed from a series of stone-plate drawings; a color lithographic print
***cire perdue*:** from the French for "lost wax," a bronze casting process used to create hollow rather than solid sculptures
clapboard: horizontal overlapping wooden boards used as house siding; also known as weatherboard
closed form: a self-contained shape or composition that does not extend into the surrounding space
coil process: rolling clay into long, narrow cylinders; attaching the ends to create a circular coil; and stacking the coils to form a vessel
Cold War: political tension and antagonism between the United States and the USSR beginning in 1945 and ending in the early 1990s

collage: art made from torn or cut pieces of paper or fabric glued or otherwise attached to a flat surface

collective unconscious: that part of the memory that predates birth and is inherited from biological ancestors, such as instinctive behavior

colonnade: a roof structure supported by evenly spaced columns

colonoware: earthenware or clay pottery created during the colonial era along the Atlantic coast of the United States

Color Field painting or Post-Painterly Abstraction: a painting composed of large areas of color in which individual brushstrokes are deemphasized

colorist: an artist who emphasizes color over line or who employs a vibrant color palette

complimentary contrasts: colors on opposite sides of the color wheel that intensify each other

constructions: works of art constructed of preexisting objects and differing from assemblage in their larger format

contrapposto: from the Italian for "counter pose," the term refers to the Classical Greek sculptural tradition of posing a standing figure with one knee bent and the figure's weight supported by the opposing leg

cornice: decorative molding along a ceiling, the top of a building, or item of furniture

cosmogram: a circular symbol representing the cyclical nature of life

crenelate: to notch the top of a wall structure in the manner of medieval castle battlements

creole: a term used in the Louisiana Territory beginning in the 17th century to refer to colonists and slaves (as well as their practices and products) who shared a fusion of French, Spanish, African, and Native-American cultural history and ancestry

Cubism: an early 20th-century European abstract art movement practiced most notably by Pablo Picasso and Georges Braque that depicted objects and space from multiple vantage points at once

cultural salon: an event at which artists, intellectuals, and literati gather to discuss issues of culture

D

Dada: a literary and visual art movement founded in Zurich in 1916 and based on expressions of irrationality, accident, and nihilism as a reaction against the supposed rational reasoning that sparked Word War I

deconstruct: to take apart or dissect something for purposes of in-depth analysis, reevaluation, or reinterpretation

deconstruction: questioning accepted meanings of an artwork and seeing multiple interpretations as equally valid

Deconstructivist: a style of Postmodern architecture marked by a rejection of the cubic shape of Modernist buildings and a discontinuity of forms and contours

De Stijl: a Dutch art movement founded by Piet Mondrian and Theo van Doesburg in 1917 characterized by the use of rectangular forms, primary colors, and black and white

diorama: a scenic representation composed of three-dimensional sculpted figures and a two-dimensional painted background

direct wax casting: sculpture created from a wax form that is covered with clay and baked, so that the wax melts away, leaving a clay mold from which a metal sculpture can be cast

Doric: a classical Greek architectural order with columns made in multiple sections (drums) with flat, square column tops (capitals) and a decorative roof support (frieze) of alternating carved figures (metopes) and vertical grooves (triglyphs)

double entendre: a word or phrase that has two meanings, one straightforward and one indirect and often sexually suggestive

drafting table: a slanted desk for creating drawings, technical sketches, or diagrams

E

ear-lug handle: a crescent- or ear-shaped handle attached to pottery for carrying
École des Beaux-Arts: a prestigious French school of fine arts first established in 1648, where many of France's greatest artists were trained
elevation: a front or side view of an architectural structure from base to roof
engraving: a form of printmaking using a metal plate on which an image has been incised with a burin or metal tool; the plate is inked, overlaid with paper, and run through a printing press to create multiple copies
en plein air: the French term for painting "outdoors" (literally, "in the open air")
entablature: the horizontal area of the façade of a classical building located above the columns and beneath the roof, consisting of a base (architrave), a section of carvings (frieze), and a molded top (cornice)
Expressionism: an early 20th-century European art movement characterized by distorted figural forms, vivid colors, and emotive content

F

Fauvism: an early 20th-century French art movement characterized by vivid and clashing colors
femmage: assemblage or collage art created by women, often with a feminist theme
figurative expressionism: art characterized by a vivid, nonliteral palette and by distorted figures and forms
fire; firing: the process of baking clay into pottery, bricks, and other forms
Fluxus: an international and interdisciplinary group of performance artists founded in the 1960s
formalism: refers to the design or composition of an artwork
found objects: preexisting nonart objects used to create works of art
French Empire style: a classical Greek–inspired furniture and fashion design style originating in postrevolutionary France in the early 18th century
fresco: a painting made with powdered pigment on wet plaster
fretwork: an openwork ornamental design cut with a narrow, fine-toothed saw (fret saw) into a thin wood panel
frieze: an extended horizontal relief sculpture usually situated high on a wall
frontal composition: an image in which figures and objects are forward facing

G

gabled: a pitched roof comprised of two slanted sides that form a triangular or pyramid shape
gallery: in architecture, a covered walkway open on one side and often supported by columns
gaze: in art, refers to how and what is seen or observed by the viewer or the sitter; suggests a particular point of view
genre: artistic portrayals of scenes from everyday life; also, a type or style of artistic representation
geodesic: in architecture, describes a type of dome constructed of openwork triangles and polygons
Georgian Revival: an early 19th century style of architecture that incorporates the Greek architectural orders
gesso: a white plaster mixture used to prepare a surface for paint application
glazed: refers to pottery that is fired after being coated with a lustrous substance (a glaze) that adds shimmer and color to the clay form
glazing: installation of glass windows and walls
Gothic Revival: a design style originating in the 1740s that revived medieval Gothic forms such as spires, pointed arches, and tracery (interlaced openwork derived from Gothic windows)

gourd: the hollow, dried, and hard shell of certain fruits, such as squash and pumpkin
graffiti: unsanctioned informal urban murals that are often expressive and abstract in form, and include elements of text
Grand Tour: an extended cultural tour of continental Europe considered vital to the education of wealthy young Americans and Europeans from the 17th to the 19th centuries
Great Migration: the migration of more than 1.5 million African Americans from the rural South to the urban North, chiefly between 1910 and 1930
griot: a West African poet-historian, storyteller, and custodian of oral tradition
***grisaille*:** from the French word for "gray," describes painting in black, white, and gray tones only
groundhog kiln: a tunnel-shaped oven often inset into the ground and used to fire alkaline glazed pottery in the 19th century
Gullah: refers to inhabitants the coastal islands of South Carolina, Georgia, and northern Florida, whose customs and language fuse English and West African elements. The term traces either to the southwestern African country of Angola, the Gola (Gula) people of Sierra Leone and Liberia, or the indigenous American Guale people who once occupied the Georgia and Carolina coasts

H

happening: a public art performance that incorporates audience participation
Hard-Edge painting: a painting style characterized by clearly defined geometric shapes and often vibrant color
hatching: creating tonal gradations in a drawing or print using multiple lines either parallel to one another or crisscrossed (crosshatching)
HBCU: acronym for Historically Black Colleges and Universities
hemp: a coarse fiber derived from the cannabis plant and used for making cloth
hieroglyphics: an ancient Egyptian alphabet consisting of letters and icons, or picture symbols
hipped roof: refers to roof construction comprised of two triangular and two trapezoidal sides that slope downward to the walls of the structure, creating a modified pyramid shape
Hoosier group: late 19th- and early 20th-century Indiana Impressionist artists
Hudson River School: a group of 19th-century Romantic painters, including Thomas Cole, Frederick Edwin Church, and Asher B. Durand, who painted the Hudson River valley landscape
humanist: refers to a belief in the supremacy of human achievement over spiritual or religious concerns

I

iconography: the study of the meaning of art and artistic symbols
icons: symbolic images
illusionism/illusionistic: refers to art that aims to replicate visual reality; see naturalism
illusionistic: see illusionism
impasto: the thick or heavy application of paint
Impressionism: a style of painting that emerged in France around 1870 and is noted for a chromatic palette and short brushstrokes to depict the changing effects of light and atmospheric conditions on a given scene
incise: to cut or carve into a surface
Indigenist Movement: a Haitian literary and visual arts movement from the late 1920s to the mid-1940s during which artists focused on uplifting portrayals of the Haitian poor rather than on the elite
installation: a form of art composed of multiple components and installed in a large interior or outdoor space
intermedia art: art created across creative disciplines and with multiple media

International Style: a style of modern architecture formulated in the United States and Europe in the 1920s and 1930s and characterized by rectilinear forms, glass façades, and a lack of exterior ornamentation

in the round: sculpture created for viewing from all sides

Ionic: a classical Greek architectural order with monolithic columns mounted on a base with scrolled tops (capitals) and a decorative roof support (frieze) of carved figures

Italianate style: a style of Neoclassical architecture popular in the second half of the 19th century characterized by a similarity to Italian Renaissance villas

J

Jim Crow: refers to the era in the 1880s and 1890s when a series of southern U.S. state laws were passed to enforce racial segregation

joiner: one who cuts and fits wood joints without the need for nails or screws

Jungian archetypes: refers to universal symbols or mental images common to humankind and first postulated by Carl Jung in his 1953 book *The Archetypes and the Collective Unconscious*

K

***kente* cloth:** a colorful silk and cotton fabric created from interwoven strips of geometrically patterned cloth by the Akan people of Ghana

***kifwebe*:** the Songye (Democratic Republic of the Congo) word for a mask representing spirits who support social order

kinetic: in art, refers to moving sculptures or visually active two-dimensional compositions

kitsch: low-quality art with mass appeal

L

lancet: in architecture, a tall and narrow Gothic-style window with a pointed arch at its apex

Light and Space Art Movement: a sculpture movement centered in 1970s Los Angeles that used light, spatial effects, and new media such as fiberglass and resin to undermine the static nature of art objects and to engage the sensory perceptions of the viewer

limner: an 18th- and 19th-century itinerant or traveling portrait painter

linocut/linoleum print: a print created by cutting an image or design into a flat sheet of linoleum for transfer to paper using ink and a printing press

linoleum print: see linocut

lithograph: an image created by first writing or drawing with a wax-based crayon on flat limestone and then inking the stone and running it through a printing press to produce multiple copies

Los Angeles Look style: a 1960s California-based predecessor to the Light and Space Movement, which popularized the use of fiberglass and resin to create glossy two- and three-dimensional abstract art

lute: any of a variety of wooden stringed instruments with a long, usually fretted neck and a vaulted, hollow, pear-shaped body

M

magic realism: fantasy or dream images rendered in a scrupulously realistic manner

maker's mark: the stamp of a ceramicist or metalsmith impressed onto pieces to identify the maker

***marbrier*:** one who carves or sculpts in marble

Marxism: a theory based on the 1949 *Communist Manifesto* by Karl Marx and Friedrich Engels that advocates the establishment of a classless society through proletariat revolution

Masonic: referring to Freemasons, an international fraternal organization originally founded by stonemasons in the Middle Ages

McCarthy era: a period characterized by political and economic persecution of American socialists and communists from the mid-1940s until 1960

memento mori: an image intended as a reminder of death

mercantile economy: a system in which the government controls foreign trade and encourages product exportation

metaethics: the study of the origin and meaning of morality, including the psychological bases for morality and whether or not morals are a human construction or a transcendent truth

metope: sections of relief sculpture carved on the entablature of a classical doric temple

***mexicanidad* style:** a nationalistic art style that embraced Mexico's pre- and post-Columbian art, culture, and history

Middle Passage: journey of slave ships across the Atlantic from West Africa to the Americas

millwork: woodwork such as doors and molding made at a mill

miniaturist: an artist who paints on a very small scale

Minimalism: a form of monochromatic painting and sculpture characterized by simple geometric forms, industrial materials, and lack of evidence of the artist's subjective input

mob cap: a gathered or pleated bonnet that is fringed and usually made of linen or cotton; it was used to cover women's hair in the 18th and 19th centuries

modeling: in two-dimensional art, shading forms to give the illusion of three-dimensionality; in sculpture, shaping forms

modiste: a French term denoting a fashion designer and stylist

mortise and tenon: a wood joint created with a notch and groove technique

N

NAACP: the National Association for the Advancement of Colored People, a civil rights organization founded in 1909

naturalism: realistic portrayals of forms and figures; art that replicates forms in nature or that creates an impression or illusion of physical reality, particularly two-dimensional art that simulates the three-dimensional world

negative space: areas of a composition that are left untouched, empty, or open

Neoclassical: art and architecture produced in the 18th and 19th century that derives from classical Greece and Imperial Rome

Neo-Gothic: a synonym for Gothic Revival, a design style originating in the 1740s that revived medieval Gothic forms such as spires, pointed arches, and tracery (interlaced openwork derived from Gothic windows)

Neo-Historicist: refers to 20th- and 21st-century architecture that utilizes premodern styles such as Neoclassicism and Gothic Revival

Neo-Impressionism: a painting style of the 1880s wherein compositions were created using small touches from the tip of a paintbrush to create a mosaic effect; sometimes referred to as pointillism

Neomodern: refers to contemporary architecture that persists in the use of monolithic cubic forms associated with 20th-century Modernism, particularly International Style high-rise construction

Neoplatonic: based on the philosophy of third-century Greek philosopher Plotinus, which suggests that the visible world is an illusory manifestation of a more transcendent reality

Neo-Pop: a 1980s and 1990s art movement inspired by 1960s Pop Art but with emphasis on more contemporary subjects and high-tech materials

Neue Sachlichkeit: a term that means "new objectivity" and refers to figurative art produced in the 1920s that critiqued German society and politics and that rejected abstraction and Expressionism for Realism as indicative of a "return to order" in the wake of World War I

New York School: a group of abstract expressionist painters living and working in New York City in the 1940s and 1950s

Nike figure: refers to the ancient Greek allegorical female figure of victory

nkondi: a sacred Kongo wood figure sculpture
nonobjective: refers to art that does not depict any known or recognizable object
***nsibidi* sign**: an ideographic or conceptual symbol used by the Ekoi, Efik, and Igbo people of southeastern Nigeria

O

oculus: a circular window in the center of a domed ceiling
oil glaze: a thin, transparent layer of oil paint applied to opaque painted surfaces to create subtle color or luster effects
Op Art: abstract or non-representational art designed to create an optical illusion such as movement, popularized in the 1960s
orientalist: refers to a 19th-century European interest in Middle Eastern and Asian motifs
orisha: a diety originating among the Yoruba-speaking people of Nigeria and Benin in West Africa
Outsider Art: art created outside of the institutions and traditions of the academic art world

P

palette: choice of colors used by an artist; the portable surface on which an artist mixes paint
Palladian style: a style of architecture inspired by the Renaissance designs of Andrea Palladio, which in turn were derived from the asymmetrical construction of antique Roman buildings
Pan-African: refers to a philosophy that promotes international collaboration among people of African descent
panorama: a large-scale work of art that depicts an epic scene such as a vast landscape, cityscape, or complex historical event, often designed in a long, horizontal format that could be mounted and viewed in the round
papier collé: paper collage
Paris Salon: in the 18th and 19th centuries, the official art exhibit of the French Fine Arts Academy (École des Beaux Arts) and the Société des Artistes Français
pass; passing: refers to when biracial African Americans self-identify as white due to their Caucasian appearance
patina: the surface color or appearance of a sculpture
patriarchy: a sociopolitical system in which men are empowered and women disempowered
patron: a financial supporter of the arts or of a particular artist
Pattern and Decoration Movement: a 1970s American art movement that reacted against Minimalism with art composed of colorful, all-over floral and geometric patterns
pediment: on a building façade, a triangular area created by and located directly below a pitched roof, and supported by columns
Percent for Art: legislation requiring that 1% of the budget for a government-funded building be spent on public art
photo essay: a series of photographs that, collectively, express a single narrative
photogram: a photograph made without the use of a camera by blocking out areas on the surface of light sensitive paper (or other photographic surface, such as metal) and exposing it to light
photomontage: a work of art composed of multiple cut or torn photographs
pickaninny: a derisive caricature of a black child, often with bulging eyes and large lips
piece; piecing: in quilt making, sewing together multiple fabric pieces to create a single large textile
Pierrot: similar to a harlequin, a French traditional performer who wears a white costume and pointed hat, white face paint and painted red lips like a clown; usually a male character, he performs with a sorrowful rather than happy expression
pinnacled: refers to an architectural tower, spire, or buttress that is crowned with a vertical, pointed form in the shape of a narrow pyramid or cone

pipkins: small cooking pots
planar: describes a two-dimensional composition or elements of its design that are rendered parallel to the picture surface
planar composition: see planar
porringers: decorative shallow bowls with one or two handles from which one could either eat or drink
portico: a covered porch set between an exterior building wall and a row of outer columns
Post-Black: a period beginning in the 1990s when many African-American artists rejected being identified by their race
Post-Impressionism: a French painting movement of the 1880s and 1890s dedicated to improving on Impressionism by adding geometric structure, arbitrary color, and emotional content
Postmodern architecture: architecture since the 1960s that rejects the monolithic austerity of modern buildings for such features as organic forms, colorful façades, and references to premodern styles
post-Reconstruction era: a period in southern U.S. history from 1877 to the turn of the 20th century, marked by legalized segregation and racial violence against and systematic disenfranchisement of African Americans
Post-Structuralism: a philosophy that sees social, behavioral, moral, verbal, and visual structures as changeable constructions rather than fixed truths or realities
poteaux-en-terre (posts-in-earth): a French term that refers to architectural construction wherein the roof is supported by posts that are embedded in the earth
primary source: original, firsthand, or direct evidence that has not been altered, concerning a specific topic
primitivism: a style of art that mimics the art of children or untrained artists
printmaker: one who creates images for reproduction using a printing press
pugmill: a device used to grind and mix clay with water to produce a consistent viscous mixture
pyrogravure: a French term referring to drawing with a metal poker or similar heated instrument onto wood or leather

Q

quatrefoil: a four-leafed clover design made up of overlapping circles

R

racial iconography: the study of racial meaning and symbolism in art
Rada *boula* drum: a peg-tuned, high-pitched drum played with sticks at Haitian-derived Vodou ceremonies in honor of the gods of wisdom, composure, and benevolence
ready-made: a work of art composed of common manufactured objects recontextualized by the artist
Reconstruction: a period in U.S. history from the end of the Civil War to 1877 when Confederate states were readmitted to the Union under northern military supervision, and African-American men were politically enfranchised by the Thirteenth, Fourteenth, and Fifteenth Amendments to the Constitution
relief: sculpture that projects from or is carved into a flat or two-dimensional background surface
reliquary sculpture: a sculpture that adorns a container of human remains such as bones, teeth, hair, and so on
Renaissance: a period in 15th- and 16th-century Europe marked by a revival of classical Greco-Roman culture, intellectual achievement, scientific advancement, and transatlantic exploration
representational art: see naturalism
revisionism: the revising or modifying of previously accepted theories, principles, or points of view

Rococo: an art and design style that originated in 18th-century France and is noted for its asymmetry, scrolls, floral elements, and elaborate ornamentation
Romanesque style: a style of medieval architecture characterized by roughhewn stones and rounded arches
Romantic era: a 19th-century visual arts period noted for emotional and imaginative subject matter and an interest in the grandeur of nature
rose window: a circular window found in church architecture
rusticate: in architecture, to decorate with large stones that feature rough surfaces and wide, deeply set joints

S

salt-glazed stoneware: ceramics with a high-gloss-textured finish created by adding salt to the firing process
Sambo: a derogatory slave-era term for an unintelligent black male
sarcophagi: plural of sarcophagus; a stone coffin decorated with relief sculpture and inscriptions
screen-printing: a printmaking technique wherein an image is painted onto mesh fabric using thinned glue and ink is pushed through the glue-free areas onto paper or other surfaces using a squeegee; differs from silk-screening in that the mesh fabric is a synthetic or other nonsilk fabric
sculpture-in-the-round: freestanding sculpture that is meant to be seen from many angles
Sea Islanders: inhabitants of a group of islands off the coast of South Carolina, Georgia, and northern Florida
secco: a fresco mural technique in which egg and water are added to powedered pigment before it is applied to a wet plaster wall
secondary source: a document or object that provides secondhand knowledge of an artwork or topic
semiotics: the study of signs and symbols, and their meaning and construction, within a universal rather than narrowly defined or individual context
Senegambian: referring to the people and culture of Senegal and Gambia
signified: the object of the meaning of a symbol or sign
signifier: a sign or symbol
silhouette art: initiated in England in the 1700s, a type of portrait made by cutting the silhouette likeness of a person from black paper
silk collagraph: also known as silk aquatint, a form of print created by painting an image onto a black, silk-covered plastic printing surface with white acrylic paint; the image is then inked and printed on an etching press
silk screen (serigraph): a printmaking technique wherein an image is painted onto a mesh fabric using water-diluted glue and then ink is pushed through the nonglued areas onto paper or another surface using a squeegee
site-specific: refers to a work of art designed for a specific physical space
sitter: one who poses for a portrait
slave codes: a series of laws enforced beginning in the 17th century that dictated the treatment of African slaves
slip: in ceramics, a viscous mixture in which clay particles are suspended in water
Social Realism: a style of art popularized in the 1930s and characterized by figurative representations that extol the working class or promote a socialist agenda
staining: a method of painting an unprimed (ungessoed or raw) canvas so that large areas of paint seep into the material of the canvas
***Stammbücher*:** from the German word for "albums," refers to friendship albums or autograph books

steel-frame construction: building design utilizing vertical steel columns and horizontal beams as a grid-shaped understructure to which the floor and walls are attached

stepping: in architecture, a graduated recession of the façade

stereograph: a double photograph of the same image meant to be viewed through a stereoscope or two-lens optical viewer to create a three-dimensional effect

stoicism: accepting the misfortunes of life without complaint, based on an ancient Roman philosophy

structuralism: the analysis of cultural structures such as art, language, literature, anthropology, and society through an examination of binaries or opposing elements within each structure

Suprematism: a Russian art movement founded by Kasimir Malevich in 1915 that used simple geometric forms and a red, black, and white palette to express and invoke transcendence and the unknown

sustainable design: the use of eco-friendly materials and systems to reduce negative environmental impact

Symbolism/Symbolist: a late 19th-century literary and visual art movement in the United States and Europe noted for macabre and decadent themes, veiled symbols, mythology and fantasy

Symbolist: see Symbolism

symmetrical balance: balance created when two sides or halves of a form or composition are equivalent or corresponding

syncopation: placing regular emphasis on sounds or forms that would otherwise be subordinate elements in a musical composition or work of art

Synthetic Cubism: the second phase of Cubism, practiced after 1912, which incorporated elements of collage and flatly painted areas of color

T

tabby foundation: an architectural foundation created from a cement-like building material made of lime, sand, water, and seashells

technoculture: culture influenced by Internet technology

tester bed: a four-poster canopied bed

text: in semiotic terms, any object or document that communicates information and exists independently of its creator

tintype: a fast-developing positive photograph exposed on a thin iron sheet

tondo: a circular-format painting

tracery: carved ornamental stonework that encases the stained glass in a Gothic church window

transept: in church architecture, a rectangular section of a building that intersects its main space

triangular trade route: Atlantic slave trade routes between Africa, the United States, and Europe

triglyph: a three-part vertical groove pattern carved on the entablature of a classical doric temple

triptych: a work of art that is divided into three components

trompe l'oeil: French for "trick the eye," refers to the practice of painting images that appear identical to actual objects

trumeau: in church architecture, a central column, often decoratively carved, that separates double doors and supports a lintel

tympanum: in church architecture, an arched decorative area above a door

typesetter: one who manually selects and assembles moveable letter forms for a printing press

U

ukiyo-e: meaning "floating world," a Japanese term that refers to colored woodblock prints of landscapes, kabuki theater, domesticity, courtesans, and entertainment created between 1660 and 1868

undressed stone: stone that has not been cut or sanded to a desired shape or surface texture

V

vernacular: in art, refers to self-trained artists and to informal or unassuming art and architecture

Victorian: associated with the art, culture, and social attitudes prevalent during the reign of Queen Victoria of England from 1819 to 1901

Vienna Secession: a group of Viennese artists led by Gustav Klimt who rejected the traditional art styles of the Association of Austrian Artists by resigning from the group in 1897

Vieux Carre: from the French "old square," the term describes the French Quarter, the oldest neighborhood in New Orleans

visual literacy: the ability to identify, interpret, and evaluate information presented in image form

Vodou (Haiti): a Haitian-based religion derived from religious practices in the Congo and Benin that fuses African beliefs with Christian icons

voussoirs: in architecture, stone or masonry wedges used to create an arch

W

Washington Color School: 1950s and 1960s non-representational art movement centered in Washington, D.C. and defined by bold colors and geometric forms

Weltanschauung: a philosophy or worldview

wet drapery: a sculptural technique developed by the ancient Greeks that creates the appearance of clothing clinging to the body

wheel-thrown earthenware: refers to pottery that is created using a potter's wheel

wheelwright: one who makes and repairs wood or metal wheels and wheeled conveyances

woodblock print: see woodcut

woodcut/woodblock print/wood engraving: a print created by carving an image into a block of wood; then inking the block; overlaying it with paper; and running it through a printing press

wood engraving: see woodcut

Y

yard artist: one who displays his or her own handmade works of art in his or her yard or garden

Yoruban: pertaining to the Yoruba-speaking people of Nigeria and Benin in West Africa

Z

ziggurat: originating in ancient Mesopotamia, a stepped temple constructed of trapezoid-shaped levels that decrease in size from bottom to top

BIBLIOGRAPHY

Art and Architecture: Books

Arnett, Paul William, and Arnett, Paul S., eds. *Souls Grown Deep: African American Vernacular Art of the South*. 2 vols. Atlanta, GA: Tinwood Books, 2000.

Arthur, Stanley. *Old New Orleans, a History of the Vieux Carre, It's Ancient and Historical Buildings*. Westminster, MD: Heritage Books, 1936.

Baldwin, Cinda K. *Great and Noble Jar: Traditional Stoneware of South Carolina*. Athens: University of Georgia Press, 1993.

Barnwell, Andrea A. *The Walter O. Evans Collection of African American Art*. Seattle: University of Washington Press, 1999.

Bearden, Romare, and Henderson, Harry. *A History of African-American Artists, 1792–1988*. New York: Pantheon, 1992.

Beardsley, John. *Gardens of Revelation: Environments by Visionary Artists*. New York: Abbeville, 1995.

Bernier, Celeste-Marie. *African American Visual Arts from Slavery to the Present*. Chapel Hill: University of North Carolina Press, 2009.

Black, Patti Carr. *American Masters of the Mississippi Gulf Coast: George Ohr, Dusti Bonge, Walter Anderson, Richmond Barthe*. Jackson: University Press of Mississippi, 2009.

Bontemps, Arna, ed. *Forever Free: Art by African-American Women, 1862–1980*. Alexandria, VA: Stephenson, 1980.

Brackman, Barbara. *Unraveling the History of Quilts and Slavery*. Concorde, CA: C & T, 2006.

Brilliant, M. Brooke. *Colonoware, Creolization, and Interactions Between African Americans and Native Americans During the Colonial Period in the South Carolina Lowcountry*. Ann Arbor, MI: UMI Dissertation Publishing, 2012.

Broude, Norma, and Garrard, Mary D., eds. *The Power of Feminist Art: The American Movement of the 1970s, History and Impact*. New York: Harry N. Abrams, 1994.

Brown, William Wells. *The Black Man, His Antecedents, His Genius, and His Achievements*. New York: Thomas Hamilton, 1862. Web. 3 Jan 2014. http://docsouth.unc.edu/neh/brownww/brown.html# brown214.

Bustard, Bruce I. *A New Deal for the Arts*. Washington, D.C.: National Archives and Records Administration, 1997.

Butcher, Margaret Just, and Locke, Alain. *The Negro in American Culture*. New York: Knopf, 1956.

Calo, Mary Ann. *Distinction and Denial: Race, Nation, and the Critical Construction of the African American Artist, 1920–40*. Ann Arbor: University of Michigan Press, 2007.

Campbell, Mary Schmidt. *Tradition and Conflict: Images of a Turbulent Decade, 1963 to 1973*. New York: Studio Museum in Harlem, 1985.

Christovich, Mary Louise, and Evans, Sally. *New Orleans Architecture: The Creole Faubourgs*. Vol. 4 of New Orleans Architecture Series. Gretna, LA: Pelican, 1995.

Christovich, Mary Louise, and Toledano, Roulhac. *New Orleans Architecture: Faubourg Treme and the Bayou Road*. Vol. 6 of the New Orleans Architecture Series. Gretna, LA: Pelican, 2003.

Collina, Lisa Gail, and Crawford, Margo Natalie, eds. *New Thoughts on the Black Arts Movement*. New Brunswick, NJ: Rutgers University Press, 2006.

Conway, Cecelia. *African Banjo Echoes in Appalachia*. Knoxville: University of Tennessee Press, 2005.

Cooks, Bridget R. *Exhibiting Blackness: African Americans and the American Art Museum*. Amherst: University of Massachusetts Press, 2011.

Cosentino, Donald. *Sacred Arts of Haitian Vodou*. Los Angeles: UCLA Fowler Museum, 1995.

Donaldson, Jeff R., and Donaldson, Geneva S. *The People's Art: Black Murals, 1967–1978*. Philadelphia: African-American Historical and Cultural Museum, 1986.

Dormer, Peter. *The Culture of Craft*. Manchester, UK: Manchester University Press, 1997.

Dover, Cedric. *American Negro Art*. New York: New York Graphic Society, 1950.

Driskell, David C. *Harlem Renaissance Art of Black America*. New York: Harry Abrams, 1987.

———. *Two Hundred Years of African American Art*. Los Angeles: Los Angeles County Museum and Alfred A. Knopf, 1976.

Duganne, Erina. *The Self in Black and White: Race and Subjectivity in Postwar Photography*. Lebanon, NH: Dartmouth College Press and the University Press of New England, 2010.

Farrington, Lisa. *Creating Their Own Image: African American Women Artists*. New York: Oxford University Press, 2004.

Fax, Elton. *Seventeen Black Artists*. New York: Dodd & Mead, 1971.

Ferguson, Leland G. *Uncommon Ground: Archaeology and Early African America, 1650–1800*. Washington, D.C.: Smithsonian Institution Press, 1992.

Fine, Elsa Honig. *The Afro-American Artist: A Search for Identity*. San Diego, CA: Holt, Rinehart & Winston, 1973.

Fortier, Jerome. *Watts: Art and Social Change in Los Angeles, 1965–2002*. Milwaukee, WI: Haggerty Museum of Art, Marquette University, 2003.

Fry, Gladys-Marie. *Stitched from the Soul: Slave Quilts from the Ante-Bellum South*. New York: Dutton Books, 1990.

Fusco, Coco, and Wallis, Brian, eds. *Only Skin Deep: Changing Visions of the American Self*. New York: Harry N. Abrams, 2003.

Gayle, Addison, ed. *The Black Aesthetic*. New York: Doubleday, 1972.

Gerdts, William. *American Neo-Classic Sculpture: The Marble Resurrection*. New York: Viking Press, 1973.

Hageman, Jane Sikes. *The Furniture Makers of Cincinnati 1790 to 1849*. Cincinnati, OH: Merten Printing, 1976.

Harrison, G. *Furniture Trade in New Orleans, 1840–1880: The Largest Assortment Constantly on Hand*. Doctoral thesis for the University of Delaware Winterthur Program. Ann Arbor, MI: UMI Reprints, 1997.

Hatch, James V., and Hamalian, Leo, eds. *Artist and Influence, 1991*. Vol. 10. New York: Hatch-Billops Collection, 1991.

Henkes, Robert. *The Art of Black American Women: Works of Twenty-Four Artists of the Twentieth Century*. Jefferson, NC: McFarland, 1993.

Hine, Darlene Clark, and McClusky, John. *The Black Chicago Renaissance*. Urbana: University of Illinois Press, 2012.

Honour, Hugh. *The Image of the Black in Western Art*. Vol. 4. Part 1. Cambridge, MA: Harvard University Press, 1989.

Huber, Leonard V., and McDowell, Peggy. *New Orleans Architecture: The Cemeteries*. Vol. III. Gretna, LA: Pelican, 1989.

James, Susan P. *The Old Plantation: The Artist Revealed*. Williamsburg, VA: The Colonial Williamsburg Foundation, 2010.

Jennings, Corrine L. *Three Masters: Eldzier Cortor, Hughie Lee-Smith, Archibald John Motley, Jr.* New York: Kenkeleba Gallery, 1988.

Jones, Kellie. *Now Dig This! Art and Black Los Angeles, 1960–1980*. Los Angeles: Hammer Museum, 2011.

Joseph, Cliff, and Harris, Jay. *Murals of the Mind: Image of a Psychiatric Community*. Boston: International Universities Press, 1973.

Joyce, Tom. *Lifeforce at the Anvil: The Blacksmith's Art from Africa*. Chapel Hill: University of North Carolina, 1998.

Kansinsky, Wassily. *Concerning the Spiritual in Art*. Trans. Michael T. H. Sadler. New York: Dover, 1977.

King-Hammond, Leslie, and Benjamin, Tritobia. *Gumbo Ya Ya: Anthology of Contemporary African American Women Artists*. New York: Midmarch Arts Press, 1995.

King-Hammond, Leslie, and Benjamin, Tritobia, eds. *3 Generations of African American Women Sculptors: A Study in Paradox*. Philadelphia: Afro-American Historical and Cultural Museum, 1996.

Kirschke, Amy Helene. *Women Artists of the Harlem Renaissance*. Jackson: University Press of Mississippi, 2014.

LeFalle-Collins, Lizetta. *Visualizing California and the Pacific Northwest*. San Francisco, CA: California Historical Society, 2003.

LeFalle-Collins, Lizzetta, and Goldman, Shifra M. *In the Spirit of Resistance: African-American Modernists and the Mexican Muralist School*. New York: American Federation of Arts, 1966.

Leininger-Miller, Theresa. *New Negro Artists in Paris: African American Painters and Sculptors in the City of Light*. New Brunswick, NJ: Rutgers University Press, 2001.

Lewis, Samella. *African-American Art and Artists*. Los Angeles: University of California Press, 2003.

Lock, Graham, and Murray, David. *The Hearing Eye: Jazz and Blues Influences in African American Visual Art*. New York: Oxford University Press, 2008.

Locke, Alain. *The Negro in Art*. Chicago: Afro-American Press, 1969.

———. *The Negro in Art: A Pictorial Record of the Negro Artist and of the Negro Theme in Art*. Washington, D.C.: Associates in Negro Folk Education; New York: Hacker Art Books, 1940.

Malpas, Simon. *The Postmodern*. New York: Routledge, 2005.

McGowan, John P. *Postmodernism and Its Critics*. Ithaca, NY: Cornell University Press, 1991.

McNaughton, Patrick. *The Mande Blacksmiths: Knowledge, Power and Art in West Africa*. Bloomington: Indiana University Press, 1993.

Moscou, Margo. *New Orleans' Free Men of Color: Cabinet Makers in the New Orleans Furniture Trade, 1800–1850*. New Orleans, LA: Xavier Review Press, 2008.

Nochlin, Linda. *Women, Art, and Power, and Other Essays*. New York: Harper & Row, 1988.

Parks, Gordon. *Camera Portraits: Techniques and Principles of Documentary Portraiture*. New York: Watts, 1948.

———. *Flash Photography*. New York, NY: Grosset & Dunlap, 1947.

Patton, Sharon F. *African-American Art*. Oxford: Oxford University Press, 1998.

———, ed. *Art by African Americans in the Collection of the New Jersey State Museum*. Trenton: New Jersey State Museum, 1998.

Perry, Regenia A. *Free Within Ourselves: African-American Artists in the Collection of the National Museum of American Art*. Washington, D.C.: Smithsonian, 1992.

Porter, James A. *Modern Negro Art*. New York: Dryden Press, 1944.

———. *Ten Afro-American Artists of the Nineteenth Century*. Washington, D.C.: Howard University, 1967.

Poston, Jonathan. *The Buildings of Charleston*. Columbia: University of South Carolina Press, 1997.

Powell, Richard J. *Black Art and Culture in the 20th Century*. New York: Thames and Hudson World of Art Series, 1997; 2003.

Powell, Richard J.; Bailey, David A.; Callow, Simon; Barnwell, Andrea D.; Stewart, Jeffrey C.; Gilroy, Paul; Attille, Martina; and Gates, Henry Louis, Jr. *Rhapsodies in Black: Art of the Harlem Renaissance*. Berkeley: University of California Press, 1997.

Prigoff, James, and Dunitz, Robin J. *Walls of Heritage, Walls of Pride: African American Murals*. San Francisco, CA: Pomegranate, 2003.

Reynolds, Gary A., and Wright, Beryl J. *Against the Odds: African-American Artists and the Harmon Foundation*. Newark, NJ: The Newark Museum, 1989.

Robinson, Jontyle Theresa. *Bearing Witness: Contemporary Works by African American Women Artists*. Atlanta, GA: Spelman College; New York: Rizzoli, 1996.

Rowley, Sue. *Craft and Contemporary Theory*. St. Leonards, Australia: Allen and Unwin, 1997.

Schulman, Daniel. *A Force for Change: African American Art and the Julius Rosenwald Fund.* Evanston, IL: Northwestern University Press, 2009.

Simpson, Bennett. *Blues for Smoke.* Los Angeles: The Museum of Contemporary Art, 2012.

Sims, Lowery Stokes. *African American Art: 200 Years.* New York: Michael Rosenfeld Gallery, 2008.

Smith, Margaret Denton. *Photography in New Orleans, the Early Years, 1840–1865.* Baton Rouge: Louisiana State University Press, 1982.

Smythe, Victor N. *Black New York Artists of the 20th Century: Selections from the Schomburg Center Collections.* New York: New York Public Library, Astor Lenox and Tilden Foundation, 1998.

Southern, Eileen. *Readings in Black American Music.* New York: W.W. Norton, 1983.

Sullivan, George. *Black Artists in Photography, 1840–1940.* New York: Cobble Hill Books, 1996.

Sweezy, Nancy. *Raised in Clay, the Southern Pottery Tradition.* Chapel Hill: University of North Carolina Press, 1994.

Taylor, William Edward. *A Shared Heritage: Art by Four African Americans.* Bloomington: Indiana University, 1996.

Tobin, Jacqueline L., and Dobard, Raymond G. *Hidden in Plain View: The Secret Story of Quilts and the Underground Railroad.* New York: Random House, 1999.

Vlach, John. *The Afro-American Tradition in Decorative Arts.* Cleveland, OH: Cleveland Museum of Arts, 1978.

———. *By the Work of Hands: Studies in Afro-American Folklife.* Charlottesville: University of Virginia Press, 1991.

Wahlman, Maude. *Signs and Symbols: African Images in African-American Quilts.* New York: Studio Books, 1993.

Willis, Deborah. *Picturing Us: African American Identity in Photography.* New York: New Press, 1994.

———. *Reflections in Black: A History of Black Photographers 1840 to Present.* New York: W.W. Norton, 2000.

Wilson, Samuel, and Huber, Leonard V. *The St. Louis Cemeteries of New Orleans.* New Orleans, LA: St. Louis Cathedral, 1963.

Zimmerman, Philip D. *American Federal Furniture and Decorative Arts from the Watson Collection.* New York: Hudson Hills Press, 2004.

Art and Architecture: Articles

Amos, Emma. "Contemporary Feminism: Art Practice, Theory, and Activism: An Intergenerational Perspective." *Art Journal* 58, no. 4 (Winter 1999): 10.

———. "Contemporary Views on Racism in the Arts." *M/E/A/N/I/N/G* 7 (May 1990), unpaginated.

———. "Some Do's and Don'ts for Black Women Artists." *Heresies, a Feminist Publication on Art and Politics* 15 (1982), unpaginated.

Aronson, Lisa. "African Women in the Visual Arts." *Signs* 16, no. 3 (Spring 1991): 550–574.

Ascher, Robert, and Fairbanks, Charles. "Excavation of a Slave Cabin, Georgia, U.S.A." *Historical Archaeology* 5 (1971): 3–17.

Brady, Patricia. "Black Artists in Antebellum New Orleans." *Louisiana History: The Journal of the Louisiana Historical Association* 32, no. 1 (Winter 1991): 5–28.

———. "A Mixed Palette: Free Artists of Color of Antebellum New Orleans." *International Review of African American Art: 19th Century African American Fine and Craft Arts of the South* 12, no. 3 (1995): 5–8.

Brown, Kay. "The Emergence of Black Women Artists: The Founding of 'Where We At.'" *Nka: Journal of Contemporary African Art* 29 (Fall 2011): 118–127.

Chase, Judith. "Afro-American Heritage from Ante-Bellum Black Craftsmen." *Southern Folklore Quarterly* 42 (1978): 156.

Cole, Diane. "Were Quilts Used as Underground Railroad Maps?" *U.S. News & World Report*, 24 June 2007. Web. 17 Mar 2013. http://www.usnews.com/news/articles/2007/06/24/were-quilts-used-as-underground-railroad-maps.

Cooks, Bridget R. "Black Artists and Activism: Harlem on My Mind, 1969." *American Studies Journal* 48, no. 1 (Spring 2007): 5–40.

Coolen, Michael Thodore. "Senegambian Archetypes for the American Folk Banjo." *Western Folklore* 43, no. 2 (April 1984): 117–132.

Donaldson, Jeff. "AfriCOBRA Manifesto: 'Ten in Search of a Nation.'" *Nka: Journal of Contemporary African Art* 30 (Spring 2012): 76–83.

———. "The Rise, Fall and Legacy of the Wall of Respect Movement." *International Review of African American Art* 15, no. 1 (1991): 22–26.

———. "10 in Search of a Nation." *Black World* 19, no. 12 (October 1970): 82–86.

Epstein, Dena J. "The Folk Banjo: A Documentary History." *Ethnomusicology* 19, no. 3 (September 1975): 352–360.

Greaney, Maura E. "The Power of the Urban Canvas: Paint, Politics, and Mural Art Policy." *New England Journal of Public Policy* 18, no. 1, article 6 (2002): 8–48.

Groft, Aaron de. "Eloquent Vessels/Politics of Power: The Heroic Stoneware of 'Dave the Potter.'" *Winterthur Portfolio* 33, no. 4 (1998): 249–260.

Harris, Juliette. "AfriCOBRA NOW!" *International Review of African American Art* 21, no. 2 (2007): 2–11.

Holcombe, Joe L., and Holcombe, Fred E. "South Carolina Potters and Their Wares: The History of Pottery Manufacture in Edgefield District." *South Carolina Antiquities* 21, no. 1–2 (1989): 11–30.

Hume, Ivor Noël. "An Indian Ware of the Colonial Period." *Quarterly Bulletin of the Archaeological Society of Virginia* 17, no. 1 (1962): 2–14.

Joseph, J. W. "One More Look into the Water—Colonoware in South Carolina Rivers and Charleston's Market Economy." *The Newsletter of the African Diaspora Archeology Network*, June 2007. Web. 8 Dec 2012. http://www.diaspora.illinois.edu/news0607/news0607.html.

Lippard, Lucy. "Sweeping Exchanges: The Contribution of Feminism to the Art of the 1970s." *Art Journal* 39 (Fall/Winter 1980): 362–365.

Locke, Alain Leroy. "The African Legacy and the Negro Artist." *Exhibition of the Work of Negro Artists*. New York: Harmon Foundation, 1931.

———. "The Art of the Ancestors." *Survey Graphic* 6, no. 6 (March 1925): 673.

———. "Enter the New Negro." *Survey Graphic* 6, no. 6 (March 1925): 631.

Nochlin, Linda. "Why Have There Been No Great Women Artists?" *ARTnews* 69, no. 9 (January 1971): 22–39.

Patton, Sharon. "Antebellum Louisiana Artisans: The Black Furniture Makers." *International Review of African American Art* 12, no. 3 (1995): 15–23, 58–62.

Perry, Rachel Berenson. "Celebrating Indiana's African-American Artists." *American Art Review* 24, no. 1 (January–February 2012): 82–127.

Shaw, Madelyn. "Slave Clothing and Clothing Slaves: Craftsmanship, Commerce and Industry." *Journal of Early Southern Decorative Arts* 34 (2012). Web. 8 Dec 2012. http://www.mesdajournal.org/2012/slave-cloth-clothing-slaves-craftsmanship-commerce-industry/.

Stavisky, Leonard. "Negro Craftsmanship in Early America." *American Historical Review* 54, no. 2 (1949): 315–325.

———. "The Origins of Negro Craftsmanship in Colonial America." *Journal of Negro History* 32, no. 4 (1947): 417–429.

Steen, Carl. "Alkaline Glazed Stoneware Origins." *South Carolina Antiquities* 43 (2011): 21–32.

Stukin, Stacie. "Unraveling the Myth of Quilts and the Underground Railroad." *Time Magazine*, 3 April 2007. Web. 9 Dec 2013. http://content.time.com/time/arts/article/0,8599,1606271,00.html.

Terry, Clifford. "Deserving Aid for African-American Artists: The Harmon Foundation's Rich Legacy Is Displayed in an Exhibit at the Cultural Center." *Chicago Tribune*, 19 August 1990. Web. 1 Feb 2014. http://articles.chicagotribune.com/1990-08-19/entertainment/9003090469_1_art-institute-minority-artists-harmon-foundation.

Thompson, Krista A. "Preoccupied with Haiti: The Dream of Diaspora in African American Art, 1915–1942." *American Art* 21, no. 3 (Fall 2007): 74–97.

Tomlinson, Glenn C., and Corpus, Rolando. "A Selection of Works by African American Artists in the Philadelphia Museum of Art." *Philadelphia Museum of Art Bulletin* 90, no. 382/383 (Winter 1995): 1, 4–47.

Vlach, John Michael. "Affecting Architecture of the Yoruba." *African Arts* 10, no. 1 (October 1976): 48–53, 99.

———. "Shotgun Houses." *Natural History* 86 (1977): 51–57.

Wright, Cherilyn C. "Reflections on CONFABA: 1970." *International Review of African American Art* 15, no. 1 (1998): 37.

Art and Architecture: Websites

AfriCOBRA: http://africobra.com/Introduction.html

Chicago Public Art Group (CPAG) Community Public Art Guide: http://www.cpag.net/guide/index.htm

Drayton Hall: http://www.draytonhall.org

Edgefield Pottery: http://www.edgefieldpottery.org

Foundation for Self Taught Artists: http://foundationstart.org/

Free Library of Philadelphia: http://libwww.freelibrary.org/

Historic New Orleans Collection: www.hnoc.org

Library Company of Philadelphia Digital Collections: http://lcpdams.librarycompany.org

Louisiana State Museum: http://www.crt.state.la.us/Museum/collections/visual_arts/

Mary and Leigh Block Museum of Art of Northwestern University; Wall of Respect: http://www.blockmuseum.northwestern.edu/wallofrespect/main.htm

National Gallery of Art African American Artists Collection Highlights: http://www.nga.gov/collection/gallery/ggafamer/ ggafamer-45955.html

Pictorial Archives of Early American Architecture of the Library of Congress Prints and Photographs Division: http: //www.loc.gov/rr/print/coll/186.html

Quilt Index: http://www.quiltindex.org

Smithsonian Institution National Museum of American History: http://collections.si.edu

Threaded Smithsonian blog: http://blogs.smithsonianmag.com/threaded/

WEUSI Artist Collective: http://www.weusiart.com/

Art: Audiovisual Resources

Edwards, Amber, and Aranow, Nila, prod./dir. *Against the Odds: Artists of the Harlem Renaissance.* 57 min. New Jersey Network, 1994. Videocassette.

Never the Same. AfriCOBRA artists videotaped interviews and transcripts. Web. 12 Sept 2015. http://never-the-same.org/interviews/.

Culture and Society: Books

Davis, Angela. *Women, Race & Class.* New York: Random House, 1981.

Davis, James. *Who Is Black? One Nation's Definition.* University Park: Pennsylvania State University Press, 1991.

Delaney, Martin Robinson. *The Condition, Elevation, Emigration, and Destiny of the Colored People of the United States.* Baltimore, MD: Black Classic Press, 1993.

Foster, Hal, ed. *Postmodern Culture.* London: Pluto Press, 1985.

Fox-Genovese, Elizabeth. *Within the Plantation Household: Black and White Women of the Old South.* Chapel Hill: University of North Carolina Press, 1988.

Friedan, Betty. *The Feminist Mystique.* New York: Norton, 1963.

Goldsby, Jacqueline. *A Spectacular Secret: Lynching in American Life and Literature.* Chicago: University of Chicago Press, 2006.

Gomez, Michael A. *Exchanging Our Country Marks: The Transformation of African Identity in the Colonial and Antebellum South.* Chapel Hill: University of North Carolina Press, 1998.

Goodrick-Clarke, Nicholas, ed. *The Western Esoteric Traditions: A Historical Introduction*. Oxford: Oxford University Press, 2008.

Holloway, Joseph E., ed. *Africanisms in American Culture*. Bloomington and Indianapolis: Indiana University Press, 1991.

hooks, bell. *Ain't I a Woman: Black Women and Feminism*. Boston: South End Press, 1981.

Johnson, Eloise. *Rediscovering the Harlem Renaissance: The Politics of Exclusion*. London: Taylor & Francis, 1997.

Jones, Jacqueline. *Labor of Love, Labor of Sorrow: Black Women, Work, and the Family, from Slavery to the Present*. New York: Basic Books, 1985.

Joseph, Ralina Landwehr. *Transcending Blackness: From the New Millennium Mulatta to the Exceptional Multiracial*. Durham, NC: Duke University Press, 2013.

Lewis, David Levering. *When Harlem Was in Vogue*. New York: Penguin Books, 1997.

Lorde, Audre. *Sister Outsider: Essays and Speeches by Audre Lorde*. Trumansburg, NY: Crossing Press, 1984.

Morton, Patricia. *Disfigured Images: The Historical Assault on Afro-American Women*. Westport, CT: Praeger, 1991.

Osofsky, Gilbert. *Harlem: The Making of a Ghetto, Negro New York, 1890–1930*. Chicago: Ivan R. Dee, 1996.

Schreiber, Rebecca M. *Cold War Exiles in Mexico: U.S. Dissidents and the Culture of Critical Resistance*. Minneapolis: University of Minnesota Press, 2008.

Tallant, Robert. *Voodoo in New Orleans*. Gretna, LA: Pelican, 1984.

Thompson, Robert Farris. *Flash of the Spirit: African and Afro-American Art and Philosophy*. New York: Random House, 1984.

Wallace, Michele. *Black Macho and the Myth of the Superwoman*. New York: Dial, 1979; reprint, Verso, 1991.

Wallace-Sanders, Kimberly, ed. *Skin Deep and Spirit Strong: The Black Female Body in American Culture*. Ann Arbor: University of Michigan Press, 2002.

Watson, Steven. *The Harlem Renaissance: Hub of African-American Culture, 1920–1930*. New York: Pantheon Books, 1995.

Windley, Nathan A. *Runaway Slave Advertisements: A Documentary History from the 1730s to the 1790s*. Westport, CT: Greenwood Press, 1983.

Yancey, William L. *The Moynihan Report and the Politics of Controversy*. Cambridge, MA: M.I.T. Press, 1967.

Culture and Society: Articles

Baker, David W. "J. Liberty Tadd, Who Are You?" *Studies in Art Education* 2, no. 2 (Winter 1985): 75–85.

Dalby, David. "The Indigenous Scripts of West Africa and Surinam: Their Inspiration and Design." *African Language Studies* XI (1968): 156–197.

DuBois, W.E.B. "The Talented Tenth." In Booker T. Washington; DuBois, W.E.B.; Dunbar, Paul Laurence; Chestnutt, Charles W.; Smith, Wilford H.; Kealing, H.T. and Fortune, T. Thomas. *The Negro Problem: A Series of Articles by Representative American Negroes of Today*. New York: James Pott, 1903.

Fennell, Christopher. "Early African America: Archaeological Studies of Significance and Diversity." *Journal of Archaeological Research* 19, no. 1 (March 2011): 1–49.

Goffe, Leslie. "Don't Call Me African-American." *New African* 517 (May 2012): 86–89.

Jones, Steven Loring. "A Keen Sense of the Artistic: African American Material Culture in 19th Century Philadelphia." *International Review of African-American Art* 12, no. 2 (1995): 9–26.

Martin, Ben L. "From Negro to Black to African-American: The Power of Names and Naming." *Political Science Quarterly* 106, no. 1 (Spring 1991): 83–107.

Metraux, Alfred. *Voodoo in Haiti*. New York: Schocken Books, 1972.

Owens, John. "Family's Racial History Comes into Focus." *Chicago Tribune*, 26 October 2012. Web. 4 Sept 2014. http://articles.chicagotribune.com/2012-10-26/news/ct-met-king-ganaway-20121026_1_photographers-ganaway-chicago-area.

Ringgold, Faith, and Mahoney, Margaret. "Higher Education and Women." *Women and the Arts* 11, no. 1 (Spring–Summer 1974): 95–99.

Rury, John L. "The New York African Free School, 1827–1836: Community Conflict over Community Control of Black Education." *Phylon* 44, no. 3 (1983): 187–197.

Singer, Lester. "Ethnogenesis and Negro Americans Today." *Social Research* 29 (Winter 1962): 419–432.

Staples, Robert. "The Myth of Black Matriarchy." *The Black Scholar* 1 (1970): 9–16.

Thompson, Robert Farris. "Black Ideographic Writing: Calabar to Cuba." *Yale Alumni Magazine*, November 1978: 29–33.

Wintz, Cary D., ed. "The Torturous Transition: Black Art in the Late Nineteenth and Early Twentieth Centuries." *Sage* IV, no. 1 (Spring 1987): 19–22.

Culture and Society: Websites

Black Gotham Archive: http://archive.blackgothamarchive.org

Black Panther Foundation: http://www.blackpanther.org/

Carolina Environmental Diversity Explorations: http://www.learnnc.org

National Humanities Center: http://nationalhumanitiescenter.org

National Park Service Park Ethnography Program: http://www.nps.gov/ethnography/aah/aaheritage

National Public Radio: http://www.npr.org

Preservation North Carolina: http://www.presnc.org/

History: Books

Allured, Janet, and Gentry, Judy, eds. *Louisiana Women: Their Lives and Times*. Athens: University of Georgia Press, 2009.

Bell, Caryn Cosse. *Revolution, Romanticism, and the Afro-Creole Protest Tradition in Louisiana*. Baton Rouge: Louisiana State University Press, 1997.

Beyan, Amos Jones. *African American Settlements in West Africa: John Brown Russwurm and the American Civilizing Efforts*. New York: Palgrave, 2005.

Brawley, Benjamin Griffith. *The Negro Genius: A New Appraisal of the Achievement of the American Negro*. New York: Biblio and Tannen, 1966.

Christian, Charles, and Bennet, Sari. *Black Saga: The African American Experience: A Chronology*. New York, NY: Basic Civitas Books, 1998.

Davidson, Basil. *The African Slave Trade*. Boston: Back Bay Books, 1988.

Desdunes, Rodolphe Lucien. *Our People and Our History: Fifty Creole Portraits*. Baton Rouge: Louisiana State University Press, 1973.

Emilio, Luis F. *History of the 54th Regiment of Massachusetts Volunteer Infantry, 1863–1865*. New York: Arno Press, 1969.

Fogel, Robert William, and Engerman, Stanley L. *Time on the Cross: The Economics of American Negro Slavery*. Boston: Little, Brown, 1974.

Gates, Henry Louis, Jr. *In Search of Our Roots: How 19 Extraordinary African Americans Reclaimed Their Past*. New York: Crown, 2009.

Gordon-Reed, Annette. *The Hemingses of Monticello: An American Family*. New York: W.W. Norton, 2008.

Gregory, James N. *The Southern Diaspora: How the Great Migrations of Black and White Southerners Transformed America*. Chapel Hill: University of North Carolina Press, 2007.

Johnson, Charles, and Smith, Patricia. *Africans in America: America's Journey Through Slavery*. New York: Houghton Mifflin Harcourt, 1999.

Johnson, Michael P., and Roak, James L. *Black Masters: A Free Family of Color in the Old South.* New York: Norton, 1984.

Jonas, Gilbert S. *Freedom's Sword: The NAACP and the Struggle Against Racism in America, 1909–1969.* New York: Routledge, 2005.

Keckley, Elizabeth. *Behind the Scenes: Or 30 Years a Slave and Four Years in the White House.* New York: G. W. Carleton, 1868. Google ebooks. Web. 17 Nov 2014. http://books.google.com/books/about/Behind_the_scenes_or_ Thirty_years_a_slav.html?id=0UsIAAAAQAAJ.

Landers, Jane. *Black Society in Spanish Florida.* Urbana: University of Illinois Press, 1999.

Lockpez, Inverna; McWillie, Judith; Thompson, Robert Farris; Mason, John; and McWillie, Judith. *Another Face of the Diamond: Pathways Through the Black Atlantic South.* New York: INTAR Latin American Gallery, 1988.

Macdonald, Robert M.; Kemp, John R.; and Hass, Edward F., eds. *Louisiana Black Heritage.* New Orleans: Louisiana State Museum, 1969.

Mills, Gary. *The Forgotten People: Cane River's Creoles of Color.* Baton Rouge: Louisiana State University Press, 1977.

Morris, Thomas D. *Southern Slavery and the Law, 1619–1860.* Chapel Hill: University of North Carolina Press, 1999.

Nash, Gary B. *Forging Freedom: The Formation of Philadelphia's Black Community, 1720–1840.* Cambridge, MA: Harvard University Press, 1991.

Onuf, Peter S., ed. *Jeffersonian Legacies.* Charlottesville: University Press of Virginia, 1993.

Peterson, Carla. *Black Gotham: A Family History of African Americans in Nineteenth-Century New York City.* Hartford, CT: Yale University Press, 2011.

Rasmussen, Daniel. *American Uprising: The Untold Story of America's Largest Slave Revolt.* New York: Harper, 2011.

Rawick, George E., ed. *The American Slave: A Composite Autobiography.* Westport, CT: Greenwood Press, 1972.

Schmidt, Nelly. *Victor Schoelcher and the Abolition of Slavery.* Paris: Fayard, 1994.

Segal, Ronald. *The Black Diaspora: Five Centuries of the Black Experience Outside Africa.* New York: Farrar, Straus and Giroux, 1995.

Spray, William A. *Blacks of New Brunswick.* Fredericton, NB, Canada: Brunswick Press, 1972.

Taylor, Joe Gray. *Negro Slavery in Louisiana.* Baton Rouge, Santa Barbara, CA: Greenwood Publishing Group, 1963.

Thornton, John Kelly. *Africa and Africans in the Making of the Atlantic World, 1400–1800.* Cambridge: Cambridge University Press, 1998.

Tyler-McGraw, Marie. *Virginia Emigrants to Liberia.* Charlottesville: University of Virginia, 2008.

White, Deborah Gray. *Ar'n't I a Woman? Female Slaves in the Plantation South.* New York: W.W. Norton, 1985.

Wiencek, Henry. *Master of the Mountain: Thomas Jefferson and His Slaves.* New York: Farrar, Straus & Giroux, 2012.

Woodson, Carter G. *Free Negro Owners of Slaves in the United States in 1830, Together with Absentee Ownership of Slaves in the United States in 1830.* Washington, D.C.: The Association for the Study of Negro Life, 1924; reprint, New York, 1968.

Yetman, Norman. *Life Under the "Peculiar Institution": Selections from the Slave Narrative Collection.* New York: Holt, Rinehart & Winston, 1970.

History: Articles

Allen, William C. "History of Slaves in the Construction of the U.S. Capitol." U.S. Congress, 1 June 2005. Web. 15 Apr 2014. http://artandhistory.house.gov/art_artifacts/slave_labor_reportl.pdf.

Brady, Patricia. "Free Men of Color as Tomb Builders in the Nineteenth Century." In Glen R. Conrad, ed. *Cross Crozier and Crucible: A Volume Celebrating the Bicentennial of a Catholic Diocese in Louisiana.* New Orleans, LA: The Archdiocese of New Orleans, 1974.

Dunlap, David W. "18th-Century Ship Found at Trade Center Site." *New York Times*, 14 July 2010. Web. 2 May 2013. http://cityroom.blogs.nytimes.com/2010/07/14/18th-century-ship-found-at-trade-center-site/?_r=0.

Haliburton, R., Jr. "Free Black Owners of Slaves: A Reappraisal of the Woodson Thesis." *The South Carolina Historical Magazine* 76, no. 3 (July 1975): 129–142.

Lightner, David L., and Ragan, Alexander M. "Were African American Slaveholders Benevolent or Exploitative? A Quantitative Approach." *Journal of Southern History* 71, no. 3 (August 2005): 535–558.

Schaffer, Matt. "Bound to Africa: The Mandinka Legacy in the New World." *History in Africa* 32 (2005): 321–369.

Sipkins, Henry. "An Oration on the Abolition of the Slave Trade." 2 January 1809. New York Public Library. Web. 24 Sept 2013. http://abolition.nypl.org/content/docs/text/oration_sipkins.pdf.

History: Websites

Amistad Research Center: http://www.amistadresearchcenter.org/beyond_the_blues/biographies.html

Archdiocese of New Orleans Archives: http://www.archdiocese-no.org/archives/

BlackPast.org: http://www.blackpast.org

Case Western University Encyclopedia of Cleveland History: http://ech.case.edu/

Colonial Williamsburg E-Museum: http://emuseum.history.org

Library of Congress: Life in the White House: http://myloc.gov/Exhibitions/lincoln/vignettes/LifeintheWhiteHouse/exhibitobjects/MTLJewelry.aspx

Massachusetts Historical Society: http://www.masshist.org

National Museum of American History Kenneth E. Behring Center: http://americanhistory.si.edu/collections

New Orleans Notarial Archives: http://www.notarialarchives.org

North Carolina Caswell County Historical Association: http://ncccha.org

PBS Africans in America Resource Bank: http://www.pbs.org/wgbh/aia

Schomburg Center for Research in Black Culture of the New York Public Library: African American Migration Experience: http://www.inmotionaame.org/texts/viewer.cfm?id=4_007T&page=1

Texas State Historical Association: http://www.tshaonline.org

Trans-Atlantic Slave Trade/Voyage Database: http://www.slavevoyages.org

United States Census Bureau: http://www.census.gov/

United States History.org: http://www.ushistory.org/

University of North Carolina, Greensboro Digital Library on American Slavery: http://library.uncg.edu/slavery/

University of South Carolina Scholar Commons: http://scholarcommons.sc.edu

University of Virginia Electronic Text Center: http://web.archive.org/

Yale University Gilder Lehrman Center for the Study of Slavery, Resistance & Abolition: http://www.yale.edu/glc

Methodology and Theory: Books

Adams, Laurie Schneider. *The Methodologies of Art: An Introduction*. New York: Westview Press, 2009.

Barthes, Roland. *Elements of Semiology*. New York: Hill and Wang, 1967.

Foucault, Michel. *The Order of Things: An Archaeology of the Human Sciences*. New York: Pantheon Books, 1970.

Freud, Sigmund. *The Standard Edition of The Complete Psychological Works of Sigmund Freud*. 24 vols. London: Hogarth Press, 1956–74.

Gombrich, Ernst. *Symbolic Images: Studies in the Art of the Renaissance*. 2 vols. London: Phaidon Press, 1972.

Jung, Carl. *The Archetypes and the Collective Unconscious: Collected Works of C. G. Jung*. 2nd ed. Princeton, NJ: Bollingen, 1981.

Kant, Immanuel. *Critique of Judgment*. Trans. John H. Bernard. New York: Cosimo, 2007.

Kristeva, Julia. *Desire in Language: A Semiotic Approach to Literature and Art*. Oxford: Blackwell, 1980.

Lacan, Jacques. *The Four Fundamental Concepts of Psychoanalysis*. New York: Norton, 1981.

———. *The Language of the Self: The Function of Language in Psychoanalysis*. Baltimore, MD: Johns Hopkins University Press, 1981.

Panofsky, Erwin, and Panofsky, Gerda. *Studies in Iconology: Humanistic Themes in the Art of the Renaissance*. NY: Westview Press, 1972.

Winnicott, D. W. *Playing and Reality*. London: Tavistock, 1971.

Monographs and Biographies: Books

Ali, Laylah. *Laylah Ali: Note Drawings*. Lincoln, MA: Decordova Museum and Sculpture Park, 2008.

Ater, Renee. *Remaking Race and History: The Sculpture of Meta Warrick Fuller*. Los Angeles: University of California Press, 2011.

Becker, Carol, and Borchardt-Hume, Achim. *Theaster Gates*. London: Phaidon Press, 2015.

Bedford, Christopher. *Mark Bradford*. Columbus: Ohio State University Wexner Center for the Arts, 2010.

Benjamin, Tritobia Hayes. *The Life and Art of Lois Mailou Jones*. San Francisco: Pomegranate Art Books, 1994.

Berger, Maurice. *Adrian Piper: A Retrospective*. Baltimore: University of Maryland, 1999.

Berger, Maurice; González, Jennifer A.; and Wilson, Fred. *Fred Wilson: Objects and Installations 1979–2000*. Philadelphia, PA: University of the Arts, 2001.

Berry, Ian. *Jeff Sonhouse: Slow Motion*. Saratoga Springs, NY: Skidmore College Frances Young Tang Museum, 2015.

Bey, Dawoud. *Class Pictures: Photographs by Dawoud Bey*. Contemporary Arts Museum Houston, 2008.

Biggers, Sanford, and Adkins, Terry. *Sanford Biggers*. Berkeley, CA: Berkeley Art Museum and Pacific Film Archive, 2002.

Binstock, Jonathan P. *Sam Gilliam: A Retrospective*. Los Angeles: University of California Press, 2005.

Bob Thompson: Heroes, Martyrs, and Spectres. New York: Michael Rosenfeld Gallery, 1997.

Booker, Chakaia. *RubberMade: Sculpture by Chakaia Booker*. Kansas City, MO: Kemper Museum, 2008.

Bruce, Marcus. *Henry Ossawa Tanner: A Spiritual Biography*. New York: Crossroad, 2002.

Buick, Kirsten Pai. *Child of the Fire: Mary Edmonia Lewis and the Problem of Art History's Black and Indian Subject*. Durham, NC: Duke University Press, 2010.

Bullock, Starmanda. *Through the Eyes of James A. Porter: American Art*. Washington, D.C., 2015.

Bundles, A'Lelia. *On Her Own Ground: The Life and Times of Madam C.J. Walker*. New York: Scribner, 2001.

Carretta, Vincent. *Complete Writings by Phillis Wheatley*. New York: Penguin Books, 2001.

Carrion-Murayari, Gary, ed. *Ellen Gallagher: Don't Axe Me*. New York: New Museum of Contemporary Art, 2014.

Cave, Nick; Foster, Kenneth J.; Eilertsen, Kate; Cameron, Dan; and McClusky, Pamela. *Nick Cave: Meet Me at the Center of the Earth*. San Francisco, CA: Yerba Buena Center for the Arts, 2009.

Charles Ethan Porter, 1847?–1923. Marborough: Connecticut Gallery, 1987.

Chase-Riboud, Barbara. *The President's Daughter*. New York: Random House, 1994.

———. *Sally Hemings*. New York: Viking, 1979.

Coleman, Floyd. *Felrath Hines*. Indianapolis, IN: Indianapolis Museum of Art, 1995.

Colwill, Stiles Tuttle, and Weekley, Carolyn J. *Joshua Johnson: Freeman and Early American Portrait Painter*. Williamsburg, VA: Abby Aldrich Rockefeller Folk Art Center; Baltimore, MD: Maryland Historical Society, 1987.

Conkelton, Sheryl, and Thomas, Barbara. *Never Late for Heaven: The Art of Gwen Knight*. Seattle: University of Washington Press, 2003.

Corbett, John; Elms, Anthony; and Kapsalis, Terri, eds. *Pathways to Unknown Worlds: Sun-Ra, El Saturn and Chicago's Afro-futurist Underground, 1954–68*. Chicago, IL: University of Chicago Press, 2006.

Cox, Renee. *Renee Cox: Raje: A Superhero; The Beginning of a Bold New Era*. New York, NY: Cristinerose Gallery, 1998.

Cummings, Hildegard. *Charles Ethan Porter: African American Master of Still Life*. New Britain, CT: New Britain Museum of American Art, 2008.

Davis, Alonzo. *Alonzo Davis: Recent Works*. Memphis, TN: Memphis College of Art, 2002.

DeCarava, Roy. *The Sound I Saw: The Jazz Photographs of Roy DeCarava*. New York: Phaidon, 2003.

DeCarava, Roy, and Hughes, Langston. *The Sweet Flypaper of Life*. New York: Simon and Schuster, 1955.

Dial, Thornton. *Thornton Dial: Image of the Tiger*. Cliffside Prk, NJ: New Line Books, 2003.

Douglas, Robert L. *Wadsworth Jarrell: The Artist as Revolutionary*. Rohnert Park, CA: Pomegranate, 1996.

Earle, Susan, ed. *Aaron Douglas: African American Modernist*. New Haven, CT: Yale University Press, 2007.

Edward M. Bannister: A Centennial Retrospective. Newport, RI: Roger King Gallery of Fine Art, 2001.

Elderfield, John. *Martin Puryear*. New York, NY: Museum of Modern Art, 2007.

Elms, Anthony, and Enwezor, Okwui. *Terry Adkins: Recital*. New York, NY: Prestel Publishing, 2015.

Eversley, Fred. *Fred Eversley: Four Decades : 1970–2010*. Santa Monica, CA: William Turner Gallery, 2010.

Farrington, Lisa. *Art on Fire: The Politics of Race and Sex in the Paintings of Faith Ringgold*. New York: Millennium Fine Arts Press, 1998.

———. *Faith Ringgold*. San Francisco, CA: Pomegranate, 2004.

Fine, Ruth. *The Art of Romare Bearden*. New York: Abrams, 2003.

Fleischner, Jennifer. *Mrs. Lincoln and Mrs. Keckley: The Remarkable Story of the Friendship Between a First Lady and a Former Slave*. New York: Random House, 2007.

Fuller, Edmund L. *Visions in Stone: The Sculpture of William Edmondson*. Pittsburgh, PA: University of Pittsburgh Press, 1973.

Gates, Henry Louis. *Trials of Phillis Wheatley: America's Second Black Poet and Her Encounters with the Founding Fathers*. Jackson, TN: Civitas Books, 2010.

Gedeon, Lucinda H. *Melvin Edwards, Sculpture*. Purchase, NY: Neuberger Museum of Art, State University of New York, 1993.

Golden, Thelma. *Bob Thompson*. Los Angeles: University of California Press, 1998.

———. *Trenton Doyle Hancock: The Wayward Thinker*. Edinburgh, UK: Fruitmarket Gallery, 2007.

Golden, Thelma; Wiley, Kehinde; Hobbs, Robert; Lewis, Sarah; Jackson, Brian Keith; and Halley, Peter. *Kehinde Wiley*. New York: Rizzoli, 2012.

Goodrich, Lloyd. *Thomas Eakins*. Boston: Harvard University Press, 1982.

Green, Renée. *Other Planes of There: Selected Writings*. Durham, NC: Duke University Press, 2014.

Hale Woodruff: Fifty Years of His Art. New York: Studio Museum in Harlem, 1979.

Hancock, Trenton Doyle. *Me a Mound*. New York: PictureBox, 2006.

Haskins, James. *Van Der Zee: The Picture Takin' Man*. Trenton, NJ: Africa World Press, 1991.

Helfenstein, Josef, and Kurzmeyer, Roman, eds. *Bill Traylor: 1854–1949: Deep Blues*. New Haven, CT: Yale University Press, 1999.

Herzog, Melanie Anne. *Elizabeth Catlett*. Seattle: University of Washington Press, 2005.
———. *Elizabeth Catlett: An American Artist in Mexico*. Seattle: University of Washington Press, 2000.
Hess, Janet Berry. *The Art of Richard Mayhew: A Critical Analysis with Interviews*. Jefferson, NC: McFarland, 2000.
Holland, Juanita, and Jennings, Corrine. *Edward Mitchell Bannister*. New York: Kenkeleba House, 1992.
Holloway, Camara Dia. *Portraiture and the Harlem Renaissance: The Photographs of James L. Allen*. New Haven, CT: Yale University Art Gallery, 1999.
Isaak, Jo Anna. *Renee Cox: American Family*. New York, NY: Robert Miller Gallery, 2001.
Janson, Peter Selz, and Janson, Anthony E. *Barbara Chase-Riboud, Sculptor*. New York: Harry N. Abrams, 1999.
Jezierski, John Vincent. *Enterprising Images: The Goodridge Brothers, African American Photographers, 1847–1922*. Detroit, MI: Wayne State University Press, 2000.
Jones, Kellie. *Lorna Simpson*. London: Phaidon Press, 2002.
Jones, Lois. *Loïs Mailou Jones: Peintures, 1937–1951*. Tourcoing, France: Presses Georges Frères, 1952.
Ketner, Joseph D. *The Emergence of the African-American Artist: Robert S. Duncanson, 1821–1872*. Columbia: University of Missouri Press, 1993.
King-Hammond, Leslie. *Hughie Lee-Smith*. New York: Pomegranate Press, 2011.
Kirscke, Amy. *Aaron Douglas: Art, Race and the Harlem Renaissance*. Jackson: University Press of Mississippi, 1995.
Knappe, Stephanie Fox, and Ater, Renée. *Aaron Douglas: African American Modernist: The Exhibition, the Artist, and His Legacy*. New Haven, CT: Yale University Press, 2007.
Kogan, Lee. *The Art of Nellie Mae Rowe*. Jackson: University Press of Mississippi, 1998.
Koverman, Jill B., ed. *"I Made This Jar . . ." The Life and Works of the Enslaved African-American Potter, Dave*. Columbia: University of South Carolina McKissick Museum, 1998.
Leeming, David. *Amazing Grace: A Life of Beauford Delaney*. New York: Oxford University Press, 1998.
Lewis, Samella. *The Art of Elizabeth Catlett*. Claremont, CA: Hancraft Studios, 1984.
Lowe, Harry; Zibart, Carl; and Sharp, Walter. *Will Edmondson's Mirkels*. Cheekwood: Tennessee Fine Arts Center at Cheekwood, 1964.
Marcesa, Frank, and Ricco, Roger. *Bill Traylor: His Art—His Life*. New York: Alfred A. Knopf, 1991.
Marshall, Kerry James; Sultan, Terrie; and Jafa, Arthur. *Kerry James Marshall*. New York: Harry N. Abrams, 2000.
Mathews, Marcia M. *Henry Ossawa Tanner: American Artist*. Chicago: University of Chicago Press, 1995.
McDaniel, M. Akua. *Edwin Augustus Harleston, Portrait Painter 1882–1931*. Atlanta, GA: Emory University, 1994.
McGhee, Reginald, and De Cock, Liliane. *The World of James VanDerZee*. Dobbs Ferry, NY: Morgan & Morgan, 1973.
Mercer, Kobena. *James VanDerZee*. New York and London: Phaidon, 2003.
Mitchell, Susan Crawley, and Ausfeld, Margaret Lynne, eds. *Bill Traylor: Drawings from the Collections of the High Museum of Art and the Montgomery Museum of Fine Arts*. New York: Delmonico Books and Prestel, 2012.
Nelson, Charmaine. *The Color of Stone: Sculpting the Black Female Subject in Nineteenth-Century America*. Minneapolis: University of Minnesota Press, 2007. [Re: Edmonia Lewis]
Norman Lewis: From the Harlem Renaissance to Abstraction. New York: Kenkeleba Gallery, 1989.
Norment, Camille. *Camille Norment: Within the Toll*. Høvikodden, Norway: Henie-Onstad Kunstsenter, 2011.
Our Own Artist: Paintings by Indiana's William Edouard Scott. Indiana State Museum, 2007.

Pace, Lorenzo. *Jalani and the Lock*. New York, NY: Rosen Publishing, 2001.

Parks, Gordon. *A Hungry Heart: A Memoir*. New York: Washington Square Press, 2005.

Parr, Ann, and Parks, Gordon. *Gordon Parks: No Excuses*. Gretna, LA: Pelican, 2006.

Patterson, Vivian. *Carrie Mae Weems: the Hampton Project*. Williamstown, MA: Williams College Museum of Art and New York, NY: Aperture, Inc., 2000.

Pope L., William. *Black People Are Cropped: Skin Set Drawings, 1997–2011*. Zurich, Switzerland: JRP/Ringier, 2012.

———. *Pope. L: Showing Up to Withhold*. Chicago, IL: University of Chicago Press, 2014.

———. *William Pope. L: The Friendliest Black Artist in America*. Cambridge, MA: MIT Press, 2002.

Post, Liza May. *Trenton Doyle Hancock*. Houston, TX: Contemporary Arts Museum, 2001.

Powell, Richard J. *Homecoming: The Art and Life of William H. Johnson*. Washington, D.C.: National Museum of American Art of the Smithsonian Institution, 1991.

———. *James Lesesne Wells: Sixty Years in Art*. Washington, D.C.: Washington Project for the Arts, 1986.

Price, Sally, and Price, Richard. *Romare Bearden: The Caribbean Dimension*. University of Pennsylvania, 2006.

Ringgold, Faith. *Tar Beach*. New York, NY: Crown Publishers, 1991.

———. *We Flew over the Bridge: Memoirs of Faith Ringgold*. Boston: Little Brown, 1995.

Robert Duncanson 1821–1872: Landscape, 1870. New York: Bill Hodges Gallery & Merton D. Simpson Gallery, 2003.

Roberts, Norma, ed. *Elijah Pierce, Woodcarver*. Columbus, OH: Columbus Museum of Art, 1992.

Robinson, Aminah; King-Hammond, Leslie; and Nil, Annegreth. *Symphonic Poem: The Art of Aminah Brenda Lynn Robinson*. Columbus, OH: Columbus Museum of Art and New York, NY: Harry N. Abrams, 2002.

Rodgers, Kenneth G. *Climbing Up the Mountain: The Modern Art of Malvin Gray Johnson*. Durham: North Carolina Central University Art Museum, 2002.

Rodman, Selden. *Horace Pippin: A Negro Painter in America*. New York: Quadrangle, 1946.

Rogerson, Ann S. *William Edmondson: Visions in Stone*. Montclair, NJ: The Montclair Art Museum, 1975.

Ross, Ishbel. *The President's Wife: Mary Todd Lincoln, a Biography*. New York: Putnam, 1973.

Rothkopf, Scott. *Glenn Ligon: America*. New York: Whitney Museum of American Art, 2011.

Rudolph, William Keyse, and Brady, Patricia. *In Search of Julian Hudson: Free Artist of Color in Pre-Civil War New Orleans*. New Orleans, LA: Historic New Orleans Collection, 2010.

Saar, Betye. *Betye Saar, Workers and Warriors: The Return of Aunt Jemima*. New York, NY: Michael Rosenfeld Gallery, 1998.

Schoonmaker, Trevor. *Street Level: Mark Bradford, William Cordova and Robin Rhode*. Durham, NC: Duke University Nasher Museum of Art, 2007.

Shaw, Gwendolyn DuBois. *Seeing the Unspeakable: The Art of Kara Walker*. Durham, NC: Duke University Press, 2004.

Simmons, Danny. *Three Days as the Crow Flies: A Novel*. New York: Simon and Schuster, 2010.

———. *I Dreamed My People Were Calling but I Couldn't Find My Way Home: The Poetry and Paintings of Danny Simmons*. New York: Moore Black Press, 2007.

Sims, Lowery S. *Hughie Lee-Smith Retrospective Exhibition*. Trenton: New Jersey State Museum, 1988.

Sinette, Eleanor Des Verney. *Arthur Alfonso Schomburg, Black Bibliofile and Collector: A Biography*. Detroit, MI: Wayne State University Press, 1989.

Sirmans, Franklin, and Lipschutz, Yael. *Noah Purifoy: Junk Dada*. New York: Prestel Publishing, 2015.

Smith, Morgan, and Smith, John. *Harlem: The Vision of Morgan and Marvin Smith*. Lexington: University Press of Kentucky, 1997.

Sobel, Mechal. *Painting a Hidden Life: The Art of Bill Traylor*. Baton Rouge: Louisiana State University Press, 2009.

Sperath, Albert; Vendryes, Margaret; Jones, Steven; and King, Eva. *The Art of Ellis Wilson*. Louisville: University of Kentucky Press.

Theisen, Olive Jensen. *A Life on Paper: The Drawings and Lithographs of John Thomas Biggers*. Denton: University of North Texas Press, 2006.

———. *Walls That Speak: The Murals of John Thomas Biggers*. Denton: University of North Texas Press, 2010.

Thomas, Mickalene. *Mickalene Thomas: Origin of the Universe*. Santa Monica Museum of Art, 2012.

Thompson, Robert Farris. *Soundings: An Exhibition of Sculpture by Ed Love*. Washington, D.C.: Howard University Gallery of Art, 1986.

Tilton, Connie, and Charlwood, Lindsay, eds. *LA Object and David Hammons Body Prints*. New York: Jack Tilton Gallery, 2011.

Tsai, Eugenie. *Kehinde Wiley: A New Republic*. New York: Prestel Verlag, 2015.

Turner, Elizabeth H., ed. *Jacob Lawrence: The Great Migration*. Washington, D.C.: The Phillips Collection and Rappahannock Press, 1993.

Turner, Justin G., and Turner, Linda Levitt. *Mary Todd Lincoln: Her Life and Letters*. New York: Alfred A. Knopf, 1972.

Vendryes, Margaret Rose. *Richmond Barthé: A Life in Sculpture*. Jackson: University Press of Mississippi, 2008.

Vlach, John Michael. *Charleston Blacksmith: The Work of Philip Simmons*. Columbia: University of South Carolina Press, 1992.

Walker, Kara Elizabeth, and Baker, Alex. *Laylah Ali: Typology*. Philadelphia: Pennsylvania Academy of the Fine Arts, 2007.

Wallace, Michele. *Faith Ringgold: Twenty Years of Painting, Sculpture and Performance (1963–1983)*. New York: The Studio Museum in Harlem, 1984.

Willis, Deborah, and Birt, Robert C. *VanDerZee: Photographer, 1886–1983*. New York: Harry N. Abrams, 1998.

Willis, Deborah, and Bernard, Emily. *Michelle Obama: The First Lady in Photographs*. New York: W.W. Norton, 2009.

Wilson, Fred; Klein, Richard; and Copeland, Huey. *Fred Wilson: Black Like Me*. Ridgefield, CT: Aldrich Contemporary Art Museum, 2006.

Wilson, James L. *Clementine Hunter: American Folk Artist*. Gretna, LA: Pelican, 1988.

Wilson, Judith. *Bob Thompson*. New York: Whitney Museum of American Art, 1999.

Wolfe, Rinna Evelyn. *Edmonia Lewis: Wildfire in Marble*. Parsippany, NJ: Dillon Press div. Simon & Schuster, 1998.

Wright, Beryl J., and Hartman, Saidiya V. *Lorna Simpson: for the Sake of the Viewer*. New York: Universe Publishing, 1992.

Yanari, Sachi. *Alma W. Thomas: A Retrospective of the Paintings*. San Francisco, CA: Pomegranate, 1998.

Zeidler, Jeanne, ed. *Elizabeth Catlett: Works on Paper, 1944–1992*. Hampton, VA: Hampton University Museum, 1993.

Monographs and Biographies: Articles

Barfield, Rodney. "Thomas and John Day and the Journey to North Carolina." *North Carolina Historical Review* 78, no. 1 (January 2001): 5.

Beeching, Barbara. "Nelson A. Primus, African American Artist, 1842–1916." *International Review of African American Art* 18, no. 4 (2002): 46–50.

Birt, Roger. "Coreen Simpson: An Interpretation." *Black American Literature Forum* 21, no. 3 (Autumn 1987): 289–304.

Brady, Patricia. "Florville Foy, F.M.C. Master Marble Cutter and Tomb Builder." *The Southern Quarterly: A Journal of the Arts in the South* 21, no. 2 (1993): 12.

———. "The Warburg Brothers: Sculptors." *The Historic New Orleans Collection Newsletter* 3 (1989): 8–18.

Bryan, Jennifer, and Torchia, Robert. "The Mysterious Portraitist Joshua Johnson." *Archives of American Art Journal* 36, no. 2 (1996): 2–7.

Bullard, Laura Curtis. "Edmonia Lewis." *The Revolution* 7, no. 16 (20 April 1871); reprinted in *The New National Era* 2, no. 17 (4 May 1871): 1.

Burgard, Timothy Anglin. "Edmonia Lewis and Henry Wadsworth Longfellow: Images and Identities." *American Art Review* 7 (February/March 1995): 114–117.

Chandler, Robert J. "From Black to White: Lithographer and Painter Grafton Tyler Brown." *California Territorial Quarterly* 86 (Summer 2011): 4–29.

Clemson, John D. "The Edward Augustus Brackett House, 290 Highland Avenue, Winchester, Massachusetts." Clemson Preservation.com, undated. Web. 5 Oct 2014. http://clemsonpreservation.com/pdf/290HighlandAve.pdf.

Conwill, Kinshasha. "Remembering Emilio Cruz." *International Review of African American Art* 20, no. 2 (2005): 63.

Cotter, Holland. "Hughie Lee-Smith, 83, a Painter of Spare, Bleak Scenes Touched with Mystery." *New York Times*, 1 March 1999. Web. 17 Aug 2013. http://www.nytimes.com/1999/03/01/arts/hughie-lee-smith-83-a-painter-of-spare-bleak-scenes-touched-with-mystery.html.

Cowan, Wes. "Sweet Dreams: Henry Boyd Tester Beds Highly Collectible." *WorthPoint Antiques*, 24 May 2010. Web. 18 June 2013. http://www.worthpoint.com/blog-entry/sweet-dreams-henry-boyd-tester-beds.

Curnutte, Mark. "Henry Boyd Built Furniture to Last." *The Cincinnati Enquirer*, 21 February 1997. Web. 9 Apr 2014. http://www.enquirer.com/editions/1997/02/21/loc_blackhistory.html.

Dawkins, Wayne. "Frederick Eversley Art, Energy and Invention." *International Review of African American Art* 23, no. 3 (2011): 28–32.

Degener, Patricia. "Ed Love's Spirited Steel Sculptures Are Tribute to Jazz." *St. Louis Post-Dispatch*, 18 May 1991: 5D.

Duncan, Pearl. "Is One of America's Leading Potters Related to the Family of Potters Who Owned Him as a Slave?" *The Art Daily*, 31 May 2012. Web. 8 July 2013. http://artdaily.com/news/55726/Is-one-of-America-s-leading-potters-related-to-the-family-of-potters-who-owned-him-as-a-slave-#.UkCkH4akqOc.

East, Charles. "Jules Lion's New Orleans." *Georgia Review* 40 (Winter 1986): 914–916.

Edwards, Bowan. "John Brown's Famous Photograph: An 1840s Image Captures an Extremist Fervor." *Smithsonian.com Magazine*, 21 September 2009. Web. 6 Jan 2014. http://www.smithsonianmag.com/history-archaeology/John-Browns-Famous-Photograph.html#ixzz2o9IlZGEn.

Edwards, Jeff. "The Long Sweep: A Conversation with Ed Clark About His 60 Plus Years in the Art World." *Art Pulse Magazine*, May 2013. Web. 16 May 2014. http://artpulsemagazine.com/the-long-sweep-a-conversation-with-ed-clark-about-his-60-plus-years-in-the-art-world.

Erickson, Peter. "Black Like Me: Reconfiguring Blackface in the Art of Glenn Ligon and Fred Wilson." *Nka: Journal of Contemporary African Art* 25, no. 1 (2009): 30–47.

Forney, Caitlan. "Richard Mayhew." Penn State University Library, 2008. Web. 17 June 2012. http://pabook.libraries.psu.edu/palitmap/bios/Mayhew__Richard.html.

"Found 200 Year Old Pitcher on the Seabed: Turned Out to Be Something of a Curiosity from 'Commeraw's Pottery.'" *Arkeologiavisa*, 14 May 2012. Web. 28 Aug 2013. http://arkeologiavisa.blogspot.com/2012/05/fant-200-ar-gammel-krukke-pa-havbunnnen.html.

Fox, Margalit. "Terry Adkins, Composer of Art, Sculptor of Music, Dies at 60." *New York Times* (22 February, 2014): D11.

Glazer, Lee Stephens. "Signifying Identity: Art and Race in Romare Bearden's Projections." *Art Bulletin* 76, no. 1 (March 1994): 411–426.

Gold, Susanna W. "The Death of Cleopatra / The Birth of Freedom: Edmonia Lewis at the New World's Fair." *Biography: An Interdisciplinary Quarterly* 35, no. 2 (Spring 2012): 318–341.

Huebner, Jeff. "An Artist's Homecoming: Chicago Painter Calvin Jones." *Chicago Reader*, 10 March 2011. Web. 9 June 2014. http://www.chicagoreader.com/chicago/calvin-jones-chicago-artist/Content?oid=3391273.

———. "The Man Behind the Wall." *The Chicago Reader*, 28 April 1997. Web. 26 May 2014. http://www.chicagoreader.com/chicago/the-man-behind-the-wall/Content?oid=894264. [Re: Calvin Jones]

Kearns, Martha. "Elizabeth Catlett: The Spirit of Form." *Sculpture Magazine* 18, no. 2 (March 1999). Web. 14 Apr 2013. http://www.sculpture.org/documents/scmag99/march99/catlett/catlett.shtml.

Ketner, Robert D. "Robert S. Duncanson (1821–1872): The Late Literary Landscape Paintings." *American Art Journal* 15, no. 1 (Winter 1983): 35–47.

Khan, Eve. "Condemning Slavery with a Paintbrush." *New York Times*, 15 July 2011: C24. Web. 1 Jan 2014. http://www.nytimes.com/2011/07/15/arts/ design/painter-robert-s-duncanson-and-2-jewelry-exhibitions.html?_r=1& [Re: Robert S. Duncanson]

Koplos, Janet. "Martin Puryear's 'Ars Poetica': Being, Rather than Meaning, Is at the Core of This American Sculptor's Finely Crafted Oeuvre." *Art in America* 89, no. 12 (Dec. 2001): 74–79.

Laduke, Betty. "Lois Mailou Jones: The Grande Dame of African-American Art." *Woman's Art Journal* 8, no. 2 (Fall/Winter 1988): 28–29.

Lando, Michal. "Oakland Photo Artist Eubanks Captures Moments." *Contra Costa Times*, 17 June 2003: A09.

"Landscape of Slavery, Mulberry Row at Monticello: John Hemmings." Monticello Museum, undated. Web. 17 Nov 2012. http://www.monticello.org/mulberry-row/people/john-hemmings.

LeFalle-Collins, Lizzetta. "Grafton Tyler Brown: Selling the Promise of the West: African American Lithographer and Painter." *International Review of African American Art* 12, no. 1 (Winter 1995): 26–45.

———. "The Spiritual Realm of Richard Mayhew." *American Visions* 15, no. 2 (2000): 16–21.

Leininger-Miller, Theresa. "An American Journey: The Life and Photography of James Presley Ball, Cincinnati Museum Center, Cincinnati, Ohio, May 1–October 24, 2010." *Nineteenth Century Art Worldwide Journal* 10, no. 2 (Autumn 2011). Web. 5 Oct 2013. http://www.19thc-artworldwide.org/autumn11/review-of-an-american-journey-the-life-and-photography-of-james-presley-ball.

Leung, Simon; Green, Renee; Kolbowski, Silvia; and Prima, Stephen. "Contemporary Returns to Conceptual Art: Renée Green, Silvia Kolbowski, and Stephen Prina." *Art Journal* 60, no. 2 (Fall 2001): 54–71.

Levy, Jane Freundel. "The Scurlock Studio." *Washington History* (Spring 1989): 41–57.

Lock, Graham. "Blues on the Brush: Musical Influence in Rose Piper's Blues and Negro Folk Songs Paintings of the Mid-1940s." *International Review of African American Art* 22, no. 1 (2008): 18–29.

Mack, Thomas. "Dave the Potter." *Maine Antique Digest* XXXX, no. 6 (June 2012). Web. 12 Mar 2012. http://www.usca.edu/aasc/davepotter.htm.

McHenry, Susan. "'Sally Hemings': A Key to Our National Identity/A Conversation with Barbara Chase-Riboud/Barbara Chase-Riboud Tells Why She Outraged the Jefferson Scholars." *Ms.* 9, no. 4 (October 1980): 40.

McQuaid, Cate. "Aesthetic and Social Concerns of John Wilson." *Boston Globe*, 16 October 2012. Web. 6 Aug 2012. http://www.bostonglobe.com/arts/theater-art/2012/10/16/what-boston-area-art-galleries/333b9XKY08DD5SHhbAl65K/story.html.

Moore, Lucinda. "America's Forgotten Landscape Painter: Robert S. Duncanson." *Smithsonian .com Magazine*, 19 October 2011. Web. 2 Jan 2014. http://www.smithsonianmag.com/arts-culture/Americas-Forgotten-Landscape-Painter-Robert-Duncanson.html.

Newton, James A. "Crow's Nest or Eagles' Aeries? The Octagon Houses of E.A. Brackett and H.P. Wakefield." *Old-Time New England* (Winter–Spring 1977): 57–72.

Pleasants, J. Hall. "Joshua Johnston, the First American Negro Portrait Painter." *Maryland Historical Magazine* 37, no. 2 (June 1942): 121–149.

Pringle, Allan. "Robert S. Duncanson in Montreal, 1863–1865." *American Art Journal* 17, no. 4 (Autumn 1985): 28–50.

Prown, Jonathan. "The Furniture of Thomas Day: A Reevaluation." *Winterthur Portfolio* 33, no. 4 (Winter 1998): 216.

Richard, Paul. "Black Artists: Their Pride and Problems: Ed Love." *Washington Post*, 15 March 1981: K1.

———. "Ed Love's Scrap Yard Spirits: At Howard, the Sculptor's Raging, Dancing Statues." *Washington Post*, 15 September 1986: B1.

———. "The Politics of Pain: Sculptor Ed Love's White-Hot Rage." *Washington Post*, 14 February 1981: D1.

Richardson, Marilyn. "Edmonia Lewis's The Death of Cleopatra." *International Review of African American Art* 12, no. 2 (July 1995): 36–52.

Rowell, Charles H. "A Conversation with Gwendolyn Knight." *Callaloo* 11, no. 4 (1988): 689–696.

———. "An Interview with Lois Mailou Jones." *Callaloo* 12, no. 2 (1989): 357–378.

Self, Robert L., and Stein, Susan R. "The Collaboration of Thomas Jefferson and John Hemings." *Winterthur Portfolio* 33, no. 4 (1998): 233–248.

Short, Alvia Jean Wardlaw. "Strength, Tears, and Will: John Biggers' *Contribution of the Negro Woman to American Life and Education*." *Callaloo* 2, no. 1 (1979): 135–143.

Smee, Sebastian. "John Wilson: Clear and Present." *Boston Globe*, 29 November 2012. Web. 30 Apr 2014. http://www.bostonglobe.com/arts/theater-art/2012/11/29/john-wilson-clear-and-present/OgFjg0uPPeO5AndFeIBi2K/story.html.

Smith, Beuford. Interview by Lou Draper. In Hatch, James; Hamalian, Leo; and Blum, Judy, eds. *Artist and Influence* XVIII. New York: Hatch-Billops Collections, 1999.

Smothers, Ronald. "Vincent Smith, 74, Painter Who Portrayed Black Life." *New York Times*, 3 January 2004. Web. 15 May 2012. http://www.nytimes.com/2004/01/03/arts/vincent-smith-74-painter-who-portrayed-black-life.html.

Thompson, Robert Farris. "Monuments to the Future: The Art of Ed Love." *Studio Potter* 17, no. 1 (4 December 1988): 3.

Thorson, Alice. "An Interview with Jeff Donaldson: AfriCOBRA—Then and Now." *New Art Examiner* 17 (March 1990): 26–31.

Tyler, Lawrence. "Reginald Gammon: The Carnal Art of the Tattoo." *International Review of African American Art* 7, no. 3 (1987): 57–61.

Wasser, Fred. "Thomas Day: A Master Craftsman, with Complications." National Public Radio, 29 July 2010, Transcript. Web. 4 June 2012. http://www.npr.org/templates/story/story.php?storyId=128849634.

Whitten, Jack. "Ed Clark." BOMB Magazine's Oral History Project, 1 April 2014. Interview transcript. Web. 11 June 2014. http://bombmagazine.org/article/1000101/ed-clark.

Wiencek, Henry. "The Dark Side of Thomas Jefferson." *Smithsonian Magazine*, October 2012. Web. 5 Oct 2012. http://www.smithsonianmag.com/history-archaeology/The-Little-Known-Dark-Side-of-Thomas-Jefferson-169780996.html.

Williams, Phil, and Williams, Linda. "Interview with Benny Andrews." *Artaxia* 4 (1975). Web. 15 Mar 2014. http://garev.uga.edu/andrewsinterview.html.

Wilson, Judith. "Lifting 'The Veil': Henry O. Tanner's The Banjo Lesson and The Thankful Poor." *Contributions in Black Studies* 9 (1992): article 4.

Zax, David. "The Scurlock Studio: Picture of Prosperity." *Smithsonian Magazine*, February 2010. Web. 8 July 2013. http://www.smithsonianmag.com/people-places/the-scurlock-studio-picture-of-prosperity-4869533/.

Monographs and Biographies: Websites

Archives of American Art Oral Histories: http://www.aaa.si.edu/collections/interviews/
The Art Story.Org: http://www.theartstory.org/
Barbara Chase-Riboud: http://chaseriboud.free.fr/index.html
Benny Andrews: http://bennyandrews.com/
Betty Blayton: http://bettyblaytonartist.com/
Betye Saar: http://www.betyesaar.net/
Carnegie Museum Teenie Harris Archives: http://teenie.cmoa.org/Default.aspx
Cliff Joseph: http://kyserpro.wix.com/cliffjoseph#!the-artist
Columbia State Community College of Delaware, Ohio Elijah Pierce pages: http://www.cscc.edu/elijahpierce/
Dana Chandler Facebook page: https://www.facebook.com/danacchandlerjr/info
Davis Brody Bond Architects: www.davisbrody.com
Duke University Nasher Museum of Art Archibald Motley Timeline: http://nasher.duke.edu/motley/
Ed Clark: http://www.artistedclark.com/index.html
Edward M. Bannister: http://www.edwardmbannister.com/
Emilio Cruz Estate: http://emiliocruz.com/home.html
Faith Ringgold: http://www.faithringgold.com/
Freelon Architects: http://www.freelon.com/
Gantt Huberman Architects: http://www.gantthuberman.com/index.php
Gordon Parks Foundation: http://www.gordonparksfoundation.org/
Harold Cousins: http://www.haroldcousins.com/biography/
History Makers: http://www.thehistorymakers.com/
Huff + Gooden Architects: http://www.huffgooden.com/architects
Jacob and Gwen Knight Lawrence Visual Resource Center: http://www.jacobandgwenlawrence.org/index.html
James Phillips: http://www.jamesphillips-artist.com/index.html
John Biggers: www.johnbiggers.com
Judith Alexander Foundation Nellie Mae Rowe page: http://www.judithalexander.org/nellie-mae-rowe/
June Kelly Gallery: http://www.junekellygallery.com/artists.htm
Kentucky Museum of Art and Craft Essential Elijah Pierce: http://www.kentuckyarts.org/the-essential-elijah-pierce/
KET Public Media Ellis Wilson pages, “So Much to Paint”: http://www.ket.org/elliswilson/
Madame C. J. Walker: http://www.madamcjwalker.com/bios/alelia-walker/
Malvin Gray Johnson Collection: http://thejohnsoncollection.org/malvin-gray-johnson/
Marie Johnson Calloway: http://artbymariecalloway.com/
Marshall/Moya Architects: http://www.marshallmoya.com/
McKissack & McKissack Architects: http://www.mckissackdc.com/
Melvin Edwards: http://www.meledwards08.com/index.php
Michael Rosenfeld Gallery artists’ biographies: http://www.michaelrosenfeldart.com/artists
North Carolina Humanities Council Thomas Day Educational Project: http://thomasday.net
Philip Simmons Foundation: http://www.philipsimmons.us/
Reginald Gammon: http://www.reggiegammon.com/index.html
Richard Hunt: http://www.richardhunt.us/
Romare Bearden Foundation: www.beardenfoundation.org
San Francisco Museum of Modern Art Raymond Saunders interview: https://archive.org/details/cocac_000011
Sharon Haggins Dunn: http://sharonhagginsdunn.photoshelter.com/
Sherry and Roy De Carava Archives: http://www.decarava.org/

Thomas Commeraw Project: http://www.commeraw.com/
Visionary Leadership Project: http://www.visionaryproject.org/
William T. Williams: http://www.williamtwilliams.com/
Winchester Massachusetts Archival Center E. A. Brackett Collection: http://www.winchester.us/index.php/departments/archival-center.html

Monographs and Biographies: Audiovisual Resources

Allport, Carolyn Jones, dir./prod. *Sermons in Wood*. Interview with Elijah Pierce. Memphis, TN: The Center for Southern Folklore, 1980. Videocassette.
Flander, David, dir./prod. *Keeper of the Gate: The Life and Works of Philip Simmons: Master Blacksmith*. Charleston, SC: Philip Simmons Foundation, 1994. Videocassette.
Gary Ames Rickson Artist Profile. Massachusetts Community College Killian Gallery, Canton, 12 March 2013. Video. Web. 12 Apr 2013. http://www.youtube.com/watch?v=czpcRwqtDn4.
Irving, David, and Freeman, Linda, dir. and prod. *Richard Mayhew: Spiritual Landscapes*. Chappaqua, NY: L&S Video, 1999. Videocassette.
Light, Allie, and Saraf, Irving, dir. *The Angel That Stands by Me: Minnie Evans Paintings*. Light-Saraf Films, 1983. Film.
Love, Kenneth, and Seamans, Joseph, dir. *One Shot: The Life and Work of Teenie Harris*. 2003. Film.
Sam Gilliam's "From a Model to a Rainbow," PBS Newshour. PBS, 18 August 2011. Video. Web. 8 July 2015. http://video.pbs.org/video/2098117627/.

INDEX